Belief and M

The Veritas Series

Belief and Metaphysics
Edited by Conor Cunningham and Peter M. Candler

Proposing Theology
John Milbank

Tayloring Reformed Epistemology: Charles Taylor, Alvin Plantinga and the de jure Challenge to Christian Belief
Deane-Peter Baker

Theology, Psychoanalysis, Trauma
Marcus Pound

Transcendence and Phenomenology
Edited by Conor Cunningham and Peter M. Candler, Jr

VERITAS

Belief and Metaphysics

Edited by
Conor Cunningham
and
Peter M. Candler, Jr

scm press

in association with

The Centre of Theology and Philosophy
University of Nottingham
2007

All rights reserved. No part of this publication may be reproduced,
stored in a retrieval system, or transmitted,
in any form or by any means, electronic, mechanical,
photocopying or otherwise, without the prior permission of
the publisher, SCM Press.

© Conor Cunningham and Peter M. Candler 2007

The Authors have asserted their right under the Copyright, Designs and
Patents Act, 1988, to be identified as the Authors of this Work

British Library Cataloguing in Publication data

A catalogue record for this book is available
from the British Library

Hardback 978 0 334 04150 4
Paperback 978 0 334 04137 5

First published in 2007 by SCM Press
13–17 Long Lane,
London EC1A 9PN

www.scm-canterburypress.co.uk

SCM Press is a division of
SCM-Canterbury Press Ltd

Typeset by Regent Typesetting, London
Printed and bound in Great Britain by
MPG Books Ltd, Bodmin, Cornwall

Contents

Veritas Series Introduction	xiii
Foreword by Archbishop Javier Martinez	xv
List of Contributors	xxiii
Acknowledgements	xxviii
Introduction	xxix

1 Belief and Metaphysics
   Louis Dupré 1

2 The Confidence of Thought: Between Belief and Metaphysics
   William Desmond 11

3 The Beauty of the Metaphysical Imagination
   John R. Betz 41

4 Metaphysics of Creation
   David Burrell, C.S.C 66

5 Metaphysics and the Question of Creation: Thomas Aquinas, Duns Scotus and Us
   Rudi te Velde 73

6 Trying My Very Best to Believe Darwin, or, The Supernaturalistic Fallacy: From Is to Nought
   Conor Cunningham 100

7 Metaphysics as Preamble to Religious Belief
   Oliva Blanchette 141

8	Truth, Time, Religion *Philipp W. Rosemann*	161
9	On the Power and Fragility of Belief: Updike, Deleuze and Lyotard *James Williams*	183
10	Can Abraham be Saved? And: Can Kierkegaard be Saved? A Hegelian Discussion of *Fear and Trembling* *Vittorio Hösle*	204
11	From Copenhagen to Cambrai: Paradoxes of Faith in Kierkegaard and de Lubac *Eric Lee*	236
12	Heidegger's Approach to Aquinas: Opposition, *Destruktion*, Unbelief *Sean McGrath*	260
13	A Defence of Anti-Conceptual Realism *E. J. Lowe*	291
14	Realism in Theology and Metaphysics *Michael C. Rea*	323
15	Deification as Metaphysics: Christology, Desire, and Filial Prayer *Patrick Riches*	345
16	Wittgenstein's *Leben*: Language, Philosophy and The Authority of the Everyday *Neil Turnbull*	374
17	Plato against Ontotheology *Paul Tyson*	393
18	Lacan, Metaphysics and Belief *Marcus Pound*	413
19	The Politics of Fear and the Gospel of Life *Daniel M. Bell, Jr*	426

20 Only Theology Saves Metaphysics: On the
    Modalities of Terror   452
    John Milbank

*Appendix   An Interview with John Milbank and
Conor Cunningham*   501

Name and Subject Index   529

In memoriam
Lucy Tyson
8 July 2006 – 14 February 2007

The births of so many humans who did not exist are each day greater miracles than the resurrection of humans who existed.

St Augustine

Centre of Theology and Philosophy
www.theologyphilosophycentre.co.uk

Every doctrine which does not reach the one thing necessary, every separated philosophy, will remain deceived by false appearances. It will be a doctrine, it will not be Philosophy.
Maurice Blondel, 1861–1949

This book series is the product of the work carried out at the Centre of Theology and Philosophy, at the University of Nottingham.

The COTP is a research-led institution organized at the interstices of theology and philosophy. It is founded on the conviction that these two disciplines cannot be adequately understood or further developed, save with reference to each other. This is true in historical terms, since we cannot comprehend our Western cultural legacy unless we acknowledge the interaction of the Hebraic and Hellenic traditions. It is also true conceptually, since reasoning is not fully separable from faith and hope, or conceptual reflection from revelatory disclosure. The reverse also holds, in either case.

The Centre is concerned with:

- The historical interaction between theology and philosophy.
- The current relation between the two disciplines.
- Attempts to overcome the analytic/Continental divide in philosophy.
- The question of the status of 'metaphysics'. Is the term used equivocally? Is it now at an end? Or have twentieth-century attempts to have a post-metaphysical philosophy themselves come to an end?
- The construction of a rich Catholic humanism.

I am very glad to be associated with the endeavours of this extremely important Centre that helps to further work of enor-

mous importance. Among its concerns is the question whether modernity is more an interim than a completion – an interim between a premodernity in which the porosity between theology and philosophy was granted, perhaps taken for granted, and a postmodernity where their porosity must be unclogged and enacted anew. Through the work of leading theologians of international stature and philosophers whose writings bear on this porosity, the Centre offers an exciting forum to advance in diverse ways this challenging and entirely needful, and cutting-edge work.

Professor William Desmond (Leuven)

VERITAS

Series Introduction

'... the truth will set you free.' (John 8.32)

Pontius Pilate said to Christ, 'What is truth?' And Jesus remained silent. In much contemporary discourse, Pilate's question has been taken to mark the absolute boundary of human thought. Beyond this boundary, it is often suggested, is an intellectual hinterland into which we must not venture. This terrain is an agnosticism of thought: because truth cannot be possessed, it must not be spoken. Thus, it is argued that the defenders of 'truth' in our day are often traffickers in ideology, merchants of counterfeits, or anti-liberal. They are, because it is somewhat taken for granted that Nietzsche's word is final: truth is the domain of tyranny.

Is this indeed the case, or might another vision of truth offer itself? The ancient Greeks named the love of wisdom, *philia*, or friendship. The one who would become wise, they argued, would be a 'friend of truth'. For both philosophy and theology might be conceived as schools in the friendship of truth, as a kind of relation. For like friendship, truth is as much discovered as it is made. If truth is then so elusive, if its domain is *terra incognita*, perhaps this is because it arrives to us – unannounced – as gift, as a person, and not some thing.

The aim of the Veritas book series is to publish incisive and original current scholarly work that inhabits 'the between' and 'the beyond' of theology and philosophy. These volumes will all share a common aspiration to transcend the institutional divorce in which these two disciplines often find themselves, and to engage questions of pressing concern to both philosophers and theologians in such as way as to reinvigorate both disciplines with a kind of interdisciplinary desire, often so absent in contemporary academe. In a word, these volumes represent collective efforts in the befriending of truth, doing so beyond the simulacra of pretend

Veritas: Series Introduction

tolerance, the violent, yet insipid reasoning of liberalism that asks with Pilate, What is truth? – expecting a consensus of non-commitment; one that encourages the commodification of the mind, now sedated by the civil service of career, ministered by the frightened patrons of position.

The series will therefore consist of two 'wings': 1, original monographs; and 2, essay collections on a range of topics in theology and philosophy. The latter will principally be the products of the annual conferences of the Centre of Theology and Philosophy (www.theologyphilosophycentre.co.uk).

Conor Cunningham
Peter Candler
Series editors

Foreword

FRANCISCO JAVIER MARTÍNEZ
Archbishop of Granada

On the wall of the beautiful Renaissance building which today hosts the offices of the Archdiocese, and that was the first seat of the University of Granada, downtown, just facing the Cathedral, there is a small statue in homage to one of the great men of the city. This man is Francisco Suárez (1548–1617), who was born in Granada and lived here before going to study philosophy and theology in Salamanca in 1564, at the age of 16.

The connection between Granada and Suárez might be one of the motifs for our being together here now. Besides the trust of John Milbank, Conor Cunningham and their co-operators at the Nottingham Centre in our capabilities to provide the infrastructure for our meeting (a trust which I can only call an 'excess'), the fact that we gather to think, to speak and to discuss 'Belief and Metaphysics' in a place like Granada is, to say the least, highly significant.

Granada is, or was, in many respects, a modern city. Rebuilt and to a great extent 'created' as a Christian city after 1492 – it is above all a late Renaissance and Baroque city. Perhaps Spain, as it was conceived after 1492, and in spite of the many traditional features of its institutions, of its culture, and of the life of its people, and in spite of the many appearances that would seem to contradict this statement – is also a peculiarly modern country, with the achievements and the limitations of modernity. Perhaps this helps to understand better some of the features of our history, past and present. It is curious, for instance, that the living memory of the Christian people in Spain (more perhaps in the South but I would

Foreword

say the phenomenon is rather general) goes back mainly to the great saints of the sixteenth and seventeenth centuries. What happened before is properly 'prehistory', in the sense that it is something left to the care of specialists, but that in no way informs the sense of belonging or the imagination of the Christian people, educated mainly by Jesuits or by feminine orders very much inspired and guided by them. No Benedictine tradition, for instance, has reached Andalusia until very recently. This simple fact would already make a great distinction between our Christian memory and that of other European Christians, including those of Italy.

Certainly, the relationship of Spanish Catholicism with modernity is extremely complex, and obviously nothing I could say here will be able to express the many nuances of this complexity. This relationship is in many ways one of both hatred and love. It has many peculiar features coming from our previous history, which can be described to a great extent as the history of some Christian kingdoms living for centuries in a changing frontier with Islam (political and economic as well as cultural), and engaged in a war of 'liberation' that at the same time assimilated quite a number of features, categories and concepts of 'the other side'. But here again, perhaps the kind of relationship with 'the other side' or 'sides' that only sees as possibilities their assimilation, their suppression or their exclusion, reflects precisely the influence of that 'other side', and would become a specifically modern idea: one that helped to generate the principle *cuius regio eius religio* ('whose rule, his religion'), and helped give birth to the modern nation-state. And perhaps this idea, deeply alien to the Christian tradition at its best – like the related conception of God as a 'being' outside creation, and whose relationship to creation is mainly one of absolute (and arbitrary) power, even if that power happens to be benevolent – owes more than we might be willing to accept to Islamic influences that have come to us by way of confrontation.

By saying this, I do not at all mean to suggest that Spain was the source of these ideas that have so deeply marked modern European culture and politics. It is simply obvious that Europe produced these ideas from many sources and circumstances, such as the presence of Islam in the whole Mediterranean region and in Southern Italy, the pressure of Islam upon the Byzantine Empire and upon Eastern Europe, the many connections created by the Crusaders, and by the commercial relationships that were maintained in spite of immense difficulties. Rather, the fact that the kingdoms of Spain were concentrated on the struggle with Islam within their own territories for so long isolated them in more than one way from what was going on in other parts of Europe.

All I intend to say is that modern Spain (or at least, modern Spanish Catholicism) is probably best understood from Granada, and that Granada is a specifically modern city, created as such at the dawn of modernity, at the very origins of the project of Spain as a modern nation-state. If this is true, and I believe it is, Spanish Catholicism is much more 'modern' and much less traditional than is commonly thought. I think that understanding the specifically modern contours of Spanish Catholicism helps us to understand better the difficulties and challenges facing Catholicism today. The end of modernity will certainly mean the end of a Catholicism (the end of a Christianity) that has strongly tied up its destiny to the destiny of a specifically modern culture. The difficulties and challenges facing Spanish Catholicism may not be, after all, so different from those facing Christianity in other parts of the world, but at least in a Catholic context, those challenges and difficulties have to do mainly with the heritage of Suárez. This heritage frustrated to a great extent the possibility of a Christian modernity, and through his thorough separation of the 'natural' and 'supernatural' orders, and his account of the 'two ends' of human life, finished with the traditional Christian teleology of human life, opened the way to an understanding of nature as 'outside God', as self-interpreting without the need for revelation or redemption – that is, without the need for Christ, and so, opened the way to the radical secularization of culture that we experience today. He created and articulated for centuries a vision of the whole world for which Jesus Christ is not necessary or significant. In fact, for Suárez, Jesus Christ has nothing to do with the world as such, as 'natural', as created, except in the initial act of creation. Whatever relationship Jesus Christ may have to 'temporal' things has to be purely 'spiritual'; it must pertain solely to the 'elevation' of the natural to the supernatural order. What remains of the traditional Christian vision of the world here, it is not for me to say now, but it is obvious that these are deep and not so subtle transformations.

Foreword

The 'creation of metaphysics', or at least, of what modern thinkers have understood as 'metaphysics', is essential to Suárez's project, a project which, one could say, ran against the deepest of St Ignatius' intentions, as shown for instance in the first lines of the *Spiritual Exercises*, named 'Principle and Foundation'. Nevertheless it is a project that was diffused very rapidly all over Europe through the powerful Jesuit system of schools.[1]

Indeed Alasdair MacIntyre has said of Suárez: 'Suarez, both in his preoccupations and his methods, was already a distinctively modern thinker, perhaps more authentically than Descartes the founder of modern philosophy.'[2] To call him the 'founder' of modern philosophy is almost the same as naming him the founder, as Conor Cunningham has put it, 'of *philosophical* metaphysics', that is, the 'positing of a reality other than God'.[3] This is something widely recognized today: on one hand, Suárez crystallized in a complete system several tendencies at work in the West since the late thirteenth century, and on the other hand, his way of understanding 'Thomism' has been and is still decisive (and I would add, decisively damaging) in the Catholic academy and in Catholic life in general. In my view, the need to move beyond (or away from) the heritage of Suárez, the need to transgress the borders between theology and philosophy as created by Suárez and modern meta-

---

1 Cf. John Montag's contribution, 'Revelation: The False Legacy of Suárez', in John Milbank, Catherine Pickstock and Graham Ward (eds), *Radical Orthodoxy. A New Theology* (London: Routledge, 1998), pp. 38–63. Cf. especially pp. 62–3.

2 MacIntyre, *Three Rival Versions of Moral Enquiry: Encyclopedia, Genealogy and Tradition* (Notre Dame: University of Notre Dame Press, 1990), p. 73. The lineage that goes from Suárez to Descartes is easily recognizable, not only because Descartes was heavily influenced by the Jesuits who taught him (they themselves strongly marked by Suárez's thought, as MacIntyre himself notes), but also because the independence of human reason 'from the particular bonds of any particular moral and religious community', which is the invention of 'reason as such, impersonal, impartial, disinterested, uniting, and universal' (MacIntyre, *Three Rival Versions*, p. 59), commonly attributed to Descartes, is already found to a great extent in Suárez's system.

3 Conor Cunningham, 'Language: Wittgenstein after Theology', in Milbank et al., *Radical Orthodoxy*, pp. 1–20; cf. p. 64.

physics, is one of the most urgent and necessary tasks for the Church to recover her own identity and tradition.

To give just one example: in his study of the encyclical *Aeterni Patris* by Leo XIII, Alasdair MacIntyre signals how Joseph Kleutgen, recognizably 'the most important influence upon the drafting'[4] of the encyclical, had misinterpreted Aquinas by reading him through Suárez. As a result, 'epistemological concerns' (perfectly at home in Suárez's understanding of the relationship between the intellect and actual existing things) were central to Kleutgen's Thomism. Although this does not appear in the text of the encyclical itself, 'Aquinas was presented as the author of one more system confronting the questions of Cartesian and post-Cartesian epistemology', and in so doing, Kleutgen and his many followers 'doomed Thomism to the fate of all philosophies which give priority to epistemological questions: the indefinite multiplication of disagreement'.[5]

I am not a professional philosopher, nor a professional theologian, my academic training having being mainly as a Semitic philologist. But as a pastor of the Church I try to keep my eyes open, and to understand as well as possible the world in which I live. I am not in a position to judge, for instance, how much the thought of Suárez owes to Duns Scotus or the Nominalists, or how much Scotus himself owes to Avicenna. But I am very much aware that the division between nature and the supernatural has made, in the long run, the event of Jesus Christ irrelevant for our real humanity: an ornament, an option, something added to this humanity. This is a tragic thing, and not only for the Church, but equally so for the world, because the destiny of the Church and that of the world are mysteriously tied up together forever since the Easter morning. I am painfully conscious, however, that most of us Catholics in Spain are not aware of this, because one almost unavoidable effect of the division between a 'natural' and a 'supernatural order' is the identification of the natural order with what is left when you take away Christianity (or what from such a division you can think Christianity is). And this means that 'nature' is identified with a particular culture, or with a particular social order. In

---

4 MacIntyre, *Three Rival Versions*, p. 73.
5 MacIntyre, *Three Rival Versions*, p. 75.

Foreword

other words, the mind is left unarmed from the Christian experience, from the Christian event, from the knowledge of God that comes from Jesus Christ as it is handed down in the sacred tradition and is lived in the communion of the Church, and from these becomes unable to 'judge' any given social order, any given 'human science', in the end, anything human – anything.[6] To put it still differently, after this division and the inability to see the world from the faith that comes from it, the Church is ready for ideological consumption, and to become, on one hand, an ideology or the institutional support for one, and on the other, the target of the best arguments in the critique of religion of the nineteenth and twentieth centuries, arguments that focus precisely in the Church being just that.

I came across the work of John Milbank in the most convoluted of ways, by reading Gavin D'Costa's work, *The Meeting of Religions and the Trinity*, which draws significantly on Milbank's thought in his analysis of the liberal concept of tolerance.[7] Fascinated by his references to MacIntyre and Milbank, and in the context of the concerns I have just put forward, you can imagine my joy when I started reading Milbank's *Theology and Social Theory*, and I could see there a *theological* critique of the Enlightenment, and of the present consequences of the Enlightenment's failure.[8] Before I had only seen something like that in the theological works of de Lubac and Balthasar, almost as a demand derived from their theological positions. I had also met many true elements of that critique (but never in such a systematic way) in some prophets of our time, such as G. K. Chesterton, Georges Bernanos and Charles Péguy. I dare say that I have also seen an attempt to recuperate the essential elements of the Christian

---

6 I honestly think that Suárez's dualism (and with it the fractures of modernity) are overcome by the Church's teaching in two key texts of Vatican II: *Lumen gentium*, §1, and *Gaudium et spes*, § 21. But this does not mean at all that these teachings have been incorporated to the Church's life, and even less that they have become a new starting point for the thinking or the daily life of the Church.

7 Gavin D'Costa, *The Meeting of Religions and the Trinity* (Maryknoll, NY: Orbis Books, 2000).

8 John Milbank, *Theology and Social Theory: Beyond Secular Reason* (Oxford: Blackwell, 1990; 2nd edn 2005).

experience beyond the fragmentations of modernity, where that critique is assumed and transformed into a positive *criterium* for a pedagogical method, in the writings of Luigi Giussani and in the Communion and Liberation movement founded by him.

You can easily understand what an immense honour it is for myself, and for the very small team of teachers and workers engaged in putting together this 'Edith Stein Institute of Philosophy' (which is only a year old; it was founded on 9 August 2005, feast day of the holy Theresia Benedicta of the Cross [Edith Stein], patroness of Europe), in having such a significant group of great thinkers, professors and students, gathered here to discuss and to talk freely about a topic as politically incorrect and seemingly uninteresting as it is necessary and urgent to get out from the 'moral wilderness' where we all live now.

I wholeheartedly want to thank first of all Professor John Milbank, who conceived this idea of gathering in Granada in the first place, and believed also in our capacity to host this conference. I thank also Dr Conor Cunningham who has put upon himself, together with Guillermo Peris, the heavy material task of putting together the programme, and dealing with registrations, and all that having to work from two bases, one in Nottingham and another in Granada. The fact that we are all here and they are both alive is, I can assure you, a proof that 'an ontology of gift' is not a utopia, and it is much more than a beautiful phrase.

Although they are not all here, I cannot but thank, and for exactly the same reason, a whole little army of volunteers that have helped or will help in many ways to make possible our gathering (and make it, I hope, also very pleasant).

I am convinced that in the advancement of the kind of inquiry we are going to be working here, a lot of things in the future of the Church and of the world are at stake. I am also convinced that friendship (real friendship, not just academic competition) is an absolute precondition for any serious theological or philosophical inquiry. My wish and my prayer at this point is exactly this: if these days that give us the blessing and the opportunity of listening to one another and working together would in the end have helped all of us to be better friends, to discuss and to debate as passionately and as freely as friends can do, our main goal will be achieved. The fruits of that friendship are not in our hands. But the reasons for a real hope, for a hope with no delusion, will have been greatly increased. In fact, those reasons are already here. Charles Péguy mentioned happiness and mercy as conditions for hope. In *Le Porche du Mystère de la deuxième vertu* he wrote, 'To be able to hope, my daughter, it is necessary to be truly happy, it is necessary to have obtained, to have received, a great mercy.' Happiness and friendship (and true freedom) go together. Our meeting these days is not just an immense privilege. Think that, perhaps only fifteen years ago, a meeting like this, so spontaneous and, I would say, in a certain sense, so informal, around such a set of questions like the ones raised by the title 'Belief and Metaphysics', in the classrooms of a Catholic Seminary in Southern Spain, would have been unthinkable, at least for many of us. It is the kind of God's gift that makes us hope.

Contributors

Daniel M. Bell, Jr. is Associate Professor of Theological Ethics and Director of Methodist Studies at Lutheran Theological Southern Seminary. He has published many articles and is the author of *Liberation Theology After the End of History: The Refusal to Cease Suffering (Radical Orthodoxy Series)* (2001), and the forthcoming *Justice* for the *Interventions* series (Eerdmans).

John R. Betz is Assistant Professor of Theology at Loyola College, Maryland. He has published many articles on theology and philosophy and is author of the forthcoming *After Enlightenment: The Post-Secular Vision of J. G. Hamann* (*Illuminations*, Blackwell), and *Beyond the Sublime: A Metaphysics of Glory and Glorification*.

Oliva Blanchette is Professor of Philosophy at Boston College. He is the author of *Philosophy of Being: A Reconstructive Essay in Metaphysics* (2003), *The Perfection of the Universe According to Thomas Aquinas: A Teleological Cosmology* (1992) and is translator of Maurice Blondel's *Action* (1893).

David Burrell C.S.C. is Theodore M. Hesburgh, C.S.C. Professor in Philosophy and Theology at the University of Notre Dame. His books include *Faith and Freedom: An Interfaith Perspective* (2004), *Freedom and Creation in Three Traditions* (1993), *Knowing the Unknowable God: Ibn Sina, Maimonides, Aquinas* (1986), *Aquinas: God and Action* (1979), *Exercises in Religious Understanding* (1974) and *Analogy and Philosophical Language* (1973).

Conor Cunningham is lecturer in Philosophy of Religion at the

Contributors

University of Nottingham and is Assistant Director of the Centre of Theology and Philosophy. He is author of *Genealogy of Nihilism* (2002), which has now been translated into Spanish, and *Evolution: Darwin's Pious Idea* (*Interventions*, 2008). Along with Peter Candler, he is the series editor of *Veritas* (SCM Press) and *Interventions* (Eerdmans).

William Desmond is Professor of Philosophy at the Katholieke Universiteit Leuven. He is the author of many books, including *Is There a Sabbath for Thought? Between Religion and Philosophy* (2005), *Hegel's God: A Counterfeit Double?*, *Ethics and the Between* (2001), *Being and the Between* (1995) and the forthcoming *God and the Between* (*Illuminations*, 2007).

Louis Dupré is T. Lawrason Riggs Professor of the Philosophy of Religion at Yale University. A graduate of the University of Louvain in Belgium, he has received honorary doctorates from Loyola College, Sacred Heart University and Georgetown University as well as the Aquinas Medal from the American Catholic Philosophical Association. Besides studies on Hegel, Marx and Kierkegaard, his books include *The Enlightenment and the Intellectual Foundations of Modern Culture* (2005), *Symbols of the Sacred* (2000), *Religious Mystery and Rational Reflection: Excursions in the Phenomenology and Philosophy of Religion* (1997) and *Passage to Modernity: An Essay in the Hermeneutics of Nature and Culture* (1993).

Vittorio Hösle is currently Paul Kimball Professor of Arts and Letters at the University of Notre Dame in the Departments of German, Philosophy and Political Science. He is the author of countless books, most notably, *Woody Allen: an Essay on the Nature of the Comical* (2007), *Darwinism & Philosophy* (2005), *Morals and Politics* (with Christian Illies) (2004), *Philosophie und Öffentlichkeit. Das Informationspotential der Röntgenstrahlen* (2003), *The Dead Philosophers' Cafe: An Exchange of Letters for Children and Adults* (2000), *Darwin* (with Christian Illies) (1999), *Objective Idealism, Ethics, and Politics* (1998) and *Hegel's System*, 2 Vols (1988).

Contributors

Eric Lee is in the Master of Arts in Religion program at Point Loma Nazarene University in San Diego, California, and plans on beginning a PhD program in the latter half of 2008. His research interests are in philosophical theology, Christian ethics, and metaphysics.

Jonathan Lowe is Professor of Philosophy at Durham University, specializing in metaphysics, philosophy of mind and action, philosophy of logic and language, and the philosophy of John Locke. His books include *Kinds of Being* (1989), *Subjects of Experience* (1996), *The Possibility of Metaphysics* (1998), *Locke* (2005) and *The Four-Category Ontology* (2006).

Sean McGrath is an Assistant Professor at Memorial University of Newfoundland. He is the author of *The Early Heidegger and Medieval Philosophy: Phenomenology for the Godforsaken* (2006), as well as articles on Heidegger, Lonergan, Aquinas and Boehme. McGrath is currently working on a new book, entitled *Heidegger. A Very Critical Introduction* for the *Interventions* series (Eerdmans).

John Milbank has taught at the universities of Cambridge and Virginia, and is currently Professor of Politics, Religion and Ethics at the University of Nottingham, and Director of the Centre of Theology and Philosophy, also at Nottingham. He is author of numerous articles and books, many of which have been translated into a number of languages. His most notable works include *Theology and Social Theory* (2nd edition, 2006), *The Suspended Middle* (2005), *Being Reconciled* (2003), *Truth in Aquinas* (with Catherine Pickstock) (2000), *The Word Made Strange* (1997) and the forthcoming volume *Proposing Theology* (*Veritas*, SCM Press). Professor Milbank is also series editor of *Radical Orthodoxy* (Routledge) and *Illuminations* (Blackwell).

Marcus Pound is a lecturer in Theology at the University of Durham. He is the author of *Theology, Psychoanalysis and Trauma* (*Veritas*, 2007), and the forthcoming *Žižek: A Very Critical Introduction* for the *Interventions* series (Eerdmans).

Contributors

Michael Rea is Associate Professor of Philosophy and Associate Director of the Center for Philosophy of Religion at the University of Notre Dame. He is the author of *World Without Design* (2002), co-author (with Michael Murray) of *An Introduction to Philosophy of Religion* (2007) and co-editor (with Thomas Flint) of *The Oxford Handbook of Philosophical Theology* (2008).

Patrick Riches is a doctoral candidate at the Centre of Theology and Philosophy at the University of Nottingham.

Philipp W. Rosemann is Associate Professor of Philosophy at the University of Dallas. He works at the intersection of medieval thought and Continental philosophy. As such, he is the author of a Lacanian reading of the thought of Thomas Aquinas, *Omne ens est aliquid: introduction à la lecture du 'système' philosophique de saint Thomas d'Aquin* (1996), and of *Understanding Scholastic Thought with Foucault* (1999). His most recent books are an introduction to the theology of Peter Lombard (2004) and a study of how medieval and early modern theology developed in the commentaries on Peter Lombard's famous *Book of Sentences*: *The Story of a Great Medieval Book: Peter Lombard's 'Sentences'* (2007). Currently, he is preparing a volume on transgression for the *Interventions* series (Eerdmans).

Neil Turnbull is Senior Lecturer in Philosophy and Social Theory at Nottingham Trent University and one of the editors of the journal *Theory, Culture & Society*. He is currently writing a book on Philosophy and Everyday Life.

Paul Tyson is a doctoral candidate at the Queensland University of Technology. His research concerns the nature of truth in Western culture, and is particularly interested in 'faith and reason' in Plato, and how that might relate to contemporary post-secular approaches to truth, in particular, to 'Radical Orthodoxy'. It is to the memory of Paul's daughter, Lucy, that this volume is dedicated.

Rudi te Velde is Radboud Professor in the relations between philosophy and Christianity at University of Amsterdam and he

Contributors

lectures in philosophy at University of Tilburg. He is the author of *Participation and Substantiality in Thomas Aquinas* (1995) and *Aquinas on God* (2006), as well as a forthcoming book, *Participation,* for the *Interventions* series (Eerdmans).

James Williams is Professor of Philosophy at the University of Dundee. His many publications include, *The Transversal Thought of Gilles Deleuze* (2005), *Understanding Poststructuralism* (2005), *Gilles Deleuze's Difference and Repetition: A Critical Introduction and Guide* (2003), *Lyotard and the Political* (2000), and *Lyotard* (1998).

Acknowledgments

This volume is the result of the Centre of Theology and Philosophy's second annual conference, which took place in September 2006, in Granada, Spain, at the Instituto de Filosofía Edith Stein – a truly wonderful place to exercise the intellect and rest the soul. We would very much like to take this opportunity to thank all those who helped to make that event the fantastic success that it turned out to be: first of all a special thanks to our colleagues at the Centre in Nottingham, Philip Goodchild and Karen Kilby. Others to whom we owe sincere thanks include Louis Dupré, David Burrell, David Cooper, Marcus Pound, Graham Ward, James Williams, Simon Conway-Morris, Merold Westphal, Oliva Blanchette, Ira Brent Driggers, Chris Hackett, Rosie Fraser, Neil Turnbull, Tony Baker, and Michael Rea. In addition, we would like to express our thanks to the indefatigable and tireless staff at SCM, particularly Barbara Laing, Mary Matthews, Laurence Osborn, and Roger Ruston; all at Red Roof Designs, especially Sara Cunningham-Bell, Murray Bell, and Eric Lee; and a special thanks to Aaron Patrick Riches and Anthony Paul Smith for all their hard work, and support. Our deep gratitude also to Guillermo Peris, whose vision, industry and patience, was essential to the entire project. Similarly, we are deeply grateful to 'the girls' at the Instituto, who tolerated us all with great grace, and in truth ran the whole show in Granada. Our profound thanks go to Archbishop Javier Martinez, without whose support, encouragement and warmth of spirit the conference would have been impossible. Mgr Martínez's stunningly intelligent faith and childlike hope remains a true inspiration to us all. Lastly, we would like to thank John Milbank, whose intelligence, support, enthusiasm, and willingness to put his hand to any task, no matter how menial, remains exemplary. And who will ever forget his 'Soup discourse'?

Peter M. Candler, Jr and Conor Cunningham

Introduction

The Return of Metaphysics

Could it turn out that nobody has ever believed anything?
Paul Churchland

Metaphysics always buries its undertakers.
Étienne Gilson

This volume is the first fruit of an ongoing research project being conducted at the Centre of Theology and Philosophy, entitled *The Return of Metaphysics*. In an effort to contextualize the motivation behind many of the chapters that follow, it may be helpful to outline the main lines of investigation that constitute this project.

As traditionally practised by Plato and subsequent philosophers, metaphysics united a range of disciplines and approaches in order to try to answer fundamental questions about the nature of being and knowing. But in a long process culminating in twentieth-century thought, philosophy, both analytic and Continental, has tended to confine metaphysical reflection to questions of method, of the precisely knowable and the a priori range of logical and cognitive possibility. Because, in the main, philosophy in the modern period has been preoccupied with epistemology, questions of ultimate reality and causality have been increasingly bracketed, thus separating philosophy from theology and science from religion. It needs to be asked again whether these developments were strictly 'critical' in character and whether some of their effects have not been deleterious for accounts of reason and faith.

Late nineteenth- and twentieth-century philosophy was characterized by an unprecedented critique and often rejection of metaphysics, above all in the works of Friedrich Nietzsche and Martin Heidegger. For the last thirty years or so however, metaphysics has shown signs of returning, within both the analytic and the

Introduction

Continental traditions. Why did this development and counter-development take place? Did metaphysics decline because of the need for philosophy to justify itself as a specific science? Was the decline also to do with the need to sustain a polite secular neutrality between the competing claims of naturalism and religion? Was the 'anti-psychologistic' rejection of naturalism by both Husserl and Frege really justified? Concomitantly, has metaphysics returned in the wake of decisive critiques of the 'scientific' mode of philosophy, whether phenomenological, logical positivist or linguistic analytical? Have these critiques also undermined 'agnosticism' between religion and naturalism? In theology, has the post-Heideggerian appeal to 'narrative' been able to prevent itself, in its more anti-metaphysical moments, from suspicions of fideistic relativism? And is this in part why we now see the return of dogmatic scientism on the one hand and more publicly expressed religious outlooks on the other?

Moreover, it might also be asked whether or not, after Nietzsche, the metaphysical ghost has really been exorcised from philosophy. It is in fact arguable that the anti-metaphysical tradition for which he is sometimes held responsible is already itself a metaphysical project. That tradition might be simply summarized by saying that we cannot know what really is; we can only know the appearances of things. All pretensions to 'reality as it is in itself', so the argument goes, are but expressions of one's own will-to-power. But even here, at its most apparently non-metaphysical juncture, it is evident that there can be no 'revaluation of all values' that is not a revaluation of being itself. And yet vanquishing God's shadow, in Nietzsche's view, meant a new story of being itself, understood now as will-to-power.

But Nietzsche was not alone in thinking that once we have gotten rid of the Christian God, then we can be done with metaphysics. For some philosophers, the latter is simply the residue of the former; Nietzsche himself quite rightly points out that many *theologians* in fact elide one with the other, neglecting the historical character of the Judeo-Christian tradition. Hence Heidegger's famous description of 'onto-theology', whereby theology has subordinated itself to a prior account of being. But in some ways it would seem that all announcements of the 'end of metaphysics' were somewhat premature. It might turn out that, as Maurice

Introduction

Blondel once wrote, 'One cannot exclude metaphysics except by a metaphysical critique.'[1] For if, as Blondel said, citing Aristotle, if we must give up on philosophy, we must still practise it.

The long-range research project of which the present volume is an important instance will have a twofold focus, evident here in these essays: historical/analytical and constructive/creative. The initial thrust of the research programme will be to identify and investigate those decisive moments in the history of philosophy – for instance John Duns Scotus's adoption of the univocity of being, William of Ockham's prioritization of will over intellect, Descartes' method of universal doubt, Cajetan's reading of Aquinas, Suárez's conception of the twofold end of humanity, or Hume's divorce of faith and reason, to name a few – when choices were made which encouraged the cultural demise of a broader conception of metaphysics. Subsequent research will then concentrate upon exploring the consequences of these choices and developing an alternative model for metaphysics. It is worth pointing out here that this involves no romantic picture of a pristine period in which theology was practiced in a 'pure' way, and after which the rot set in. Theology as practised by Thomas Aquinas may be in many ways paradigmatic, but it is not immune to criticism, and it is possible that even within his work there are certain *aporiai* that make possible – in lesser minds – the fissures which were to open up later.

It is nevertheless true that there is no *single* moment in intellectual history which could account for the shifts – seismic in proportion but perhaps so slight as to be undetectable at the time – from, say, the Middle Ages to the modern or post-Christian period. To affirm that such a shift or series of shifts has taken place is not, however, to deny that there is a certain historical continuity at work here as well; hence one may describe such historical as shifts and not breaks, even if, in retrospect, what separates our philosophical presuppositions from those of Plato or Aquinas is a chasm, the fruit of generations of subtle shifts in thought, resulting, to put it one way, a rupture in being. Still, having said all this, we can say with confidence that some of the moves mentioned above have been more decisive than others.

---

1 Maurice Blondel, *Action (1893)*, tr. Oliva Blanchette (Notre Dame: Notre Dame University Press, 1984), p. 358.

Introduction

This is perhaps most apparent in the rupture between faith and reason. In relation to God, faith cannot abandon reason, nor theology, philosophy. But when theology properly makes use of philosophy, the latter becomes transformed. For as Aquinas says, 'Those who use philosophical texts in sacred teaching, by subjecting them to faith, do not mix water with wine, but turn water into wine.'[2] Indeed he says further that 'It is necessary that natural reason be subservient to faith'.[3] Why must it be? Well, as Rudi te Velde has said, 'If reason were justified in its claim to autonomy the only way Christianity could affirm its faith would be by rejecting reason.'[4] For such autonomy would then become a counterfeit God, so to speak,[5] as reason would offer itself as a competitor to God. But also, reason left to its own cannot cope with what is most fundamental in life. This is why we see a great deal of philosophy do away with many phenomena, rather than remain in a state of unknowing with regard to their possibility, and the complexity of their existence. From consciousness to colour, we witness a wholesale cull in the name of parsimony – the economy being here one of philosophy's own ability. The consequences of leaving reason to itself are epitomized by the philosophy of Paul Churchland – an advocate of eliminative materialism, who asks: 'Could it turn out that nobody has ever believed anything?'[6] Here we see why we cannot simply ask philosophy if it believes in the existence of God, when it does not even believe in belief!

During the last 30 years, historians of thought have transformed our understanding of the history of metaphysics. Phenomenologically inclined historians tend to trace the genealogy of Heidegger's diagnosis of metaphysics as 'onto-theology', meaning the circular co-implication of 'being' defined as the general fact of being on the one hand, and 'being' as defined in terms of a supreme being and causal source of all finite being on the other. Analytically

---

2 *Commentary on the* De Trinitate *of Boethius*, 2.4, ad 5.

3 *Summa Theologiae* I, q. 1, a. 8, ad 2.

4 Rudi te Velde, 'Natural Reason in the *Summa Contra Gentiles*', *Medieval Philosophy and Theology* 4 (1994), pp. 42–70, at p. 58.

5 On the notion of a counterfeit God, see William Desmond, *Hegel's God: A Counterfeit Double?* (London: Ashgate, 2003).

6 Paul Churchland, *Matter and Consciousness*, revised edition (Cambridge, MA: MIT Press, 1988), p. 43.

Introduction

inclined historians, by contrast, tend to focus on the issue of 'modality' and in particular the supposed 'liberation' of possibility from the assumption of the priority of actuality in Aristotle. Yet in either case there is now widespread agreement that the pivotal figure in the history of Western philosophy is Duns Scotus rather than Kant. Crucially, his theses of the univocity of being, the formal distinction, and individuation by *haecceitas* together established both onto-theology and the primacy of the possible over the actual. However, the question so far not fully explored is the degree to which this shift was less a matter of pure philosophical argument and more a matter of theological discussion. Moreover, what requires examination is the extent to which this theological change was reinforced by shifts in religious and cultural sensibility, which tended to think of the world as now more alien from God, and of God himself as more the exerciser of will-power than as triune charity, both the ground and the beyond of reason. While these philosophical shifts encouraged the growth of secularism, there is a need to probe further the paradox that they may, nevertheless, have been decisively encouraged by changes in theological outlook.

It seems that we now live in a period marked by both (strict) naturalism and fideism and the struggle between the two. It is worth asking whether this is in part because of a need to fill a void left by the neglect of metaphysics in the twentieth century. Is there actually a social and cultural requirement for metaphysics in the sense of an unavoidable imperative to express fundamental presuppositions about human and natural existence? Is human culture as such based upon such expressions? Hence, today, by default, has this task fallen to over-speculative scientists on the one hand and religious extremists on the other? One could interpret these groups in terms both of the return of metaphysics and the emergence of an *ersatz* metaphysics in the face of the absence of something more sophisticated.

It is also worth asking whether there is a crucial need for metaphysics to mediate between pure reason and pure faith. Perhaps the notion that reason does not need to be supplemented by faith has led to a dangerous dogmatism of reason. On the other hand, a refusal of the idea that religious intuition can still be guided by rational discussion may encourage fanatical and violent modes of religiosity. We may need metaphysics both to mediate between

Introduction

different faiths and to discriminate between wise and unwise modes of religiosity. Equally though, we may need metaphysics in order to defend certain features of our commonsense perception of the world against the ravages of a dogmatic science which would claim that the things we perceive, besides human will and consciousness as such, are in some sense illusions. This equally threatens to undermine an ethical humanism.

The essays in this collection betray a wide variety of approaches to the relation between belief and metaphysics, from the phenomenological to the analytic, the literary to the scientific, the strictly philosophical to the more explicitly theological. The diversity of this collection is emblematic of the work of the Centre more broadly, and especially of the character of its conferences, which bring together a broad range of thinkers from different traditions, but all of whom are committed in one way or another to the ongoing task of thinking theology and philosophy together. Many of these essays also illustrate differences of thought on the aforementioned genealogy of modern philosophy, but are also generally united in their common suspicion of the modern divorce between reason and faith.

In a paper presented at the Granada conference, Angel Mendez, OP offered a critique of Isak Dinesen's short story, *Babette's Feast*, in the service of what he calls a theology of alimentation.[7] He argued that theology, properly understood and properly done, involves (indeed, *is*) a kind of nourishing festivity, because of the central Christian doctrine of creation, which proposes that everything that is is the gift of a superabundantly generous God, who creates out of no need of his own. In the story, a guest and old friend of the Lutheran community comes to visit his old friends, and enjoy the sumptuous feast prepared by Babette with the ten thousand francs she has recently won in the Paris lottery. After dinner – a meal as unnecessary and gratuitous as it is generous – General Lowenhielm rises and quotes the Psalmist: 'Mercy and truth, my friends, have met together . . . Righteousness and bliss shall kiss one another.'[8]

---

7 Isak Dinesen, 'Babette's Feast', in *Anecdotes of Destiny and Ehrengard* (New York: Vintage, 1993), pp. 19–59.
8 Dinesen, 'Babette's Feast', p. 52.

Introduction

That alimentary spirit, we believe, animated the gathering in Granada, and animates this collection as well. We hope that this is a fortunate sign of the future of the meeting of theology and philosophy. It is perhaps more than an odd coincidence that, during lunch on 16 September, in the middle of the conference, Guillermo Peris – who did so much to imbue the event with his joyful spirit – announced that the speech which Pope Benedict had given in Regensburg a few days before, on the 12th, had caused something of a firestorm of negative reaction across Europe, resulting in a variety of dangerous threats to Christians around the world, including the Pope himself. After lunch, copies of the speech were made available to the conference participants so that we could read for ourselves the controversial address.

Standing in the hallway of the seminary, reading the Regensburg address, one could not help but be struck by the uncanny sense of synchronicity between the Pope's injunction for the re-hellenization of Christian faith and of reason and the common conviction of participants of our own conference. The Holy Father particularly seemed to hit a common nerve in his plea for the 'courage to engage the whole breadth of reason' beyond the voluntarism he diagnosed, not only in certain forms of Protestant Christianity and in Islam, but also in the Catholic nominalism of Scotus (whom he explicitly named in the address). The reduction of reason to the 'empirically falsifiable' on the one hand, and religion to pure fideism on the other, so Benedict argued, had lead to unmediated conceptions of 'truth' that had necessarily foreclosed dialogical communication, giving way simultaneously to the dictatorship of relativism in liberal 'secular' sphere, and fundamentalist religion in the now purely 'sacred' sphere. Thus the Pope's charge: only the mediation of the grandeur of reason could make possible the genuine dialogue of cultures and communication between peoples that our world so desperately needs.

Needless to say, much of the conversation about the Regensburg address in the halls of the seminary, under luminous, Goya-esque skies outside the café down the street, and in the tapas bars around the Plaza de Toros after the sessions was vigorous, though hardly contentious (they even provoked an op-ed piece on the speech in *The International Herald Tribune* by Phillip Blond[9]). It is difficult to imagine theology being more, in Jean Daniélou's terms, *actuelle*.

Introduction

Many who were there found the kind of conviviality a refreshing respite from the often more mundane activities of professional academic life; but more than that, such a level of philosophical and theological reflection and of festivity necessarily go together. We mention these episodes as examples of the kind of intellectual community that can arrive, however briefly, under such conditions. Just as one cannot do metaphysics without theology, and vice versa, there is no real knowledge where there is not at least a form of real friendship. One cannot feast alone.

In his Foreword to this volume, Archbishop Javier Martínez writes that 'friendship (real friendship, not just academic competition) is an absolute precondition for any serious theological or philosophical inquiry'. We are pleased to say that in many ways, his hopes that 'the blessing and the opportunity of listening to one another and working together would in the end have helped all of us to be better friends, to discuss and to debate as passionately and as freely as friends' proved to have been, in some small part, realized. It is, of course, for the reader to decide the extent to which this spirit is similarly realized in the chapters that follow. The fruitful conversation for which the Archbishop expressed his hopes in his Foreword did indeed emerge, and will, *deo volente*, go on, specifically at the next conference of the Centre – in Rome 2008 – which will address itself to the challenges put forward by the Pope's speech in Regensburg. But at the very least, the event in Granada, and the pages which follow, we believe, are grounds for hope in a new form of life – intellectual, carnal and spiritual – of which we were honoured to partake in the warm company of Andalucía.

To gloss the Psalmist, we hope that reason and faith might meet together, in a new way.

Peter Candler and Conor Cunningham
The Feast of St Dominic, Priest and Friar
8 August 2007

---

9 Phillip Blond, 'It's all about faith and reason', *International Herald Tribune*, 19 September 2006, online at http://www.iht.com/articles/2006/09/19/opinion/edblond.php

1. Belief and Metaphysics

LOUIS DUPRÉ

I shall use the term 'belief' in the religious sense, as an equivalent of faith, even though belief has a more cognitive connotation than faith, which includes trust and confidence. A second preliminary principle concerns the relation between religious belief and theology. To be comparable with or related to metaphysics, religious belief needs to be at least minimally interpreted and justified. The believer must have some notion of what it implies and ought to conceive of it as logically coherent. All of this requires some theological interpretation. Hence, in the following discussion I shall focus on faith as raised to the level of theological reflection.

The Unity of Theology and Metaphysics in the Past and their Separation in the Modern Age

When Kant in the *Critique of Pure Reason* reduced philosophy to epistemology he not only eliminated metaphysics from its scope but theology as well. As he stated in the Introduction, he intended to leave to faith what previously had belonged to science. Already Descartes had separated philosophy from any kind of theological speculation. In a letter concerning the dogma of the Eucharistic presence, he wrote: 'I abstain as far as I can from questions of theology'.[1] In this respect the father of modern philosophy merely drew the conclusions from late medieval, nominalist theology,

---

1 *Oeuvres*, ed. Adam & Tannery (Paris: Vrin, 1964), Vol. IV, pp. 162–70.

which had sharply distinguished the natural order of things, to which philosophy belonged, from the supernatural one dealt with in theology. God's transcendence and unrestricted power excluded any possibility of predicting or understanding his ways with creation. The present world order was the outcome of a divine decree that had no intrinsic necessity and could be changed as arbitrarily as it had been initiated. Theology had to rely entirely on revelation and received no more than logical support from philosophy.

1   In high scholasticism no such separation between philosophy and theology had existed. Aquinas had called his synthesis of revelation with Aristotelian, Neoplatonic and Arabian philosophy *Summa Theologiae*. He had distinguished 'natural' virtues from supernatural ones and had even recognized a natural end to the person, which he described in Aristotelian and Stoic terms. But 'natural' virtue is incomplete and the 'natural' end of human beings remains subordinate to the more comprehensive, supernatural one. Yet this distinction between the natural and the supernatural is purely functional. Taken by itself the 'natural' is an abstraction. The great Franciscan teachers Bonaventure and Scotus integrated the two orders of discourse even more intimately.

2   For the ancient philosophers, Plato, Aristotle and Plotinus, distinction between natural and supernatural had, of course, not existed. We may nevertheless compare the continuity between the human and the divine order as conceived by those pre-Christian philosophers with the one that prevailed in the Greek fathers and the scholastics. For Plato and Plotinus, the erotic drive of thought originates in an attraction derived from a transcendental source. Aristotle in *De anima* describes the active principle of the human intellect as divine. In order to think, he argues, the mind needs the impulse of a principle that has never ceased thinking. This can only be divine. Indeed, the soul itself, once freed from the passivity of the body, will become divinized. In the tenth Book of the *Nicomachean Ethics*, Aristotle describes contemplation, the goal of philosophy, as a properly divine activity. Beyond the internal dialogue that the mind entertains with itself, it aims at an intuitive state, which reasoning merely prepares. Again, he insists that such

a state surpasses human capacity. The person attains it only 'insofar as something divine is present in him; and by so much as this is superior to our composite nature, its activity is superior to the exercise of the other kind of virtue. If reason is divine in comparison with man, the life according to it is divine in comparison with human life' (*Nic. Ethics*, X, 7, 5 (1177B)).

3   The highest state of consciousness, then, for classical philosophers as well as for Christian thinkers of the High Middle Ages, implied some kind of divine communication with human nature. The very possibility of communicating with God arouses a 'natural' desire for God. Yet the alleged object of this desire, the *religious* idea of God, originates neither in philosophy nor in any other natural mode of cognition, but in a divine *revelation*. Philosophy merely encounters this idea, which precedes philosophical reflection. But then the problem occurs: How can we speak of a 'natural' desire for a 'revealed' idea?

(a) If philosophy ought to be an autonomous science that tolerates no interference from other sources, as modern thinkers have increasingly emphasized, a revealed idea of God should have no place in philosophy. At most, philosophy may admit some notion of transcendence. The religious idea of God, derived from a pre-philosophical source, appeared perfectly acceptable to pre-modern thinkers, who distinguished the natural from the supernatural but did not separate them. In the *Summa contra Gentiles* Aquinas argues that each being seeks to achieve the fullness of its nature. Thus a spiritual being naturally desires the divine qualities of goodness and truth but its limited capacity prohibits it from ever fully attaining them. The desire, then, Thomas concludes, is natural, but its full realization surpasses natural human power.

(b) One might think that Platonic philosophy makes a similar claim. But the object of Platonic desire differs from Aquinas's supernatural object. Plato's idea of the Good, as well as Aristotle's Unmoved Mover and Plotinus' One attract the mind, not because they have been *revealed*, or because they intend to attract. The object of the desire they evoke remains wholly indifferent to that desire. The Good or the One entertains no active relation to our world – nor has it freely created that world.

(c) Modern thought finds it exceedingly difficult to conceive of a natural desire for a revealed and hence supernatural Absolute. Both philosophical and theological reasons prevent it from doing so. Philosophy tolerates no interference from non-philosophical sources. The resistance is equally strong in modern theology, which has separated nature and the supernatural. If the notion of a natural desire of God nevertheless occurs in such modern philosophers as Nicholas Malebranche or in the Cambridge Platonists, it could do so only because these authors ignored the restrictions of modern philosophy as well as those of a theology influenced by nominalism. With Kant these restrictions became even tighter: not only would revealed concepts not be admitted into philosophy (unless previously converted into philosophical ones) but metaphysics itself, which made the communication possible, was exorcized from critical philosophy.

The Way to Reunion

1   On this last point three of Kant's wayward followers disagreed and with them begins a new attempt to reintroduce religious and even revealed ideas into philosophy. J. G. Fichte attacked what he considered an inconsistency of his master who, on the one hand, denied the possibility of an intellectual intuition (the basic condition of metaphysics) and, on the other, grounded his ethical theory in the intuition of an absolute ethical imperative. Schelling shared Fichte's concern, and, in addition, objected to Kant's position that the mind has no intuitive knowledge of nature. Both idealists re-established the legitimacy of metaphysics. Yet they all the more strongly stressed the autonomy of philosophy. They did not formally exclude divine revelation from philosophy, but they submitted the concept of revelation to such stringent philosophical conditions that they practically transformed it into an intrinsically philosophical one.

Hegel may have come closest to recognizing revealed faith on its own terms. He claimed to have derived the entire content of his philosophy from Christian faith. Yet that faith, he argued, does not attain full self-understanding until it has transferred to *thought* what religion merely *represents*. His position may appear to apply

Belief and Metaphysics

Augustine's rule that faith must seek understanding (*fides quaerens intellectum*). For Hegel, however, philosophy does not merely reflect on faith: he transposes its content into a different mode of consciousness. It thereby loses its receptive capacity altogether and returns philosophy to its purely autonomous status.

2   None of the proposed attempts, then, to reunite metaphysics with religious belief while preserving each one's identity succeeded. In the twentieth century two developments changed the situation. First, the birth of phenomenology, especially after it developed into the hermeneutic philosophies of Heidegger, Gadamer and Ricoeur. The issue was no longer whether metaphysics could incorporate faith or be incorporated by it. Phenomenologists remained acutely aware of the methodological limits of philosophy. Yet they felt that the Kantian rules unduly restricted philosophy's ability to fulfil its proper task, namely, a systematic, yet comprehensive search of meaning. In his *Critique*, Kant had limited the field of meaning to a justification of morality, aesthetics and the natural sciences. But all these sciences raise more general and more fundamental questions which philosophy ought to address.

Metaphysics investigates the meaning-giving fact on which all meanings depend, namely the self-disclosure of Being. This must be done through an analysis of human existence in which Being reveals itself. Metaphysics, then, has as its task to investigate all forms of meaning, including the one of religion, which opens a unique problem. Unlike the positive sciences or even, in a different way, ethics and aesthetics, religion can claim no incontrovertible empirical certainties. To be sure, Christian faith may refer to the historical, established facts of its origin. But, as Lessing had objected, how reliable are alleged facts recorded centuries before historical critique had fully developed?

To be sure, the hermeneutical principle that fact and interpretation are indissolubly united definitely applies in religious matters, where all 'facts' carry a symbolic meaning. But what are the facts of the Christian faith? Kierkegaard, a committed Christian believer, once wrote that historically they amount to a footnote: during the reign of Emperor Tiberius a Jew in Palestine died for his religious beliefs and on the basis of his deeds and doctrine was believed to be divine. All the rest is interpretation. But how far can we stretch religious interpretation without breaking the meaning altogether? More importantly, do those facts justify the transcendent significance faith attaches to them? Even if I accept Christ's resurrection as a proven fact, why should that affect my entire philosophical outlook?

The author of a recent essay on 'Philosophy and Theology' suggests a possible answer to these questions in Paul Ricoeur's late philosophy.[2] The Christian philosopher ought to treat the content of faith as a hypothesis and then investigate how much this hypothesis contributes to a deeper understanding of human existence. Of course, this approach does not disclose the ultimate meaning of faith. Religious mysteries furnish conceptual paradigms to philosophy. Philosophy does not try to 'prove' them. Metaphysics belongs to a different kind of intelligibility than the discourse of religion. Above all, metaphysics does not attempt to demonstrate their truth, because they have nothing to do with demonstrations.[3] But at least such a *Daseinsanalyse* forces metaphysics to take religious belief seriously.

Once the question of meaning is raised at an existential level, the epistemic difference that distinguishes modern philosophy from theology ceases to be a prohibitive separation. Hermeneutic philosophy is open to any source of existential meaning. To the believer, faith is the most fundamental source of meaning: he or she must adopt it within the metaphysical quest of meaning. Since this source is not available to the non-believer, it stands in need of a particularly critical examination. Even the non-believer is not qualified a priori to rule out a source of meaning which he or she does not know from within. The believing philosopher cannot dispense with a critical examination of his faith. Yet once he or she has successfully accomplished this task, it cannot but constitute a primary factor of existential meaning.

3   Yet another innovation in contemporary philosophy has reopened the road to belief. During the first half of the twentieth

---

2 James Pambrun, 'The Relationship Between Theology and Philosophy: Augustine, Ricoeur and Hermeneutics', *Theoforum* 36.3 (2005), pp. 293–319.

3 Miklos Vetö: 'Jalons et moments', *Iris: Annales de philosophie* 27 (2006), pp. 1–11 (quote on p. 11).

century a few French and Belgian philosophers steered Thomist philosophy in a new direction. Pierre Rousselot, a French Jesuit killed in World War One, argued that an intellectual dynamism moves the cognitive act beyond its immediate objects toward a transcendent goal. It implicitly co-affirms this goal, even though its nature lies beyond our cognitive capacity. In a celebrated dissertation published in 1893 entitled *L'Action*, Maurice Blondel argued that all human acting implies a transcendent goal. All human acting receives its impulse from a fundamental desire that surpasses the immediate object of choice. The motive of my acting moves well beyond its actual and even its possible achievements. Will this self-transcending aspiration ever be fulfilled? To this question philosophy shows at least the openness to a transcendent response, if this ultimate goal were ever to reveal itself.

Joseph Maréchal, professor at the Philosophical Faculty of the Belgian Jesuits in Louvain, completed the work of these predecessors in a masterly five-volume reinterpretation of Western epistemology and, indeed, of Thomist metaphysics in its entirety. With Kant, whose influence continues to dominate his work, he excludes the possibility of an intellectual intuition. Yet he shows that a number of Western philosophers have recognized an *implicit* intuition of the absolute in the self-surpassing drive of all thinking. The intuition remains implicit, because it conveys no metaphysical 'knowledge' of God. Still the active *presence* of transcendence within the act exceeds Kant's reductionist analysis of religion.

Transcendental Thomism has from the beginning provoked much controversy. Can a medieval system ever be integrated with Kantian philosophy? Even if Maréchal presents a valid reinterpretation of metaphysics, as I believe he does, the distance between actual faith and intellectual dynamism remains considerable, apparently greater than in the hermeneutic philosophy we have just discussed. In comparing the two, however, we must not forget that precisely the theory of intellectual dynamism creates a necessary condition for hermeneutic philosophy to be existentially meaningful. Without an ontological desire in thinking and acting, the possibility of existential meaning derived from a transcendent source, remains unintelligible. Gabriel Marcel has shown the riches of meaning to be drawn from the theory of transcendental desire.

Veritas: Belief and Metaphysics

Does Faith needs Metaphysics?

1   So far we have discussed how transcendental philosophy and hermeneutic thought may have opened a new way toward integrating transcendent meaning with a metaphysics of Being. But does religious faith need metaphysics? We know that one of the important theologians of the past century, Karl Barth, vehemently denies this. According to his *Church Dogmatics*, any attempt to mediate biblical revelation through metaphysics corrupts the divine message. Like a meteor fallen from heaven Christ touches this world at one tangential point. His revelation needs no philosophical support, nor does it fit our categories of thinking. The Christian message cannot even be ranked under the general concept of religion.

Against this position I hold, with most theologians, that a faith conceived in human ideas, expressed in human words, requires some *praeparatio fidei*, to be received, cultivated and practised. As Romano Guardini describes the process, we must first *see* something and then risk the plunge. *Etwas sehen und es dann wagen*. Metaphysics leads us to that insight in the human condition, where alone the need for transcendent meaning can be felt.

2   Yet metaphysics must be more than a *praeparatio fidei*. In concluding the volume on modern metaphysics of his monumental *The Glory of the Lord*, Hans Urs von Balthasar wrote:

> A Christian has to conduct philosophical enquiry on account of his faith. Believing in the absolute love of God for the world, he is obliged to understand Being in its ontological difference as pointing to love, and to live in accordance with this indication ... The mystery that anything exists at all becomes for him yet more profound and in the most comprehensive sense more worthy of enquiry than it does for any other kind of philosopher.[4]

For the believer, the ontological difference consists in the insight that Being possesses no intrinsic necessity as it did in ancient

---

4   Hans Urs von Balthasar, *The Glory of the Lord.* Vol. V: *The Realm of Metaphysics in the Modern Age*, trans. Oliver Davies, Andrew Louth, Rowan Williams, et al. (San Francisco: Ignatius Press, 1991), p. 646.

thought, when the cosmos and the gods possessed an equal necessity. The believer experiences Being as a gift.

This means more than that God created all things. To claim that, since God created all things, God created Being evades the fundamental metaphysical question: Why is there something rather than nothing? It merely raises the further question: And what about God? Is God not Being? Heidegger repeated Leibniz's question in his *Introduction to Metaphysics* (1935). He continued to struggle with it for years and finally, in the *Letter on Humanism* (1949), repeated what all philosophers since Kant had claimed, namely, that philosophy is incapable of adequately dealing with the idea of God.

Still, faith requires some insight in this metaphysical question to understand the mystery of creation. In my view, there is only one way to reconcile the scholastic position that God is Being – *esse substantiale subsistens*, as St Thomas defines divine Being – with the notion of creation, namely, in positing that all created things exist in God, as all beings are *in* Being. Heidegger himself tentatively suggested a somewhat related analogy in a 1960 meeting with theologians: philosophy is related to Being as theology is related to God.[5] Creation, then, would consist in an unfolding of divine Being, as Nicolas of Cusa had argued in the fifteenth century. God thereby becomes the very Being of all beings, distinct from them by nothing but their finitude.

This panentheistic position differs from the pantheistic one that God is the sum total of all beings. First, because God in Christian theology is discussed as *substantial* Being, which means that God, while including all beings within the divine Being, transcends them. This presupposes that the relation between Being and all beings be conceived as a dynamic, unfolding of Being, a process which monotheist theology calls *creation*. Precisely this dynamic aspect of creation distinguishes Cusanus' metaphysics from Spinoza's static one, in which God is the *substance* of all things. Scholastic metaphysics, inspired by Neoplatonism, was particularly well-equipped for expressing the self-communication of Being represented by the mystery of creation. The adage *bonum est divisum sui* supported the mysterious description of the First

---

5 James N. Robinson, 'The German Discussion', in *The Later Heidegger and Theology* (New York: Harper & Row, 1963), p. 43.

Epistle of John, that God is *Love*, which I would translate as goodness that communicates itself.

3   If God is Love, we understand that all God's manifestations, all created beings, are gratuitous, not intrinsically necessary, yet freely dispensed as a gift. This still does not exhaust the meaning of the Christian belief that *Being* itself is a gift. How can the Giver also be gift? What the Creator gives is nothing but himself: God is the very Being of all beings. To this metaphysical truth, indispensable to faith for understanding its own mystery, theology has added yet another one, which deepens metaphysics' own insight. In the mystery of the blessed Trinity, inscrutable to philosophy yet completing its self-understanding, the relation of *fides quaerens intellectum* reverses itself into the equally Augustinian *intellectus quaerens fidem*.

Balthasar, then, has rightly called the Christian the guardian of that metaphysical wonderment in which philosophy originates.[6] Religious believers deepen their faith through metaphysics, while at the same time keeping the metaphysical flame alive. During two and a half centuries of Western philosophy, the wonderment before the religious mystery has stimulated metaphysical thought, from Parmenides to Plato and Plotinus; from Augustine to Aquinas and Scotus, from Nicolas of Cusa to Leibniz and Hegel.

The forgetfulness of Being denounced by Heidegger is, not coincidentally, accompanied by a forgetfulness of God. Metaphysics has risen from mythology and religion. Without a religious sense of wonder the philosopher is rarely inclined to raise the question of Being in its totality, against the horizon of nothingness. In an essay 'On a Certain Blindness', William James identified the lack of perceptiveness for the significance of things as one of the principal shortcomings of our time.[7] We have lost our ability for being surprised by their *being there*. Today it is among poets, rather than philosophers, that we most commonly find the sense of wonder from which metaphysics springs.

---

6   von Balthasar, *The Glory of the Lord*, Vol. V, p. 656.

7   William James, 'On a Certain Blindness in Human Beings', originally published in *Talks to Teachers on Psychology and to Students on Some of Life's Ideals* (New York: H. Holt and Co., 1899); republished in *Writings, 1878–1899*, ed. Gerald Myers (New York: Library of America, 1992), pp. 841–60.

2. The Confidence of Thought: Between Belief and Metaphysics

WILLIAM DESMOND

Between Metaphysics and Believing

The term 'metaphysics' has diverse meanings for different thinkers. While this is not the place to go into these meanings, in the popular mind metaphysics deals with matters beyond the realm of ordinary experience. In minds schooled with some smattering of philosophy, metaphysics might mean something like a caricatured version of Platonism: there is an other world, up there beyond, and metaphysics gets us there, into outer space, not through experience, but by pure thinking. A caricature is not something untrue, but it exaggerates a true feature, and it does make something evident, but in the exaggeration it distorts, hence in being true it is also false. We have been dealing in caricatures of metaphysics, in perhaps a minor key since Kant, in perhaps a major key since Nietzsche. There is something both intimate and transcending about metaphysical thinking. We can so stress the transcending that we forget the intimacy, thus lending credence to the caricature of the unworldly, aboveworldly, otherworldly thinking. We can so stress the intimacy that we stop the self-surpassing of transcending thought, and perhaps with the well-intentioned desire to secure what we can know within the boundaries of immanence itself. But there is more. Metaphysics does have something intimate to do with what is above, what is other, what is beyond, but not in such a wise that it tramples on what is intimate to the world as given to us and as we come to know it. Metaphysics is metaxological:

between the strangeness of being and the intimacy, between the robustness of immanent givenness and the elusive mystery of what is more than just the given immanence.[1]

What of believing? Metaphysical thinking asks such questions as: 'What does it mean to be?' 'What is the meaning of the "to be"?' Such questions necessarily are bound up with such questions as: 'What does it mean to be good?' 'Is there something about the "to be" that might be called good in a fundamental sense?' The issues of nihilism are here at stake. If the 'to be' comes to nothing, 'nothing' then has the primordial place and the last word. Such questions are both metaphysical and ethical, in that for human beings the good of the "to be" is in question in a radically intimate way. To what does it all come? Every human being lives a response to this question, even let nothing be said about it, or nothing be said in response to it. The questions 'What is the meaning of the "to be"?' 'Is there a good about the "to be"?' inevitably bring us to the question of origin: origin of the 'to be' itself, and its worthiness to be mindfully affirmed and not only lived. Religious traditions have called that origin God. Thus the above questions dovetail with the question: 'What is God, what is it to be God?'[2]

In the longer tradition of thought we find a companionship of the religious and metaphysics. This companionship is disturbed, if not broken, in modern thought, with repercussions for the nature of metaphysics, as well as the hospitality of thought to religious belief. Modern thought, after all, claims to begin anew with doubting, not with believing. I will argue that this companionship is crucial for both the confidence of thought and the faithfulness asked of religious belief. An entire rethinking of metaphysics is needed in the light of the promise of a postmodern renewal of this companionship. The breach of companionship in modernity is an interim: between a pre-modernity where the companionship was

---

1 See my 'Neither Deconstruction or Reconstruction: Metaphysics and the Intimate Strangeness of Being', *International Philosophical Quarterly* 40:1 (2000), pp. 37–49.

2 I have tried to address these three questions in *Being and the Between* (Albany, NY: SUNY, 1995), *Ethics and the Between* (Albany, NY: SUNY, 2001) and *God and the Between* (Oxford: Blackwells, 2007).

The Confidence of Thought

perhaps so taken for granted that its enabling power was not always appreciated, and sometimes abused; and a postmodernity when the idea of philosophy enabling itself through its own immanent resources alone has run into the ground. In the night of nihilism philosophy can rediscover that without acknowledgement of its relation to what is other to itself, so-called autonomous self-determining thinking revolves around itself as its own void, avoiding or even voiding the ontological robustness of its intermediation with the full givenness of worthy being.

But is it not just the *lack of confidence* in reason that is most notable in postmodern thought? I would say that modern doubting seems to express a confidence in autonomous reason, but a kind of overconfidence can swell and prepare a fall. There is an overconfidence that produces a bubble of inflation, but the bubble bursts, and long thereafter we must pay for the afflatus that, after all, was not so divine. The situation is perhaps still more equivocal. For the confidence of modern reason is also coupled with a belief in the powers of critique. But these powers, handled in a certain way, produce a lack of confidence in reason, and not least in metaphysical thinking. I think of Kant. True, there were idealistic reactions that again stressed even more the confidence of autonomous reason, for even the negating powers of critical reason seem amenable to redirection in terms of this confidence. I think of Hegel's confidence, overconfidence: every negative can and will be harnessed to the triumphant benefit of self-determining reason.

This peculiar combination of the lack of confidence in reason and the overconfidence falls away from the in-between character of human thinking. The *eros* of thinking might be said, *pace* Plato, to mingle *poros* and *penia*. Stress the *penia* only and there is no movement of transcending. Stress only the *poros* and the plenty overflows into perhaps thinking's exultation in itself as if it were a God, and not a finite participation in something divine. Too little, and there is no thought. Too much, and there is a kind of thought that is also no thought, for it deserts our in-between condition. Too little confidence and overconfidence are both to the detriment of the middle way of metaxological metaphysics. Too little and too much confidence are also bound up with the projects of critique and self-determining thought. I will raise questions about both from the standpoint of a considered confidence in the metaxological character of metaphysics.[3]

There is also the question of the recessed roots of metaphysical thinking – again understood in this metaxological way. These recesses are not necessarily in this or that belief but in a more primal trust in the intelligibility of what is. The confidence of thought asks a willingness to hearken to what is worthy in the beliefs of religion. Once again an old companionship calls for a renewal, after the great divorce of modernity. Like many divorces, there is often something equivocal here too. For the virtues of the abandoned companion are often called on, or sneaked back in, though under names not sanctioned in terms of the old companionship. Philosophy will try to do what properly only religion can do – as we see with Hegel. Or philosophy might ask art to do what properly only religion can do – as we see with Nietzsche. In my view we need a new postmodern porosity between the religious and the metaphysical. Of old in modernity we knew the self-understanding of the philosopher as a scientist or technician or revolutionary and latterly as perhaps even a poet after his or her own fashion.[4] But the more archaic companionship of the philosopher with the religious and its vocation is worth new thinking and renewal.[5]

Believing: What to Credit

There are different senses of belief. The most immediately striking has perhaps to do with what one holds to be reliable in terms of this or that state of affairs. When one is asked: 'What do you believe?' one might answer: 'I believe in one God, Father Almighty, maker of heaven and earth and so on.' Of course, there are everyday beliefs: I believe I have competent colleagues; I believe my fellow card-players will play straight; I believe fruits and vegetables are good for my health; and so on. Belief seems to be bound to

---

3 On this metaxological character, see *Being and the Between*.
4 See William Desmond, *Philosophy and its Others: Ways of Being and Mind* (Albany, NY: SUNY, 1990), chapter 1.
5 See William Desmond, 'Consecrated Thought: Between the Priest and the Philosopher', *Louvain Studies*, 30 (2005), pp. 92–106.

a determinate this and that. Religious belief also seems to be so directed to such a determinate state of affairs. It is perhaps here we encounter beliefs in the sense of doctrines, articulated in terms of institutionally sanctioned formulations or propositions. Needless to say, doctrines in that sense are very important. They articulate with some determinacy what a believing community holds to be centrally significant in defining how it understands itself, and not only in terms of itself, but in relation to God as above and more than it.

Of course, we can become so fixated on the letter of the doctrines that the spirit is forgotten. The question is important here, for the issue arises as to whether more determinate doctrines are to be seen as coming to articulation out of (sometimes) recessed communications, or community, marked by what I will call a reserve of overdeterminate trust: not just trust in this or that, but a more primal trust which enables the investment of determinate trust in this and that. This reserve is not the possession of any individual, but rather enables the individual to be trusting. Likewise the written determinacy of doctrines is, so to say, underwritten by that reserve and its communication with the more original source of creditworthiness. Against fundamentalist literalism, the determinacy of religious articulations is not simply univocal. Often redolent of suggestion and evocative ambiguity, these articulations call for finessed interpretation. If the reserve of faith is not intimately available, one might play cleverly with propositions, but there is a foolish cleverness. Something analogous might be found with philosophical thinking. It is especially important for metaphysics to remain mindful of these reserves that enable thought to think at all.

What we believe shows itself as what we can credit or do credit. Belief seeks a bond with the creditworthy. We often invest the word 'credit' with an economic meaning, but the economic meaning itself emerges out of a more basic meaning. There is economic credit because there is more than the economic, in the sense of utilitarian exchange. What we credit is what is worthy of trust. We credit a person who is worthy of trust. What constitutes trustworthiness? A creditworthy person is not one with a big bank account but one we can rely on, someone of integrity who answers for himself or herself. The trustworthy person is one on whose

Veritas: Belief and Metaphysics

word we can count, one whose promises will be kept.

We are not far off from religious connotations. The word credit comes from *credere* – to believe. We say '*credo*' – I believe – and we announce what we consider to be worthy of trust. Being worthy of trust is not just our *projection* of anticipation onto some receiving other. It comes out of something already enigmatically received from the other: some witness of reliability already intimated. Trust ventures something about the integral reliability of the one or the source trusted. The venture is an adventure, in the sense of a venture towards (*ad*), but also an advent, in the sense of something coming towards us in the venturing of expectation. This has an ontological intonation. Something about the *being* of the trustworthy is at issue: what they *are* is thought trustworthy. This is especially the case with the human person. Ultimately it is not this or that characteristic that we consider trustworthy: it is the integral person who is deemed worthy of credit. An integral person is a witness to trustworthiness.

Of course, we also come across the language of economics when we speak of the investment of credit. It seems we are dragged back to a calculated venture of exchange where, in the end, nothing is an end in itself, and everything a means. Once again I think this is not the primary meaning of the investment of credit. Rather one might say that investment reflects an investiture. What is an investiture? It is a granting of enabling power – a granting by a source that is capable of properly re-sourcing the one invested. The reserve of enabling power is passed over, communicated from a source to a recipient, and the creditworthiness of the recipient is so, not first in virtue of itself, but in terms of the communicating source, and derivatively in terms of the re-source vested immanently in it. Thus for us the first issue is not a matter of that wherein we invest our credit – this comes later. More primally, it is a matter of what it is that we find about ourselves as already invested with certain powers. We are the recipients of investitures. We are endowed. We are endowments. Our very being, our 'to be' is an endowment. There are enabling powers, re-sources, first given before they can be invested in something further.

One thinks of the parable of the talents: the gift of the talents is first; the investiture of talent is a promise of fruit; credit is given to beings considered creditworthy; we are ourselves invested in, we are the investment. What is the return? It is not quite the economic profit of God as a speculative creditor. It is the generosity of the endowing God who calls to agapeic return. This is not a surplus profit in the sense of adding this or that to a determinate store. It is simply generosity and thankfulness lived as both self-enabling and more than self-enabling. The return is to give away the gift, in the sense of passing on the endowment with the generosity fitting to the gift. We own nothing, and we are most profitable, when we make no profits for ourselves, but pass on the increase in generosity that cannot be increased, and that is itself nothing but increase of participation in the good of the 'to be'.

Believing and Determinate Knowing: From Epistemic Deficiency to Revolutionary Ardour

This way of thinking about believing stands in contrast with the notion of belief as bound to a set of determinate propositions. To speak properly of the creditworthy, of the sources of the trustworthy, I believe we need to speak of more than the indeterminate, the determinate and the self-determining. We need to speak of the *overdeterminacy* of the endowing source. Let me first remark on how we might look on indeterminacy, determinacy and self-determination.

To know, it will be said, is to know something – something determinate. If we hold belief to be bound to a set of determinate propositions, the philosopher is immediately tempted to ask about their warrant, rational and evidentiary. What we believe is defined as a set of potentially epistemic determinations to be judged on the grounds of rational argument and empirical evidences. There is nothing wrong with asking the warrant of determinate positions or propositions, of course, but this is not the end of the matter. What constitutes the epistemic ground of the creditworthy is not simply epistemic, in the sense of something entirely separable from metaphysical and ethical considerations, nor indeed from religious. Calling on Pascal's distinction between *l'esprit de finesse* and *l'esprit de géométrie*, I would say the creditworthy is more a matter of 'finesse' than of 'geometry'. 'Geometry' is not at all to be looked at askance; nevertheless, the appropriate philosophical relevance of geometry is not itself determined by geometry itself. It is finesse that determines the fitting intervention of geometry. And it may not be fitting to intervene geometrically, as if this were the one and only way, or the finally determinative orientation, when the matter at issue is the investment of ultimate metaphysical and ethical credit.

The danger with an overweening intrusion of geometry is that the matter of belief now seems to be defined in terms of deficiencies rather than resources. The deficiencies are epistemic: I believe when I do not know, when perhaps I cannot know. To believe and to know become disjoined. In believing, the evidences are not fully forthcoming. Were they fully forthcoming I would know and not believe. When one believes, one does not yet know. When one does know, one no longer believes.

The stress on determinacy plays here an important role. Belief may entail a determinacy that is more or less successful with respect to this or that state of affairs but by its nature cannot be fully successful with respect to full determinate evidences. Further, if belief is a determinacy, it is one now seen in the light of an indeterminacy. Our ignorance shows the indeterminacy: we know not; and the indefinition of our not-knowing should properly be overcome with more and more univocal determinacies; otherwise we remain epistemically deficient. There would seem to be no such thing as indeterminate knowing. To know is to know a determinate somewhat. By contrast, it is out of indeterminacy that belief is said to sprout. It is a supplement to ignorance that claims to substitute for knowing. It turns out to be an indeterminacy when subjected to closer scrutiny. I believe this or that to be the case, but when I inspect the determinacy of belief, it dissolves because it cannot be fully warranted by the determinate evidences.

The resulting tendency to separate knowing and believing is fateful for the relation of belief and metaphysics. Thus in modern philosophy, belief tends to be seen as extraneous to knowing. To believe is to project beyond ignorance, and claim unwarranted knowing beyond the evidences. To know is to submit to immanent justifying warrant. Knowing comes to its truth through itself, not through anything other that remains beyond its scope. For knowing, there is nothing beyond its scope. To extend the scope of knowing is to contract the space into which we can project belief.

The Confidence of Thought

There is a certain univocity to the claim here: belief and knowing are homogeneous. I will indicate more fully that this kind of homogeneity of determinacy is appropriate neither to the sources of religious believing, nor to the sources of metaphysical thinking, sources bound up with the nature of the ontological, religious and ethical confidence that is intimate to what we are. With this homogeneity, however, metaphysics becomes defined in terms not of the indeterminate but in terms of the quest for determinate knowing first, and then for self-determining knowing. Metaphysics ought to be determinate knowing via the methods of immanent knowing. It must determine the field of the knowable through itself alone (rationalism), or via perhaps the acknowledgement that another determinacy is needed from sensory evidences (empiricism). If the latter is the paradigm of knowledge we seem to end up with scepticism about metaphysics – the evidences of sensory experience cannot deliver rational necessity (as we see with Hume). Kant clearly sought a togetherness of these two – rational necessity and experiential evidences. But with Kant, no less than with Hume, metaphysics clearly dies a death as transcendent metaphysics, even if it is resurrected, in a very qualified way, as bearing on transcendental knowing, or the immanences of practical reason in the form of moral autonomy.

Here the stress on determinate knowing passes over into self-determining. For the transcendent entails a reference to the 'beyond', and self-determining reason issues its negation to this reference. This negation is also reason's prohibition *to itself* as tempted to claim to know the beyond. By contrast, transcendental knowing, in Kant's sense, is concerned with the conditions *immanent* in knowing itself. Once again claims to know the transcendent must be abjured. For Kant this is entirely compatible with the ideal of knowledge as overcoming the overclaimed determinacies of belief, as well as the indeterminacy of faith. Of course, Kant famously spoke of sacrificing knowing to make room for faith. But this is equivocal relative to the issue here at stake. It is moral faith to which Kant refers, and so we remain within the immanence of self-determining reason, even if it is now practical rather than theoretical. Faith in what is beyond reason: this is not what Kant offers. There is perhaps something beyond the employment of reason in natural science but this is not faith beyond reason.

Veritas: Belief and Metaphysics

Kantian faith credits the trustworthiness of the rational self-determining powers of practical reason. This alone is what Kant considers creditworthy in an ultimate sense. If there is something like an equivocal opening to God in Kant, this has not to do with religious faith as such. Every faith, religious or otherwise, must be judged creditworthy by practical reason. Moral faith, in the light of the idea of autonomous reason, be it theoretical or practical, is the faith that reason has in itself. We come back to the moral self-confidence of practical reason in itself.

Kant's metaphysics of morals might seem to be the resurrection of metaphysics in light of moral faith, but the issue here too is very equivocal. The end of metaphysics in a more traditional sense is bound up with a certain understanding of determinate knowing and experience. For Kant we can invest qualified trust in determinate knowing, but not in the traditional metaphysics. Similarly with respect to religious belief, this too offers only a slender warrant; any creditworthy warrant must come from the reconfiguration of religious belief in moral terms. Religious belief offers nothing trustworthy at all if it claims to go beyond empirical experience and moral reason. The faith Kant allows may have the same name as religious faith, but what carries the identifying name is a changeling – or if you agree with Kant, it is the legitimate child and true heir. To the end of traditional metaphysics seems to be added the end of traditional religious faith. In fact, Kant's line of thinking leads to permanent *suspicion* of belief in terms of critique. Kant is the rationalistic fussy grandfather of critique in this sense, but he will generate children and grandchildren who are not fussy in his sense. Brimming with rational (over)confidence, some will colonize all reality with system; others, full of suspicion about things traditional, will turn with revolutionary vehemence from speculative theory to the 'terrorism of theory' (Bruno Bauer). From moral action honouring old decencies and duties, practical reason, alternatively (over)suspicious and (over)confident, will set to work in overturning it all, in favour of its belief in itself as the womb of a new world or epoch.

The Confidence of Thought

Critique, Self-determining Thinking, Believing

Is there metaphysics after critique? I have addressed this question elsewhere,[6] but it is worth dwelling on the fact that the project of philosophical thinking as critique emerges with respect to a certain rational dissatisfaction with epistemic fixation on determinacies. If thought is to be self-determining, everything that appears other to thought must be subject to the determination of thought. But this means the displacement of this other from any position of being in the original place and its reformulation in terms that compel it to come before the tribunal of self-determining reason – on the terms of the latter. These terms first and foremost determine the truth of the matter. The project of critique emerges from a sense of distrust about determinate propositions, seen in the light of a scepticism concerning putatively dogmatic determinacies. If religious beliefs are made up of such dogmatic determinacies, they must be put to the test of the tribunal of critique. Need I say that Kant especially comes again to mind here? I confine myself now to the general point.

Though critique presents itself as somehow more than scepticism, it is the sceptical impulse that is energetic at its core. What is given is not self-justifying. It must justify itself before critical thought, thought as reflective not immediate, thought as questioning and not assenting without further ado. Thus religious beliefs or political allegiances must be justified, not through themselves but through critical reason. Since they possess elements that are other to reason, a negative judgement seems always a real possibility, if not predetermined from the start. Recall here the critique of faith by the Enlightenment, critique not separable, in the end, from certain political commitments. This example is not merely of antiquarian interest, since some current characteristic attitudes often mimic this earlier critique. Of course, we find here faith protecting itself by jettisoning doctrinal claims. For just such claims as *determinate* invite the scepticism of critique. Seeking to escape this by such jettisoning, faith risks becoming a vague belief in a something 'other' that 'somehow' is beyond critique. It is as if the alternatives

---

6 William Desmond, 'Is there Metaphysics after Critique?', *International Philosophical Quarterly*, 45:2 (2005), pp. 221–41.

were either strong determinacy or weak indeterminacy. Strong determinacy of faith brings forth the oppugnancy of sceptical critique. Reactive to this, a weak indeterminacy of faith seems so fluid that determinate thought cannot step twice, in a definite way, into its fluid waters. As Hegel saw, faith and enlightenment are here in a kind of collusion.[7] In a sense, they are one and the same, since all determinate content becomes vaporized, whether in the negativity of critique or the weak indeterminacy of undefined faith.

Hegel did not like this outcome. He has a point, even if, as we shall see, one need not embrace his response, which is an intensification of the claims of self-determining reason. It is the abstraction of reason that is to blame, he claims, not reason as such. True reason entails a negativity of thought that produces a positive outcome. In his singular way, Hegel is a more thorough rationalizer of faith: more truly self-determining reason can take the entire measure of full religious belief. From determinacy and indeterminacy and the oscillation between the two, the dialectic of reason will prove self-determining. I think this is not the end, or the beginning of the matter. As already suggested, there is an overdeterminacy more than indeterminacy, determinacy and self-determination. Hegel offers a reconfiguration of indeterminacy and determinacy in terms of self-determining thought. He passes over the overdeterminacy – something revealed in both faith and thought, and shown not in weak indeterminacy but in true confidence. I will come to this.

The main point now: critique as negating thinking cannot produce any content on its own. Every determinacy may be deconstructed, but the end result is not something creditworthy as determinate. For all determinacy lacks credit – credit ultimately justified. We are left with indeterminacy. If this might seem to allow us to be open to 'something other', nevertheless we find ourselves here forbidden from determining this other. For then we are back with the determinate, which then must be critiqued – and so on and on. We might say it is a 'something', an X. Even this is too determinate, and can set off another bout of hand wringing

---

7 G. W. F. Hegel, *Phänomenologie des Geistes* (Hamburg: Meiner, 1952), pp. 376ff.; *Phenomenology of Spirit*, trans. A. V. Miller (Oxford: Clarendon Press, 1977), pp. 321ff.

about the fixation of determinacy as such. I find something of this anxiety of determinacy at work in deconstructive critique. We pass back and forth between fixed univocity and unfixed equivocity. I have argued elsewhere more extensively that the affirmative cannot simply come from thought as negativity, whether understood in Hegelian, in post-Hegelian, or indeed post-Nietzschean, post-Heideggerian deconstructive form.[8] Thought must open to something other than thought thinking itself. I have also argued that it cannot do this truly without its companionship with the religious – though great art can also be a worthy, enabling companion.

Critique may demand that the determinate others justify any confidence in them, and critique may have confidence in its own deconstructing powers but this self-confidence will eviscerate itself in the long run, when critique is turned back on itself and it finds no reason why it should not devour itself in self-negation, where before it devoured the fixity of the determinate others. Such self-devouring critique is not really remedied by what Hegel in his *Phenomenology of Spirit* calls 'self-completing scepticism (*sich vollbringende Skeptizismus*)'.[9] For this too presupposes something more than thinking as negativity, and this 'more' is not something that Hegel explores well enough, if at all. This 'more' bears on the overdeterminate. For Hegel thinking is a matter of the negation of both the indeterminacy and the determinacy: of the indeterminacy, because it is too empty; of the determinacy because it is too fixated. One is a poverty that generates nothing as such; the other is a fixation that prevents the fluid unfolding of the process of thinking qua process. Thinking as negating must deconstruct the fixations but in this, Hegel holds, thinking *comes to itself* as thinking; *comes to itself* as self-determining; *comes to itself* as overcoming the indeterminacy of its starting point; and ends up *beholden to nothing but itself alone*, and its own immanent resources. Hegel has no mind for, does not keep in mind, the overdeterminacy as such.

In some such manner, we move from extreme critique to what presents itself as the robust self-confidence of reason in itself. We move from Kantian timidity to Hegelian hubris. The timidity and

---

8 In 'Consecrated Thought'.
9 *Phänomenologie des Geistes*, p. 67; *Phenomenology of Spirit*, p. 78.

the hubris are defined along a homogeneous line of consideration. Indeed the Hegelian hubris is quite intelligible if this line of consideration exhausts the matter. I think it does not. As already suggested, the gift of the overdeterminacy is overlooked in all this. There is a confidence of thought prior to and beyond critique and it is not adequately described by Hegel's self-determining thought. It is worth noting that the latter is defined by a dialectic with religious belief, presented as a set of representational determinations which must be conceptually overcome, *aufgehoben*. This overcoming is determined entirely through a reason oriented to the *telos* of being absolute self-determining. My point is not that religious representation is immune from critique – not at all – clearly it calls forth critique. My focus is on an issue that does not even get acknowledged, much less explored, if indeterminacy, determinacy and self-determination are held to exhaust the matter.

The matter is not one of defining faith over against Enlightenment reason. It is not a matter of sublating faith into speculative reason. For faith in both these instances is either a set of determinations or bare indeterminacy. There is a more basic sense of confidence, and this must be explored – and not to be either critiqued or sublated but to open a porous dialogue between it and the adventure of thought. This adventure of thought is as much endowed by this other confidence, as it finds itself perplexed by it, as it finds that it peters out in nothing if it does not constantly return to this reserve of confidence. It is an overdeterminate reserve that invests reason with the power to be true to what is: to be true, to be faithful, not only to itself but to what is beyond itself. This issue transcends the difference of inner and outer, the immanent and the transcendent. It bears on a transcendence that is as much intimate to immanence as beyond its full resources when immanence makes claim to a self-determining self-sufficiency.

Thinking and Trusting

We are right to believe what is trustworthy, but what is trustworthy is beyond critique. It offers itself from a source that is not captured by critique. The connection of the trustworthy and the true is important. The true is what shows itself trustworthy. Here we need to acknowledge the intimate inseparability of being true with our own being truthful. There is no truth for us without our being truthful, which does not mean that being true is exhausted by our being truthful. We can be truthful not only to ourselves but to what as other is shown to us, to what is communicated to us. Being truthful opens to what is beyond itself in its own most intimate integrity of honesty. The trustworthy, the creditworthy alerts us to what is worthy to be believed in this intimate sense.[10]

In this connection thought and belief cannot but be regarded as companions. Thinking truthfully about something is crediting it, or being credited by it, in such a wise that the relation between us and it is rendered trustworthy. The relation itself embodies a kind of ontological trust. It will hold, we think. We hold to it, because we trust it will hold.

What is at issue is not only a trust in this or that determination. We are pointed to a trust that is more basic than trust in this or that. Our being truthful itself testifies to something of this more basic trust. Why should we be truthful? There is no answer to this question in terms other than truthfulness itself. There is something basic about being truthful. We are called to be truthful even when we do not know the truth, and even when we have to confess we do not know it. A confession of ignorance or being wrong testifies to the spirit of being truthful. For to pose the question of truth is to find oneself in a relation that holds one to being truthful. This is even true if our purpose is to mock truth, as Pilate (in)famously did. This call to be truthful is something immanent in thinking itself, and is not exhausted by a relation between thinking and some fixed state of affairs external to it. This does not mean there is not an otherness at work but it is not one that can be simply objectified in terms of any such fixed externality. Being truthful testifies to a trust that to be true will bring us into the company of the true or truth.

In this light, suppose we look again at critique, in the mode of posing questions. No matter the severity of the posing of a

---

10 See William Desmond, *Being and the Between*, chapter 12 on different senses of being true; also 'Pluralism, Truthfulness and the Patience of Being', in *Health and Human Flourishing: Religion, Medicine and Moral Anthropology*, edited by Carol R. Taylor, Roberto Dell'Oro (Washington, DC: Georgetown University Press, 2006), chapter 3.

question, the very posing is not just a position or the positing of this or that truth. It is an ontological-epistemic orientation to what puzzles, perplexes, baffles us. Nevertheless, it is one in which there is an anticipation that an answer will respond one way or other to the question posed. The matter is not one of the 'what' about the posing of the question, and the definite propositions or positions that would answer the posing. It is the very posing itself as the embodiment of an orientation to what is true. This orientation to the true is the living enactment of trustfulness that there is a true to be known. And this is true, even when the question is posed in the spirit of suspicion.

Even finally to be confronted with the absurd is still to go towards it with the anticipation of trustworthy truth. True, when we meet the absurd our expectation is defeated or disappointed, but the expectation is more primal than the defeat, and since we know the defeat, expectation already resurrects itself in the disappointment. We cannot but be beings that live in a trust in the true. It makes us the kinds of being we are. We live between the question and the true and the question itself reveals a prior relation to the true – not only with respect to its own truthfulness but with respect to the possibility of truth as other to our expectations. Living this primal trust, we are the expectation of the unexpected.

The search for the true is never a matter of self-confirmation simply. Something is confirmed for us, but there is also an ingression of something other that, so to say, takes us out of ourselves. This exceeding of ourselves is not just with respect to this truth or that truth as other, but with respect to a more primal relation between us and the true. This relation is intimate but not merely immanent; it is transcending and relates us to what transcends us; this other beyond or above us is not a fixed objectivity over against which we stand in a relation of something like dualistic opposition. The intimacy and otherness mean also that it is not a matter of us either sublating this truth or of our being sublated by it. We always move in the between of communication where otherness and intimacy are both inseparable and irreducible.

This prior sense of being truthful cannot be articulated fully in the language of the autonomy of thought. Quite the opposite: it shows all thought to be already implicated with something other to itself. And it shows this, whether we approach the matter from the intimacy of thought seeming to communicate with itself, or of thought in relation to something beyond itself which communicates with it. The posing of a question is a between, is an intermedium of communication, already underway before the posing wakes up to itself, either in self-enjoyment, self-critique, other-enjoyment or other-critique. This between-being of the question makes it impossible to claim the posing to be ruled by the *nomos* of *to auto*, the law of itself. There is a heteronomy at work here but it is no squashing otherness. It is releasing and enabling of the very search for truth. We are enabled to seek the truth before we possess the truth, and this prior enabling is not determinate thought, nor determined through ourselves alone, hence it cannot be defined in the logic of autonomy. This prior enabling is just what allows us to be relatively autonomous at all. We would not be autonomous were not autonomy enabled by something prior to and other to autonomy. Self-determining thinking is released into its own freedom to think for itself by an enabling resource that is not itself, a source not to be captured in terms of this or that determinate thought, or by thought's own determination by and for itself. There is more that allows thinking to be itself more than itself.

The Confidence of Thinking

This prior sense of being truthful in relation to the true throws light on the confidence of thinking. What does confidence mean? We notice the reference to *fides* in confidence – there is a *con-fides* – a faith with. One might say there is a companionship of faith, companionship marked by a fidelity. Confidence thus enfolds within itself relationality to something beyond self. It is like trust: even when one trusts in one's own power, there is more than what one can empower, or own, completely through self-trust alone. I trust because I am trusted, because I am entrusted.

In practice, I trust I can do this or that, but I must hazard my talent to confirm my trust in myself, hence I must always open myself to what is beyond me. But even before the confirming hazard that redounds to the adventurer, there is already a confidence in the adventuring, and hence an opening to what is other to me before there is an opening of me to what is other. My trust in myself is impossible to determine purely through myself alone. The confidence that is invested in my trust is enigmatically related to what is not of itself alone. Trust in oneself would seem to come down to oneself alone, but in trying to come down to itself alone it draws from a reserve that cannot come down to itself alone.

That said, this entails no reason at all to eradicate this intimate reference to oneself. The most intimate reference to oneself shades into a porosity to what exceeds oneself alone. This may not always be acknowledged. Non-acknowledgement can be paradoxically greater *consequent* to the confirmation of the trust in oneself through the venturing that hazards itself on the other. Blithe ingratitude too often follows enjoyment of something given to one. For the nine lepers among the ten healed, restoration overwhelmed thanks, and we must count ourselves mostly among these nine. There seems an inevitable tendency to elide thanks to the source that gives courage to the trust in self. Ingratitude is not a helpful companion of mindful granting.

I would say there is no confidence in self without this other to self confiding in one. Confiding in one: again there is the note of intimacy. When a companion confides in me I am invested with a trust. I am answerable to the trust of the other because I am endowed with the promise of being trustworthy. I do not constitute this trustworthy promise or character through myself alone. This is impossible in the nature of the case. It is not only this or that secret, or item of information that is confided in me. Being confided in by the companion extends to the totality of what I am, and seems nothing, in a way, for it is not quite this or that. Being confided in enters into, permeates the integrity of what I am. We are integrities of being not totally self-constitutive but constituted in virtue of a relation of reception to what is other and beyond us – a beyond that, nevertheless, communicates intimately to the very being of what we are.

I am worthy of confidence in being thus confided in. This is a kind of ontological confiding that makes possible my confidence. It comes to me from an other who releases me as the recipient of communication into my own being for itself, capable of itself, and confident in its power, its own powers but not just power that is its own. On the basis of this confidence I can set out to determine myself this way or that, or indeed to determine if such and such is or is not the case. In other words, this prior confidence, this prior communication of confidence is not a determinate confidence which tells me this or that, it is not a self-determining confidence, but something more than both. And it is not merely indeterminate, thenceforth to be made either determinate or self-determining. In language introduced earlier, I would say it is overdeterminate, over self-determining also, in the sense that it is more than determinate and self-determining confidence. 'Over' here means: not overpowering – but power that, though over one, releases; 'over' in the sense in which (in an immemorial image) a guardian angel might watch over its mortal charge, let it to seek the fullness of its own promise. In being let go, we are kept in mind. We are mindful, and capable of minding, because we are kept in mind: already minded before we mind this or that, or determine our minds thus and thus.

The case is analogous to courage, and I have discussed this elsewhere.[11] There is no courage without being encouraged; just as there is no love without first being loved, or speaking without being addressed. There is no communication from us without our being in communication. We are in what enables us to be ourselves as wording our being, but what we are in is not just our own being, and the wording of it is more than words we can simply call our own. The first word comes to us in the woo of the mother who coaxes us into our own words. We arrive in a communication long underway without us, and we come into it as recipients of its resources and reserves, though also in time we come to complain, and alas, like Caliban, being taught to speak, we also learn quickly to curse. Words, of course, are the most intimately personal but no word is owned by us exclusively. Words, intimately personal, enable the universal, enable the intimate universal. This is how I have described the community of being religious.[12]

This prior confidence has implications for the practice of thinking, in a general sense, and in its current forms. As briefly suggested at the beginning, one aspect of postmodern times is a lack of

---

11 'The Secret Sources of Strengthening: On Courage', *Is There a Sabbath for Thought?: Between Religion and Philosophy* (New York: Fordham University Press, 2005), chapter 7.

12 E.g. in *Is There a Sabbath for Thought?*, pp. 1–32.

confidence in the affirmative powers of thought, coupled with a hypertrophy of suspicious critique. One might see this as a reaction to the confidence of modern reason which, in Enlightenment form, assumed the face of a certain self-confidence. Since this self-confidence was formed in rejection of religious belief, it tended towards an *assertive* self-confidence. We do not submit ourselves to heteronomous religious sources; we insist on thinking for ourselves; there is to be no self-incurred tutelage and so on. Call this the assertiveness training of modern reason, building up its post-religious confidence in itself.

There is something not entirely happy about this. There is a self-confidence which, when self-assertive and under the aegis of a certain autonomous self-determination, is simply untrue to what it itself is, as already the beneficiary, indeed beneficence of a confiding. We have already received such beneficences before we think for ourselves. They are confided to us. This is true of a people, of a religious tradition, and it is no less true of an individual. One might ask, for instance: Who was the mother of the *cogito*? The *cogito* has no mother. How then was it wooed into words? It is as if the *cogito*, masking Descartes, would be self-born. Consider the later Nietzsche, not always masking himself: he would be mother and father and offspring of himself, all in one. Far from being serenely confident this strikes one as an assertiveness that feels it has to create a space for itself by negation or subsumption of another. Its self-assertiveness has to continue to assert itself, lest it collapse back into the other(s) from which it wants to distance itself or against which it wants to revolt. The determinate other has to be overcome, the indeterminate formlessness has to be overtaken. Self-determination becomes self-wording self-assertion in the case of overconfidence; it becomes indeterminate self-negating in the case of reactive under-confidence. Over-projection produces its boomerang in the twin that is its *incognito* understudy, namely, abjection. Are there strains of postmodern thinking which fear collapse in this sense: the confidence of reason cannot truly be restored by self-assertion, once that confidence has turned against itself? And what trustworthy truth is confided, can be confided, in reactive abjectness?

I return again to Hegel as representing the acme of a certain Enlightenment self-confidence of reason. His hyperinflation of our reason's claims produced a speculative bubble and a long anti-philosophical deflation from which we have not yet fully recovered. Recovery asks something like a fuller résumé of the prior reserve of confiding. This entails a self-confidence that knows its power to be always, in the primal place, second; self-confidence grateful to have received what it has been granted; confidence not rancorous against external limitation, nor against itself for being finite; confidence that yet, as being confided in, is released into an adventure of seeking what is intimately of itself and more than itself; confidence purged of rancour against God.

For there are different forms of self-confidence, and the wrong self-confidence overtakes the 'con' of con-fidence. It lets the self override the relation to the other hidden in the con-fidence. It overtakes any *passio essendi*, as it wills itself to become a *conatus essendi* that takes over. I mean a *con-natus* that in its endeavour to be itself occludes the 'con' of its own being 'born with', for it would be self-born. No longer would there be anything over it; it would overtake whatever it receives, claiming it for itself. Taking all over, it would come to be, in a self-birthing, its own absolute self-confidence. This certainly is a temptation of reason understood in the modern sense of self-determining. Consider Hegel's overtaking of religion, though it might be dressed up in the language of a certain companionship of the *Begriff* and *Vorstellung*. This is a companionship of a provisional sort, since the religious friend must cede to philosophy the ultimate place of ultimacy, just because it fails to be absolutely self-determining. Religion does not have the requisite absolute confidence in reason's own power of self-determination. The kernel of the matter remains an overtaking, for all the pious Hegelian talk about preserving the religious. There is a conceptual reconfiguration of the *passio* of religion, and the community of the intimate universal, in favour of a self-absolutizing *conatus* of thought which claims to be the concrete universal. The intimate universal is not this concrete universal.

I recall Hegel's very confident remarks about the courage of truth (*der Muth der Wahrheit*) in his inaugural lecture in Heidelberg, repeated at Berlin: 'The human being . . . should and must deem himself worthy of the highest . . . The initially hidden and concealed essence of the world has no power to withstand the

Veritas: Belief and Metaphysics

courage of knowledge.'[13] This is very definitely a rousing call against any abjectness of the human spirit. We may be initially perplexed, but hold fast, call upon courage, and the initially hidden essence of the world will show its impotence to hold out. We must not be discouraged; knowing will triumph! This is self-confidence without apology.

What of the courage itself? We call upon courage, but how *call* upon courage? Can we call upon courage as if it were a resource within our command? Is there not something to courage that exceeds determinate command? Courage surges forth from sources hard to pin down to determinacy or to encapsulate in self-determination. We do not so much call upon courage as that something is called forth from us in courage. Courage suggests a resource, a source, at once deeply intimate to our being, and yet other to our total self-command, even when we are commanding persons, and in self-command. We call on courage and something is *held out to us*, and only then we find that the recalcitrance of what holds out against us may no longer hold. This means that our courage can never just be ours alone. Our courage comes out of sources that involve our *'being encouraged'*. There is a 'being en-couraged' before 'being courageous'.

Suppose Hegel is right: because we have had courage, knowledge comes. But from where then does the courage come? It does not come from the knowledge; for we must have the courage to have the knowledge. If knowledge comes from the courage, from where does the courage come? Is there a courage of knowing

---

13 'Der Muth der Wahrheit;- der Glaube an die Macht des Geistes ist die erste Bedingung der Philosophie; der Mensch, da er Geist ist, darf und soll sich selbst des Höchsten würdig achten, von dem Grosse und Macht seines Geistes kann er nicht gross genug denken; und mit diesem Glauben wird nichts so spröde und hart seyn, das sich ihm nicht eröffnete; das zuerst verborgene und verschlosse Wesen des Universums hat keine Krafft, die dem Muthe des Erkennens Widerstand leisten konnte; es muss sich vor ihm aufthun, und seinen Reichthum und seine Tieffen ihm vor Augem legen und zum Genusse geben.' This is the Heidelberg version, *Gesammelte Werke* (Hamburg: Felix Meiner, 1968), vol. 18, 6; the Berlin version, vol. 18, 18 is slightly more clipped and direct. Hegelian courage tries to enact more audaciously the Enlightenment motto of Kant: *sapere aude!*

The Confidence of Thought

before knowledge? If so, how then is it a courage of *knowledge*? Is the courage of knowing encouraged by sources it cannot know in advance, maybe can never know in a fully determinate manner, since these sources are what make determinate knowledge itself possible? Does knowledge presuppose a courage that knowledge itself cannot make fully determinate, whose secret source it cannot completely comprehend? If this is so, knowing is successful on the basis of a courage it invokes but that it neither fully understands nor can explain. This line of argument suggests that our coming to know is a *being given to understand*, with emphasis on (unknown) sources of knowing that release us, free us into understanding. Knowing is possibilized by an empowering of understanding, an *encouraging of knowing* quite different from the courage of Hegelian knowing that claims to be self-determining, self-encouraging.

I do not believe abjectness of thought is the true response to the Hegelian self-confidence of reason. This self-confidence becomes overconfidence, in occluding the more original, confiding source of courage. When such overconfidence becomes confidence over all, this is spiritual hubris for the human being. One would not even attribute such confidence to a God, and especially not if that God is agapeic, which Hegel's is not. The agapeic God is a God of releasing the other into its own being for itself.[14] The agapeic God is the God of the most ultimate confidence – confiding freedom to the mortal creature, to the finite human. This is a venture on the mortal creature, full of the hazard of an extraordinary confidence, the confiding that is the investiture of freedom to be at all, and to be oneself. This confiding is an endowing: a giving that gives resources that can be put to work and enjoyment – with a promise that is to be redeemed, but that is not exhausted in self-satisfied self-determination.

In this light, the truer sense of confidence is not the self-confidence, not the overconfidence, but the confidence that is between. The '*con*', '*cum*', 'with', of con-fidence opens the between space of communicating difference which it also crosses. The confidence of

---

14 On this more fully, see *God and the Between*; on Hegel's God as erotic rather than agapeic, see William Desmond, *Hegel's God: A Counterfeit Double?* (Aldershot: Ashgate, 2003), *passim*, but especially chapter 4.

our endowment can grant its (re)sources in itself and its source in more than itself. This confidence can grant a superior other, a God over it. It does not have to overtake everything to be itself. It knows the mutilation involved when this kind of self-confidence takes over. There is tyranny of faith in oneself which is lack of faith in anything else. This becomes in turn a suspicion, a distrust that can turn into destruction of the other. For every other is a reminder of the lie that this self-affirmation is: a lie that is not truthful with itself, much less with the other.

In such a world the sources of a more original trust are blocked up, and the soul cannot look up. The ontological porosity that goes with confidence as a between is clogged. Confidence as a between condition is both confident and the recipient of confidences. I see this in the light of the intimate universal. In our hearts we know something of being the recipient of confidences, even if the confiding power is often enigmatic and nameless. Our confident heart, having being confided in, participates in the intimate universal. Often we have to silence the clamour in and around us to hear such confidences. We live in a world full of shouting. Wording the between becomes harder in this world of shouts.

In Confidence: Metaphysics and the Intimate Universal

Wording the between, that is to say, giving a *logos* of the *metaxu*: such is the task of a metaxological philosophy. This, one can now say, endorses a proper affirmation of the confidence of thinking. True, this affirmation has to be in the right register and with the right note. Much hangs on the 'how' of the affirmation. The extremes of overconfidence and abjectness are to be avoided. We can be confident in thought because we are recipients of confidence(s). There is an intimacy and patience here beyond critique. In this intimate patience a communication of metaphysical astonishment may also come. One cannot project astonishment; one cannot project surprise; one must be opened, or become open to its happening. Astonishment comes to us before we go from it towards what is beyond us.

There is a confidence both prior to and beyond nihilism that can never be entirely exhausted, as long as we remain the beings we are. This means that there is a future for metaphysical thinking. This is not first a question of particular doctrines to be renewed or taken over from the tradition – though respect for modes of thinking showing reliable constancy over time is very important. Even less is it a matter of thinking that all thought hitherto is something to be deconstructed. It may well be true that there are fixations that have to be made fluid and porous again. But if the undoing of the fixity does not lay itself open to the deeper source of confidence, it risks being merely an updated version of thinking as negation. This too ends up with almost nothing, in the end. It does not come again into confidence but vacillates between saying something and saying nothing, with the tilt towards saying nothing, even while seeming to say something. The primal confidence can indeed cause us to look with diffidence on some fixations but there are different ways of looking, and it is all important that the looking be informed by truthful love. The determinacies of thought may hide their own recession of the deeper confidings of thinking. Wording the between asks of us finesse for discernment concerning these recessions. The ontological love that is present in being truthful is not to be betrayed. There can be a knowing that glories in supposedly telling the truth, but if this telling is informed with secret traces of hatred, the spirit of truth is itself corrupted.

Consider how we might correct the conduct of another that is amiss: the correction can be communicated in a spirit of less than love. The exact same things might be said in correction, but the 'how' of the saying, reflecting the 'who' of the sayer, might fulfil the truth of the situation, and its promise, or else might betray it, turning truth-telling into an ontological violence. Such truth-telling tells the truth, in one sense, but since the 'how' of the telling, and the 'who' of the one who tells, are lacking in the love of truth revered by truthfulness, the telling warps the spirit of truthfulness. Of course, traditional metaphysics has been charged with an ontological violence, but one has to be very qualified about this. There is an indictment of metaphysics that tells us as much about the indictor as the indictee – the indictor who cannot see the tradition in any other light except that of an erring. Such a teller cannot invest any trust in it. In the name of what is this refusal of trust? In the name of truth, or truthfulness, one might say. Of its own truthfulness? But the deeper we know this, the more we know that we must be finessed in diffidence about judgement on the other as putatively not in the truth. The truth of something 'other'? Well then, hewing to the path of truthfulness must continue. And on this path the best of metaphysical thinking has always passed.

I am not saying this in merely reactive exoneration of traditional metaphysics. The true confidence of thinking is beyond self-assertive indictment and reactive exoneration. There is one great circumstance that calls again for mention: the companionship of religion and metaphysics in the past. To my mind this provides a source of affirmation that gives a confidence, as much expressed in religious faith as in the trust in reason itself, as much admonitory of the overreaching ambitions of human power as in solidarity with human poverty, as much rejoicing in the excellence of human nobility as compassionate in sight of the tragedies of failure, as much tender to human limitations as laughing with its folly. Of course, the distrust of traditional metaphysics is often coupled with a distrust of, disdain for, even violence to religion. But this reveals the extremity of the situation. What is most needed is what is least acknowledged as so needed. To confess this need would be to seek release from the scientistic bewitchments of fixated determinacy, as well as de-idolize the idea of self-determining thinking. It would be to move beyond the deconstruction of both the determinacy and self-determinacy, not so much in the direction of a new construction as towards a renewed patient mindfulness of the intimate strangeness of being.

The confidence of thought entails an ontological trust and epistemic fidelity without which the very enterprise of thinking, and of all our seeking for knowledge, can only come to nothing. We know the seeking can turn against the search itself. Yet this turn against itself of searching thought reveals the same deep-down companionship of the confiding. Patient mindfulness must open itself again to this passion of thinking – passion as an under-going and a receiving – passion, one might also say, as an inspiration that already carries us in an at first unchosen arc of transcending. This patience is *ecstasis* into a darkness that is not grim but lightening. In this we see the family resemblance to religious faith. This is no univocal light but a trust that comes to hold steady, to be held steady in the play of light and darkness, in the equivocal twilight, or dawn, that marks our metaxological condition. There is a going into the cave of our own ignorance, but we must be vigilant that our own hugging of ourselves against the darkness does not become also our self-retraction against the communicating light.

The confidence of which I speak is not a matter of fideism, just as the trust of faith is not simply a sacred 'say so' – as can happen with fideistic interpretations. Reason and faith are in a darkness that is not dark. It is the darkness of a mystery that is not alone enveloping but intimate to our undergoing of metaphysical astonishment and perplexity at our middle condition. When all things are considered, this mystery is what, in our heart of hearts, we love as ultimate. Love is in confiding. We are loved when another takes us into their confidence. We love another when we are taken into confidence. We are by our very being taken into confidence. The call on our being is to take what is given into our own confidence.

This is reflected in the task of metaphysics as a mindful love of being, as a knowing fidelity to what being shows itself to be. This is reflected in the consolation of being religious: in the dark night of the seemingly absent God, trust is confided, dark trust that grows lighter with love as it dwells more and more with its own darkness. There is nothing of escapism in this. There is a mysticism of deeper communication, and it is in love with the good of mortal things because secretly the divine love of mortal things has been confided to them. This issues in a service which I think can only be called agapeic – generous giving, surplus to determinacy, and self-determinacy, and no mere indeterminacy but an overdeterminacy of availability. What is confided to us is the confidence to lay ourselves open, even in the attack of the hostile other, for even there, there is the promise of good, more always than the face of oppugnancy turned towards us. What turns towards us has buried deep in itself the ontological confidence which can be resurrected over there only by seeing it already invested in the neighbour who smiles its gift towards the retracted one, unasked. This is an ethical-religious service – enacting an idiotic smile of the love of God that has set us on the way and that does not go away even when we are away, even astray.

Deprived of the worthy, we cannot still but desire the worthy. We desire what is worthy for itself, what is worthy of ourselves, what is worthy of the promise of truth that has been confided to us.

Veritas: Belief and Metaphysics

We love the trust that has been confided in us. Metaphysics can be a form of this thinking love. The love of the trust is not just our own love, or our own trust. When we are loved we are trusted. When we love we trust. When we think, we trust that there is truth to be heard and communicated. When we truly think, we are in love. Trust in thought is our participation (sometimes even thoughtlessly) in the agapeics of being.

What do we trust? This question has to be asked about the confiding: could a neutral causality or valueless process or mechanism confide? If such neutered being or valueless process were the final answer, could there be any confidence at all in thought, such as we have discovered it to be? Were being a neutral mechanism or valueless process, of which we too would be instantiations, the confidence, being called on, and put to work fruitfully, would finally come to the truth which would show us that there is no ground for confidence at all. We would then be theorizing on the same branch that we are confidently sawing off with our own thoughts.

One might say: This power of the process of being is in one, is one and is over against one – and this process is power and nothing but power. But what kind of power? Will to power? But devoid of reference to what is worthy to be trusted, to the trustworthy, how relate to this power? How affirm it, in the sense at issue, if it too is nothing but valueless happening? Would not our own affirmation of it, or of ourselves, be then too a valueless happening? And would not then the self-confidence of this power be also strangely out of place? Out of place, since if this too were a neutered process, there is no explanation for the stress of singularity, singularity of a personal character, that is expressed in self-confidence.

'Being out of place' is itself hard to make intelligible, if there is not something to the confidence that can shed light on the possibility of the *betrayal*, as well as the redemption of promise. For confidence communicates the promise of some good. To speak of the betrayal or redemption of promise ultimately can have no meaning in a world of worthless process or valueless being. Similarly, the courage of knowing makes no sense in any such neutralized world. Would not the extremity of such a way of thinking point towards a totally deconsecrated world? From where comes such confidence in an entirely deconsecrated world? Such confidence could not be endowed in such a world. Yet we continue to enjoy its benefit – though, properly speaking, on this view the confidence should not be at all. It is warped confidence that deconsecrates the world.

Think here of the example of the torturer and trust. The torturer lives in a world that seems quite different to that of the neutralized world of valueless being. Torture is an activity saturated with value – though it is hatred, whether hot or cold, that drives it. Yet there is a connection between the torturer and valueless being. The torturer takes the next step to deconsecration – he desecrates the other. The torturer tries to gain access to the mortal intimacy of the idiotic soul. He seeks access, by force or guile, utterly to destroy trust in the victim. He desecrates the soul's place of intimate confiding. He tries to destroy trust in God. His violation says: Your God is dead; you too will die, and deeper than the death of your body will be the destruction of your spirit – and its confidence. Without trust life is impossible for us. When nothing confides in us, nothing communicates with us, we are as nothing. When confidence dies or is killed, we are condemned to be nothing. That we *are at all* means that the intimate confiding is communicated into the secret chambers of the soul. The torturer wants to ransack these secret chambers, perhaps kill God in the soul. All too often we are our own torturer. We kill God in ourselves.

Bist du bei mir: the haunting music sings of the love that is confided, even in the meeting with death. It seems reasonable to suggest that the source of a confiding must in some measure be proportionate to the character of the confidence. A liar does not confide the truth. A source of truth does not confide a lie. A liar may betray the truth, in telling a lie. Even the lie is told with the confidence of truth. If we are confided trust in truth, in our being truthful, what does this say of the source of the confiding, the confidence? The source of our confidence must reflect something of the nature of that confidence, confided both as trust that the world can be truly known, or as self-confidence that we can trust the powers entrusted to us. At its deepest, confidence is personal, both as singular and as communal. If our confidence reveals something both intimate and universal, in a personally stressed singularity that opens to all that is beyond itself, we might expect that the source of the confiding too will have something of the nature of the intimate universal.

Between ourselves, and speaking now in confidence, there is something entirely fitting if we think of God as the endowing source of the confiding. You object that this is a leap. But must philosophy slouch? And as it slouches, oddly strut with self-confidence? Slouching towards what? You say: walking is enough. But walking lifts us up. In confidence we leap. Even though we are tested in our confidence in the divine, the confidence is endowed by the divine. God confides the promise of the intimate universal. Trust is invested in what is worthy to be trusted – but what most is worthy to be trusted is what loves us in the proper measure. This measure for us is an infinite measure. We would be infinitely loved. In our most idiotic intimacy, we live ourselves never as a neutral replaceable but as intimately singular. God is the endowing source of the intimate universal. Only the personal, transpersonal God could endow the trusted singular with the universal as the intimate universal. *Bist du bei mir*: the air quickens our confidence, heartens it, but it is love that the air consecrates.

3. The Beauty of the Metaphysical Imagination

[I would like to dedicate the following to John Milbank]

JOHN R. BETZ

It seems *de rigueur* today to say that we live in a post-metaphysical age, or so we have been told, and that any discussion of metaphysics, even among theologians, will likely be received as an anachronism. Indeed, scepticism of metaphysics is almost as standard a feature of academic theology today as it is of the dominant trends of postmodern philosophy. This circumstance may be attributed, on the one hand, to the inevitable influence of modern philosophy: from the dubious thought-experiment of Descartes, to the anti-metaphysical scepticism of Hume, to Kant's 'island of illusion' and doctrine of the unknowability of the *Ding an sich,* to Nietzsche's doctrine of the will to power, to the *Verwindung* (though not *Überwindung*) of metaphysics in Heidegger, to the logical positivism of the Vienna circle, to American pragmatism and Anglo-American analytic philosophy, to the linguistic turn of the late Wittgenstein, not to mention the surd of crass materialism, divorced from any notions of formal and final causation, that still informs so much of modern natural science. On the other hand, there have been significant contributing factors within the theological tradition itself: from the Reformation's suspicion of natural theology (Luther more so than Calvin), to Karl Barth's rejection of the *analogia entis* in favour of a narrative-based dogmatic theology, to the cultural-linguistic model of Christianity proposed by George Lindbeck and popularized (with an admixture of Barthianism) by the Yale school.[1]

---

1 See George A. Lindbeck, *The Nature of Doctrine: Religion and*

Veritas: Belief and Metaphysics

In the following, however, I wish to argue (however anachronistically) for the indispensability of metaphysics to theology – at the very least, as Nicholas Lash has argued, as having a regulative function that keeps Christian discourse (first and foremost of the incarnate *Logos*) from degenerating into mere mythology or, what amounts to the same thing, simply the 'language game' of this or that community.[2] This is true, for example, not only of the doctrine of the incarnation, but also of the doctrine of creation, which in the absence of an objective metaphysics and proper distinctions between act and potency, being and becoming (and given especially the contemporary dominance of modern scientific, that is, merely material and efficient, accounts of causation) similarly threatens to be taken for mere mythology. This is not to say that a theologically neutral metaphysics has pre-eminence over Christian discourse; for a *Christian* metaphysics will be decidedly determined by *Christian* revelation, which retains its due priority. Rather, it is to say that without a theological metaphysics, the transcendent perspective, which metaphysics holds open, threatens to collapse into the 'way of speaking' of this or that 'faith community' – and with it the reverence apart from which the worship of the one, true God all too readily degenerates into idolatry. Indeed, in this respect, metaphysics (without which there would have been no apophatic tradition of the Areopagite) serves precisely to safeguard the transcendence of the God who 'dwells in unapproachable light' (1 Tim. 6.16).

Of course, one might conceivably claim that metaphysics adds nothing to what Scripture itself already reveals. For here too we are informed of God's eternity, transcendence, goodness, and beauty –

Theology in a Postliberal Age (Philadelphia: Westminster Press, 1984). For a discussion of the fate of metaphysics in light of these influences, especially Barth and Heidegger, and for a fuller treatment of the concerns addressed here, see John R. Betz, 'Beyond the Sublime: The Aesthetics of the Analogy of Being (Part One)', *Modern Theology* 21.3 (July 2005), pp. 367–411; 'Beyond the Sublime: The Aesthetics of the Analogy of Being (Part Two)', *Modern Theology* 22.1 (January 2006), pp. 1–50.

2 See, for example, Nicholas Lash, 'Ideology, Metaphor, and Analogy', in Stanley Hauerwas and Gregory Jones (eds), *Why Narrative?: Readings in Narrative Theology* (Grand Rapids, MI: Eerdmans, 1989), pp. 113–37.

indeed, of something new and metaphysically unforeseen: his indwelling *Shekinah* glory [*kābôd*]. Yet one must admit that, for all that Scripture contains and reveals, one's understanding of these concepts has been informed by the metaphysical tradition in ways that we need not disparage or regret. One must admit, furthermore, that certain aspects of Scripture are explicitly metaphysical in content (it would be impossible, for example, to separate out the metaphysical implications of the Logos metaphysics of the prologue of John, and one could make a similar case for the matter of Stoicism in Paul).[3] But not only is metaphysics *in* Scripture, and inextricably woven into its fabric. As Matthew Levering has recently argued, for the Church fathers (e.g. from Origen to Gregory of Nyssa to Augustine to that quintessentially metaphysical theologian, Maximus) and Aquinas, the appropriation of sacred teaching has always demanded metaphysical questioning, which in turn serves heuristically to illuminate scriptural revelation.[4]

A strong case can thus be made for the importance of metaphysics to theology: on the one hand, as having a regulative function *vis-à-vis* Christian discourse; on the other hand, as a heuristic aid to illuminating Scripture's inherent metaphysical depth. In any case, it would seem that the role of metaphysics in theology is not only legitimate, but at some level indispensable; that, *contra* Tertullian, there must be a connection between Athens and Jerusalem, between the wisdom of the philosophers and the incarnate wisdom revealed in Christ[5] – and not least of all because

---

3 See, for example, Troels Engberg-Pedersen, *Paul and the Stoics* (Louisville: Westminster John Knox Press, 2000). Of course, from the eighteenth century (e.g., Matthew Tindal, J. D. Michaelis, H. S. Reimarus, and Thomas Jefferson) to the nineteenth (e.g., D. F. Strauss and A. von Harnack) to the Jesus Seminar and not a small number of theologians of the twentieth, it has been characteristic of the liberal Protestant tradition to weed out what its various representatives have deemed accidental and therefore dispensable accretions to Scripture (whether this be the 'mythological' accounts of miracles or the apathy axiom of Greek metaphysics).

4 Matthew Levering, *Scripture and Metaphysics: Aquinas and the Renewal of Trinitarian Theology* (Oxford: Blackwell, 2004), pp. 8–9.

5 To be sure, philosophy will be transformed by this encounter; it will initially be baffled, stupefied, as the apostle says of the Word of the Cross

without metaphysics theology tends to become boring, *unimaginative*, and ultimately uninspiring. As Stephen R. L. Clark aptly puts it,

> Once religion is reduced to the level of sentimental moralism on the one hand, and equally sentimental ritualism on the other, it is hardly surprising that a lot of people lose interest. When it is understood that there is something to be said for a hard metaphysical theism we can at least get a sensible discussion going.[6]

That is to say that without a metaphysical vision something of the *aesthetics* of Christian truth is also lost, and with it something of the beauty of the God who would draw or attract all things to himself.

My ultimate aim in the following, therefore, in the interest of an undiminished Christian aesthetic, is to explicate the relevance of a specifically *Christian* metaphysics to the project of a *Christian* aesthetics. In other words, I wish to argue that metaphysics (an analogical metaphysics, in particular) is indispensable to an articulation of the beauty of the God that Christianity proclaims. To some, admittedly, this might seem far-fetched. One might dispute, for example, that there is any necessary connection between metaphysics and aesthetics. One might even consider it obligatory, as a matter of aesthetic appreciation, precisely to avoid metaphysical abstractions when speaking of something as ineffable as divine beauty or as concrete as the presence of God in Christ. And yet, it is no accident that Hans Urs von Balthasar devotes two volumes of *The Glory of the Lord*, without question the most important work of theological aesthetics in our time, to the topic and history of metaphysics. And surely it is also of note that from its historical inception the metaphysical imagination, in Plato and Aristotle

---

(1 Cor. 1.18ff.). But if it should receive the novelty of revelation (cf. John 1.12), such reception is not unto its abrogation (according to the modern model of philosophy as *autonomy*), but unto its fulfilment in cognitive *union* with the divine to which it naturally aspires. Which goes to say that philosophy is not true philosophy apart from the loving admission of something beyond its native grasp.

6 Stephen R. L. Clark, *The Mysteries of Religion* (Oxford: Basil Blackwell, 1986), p. 247.

especially, has been concerned, almost preoccupied, with the question of beauty. By contrast, one could characterize the inception of modern philosophy (and modernity in general) precisely in terms of *the loss of the metaphysical imagination* and a corresponding boorish failure to appreciate beauty's transcendent significance.

Metaphysics and Aesthetics in Historical Perspective

When Plato and Aristotle spoke of beauty, it is notable that they did so in explicitly metaphysical terms. Indeed, for them, the very pursuit of philosophy itself, which commences with wonder (θαῦμα), could be described, quite simply, as a response to an *aesthetic* experience. As Plato says in the *Theaetetus,* 'For truly, this experience of wonder is the mark of the philosopher. Indeed, philosophy has no other origin' (μάλα γὰρ φιλόσοφον τοῦτο τὸ πάθος, τὸ θαυμάζειν. Οὐ γὰρ ἄλλη ἀρχὴ φιλοσοφίας ἡ αὐτή).[7] And as Aristotle similarly says in the *Metaphysics*: 'It is on account of wonder that now and from the beginning human beings began to philosophize' (διὰ γάρ τὸ θαυμάζειν οἱ ἄνθρωποι καὶ νῦν καὶ τὸ πρῶτον ἤρξαντο φιλοσοφεῖν).[8] Along the same lines, therefore, Aristotle affirms against the Pythagoreans and Speusippus that a 'supreme beauty' was present (in the order of being) from the beginning.[9] For Plato and Aristotle, however, beauty stands not only at the theoretical beginning of philosophy, but also at its theoretical *and* practical end. Thus Plato has Diotima say to Socrates in the *Symposium,* 'the quest for the universal beauty must find him ever mounting the heavenly ladder . . . until at last he comes to know what beauty is' (211c); thus in the *Metaphysics,* Aristotle's prime mover moves all things by being loved, as that which is beautiful and desirable in itself (1072a); thus in the *Republic,* Plato, the Pythagorean, conceives of the moral life ultimately in terms of a beautiful harmony of the soul (400d); and thus in the *Nicomachean Ethics* – though this is something often mistranslated and therefore overlooked – Aristotle conceives of the

---

7 *Theaetetus,* 155 d.
8 *Metaphysics,* 982 b.
9 *Metaphysics,* 1072b.

end (*telos*) of virtue, remarkably enough, in terms of beauty (τὸ καλόν) as the very thing at which the moral life consistently aims.[10]

By the time Alexander Gottlieb Baumgarten coined the term 'aesthetics' in the middle of the eighteenth century, however, beauty no longer had so immediate a metaphysical or practical import, notwithstanding his avowedly metaphysical philosophy. Nor, increasingly, did it enjoy its former rapport with the other transcendentals, but was gradually sequestered from its sisters, relegated to the domain of mere sense perception, as the term aesthesis (from ἀισθεσις) would suggest. On the one hand, certainly, this development was the inevitable result of the anthropological turn at the beginning of modern philosophy in Descartes, and of the same scepticism regarding the phenomenal world that proved so inimical and fateful to metaphysics. At the same time, once the phenomenal world had been depersonalized and reduced to non- or sub-rational status (as opposed to the classical vision of the phenomenal world's participation in and expression of the eternal *Logos*), it can be seen precisely as the result of the various mechanistic and neo-Epicurean materialist cosmologies of the Enlightenment, for which the realm of the senses no longer constituted, in any necessary sense, a revelation of transcendent significance. And, finally, with Kant's transcendental gutting of the theoretical realm in the first *Critique*, the transcendentals had been so radically sundered that a monumental and arguably unsuccessful effort was required (in his second and third *Critiques*) to put them back together again.

From a theological perspective, however, which cannot fail to see that 'the heavens declare the glory of God' (Ps. 19.1) – not even for the sake of a methodological *epoché* or a phenomenological reduction to consciousness – the history of modern philosophy cannot help but appear as the history of a mistake, one that could not be corrected without going back to its *proton pseudos*, that is, its founding separation of the sensible and the metaphysical (or, in Descartes' case, the sensible and the certain). Accordingly, the task of restoring philosophy, healing it from its self-incurred wounds, and salvaging it from the service of purely immanent, technological ends, would seem to depend upon the discovery of the 'clear

---

10 *Nicomachean Ethics*, 1115b.

and distinct' *within* the sensible, of the ideal *in* the real – however much 'through a glass darkly'. In short, it would seem to require a rethinking of the metaphysical implications of the aesthetic realm, of beauty itself, not as merely one subject among the philosophical disciplines, but as the *principium* and *finis* of philosophy's investigations.

To be sure, one cannot undo the history of philosophy; one cannot simply return to Plato and Aristotle. One can, however, validate their philosophical intuition (and certain intuitions of German idealism, those of Schelling, in particular) with the credibility of revelation. Indeed, following a certain reading of the Thomistic maxim, *fides non destruit sed supponit et perficit rationem*, theology can lend support to philosophy, which, left to its own devices, inevitably succumbs to scepticism and – as history bears out – nihilism.[11] Specifically, in confirmation of philosophy, theology can say that the reason why Plato and Aristotle began with wonder is that the sensible world *is* a revelation. This is why one *can* begin with the senses, and why one can – and *should* – begin with the experience of wonder. Moreover, one can say that Christianity fulfils philosophy by enabling one to see the unseen *in* the seen, the metaphysical *in* the sensible (John 1.18; 14.7f.). Admittedly, the novelty of revelation exceeds rational comprehension – just as the incarnation eclipses the wonder of Greek philosophy, and just as the Word of the Cross is 'foolishness' to the Greeks (1 Cor. 1.18). And yet, in some sense, the revelation of the invisible God in Christ (Col. 1.15) also confirms the Greek

---

11 Cf. *De Veritate*, q. 14, a. 10 ad 9; *Summa Theologiae* I, q. 1, a. 8 ad 2; ibid., I, q. 2, a. 2 ad 1. I am reading *supponit* here not as it is usually translated, as 'supposes' (in the sense that faith 'supposes' reason, just as grace 'supposes' nature), but more tendentiously, in an etymologically legitimate sense of 'supports'. The upshot of this ambiguity is that the maxim can be taken to contain both a *warning* and a *promise* to reason. The warning is that apart from faith, autonomous reason can secure for itself no foundation (as the history of philosophy's failures in this regard amply demonstrate), and thus collapses either into nihilism or the service of the purely immanent ends of technology. The promise, on the other hand, according to the traditional reading, is that reason is perfected by faith, and is thus able to see more and understand more than was hitherto possible.

philosophical intuition of a connection between metaphysics and aesthetics, even as it radically transforms this connection into an hitherto inconceivable Christological commingling and saturation of the one with the other.

Metaphysics and *The Glory of the Lord*

Having established the historical connection between metaphysics and aesthetics – a connection that in modern philosophy, in the interest of certainty apart from faith, was radically severed – we are now in a position to state, from a Christian perspective, that metaphysics and aesthetics do, in fact, imply one another; moreover, that this itself is in some sense the mystery of the incarnation as the *aesthetic* revelation of the *metaphysical* God. Indeed, because of this mutual implication, a theological aesthetics is necessarily concerned with metaphysics. As von Balthasar programmatically puts it, 'The specific theological task of treating the glory of the Christian revelation cannot be completed without constant concomitant reflection on the subject of metaphysics.'[12] The only question at this point, as we proceed from the general to the specific, is what kind of metaphysics is best suited to articulating a specifically Christian aesthetics. And to this end, loosely following von Balthasar, I would argue that 'the glory of the Lord' cannot be separated from, and indeed in some sense depends upon, a metaphysics of *analogy* – the *locus classicus* for which is Erich Przywara's *Analogia Entis*.[13] Indeed, following von Balthasar's suggestion in his treatment of Aquinas, I would argue that there can be no glory – no *Herrlichkeit* – without it.[14]

In order to get to this point, however, one must acknowledge that the *analogia entis* has been the target of much criticism, philo-

---

12 Hans Urs von Balthasar, *Herrlichkeit: Eine Theologische Ästhetik*, III/1 (Einsiedeln: Johannes Verlag, 1965), p. 14.

13 Przywara, *Analogia Entis*, in *Schriften*, vol. 3 (Einsiedeln: Johannes Verlag, 1962). Hereafter cited as *AE*. The original text of *Analogia Entis: Metaphysik*, which is reprinted here with a few emendations, was published in 1932. An English translation of *Analogia Entis*, translated by myself and David Hart, is soon to appear with Eerdmans.

14 *AE*, p. 365.

The Beauty of the Metaphysical Imagination

sophical as well as theological, beyond the general criticisms of metaphysics that were indirectly addressed above: on the one hand, the standard postmodern charge, stemming from Heidegger, that the *analogia entis* is a species of 'ontotheology', and therefore must be rejected; on the other hand, criticism from within the Christian tradition itself, most notably Karl Barth's hyperbolic verdict in the preface to the *Church Dogmatics* that the *analogia entis* is '*the* invention of Antichrist' and the reason why one 'cannot become Catholic'.[15] The result of this strident declaration, which amounted to a Protestant *anathema sit*, was that from then on the *analogia entis* became, as Przywara once put it with chagrin, 'the favourite puppet' in the carnival of ecumenical debate.[16]

In order to get beyond these criticisms to the aesthetic implications of the *analogia entis*, certain steps will therefore be required. I will argue *first* that the *analogia entis*, as a particular metaphysics, far from being a metaphysical chimera, is, at the end of the day, simply a consistent development and philosophical clarification of the Church's doctrine of creation. *Second*, given that the term *analogia entis* is notoriously employed far more often than it is understood (of which Barth's use of the term is a prime example), I will sketch out what Przywara himself actually understood by it. *Third,* I will briefly address Barth's and Heidegger's specific objections to the doctrine. *Finally,* having argued for the legitimacy of *this particular metaphysics*, I will sketch out the kind of theological aesthetics that might go along with it – with the additional hope of shedding some light on why von Balthasar held Przywara in such high regard, referring to him at one point as the 'old master', who remains strangely 'younger' than his disciples.[17]

---

15 *Kirchliche Dogmatik*, I/1 (Zurich: Evangelischer Verlag, 1932), p. viii.
16 *In und Gegen: Stellungnahmen zur Zeit* (Nürnberg: Glock und Lutz, 1955), p. 278.
17 See Leo Zimny (ed.), *Erich Przywara: Sein Schrifttum (1912–1962)*, with an introduction by Hans Urs von Balthasar (Einsiedeln: Johannes Verlag, 1963), p. 18.

Toward a Metaphysics of Creation

As Newman famously observed in his *Essay on the Development of Christian Doctrine*, one of the characteristics of the doctrines of the Church is that they were never defined all of a sudden, but developed over time, typically in battle with heresy – and, oddly, thanks to it. And in this vein he compares doctrines to rivers, which only gradually, over the course of their winding and tentative beginnings, strike out in a definite direction, at which point they begin powerfully to determine the intellectual landscape of the Church. The only problem with Newman's analogy, as he himself admits, is that rivers tend to be clearer the nearer they are to their source. In view of Church history, however, he says that doctrine develops precisely in the opposite direction, from lesser to greater clarity. As he explains it,

> It is indeed sometimes said that the stream is clearest near the spring. Whatever use may fairly be made of this image, it does not apply to the history of a philosophy or belief, which on the contrary is more equable, and purer, and stronger, when its bed has become deep, and broad, and full.[18]

The point of this reflection is to say that what has been true of other doctrines, like the Trinitarian doctrine of the fourth century and the Christological doctrine of the fifth, has also been true of the Church's doctrine of creation. For it too has undergone development (or, more precisely, clarification), under the varying influence of Plato (as modified by Augustine, among others) and Aristotle (as modified by Aquinas, among others); and it too has been shaped by challenges – from Augustine's early battles against the Manichees to John Milbank's and David Hart's more recent responses to Nietzsche's and Deleuze's similarly violent ontologies.[19] Indeed, from antiquity to postmodernity the Church has

---

18 Quoted in Ian Ker, *Newman on Being a Christian* (Notre Dame: University of Notre Dame Press, 1990), p. 34.

19 See John Milbank, *Theology and Social Theory: Beyond Secular Reason* (Oxford: Blackwell, 1990); David Hart, *The Beauty of the Infinite: The Aesthetics of Christian Truth* (Grand Rapids: Eerdmans, 2003).

The Beauty of the Metaphysical Imagination

often been obliged to defend its doctrine of creation, especially its ultimate goodness and peacefulness. And in its effort to do so, it has typically – and I would argue necessarily – presented its doctrine of creation in terms of *analogy*, which has the advantage of allowing the Church to speak of the being, goodness and beauty of creation as a positive *participation* in the being, goodness and beauty of God, *while at the same time* affirming God's radical transcendence of creation and his abiding difference from it. In short, it allows the Church to avoid both the Scylla of univocal identity (which would collapse the distinction between Creator and creature) and the Charybdis of equivocal alterity (which would foreclose the possibility of any relation between them).

What is the *Analogia Entis*?

The term *analogia entis* seems to have originated with Cajetan, but what it describes is more or less original to Aquinas.[20] That being said, one must acknowledge that there are many today, some of them distinguished scholars of Aquinas, who would dispute that Thomas ever had a doctrine of the analogy of being, seeing his use of analogy as applying merely to theological judgements regarding the use of certain words.[21] And one must grant that Thomas never used the term *as a term*. For Przywara, however, even if it is nowhere explicitly stated, the *analogia entis* (i.e. an ontological and not merely linguistic doctrine of analogy) is implied by Aquinas's doctrine of divine simplicity and his corresponding doctrine of a real distinction in creatures between essence and existence.

---

20 See Julio Terán-Dutari, 'Die Geschichte des Terminus 'Analogia Entis' und das Werk Erich Przywaras', *Philosophisches Jahrbuch* 77 (1970), pp. 163–179. As Terán-Dutari shows, *analogia entis* was long a *terminus technicus* among the Jesuits and can readily be found, for example, in Suarez, de Rhodes and Franzelin.

21 See, for example, Herbert McCabe in his translation of the *Summa Theologiae*, vol. 3: *Knowing and Naming God* (London: Eyre and Spottiswoode, 1964), p. 106: 'Analogy is not a way of getting to know about God, nor is it a theory of the structure of the universe, it is a comment on our use of certain words.'

Veritas: Belief and Metaphysics

Thus, following scholars like W. Norris Clarke, one might say that the difference is one between an implicit and an explicit doctrine – in this case a doctrine that is implied by Aquinas's understanding of creation.[22] Indeed, not just for Aquinas but for medieval theology in general, analogy is implied by the causality of creation.[23] As Gilson puts it, 'every cause produces an effect that resembles it: *omne agens agit sibi simile* . . . If then, as the idea of creation implies, the Christian universe is an effect of God, it must of necessity be an *analogue*.'[24] Or, as Aquinas himself puts it, 'Since every agent reproduces itself so far as it is an agent, and everything acts in accord with its form, the effect must in some way resemble the form of the agent.'[25] And this is why Gilson says that 'every Christian metaphysic involves the conceptions of participation and similitude . . . '[26]

But if creation is necessarily an analogue, one must be clear that for Przywara (as for Thomas and Gilson) it is *only* an analogue. For, notwithstanding a certain relationship based in similarity, God and creation are ultimately *incommensurable*. Indeed the

---

22 See W. Norris Clarke, *Explorations in Metaphysics* (Notre Dame: University of Notre Dame Press, 1994), p. 45.

23 See Kenneth Surin, 'Creation, Revelation, and the Analogy Theory', in *The Turnings of Darkness and Light* (Cambridge: Cambridge University Press, 1989), pp. 1–19, where he makes a helpful distinction within Aquinas's theory of analogy between a *linguistic* subthesis (regarding the rules of proper theological predication, as governed, respectively, by an analogy of attribution and an analogy of proper proportionality) and a *metaphysical* subthesis, which is the ground and *sine qua non* of the former (and consists, ultimately, in an analogical 'isomorphism' between God and creation on the basis of divine simplicity and causality). Cf. David Burrell's observation: 'since any warrant we have for using human language at all – even perfection terms – turns on the grounding fact of creation, such terms cannot be univocal, since they must be able to span "the distinction" of creatures from creator without collapsing it' ('Analogy, Creation, and Theological Language', in *The Theology of Thomas Aquinas*, ed. Rik van Nieuwenhove and Joseph Wawrykow (Notre Dame: University of Notre Dame Press, 2005), p. 78; cf. p. 83).

24 Etienne Gilson, *The Spirit of Medieval Philosophy* (Notre Dame: University of Notre Dame Press, 1936), p. 95f. My emphasis.

25 *ST* I, q. 4, a. 3.

26 *The Spirit of Medieval Philosophy*, p. 96.

proportion between them *must* be disproportionate, because in creating God adds nothing to himself; and because the being of the creature – being utterly gratuitous – has no claim on its being. Of course, one might ask, how can the being of creation be an *incommensurable analogue* of the being of God? Is this not a case of wanting to have one's cake and eating it too? Is this not attempting to do the impossible – to speak of similarity and difference without compromising either? And in a sense it is. But in Przywara's case it is never a simple balancing act. For the all-important qualification here, as with every negative theology, is that the emphasis is always upon the ultimate and abiding *difference* – the '*ever greater dissimilarity*', as he tirelessly puts it – between God and creatures *within* every similarity and *exploding* every similarity, however great. Indeed, the *analogia entis* is precisely this *unstable* rhythm between similarity and an ultimate dissimilarity; and this is why Przywara summarizes the *analogia entis* (explicitly against Hegel) as a methodological *reductio in mysterium*.

To spell out the difference between God and creatures in terms of the real distinction, which lies at the basis of Przywara's doctrine, the difference is that whereas God IS (being a simple identity of essence and existence), creatures are forever becoming who they 'are'. Thus, not only is the existence of the creature gratuitous, but even its essence is something fundamentally incomplete (which is all the more so the case to the extent that one is talking not about rocks or plants or animals, but about free rational creatures who are made to find fulfilment in God). As the first epistle of John puts it in reference to Christ, 'What we will be has not yet been revealed. What we do know is this: when he is revealed, we will be like him, for we will see him as he is' (1 John 3.2). Or, as that quintessentially metaphysical thinker, C. S. Lewis, might have put it, in comparison to Christ we in our pre-eschatological and thus pre-transfigured state are but 'shadows of men'.[27] And this is why, in view of such metaphysical incompleteness, Przywara defines

---

27 Consider, for example, the conclusion of *Perelandra*, or the title of *Till We Have Faces,* or the whole story of *The Great Divorce* as a story, on the one hand, of minuscule 'shadows' and 'ghosts', who are either in hell or purgatory, and the life-size, bright, solid people of heaven, on the other, who have been solidified (and made real) by grace.

creaturely reality in terms of the dynamic formula: 'essence-in-and-beyond-existence' (*Sosein-in-über-Dasein*).[28]

This, then, in the briefest of terms, is what Przywara means by the analogy of being: an analogy between an absolute identity of essence and existence in God and an utterly contingent and gratuitous relation of essence and existence in creatures. What is unique to his doctrine, one could argue, is the dynamism that he introduces into the real distinction – a dynamism that registers at once both the radical dependence of the creature (whose existence is a gift) and the radical mutability of the creature (since the creature is not self-identical or in possession of itself, but fundamentally 'stretched', to use Gregory of Nyssa's favourite image from Paul (Phil. 3.13) – which also gives new meaning to Paul's dictum, 'ye are not your own' (1 Cor. 6.19). At the same time, for all its originality and subtlety, Przywara's doctrine is but an intentional synthesis of Augustine, Thomas and pseudo-Dionysius: of Augustine in so far as he speaks of the creature in terms of restlessness, in terms of a radical mutability, in terms of a cascading torrent driven along by its own insufficiency;[29] of Thomas, in so far as he articulates the being of the creature in terms of a 'non-identity' between essence and existence; of pseudo-Dionysius (who, of course, is not alone in this), in so far as he speaks of God's radical transcendence as *Deus excessus*, as *Deus semper maior*, as '*Gott Überschwang*' even in the face of God's positive self-revelation.

On the one hand, the *analogia entis* is thus intended to show that the creature has no metaphysical claim upon God, since every creaturely ascent is but an asymptotic approach *in infinitum*; and since even this ascent is itself powered by a humility before an inscrutable identity – which the creature never is nor can hope to be – between essence and existence. This is why Przywara so frequently cites Augustine, saying: 'He is hidden in order that you

---

28 *AE*, p. 28.

29 See *AE*, p. 167: 'Creaturely being is a "cascading torrent" (*torrens . . . colligitur, redundat, perstrepit, currit et currendo decurrit* – in Ps. 109, 20); indeed, one could even say that it only "was" and "will be", but never "is" (*antequam sint non sunt, et cum sunt fugiunt, et cum fugerint non erunt* – *De liber. arb.* III 7, 21).'

The Beauty of the Metaphysical Imagination

might seek him; and in order that you might not cease in your search, once you have found him, he is infinite. Thus it is said . . . "Seek his face evermore."[30] On the other hand, the *analogia entis* is intended to show that the creature does not even have any ultimate claim upon itself. Thus, employing yet another sense of analogy as a *meson*, or something 'in-between',[31] Przywara speaks of the creature as a 'suspended *middle*' between its own potentiality and end, and, ultimately, as a 'suspended middle' between nothing and the Creator out of nothing (as Augustine puts it along these lines, the creature simultaneously 'is and is not', *est non est*).[32]

Such is the tenuous 'status' (one might better say 'instability') of the creature that the *analogia entis* seeks to describe. And this is why, in view of the creature's radical non-self-sufficiency, Przywara can say that his doctrine is simply a philosophical explication of the doctrine of *creatio ex nihilo*.[33] It is also why the ultimate sense of analogy, as Przywara employs it, is *not* that of any analogy of attribution (which would highlight creaturely similitude to God as the *cause* of creaturely perfections), still less popular misunderstandings of analogy as some kind of metaphysical super-glue that binds God to his creation, but that of an analogy of proportionality (*analogia proportionalitatis*), understood not as requiring 'a measurable distance between the analogates',[34] but in Przywara's somewhat idiosyncratic use of the term, as a proportion of one alterity to another (ἄλλο πρὸς ἄλλο).[35] As Przywara once

---

30 *Jo. ev. tract.* 63,1.

31 *AE*, p. 149f. Cf. *Nicomachean Ethics*, 1131b10: τὸ γὰρ ἀνάλογον μέσον; cf. *AE*, p. 149f. Cf. William Desmond's 'metaxalogical' metaphysics as developed chiefly in *Being and the Between* (Stonybrook, NY: State University of New York Press, 1988), which is comparable to Przywara's metaphysics in scope and depth.

32 See Augustine, *In Ps.* 121, 12; *Confessions*, XII, 6; cf. Augustine's account of his vision at Ostia, and, in particular, his account of the collective witness of creation in Book IX.

33 See *Schriften*, vol. 2, p. 403f.

34 As described in Peter Oh's admirable work, *Karl Barth's Trinitarian Theology: A Study in Karl Barth's Analogical Use of the Trinitarian Relation* (London: T & T Clark, 2006), p. 7.

35 See *AE* § 6, 8, pp. 135ff. Because the analogy of proper proportionality is associated most directly with Cajetan, it is important here to

put it, confounded by so much misunderstanding of his doctrine, even, he thought, on the part of von Balthasar, 'My dear friends – from Karl Barth to Söhngen to Haecker to Balthasar – have apparently never grasped that "*analogia*", according to Aristotle, is a "proportion between two X" (see my *Analogia Entis*!).'[36]

Common Objections to the *Analogia Entis*

In view of the foregoing, we now have a basis for responding to the more common objections to the *analogia entis*. As for modern philosophy's suspicion of metaphysics in general, deriving from its anthropological starting point, the first sections of Przywara's *Analogia Entis* constitute a sufficient response.[37] Beginning from a phenomenological standpoint, Przywara demonstrates the inadequacy of any purely subjective, transcendental, 'meta-noetic', starting point (e.g., in Kant and Husserl), as well as any purely objective, 'meta-ontic' starting point (in Scheler, for example, or in Heidegger's beginning with the forgotten question of being qua being). In other words, while each approach has its merits, neither is sufficient in itself. Instead, according to Przywara, a genuine phenomenology reveals an inevitable correlation of both: in terms of what he calls a 'metaphysical transcendentalism' (e.g. in Kant and Husserl) and a 'transcendental metaphysics' (e.g. in Plato and Aristotle).

In any event, as these terms themselves suggest, there is no escaping from metaphysical questions, neither in modern epistemology, which retreats into the fortress of pure reason and its essential, transcendental determinations, nor in Heideggerian ontology, which begins in quite the opposite fashion, with the 'thrownness'

---

emphasize that Przywara views the analogy of proper proportionality as the apophatic moment or 'apophatic' analogy *vis-à-vis* the 'kataphatic' analogy of the analogy of attribution. In other words, the former emphasizes difference and mutual alterity; the latter emphasizes participation and likeness. Though Przywara gives it a new, apophatic sense, the phrase ἄλλο πρὸς ἄλλο comes from Aristotle (see *Metaphysics*, 1016b35).

36 *In und Gegen: Stellungnahmen zur Zeit* (Nürnberg: Glock und Lutz, 1955), p. 278.
37 See *AE*, §§ 1–4.

The Beauty of the Metaphysical Imagination

(*Geworfenheit*) of *Dasein* and its radical, existential *in-der-Welt-sein*, from which perspective to raise anew the question of *Sein*, of the Being of beings. For what lies at the bottom of this historical, philosophical tension between a 'meta-noetics' and a 'meta-ontics' (which one may roughly identify with the tension between Cartesian essentialism and Heideggerian existentialism) is none other than the age-old *metaphysical* tension between essence and existence. To be sure, both modern epistemology and Heideggerian ontology are commonly presented as post-metaphysical, even as spelling the end of metaphysics. From Przywara's perspective, however, they are simply dialectical flipsides of the same *metaphysical* problem. Indeed, it turns out that, instead of advancing beyond scholasticism, modern and postmodern philosophy – under the banners, respectively, of a transcendental essentialism and an ontological existentialism – in some sense never got beyond, but merely transformed into a *dialectic* of historical periods what for the scholastics, however much they may have differed, was always a mysterious *relation* between essence and existence.[38]

As for Barth's more specific criticisms, one seems to be dealing with an unfortunate and – for Przywara's reputation – rather costly misunderstanding. What Barth appears to have seen in the *analogia entis* was yet another instance of human pride and Prometheanism: a metaphysics that compromised divine transcendence by establishing a correspondence between God and creatures independently of faith in Christ. He seems to have concluded that the *analogia entis* gives Christ short shrift, such that Christ comes into view only once a pre-Christian metaphysics is already in place. These I take to be the main objections. What he *failed* to see, however – as plain as it is, once one looks past the title – is that the *analogia entis* is a full-blown *negative* theology in the tradition of the Areopagite. In fact, far from being a tidy natural theology that puts God into some kind of theoretical box, the *analogia entis*,

---

38 Of course, even if he came to different conclusions, it cannot be said that Heidegger was unaware of this connection or did not thoroughly consider it. See, for example, his *Grundprobleme der Phänomenologie*, in *Gesamtausgabe*, vol. 24 (Frankfurt am Main: Vittorio Klostermann, 1975), § 10, pp. 108–39.

as Przywara formulated it, was intended precisely to explode all fixed systems, to the point of relativizing not only natural, but even supernatural knowledge of God. Thus, Barth's main objection may be disregarded. His other objection is less easily answered, but the quickest response would be to say that, if the *analogia entis* does not treat Christ directly, then neither do the first two parts of Aquinas's *Summa*; that if the *analogia entis* is to be condemned, then one must be consistent and condemn Aquinas too; and that, in attacking the *analogia entis*, Barth was ultimately pitting one legitimate doctrine against another (even if, against the Catholic tradition of natural theology, he would claim that one cannot treat creation independently of Christ).

As for Heidegger, it is notable that his criticisms of analogy seem to be based upon a conception of analogy similar to that of Barth, namely, as a rationally envisaged system of correspondences, in which God appears within a hierarchy of beings as the highest being to which beings necessarily correspond. As a result, so the argument goes, we end up thinking of being primarily in terms of causation, and thereby occlude a more primordial and, for Heidegger, more authentic experience of being (*Sein* or, more archaically, *Seyn*) and the difference between being and beings (*Sein und Seindes*). Heidegger's criticisms, one must admit, have a point: they apply, for instance, to the mechanistic deism of the eighteenth century and to theological conceptions of God as the *direct* cause of all things, whereby everything that happens is necessarily and rather frighteningly a pristine mirror of the divine will (as is more or less the case with Reformed Calvinism and Dominican Banezianism).[39] And, as far as the *analogia entis* is concerned, one would have to take these criticisms seriously *if* this were what Przywara's doctrine actually entailed.

In point of fact, however, Przywara's doctrine of the *analogia entis* is meant precisely to uphold the difference between primary and secondary causation (*causae secundae*), and therewith the

---

39 Thanks to David Hart for a fruitful conversation in this regard. As far as these theologies of the divine will are concerned, the question would seem to be if the mirror in which they look is not, in fact, more akin to Galadriel's well in Tolkien's *The Lord of the Rings*, in which the dread eye of Sauron is seen staring back.

The Beauty of the Metaphysical Imagination

mystery of creation as a granting of freedom. To be sure, for Przywara, God remains the *cause* of creation (how could it be otherwise?); but in no sense is he a mechanistic hinge of the universe.[40] Rather, in a way that recalls Heidegger's own notion of *Bewëgung* (sic), God is more like a kenotic giver, who gives way in what he gives – which is as true of creation as it is of the Passion (from which creation itself, as the work of the *Ars Patris* 'by whom all things were made,' should be understood). And so Heidegger's criticisms of the Christian doctrine of creation, and of a doctrine of analogy that supposedly grounds it, apply only to those versions of it that neglect its kenotic, Christological stamp (cf. Phil. 2.6f.).

Finally, as an explicitly *negative* theology, first appearances notwithstanding, the doctrine of the *analogia entis* points to a God who is explicitly *beyond* all analogy. Indeed, the final word of the *analogia entis* is not any similarity or correspondence, but, as Przywara puts it, an *'ever greater'* dissimilarity, in view of a God who is himself *semper maior*. This is why Przywara repeatedly says that his doctrine is nothing but a metaphysical articulation of what the fourth Lateran council affirmed in 1215 against the heretical immanent Trinitarianism of Joachim of Fiore: 'One cannot posit any similarity between Creator and creature, however great, without noting a greater dissimilarity [between them].'[41] This is why, as a matter of *principle* (would that Barth had grasped it), every grasp of God is necessarily broken (as Przywara frequently puts it, citing

---

40 On the other hand, from Przywara's perspective, Heidegger's *Seyn als Nichts* is a disingenuous side-stepping of the problem. Though his *Seyn* allegedly does nothing, and is therefore not to be confused with a *causa prima*, it nevertheless does something quite theological, in fact, quite Christological: it gives, as the kenotically hidden *'es gibt'* in all that is (*Seiendes*). Thus, as Przywara already pointed out in 1932, Heidegger's nothing is not really nothing but an 'all-determining' 'productive nothing', which is to say, a nothing that functions as God without God. See *AE*, p. 109. For an account of this secular logic of 'nothing *as* something', see Conor Cunningham, *Genealogy of Nihilism: Philosophies of Nothing and the Difference of Theology* (London: Routledge, 2002).

41 *Inter creatorem et creaturam non potest tanta similitudo notari, quin inter eos maior sit dissimilitudo notanda* (Denz. 432). See in this regard especially Przywara, 'Die Reichweite der Analogie als katholischer Grundform', in *AE*, pp. 247–301.

Augustine, *si comprehendis, non est Deus*).⁴² This is why every 'resonant' analogy ultimately gives way to a 'silent' analogy.⁴³ And this is why the final, definitive image of the *analogia entis*, following Augustine and John of the Cross, is that of a dark 'night'.⁴⁴ Thus, as Eberhard Jüngel, arguably the most important Barth scholar today, has noted, in a complete reversal of Barth's and the typical Protestant view, if Przywara is to be faulted, then he is to be faulted for too greatly emphasizing God's *alterity*.⁴⁵

The Aesthetics of the Analogy of Being

Thus far, I have argued for the importance of metaphysics to theology, for a connection between metaphysics and aesthetics, and for the importance and warrant of the metaphysics of the *analogia entis* in particular. What now remains is to spell out the implications of the *analogia entis* for a properly *theological* aesthetics. And to this end, one might begin by considering the aesthetic implications of the metaphysical term 'essence', which may also be translated as 'form' (either as Plato's *eidos* or Aristotle's *morphē*, or simply as the Latin *forma*), since it is the *forms* of things that we perceive, and beautiful things in particular that stand out because of their 'formliness', one might even say, in translation of Aristotle's *morphē*, their 'shapeliness'. In fact, as Aquinas puts it, the form of a thing *is* its beauty: '*forma rei est decor eius . . . decor resultans ex forma et proportione partium*' ('the form of a thing is its comeliness [or beauty], resulting from the form and proportion of its parts').⁴⁶

What is properly meta-physical about beauty, however, is its display of depth, its revelation of something *in* a thing that at the same time *exceeds* or goes *beyond* the thing, so that the thing itself becomes a mysterious index of something beyond it (as is espe-

---

42 Sermon 117, 3; cf. Sermon 52, 16. See *AE*, p. 170; cf. p. 435f.

43 *AE*, p. 210.

44 *AE*, p. 170.

45 See *Gott als Geheimnis der Welt*, 6th ed. (Tübingen: Mohr-Siebeck, 1992), p. 357.

46 Quoted in von Balthasar, *Herrlichkeit*, p. 358. See Thomas Aquinas, *Super Sent.*, lib. 3 d. 23 q. 3 a. 1 qc. 1 s.c. 2; d. 1 q. 1 a. 3 arg.

The Beauty of the Metaphysical Imagination

cially clear in the saints, in whom the diaphanous nature of creation is restored); moreover, so that the visible, as John Milbank has suggested, becomes a site of the appearing of the invisible – to the point that the visible is seen epiphanomenally (*sic*) for what it is: as the site of a 'wondrous exchange' between the visible and the invisible.[47] Indeed, according to this rich image of a 'wondrous exchange' (*commercium admirabile*), one could say that every experience of beauty bears a Christological stamp, whereby the perception of a mysterious reciprocity between the visible and the invisible, the immanent and the transcendent, points beyond itself, analogically, to an ultimate reciprocity of profundity and visibility in Christ, the primary analogate and measure of all beauty, indeed the measure of all creation whatsoever, since in him the resplendent *depths* of the Father (cf. Jas. 1.17) are precisely and fully *seen* (John 14.7f.).

In any event, *in* their appearing, beautiful things – more so than ordinary things – display an *excess* of their appearing. In short, they daze us with their depth. And it is in this Platonic vein, in his commentary on Dionysius' *Divine Names*, that Aquinas says, '*omnis forma . . . est participatio divinae claritatis*' ('every form is a participation in the divine clarity', which one might also translate as 'participation in the divine beauty').[48] Clearly, then, for the Platonic tradition and its assimilation by the Church – from Augustine to Dionysius to the Chartres Platonists to Thomas – metaphysics and aesthetics go together, to the point of implying one another. And in this regard one could even rephrase Keats's now clichéd phrase and say that '"Beauty is Being, Being Beauty," – That is all ye know on earth and all ye need to know.'

But what about the *analogia entis*? What does it have to do with a theological aesthetics, and what in particular does it introduce into what thus far has been an essentially Platonic picture of things? Let us first recall Przywara's cryptic formula, 'essence-in-and-beyond-existence'. At face value, it would be hard to say what this formula has to do with aesthetics or with any particular notion

---

47 See Milbank, 'Beauty and the Soul', in *Theological Perspectives on God and Beauty* (Harrisburg: Trinity Press International, 2003), pp. 1–34.
48 Aquinas, *Commentary on the Divine Names*, 4, 5. Quoted in von Balthasar, p. 359.

of beauty (it is, after all, a cumbersome and rather unattractive formula). But if we make a legitimate substitution of 'form' for 'essence', since in the metaphysical tradition the two are more or less synonymous, we come up with the formulation: 'form in-and-beyond existence'. And if, following Thomas, we make the further substitution of 'beauty' for 'form', we suddenly come up with the formula, 'beauty in-and-beyond existence'. In other words, what we discover is that what the *analogia entis* seeks to describe (at least in this partial formula) is altogether akin to what we feel in the face of beauty. One could even say that 'essence-in-and-beyond-existence' is simply a metaphysical expression for aesthetic experience: of the fact that there is an alluring depth to things that is never reducible to the things themselves. It is, one could say, a legitimate and altogether appropriate philosophical formula for a world we encounter as *art*.

Thus far I have not introduced any distinction between the beautiful and the sublime, but here is where it would come into play. For postmodern aesthetic theory, the sublime is antithetically *opposed* to the beautiful, just as for postmodern ontology existence is *opposed* to essence, according to the terms of its characteristically violent cosmology. For Christianity, however, this can never be so; rather, creaturely being and experience are defined precisely by a dynamic *relation* between essence and existence, the beautiful and the sublime. Admittedly, the sublime may be distinguished from the beautiful; for there are some things in aesthetic experience – typically oceans, mountains, the starry host – that elicit feelings of the sublime, and not the beautiful. But if one wanted to be more precise about the excess *'in'* the beautiful, one could speak of this excess as a moment of the *sublime* '*in*' the beautiful: namely, as the inexhaustible depth that one experiences *within* every limited form, as though there is always something *more* to see. Indeed, one could say that the sublime is ever more present *within* the beautiful to the degree that *in it* one is confronted with the *transcendent*; to the degree, moreover, that, in being *transfixed* by the beautiful, in being unmistakably *held* by it, one is simultaneously, and paradoxically, *moved* by it.[49]

---

49 The ultimate theological pericope for this would be John 21.7, where Peter, seeing the resurrected Christ, seeing, that is, the glory of the

The Beauty of the Metaphysical Imagination

But this is not the only site of the sublime within the kind of theological aesthetics opened up by the *analogia entis*. In fact, properly speaking, none of this is peculiar to a *theological* aesthetics at all. For as of yet I have spoken merely in Platonic terms of essence or essences and not yet discussed what difference it makes that finite reality is also a *creaturely* reality, and as such 'composed', for lack of a better word, of essence *and* existence. In other words, to get at a specifically theological aesthetics, one needs to ask the following question: What are the aesthetic implications of Thomas's real distinction (which lies at the heart of the *analogia entis*), and what is added thereby to an otherwise strictly Platonic picture of finite reality participating in and showing forth a reality that exceeds it?

The simple answer to this question is the vision of gratuity and generosity it affords – a generosity that exceeds the Platonic conception of the good diffusing itself (*bonum diffusivum sui*), because it is a generosity that is altogether without need: it is sheer gift. In fact, it is precisely this difference that allows us to see the world not merely as a hierarchy of being or beauty, but as a manifestation of divine *glory*, of God's *lordliness* over creation – of God's *Herr-lichkeit*.[50] In other words, the *analogia entis* leads directly to a perception (to an aesthetics!) of creation *as creation*, which is to say, as a display of *gratuitous excess and depth* – gratuitous, inasmuch as its very reality is a gift; excess and depth, inasmuch as the essence of anything transcends its instantiation in any given moment. One might even say that God's glory does not properly appear except when both of these moments – the gratuity and the excess – are perceived at once: when it is seen in the *non-necessity* of anything at all, and in the *excess* of everything that is (in reflection, as it were, of God's own freedom and infinity).

Lord, casts himself wholeheartedly and without hesitation into the sea (of the divine infinity).

50 As von Balthasar puts it, 'Thomas' doctrine of the real distinction between *esse* and *essentia* is a philosophical thesis, but it allows us . . . to make a clear distinction between the "glory" [*Herrlichkeit*] of God and the beauty of the cosmos; indeed, it allows us . . . to recover the meaning of this glory not only for the theologian, but even for the believer in general.' See *The Glory of the Lord. Volume IV: The Realm of Metaphysics in Antiquity*, p. 395.

Veritas: Belief and Metaphysics

Thus far we have registered the sublime *in* the beautiful as the *excess* of essence. Now we can register the sublime in terms of the sheer *gratuity* and inexplicable *novelty* of existence itself. In other words, whereas the essence of a thing is the beauty of the thing, the sublimity of a thing is both the *excessiveness* of its beauty and the *novelty* of its gratuity. Thus, just as one may speak of a 'composition' of essence and existence in creatures – the one being irreducible to the other – so too one might speak of an aesthetic accord, even a reciprocity, between the beautiful and the sublime, such that the one who has true perception, the true aesthete, invariably sees both (and thus allows himself or herself to be carried away by the transcendence, the excess *and* the sheer gratuity, *in* what he or she sees). All of which is a way of saying that salvation, understood as the ecstatic, meta-physical transformation of the human being by the Spirit from glory to glory (2 Cor. 3.18), is itself an aesthetic experience, since the only conceivable response to grace, to the 'sheer gift' of endless participation in the infinite excess of the divine nature (2 Pet. 1.4), is the aesthetic transport of love.

Such are the imaginative possibilities opened up by the *analogia entis*. It begins by helping us to see creation as something infinitely beautiful, wondrously deep and, at the same time, wholly gratuitous – in which regard creation itself is a mirror of God's work in salvation, Indeed, it registers not only the excess of beauty in all beauty (in accordance with a merely Platonic metaphysics), but reveals the world as the gift *of* beauty – behind which stands nothing but the inscrutable will of the Creator and his sublime (because utterly unnecessary) utterance: *fiat lux*. And since both of these aspects are what we appreciate in a work of genius – both the depth, the 'more' there is to see, *and* the novelty – we may conclude by saying that the *analogia entis* provides us with sound reason, a metaphysical foundation, as it were, for seeing the world as *art*.

As of yet, however, I have not yet stated the implications of the *analogia entis* for a specifically *theological* aesthetics. That is to say, we have not yet stated what this means for our understanding of God himself. But we are now ready to do so. For if one recalls that, for Thomas as for Przywara, God is a simple identity of essence and existence, and if one recalls, furthermore, that for Augustine God is *Ipsa Forma* ('Form or Formliness or Beauty

Itself'), and if, following Gregory of Nyssa, God is at the same time *infinite*, then God appears in aesthetic terms, in a way transcending every analogy, as at once beautiful and sublime, or, to be more precise, as an inscrutable identity of beauty and sublimity: as beautifully sublime and sublimely beautiful.

4. Metaphysics of Creation

DAVID BURRELL, C.S.C.

In this brief chapter, I shall use Aristotle's *Metaphysics* as our starting point, occasionally employing what contemporary analytic philosophers call 'metaphysics', as in 'metaphysics and epistemology', as a foil. For each exemplifies Heidegger's charge of '*forgetfulness* of being', though Aristotle's deficiency could better be dubbed '*not yet mindful* of being', as we shall see. Meanwhile contemporaries would better be charged with obtuse *obliviousness* of being – so ugly a charge that we will no longer use the phrase; it is better left in oblivion itself! I shall nevertheless try to unpack the charge, highlighting crucial grammatical turns of the discipline, then attempt to offer a constructive articulation of creation as a paradigmatic exemplification of these strategies.

Anyone who has attempted to negotiate Aristotle's *Metaphysics*, especially to lead students through it, cannot but feel let down as he concludes his extensive dialectical search for the proper sense of *substance*, the paradigm for what-is, or *being*. After rejecting various candidates as inadequate, he lights hesitantly on *form* as the best rendering. So what happened to his sometime intemperate critique of Plato, when Plato emerges victorious at the tentative finish line? Some may object to the metaphor of 'finish line', since Aristotle will undertake another dialectical probe to articulate the 'prime mover'. Yet what emerges is the 'principle of *motion*', not of *being*. For still following the lead of Plato, the universal cause of all motion could find a place among Aristotle's celebrated four causes, as the final cause (reminiscent of Plato's *good*), while, as we shall see, none of them could qualify as a 'cause of being'. That impasse resulted in an enduring *aporia*, fully elaborated by Edward Booth (in his *Aristotelian Aporetic Ontology in Islamic and Christian Writers*[1]) yet identifiable to any introductory student: Aristotle failed to articulate what made individual existing things the paradigm for *substance*. Or put another way: he could not show how or why his conviction that *substance* is primarily displayed in individual existing things had to be true.

Booth details how one commentator after another attempted to 'paper over' this recurring crack in Aristotle's treatment of *substance*. Only when Plotinus began to employ Platonic strategies to articulate Aristotle's concerns did the extended metaphor of 'emanation from the One' emerge, to begin to broach the question of the 'cause of being'.[2] (*Emanation*, as we shall see, is not far from *participation*, which Aristotle had eliminated as 'mere metaphor'.) But we may well find metaphor to be indispensable when we are pressed beyond Aristotle to complete his causal enquiry into *being itself*. For however one may assess his success in the matter, Plotinus's emanation scheme did broach the question (of the cause of being) while his insisting that the One must be 'beyond being' could well be his way of introducing the 'infinite qualitative difference' between beings and *being*.

So encouraged by his boldness, Islamic, Jewish and Christian philosophical theologians began to read Aristotle's apparently crowning achievement of the 'prime mover' as the origin of the universe itself; that is, of all-that-is (*being*), and not simply of motion of things.[3] From a purely exegetical perspective, their efforts move well beyond the contours of Aristotle's enquiry in the *Metaphysics*, yet could also be said to blaze trails already proposed by his unrelenting enquiry into the 'causes of substance'. So they were impelled, is it were, by the *élan* of enquiry itself, much as Aristotle found his predecessors heading towards his account of *substance* by 'attending to the things themselves'. For it certainly

---

[1] Cambridge: Cambridge University Press, 1987.

[2] Lloyd Gerson, *God and Greek Philosophy* (New York: Routledge, 1990); *Plotinus* (New York: Routledge, 1994).

[3] Isabelle Moulin's dissertation: 'La question Aristotelicienne de Dieu et sa reception chez les commentateurs grecs et medievaux', Sorbonne 2004.

seems utterly natural that a sustained enquiry into the causes of things (or reasons for things) would have to ask about the cause of their very *being* – following the contours of Aristotle's original isolation of 'being qua being'. (A parallel can be found in early Christian theological attempts to establish the identity of Jesus Christ. Thomas Weinandy has shown how the positions that emerged on the way to Chalcedon display the contours reason would have to take to reconcile Christian practice of praying to Jesus with the *shema*.[4])

Yet an Islamic thinker supplied the indispensable step in showing how beings might relate to *being*, by accentuating Aristotle's semantic distinction between the way two basic questions would have to be answered: 'what is it?' and 'is it?'. Yet after identifying these questions as basic and distinct from one another, Aristotle focused – as philosophers are wont to do – on the first: 'what is it?', thereby obscuring the natural thrust of reason to identify the 'cause of being'. Ibn Sina (Avicenna) was the first, it seems, to see (however obscurely) the metaphysical import of this distinction between 'what something is' and 'whether it is', suggesting that the principle accounting for things' very existence would have to lie outside them, in the One who bestows being on essences.[5] It is easy for us to read this as a philosophical attempt to structure Plotinus's metaphor of 'emanation' (or 'overflow') by identifying a 'giver of forms' (Ibn Sina) whose act of giving would see to it that such forms actually exist. Yet the intent of this crucial distinction is rather to identify the lineaments of Plotinus as they emerge in each being in its relation to what gives it being: the One which cannot be one of those beings.

Yet even if Aristotle had followed the natural thrust of his metaphysical enquiry to ask about a cause of being, he would not have been able to express it, since none of his four causes could do the job. Yet philosophical enquirers following in his wake were moved

---

4 Thomas Weinandy, *Does God Change?* (Still River, MA: St. Bede's, 1985).

5 See my *Knowing the Unknowable God* (Notre Dame IN: University of Notre Dame Press, 1986), and Harm Goris, *Free Creatures of an Eternal God: Thomas Aquinas on God's Foreknowledge and Irresistible Will* (Leuven: Peters, 1996) for an illuminating contrast between Avicenna and Aquinas on this issue.

ineluctably to press his 'prime mover' into that very role. As the example of Ibn Sina suggests, the advent of a revealed Creator inspired these thinkers to pursue Aristotle's enquiry beyond the parameters his categories had set. Can we say here that revelation was needed, since the very logic of an enquiry into causes should tell us that we cannot hope to identify such a cause (of being itself) among beings, all of whom are caused by it? (Nor can we locate *form* as a thing in this way either, of course, yet it can be identified as an enduring feature of anything that is.) So this seems to be a case – perhaps the paradigm case – where the causal enquiry peculiar to metaphysics – into what-is in so far as it is – will not be able to be carried to its natural intentional conclusion without a revelatory impulse. It may be that not even Plotinus is an exception to this contention, since his enquiry was conceived as a home-grown response to Jewish and Christian promulgation of the resounding opening assertions of Genesis: 'In the beginning god created heaven and earth.' However one might interpret 'beginning', a causal enquiry into the being of beings would have to attend to it. So the fact that Aristotle did not follow his own enquiry to this point remains puzzling, unless it were a premonition of the perceived oddity of such a One – not *a* being, certainly, but in some way that escapes articulation, *being itself*; or as Plotinus was led to insist: One 'beyond being'.

As Edward Booth articulates the development, Aristotle's lingering *aporia* found a respectable resolution in Aquinas's recasting of Ibn Sina's essence/existing distinction as a fresh exemplification of Aristotle's master analytic tool of potency/act, whereby the *essence* of each thing becomes *potential* to its *act of* existing, bestowed by the One. Booth argues that Aquinas was led to this resolution by his reading of pseudo-Dionysius, while similar influences can be detected in Aquinas's commentary on the *Liber de causis*, an Islamic adaptation of Proclus.[6] But that story is either familiar or readily recoverable. We are intent on a meta-version here: why and how does the effective execution of metaphysical inquiry demand

---

6 See my 'Aquinas' Appropriation of *Liber de causis* to Articulate the Creator as Cause-of-Being', in Fergus Kerr (ed.), *Contemplating Aquinas: On the Varieties of Interpretation* (London: SCM Press, 2003), pp. 55–74.

that it grapple with the One who is the source of all-that-is, a Creator?

Toward a More Proper Articulation of the 'Cause of Being'

Let me essay an answer. Nothing less will respond to the existential promise of metaphysical enquiry, a promise animating Aristotle's valiant attempts, and source of the disappointment we noted at his failure to fulfil it. Put another way by my Jerusalem colleague, Avital Wohlman: pressed to this limit, essentially contestable philosophical questions become existential theological issues, as the universe emerges as intelligently ordered by the One. Already intimated in Plato's *good*, the presence of the One emanating all-that-is invites us to enquire into the order of the universe as all-that-is activates our distress at the disorder we find in it, eliciting the so-called 'problem of evil'. In short, when metaphysics allows itself to be drawn to the goal natural to a causal enquiry, it begins to display its inherent *élan* towards 'the good', and fully engages us as enquirers.

Short of this critical point, metaphysical enquiry will remain as it often appears in contemporary philosophy: an endless consideration of possible structural configurations, with ample room for clever modal permutations, yet without a discernable goal. For nothing, it seems, is able to entice philosophers beyond formal or essential considerations except a causal enquiry that leads beyond structure to *existing*, and thereby to One which defies structural articulation. Yet even while remaining within what is rationally articulable may satisfy 'professional philosophers', it will inevitably fall short of eliciting that full intellectual engagement traditionally seen to be the goal of philosophical enquiry, so will soon be boring to those drawn to an intellectual goal exceeding displays of cleverness. Yet it remains that to venture beyond what is rationally articulable, so as to arrive at a One whose very essence is to-be, can and will strike the philosophically inclined as irrational.

Here is where revelation appears as an indispensable prod and even partner to attempts to articulate what theology has always insisted will exceed our understanding: a source of all-that-is, One who must therefore be distinct from everything, yet whose very

Metaphysics of Creation

subsistent being sees to it that whatever-is exists. But how? If we could directly respond to that question, we would be treating the One as another item in the universe. Instead, to be faithful to the logic (as well as the revelation) that brought us to this point, we are drawn to return to Plotinus's metaphor of *emanation*, enriched by Dionysius's use of Plato's original 'participation', to try to do justice to a relation between the One and all-that-is which is explicitly 'non-contrastive' yet sustaining.[7] This relation is 'non-contrastive' in that the relation itself is beyond customary interpretation as between two things. Moses Maimonides insists that there is no way in which God can be said to be related to the universe, which sounds oxymoronic in that the couplet – creator/creature – until we notice that any relation (for him) must be reciprocal. So he is asserting – *avant la lettre* – Aquinas's insistence that the creator, to be creator, cannot be 'really' – that is, reciprocally – related to creatures.[8] It is sustaining, in that everything-that-is will be related to the One by a 'non-reciprocal relation of dependence', the prescient phrase that Sara Grant employs to introduce Shankara's notion of *non-duality* as a way of attempting to express this inexpressible relation.[9] Her strategy should manage to remind us that any attempt to express what creating 'is like' will inevitably turn this *sui generis* relation into a reciprocal one between two items in the world. So much for a 'metaphysics of creation', which can only be a grammar of these matters, laid out as best we can. To

---

7 On the relation of creator to creation, see Robert Sokolowski, *God of Faith and Reason* (Washington, DC: Catholic University of America Press, 1995); for the use of 'non-contrastive', see Kathryn Tanner, *God and Creation in Christian Theology* (Oxford: Basil Blackwell, 1988); and for *participation*, see Rudi teVelde, *Participation and Substantiality in Thomas Aquinas* (Leiden: Brill, 1995).

8 On Aquinas's fascinating relationship with Maimonides, see Alexander Broadie, 'Maimonides and Aquinas on Names of God', *Religious Studies* 23 (1987), pp. 157–70, and my 'Aquinas' Debt to Maimonides', in Ruth Link-Salinger and Jerome Hackett (eds), *A Straight Path: Studies in Medieval Philosophy and Culture* (Washington, DC: Catholic University of America Press, 1989), pp. 37–48; reprinted in *Faith and Freedom* (Oxford: Blackwell, 2005).

9 Sara Grant, *Towards an Alternative Theology* (Notre Dame IN: University of Notre Dame Press, 2002).

resume: if the creator is to be a cause, it cannot be one of Aristotle's celebrated four (nor, a fortiori, any current simplistic version of *efficient* cause), and the strategy which moves us beyond these options towards a better way will profit from revelation, be it biblical or Qur'anic. And should our enquiry feel as unsatisfying as Aristotle's, it has at least explained why a metaphysics that falls short of these paradoxical results soon bores us, suggesting why so much satisfying philosophy can be found today in the pages of *Modern Theology*.

5. Metaphysics and the Question of Creation: Thomas Aquinas, Duns Scotus and Us

RUDI TE VELDE

Introduction: The Question of Creation

Within the intellectual horizon of modern secular culture, religious belief in creation meets with a certain difficulty of intelligibility. For many, the word 'creation' sounds a little old-fashioned, reminiscent of former 'more religious times' in which we were still able to experience the hidden presence of the divine in nature. But now, with the rise of natural science and the prevalent naturalistic worldview, 'creation' has become more and more an anomaly, a mythical and anthropocentric remainder which can survive only in the weakened and non-cognitive sense of a metaphor expressing the religious and ethical attitude towards nature as something that is not of our own making and which in its greatness and vulnerability (cf. the phrase 'poor creature') *seems* to refer to something greater than us. We generally feel that 'creation' does not posit any demonstrable truth about nature, that it is not an objective fact of the physical universe (except perhaps for those 'creationists' who assert it as a literal truth against the nihilism of the Darwinist view of nature).

But is our choice simply between the immanent metaphysics of naturalism and creationism? Between a logic according to which all there is can be sufficiently explained, on the one hand, by means of the methods and principles of natural science, and on the other, by the creationist belief that (human) nature is the immediate work of a divine intelligence?

It is not only that, from the conceptual horizon of natural science, the workings of a 'supernatural agent' cannot be recognized as a genuine and acceptable scientific explanation; but what is more, such a 'supernatural agent' must necessarily appear as an additional explanatory factor that concurs with other 'natural' factors. In traditional language: it is as if one calls upon the 'first cause' within the domain of the 'second causes' of nature in order to explain particular features of natural processes and facts. 'God' versus 'natural evolution' is only an alternative when the immanent sphere of nature counts as the ultimate horizon of human self-understanding; but if this is so, 'God' is reduced to 'playing a part in the game' as nothing more than an additional factor within the one natural playing-field.

The problem of the meaning of 'creation' in the modern world attests to the fact that current philosophical discourse remains silent about the metaphysical background of our experience of the world. The existence of the world, including the existence of human beings who know about the world as a whole, is taken for granted without asking further whether human beings can reach an adequate self-understanding within the horizon of the natural world. Much of contemporary thought, so it seems, prefers the brute facticity of existence as the ultimate truth of the world. The implicitly nihilistic message of naturalism – 'there is no higher meaning or purpose in nature' – allows us to regard ourselves as the only source of meaning and freedom. We want to be master of our own freedom and existence; within a naturalistic world-view the human ethical life of self-responsible freedom can only assert itself, so it seems, by a original act of self-constitution (*causa sui*).

In modern philosophy, in its paradoxical intertwining of naturalism and existentialism, there is a strong tendency to maintain an immanent human perspective of truth and reality. Whatever truth we may assert, that truth must be wholly intelligible in reference to the human perspective, to the human way of knowing; otherwise it would not be accounted as truth. We feel that there cannot be a 'view from nowhere' (Nagel), since from such a vantage nothing could be seen at all. Realism seems only to be acceptable if it is a realism 'with a human face' (Putnam). To speak of knowledge, meaning or truth is essentially to speak of a human affair. The dismissal of a metaphysical position is often motivated by the fear that we would forget about the inevitability of this 'human face'. Metaphysics is, therefore, generally associated with a non-human foundational stance outside the realm of history and human experience. It is as if, from such an ontotheological point of view, the contingent and temporal character of the human perspective on truth and being is ultimately resolved into a self-identical reality in which everything is what it is.

It is true that creation, understood in its metaphysical sense, implies a sort of transcendent perspective, a divine subjectivity, which is the absolute ground of human freedom and nature alike. But it is not necessarily the case that such a divine perspective would cancel the radical openness of the human experience of the world, as if we now have to play a part in someone else's game – someone who has laid down the rules and set the goals of our lives. Talk of 'creation' may, in fact, be seen as expressive of the fundamental experience that in all of our practical and theoretical dealings with the world, in all our self-responsible concerns for the ethical and political orderings of our freedom, the very being of reality takes the initiative. For in all cases, prior to what we decide to do with our life, we already exist, and that we exist and find ourselves to live in the world with a rich diversity of other creatures is not a neutral fact but something to which we must respond. To be a creature, one might say, means to exist in response to an initiative prior to ourselves; and that initiative we may think of as a source of being from which we receive our existence and from which our existence receives its *telos*.

Metaphysics and the Modern Turn to Immanence

The preceding rudimentary sketch of the actual situation in which we find ourselves with respect to the issue of creation serves as the background against which I want now to discuss how Thomas Aquinas explicates the truth of creation on the basis of his metaphysical understanding of being. It is not my intention to explicate or defend here in all respects the Thomistic doctrine of creation.[1] Rather, what I want to do is to offer a sympathetic reconstruction of Aquinas's thought about 'being', to rethink the basic insights behinds his metaphysics, and to do so in view of the actual possibilities of a metaphysical understanding of creation. The assumption here is that the meaning of 'creation' is not restricted to religious belief or to the pre-modern experience of the world (which is of course no longer accessible to us moderns), but that its alleged truth and meaning is open to a genuine philosophical articulation. What people may assert in faith is not necessarily without a *fundamentum in re* – that is, not without an intelligible basis in the general structure of human experience of reality.

For Aquinas, creation refers to a 'higher origin' beyond the sphere of natural causation within this world. Such a higher origin can only be conceived, he says, when the human intellect raises itself, from its habitual 'physical' attitude to the world of sensible things, to a metaphysical level of thought (cf. *ST* I, q.44, a.2). The notion of creation, together with that of a universal cause of being (*causa universalis totius esse*), occupies a central place in Aquinas's philosophical enquiries. It may be argued that the Aristotelian conception of first philosophy as the study of being qua being has been interpreted and transformed by Aquinas especially in view of making the idea of creation – the very becoming of the whole of reality under the aspect of being – understandable. In what follows I want to highlight in particular two characteristic features of his conception of metaphysics, which I think are valuable and of

---

[1] For a full presentation and analysis of the Thomistic doctrine of creation, see my dissertation *Participation and Substantiality in Thomas Aquinas* (Leiden/New York/Köln: Brill, 1995). Cf. also chapter 5 of my *Aquinas on God* (London: Ashgate, 2006). The most up-to-date and comprehensive study of Aquinas's metaphysics is John Wippel, *The Metaphysical Thought of Thomas Aquinas. From Finite Being to Uncreated Being* (Washington DC: CUA, 2000). A valuable study of the idea of creation in the three monotheistic traditions is David Burrell, *Freedom and Creation in Three Traditions* (Notre Dame: University of Notre Dame Press, 1993). What I find still missing in the recent literature about Aquinas is an immanent philosophical critique of his metaphysics of being. A not very satisfying attempt at such a critique, from the point of view of analytical philosophy, is Anthony Kenny, *Aquinas on Being* (Oxford: OUP, 2002).

special interest inasmuch as they bear directly on the idea of creation. I mean his notion of being as actuality (*actus essendi*) and his interpretation of the phrase 'being as being'. With respect to both points Aquinas's understanding of metaphysics deviates from what has become more or less the standard view of metaphysics in the history of Western philosophy.

What then is this standard view of metaphysics? According to a generally accepted view, metaphysics may be described as that part of philosophy that asks the most general questions about the most general nature of reality. The editors of a recent anthology of key texts from the Western metaphysical tradition explain in their foreword that metaphysical enquiries deal with the nature of what there is, in abstraction from the particular details of the goings of the world, in an attempt to uncover the underlying structure of reality.[2] It is an informal and general description, but it definitely reminds one of the classical passage in Aristotle's *Metaphysics* where a science is introduced that studies being qua being and the properties which belong to being as such (*Met.* bk. VI). Metaphysics is conceived of in the manner of general ontology, which investigates the 'nature of reality' or the 'underlying structure of reality'. Metaphysics, one might say, studies the most general features of the world and attempts to find out what sorts of things the world does contain, where 'world' is taken as a collective name for everything there is.

Although Aquinas's view of metaphysics does to some extent fit into the above description of metaphysics, I think, nevertheless, that this standard view is somehow more in line with John Duns Scotus, and his definition of the subject and nature of the science of metaphysics. Duns Scotus inaugurated an ontological conception of metaphysics which – via Suarez (*Disputationes metaphysicae*) and Wolff – became the dominant view of metaphysics in early modern philosophy.[3] According to this conception, metaphysics

---

2 Tim Crane and Katalin Farkas (eds), *Metaphysics. A Guide and Anthology* (Oxford: OUP, 2004).

3 See especially the impressive study of Ludger Honnefelder, *Scientia transcendens. Die formale Bestimmung der Seiendheit und Realität in der Metaphysik des Mittelalters und der Neuzeit (Duns Scotus – Suárez – Wolff – Kant – Peirce)* (Hamburg: Felix Meiner Verlag, 1990). Honnefelder argues that, among the widely different interpretations of the Aristotelian

investigates the general nature of reality from the perspective of the universal concept of 'being', which embraces everything there is, all different kinds of reality, substance and accident, creature and God alike. 'Being', so one might say, stands for that primary and foundational concept that signifies all things in their minimal common structure, as distinguished from sheer non-being. As such, it guarantees the objective unity of whatever falls under the range of conceptual knowledge. According to this view one must say that the consideration of being as being is logically prior to the distinction between created being and uncreated being. Seen thus from a metaphysical point of view, even God – the infinite being – falls under the objective unity of the concept of being, since 'being' in its conceptual indifference is prior to the distinction between finite and infinite. In this ontological version of metaphysics 'being' is interpreted in the minimal sense of a 'formal' structure common to all things, required by the logical unity of conceptual thought.

In contrast to this ontological metaphysics of the *concept* of being, the metaphysics we encounter in Aquinas is a genuine metaphysics of *being*. What this means, what is attractive about this metaphysics and what are its inherent problems, will be presently discussed; let us, however, begin by saying something about the two characterizing features of this metaphysics, features especially relevant to our theme of creation. First, instead of being as a

---

metaphysics in the thirteenth century, Duns Scotus's conception of metaphysics stands out as being systematically the most coherent and historically the most successful one. In his study he traces the dominant influence of Scotus's formal and conceptual approach to the issue of being in the metaphysics of the early modern period before Kant. The same historical thesis but conjoined with a philosophical evaluation which is the opposite of Honnefelder's can be found in the famous study of Etienne Gilson, *Being and Some Philosophers* (Toronto: PIMS, 1952). A few other items of the literature worth mention here are: L. Honnefelder, 'Der zweite Anfang der Metaphysik. Voraussetzungen, Ansätze und Folgen der Wiederbegründung der Metaphysik im 13./14. Jahrhundert', in J. P. Beckmann (ed.), *Philosophie im Mittelalter* (Hamburg: Felix Meiner Verlag, 1987), pp. 165–86; Honnefelder, 'Transzendent oder transzendental: Über die Möglichkkeit von Metaphysik', *Philosophisches Jahrbuch* 92 (1985), pp. 273–90; Jean-François Courtine, *Suarez et le système de la métaphysique* (Paris: PUF, 1990).

Metaphysics and the Question of Creation

minimal conceptual structure Aquinas understands being from the perspective of actuality (*actus essendi*). For him, 'to be' primarily means 'to be in act'. 'Being' refers to the whole of what is (*omne quod est*), the concrete totality of everything that in whatever way shares in the actuality of being. And act entails the character of perfection. Whatever has being shows, in a certain degree, the perfection of being and is, therefore, related to a maximum of perfection. Second, the phrase 'being qua being' stands for a consideration of the whole of reality under the aspect of the intelligibility proper to it in so far as it is being. In contrast to Scotus, the metaphysical consideration of being qua being does not prescind from the difference between the finite and the infinite; it rather reveals the infinite within the finite, the transcendence of perfection in the immanence. Considered precisely as being no finite thing is simply finite, existing *in se*, but is something that appears as a finite expression (*similitudo*) of the infinite perfection of being in which it participates. In this sense, the being that is God is not so much included within the universal conceptual horizon of 'being qua being'; God is the name of the cause of all beings in so far as they are being. In other words: God is conceived of as the universal principle and origin of that concrete totality of all things sharing in the common perfection of being (*ens commune*). In so far as the totality of all beings is not intelligible in itself, it must be understood as the multiplied and differentiated effect of that original fullness of being in relation to which the whole of reality becomes intelligible as being. The differentiated *esse* of the many things, constituting the world, is not intelligible unless as derived from that which is *ipsum esse*. So it is from this perspective that one can affirm and uphold the concrete substantial reality of the world without identifying it with the ultimate reality.

In the long run, Scotus's definition of metaphysics as the science of the transcendental concept of being has been more successful and has ultimately led to the notion of a *metaphysica generalis* (Wolff), the study of the structure of reality from the conceptual horizon of being as such (*ens ut sic*). As a consequence of this development the ontological consideration of being in general has lost its intrinsic relation to the theological transcendence of being itself. I think this is a real loss. One might say that metaphysics in its historical development became more and more 'secularized' in the profound sense that the very being of reality no longer points beyond itself to a transcendent source of being. In this regard the position of Suarez is exemplary of the modern turn to immanence. According to Suarez, metaphysics considers things precisely in so far as they are being, and this perspective formally differs from considering things in their character as created, as related to their extrinsic cause of being. Considered as a being (*ut ens*), a creature is not defined in terms of its relationship to God, since anything said to be is said to be by reason of what it is in itself. To be created is an added qualification of a thing's being, a qualification by which it is explicitly related to the divine principle from which it receives its being.[4] So when a thing is considered formally as a being, it is posited *in se*, that is, *extra nihil*, but not yet as created. The ontological consideration of being as such favours a stance of immanence according to which reality is defined by its intrinsic character of beingness (or *realitas*), without any reference to a higher and more perfect being. This prepared the way for the typical modern immanent approach to the different spheres of reality, each with their own lawfulness and rules of explanation.

In what follows I want to explore Aquinas's conception of metaphysics in view of the question of creation. I will focus especially on the two characteristics mentioned above, first, the primacy of actuality in his conception of being; and second, his interpretation of the formula 'being qua being'. In order to highlight the unique

---

4 Cf. *Disputationes metaphysicae*, XXVIII, 3, 15: *Nam constat, creaturam non denominari ens extrinsece ab entitate aut esse, quod in Deo est, sed a priori et intrinseco esse, ideoque non per tropum sed per veritatem et proprietatem ens appelari. Item constat, creaturam, ut ens est, non definiri per creatorem aut per esse Dei, sed esse ut sic, et quia est extra nihil; nam si addatur habitudo ad Deum, v.g. creaturam esse ens, quia est participatio divini esse, sic non jam definitur creatura ut ens est, sed ut tale ens est, nimirum creatum.* This is a crucial text which bears witness of the modern turn to immanence. In so far as a creature is a *being*, it is considered absolutely and defined by its proper and intrinsic being, as distinguished from nothing. Metaphysics considers things in so far as they are *in se* and abstracts from the difference between created and uncreated. Aquinas endorses the opposite view: *nam eo dicitur aliquid creatum, quod est ens, non ex eo quod est hoc ens* (*S.T.* I, q.45, a.4 ad 1).

and characteristic position of Aquinas with respect to metaphysics I shall often refer to the contrasting position of Duns Scotus.

'Being' as the First Concept of the Intellect

In the Aristotelian tradition, metaphysics is distinguished from the other speculative sciences, mathematics and physics, by being universal in its scope. While mathematics and physics are both particular sciences, extending their consideration to a particular domain of being (since not every being is a mathematical being or a physical being), metaphysics is a universal science in that it considers being universally, *in so far as it is being*. Metaphysics is called a 'common science' (*scientia communis*) because it considers those notions and principles that are common to the knowledge of the special sciences, such as 'being', 'one', 'many', 'potency' and 'act'. These common notions are presupposed by the more specific forms of knowledge; they are known only as adapted and restricted to the particular domain of any of the special sciences. Metaphysics is, therefore, the science of the common presuppositions of the special sciences, among which is 'being', the first and most universal notion of the human intellect. Any science is a science of being, but under some particular aspect, for instance, 'being-in-motion' (*ens mobile*), which is the subject-matter of physics. That a science is a particular science, extending its consideration to only a part of being (thus having a partial view of reality), means that the intelligibility of its object depends on principles or presuppositions which it cannot make understandable within its own restricted horizon. For instance, the science of physics depends on a prior and more universal science because and in so far as the intelligibility of physical (movable) objects depends on a first principle of motion which, in itself, transcends the domain of nature (see the last book of Aristotle's *Physics*). The subject of physics does not have a self-sufficient (per se) intelligibility in the sense that the whole of nature cannot be explained adequately from within, in its own terms. In so far as physics is still a *particular* science, nature is not the ultimate reality and does not coincide with being as being.

Metaphysics is, for Aquinas, the most intellectual science, that is, the science of the most intelligible objects.[5] Among these most intelligible objects are the universal principles, such as 'being' and the properties that belong to 'being' as such. These universal principles are per se intelligible, that is, their intelligibility does not depend on something else. In contrast to physics, which studies intelligible aspects of reality as falling under the senses, thus in supposition of matter, metaphysics studies intelligible aspects of reality as such, whether material or not. In relation to these objects (reality under the intelligible aspect of 'being') the intellect realizes itself most adequately in conformity with its intellectual nature; in relation to these most intelligible objects the intellect, one can say, has returned completely to itself and has become most intellectual in its act. For Aquinas, 'being' is the first notion of the intellect. The process of knowledge consists in a reduction to this first notion of 'being', in which the intellect comes to rest. 'Being' is said to be the *primum intelligibile* and is as such *notissimum*, something in which the intellect is most at home. If we characterize metaphysics as the science of the ultimate reality, then this means that metaphysics considers reality in the light of the *primum intelligibile* and aims to conceive the whole of reality according to its intrinsic intelligibility as being.

Thus metaphysics considers reality in the light of the *primum* of the intellect. A similar relation between metaphysics and the first notion of the intellect we encounter in Duns Scotus. For him, 'being' is the first concept of our intellect in the sense that all other concepts must be resolved into this most simple and universal concept of being. Metaphysics is, for Scotus, the 'first science' in so far as it considers the whole of reality from the conceptual perspective of what is primary in the order of our knowledge. Metaphysics is the science of the concept of being as such, which underlies the whole range of what can possibly be known by us. This same idea of the primacy of 'being' in the order of knowledge allows, apparently, for different interpretations, leading to different conceptions of metaphysics. Let us try, therefore, to clarify in what sense Aquinas understands this primacy of 'being' and why he, in contrast to Scotus, does not speak of it in terms of a 'concept of being'.

---

5 See the Foreword to his Commentary on Aristotle's *Metaphysics*.

Metaphysics and the Question of Creation

Aquinas often quotes Avicenna saying that the first thing that falls in the intellect is 'being', *quod primo cadit in intellectu est ens.*[6] 'Being' is the *primum* of the intellect in the sense that any thing is but knowable in so far as it is being. It is the formal reason of the intelligibility of any object, the *ratio intelligibilitatis*. How must we understand this thesis? For Aquinas, the basic idea seems to be quite evident and not in need of much clarification. What the intellect first of all conceives, when it opens itself to the world, is 'being'. One should resist here, I think, an epistemological interpretation in the sense that the intellect becomes first of all aware of the fact that 'there is something', a general and confused knowledge concerning a concrete individual object present within the field of experience. That is not what Aquinas has in mind. It is not what the intellect first conceives from any object in presupposition of its universal openness to the world. One should rather say that 'being' expresses the initial unity of the intellect with the whole of what exists. The notion of 'being' opens the infinite and absolute horizon within which the intellect operates and can come to conceive any object in particular. Before it comes to a distinct conceptual expression of what it knows or perceives, the intellect already is 'in touch' with reality, and this 'being-in-touch' is what is expressed by the notion of 'being' in a still unreflective and immediate sense. Any reflective awareness of the distinction between the world and what the intellect conceives from it is not yet in order.

However, the problem arises when we feel it necessary to use inverted commas and speak of 'being' in the sense of the concept the intellect forms and by which it gives expression to what it formally and distinctively conceives from any thing when it conceives it as being. Aquinas never speaks of the 'concept' of being as something with a distinctive logical unity, resulting from its act through which it grasps real beings existing outside itself. Here, I think, lies a fundamental obscurity in Aquinas's thought about being. The question of how the intellect itself is involved in its first conception is not taken into account. Aquinas does not distinguish between being (object) and the conceptual form under which it is

---

6 See, for instance, *De veritate* q.1, a.1; q.10, a.11 ad 10; *ST* I, q.5, a.2. The reference is to Avicenna, *Metaphysica* I, c.5 (*Liber de Philosophia Prima*, ed. S. van Riet (Leuven: Peters, 1977), p. 31).

Veritas: Belief and Metaphysics

conceived. Taken as a concept 'being' enjoys a universality that is the result of its being conceived by the intellect: it is the single common predicate that can be attributed indifferently to everything that in whatever way is. If we approach the matter under this angle, we might assign to 'being' a conceptual universality which consists in its ability to represent to the intellect the many real beings in their common character as being. This is what Duns Scotus seems to have in mind. 'Being', he says, is the first object of the intellect in the sense that it corresponds to the universal extension of the intellectual faculty. 'Being' embraces the whole object domain of the intellect. Under the conditions of present life, however, the first object is disclosed to the intellect according to its restricted receptivity on the basis of sense perception. The human intellect, as it operates in this life, does not have an immediate access to the being of reality in itself, but knows reality by means of abstract and universal concepts formed on the basis of sense perception. Departing from the experience of sensible things the intellect conceives 'being' in its distinct character by way of an abstract concept, the first distinctively knowable concept included in all other concepts that the intellect forms with respect to reality as present to the senses.[7] Scotus distinguishes between 'being' as something that is indifferently present in all beings (*ens secundum totam indifferentiam ad omnia in quibus salvatur*[8]), which corresponds to the universal inclination of the intellect as such, and the abstract concept of 'being' that underlies the unity of our experience of the world as a whole. The *conceptus entis* formulates the minimal condition under which any object of experience can be identified as a being. It is that conceptual minimum which guarantees the unity of reality as object of conceptual thought. What, then, does this concept formally express of any object? In this concept each thing is conceived in its minimal structure as something to which being is not inconsistent (*hoc cui non repugnant esse*). It is included in all other concepts signifying 'what' a thing is, inasmuch as each real concept presupposes with regard to its

---

7 Cf. Honnefelder, 'Der zweite Anfang der Metaphysik'.
8 Scotus, *Ordinatio* I, d.3, p.1, n.124, ed. Vat. III, 76f. See Honnefelder, 'Der zweite Anfang der Metaphysik', p. 178.

object that it has a proper consistency by reason of which it can possibly exist.

Let us now look at how Aquinas explains the primacy of 'being' and where the difference with Scotus lies. Where he comments on the primacy of 'being' Aquinas follows a twofold line of reasoning. At some places he points out that 'being' is the commonest predicate and therefore logically prior to the less common predicates which add to being. 'Being' is said to be *primum per communitatem*: all conceptions of the intellect are resolved into this first one which is 'being', because in whatever the intellect conceives, some being is known. This approach suggests that 'being' is universal in the sense of the thinnest predicate which is common to all things (or to all concepts?) without specifying their distinct and determined character. 'Being' stands for the most empty and indeterminate concept in the sense that it does not express with respect to any concrete thing what its being consists in.

However, at other places we see Aquinas explaining the primacy of 'being' in terms of actuality:

> The first thing conceived by the intellect is being, because everything is knowable only inasmuch as it is actually. Hence, being is the proper object of the intellect, and is thus the first intelligible, as sound is the first audible.[9]

This seems to me to be the most definitive and complete explanation. 'Being' constitutes the intelligibility of any object in so far as its proper *ratio* consists in actuality: 'being' signifies primarily 'being-in-act'. But what has actuality to do with intelligibility? Should we not say that a thing is knowable in so far as it has a definite essence which can be grasped or represented by the intellect? Whether a thing actually exists or not does not seem to make any difference to the intelligible content of its essence. What is more, actual existence seems to be a matter of contingent actualization of a possible essence that in itself has a determinate and necessary character. On the other hand, it is not unreasonable to grant actuality the priority over the merely possible. One can argue, with Aquinas, that the possible is said in relation to the

---

9 *ST* I, q.5, a.2.

actual. Possible is what can be actual. And it is only the actual as such that exists in the proper sense. What is possible does not exist, at least not *in itself*; it is not a complete and subsisting being. It may exist in the conception of the intellect or in the power of the cause (e.g. the weather of tomorrow) or even in the potentiality of matter (e.g. the statue, which pre-exists in a piece of marble), but only in so far as it has being, does it actually exist.[10] And only then do we have a complete being (a complete individual thing that subsists in its being, *subsistit in suo esse*). Here we see another difference with Scotus. For Scotus the essential mark of reality is the inner *ratitudo* (firmness, stability) or *certitudo* (certainty) by which it is a possible (non-contradictory) object of a concept, even if it does not actually exist. For Aquinas, on the contrary, reality is first of all characterized by actuality.

Without actual existence nothing is left in the thing, since it does not exist any longer in itself. Actuality is regarded as the completion, the fulfilment of any form or substance by being actually what it is. So a good case can be made for the primacy of actuality. Still the question remains: In what sense is intelligibility constituted by actuality? It must be by reason of the fact that 'being' grounds the very *actual* unity of the intellect with its object. In the passage cited above, Aquinas draws a telling comparison with the sense of hearing. Just as 'being' is the proper object of the intellect, so is 'sound' the proper object of the ear. The comparison throws light on the relation between actuality and universality. Sound is common to everything that can be heard by the ear. It is the common actuality of every particular specimen of sound by reason of which it is an audible object united with the actual hearing. The ear is receptive of whatever particular sound by reason of its sounding. Likewise the intellect is receptive of whatever is being by reason of its actual be-ing. Actuality constitutes intelligibility in so far as it formally grounds the unity of the object with the intellect in its act.

We can conclude that the argument from universality is qualified by actuality which is the proper *ratio* of being. Being is common to

---

10 Cf. *De potentia*, q.7, a.2 ad 9, where Aquinas speaks of *esse* as the 'actuality of all acts' and the 'perfection of all perfections'.

all things in the sense that *esse* is the common actuality of all that is. This means that Aquinas puts the emphasis on universality in the ontological sense; 'being' is conceived in a yet-undifferentiated unity with the object. Just as sound is the common form and actuality of all the particular instances of sound by reason of which they are audible to the ear, so is being the common form and actuality of all particular beings by reason of which they are knowable by the intellect. But here lies a crucial problem, as the alternative reasoning of Duns Scotus makes clear. A certain ambiguity can be noticed in Aquinas between *conceptual universality* – the universality that follows upon being conceived by the intellect – and the universality that is proper to reality in itself, the *common actuality* of all things. Aquinas speaks in a rather unreflective and direct way of 'being', *esse*, as something that is *found* in things in a contracted way. In each particular being *esse* is contracted to a particular nature, in such a way that the particular nature does not coincide with the being it has. In his typical quasi-empirical way of speaking, Aquinas says that in each thing 'being' is found as something which is in itself infinite and pure actuality, and which, therefore, cannot explain by itself the particular and finite manner in which 'being' is found in this thing. Of course this is not meant in a strictly empirical sense, as if the intellect is just looking at how things present themselves. The thing in which 'being' is found in a particular and limited manner is the thing as it is posited within the infinite horizon of the intellect conceiving it in the light of the idea of being. However, the proper logical dimension of the conception of the intellect (this 'idea' of being) remains implicit. It is as if the intellect is immediately present to reality, making in it the distinction between reality's being and the particular manner by which it has being, and this without being reflexively aware of its own doing. Instead of saying that our concept of a horse expresses a particular being, as such distinguished by its proper content from other concepts, Aquinas contends that a horse – that being which is a horse – must be understood as the particular manner in which it relates to something universal. It participates in being which is in itself something universal. The *transcensus* of the intellect takes place from the side of the object: in so far as the object incorporates the universality of being in a particular manner, it points beyond itself to the original fullness of being. But this pointing beyond itself of any finite being can only be recognized by the intellect by reason of its universal openness.

It may be clear where my sympathy lies. However, I think that Duns Scotus indirectly puts his finger on a weak spot in Aquinas's view inasmuch as he seems to pass over the role of the conceptual expression of our knowledge of 'being'; consequently a certain ambiguity can be noted between the universality from the side of the object (the *esse* which is common to all things) and the universality which results from our conceiving *ens* as such, apart from its concrete determination. This ambiguity runs through the whole tradition of Thomism, for instance in the ongoing discussion about how the expression 'common being' (*esse commune*) must be understood. Even the phrase *cadit in conceptione intellectus* attests to this ambiguity in so far as the act of conception seems to be purely passive with respect to 'what falls in it' without playing a proper role. It is as if the human mind, when it starts to exercise its openness with respect to reality, becomes first of all aware of being in such a way that Aquinas does not yet distinguish between this initial awareness of the whole of what is and the conceptual expression of this awareness by means of the term 'being'. That is why terms like 'initial awareness' suggest themselves as describing the implicit dimension of what the intellect conceives as being.

Duns Scotus describes the concept of being as the first and simplest concept in the order of conceptual knowledge by which the objects of sense experience are represented to the intellect. By means of a resolution of our distinct concepts we reach the simplest, not further analysable element, the rock bottom of all our conceptual knowledge of reality, by which I am certain to grasp something as a being without knowing whether it concerns such or such a being. Through this first concept a distinctive intelligibility in things is conceived, their formal structure of being-ness, which conceptually transcends all its categorical and modal differences. Any real being must be necessarily either a substance or an accident, either finite or infinite, but what I conceive when I conceive a thing in its being-ness is something common and prior to these differences. For Aquinas, this would be quite unthinkable. 'Being' (*ens*) is said of things according to their relationship to being (*esse*) and therefore cannot be conceived in its unity prior to, or independent of, the difference in the manner by which something relates to the same *esse*, by which *esse* becomes differentiated in different things. 'Being' signifies something common in the sense that in each thing the principle of *esse* relates to that other principle that accounts for the determinate (and limited) character of a thing's *esse*. *Ens* does not signify the 'what' of things prior to the determinate character of that 'what' – the common factor of all 'quiddities' – but it signifies the determinate 'what' as related to the *esse* they all have in common. 'Being' is always a determinate something (a 'quid') which has *esse*. It signifies, so to say, each thing as differently related to the same of being. This is why one must say that, for Aquinas, 'being' is not so much the first thing I know from any object in the sense of that minimal conceptual content I conceive distinctively when I conceive a thing in its being; it is rather so that 'being' expresses the absolute and comprehensive unity of the intellect and the whole of what is (= *ens*) in such a way that the proper and distinctive conceptual expression of this unity remains implicit.

To some extent the scholastic notion of proper object (or formal object, *obiectum formale*) can be compared to the Kantian notion of a priori. It is like an a priori form in that it grounds the universal relationship of the cognitive power to all the objects to which its operation extends, not something the knowledge of which must be acquired. At the same time, however, 'being' is not a *formal* a priori of the intellect in the sense of an 'empty form' without a content of its own, which structures the empirical data delivered by the senses. 'Being' is the first thing the intellect knows in the sense that it is known directly and naturally in the first contact of the intellect with reality, and this 'contact' is mediated by the senses. Within the sense-mediated relationship to reality the first thing that 'falls' in the intellect is 'being'. And this not in the sense that it is the first thing the intellect conceives from any particular object in presupposition of this 'contact', but one should say that 'being' expresses this 'being-actually-in-contact-with-reality' as such. In other words: 'being' expresses the a priori of the intellect in relation to an a posteriori, because sensory, given object. The intellect exercises its a priori openness to being in relation to what is apprehended by the senses. Now we can also understand why 'being' oscillates between fullness and emptiness. The unity of the intellect with being is mediated through the senses, with the consequence that its first apprehension of reality in its being on the basis of the senses is still abstract and, as it were, from the outside. The intellect, beginning its search for knowledge from sense perception, relates to its transcendental and comprehensive unity with being in a yet external manner and so it does not yet understand being in its proper determination from within, *as being*. 'Being', I said above, is not just a formal a priori; it has its proper content or determination. But what this proper determination is requires a process of mediation. The intellect, starting from the senses, apprehends being firstly in its accidental and external determination. Now, the process of mediation consists herein that being as accident cannot be understood as being unless it is reduced to being as substance; and that material substance cannot be understood as being unless it is reduced to immaterial substance; and finally, that immaterial substance cannot be understood as being unless it is reduced to the very first being which is being in identity with itself (*ipsum esse*). Here we see the crucial difference with Duns Scotus. For Duns Scotus, the first concept of being expresses in itself a formal determination which is univocally common to accident and substance, to finite substance and infinite substance, while for Aquinas 'being' is conceived in an – at first – undifferentiated unity with its object in such a way that the unity of being with the determination it has in its object requires a process of mediation and differentiation which is brought to its final conclusion in the *primum ens*.

In the next section we will see how Aquinas interprets the expression 'being qua being' and in which sense it might be said that the metaphysical perspective of being qua being reveals the whole of reality as created.

Towards a Metaphysical Understanding of Being

For Aquinas as well as for Scotus, the Aristotelian phrase 'being as being' defines the universal scope of metaphysics. Metaphysics is the science of being as being, *ens inquantum est ens*; it treats of the whole of reality under the universal aspect of being. However, their respective interpretations of this formula radically diverge. For Scotus, metaphysics considers the transcategorical and univocal concept of being. This univocal concept of being is arrived at by way of *resolutio*, that is through analysis of our distinct and categorical concepts into the most simple and universal notion which underlies our conceptual knowledge of reality. By way of resolution, the conceptual horizon of whatever is knowable by us is made explicit – the finite objects of human experience as well as the infinite being of God. In so far as the concept of being transcends the finite mode of created beings, it can function as a conceptual bridge between the finite and infinite. In this sense metaphysics is called the *scientia transcendens*, the science of the concept of being and its transcendental properties by which the first and most common condition of any possible object of knowledge is articulated.[11]

This same notion of *resolutio* plays a crucial role in Aquinas's understanding of the phrase 'being as being'. For Aquinas, human thought is raised to the sphere of the metaphysical through a process of *resolutio* by which the particular is resolved into the more universal, and ultimately into the most universal, that is, the principles of being qua being. In order to clarify how this method of *resolutio* is applied by Aquinas and what this means for his interpretation of the phrase 'being qua being', here I want to draw attention to an article in the *Summa Theologiae*.[12] It is a rich and important text in which the phrase 'being as being' occurs in direct connection with the theme of creation. The immediate issue of discussion is the question whether prime matter is created by God or rather presupposed to the effect of creation. From the Aristotelian point of view, prime matter is the uncaused substrate of the physical processes of generation and change. Within the conceptual horizon of nature, prime matter appears to be an irreducible presupposition, an absolute given. For Aquinas the position of prime matter marks the crucial difference between a physical understanding of being in terms of nature (form and matter) and the meta-physical understanding of being in so far as it is

---

11 Duns Scotus, *Met.* Prol. n.5, ed. Viv. VII 5. Cf. Honnefelder, *Scientia transcendens. Die formale Bestimmung der Seiendheit und Realität in der Metaphysik des Mittelalters und der Neuzeit.*

12 *ST* I, q.44, a.2. I have treated this text extensively in my *Aquinas on God*. At several other places in his writings Aquinas comes to speak about the advancement in the philosophical enquiry into the nature of things towards the metaphysical consideration; cf. *De potentia*, q.3, a.5; *De substantiis separatis* c.9; *Summa contra Gentiles* II, c.39.

being. The general idea is that the conceptual horizon of 'nature' must be transcended towards a metaphysical consideration of reality *as being* in order to be able to conceive, beyond nature and its principles, a 'higher origin' according to which the whole substance of reality, including its matter, is created. Matter is external to the intelligibility which resides in the principle of form, but not to being (*esse*), since even matter *is*.

It is important to realize that this notion of 'physics' is taken in a sense other than that of a specialized scientific enquiry into natural phenomena and their causes. 'Physics' here is the knowledge of physical objects, which in their categorical structures are defined as 'forms existing in matter'. The mode of knowing in physics therefore corresponds to the rational, discursive character of human thought. The human rational mode of understanding, based on sensory experience of its object, is first and foremost 'physical'. From the perspective of physics, one might say, the world is conceived of as a manifold of particular things, each of which are identifiable as 'this' distinguished from 'that'. For Aquinas, the conceptual perspective of physics, in this sense, is still *particular* in character. It focuses on the form and species of things. Metaphysics, then, comes after physics in the sense that the more universal is known after the less universal by way of resolution. Physics deals with particular realities, horses, trees, human beings, etc.; metaphysics considers the same realities but considers them in so far as they are beings. Let us now turn to how Aquinas describes this process of *resolutio* by which the philosophical enquiry into being passes from a still 'physical' approach to reality to a metaphysical approach.

In the history of philosophical thought, from its very beginning with the Presocratic philosophers, one can observe, so Aquinas contends, a progressive development with respect to how the nature of reality has been conceived by philosophers. The philosophical study of the general nature of reality (the question of being) is characterized by a developmental logic, which follows from the rational-discursive nature of human thought. In order to arrive at knowledge of the truth, Aquinas says, the intellect must go through a discursive process of reason that takes its starting point in the senses. And philosophical thought underlies this same discursive process, which goes from the senses via the *ratio* to the intellect, from the particular to the universal. Therefore, Aquinas says, 'it is only gradually, and as it were step by step, that the ancient philosophers advanced in the knowledge of truth'.[13]

From its very beginning, philosophy questions the general nature of what there is. For Aquinas, philosophy is just that kind of intellectual enquiry that aims to explicate the intelligible structure of being. And this intelligible structure is articulated in terms of principles and categories of being (substance, accident, form, matter, essence, being/*esse*). Now, in so far as the human intellect does not grasp the truth of reality immediately, it begins with an understanding of being that appears to be inadequate and which, therefore, must be passed over in a further, more adequate conception, until finally being is conceived adequately as being. This suggests a sort of dialectical process by which human thought mediates its more or less particular conception of being (how it thinks about being) with being as the *primum* of the intellect.

In *Summa Theologiae* I, q.44, a.2, Aquinas distinguishes three phases in the historical development of the question of being. In the first phase (Presocratic philosophy) 'being' is understood according to the relationship of substance and accident. In this phase, Aquinas says, the philosophers recognized no other beings except sensible bodies. 'Accident' pertains here to the sensible qualities by which the changing and multiple reality of nature appears to the senses. These sensible qualities are modifications of the material substratum that counts as the 'substance' of reality. 'Substance' is then taken in the sense of the ultimate reality that underlies the changing phenomenal qualities of things, the primary 'stuff' of which things are made. How must we think of this conception of being? Aquinas calls the way the first philosophers thought about the nature of reality 'undeveloped' (*grossiores*). They represent the primitive beginning of philosophy. And this beginning can be understood from a systematic point of view as the attempt to interpret being from the first and immediate apprehension of being on the level of sense-perception. It rests upon the immediate identification of 'being', as the *primum* of the intellect, with the objects of sense-perception. This first phase represents an ontology in which 'being' is conceived of in an extrinsic way; the

---

13 *ST* I, q.44, a.2.

one substance of reality is but the extrinsic unity of the many accidental forms. But it must be said that it is, nevertheless, a first step and as such the ontological relationship of substance–accident remains a systematic part of the more developed conception of being. In the next step the substance (matter) of reality becomes essence, composed of matter and (substantial) form, and in the final step essence (or nature) becomes being, composed of essence and its act of being (*id quod est – esse*). So in each step we see Aquinas introducing a new composition, by which a deeper and more intrinsic intelligibility of being is articulated. The advancement in the subsequent conceptions of being goes from the categorical level of accidental forms via substantial form to the transcendental level of being as such.

The second phase is marked by the introduction of a distinction between matter and substantial form. While substance was initially conceived of as undetermined matter, without an inner essence and form of its own, substance is now understood as composed by the essential parts of matter and form. The distinction between substantial form and matter is made by the intellect, Aquinas says. It is here that the intellect is raised above the level of immediate sense-perception and begins to operate in its rational mode. One can formulate this as follows: by distinguishing substantial form from matter, the intellect distinguishes itself from its immediate unity with sense-perception so that it becomes rational reflection (*ratio*), which, by means of abstraction and comparison, collects the many particular appearances in the unity of the essence. By becoming reason, the intellect transcends the immediate sensory appearance of things towards its inner non-perceptible essence. 'Being' is now conceived of as *essential being*, constituted by a form of its own.

As we said, the historical advancement of philosophy is determined by the reductive process of reason according to which the intellect begins on the level of the senses and then returns, step by step, via *ratio*, to itself as intellect. Only then, in the relation to its object, does it completely return to itself and reach the level of intellect, and thereby is raised to the consideration of being as being.[14] Philosophical thought has then become most 'intellectual',

---

14 Cf. *ST* I, q.44, a.2: *Et ulterius aliqui erexerunt se ad considerandum*

that is, has become most conformed to the intellectual dimension of knowledge in which it relates in a purely intrinsic way to the intelligibility of its object without a presupposed substratum. While the philosophers of the first two phases still considered being in a particular manner, from a categorical perspective, namely as *such* a being (according to accidental forms) or as *this* being (according to substantial forms), in the final phase being is considered in a universal manner in so far as it is being.[15]

In the third and final phase of the development of the philosophical understanding of being, being is no longer identified with the particular species and forms of things, but now the essence is understood as related intrinsically to the *being* it has. The essential relationship of matter and form, constituting the essence, is superseded by a new relationship, that is, the metaphysical composition of essence and its act of being. What is new in this composition of being is that it no longer includes matter as the presupposed substrate of form. Of course, matter may be still be part of the essence of a thing (there are material beings), but the relationship between essence and being is neutral with respect to the presence of matter (there might, therefore, exist immaterial beings). This is why the metaphysical object is no longer based on abstraction – abstraction from matter in order to disclose the intelligibility of the object to the intellect – but on what Aquinas calls *separation*.[16] 'Separation'

---

ens inquantum est ens. This is the end of the process of *resolution* by which the particular is resolved into the universal. Cf. *In de trinitate*, q.6, a.1: *Et ideo terminus resolutionis in hac via ultimus est consideratio entis et eorum quae sunt entis in quantum huiusmodi.* For the method of *resolutio* in metaphysics, see J. Aertsen, 'Method and metaphysics. The *via resolutionis* in Thomas Aquinas', in R. Työrinoja Anja Inkeri Lehtinen and Dagfinn Follesdal (eds), *Knowledge and the Sciences in Medieval Philosophy* [Proceedings of the Eighth International Congress of Medieval Philosophy (S.I.E.P.M.), Helsinki 24–29 August 1987], Bd.3, (Helsinki 1990), pp. 3–12.

15 Cf. *ST* I, q.44, a.2: '*Utrique* [the philosophers of the first two phases] *igitur consideraverunt ens particulari quadam consideratione, vel inquantum est hoc ens, vel inquantum est tale ens.*'

16 For the negative judgement of separation, see *In de trinitate*, q.5, a.3. The theory of *separatio* is a further development of the Aristotelian doctrine of the three degrees of abstraction.

refers to the negative judgement by which something is said to exist without something else, in this case: being, as understood according to the relationship of essence and *esse*, is completely intelligible from within, and this without presupposing the uncaused matter. When the intellect, in the relation to its object, has returned completely to itself, and thus considers being as being, it has overcome all externality (materiality) in the way it conceives reality.

We are now in a situation to explain more fully what Aquinas means by *resolutio*. It appears that metaphysics comes after physics in so far as the more universal is reached after the particular by way of resolution. The first two phases in the philosophical enquiry into the nature of reality exemplify what one may call a 'physical' perspective of reality. In both phases the consideration of being is still particular in character in so far as being is considered under a particular aspect, namely either as *this* being or as *such* a being. One might say that 'being' here is identified with nature, thus the universal is identified with the particular. In Aquinas's view, one passes over from the second phase to the third phase by resolving 'nature' into its metaphysical principles, that is by conceiving 'nature' *as* the particular manner in which a thing has being (*esse*) which is, in itself, something universal. Resolution pertains to the process of reason by which a given reality is reduced to its principles, through which it becomes intelligible as such. The movement of *resolutio* proceeds from the particular to the universal by showing that something particular ('man' or 'tree') must be understood as the particular manner in which it relates to something universal. The idea is that to consider reality as the sum of all particular entities such as 'man', 'tree', etc. is still an abstract way of considering reality. Through resolution it is shown that 'nature' is a *part* of being in general, and therefore the conceptual perspective of physics is but a partial and abstract perspective on being. The transition to each following phase is effected by means of resolution in the sense that the unanalysed and uncaused given in the prior phase is resolved in the next phase into its principles. What in the first phase is assumed to be the uncaused substance of reality is in the second phase analysed into the principles of substantial form and matter; then, in passing over from the second phase to the third, being as essence or nature is resolved further into the principles of being as such, namely into 'that which is' and its 'act of being'. In this final step the physical horizon of 'nature', the physical universe of generation and corruption is transcended towards a metaphysical conception of the same reality now understood as the concrete and differentiated totality of all things that actually exist (or: have *esse*), that is, each thing considered according to its own (particular) essence. It is only from this metaphysical point of view that one is able to conceive a higher origin, beyond the natural origination of things, according to which the whole substance of reality in its being can be said to be *created*. Therefore to conceive creation as a way of becoming under the aspect of a thing's being necessarily presupposes a metaphysical understanding of reality.

Conclusion: Creation is not a Truth of Physics

In the foregoing I have discussed and analysed some aspects of Aquinas's understanding of metaphysics in view of the theme of creation. My interest in Aquinas is not purely historical but is rather motivated by the conviction that the truth of the religious idea of creation can only be made understandable from a metaphysical perspective. Within a purely immanent horizon, characteristic of current naturalism, the belief in creation can only be upheld in contradiction to the truths of natural science. It is often assumed, and not only by 'creationists', that creation concurs with the natural explanation of the world. Many think of God as an additional factor we need in order to explain the essential features of nature and man or, alternatively, we can dismiss as a superfluous hypothesis. Regarded as an additional factor, we may decide, with Hugo Grotius, to consider the general order of nature 'as if God does not exist'.[17] Without God, the world and the whole of physical facts in the world remain the same (or so at least it seems to many). But it might be that in this case we precisely fail to account for the very concrete existential character of the world itself.

---

17 *De iure belli ac pacis*, curavit B. J. A. de Kanter-van Hettinga Tromp (Aalen: Scientia Verlag, 1993), prolegomena, 11.

Veritas: Belief and Metaphysics

We can learn from Aquinas that creation is not a truth belonging to the domain of physics, as a way of explaining particular features and goings on in the natural world. Creation, rather, is a truth of metaphysics, a 'divine' truth which as such is not directly and positively accessible by human reason. Creation can only be affirmed on the basis of the insight that the world we live in is not the ultimate reality. This insight may arise when 'nature', as the correlate of the categorical sphere of human (rational) experience, is resolved into its metaphysical principles by understanding nature as the particular way a thing shares in being. Then it becomes evident that the whole of nature cannot be understood *as being* unless it is reduced to a universal principle from which it takes it origin. But how can we make it plausible that the world we live in is not the 'ultimate reality'? I think this is exactly what is behind the religious notion of creation.

Metaphysics raises the question of the ultimate reality of being qua being. Returning to the first notion of the intellect, metaphysics extends its consideration to the whole of what exists and tries to understand it in the light of being. The whole of what exists is not an abstract totality, the totality of God and creatures as conceived under the univocal concept of being. On the contrary: it is a concrete and differentiated whole of many beings, each of which is mediated in a particular way with the common universality of being. If we talk about 'being' in its metaphysical sense, it comprises the concrete differentiated whole of what in whatever way is. Now one must say that neither the concrete whole as such (consisting of many and diverse parts), nor any part of the whole, can be fully understood as being. Each part simply exists within the whole and depends on it, while the whole depends on its parts, each of which is a subsisting and complete thing in so far as it is mediated in a particular way with the common universality of being. There exists a mutual dependency between the whole and its parts. What subsists in the proper sense of the word are the parts of the concrete differentiated whole; each of which is a subsistent and concrete being, but only as being *this* and *not that*, thus as differentiated from other things and mediated in its own distinctive and particular way with the being all things have in common. Each subsisting thing is a being, but it cannot account by itself for its mediated (composed) unity with being within the whole of what

Metaphysics and the Question of Creation

exists. It is as if each thing, each part of reality that enjoys being in a particular way, is given to itself, given to exist in a determinate way.

This, I think, is essentially the Thomistic view of creation. One might draw out the reasoning a little further and make a link to a spirituality of creation. To be created means, for every creature but particularly for humankind, to exist in response to the gift of being, a gift that is neither of our own making nor of an external and meaningless given. To be created means to exist in response to a meaning that does not originate in oneself but that can only be acknowledged in one's own freedom.

6. Trying My Very Best to Believe Darwin, or,[1] The Supernaturalistic Fallacy: From Is to Nought[2]

CONOR CUNNINGHAM

> *Materialism is really our established Church.*
> G. K. Chesterton[3]
>
> *There is a sense in which materialism is the religion of our time.*
> John Searle[4]

What I shall try to do in this chapter is outline, however briefly, Darwin's theory of evolution and then present some rather broad consequences – scientific, philosophical and theological – that arise from its logic. Most of all, and throughout, I will try my very best to believe Darwin, that is, to believe what he says about the natural world, something which, as we shall see, becomes increasingly difficult, not because I seek to dispute his theory. No, not at all; rather, because under the influence of some of his disciples, a

---

1 For very helpful questions, I would like to thank audiences at Edinburgh University, University of Nottingham and the Edith Stein Institute, Granada, Spain. For a much more developed assessment of Darwinism, see my *Evolution: Darwin's Pious Idea (Interventions)* (Grand Rapids: Wm. B. Eerdmans, forthcoming 2008). I would also like to thank Patrick Riches for his very helpful comments.
2 I am here playing on the 'naturalistic fallacy', which consists in any move from is to ought.
3 *Eugenics and Other Evils* (London: Cassell & Co., 1922), p. 77.
4 *Mind: A Brief Introduction* (New York: Oxford University Press, 2004), p. 48.

fairly simple, and in one sense largely inoffensive, biological theory becomes hijacked, being co-opted as a vehicle for something else.[5] And for what does it become a vehicle? Well, quite simply, for one more version of reductive materialism or, better, nihilism.[6]

In 1873, Sir Charles Sherrington was given a copy of Charles Darwin's book: *The Origin of Species By Means of Natural Selection, or the Preservation of Favoured Races in the Struggle For life* (1859) when his mother handed the book to him, she said that 'it sets the door of the universe ajar'. Why, we might ask, does it do this? Before we can hope to answer this, I shall outline that for which Darwin argued. After reading Thomas Malthus's Essay *On the Principle of Population* (1798), Darwin tells us plainly what he sees:

> A struggle for existence inevitably follows from the high rate at which all organic beings tend to increase . . . [A]s more individuals are produced that can possibly survive; there must in every case be a struggle for existence, either one individual with another of the same species, or with individuals of distinct species, or with the physical conditions of life. It is the doctrine of Malthus applied with manifold force to the whole animal and vegetable kingdom.[7]

So, according to Darwin, nature is caught in a bind between geometric growth and competition for what are now scarce resources, and this initiates a war between species and within species as they compete to survive. Hence the famous phrase, 'the

---

5 I use the word 'vehicle' deliberately, it being Richard Dawkins' term, which shall be discussed below.

6 For an intepretation of Darwinism as nihilism, from advocates of it, see Tamler Sommers and Alex Rosenberg, 'Darwin's nihilistic idea: evolution and the meaninglessness of life', *Biology and Philosophy* 18 (2003), pp. 653–68. For an extended analysis of nihilism, see my *Genealogy of Nihilism* (London and New York: Routledge, 2002).

7 Charles Darwin, *On the Origin of Species, and other Texts*, ed., Joseph Carroll (Ontario, Canada: Broadview Texts, 2003), p. 134; all references will be to this edition. This volume also contains excerpts from *The Descent of Man*, and from Darwin's *Notebooks*.

survival of the fittest' – a phrase that does not appear until the fifth edition of the *Origin of Species*, and is borrowed from Herbert Spencer's *Principles of Biology* (1864).[8] But in fact, Darwin's theory does not argue for the survival of the fittest; rather, it is more accurate to say that it is a matter of the survival of the *fitter*, because the field upon which the struggle for existence is fought is relative – so what is beneficial today may well be a hindrance tomorrow. And it is important to remember that fitness, for Darwin, is simply about the variable success at breeding: those who procure resources enough to breed are fit, while those who procure more resources and so breed more than a conspecific are deemed fitter. Here we come to Darwin's central insight:

> If variations useful to any organic being do occur, assuredly individuals thus characterized will have the best chance of being preserved in the struggle of life; and from the strong principle of inheritance they will tend to produce offspring similarly characterized. This principle of preservation, I have called, for the sake of brevity, Natural Selection.[9]

Thus, Darwin's theory of evolution is a theory of evolution by natural selection, one that depends on three crucial principles: variation, reproduction and heritability, all of which give rise to what is termed 'descent with modification', and any such modification is gradual, incremental and additive.

So far, so good then; so what's all the fuss about, we might ask? Well, there are a couple of radical implications bobbing around in his theory; or, if not radical, at least counter-intuitive, depending on whose intuition, of course. One such implication is the transmutation of species, in other words, species change. We tend to think that a dog is a dog, and a cat is a cat, and that's that – separate and immiscible they remain. But after returning from his voyage on the *Beagle* (in 1836) Darwin gave up his belief in the fixity of species, a belief that is underwritten by an essentialism that has been around since Plato, if not before. Such essentialism

---

8 But to be fair to Darwin, Spencer himself only thought of this phrase after reading Darwin.
9 *On the Origin of Species*, p. 175.

argues that species have an essence, and that any such essence is immutable. In addition, such species are nested within a natural hierarchy – the great chain of being, or *scala naturae* – from the inanimate, to the vegetative, to the worm, all the way up to humankind, and from there to the angels, and lastly God. And accompanying this hierarchy of essences is of course ascending importance or significance. We do in a sense still assign importance in a similar manner – we don't hesitate to cut the grass, but we are unlikely to cut the dog; likewise, we eat the chicken, but not our neighbour's child. But according to Darwin's theory, the natural world is not fixed, but fluid; accordingly all points of significance, or indeed reference are set adrift.[10]

Before coming back to this notion of fluidity, let me quote Darwin again, but doing so from his other major work, the provocatively entitled *The Descent of Man* (1871):

> Man with all his noble qualities . . . with his god-like intellect, which has penetrated into the movements and constitutions of the solar system – with all these exalted powers – man still bears in his bodily frame the indelible stamp of his lowly origin.[11]

These origins are, according to Darwin, one of common descent, or ancestry, not only with the great apes but, crucially, with all life. For all animate, organic creatures have, it seems, crawled out from the same primordial swamp. Indeed, Darwin refers to 'some one primordial form'[12] from which all life started, and it in turn appears to have developed in what he called 'some warm little pond' – thus life is monophyletic – that is, it has one lineage. So,

---

10 Though this fuss about transmutation of species may be the result of something approaching a category mistake. Thus I am in agreement with E. J. Lowe when he says, 'I do not accept the doctrine that biological natural kind terms have their extension fixed partly by evolutionary descent. What I do accept is that the *dog species* that exists on Earth has its membership fixed by evolutionary descent . . . However, I do not identify species (in the biological sense) with kinds. Species have members, whereas kinds have instances: species are collectives, whereas kinds are universals', *The Possibility of Metaphysics* (Oxford: OUP, 1998), p. 187.
11 *On the Origin of Species*, p. 561.
12 *On the Origin of Species*, p. 394.

just as post-Galilean science apparently tells us that the heavens have fallen to earth – there being no hierarchical difference between up and down[13] – it appears that for Darwin, there is no irreducible difference between human beings and animals, and by extending this insight, as we shall hear, mind and matter likewise inhabit a continuum (if indeed there is really such a thing as mind). First we discover that species – including *Homo sapiens* – are somewhat arbitrary, and second that man shares a common ancestor with the great apes, and lastly, that man and the apes share a common ancestry with all life, and in so doing, inhabit a continuum right back to inanimate matter. If we translate this biological insight into ontological terms, we are, it seems, left to chase a cognitive will-o'-the-wisp. For this Darwinian paradigm of species transmutation, conjoined to common ancestry, renders change, or becoming, normal (it being somewhat analogous to Newtonian inertia); and stability is then a deviant situation, one that is the product of temporal parochialism.[14] As Olivier Rieppel puts it,

> Under the aspect of continuity, the species cannot be objectified except by arbitrary delineation of some segment of genealogical nexus . . . Continuity dictates a nominalistic view of species – it emphasizes *process*, thus rendering pattern a matter of arbitrary lines of demarcation.[15]

Think of a green apple. We picture it as a real and stable entity, as something that can be qualified as 'real'. But the truth of the apple, hidden behind a veil of mere minutes (no matter how many), is nothing more than a mound of dust: *from dust you came, and*

---

13 As Quine says, 'there is no up'; W. V. O. Quine, 'Designation and Existence', in *Readings in Philosophical Analysis*, eds T. Friegl and W. Sellars (New York: Appleton-Century-Crofts, 1949), p. 46.

14 Cf. Timothy Shanahan, *The Evolution of Darwinism: Selection, Adaptation, and Progress in Evolutionary Biology* (Cambridge: CUP, 2004), p. 19. Also, see David Depew and Bruce Weber, *Darwinism Evolving: Systems Dynamics and the Genealogy of Natural Selection* (Cambridge, Massachusetts: A Bradford Book, MIT Press, 1995), p. 120.

15 Olivier Rieppel, 'Species as Individuals: A Review and Critique of the Argument', in *Evolutionary Biology*, ed. Max Hecht (New York: Plenum Press, 1986), pp. 283–317, at pp. 312–13; emphasis mine.

dust you remain. Ontologically speaking, we still bathe in our ancestral swamp. Entities, and by extension species, are merely slices of time, thus they are only cross sections of history, bearing no permanency or real identity. As John Dewey comments, Darwinism amounts to 'laying hands on the ark of absolute permanency'.[16] Consequently, when we cognize an apple, such cognition is, it seems, founded on perpetual lack – for we only manage to bestow reference by forcefully, and as said, parochially, bracketing the sheer continuity of history. Thus each would-be manifestation or cognition – like some Derridian signifier – points us endlessly away, back into the depths of a pre-history, just as our own thought processes likewise do (a theme we will return to below). Hence we are endlessly chasing after, seeking to collect, both sense and reference. This means that all appearance is strictly epiphenomenal (another issue to which we will return below).

Here let us up the ante a little. Daniel Dennett characterizes Darwin's theory as a 'dangerous idea'. He does so because

> Darwin's idea – bears an unmistakable likeness to universal acid: it eats through just about every traditional concept, and leaves in its wake a revolutionized worldview . . . Darwin's idea had been born as an answer to questions in Biology, but it threatened to leak out, offering answers – welcome or not – to questions in cosmology (going in one direction) and psychology (going in the other direction) . . . Darwin's idea thus also threatened to spread all the way up, dissolving the illusion of our own authorship, our own divine spark of creativity and understanding.[17]

(Incidentally, the philosopher John Dewey had already referred to Darwin's theory as the 'greatest dissolvent'.[18]) Here, then, it gets a little harder to believe Darwin. But to be fair to Dennett, Darwin

---

16 John Dewey, 'The Influence of Darwin on Philosophy', in *Darwin*, Norton Critical Edition, ed., Philip Appleman (New York: W. W. Norton, 1970), p. 393.

17 Daniel Dennett, *Darwin's Dangerous Idea: Evolution and the Meanings of Life* (New York: Simon and Schuster, 1995), p. 63.

18 See John Dewey, *The Influence of Darwin on Philosophy and Other Essays* (New York: H. Holt and Co., 1910), p. 19.

did sometimes seem to invite the extension of his theory beyond the realms of the strictly biological. Here is a passage from his notebooks: 'Origin of man now proved – Metaphysics must flourish – He who understands baboon – will do more for metaphysics than Locke.'[19]

We shall return below to the extension of Darwinism beyond biology. First let me outline my notion of the supernaturalistic fallacy. Following a line of thought firmly established by Wilfrid Sellars, Richard Lewontin states that 'Science is the only begetter of truth'.[20] Leaving aside the fact that this proposition is extra-scientific – that is, it is a philosophical thesis, and not a scientific one – we might be inclined to enquire why he asserts something so question-begging? Well, Lewontin gives us an answer of sorts:

> We take the side of science in spite of the patent absurdity of some of its constructs, in spite of its failures to fulfill many of its extravagant promises . . . in spite of the tolerance of the scientific community for unsubstantiated just-so stories, because we have a prior commitment to materialism . . . Moreover that materialism is absolute, for we cannot allow a Divine foot in the door.[21]

In light of such dogmatism, figures as disparate as G. K. Chesterton and Thomas Nagel seem to be correct when they tell us that, 'Fear of religion has had large and often pernicious consequences for modern intellectual life'.[22] Here we have a perfect example of this pernicious effect: if a phenomenon does not meet the sole *elected* scientific criteria, it simply does not exist. Thus, this fallacy moves from *is to nought*. For in our somewhat scientistic modernity, we are instructed to abandon what is referred to as the 'manifest image' (Sellars), instead adopting the 'scientific image'.[23] Take Sir Arthur Eddington's two tables: on the one hand, we have the

---

19 *The Origin of Species, and other Texts*, p. 468; see also, p. 397.
20 Richard Lewontin, 'Billions and Billions of Demons', in *New York Review of Books* 44 (9 January 1997), p. 31.
21 Lewontin, 'Billions and Billions of Demons', p. 31.
22 Thomas Nagel, *The Last Word* (Oxford: OUP, 2003), p. 130.
23 See Wilfrid Sellars, 'Philosophy and the Scientific Image of Man', in *Science, Perception and Reality* (London: Routledge and Kegan Paul, 1963).

'solid' table in front of us, and on the other, we have the table according to physics, one which is composed of, say, atoms and empty space. This seems fair enough, of course physics is going to look at a table this way, and of course we are going to rest our cups and saucers – with some confidence, on the back of the table. But it is suggested that when it comes down to it, the only real image is the one that belongs to physics. Why? Because *fundamental* particles, for example, are really real (*ontos onta*), while granny's table is just a folk tale, that is, it is a manifestation of what is termed, pejoratively, 'folk psychology'. We might possibly be able to stretch our credulity thus far, after all, what's in a table? – does it really matter? But of course when we abandon the manifest image, or better, when the manifest image surrenders its rights, things get a bit trickier, as it is now not really a question of tables. For instance, the world of colour must be given up, too. From Democritus to Galileo, and later John Locke, what are termed secondary qualities have been relegated to the cheap seats, and then forcefully expelled from the building. Rather prophetically, W. B. Yeats once said that Newton's science, with its acceptance of only primary qualities, had left us in a world akin to 'excrement'.[24] But as Anthony O'Hear says (following George Berkeley), 'Sauce for the secondary goose, is sauce for the primary gander'.[25] In other words, the reasons one might relegate a secondary quality are equally applicable to primary qualities, for the simple reason that they, too, depend on the status of the perceiver – they are mind-involved, so to speak.

But this wish to reduce the complex to the simple does not stop at colour. No, as Paul Churchland says:

> Consider sound. We know that sound is just a train of compression waves traveling through the air, and that the property of being high pitched is identical with the property of having a high oscillatory frequency. We have learned that light is just electro-

---

24 See W. B. Yeats, *Explorations* (New York: Macmillan, 1962), p. 325. This Newtonian excrement is reminiscent of David Lewis's atomless gunk, and Alain Badiou's inconsistent multiplicity, and as we shall see, the ultra-Darwinian 'swamp'.

25 Anthony O'Hear, *Beyond Evolution* (Oxford: OUP, 2002), p. 87.

magnetic waves . . . We now appreciate that the warmth or coolness of a body is just the energy motion of the molecules that make it up. . . . What we now think of as 'mental states' . . . are identical with brain states in exactly the same way.[26]

Here we have gone from colour all the way to thought, itself. Again to quote Churchland, 'Could it turn out that nobody has ever believed anything?'[27] According to him, 'common sense psychology' (hereafter CSP) consists in proto-scientific theories, which for the sake of exactitude (think of Borges's 'On Exactitude in Science') should be reduced to neurophysiological explanation, and since CSP does not reduce to such a neurophysiological explanation it (by its own criteria) must therefore be eliminated. Of course if neurophysiology is contextless, ahistorical and completely extensional then how could CSP fit such a reduction? It is a round peg in a square hole! Moreover, to believe that CSP is false is still to employ CSP; such are the ways of these self-cancelling thinkers. So we are in a situation, it seems, where we do not even have *beliefs*, that is, an intentional life (this seems an eminent example of Bill Livant's cure for baldness: you just shrink the head until the remaining hair covers what's left).[28] And why would that be the case? Because of the *astonishing hypothesis*, as Francis Crick explains:

The astonishing hypothesis is that you, your joys and your sorrows, you memories and your ambitions, your sense of identity and free will, are in fact no more than the behaviour of a vast assembly of nerve cells and their associated molecules.[29]

But what would it take for him for it to be otherwise? In other words, is this position falsifiable, and if indeed it is, what would

---

26 Paul Churchland, *Matter and Consciousness*, revised edition (Cambridge, MA: MIT Press, 1988), p. 26.
27 Churchland, *Matter and Consciousness*, p. 43.
28 William Livant, 'Bill Livant's Cure for Baldness', *Science and Society* 62 (1998), pp. 471–4; Dawkins' notion of the gene is a similar cure.
29 Francis Crick, *The Astonishing Hypothesis: The Scientific Search for the Soul* (New York: Charles Scribner's Sons, 1994), p. 3.

such falsification look like? We shall return to the question of falsification below.

It seems fair to suggest, then, that the supernaturalistic fallacy certainly involves what Lynne Rudde Baker, Thomas Nagel, and Chesterton call 'cognitive suicide'.[30] And ironically, this leaves us in a much more mysterious world than that of the theist, for in an almost Humean sense everything is now 'miraculous', as it is beyond explanation. In light of 'physicalism',[31] Baker argues that lived-life has become mysterious, almost miraculous, this is what she refers to as the bizarre, 'spiritualism' of the everyday. For example, in the absence of intentional agents (which physicalists argue is indeed the case), social practices that depend upon ordinary explanation and prediction of behaviour become unintelligible.[32] Indeed the mind–body problem, so-called, is itself a result of physicalism. We often hear that methodological naturalism is there to safeguard science from the intrusion of mystery; for instance, it is surely unhelpful if when seeking to explain a kettle of boiling water we were entranced by the emission of steam, endeavouring to describe this phenomenon in supernatural terms. But here, maybe unexpectedly, we are left in a secular world of perpetual mystery. Moreover, the absurdity, or at least danger, of this mysterious world – one that has abandoned the manifest image – increases when, from an evolutionary perspective, we start to question all formal thought-logic, etc., and so all objectivity. Doing so because thought is no longer abstract, or immaterial, instead thought is a meaty mechanism, so to speak, one formed, say, on the savannah (during the Pleistocene period) many millions of years ago, and was put in place for reasons other than trigon-

---

30 Cf. Lynne Rudder Baker, *Saving Belief: a Critique of Physicalism* (Princeton, NJ: Princeton University Press, 1987), chapter 7; Thomas Nagel, *The View From Nowhere* (Oxford: OUP, 1986), p. 52; also see G. K. Chesterton, *Orthodoxy*, chapter 3.

31 I am here using materialism, naturalism and physicalism interchangeably. Doing so because in truth they are historically speaking what we might call successor terms. For instance, materialism became naturalism only because according to physics matter was no longer simply inert, so the materialists had to change their name in a desparate bid to save their secularism.

32 See Rudde-Baker, *Saving Belief*, p. 130.

ometry; being so because our minds are mechanisms for survival. Consequently, according to the ultra-Darwinian advocates of evolutionary psychology, when you feel hungry and so eat, or are cold and so put on a coat, the reasons you give yourself are proximate reasons – while the ultimate cause is survival; in other words, you put your coat on or eat ultimately in order to be able to breed. This approach to reality has potentially enormous consequences.

With regard to formal thought, for instance, Nagel makes the point well, when he says, 'If we came to believe that our capacities for objective theory were the product of Natural Selection that would warrant serious scepticism about its results'.[33] Darwin already worried about this very possibility:

> With me the horrid doubt always arises whether the convictions of man's mind, which has been developed from the mind of the lower animals, are of any value or at all trustworthy. Would anyone trust the convictions of a monkey's mind if there are any convictions in such a mind?[34]

Thus it seems Jerry Fodor is correct when he says, 'Darwinism of all things, undermines the scientific enterprise. Talk about biting the hand that feeds you.'[35] Why? Because, as Fodor tell us, 'There is ... no Darwinian reason for thinking that we're true believers.'[36] In other words, in light of natural selection belief is no longer incorrigible. C. S. Lewis makes the same point: 'The assumption that things which have been conjoined in the past will always be conjoined in the future is the guiding principle not of rational but of animal behaviour.'[37] In addition, 'The relation between response

---

33 Nagel, *The View From Nowhere*, p. 79.
34 Letter to W. Graham, July 1881, *The Life and Letters of Charles Darwin*, ed., Francis Darwin (New York: Basic Books, 1959), p. 285. Chesterton echoes this concern: 'Why should not good logic be as misleading as bad logic? They are both movements in the brain of a bewildered ape', *Orthodoxy*, p. 33.
35 Jerry Fodor, *In Critical Condition* (Cambridge, MA: MIT Press, 1998), p. 190.
36 Fodor, *In Critical Condition*, p. 201. Also see also Alvin Plantinga, *Warrant and Proper Function* (New York, Oxford University Press, 1993), chapter 12.
37 C. S. Lewis, *Miracles* (London: Harper Collins, 2002), p. 30.

Trying My Very Best to Believe Darwin

and stimulus is utterly different from that between knowledge and the truth.'[38] Hence we cannot explain why or how we can see that an inference follows. William Provine states that 'in order to accept both Christian faith and Darwinian biology, you need to check your brains at the church-house door'. But in truth, for ultra-Darwinism, you need to check your mind at the door. According to Richard Dawkins, 'Although atheism might have been logically tenable before Darwin, Darwin made it possible to be an intellectually fulfilled atheist.'[39] The problem with this logic is that it retains a strong notion of *belief*, one that is just not available to the ultra-Darwinist, because atheism is to theism nothing more than the other side of the same coin (at least in this particular sense). For this very reason Nagel appears to think that the human intellect is an exception to the Darwinian view that natural selection explains everything (what is known as the 'adaptationist programme'[40]); in other words, biological phenomena – and by extension, social phenomena – are examined under the presumption that they are adaptations, that is, they have arisen as a response to selection pressures presented by the natural environment. In this way, Darwinian analysis moves from the identification of homologous physical traits shared by different species, to the identification of homologous psychological traits.[41]

So, our intellectual and social activities become subject to evolutionary analysis. Not to worry, argues Michael Ruse. For biological fitness, he tells us,

> is a function of reproductive advantage rather than of philosophical insight. Thus if we benefit biologically by being deluded

---

38 Lewis, *Miracles*, p. 28.
39 Richard Dawkins, *The Blind Watchmaker* (New York: W.W. Norton, 1986), p. 1.
40 Nagel, *The View From Nowhere*, p. 79.
41 Though one must ask, if in the latter, the difference between an analogous trait and a homologous one can be discerned – the former can as it is physically grounded in common ancestry, but can the same be said for psychology? In other words, can we really separate homology and analogy when it comes to the mind, at least without begging the question?

about the true nature of formal thought, then so be it. A tendency to objectify is the price of reproductive success.[42]

What must be realized is that such an interpretation arises from the strict dualism of *replicators* and *vehicles*. Very briefly, replicators are the genotypes, because they can actually replicate themselves – mammals can't of course, because due to *meiosis*, we can only ever get half our genetic material across the generational barrier. This division is based on the work of August Weismann,[43] who divided genetic material into the germ plasm and the *soma*: the former is immortal and the latter, which is the body as such, perishes (this of course repeats the Orphic notion that the body is a prison for the soul: *soma–sema*). Consequently, phenotypes – bodies – are never repeated again; our bodies as they are, are completely and utterly unique. Thus Socrates' nose only walked this earth once (I will return to noses later, doing so to illustrate a real irreducible relation). Weismann's barrier, as it is called, also grounds what is known as the 'central dogma' of molecular, genetic biology: information flows from DNA to proteins, but never from proteins to DNA.[44] If organisms aren't replicators, then they are vehicles; and from the Dawkinsian point of view, replicators build the vehicles. The unfortunate thing for us is that they built vehicles that *woke up* – that is, we attribute to our consciousness an ultimate validity,

---

42 Michael Ruse, *Taking Darwin Seriously: a Naturalistic Approach to Philosophy* (Oxford: Blackwell, 1986), p. 188.

43 August Weismann's views were made available to the English speaking world with the translation of his work, as *Essays Upon Heredity and Kindred Biological Problems* (Oxford: Clarendon Press, 1889). Yet his argument was disseminated much more widely when he published an article entitled 'The All-Sufficiency of Natural Selection: A Reply to Herbert Spencer', *Contemporary Review*, 64 (1893), pp. 309–38.

44 Here is how Francis Crick defines it: 'this states that once "information" has passed into protein it cannot get out again. In more detail, the transfer of information from nucleic acid to nucleic acid, or from nucleic acid to protein may be possible, but transfer from protein to protein, or from protein to nucleic acid is impossible', Francis Crick, 'On Protein Synthesis', quoted in *Genes in Development*, eds Eva Neumann-Held and C. Rehmann-Sutter (Durham, NC and London: Duke University Press, 2006), p. 79. It should be noted that Weismann's own stance is not actually equivalent to what is perpetrated in his name.

when really it is only of proximate interest. Yes, we can write poetry, form religions, be altruistic, but in the end these are mere behavioural froth on the substantial sea of genotypes; and if they are not wholly froth, they are certainly epiphenomenal, as they are, then, oblique roots to evolutionary fitness. It is for this reason that Wilson tells us that 'Theology is not likely to survive as an independent intellectual discipline'.[45]

Due, then, to the explanatory reach of evolutionary psychology, $E = mc^2$ is a roundabout way of getting someone to breed with you. As Fodor says, 'Have you heard the joke about the lawyer who is offered sex by a beautiful woman? "Well, I guess so", he replies, "but what's in it for me?"'[46] All our thoughts, then, cast a shadow, so to speak, over our would-be intentions, our conscious lives are shadowed by their evolutionary past – their formative years. There, just out of sight, at the peripheral of thought lies the dull meat of sheer animality (though we will see below, that for Aquinas, 'pure animality' is a vicious abstraction). In contrast to the casualness of someone like Ruse, Emmanuel Levinas says, 'Everyone will readily agree that it is of the highest importance to know whether we are duped by morality.'[47] Here is an answer from Ruse and Wilson: 'Ethics is an illusion fobbed off on us by our own genes to get us to co-operate, thus morality ultimately seems to be about self-interest.'[48] Indeed, 'Humans function better [that is, function better as vehicles for genes] if they are deceived by their genes into thinking there is a disinterested objective morality, binding upon them, which we should obey.'[49] Like the man who has an affair, saying he is doing so because he 'loves' the woman, yet six months later the affair has broken down. But when asked why he abandoned fidelity, he still responds, 'well, I thought I

---

45 E. O. Wilson, *On Human Nature* (Cambridge, MA: Harvard University Press, 1978), p. 192.

46 Fodor, *In Critical Condition*, p. 212.

47 Emmanuel Levinas, *Totalité et infini: Essai sur l'extériorité* (The Hague: Martinus Nijhoff, 1961), p. 21.

48 Michael Ruse and E. O. Wilson, 'The Evolution of Ethics', in *Religion and the Natural Sciences: The Range of Engagement*, ed. J. Huchingon (San Diego: Harcourt Brace, 1993), p. 310.

49 Michael Ruse and E. O. Wilson, 'Moral Philosophy as Applied Science', *Philosophy* 61 (1986), pp. 173–92, at p. 179.

loved her'. The point being that such activity works better if we can successfully lie to ourselves. Societies and communities are products of this co-operation, co-operation being proximate, biological survival being ultimate. Ruse and Wilson continue:

> It is easy to conceive of an alien intelligence species evolving rules its members consider highly moral but repugnant to human beings, such as cannibalism, incest, the love of darkness and decay, parricide and the eating of faeces.[50]

Proximately such counterfactual sojourns may appear as philosophical argumentation, but ultimately they are more than a bit silly. First, the above modes of behaviour, repugnant to 'humans', are behaviours actually practised by some humans, hence he is actually able to pick them out; so, these 'aliens' probably live next door to both Wilson and Ruse. Second, and more importantly, they speak of cannibalism as being one of these repugnant behaviours, but as Peter Koslowski says, 'before the categorical imperative of gene survival, all other imperatives become hypothetical imperatives. To be consistent this would lead to the justification of cannibalism.'[51] Thus, Wilson's repugnant practices are not only already in human society, they are actually advocated by his own theory. But crucially this Darwinian theory finds it extremely hard to even pick out any such behaviour, at least when using its own terms, which means that they must borrow the sense of the terms used from other discourses, doing so without any justification. As O'Hear says, 'From a Darwinism point of view, we may indeed wonder what is so wrong with rape.'[52]

This is so for two reasons. First, the apparently epiphenomenal status of actions – at least according to ultra-Darwinian inspired materialists – undermines any notion of *mens rea*, first-person language having being eliminated. Second, there is a lack of robust identity attributable to humans in light of materialism, because

---

50 'Moral Philosophy as Applied Science', p. 186.
51 Peter Koslowski, 'Sociobiology as Bioeconomics', in *Sociobiology and Bioeconomics*, ed. P. Koslowski (Berlin-Heidelberg-New York: Springer, 1998), pp. 301–28. p. 307.
52 O'Hear, *Beyond Evolution*, p.140.

identity seems somewhat arbitrary, as does individuation, if it is indeed true that all is matter, and that matter is construed as being prohibitive because it is inert (an understanding shared by creationists and materialists). All that can now be accommodated are arrangements and agitations of some fundamental 'stuff', whether it is Thales' water, Descartes' *res extensa* or Dawkins's highly contrived understanding of DNA. Moreover, materialism loses matter, or its prime 'stuff'. As John Peterson puts it, 'If matter is the ultimate substrate and is identified with some actual thing, then all differences within matter must come from something besides matter.'[53] Consequently, the materialist must admit that their description is metaphysical, and in being so invokes something that transcends what is basic at the level of immanence, or the merely physical. The only other option is to deny all change, just as they must, it seems, deny objects. As Peter van Inwagen says,

> One of the tasks that confronts the materialists is this: they have to find a home for the referents of the terms of ordinary speech within a world that is entirely material – or else deny the existence of those referents altogether.[54]

Or more simply, in light of Darwinism, Chesterton tells us, 'there is no such thing as a thing'.[55] And this includes persons, for as David Chalmers says, 'you can't have your materialist cake and eat your consciousness too'.[56] But, of course, Hegel had already pointed to the vacuous nature of materialism, arguing that the word 'matter' remains an ideal unless you pick out something material – but as we now know, materialism appears to preclude identity. And this becomes clearer when we realize that ontological naturalism cannot on its own terms identify what are called *persistence conditions* for an object – that which an object requires

---

53 John Peterson, 'The Dilemma of Materialism', *International Philosophical Quarterly* 39:4 (1999), pp. 429–37, at 430.
54 Peter van Inwagen, *Ontology, Identity, and Modality* (Cambridge: CUP, 2001), p. 160.
55 G. K. Chesterton, *Orthodoxy*, p. 59.
56 David Chalmers, *The Conscious Mind* (Oxford: OUP, 1996), p. 168.

to be what it is.[57] Naturalism, then, remains forever barred from such discernment because such conditions are necessary truths, and so are normative in a manner that resides outside naturalism's remit because its ontology, not to mention its methodology, cannot cope with such non-empirical concepts. Furthermore, it is arguable that naturalism cannot identify nature itself, for that would require real intentions, and these are not available.[58] Indeed, and more paradoxically, Michael Rea argues that naturalism is forced to adopt constructivism, for the simple reason that it cannot locate intrinsic modal or sortal properties;[59] again, these are normative. Consequently, objects must be made rather than discovered. But this means that it must abandon materialism. Why? Because according to materialism, a mind is a material object or event, but naturalism cannot identify objects, except in terms of constructivism. Yet this means that a mind as an object cannot exist unless some non-physical mind has thought it – hence materialism is refuted.[60] More importantly, it seems materialism, naturalism or physicalism (I am here using them interchangeably, for they are in truth mere 'successor terms') is simply a default argument, that is, it is wholly vacuous and question-begging (as David Mellor and Tim Crane argue[61]). Consequently, they continue, support for physicalism owes more to emotion than to argument,[62] a bit like saying one believes in world peace.[63] Moreover, Barry Stroud makes the crucial point that the one thing that

---

57 See Michael Rea, *World Without Design* (Oxford: Clarendon Press, 2002) – this is a brilliant refutation of ontological naturalism; also see Charles Taliaferro and Stewart Goetz, *Naturalism (Interventions)* (Grand Rapids: Wm. B Eerdmans, 2007), this is an excellent analysis of all the pertinent debates surrounding naturalism.
58 Cf. Joseph Catalano, *Thinking Matter* (London and New York: Routledge, 2000), p. 77.
59 The notion of a sortal term was first coined by John Locke.
60 Cf. Rea, *World Without Design*, pp. 162–3.
61 Cf. David Mellor and Tim Crane, 'There is no Question of Physicalism', in Paul Moser and J. D. Trout (eds), *Contemporary Materialism: A Reader* (London and New York: Routledge, 1995), p. 65.
62 Mellor and Crane, 'There is no Question of Physicalism', p. 85.
63 Cf. Barry Stroud, 'The Charm of Naturalism', in *Naturalism in Question*, eds. Mario De Caro, and David Macarthur (Cambridge, MA: Harvard University Press, 2004), p. 22.

has not been naturalized is naturalism itself, hence it remains dogmatic, yet empty of real content,[64] a mere promissory materialism.[65] This being the case it is something of an intellectual cop-out. And any veracity physicalism does manage to maintain amounts to a merely negative, regulative judgement, namely, 'no theology'.

The dubious status of materialism comes even more to the fore with Dawkins's interpretation of Darwinism, for there, the ontological fragility of all identity is reinforced by the merely accidental character of phenotypes, being themselves mere cross sections of history, as already mentioned. Consequently, phylogeny is in the ascendancy over ontogeny. But this means that any notion of functionality, for the Darwinian, is purely diachronic. This being so, there is a problem, as Fodor points out: 'My intuition . . . is that my heart's function has less to do with its evolutionary origins than with the current truth of such counterfactuals as that if it were to stop pumping my blood, I'd die.'[66] This brings to the fore the static nature of evolutionary theory; for instance, the common ancestor acts as the new essence, in other words, everything is essentially its static past.[67] For what is evolutionary psychology's veneration of the Pleistocene period but an anti-evolutionary move?[68] And where's the Darwinism in that? Consequently, the monophyletic origins of life refuse to let anything crawl out of its inanimate swamp. As Hans Jonas says, 'If mere assurance of permanence were the point that mattered, life should not have started out in the first place. It is essentially precarious and corruptible being, an adventure in mortality.'[69] But crucially for Dawkins, this

---

64 Stroud, 'The Charm of Naturalism'.
65 Cf. Karl Popper and J. Eccles, *The Self and its Brain* (Berlin: Springer, 1977), pp. 96–8.
66 Jerry Fodor, *The Mind Doesn't Work That Way* (Cambridge, MA: MIT Press, 2001), p. 85.
67 Cf. John Haught, *Is Nature Enough?* (Cambridge: CUP, 2006), p. 31.
68 Cf. Kenan Malik, *Man, Beast and Zombie* (London: Phoenix Press, 2001), p. 249.
69 Hans Jonas, *The Phenomenon of Life* (Evanston, Illinois: Northwestern University Press, 2001), p. 106. Likewise, as Peter Koslowski says, 'If the survival of genes is the purpose and this survival programme directs the actuality of what is alive, then the actuality perceptible by us,

election of the gene[70] as the sole unit of natural selection is a stance reinforced by his notion of the meme, which is itself homologous to the gene,[71] which generates three important consequences. First, organisms become merely epiphenomenal, as they are but aggregates of genes, bearing an identity on par with a cloud. Interestingly, Dawkins tells us that 'the human psyche has two great sicknesses: the urge to carry vendetta across generations, and the tendency to fasten group labels on people rather than see them as individuals'.[72] He then goes on to attribute these great sicknesses to Abrahamic religion, but arguably, the above quote is an apposite characterization of the adaptationist programme, one entailed by a gene-centred view of evolution. Because organisms are denied their individuality, and the 'selfish gene' conducts its own vendettas across generations. Second, again the scientific

---

is in great measure non-functional ... it would be more economical for the genes, to swim eternally in a primeval soup and to keep their data content in a state of potentiality without ever transforming this data into actuality with form – materialization of the DNA information is ontologically superfluous', in 'Sociobiology as Bioeconomics', in *Sociobiology and Bioeconomics*, ed. P. Koslowski (Berlin-Heidelberg-New York: Springer, 1998), p. 310.

70 The term 'gene' was coined by the Danish botanist Wilhelm Johannsen; it was a derivative of what Hugo de Vries called 'pangenes', which was itself a play on Darwin's notion of 'pangenesis'.

71 The word meme is meant to be a combination of 'gene' and 'memory'. The idea stems from the work of Donald T. Campbell, who back in the 1960s spoke of a 'mnemone', which was equivalent to a 'culturgen'; see Donald T. Campbell, 'A General "Selection Theory" as Implemented in biological Evolution and in Social Belief-Transmission-with-modification in Science', *Biology and Philosophy* 3 (1998), pp. 413–63; also see Charles J. Lumsden and Edward O. Wilson, *Genes, Mind, and Culture: The Coevolutionary Process* (Cambridge, MA: Harvard University Press, 1981). A meme is a 'unit of cultural transmission, or a unit of imitation ... Examples of memes are tunes, ideas, catch-phrases, clothes fashions, ways of making pots or of building arches. Just as genes propagate themselves in the gene pool by leaping from body to body via sperms or eggs, so memes propagate themselves in the meme pool by leaping from brain to brain via a process which, in the broad sense, can be called imitation,' Susan Blackmore, *The Meme Machine* (New York: OUP, 2000), p. 192.

72 Richard Dawkins, *A Devil's Chaplin. Selected Essays by Richard Dawkins* (London: Weidenfield and Nicholson, 2003), p. 160.

project comes under the threat of scepsis. And it does so because we really cannot be sure if our 'promissory materialism' is real; in other words, we cannot know if materialism itself, like world peace, is just an ideal, a meme, a strategy for the survival of atheism. Third, quite simply, genes do not exist in the manner that would allow anyone (anyone of intelligence that is) to adopt an ultra-Darwinian, or adaptationist position – and this on both biological and philosophical grounds. Indeed the ultra-Darwinian notion of the gene is guilty of what Alfred North Whitehead called the 'fallacy of misplaced concreteness'.[73] We must then, to use Dawkins's own words, however ironically, 'cut the gene down to size'.[74] Or again, 'we must begin by throwing out the gene as the sole basis of our idea of evolution.'[75] But as we shall see, Dawkins needs to make this move because his own gene-centred version of evolution undermines Darwinism. Yet this move only compounds the problem. We shall come back to this below.

Before doing so, it is worth noting that the now problematic nature of individuation, or in truth the lack of a complex nature, is compounded by the pervasiveness of extensional logic.[76] We should recall that an extensional logic stipulates that a class is the collection of all its elements only, and that there is no idea behind a class that is satisfied by all the elements. Thus, it struck Quine back in the 1930s that anti-Semitism did not make sense because there was no idea behind the concept *Jew* that could pick out Jews – it was, for lack of a better word, nominal. But one surely starts to witness water, baby and bath disappearing over the fence. Subsequently, and certainly under the influence of Quine, Nelson Goodman tells us, 'Any two things have exactly as many properties in common as any other two.'[77] This seems to be somewhat

---

73 See Alfred North Whitehead: *Science and the Modern World* (New York: Free Press, 1967), p. 64.

74 Richard Dawkins, *The Selfish Gene*, 30th anniversary edition (New York: OUP, 2006), p. 323.

75 Dawkins, *The Selfish Gene*, p. 191.

76 See W. V. O. Quine, *The Time of My Life* (Cambridge, MA: MIT Press, 1985), p. 32.

77 Nelson Goodman, 'Seven Strictures on Similarity', in *Experience and Theory*, eds L. Foster and J. Goodman (Amerhurst: University of Massachusetts, 1970), pp.19–29, at p. 26.

counter-intuitive, to say the least. But in the Continental tradition, Alain Badiou says much the same: 'There are as many differences, say, between a Chinese peasant and a young Norwegian professional as between myself and anybody at all, including myself.'[78] Now the absurdity of Badiou's and Goodman's position is that, given a universe consisting only of two identical zebras (clones) and a cockroach, only a philosopher would claim that any two objects have as exactly as many properties in common as any other two of them.[79] It is little wonder, then, that Michel Henry tells us 'there is no person in science'.[80] Dawkins makes the bizarre claim that 'the universe presented by organised religions is a poky little medieval universe and extremely limited'.[81] But surely it is more fair to argue that under the light of scientism, and under the cosh of the supernaturalistic fallacy, we are now made to inhabit a 'poky little universe'. As Whitehead says, on the result of reductionism, 'Nature becomes a dull affair, soundless, senseless, colorless; merely the hurrying of matter endlessly meaningless.'[82] To me this certainly sounds like a more limited universe than the medieval cosmos.

If there is no person in Dawkins' puddle of genes, there may well be persons in ours, and indeed in Darwin's. And what is interesting about the notion of a person is that it begins to signal a way past the ontological reductionism of ultra-Darwinism, the modernity of logical positivism and its progeny, scientism, not to mention postmodernity. Nagel, in a seminal essay, asks what it would like to be a bat,[83] the point of which is to bring to our attention the irreducibility of a point of view – not an opinion as such, but a perspective. Thus, a perspective is an ontologically rich notion, and cannot be discounted; in other words, for him, consciousness is

---

78 Alain Badiou, *Ethics*, trans. Peter Hallward (London and New York: Verso, 2001), p. 26

79 Cf. David Stamos, *The Species Problem* (Langham, New York and Oxford: Lexington Books, 2003), p. 343.

80 Stamos, *The Species Problem*, p. 262.

81 Richard Dawkins, 'A Survival Machine', in *The Third Culture*, ed. John Brockman (New York: Simon & Schuster, 1996), pp. 75–95.

82 Alfred North Whitehead, *Science and the Modern World*, p.54.

83 Thomas Nagel, 'What is it Like to be a Bat?', in *Mortal Questions* (Cambridge: CUP, 1979), pp. 165–80.

discernable as an irreducible event when we realize *there is something it is like to be this or that being.* Consequently, as E. J. Lowe tells us, 'Thought can no more be (or be constituted by) a brain-process than a chair can be (or be constituted by) a set of prime numbers.'[84] For thoughts must be owned; they must belong.[85] A variant of this argument is sometimes called the 'knowledge argument'. Very briefly, there's a girl called Mary, who is confined to a black-and-white room. There, she learns everything there is to know about the physical world. But upon finally leaving the room, Mary sees a red rose, something she of course had never encountered before.[86] The point is that if physicalism is true, she knows everything about the world already, because the world is purely physical, but then if Mary in seeing the rose, learns something new, then the world is not only physical, thus physicalism is refuted. Another way of putting this is to say that our lives consist in a psychological world and a phenomenal one, and if this is the case then consciousness does not logically supervene on the physical. For example, do we think there is a difference between 'me' and a 'zombie-me', who of course lacks a phenomenal world? In other words, if the subjective is reducible to the objective – such as my pain and a C-fibre firing – then no difference can obtain between the two. Sometimes philosophers point to the logical possibility of an inverted spectrum to illustrate this point; there, we imagine two physically identical beings that have nonetheless inverted conscious experiences, thus the physical cannot dictate the phenomenal.[87] To some degree this is not all that controversial, for we see that the reaction of many is to agree, but then simply

---

84 E. J. Lowe, *Subjects of Experience* (Cambridge: CUP, 1996), p. 44; also see Lowe's essay in this volume.

85 Lowe, *Subjects of Experience*, p. 25.

86 Cf. Frank Jackson, 'What Mary Didn't Know', *Journal of Philosophy* 83 (1986), pp. 291–5; also see *There's Something About Mary*, eds P. Ludlow, Y. Nagaswa and D. Stoljar (Cambridge, MA: MIT Press, 2004).

87 See David Chalmers, *The Conscious Mind* (Oxford: OUP, 1996). Chalmers has done us all a great service in challenging the orthodoxy of materialism in the philosophy of mind, nonetheless, there is still a worrying sense of epiphenomenalism with regard to mental causation in his solution.

embrace the opposite side of the proposition; in other words, they accept that our world is epiphenomenal, a mere folk-tale, and so consequently there is no person (here again we witness the supernaturalistic fallacy).

Now, if brain processes do not constitute thoughts, we must also realise that perception does not equal sensation, for there is always more – qualitatively and irreducibly more – in the former than the latter. Take the example of the *Gestalt* figure of the duck/rabbit; sensation cannot explain the aspectual switch between the two aspects – duck or rabbit. Indeed this leads us to what is called *multiple realization*, something that no doubt disturbs the dream of reductionism, at least in biology.[88] Put simply, there are many ways to say the same thing.[89] Consequently, the one-to-one relation required by reductionism is not present. Instead there is a one-to-many relation: one thing can be caused or generated by many different, say, physical constituents – leaving aside the question of bridge laws, as proposed by Nagel, that connect higher-level phenomena with their lower base, for what we need is an explanation of the bridge laws themselves. In other words, the bridge laws ought to be the explananda.[90] So, due to lack of a one-to-one relation, a macroscopic feature to a large degree does not have an isomorphic relation with a microstructural base: again, divergent base conditions are capable of giving rise to identical higher-state phenomena.[91] But more radical still, the higher-level phenomena are in some sense set free, that is, they are strongly emergent.[92] The same mental phenomena may well be realizable in physical systems other than those with human neurophysiology or perhaps even in

---

88 It is certainly true that multiple realization can itself be consistent with reductionism in physics. For instance, temperature is realized in different ways in different states of matter.

89 Cf. Richard Jones, *Reductionism* (Lewisberg and London: Bucknell University Press, 2000) p. 53.

90 Cf. Jaegwon Kim, 'Being Realistic about Emergence', in *The Re-emergence of Emergence*, eds P. Clayton and P. Davies (Oxford: OUP, 2006), p. 195.

91 Cf. Jones, *Reductionism*, p. 56.

92 In other words, such phenomena are neither reducible to nor determined by lower levels, this being the case, they possess genuinely new causal powers. See Lowe, *Subjects of Experience*, p. 80.

systems with no biological level at all. The higher-level events do not tell us *anything* about the underlying neural or other mechanisms, and accounts of the latter in no way constrain accounts of the former. As Lowe says, 'the most we can really say is that there seems to be an empirical correlation between mental states activity and brain function . . . but the capacity for perception and agency does not of its nature reside in any sort of cerebral condition. Indeed there is nothing whatever unintelligible about supposing the existence of a capacity for perception and agency in a being lacking a brain.'[93] Consequently, biological systems, including the brain, are not even necessary conditions for higher-level phenomena. But let us take such analysis beyond the dizzy heights of higher-level mental phenomena, and instead focus on colours and noses. For there, too, we see multiple realizations, and of a kind that suggests the possibility of a world composed of irreducible real relations – in this case the real biological relation of similarity.

Now, for someone like William of Ockham relations are all or nothing. Hence for him relations are analogous to things. But such a position lands Ockham having to defend the view that, in terms of real similarity, one shade of blue is no more similar to another shade of blue than it is to a completely different colour – here we are back with our zebras and cockroach.[94] Instead, we would say that the two shades share a degree of similarity with each other that they do not share with another colour. Likewise, phenotypic similarity is arguably a real relation, because it cannot be reduced to genotypic similarity, on the one hand, yet it cannot be reduced to empirical observation, on the other. The first case is true because of the supervenience of amino acids on codons – a codon being a triplet of the four-letter genetic code.[95] This simply means that different triplets (a subvenient base) can code for the same amino acid, which in turn gives rise to the phenotypic property – conse-

---

93 Lowe, *Subjects of Experience*, pp. 42–4. Jones says something similar; 'We may be an evolved, complex form of animal life ceasing at death, or there may be more levels of reality working in us, some of which will survive death in some way – the scientific study of the body . . . or the correlation of physical and mental states will never prove either possibility', Jones, *Reductionism*, p. 351.
94 See Stamos, *The Species Problem*, p. 38.
95 See Stamos, *The Species Problem*, p. 46.

quently a nose, for example, does not have a genetic base, in reductionist terms. As Jonathan Marks puts it, 'we map genes for the body's breakdown ... we don't map genes for noses.'[96]

Indeed, because the genetic code is not the only one possible, any particular phenotypic trait we care to notice will supervene on an indefinite disjunctive molecular base.[97] In other words, many genes are polyphenic, and most characteristics are polygenic; in other words, the relation between genotype and phenotype is utterly heterogeneous.[98] Turning to the second case: Surely, a nose is more similar to another nose than an ear. But to repeat, we cannot anchor similarity empirically, for the simple reason that no two noses are the same, yet there is real similarity.[99] Consequently, relations must be real, generally, and the relation of similarity, specifically.[100]

Returning to the supernaturalistic fallacy, Nobel Prize winner François Jacob tells us that 'Biology no longer studies life'.[101] And

---

96 Jonathan Marks, *What it Means to be 98% Chimpanzee* (Berkeley, CA: University of California Press, 2002), p. 105.

97 See Stamos, *The Species Problem*, p. 47, fn., 8.

98 We could also mention two immediate objections to the veneration of the gene to the unit of selection, namely, the 'directness objection', and the 'context dependence objection'. The former simply argues that natural selection simply cannot see genes; while the latter argues in turn that no gene has a fixed selective value, so how could it then be selected for? On this see Eliot Sober, *The Nature of Selection* (Chicago and London: University of Chicago Press, 1984), p. 227.

99 As G. K. Chesterton says, 'the mere repetition of things made the things to me appear rather more weird than more rational. It was as if, having seen a curiously shaped nose in the street and dismissed it as accident, I had then seen six other noses of the same astonishing shape. I should have fancied for a moment that it must be some local secret society. So one elephant having a trunk was odd; but all elephants having trunks looked like a plot,' *Orthodoxy*, p. 36.

100 Here, we might beneficially appeal to Bertrand Russell's dichotomy of internal and external relations. A relation is internal if a change in the relation entails an intrinsic change in at least one of its relata, while an external does not affect its relata, intrinsically. Similarity would in this case qualify as an internal relation; see Stamos, *The Species Problem*, pp. 289–91.

101 François Jacob, *The Logic of Life: A History of Heredity*, trans. B. Spillman (New York: Pantheon, 1973), p. 299.

Michel Henry says we should take him at his word: quite literally, there is no life in biology. Indeed, a cadaver is exactly the person reduced to their exteriority, but conversely there is no death either, because materialism dissolves any chance of picking out any such referent.[102] As Sigmund Freud warned us, 'We may be astonished to find out how little agreement there is among biologists on the subject of natural death and in fact that the whole concept of death melts away under their hands.'[103] Now, there seems to be a strange combination of Cartesian dualism and Platonism at work here. We can better discern this if we begin to realize that the notion of mere matter, or that some thing is nothing but an aggregation of the Darwinian 'swamp' of pure becoming (our ever-contemporary origin, as it were) is itself a product of a Cartesian presumption, namely, the dualism of *res extensa/res cogitans*; the latter only being there to accommodate the conceptual possibility, and articulation of the former.[104] And do we not see Dawkins et al. reproduce this 'Cartesianism' in their strict division between genotype (*res*

---

[102] Michel Henry, *I am The Truth: Toward a Philosophy of Christianity*, trans. Susan Emanuel (Stanford: Stanford University Press, 2003), p. 59.

[103] Sigmund Freud, 'Beyond the Pleasure Principle', in *The Freud Reader*, ed. P. Gray (New York and London: W. W. Norton & Company, 1989), p. 617. Lynn Rothschild makes much the same point: 'it is impossible unambiguously to determine death in a reductionist way', 'The Role of Emergence in Biology', in Clayton and Davies, *The Re-Emergence of Emergence*, p. 159; and Wilford Spradlin and Patricia Porterfield seemingly concur, though doing so rather happily: 'With the dissolution of absolutes, we may speculate that old concepts like God and man died into each other or dissolved into each other to form a uniform continuum. From this point of view, the merger of God and man is a conquest of death, which moved from a definitive event or entity to a fluid process in which life and death are relative organizational patterns'; W. Spradlin and P. Porterfield, *The Search for Certainty* (New York-Berlin-Heidelberg-Tokyo: Springer, 1984), p. 236.

[104] Cf. Hans Jonas, *The Phenomenon of Life: Toward a Philosophical Biology* (Evanston, Illinois: Northwestern University Press, 2001), p. 54, fn. 7. Cf. Karl Rahner, *Hominisation: The Evolutionary Origin of Man as a Theological Problem* (New York: Herder and Herder, 1965), p. 45, and David Braine, *The Human Person: Animal and Spirit* (London: Gerald Duckworth, 1993), p. 23.

extensa) and phenotype (*res cogitans*).[105] So, the materialist, so-called, appears to operate in Cartesian terms, terms that generate a homunculus fundamentalism, so to speak, which will be discussed below.

For the moment, it is important to realize that pure matter, that is, mere matter, is articulated within the constitutive shadow of pure mind. Indeed, it is this Cartesian notion of pure mind that allows for what Jonas calls the 'Cartesian treatment of the remainder'.[106] The smirk of the ultra-Darwinist or the eliminative materialist is fuelled and held captive by the picture of a mind inside the brain, or a soul inside or outside the body. They keep pulling up our skirts, raising the curtains so as to reveal an absence – the missing homunculus. But then, if we take a closer look, we might notice that there is something decidedly old-fashioned about this approach. Jonas makes the point that because of evolution common sense is restored: 'If man was the relative of animals, then animals were the relatives of man and in degrees bearer of that inwardness of which man, the most advanced of their kin, is conscious in himself.'[107] Gone, then, is the Cartesian treatment of animals, wherein even pain is denied of them (as it is now denied of us), because they lack pure mind (as now do we) being merely *res extensa*. And what is the upshot of this? In precise terms, we cannot, on pain of crass dualism, or matter-hating Gnosticism, locate mere matter. In other words, the swamp cannot be found, at least not innocently. We cannot find mere matter because to do so is to presume its opposite. For as God asks in Genesis: 'who told you that you were naked?' (3.11).[108] Or, we can translate the question: 'who told you that you were merely matter? – or that matter was mere?'[109] Thus to argue that because man is continuous with

---

105 Robert Spaemann makes an identical point, arguing that materialist monism is dualist *malgré lui*; *Persons*, trans., Oliver O'Donovan (Oxford: OUP, 2006), p. 49.

106 Jonas, *The Phenomenon of Life*, p.57.

107 Jonas, *The Phenomenon of Life*, p.57.

108 I would like to thank Aaron Riches, Peter Candler, and Ira Brent Driggers for helpful discussion on this notion of nakedness.

109 Jane Bennett rightly points out a problem with such a negative reading of materiality: 'The problem of meaninglessness arises only if "matter" is conceived as inert, only as long as science deploys materialism

animals, and so is merely animal, is to employ a logic that presumes mind to be *res cogitans*; indeed to approach matter or animality in this way is strictly pre-Darwinian. What logic governs such a reading? Returning to the question of colour may help us answer. What is interpreted as secondary, or as being epiphenomenal, can be so only if a falsifiable account of what it would take for it to be otherwise and still be itself, is forthcoming. To find colour you do not look for the colour of colour, and so on.[110]

Merleau-Ponty argues that what is proper to colour is to be the 'the surface of an inexhaustible depth'.[111] And for this reason he compares colour to the Eucharist:

> Just as the sacrament not only symbolizes in sensible species, an operation of Grace, but is also the real presence of God, which it causes to occupy a fragment of space and communicates to those who eat of the consecrated bread . . . in the same way the sensible . . . is nothing other than a certain way of being in the world suggested to us from some point in space, and seized and acted upon by our body . . . so that sensation is literally a form of communion.[112]

But the metaphysics, if not ideology, governing the election of physicalism in a sense demands that the bread and wine of the *Eucharist* sprout arms so that the notion of *real presence* can be

---

whose physics is basically Newtonian . . . [But] matter has a liveliness, resilience, unpredictability, or recalcitrance that is itself a source of wonder for us', *The Enchantment of Modern Life: Attachments, Crossings and Ethics* (Princeton: Princeton University Press, 2001), p. 64.

110 Barry Stroud makes the crucial point that 'it is only because we can make intelligible nondispositional ascriptions of colors to objects that we can acknowledge and identify perceptions as perceptions of this or that color. But if that is so, it requires our accepting the fact that objects in the world are colored, and this is what the restrictive naturalist who denies the reality or the objectivity of color cannot do', *Naturalism in Question*, p. 30.

111 Maurice Merleau-Ponty, *Themes From the Lectures*, trans. John O'Neill (Evanston, IL: Northwestern University Press, 1970), p. 138.

112 Maurice Merleau-Ponty, *Phenomenology of Perception*, trans. Colin Wilson (London: Routledge and Keegan Paul, 1962), p. 212.

empirically verified, but then these arms would also have to sprout arms and so on, *ad infinitum*. Maybe in this way, liturgy and the sacraments exemplify in an eminent fashion the very form of life itself, for they bid us to remain at the level of reception: 'this is my body.' And when such activity is viewed sceptically, or as something odd, maybe we have missed the point, for common sense does not in truth stray from this event. Indeed it is arguable that it is the ordinariness of the Mass that is extraordinary – and it is arguable that colour, time, consciousness, etc., all exhibit similar logic; just as we say 'this is my pain', that is, 'this is my phenomenal life'. But ultra-Darwinism and eliminative materialism, etc. are despisers, for their logic belies a hatred of matter; indeed hating nature to the point of its abolition, as they propagate a homunculus fundamentalism; they do, because for them, for colour to be colour, for life to be lived, for there actually to be creation, it must be on the literalist model of the seven days of the book of Genesis; and there must only be perfection, indeed the book of nature must be inerrant. This is why we find someone like Dawkins employing what we might call the 'imperfection argument'. Very briefly, this argues that for any property P, if it were designed by God it would be perfect; but it is not perfect, so it was not designed by God. But how much better should it be, just a little better? Indeed, the only non-arbitrary degree of goodness of design is perfection. But is that even possible, or coherent?[113] In this way, the ultra-Darwinist resembles the fundamentalist who goes to Bible college, only to discover that Moses may not indeed have been the author of Exodus (which should not come as that much of a shock, since it contains an account of his death!), and subsequently loses faith. But they remain a fundamentalist by default in so far as they have not thought to question the original model of truth that governs their approach to existence. For example, because they cannot find people in a pure, objectified mode, they presume – as a behaviourist would, a merely symbolic reality (think of Walter Gilbert's comments about being able to carry a person on a CD in his back

---

113 Cf. Timothy Shanahan, 'Darwinian Naturalism, Theism and Biological Design', in *Perspectives on Science and Christian Faith*, 49 (1997), pp. 173–4. I would like to thank Professor Shanahan for sending me a copy of this article.

pocket).[114] In other words, the person, or the person's reality, is not real; instead when we witness consciousness, pain, etc., there is no real presence as such – this, then is their Zwinglian metaphysics.

In contrast, theology does not limit truth, for it does not operate by way of a dualism. In keeping with the relation between Cartesianism and materialism, John McDowell refers to human infants as 'mere animals, distinctive only in their potential'.[115] But for someone like Aquinas 'mere animal' is an abstraction; as John O'Callaghan says, it is a vicious abstraction 'if it is then projected back on to reality'.[116] O'Callaghan continues, 'McDowell's mere animal is unique in reality, a living animality that is a member of no species, who yet stands waiting to be granted admittance by the members of one particular kind of animal.'[117] According to Aquinas,

> Something is one simple thing only through one form through which it has being; since it is from the same principles that a thing is a being and is one thing. And so things that are described by diverse forms are not one simple thing ... If, therefore, a man were to live on account of one form (the vegetative soul), and to be an animal on account of another form (the sensitive soul), and to be a man on account of still another form (the rational soul), it would follow that he would not be one simple [substantial] thing.[118]

Consequently, the intellect is not discontinuous with the sensitive and the vegetative, thus there is no mere animality. Human beings share a common ancestry with all life, yes, and this, rather than being an ontological slight, is instead all the more amazing, central to the mystery of humankind. But there is no doubt an important lesson to be learned from this discovery. And that is to accept creation as a gift. As St Paul writes in his epistle to the Philippians:

---

114 See Walter Gilbert, 'A Vision of the Grail', in D. Kelves and L. Hood, eds, *The Code of Codes* (Cambridge, MA: Harvard University Press, 1992), p. 96.
115 John McDowell, *Mind and World* (Cambridge: CUP, 1994), p. 123.
116 John O'Callaghan, *Thomist Realism and the Linguistic Turn* (Notre Dame, IN: University of Notre Dame Press, 2003), p. 296.
117 *Thomist Realism*, p. 296.
118 Thomas Aquinas, *Summa Theologiae* I, q.76, a.3, *resp*.

Veritas: Belief and Metaphysics

'Though he was in the form of God, he did not deem equality with God something to be grasped at; rather, he emptied himself and took the form of a slave, being born in the likeness of man' (2.6–7). And in light of the incarnation, human beings, in terms of the Darwinian notion of common ancestry, reflect this divine truth.[119] And it is those who endeavour to grasp the importance of humankind, in terms of an essence, pure and simple who display their Luciferian link with Gnosticism. This then is our ontological temptation.

The kenotic, emergent nature of man is captured well by Dobzhansky:

> The biological evolution has transcended itself in the human 'revolution'. A new level or dimension has been reached... The transcendence does not mean that a new force or energy has arrived from nowhere... no component of the *humanum* can any longer be denied to animals, although the human constellation of these components certainly can.[120]

Accordingly Dieter Wandschneider says, 'man is the crown and the cross of creation';[121] and he means this in evolutionary terms; moreover, in being the product of natural selection, humankind is the 'end of Natural selection' (Wandschneider).[122] And we can realize how important this is when we read Peter Godfrey-Smith

---

119 Similarly, the Church in being a perpetual participation in the body of Christ imitates the form of creation *ex nihilo*, for it retains nature's integrity or indeed culture's – call it secondary causality, if you will, just as God gifts difference to creation. Further, it may well be more accurate, theologically speaking, to translate the participle *huparchon* of Philippians 2.6 in a manner that renders the passage 'because he was in the form of God' rather than 'though he was in the form of God'. This means that being authentically human (reflecting both the divine likeness and the reality of creation *ex nihilo*) must necessarily involve an ontology that does not seek to 'grasp' at any ontic 'ground' of being. I would like to thank Professor Marcus Bockmuehl for discussions on this matter.

120 Theodosius Dobzhansky, *The Biology of Ultimate Concern* (New York: New American Library, 1967), p. 58.

121 Dieter Wandschneider, 'On the Problem of Direction and Goal in Biological Evolution', in *Darwinism and Philosophy*, eds Vittorio Hösle and Christian Illies (Indiana: University of Notre Dame Press, 2005), p. 206.

122 Wandschneider, 'On the Problem of Direction and Goal', p. 204.

admit that '[Natural] Selection is seen as a critically important part of a larger intellectual enterprise, the enterprise of developing and defending a secular worldview'.[123] But even Dawkins is forced into a rather precarious position: 'A cultural trait may have evolved in the way that it has, simply because it is advantageous to itself.' But this is an extraordinary concession.[124] And in light of such a concession, we can see why the anthropologist Helmut Plessner called man an 'ex-centric being', thus he is 'unhinged' (*ausgehängt*).[125] Similarly, Herder refers to man as 'Nature's liberated captive'. In other words, man has freed himself from his central adjustment to his animal environment, doing so because man is a symbolic species.[126] Consequently, this means that biology is a semiotic science; a science where significance and representation are essential elements. Thus, evolutionary biology stands at the border between physical and semiotic science,[127] just as man does. In this way, somatic culture, especially the emergent phenomenon of language, both reveals and in some sense ends evolution by natural selection. Now, in a manner similar to Jonas, Aquinas argues that '[t]he human soul is a kind of horizon, and a boundary, as it were, between the corporeal world and the incorporeal world'.[128] Likewise, the soul 'exists on the horizon of eternity and time'.[129] Accordingly, the human is for Aquinas a little world (*minor mundus*); and importantly, the human is not just a horizon, but also a frontier (*horizon et continuum*). But again, any such horizon cannot be grasped.

---

123 Peter Godfrey-Smith, 'Three Kinds of Adaptationism', in *Adaptationism and Optimality*, eds S. Orzack and E. Sober (Cambridge: CUP, 2001), p. 350.

124 Cf. Joseph Margolis, *The Unraveling of Scientism* (Ithaca and London: Cornell University Press, 2003), p. 38.

125 See Helmut Plessner, *Laughing and Crying; A Study of the Limits of Human Behavior*, trans. James Spencer Churchill and Marjorie Grene (Evanston, IL: Northwestern University Press, 1970); Johann Gottfried von Herder, *Reflections on the Philosophy of the History of Mankind 1*, in *Sämtilche Werke*, ed. B. Sauphan (Berlin: 1887–), xiii, p. 146.

126 Cf. Terrence Deacon, 'Emergence: The Hole at the Wheel's Hub', in *The Re-emergence of Emergence*, eds P. Clayton and P. Davies (Oxford: OUP, 2006), p. 149.

127 Deacon, 'Emergence', p. 18.

128 *In III Sent*. Pro.

129 *Summa contra Gentiles*, II, c.86. n.12.

Veritas: Belief and Metaphysics

So, we must ask, what about Darwin? Well, it seems we must save him from the ultra-Darwinists, who dismantle his theory, doing so by ontologizing it, thus ushering in the destruction wrought by ontological reductionism. Surely Vittorio Hösle is correct when he tells us that, 'We honor (Darwinism) better if we recognize its limited ontological relevance and do not make a first philosophy out of it'.[130] Otherwise, we end up not believing Darwin, as indeed one of his disciples, E. O. Wilson, admits: 'The epic story of evolution is as much mythology as the laws of evolution are ... a matter of faith.'[131] So how do we stop mythologizing Darwinism? Quite simply, by abandoning reductionism, which is in the end, nothing but a security blanket.[132] How do we do this? First, by resisting the temptation to universalize a biological theory; because if we do not resist, biology literally eats itself, as it becomes like a racing driver, who to avoid friction chooses tyres that are so smooth they offer no resistance. But then the driver will remain at a standstill, unable to move. Likewise, if Darwinism dissolves other discourses it comes to a standstill itself. As Stroud says:

> There is an embarrassing absurdity in [ontological naturalism] that is revealed as soon as the naturalist reflects and acknowledges that he believes his naturalistic theory of the world ... I mean he cannot say it and consistently regard what he says as true.

And this also applies to universalized Darwinism.[133] Thus, ultra-Darwinism is like the proverbial drunk man on a moving train who appears to walk straighter than his fellow passengers. So, as said, if we are not to fall into myth, we must abandon the reductionist image.

But by way of conclusion, let us return to ultra-Darwinism, one last time. Thus far, it has been suggested that this reading of

---

130 Vittorio Hösle, 'Objective Idealism and Darwinism', in Vittorio Hösle and Christian Illies (eds), *Darwinism and Philosophy* (Notre Dame: University of Notre Dame Press, 2005), p. 218.
131 E. O. Wilson, *On Human Nature*, p. 201.
132 Cf. Dennis Noble, *The Music of Life* (Oxford: OUP, 2006), p. 66.
133 Stroud, *Naturalism in Question*, p. 28.

Darwinism leaves us in a pokey universe. In addition, it is anti-evolutionary as it is predicated on a static picture of the natural world. Moreover, it espouses a view of the gene that is simply fictitious. Let us unpack this a little, so as to show the wholly arbitrary and anti-Darwinian nature of this pernicious ideology. First, we must realize that the ultra-Darwinian construal of genes is a historical selection, that is, it is contrived, and thus we can quite freely employ another one from the domain of possible selections.[134] And in so doing maybe we will save the phenomena, including Darwinism. There are no reasons (except maybe ideological ones) why we cannot advocate a more expansionist project, and this is just what many biologists do. The whole movement of developmental biology, for instance, begins its analyses by means other than a gene-centric perspective. Quite right too, for if there is one governing meme that dominates biological reductionism it is the 'gene'; for there is little doubt that the gene required by such reductionism just simply does not exist.

Let us imagine this ultra-Darwinian selfish gene as a castle. There it is, a discrete entity, hidden away from the vicissitudes of the phenotype, safe behind Weismann's barrier, its role protected by the central dogma; all it must do is wait for nature to select it. And in that eventuality its bid for immortality, so-called, will be closer to being realized. Such a notion is itself based on the already mentioned dichotomy of replicators and vehicles. But this is again arbitrary, and in being so does Darwinism a disservice; it does because any such account is wholly circular, and so question-begging.

First, as we know, Darwin did not know about genetics, so if that had not been forthcoming, and a notion of blending was all that pertained, his theory would not have collapsed. In other words, the replicator/vehicle divide is not essential, but merely historical.[135] Consequently, all that is needed is parent–offspring

---

134 Cf. Gary Webster and Brian Goodwin, 'The Origin of Species: a Structuralist Approach', in Eva Neumann-Held and C. Rehmann-Sutter (eds), *Genes in Development* (Durham, NC and London: Duke University Press, 2006), p. 130.

135 Cf. Stephen J. Gould, *The Structure of Evolutionary Theory* (Cambridge, MA: Harvard University Press, 2002).

resemblance. Indeed, inheritance is itself a loose concept, in that it does not matter how inheritance occurs – behavioural, genetic, cultural and so on.[136] In addition, the highly evolved notion of replication, in terms of fidelity, would not of course always be the case, so again we cannot pick out a phenomenon that turned up late in the game, as if it were the norm, at least without forcing the issue. And crucially, replication is itself thrown into a 'black box', for the simple reason that no reasons at all are given for the very development of replication as a process.[137] As Griesemer says,

> replication is treated as the paradigm case of a causal process of reproduction which operates at the level of DNA. But the particular mechanisms by which reproduction in any species occurs are themselves products of evolution, so an analysis of the replication process that relies on features of biologically contingent mechanisms cannot provide necessary conditions for the process as such.[138]

Put differently, if evolution depends necessarily on DNA, then the DNA mechanism cannot have evolved.

Second, apparently, basal concepts such as individuality are highly derivative, that is, they are evolved.[139] So selection is itself derivative, for the simple reason that selection cannot occur until there are entities to select. This means, then, that we must also take into consideration evolutionary transitions, and Dawkins et al. do not do this. In this way, 'Darwinian individuals' are not nearly the whole story, and for the sake of evolution, we must not pretend they are. Indeed some argue that they are not part of the story at

---

136 Cf. Samir Okasha, *Evolution and the Levels of Selection* (Oxford: Clarendon Press, 2006), p. 15.

137 James Griesemer, 'Genetics from an Evolutionary Process Perspective', in Eva Neumann-Held and C. Rehmann-Sutter (eds), *Genes in Development* (Durham, NC and London: Duke University Press, 2006), p. 218.

138 James Griesemer, 'The Informational Gene and the Substantial Body', in Martin Jones and Nancy Cartwright (eds), *Idealization XII* (Amsterdam/ New York: Rodopi, 2005), p. 96.

139 Cf. Leo Buss, *The Evolution of Individuality* (Princeton, NJ: Princeton University Press, 1987), p. 25.

all, or at the very most are but a subset of, say, 'inheritors'.[140] Again, any generalized theory of evolution must be able to account for the emergence of such individuals, for at a lower level, they weren't individuals at all. So Dawkins is being wholly anachronistic, and in being so, dramatically curtails the explanatory power of Darwinism.

Now, we mentioned earlier that ultra-Darwinism subjects the natural world to diachronic analyses. This is true, but it's only half the story. This situation is itself a by-product of a previous endeavour, namely, to offer a purely synchronic account of replicators and vehicles – in other words, a wholly abstract, functionalist one.[141] Replicators and vehicles are defined in purely functional terms, a consequence of which is that nearly everything else is ignored, and thus cast into the diachronic sea of phylogeny. But this is itself highly contentious, for any such account rests on level-specific hierarchies that are then extrapolated to the general concept of replicator. Dawkins makes inferences from the notion of hierarchy, that is, he relies on a hierarchical picture that allows genes to be king, but at the same time, the abstract nature of his generalization cannot explain hierarchy. So, replicators are in truth particular, only one animal in the zoo, so to speak, and not the whole zoo. Moreover, the selfishness tag is highly problematic, and not for the usual reasons, namely, the imputation of intentional language. Much more importantly, it is completely arbitrary, Gnostic even. It is because we could just as easily replace the word 'selfish' with 'self', or individual. And this helps bring to the fore the circular nature of his generalization; in effect, to avoid 'selfishness' Dawkins requires that there simply not be a self. Now, an evolutionary transition is one in which that which could live on its own, freely, as it were, subsequently cannot; it now forms a new individual.[142] And this can only be accomplished when mechanisms of conflict suppression evolve – think of a transplanted organ that may or may not be rejected. Co-operation is now exported

---

140 Cf. Griesemer, 'Genetics from an Evolutionary Process Perspective', pp. 218-19.
141 Cf. Griesemer, 'The Informational Gene and the Substantial Body'.
142 Cf. Griesemer, 'Genetics from an Evolutionary Process Perspective', p. 215.

from a lower level to a higher one.[143] The important point for us is the almost Levinasian or Derridian nature of Dawkins's understanding of identity. For him we would have to be otherwise than being, if selfishness were to be avoided, thus all gifts are impossible. But this is all a bit of nonsense.

Let us take an analogy, E. O. Wilson once famously said that genes hold culture on a leash. Maybe, but the converse is also true. If we go back in time, we can understand that genes themselves, among many other natural entities, stabilized the chaos of the Precambrian world, that is from the apeirontic depth arose individuals, and this became a cumulative effect, as lower levels gave way to new individuals, the selfishness of which is only another name for individuation. Indeed, natural selection itself only evolved, or emerged in the wake of this, and this is one reason why natural selection is itself not the cause of evolution but an effect;[144] indeed, it may even prevent evolution because it retards novelty, due to its highly conservative activity. And now, just as genes kept a leash on 'chaos', so to speak, so the nested hierarchies kept a further leash on bare simplicity – the very thing reductionism is endeavouring to return us to – culture keeps a leash on genes, exporting co-operation to ever higher levels. And if it is true that with the advent of language new forms of causality emerge, then we can see that nature has selected something it cannot control. Thus, evolutionary psychology's dichotomy of proximate and ultimate causes can now be reversed. The proximate is our evolutionary past, the ultimate is what the new level dictates, and would this not explain a great deal of human activity, doing so in a much more enlightening manner? So just as biological levels involve crucial transitions, the Darwinian paradigm is subjected to innovation of an ultimate nature. Even Dawkins admits as much. In relation to evolution,

> Darwin may have been triumphant at the end of the twentieth-century, but we must acknowledge the possibility that new facts

---

143 See R. E. Michod, 'Cooperation and Conflict in the Evolution of Individuality', *American Naturalist* 149 (1997), pp. 607–45.

144 Cf. Robert Reid, *Biological Emergences: Evolution by Natural Experiment* (Cambridge, MA: MIT Press, 2007).

may come to light which will force our successors of the twenty first century to abandon Darwinism or modify it beyond recognition.[145]

Earlier we characterized Dawkins's gene-centric view as a castle. Well, Noble makes the point that we must realize that the DNA code for a gene is nonsense until it is interpreted functionally, 'first by the cell/protein machinery that initiates and controls transcription and post-transcriptional modifications, and then by the systems level interaction between proteins that generate higher-level function'.[146] So, the gene's castle loses its floor, because it fails to control the lower levels upon which it relies, namely, the requisite chemical conditions for its environment; for instance, there are no genes for the properties of water, or for the fatty lipids that form cell membranes. And then it loses its roof, as it is what lies above it that provides any shelter, so to speak, as it is the systems-level that accommodates every biological articulation. Thus, a gene can only be functionally defined in a specific developmental context.[147] Consequently, as Neumann-Held says, 'there are no component particles (domains, regions, regulatory sequences) on the DNA apart from some developmental context.'[148] And then the castle loses its walls, for again it is that which lies around it that provides the last vestiges of structure – for there are no genes for interaction – thus the 'semantics' come from elsewhere. To make matters worse, the claim to heredity, or ownership of the castle's deeds is under threat, for inheritance does not just pass through genes, for we also inherit the egg cell from our mother with all its machinery, including mitochondria, ribosomes and other cytoplasmic components, such as the proteins that enter the nucleus to initiate DNA transcription, and lastly we inherit the environment –

---

145 Dawkins, *A Devil's Chaplain*, p. 81.
146 Noble, *The Music of Life*, p. 21.
147 Cf. R. Gray, 'Death of the Gene: Developmental Systems Strike Back', in P. Griffiths (ed.), *Trees of Life* (Dordrecht, Boston and London: Kluwer, 1992), p. 176.
148 Eva Neumann-Held, 'Conceptualizing Genes in the Contructionist Way', in P. Koslowski (ed.), *Sociobiology and Bioeconomics* (Berlin-Heidelberg-New York: Springer, 1998), p. 130.

or better, the world – with its chemical and physical laws, not to mention cultural laws.[149] Moreover, hereditary mechanisms must already be in place; thus, they are highly evolved, so natural selection cannot explain them, but is instead explained.[150] With regard to Dawkins's notion of the gene, as Carlson says, 'It is important that geneticists recognize the many levels at which genes can be perceived, but it is not helpful to select one of these levels and arbitrarily designate that as the universal definition of the gene'.[151] And Portin makes the even stronger claim that 'it is arguable that the old term gene ... is no longer useful' (the work of Lenny Moss is crucial here).[152] So this castle is certainly one built on sand; that of ideology, or at best convenience. For such a castle even loses its architectural plans – the very 'syntax' for its construction. The genotype/phenotype, for instance, is a derivative condition, and so is it not primitive, as it were.[153] Likewise, as we know, the vehicle/replicator dichotomy is ultimately misleading. For yes, it is true that no (token) body survives death, it cannot replicate, but in the same way neither can the genotype, for any replication there is at the level of type, because no token DNA chemicals survive. But if that is the case, then we can say that phenotypes also survive – doing so as types – are these not what we call species? It seems true

---

149 See Noble, *The Music of Life*, p. 41.

150 Lowell Nissen, *Teleological Language in the Life Sciences* (Lanham, New York, Boulder and Oxford: Rowman and Littlefield, 1997), p. 110.

151 E. A. Carlson, 'Defining the Gene: an Evolving Concept', *American Journal of Human Genetics*, 49 (1991), p. 475.

152 P. Portin, 'The Concept of the Gene: Short History and Present Status', in *The Quarterly Review of Biology*, 68 (1993), p. 208. Lenny Moss has argued that the model we have of the gene today is based on the conflation of two types, namely, Genes-D (developmental resource), and Gene-P (preformationist). The latter is defined with respect to the phenotype but indeterminate with respect to DNA, while the former is defined with respect to DNA sequence but indeterminate with respect to the phenotype. Only by forgetting this difference can the gene of what he calls 'vulgar Darwinism' be conjured up; see *What Genes Can't Do* (Cambridge, MA: MIT Press, 2004).

153 See Gerd Müller and Stuart Newman, *Origination of Organismal Form* (Cambridge, MA: MIT Press, 2003), p. 9.

to say that, for instance, the dragonfly has been around for quite some time.

Lastly, instead of reductionism, with its love of randomness, we should it seems, concentrate on the evident inherency in nature; for example, the phenomenon of convergence or homoplasy. Here we must ask (paraphrasing Gerd Müller and Stuart Newman): Why do similar morphological design solutions arise repeatedly in phylogenetically independent lineages that do not share the same molecular mechanisms and developmental systems? Or why did the basic body plans of nearly all metazoans arise within a relatively short time span, soon after the origin of multicellularity? And again, why do building elements fixate into body plans that remain largely unchanged within a given phylogenetic lineage?[154] Moreover, chemistry cannot pick out any difference between inanimate and animate entities, and DNA is just ordinary chemicals, thus without appeal to structure, or, better, form life is a non-starter; as Deacon says, 'form matters'.[155] A crucial example of the importance of form is that of the organism. But alas, the ultra-Darwinism advocated by, say, Dennett, is substrate neutral. Yet as Mario Bunge points out: 'such a formalist and immaterialist conception of biology seems attractive to some, sparing them the task of learning anything about biology' – again nature is lost.[156] Consequently, there is not any biology without form, but as we know ultra-Darwinism has no theory of the generative;[157] just as reductionism cannot speak of form, thus it cannot speak of nature, and indeed it cannot speak.

Against the reductionist image, then, Nagel seems to be correct:

> The recognition of logical arguments as independently valid is a precondition of the acceptability of an evolutionary story about the source of that recognition. This means that the evolutionary

---

154 See Müller and Newman, *Origination of Organismal Form*, p. 4; also see Simon Conway-Morris' excellent book, *Life's Solution* (Cambridge: CUP, 2003).

155 Deacon, 'Emergence: The Hole at the Wheel's Hub', p. 128.

156 Mario Bunge and Martin Mahner, *Foundations of Biophilosophy* (Berlin and Hedielberg: Springer, 1997), p. 362.

157 See Müller and Newman, *Origination of Organismal Form*, p. 7.

hypothesis is acceptable only if reason does not need its support
... the basic methods of reasoning we employ are not merely
human but belong to a more general category of mind. Human
minds now exemplify it.[158]

At least now, we can maybe begin to believe Darwin, for we no longer relegate his theory – along with nature, death, intentional-life and all ratiocination – to the realm of myth, mystery and superstition.

---

158 Nagel, *The Last Word*, pp. 136 and 140.

7. Metaphysics as Preamble to Religious Belief

OLIVA BLANCHETTE

My focus in this chapter is on the necessity of distinguishing between philosophy and theology as intellectual disciplines of the mind, and of keeping them joined together in the exercise of one's spiritual activity. Keeping them together often means reducing the one to the other, as in certain forms of classical theology, where questions of being and of ethics are pre-empted by myths of creation and divine law, or certain forms of systematic philosophy, where the truth of religion is either absorbed into the philosophical spirit, as in Hegel, or treated as irrelevant to the human spirit in nihilistic or atheistic fashion, as in Heidegger and other would-be postmodernists.

The Idea of Beliefs in Rational Discourse

Let me begin with the idea of belief, which is set off from metaphysics in the title of this volume. Belief, I think, is a term that is inclusive of all sorts of mental attitudes, all the way from the most uncritical and naïve to utter disbelief, in one thing or another, or even in everything altogether, as in universal scepticism. Even nihilism can be thought of as a belief that reflects a purely negative attitude toward whatever might be. As something positive, belief is something we acquire in becoming rational, in communion with other rational beings.

Beliefs are not opposed to reason, but formed by reason within human traditions, where different kinds of reasoning take place, whether that be in practical matters, such as making things or exchanging them, or in theoretical matters, such as doing physics, biology or economics. It even takes a certain kind of belief to get started in critical reasoning about metaphysics. Newcomers to any sort of rational discipline, including language itself, always begin with a sort of faith in those who are already advanced in the reasoning process, trusting them as guides in their more critical learning. Without faith in other human beings, presumably more learned than we are in one respect or another, we would never enter into any process of learning, any process of enquiring about the world or ourselves. That is why teachers and their ideas, which are taken only as beliefs by those beginning in a discipline, are so important in the critical, rational learning process. Without them, we would never have any idea of what there is to learn about, nor any beliefs that would make us wonder.

To explore the relation between philosophy and theology, or between humanism and religion, we cannot stay with just this generalized notion of belief that pervades human intersubjectivity and historical tradition of every kind, whether in the sciences or the humanities of different cultures and civilizations. We must raise the level of discourse to a higher kind of learning than the one that typically takes place in different human traditions, in relation to a more transcendent interlocutor, one who may not appear in person, so to speak, but who may have something more significant for us to learn about, and who could be revealing to us what we would have to call new beliefs that human beings have not come up with, and that perhaps they could not come up with on their own, but that would give us pause for a new kind of wondering about ourselves and about the world. These new beliefs would entail another kind of belief, a supernatural kind of belief, distinct from those we take to be natural or human beliefs, presupposing a God who transcends all human intersubjectivity and who somehow reveals Godself in a way that can be identified as transcendent in human intersubjectivity.

These are what we call religious beliefs, as distinct from other more strictly human or rational beliefs, and it is with reference to such beliefs only – that is, religious beliefs – that I wish to discuss the question of metaphysics as a preamble. Other forms of human belief (or disbelief) have preambles of their own leading up to them, which can be studied phenomenologically as a part of human experience. My contention here will be that properly religious beliefs require a more rational kind of preamble that comes only with what the French would call a metaphysical *démarche* of one kind of another, to enter into the meaning as well as the fact of a new level of discourse instituted by the God who is totally transcendent and whose word must be taken most seriously by human beings.

Stating the Problem

My way of presenting the problem reflects my way of understanding it in the context of a strong Christian tradition that has become most explicit in distinguishing at least some of its religious beliefs and aspirations as quite supernatural, in their relation to a God who is totally transcendent, so that its theology, if there is one, has to be something quite distinct or heterogeneous from any other human form of enquiry, whether in natural or social science.

I would not, however, restrict the problem to what has become explicit about religious beliefs in the Christian tradition. Like Blondel, I see this as a universal problem for any human being with authentically religious beliefs and consciousness, no matter how vaguely these may arise in traditions with a genuinely religious component, relating to a God who is taken to be transcendent in God's own being, as well as omnipotent. Such traditions may not always be as clear as the Christian tradition has become in articulating their beliefs about God and how we have to relate to God, but there is in all of them the same dynamic of a religious spirit relating to the same transcendent God.

Here we are only taking advantage of the clarity that has been brought to the problem in the Christian tradition in stating the problem for ourselves, as well as in presuming that there have been or are authentic and genuine religious beliefs in other traditions, relating to a God who is totally transcendent, but which we shall not go into here. We shall discuss the problem of the relation between philosophy and theology mainly as it has come up in the context of Christian religion or Christian beliefs, with a clear consciousness of something supernatural as well as metaphysical about the divine, as well as a consciousness that rational discourse on human beliefs about reality ultimately leads to the affirmation of the reality of God as totally transcendent.

Like Blondel and Hegel in the context of modernity, I will not make much of the distinction frequently made among Christian theologians between a theology based on supernatural faith in certain revealed articles (or on principles thought to be beyond the power of reason to investigate, as Aquinas puts it), and a theology based on principles known to reason in its own power to investigate, or a 'natural theology', which can issue forth in a 'natural religion'. While recognizing some sense in making such a distinction within a framework of beliefs thought to be supernatural, where others are thought to be natural and perhaps closed in on themselves, I do not think it is very helpful in discussing how philosophy and theology, even as distinct, have to relate to one another in articulating questions about God or about religion. In fact, I think the idea of total transcendence regarding God is enough to keep the distinction clear between philosophy and theology, without separating them from one another as operations of one and the same spirit concerning reality and the divine.

Distinction between two kinds of religion, one philosophical and one theological, or one natural and one supernatural, has the tendency to solidify each kind in isolation from the other, and systematically separate them from one another, if not oppose them to one another altogether. The distinction I wish to maintain between philosophy and theology is not one of separation that leaves the two disconnected. Nor is it one that leaves them in a state of confusion, where superstition or the loss of transcendence can creep into both theology and philosophy. It is a distinction based on recognition of the total transcendence of God and the two kinds of rational discourse that can follow from this recognition: one based on the use of human reason alone in history, and the other based on a positive revelation from God in his transcendence in what I have called religious beliefs. The problem I wish to discuss is how we bring these two kinds of rational discourse together as part of one and the same narrative on the course of a human history that is at once immanent and transcendent, or natural and supernatural.

Metaphysics as Preamble to Religious Belief

Metaphysics as Hinge in the Question of Transcendence

This is where I think metaphysics comes in for special consideration in the relation between philosophy and theology. Metaphysics, more than anything else in philosophy, has to do with the question of transcendence, especially the kind of transcendence that is presupposed in properly religious belief. As such it is the hinge on which the relation between theology and philosophy turns in any rational reading of how the spirit moves in the world. This is evident, to begin with, in the way metaphysics ends up serving as necessary preamble to any discourse about God or to any religious belief. Metaphysics may not begin with any idea of God in mind, but pushed to its ultimate limit, metaphysics ends up with such an idea, as of something that is totally transcendent to anything that can be given in our experience.

As a rational discourse it is an ontology, a science of being as being, not a theology, much less an ontotheology. If the idea of God or of first universal Cause enters into its discourse, it is not as part of what is taken to be its subject, namely, being, which is inclusive of all that we can know immediately in experience, or mediately by reasoning from effect to cause. God is not known as another thing we can know in the universe, nor can be numbered among the things or the finite spirits we do find in the universe. Metaphysics knows God only as totally transcendent to the universe, and as otherwise unknown in what God is in Godself as transcendent. Even in affirming this total transcendence of God at the summit of being, however, metaphysics does not become a theology, because that would imply that the transcendent ceases to be considered as transcendent, only to be taken in as part of the whole to which it is said to be transcendent. The only way ontology can become theology is in God himself, who is the subject of his own science, the Being where metaphysics cannot take us.

The important thing about metaphysics as preamble to any sacred teaching is that it affirms a transcendence that cannot be immanentized, even when God reveals something of Godself that we cannot otherwise know, or when God incarnates Godself as a human being. To appreciate all this as theology flowing from religious belief, we have to have a keen metaphysical sense of a transcendence 'coming into the world', to use the expression from

John's Gospel, but not as becoming part of the world, to use another phrase from John's Gospel. It is a coming into the world in order to raise it, or to assume it, as the fathers of the Church used to say, at least with regard to human beings, to something higher than the world of being as we know it metaphysically as well as historically.

It is this metaphysical affirmation of transcendence that enables us to distinguish theology and authentic religion rationally from philosophy and humanism of every sort, without falling back into the kind of superstition or nihilism that has marked recent attempts to destroy metaphysics. To deny or to ignore metaphysics as science of being as being is to leave us with nothing to consider as real, not even ourselves, at the same time as it reduces us to some form of autolatry in the very act of denying, in a complete perversion of the metaphysical and the religious sense that relates us to the transcendent Creator of all things.

The metaphysical affirmation of God as transcendent, on the other hand, not only orients us to the transcendent ground of all being, but also makes us ready to learn more about this totally transcendent Ground and what it is actually doing in the world through the way it discloses itself, whether as Creator of a universe in a full natural deployment of its own active potency, with free spirits operating within it, working toward their own destiny, or as Redeemer and Saviour challenging humankind to rise to a higher life through other means of revelation and grace in what we are calling authentic religious beliefs and practices. This is a lot to say all at once about the way God might be acting in what Hegel calls 'manifest religion', but I mention it only to bring out how much metaphysics opens us to in affirming the total transcendence of God. Far from closing us up in our world of finitude and difference, not to say just plain violence, metaphysics as preamble to religious belief opens us up to a world of transcendence, where communion of all is made possible in the trinitarian life of the Transcendent.

Metaphysics as Preamble to Religious Belief

Other Sciences as Preamble

Of course, it is possible to think of all the particular sciences and of phenomenology as also preambles to religious belief, at least when they are not closed in upon themselves in a nihilistic disposition toward anything that does not enter their field of consideration. There are many more 'scientists', social as well as natural, who are open to questions of religious belief than those who remain strictly agnostic or even militantly atheistic in this regard, usually due either to a very dim and uninformed view of religious beliefs of any kind, or to an antagonism they experience from purportedly religious figures in society. There are also many phenomenologists of religion, from Hegel to the representatives of Husserlian and Heideggerian scholasticism, who speak of religion in a positive fashion and who even purport to be theologians in their own right, even though they seldom get beyond a negative theology that remains very ambiguous as theology, not to say simply untheological. Along with these more religiously oriented phenomenologists, there are also those who are opposed to any such orientation in phenomenology, and who claim to be the only true phenomenologists, for whom the question of God, let alone a totally transcendent God, does not even arise.

The idea of the particular sciences and of phenomenology as preambles to religious belief remains a very dubious one. I would not, however, dismiss it altogether. There are enough seriously reflective scientists and phenomenologists who advance their craft as preamble to religious belief to convince me that it is worth considering. I would, however, say that they are not directly preambles to religious belief as such. They are rather preambles to metaphysics, which is the only science that is directly preamble to religious belief as such. In other words, if the particular sciences and phenomenology are to be taken as preambles to authentic religious beliefs, they can only be so through the mediation of a metaphysics that affirms the total transcendence of God, even as it recognizes some action of God in the world as the action of a God who remains totally transcendent in God's dwelling among us.

This is where I think Hegel falls short as a philosopher or as a phenomenologist of religion. He has a logic, which he claims is the logic of absolute spirit, the content of which, he writes, 'is the exposition of God as he is in his eternal essence before the creation of nature and a finite spirit'.[1] He calls this logic a 'science of logic', which certainly has some metaphysical overtones, but he has no metaphysical science as such distinct from his logic. With regard to 'the older metaphysics and logic' he mentions in passing, he says 'that in the main there was available for the contents of the science only external material'.[2] But he showed no inclination to pursue any such science of 'external material' on his own account, though he had a very high esteem for ancient metaphysics as getting to the essence of things in the form of thought.[3] He was content with his own science of logic, for which the content would come only from the realm of human thought exhibited 'in its own immanent activity or what is the same, in its necessary development.'[4] That was all the metaphysics he was interested in, one reduced to a self-propelling logic in the realm of thought.

Interestingly enough, however, the spirit Hegel spoke of as absolute is not what one would think of as totally transcendent, even though he does not shrink from referring to it as God and Creator. Absolute spirit for him is never more than the spirit of a people. That is how he characterizes even the logic he is about to embark upon in the Preface to the First Edition of his *Science of Logic*, a 'spirit which contemplates its own pure essence', even though it has not yet come to an actual *Dasein* in a people that has 'lost its metaphysics'.[5] Germany 'is a cultured people without metaphysics', he writes, as a result of the Kantian critique,

> like a temple richly ornamented in other respects but without a holy of holies. Theology, which in former times was the guardian of the speculative mysteries and of metaphysics (although this was subordinate to it) had given up this science in

---

[1] G. W. F. Hegel, *Science of Logic*, tr. A. V. Miller (London: Allen and Unwin, 1969), Introduction, p. 50.
[2] Hegel, *Science of Logic*, Preface to Second Edition, p. 31.
[3] See his remarks about ancient metaphysics in *Science of Logic*, Introduction, p. 45.
[4] Hegel, *Science of Logic*, p. 31.
[5] Hegel, *Science of Logic*, Preface to the First Edition, p. 26.

Metaphysics as Preamble to Religious Belief

exchange for feelings, for what was popularly matter-of-fact, and for erudite historicism.[6]

Hegel's intent was not to restore that former view of theology, to which metaphysics was supposedly subordinated, but rather to rectify the lack of metaphysics for the German people with his science of logic, without reference to anything like theology or the affirmation of God as totally transcendent. His metaphysics, or his logic, was to be the metaphysics or the logic of a people, much as ancient metaphysics and logic had been for him nothing more than the metaphysics and logic of the Greek people. That is as far as Hegel got in restoring a metaphysics or a logic of absolute spirit. There was no higher degree of being to be contemplated for him, nothing totally transcendent. Whatever logic or metaphysics he had was confined to the immanent order of peoples in history, the same order to which religion and theology would now be confined as lesser forms of thought than philosophy or absolute knowing.

The evidence for this confinement of absolute spirit to the immanent order of a people is all over Hegel's early writings, which have been called 'theological', but which are far from recognizably theological in any traditional sense. He criticizes the spirit of Judaism for believing in a God who is above his people (even alien to his people as lord and master), in contrast to the spirit of the Greeks, who saw their gods as one with them in a harmony with nature as well as with and among themselves. He rejects every sign of positivity in early Christianity – including that of the resurrection of the individual Christ – that would point to anything transcendent in the new spirit that was emerging. He presents Christ as the teacher of a new spirit, a spirit of love that is to replace the spirit of the law, but not as himself the divine model for that spirit who reveals Godself more fully in the mystery of the resurrection.

In the *Phenomenology of Spirit*, which Hegel describes as the deduction of the concept of pure science or of absolute knowing as the truth of every mode of consciousness (including that of religion as the capping form just before absolute knowing),[7] he leads up to

---

6 Hegel, *Science of Logic*, Preface to the First Edition, p. 26.
7 See Hegel, *Science of Logic*, Introduction, p. 49.

an account of religion as nothing more than a final resolution of the struggle for recognition that begins in a master/slave relationship and culminates in a sinner/self-righteous relationship.

> The reconciling *Yea*, in which the two 'I's' let go their antithetical *Dasein*, is the *Dasein* of the 'I' which has expanded into a duality, and therein remains equal to itself, and, in its complete externalization and opposite, possesses the certainty of itself; it is God appearing in the midst of those who know themselves as pure knowing.[8]

The use of the term *Dasein* (the consecrated term employed in German when discussing proofs for the *existence* of God), concerning the 'I' that has expanded into a duality and has thereby regained identity with itself in a pure certainty of itself at this point of transition from 'Spirit' to 'Religion' in the *Phenomenology* suggests that Hegel thinks that he has proven the existence of God in proving the existence of a reconciliation between antithetic 'Is'. That is why he immediately proceeds to speak of God as appearing among them, *mitten unter ihnen*, who now know themselves to be the pure knowing – *das reine Wissen*.

Now, that is a remarkable way of introducing God into the human dialogue of mutual recognition, but it is hardly one that recognizes the total transcendence of God that metaphysics affirms and that authentic religious belief presupposes, even in the case of belief in God made man, where religion presumably, even for Hegel, is made most manifest. That is why Hegel takes all the mystery out of the central beliefs of Christianity, or rather leaves the mystery out of them, when he comes to treat of these beliefs in his treatment of what he calls *manifest* religion, in the sense of most manifest to the human understanding. He makes good sense of the Trinity, but only as a threefold function of spirit making, managing and promoting a world in which the spirit itself can advance toward its perfect reconciliation with itself. He makes good sense of the incarnation, but only as spirit embodying itself in every man, or any man, but not in any single man, as in Jesus

---

8 Hegel, *Phenomenology of Spirit*, tr. A. V. Miller (Clarendon Press, 1977), p. 409.

Metaphysics as Preamble to Religious Belief

Christ. He makes good sense of the spirit that comes from this embodiment, but only as the spirit of a community. Any intimation of positivity in the Christian mysteries as found in the early Church was treated as a betrayal of the harmony or reconciliation that had to prevail in a human community deemed religious within the limits of reason, or as a return to the spirit of the law and alienation in the spirit of Judaism.

All this is excellent philosophizing on the Christian Spirit, and it is laudable as an exposition of the rational lines one can draw from Christian beliefs about the social spirit that can develop in any people. But it is not an exposition of the Christian Spirit itself according to the religious belief from which it comes. It is not theology in any proper sense of the term, at least not in the sense of a theology that starts from an affirmation of the total transcendence of God and belief in such a God, who speaks to us somehow or other, interiorly or exteriorly. Hegel's phenomenology of manifest religion purports to be nothing more than an exposition of the best, the most manifest way we have of representing how a supposedly absolute spirit works toward its own reconciliation with itself in history. However, in this exposition, religion is not yet in the form of absolute knowing, even though it represents the same content as absolute knowing itself. What Hegel has in mind when he speaks of absolute knowing sounds a lot like what theologians speak of as beatific vision, except that there is no vision in it of anything truly transcendent.

The question remains, at the end of the *Phenomenology*, whether absolute knowing as conceived by Hegel has anything to do with a God who is totally transcendent. Hegel's ambiguity in this regard leaves him open to the charge of atheism, a charge against which he undoubtedly would have vigorously protested, leaving us to wonder what kind of theism or religion he was advocating in his reading of the form of manifest religion in human consciousness. Without a properly metaphysical discourse on being, Hegel has no way of resolving this ambiguity in his thinking. Perhaps we could say that his *Phenomenology of Spirit* is a preamble to a metaphysics of total transcendence, if, that is, we leave out the final chapter on absolute knowing, which seems to close the door on true transcendence in being. But we could not say that it is a preamble to authentic religious belief, because the only religion it puts forth is one confined to the immanent order of a community or a people. With all its Christian trappings, it is reminiscent more of a pantheistic mode of religion found in ancient paganism, as Kierkegaard so aptly pointed out in his own revaluation of the spirit of Judaism in Abraham, the Father of Faith, in *Fear and Trembling*.

The Preamble to Nihilism and Atheism

Leaving Hegel aside for a moment, consider Heidegger: we could not say that there is in him any sort of preamble to metaphysics, let alone religious belief, given his resolve to destroy the tradition of metaphysics, which, he says runs all the way from Plato to Hegel. We could say that he has not adequately understood this tradition, especially as it antedates the onset of the ontotheology that distorted the more ancient tradition (with Duns Scotus and Suarez and their legacy in modern essentialist metaphysics), but that would not remedy his own philosophy of being or his phenomenology of *Dasein*, which is a preamble to nothing, or nihilism, apart from the univocal finite being he takes as the subject of his consideration. There was a time, early in his career, when Heidegger did admit of something like a 'theological difference', but he did not long pursue the line of reasoning that this implied. He chose instead to focus all his attention on the so-called 'ontological difference', expressed in German as *das Sein des Seienden*, which literally translates into English as *the be of being*, a puzzling expression at best in any language.

Now, I do not propose to try to unravel this puzzlement here.[9] But I would point out that, with his exclusive focus on what he calls ontological difference, Heidegger abandons all idea of analogy in being, where *be* or the act of being can never be taken in a univocal sense, to focus on *Sein* as some kind of *difference*, or some essence in a univocal sense that presumably *differs* from

---

9 I have tried to do that elsewhere, in my *Philosophy of Being: A Reconstructive Essay in Metaphysics* (Washington, DC: CUA Press 2003), and in 'Suarez and the Latent Essentialism of Heidegger's Fundamental Ontology', *Review of Metaphysics* 53.1 (September 1999), pp. 3–19.

Metaphysics as Preamble to Religious Belief

being or *das Seiende*, which is itself an essence. In other words, *das Sein* seems to be taken as essence of an essence, even in the case of *Dasein*, as the one raising the question of *Sein*, or *be*, over and above raising the question of its own being, or *des Daseienden*.

True Kantian that he is, Heidegger does not think that he can pursue this intricately contrived question of *be*, without first pursuing the question of the one raising the question, which explains why he launches on his phenomenology of *Dasein* in anticipation of a phenomenology that was supposed to go from *Sein und Zeit* to *Zeit und Sein*, but which never got off the ground in any flight of reason. The reason why this never happened, I would venture to say, is that Heidegger brought into his phenomenology of *Dasein* an ontology that could not but remain stuck in finite being as such, or in the difference that separates one finite essence from another finite essence. There is no outlet into anything but difference in such an ontology, not even for a subject who wants to raise the question of *being*, let alone the question of *be*, in its most universal sense. That is why I would say Heidegger's fundamental ontology, or his fundamental conception of ontological difference, is a preamble to nothing, or to nihilism, not only concerning the divine, but also concerning the enquiring subject and every being he might stumble on in his enquiring.

I would also point out that anyone operating with such an antimetaphysical conception of being in theology, or in the exposition of religious beliefs, is bound to betray the very beliefs one is speaking of, for lack of having any preamble for speaking of anything as being, let alone as totally transcendent. Deconstruction of being, as conceived by Heidegger in the ontological difference, leads nowhere conceptually, unless one uses it as an occasion for raising anew the question of being. If one does not turn the question of being around on Heideggerian nihilism, one is left with an essentialist conception of finite being, or a finite conception of being *tout court*, that cannot in any sense be used to refer to anything transcendent and infinite, as we see in Jean-Luc Marion's attempts to speak about 'God without Being.'

For Marion, language about God can only be either *iconic*, that is, pointing to God in his transcendence, or *idolatrous*, reducing God to something immanent as conceived by human reason, which is precisely what we do when we conceive of God as a being. The only way we can speak of God properly, in the iconic way, is by leaving out every thought of being and staying in a pure mode of reference. But the question that has to arise for the religious thinker is this: reference to what, something or nothing? If we affirm the Heideggerian conception of being, we have to say: reference to nothing, which Marion surely does not want to say. That would be to verge into atheism. But if he has no other conception of being, what else can he do? How can he explain the difference between iconic reference to God as something transcendent and idolatrous reference to anything that is not God, without coming back to some conception of being that will allow for affirming the proposition that God *is*? In other words, he has to come back to a metaphysics of being that opens the way to affirming God as totally transcendent. Otherwise he has no way of distinguishing his iconic language from that of an atheist or an idolator, both of whom coalesce with one another as unreligious. In this sense, we have to say that a proper metaphysics of transcendence is a necessary premise for what he wants to articulate in terms of religious belief.

The same would have to be said for theologians in the business of interpreting what are thought of as religious beliefs and religious facts, such as the Incarnation of the Word of God and the resurrection of Jesus Christ, as narrated in sacred texts. Without a properly metaphysical sense of the total transcendence of God, they will have no clue as to what is sacred about these texts, or to what is religious about them, as distinct from what is merely secular, as so many other texts that narrate bare facts, so to speak, and speak of no more than human beliefs and disbeliefs. They will be left only with what Blondel, in his criticism of modernist biblical scholarship, has called 'historicism', which has access only to what is discernible to the method of modern historical research, unable to discern anything divine in these texts or in the facts to which they attest. Or else, if they are more speculatively inclined, they will either deny that there is anything divine in these texts or in the facts to which they attest. Or they will rationalize it away in the manner of Spinoza or Hegel, both of whom did much of their philosophizing with the sacred texts of their respective religious communities in mind, and both of whom were perceived as somehow irreligious or atheists by these same communities.

Metaphysics as Preamble to Religious Belief

Now, I would not claim that these communities had a fully articulated metaphysics of transcendence in their suspicion of these philosophers, or of the modern historical exegetes interpreting their Scriptures in purely secular terms. Nor would I say that they were fully justified in their suspicion that these philosophers and historical writers were simply contravening religious beliefs. I would only say that the failure of these philosophers and historians to grasp the properly religious dimension of the texts and the facts they were examining was due to their lack of any metaphysics of transcendence. That is why they could not think of Jesus Christ as anything more than an extraordinary human being, or of God as anything more than nature, or of the Trinity as anything more than a function in creating human community.

They had no way of entering mindfully or rationally into what religious belief speaks of as *mysteries*: Trinity in the very selfhood of God, independently of whether there is creation or not, creation itself as freely willed by God out of sheer love for the created, the incarnation as a higher form of mediation between the human and the divine out of even greater love for a sinful humankind, or the Eucharist as the way of extending the newly formed mystical body of Christ to all generations, of whatever culture or civilization. Blondel himself achieved a good measure of this kind of reflection on the Christian mysteries at the end of his philosophical career, without reducing the transcendence of God to any sort of immanence, but only after he had made a greater place for a metaphysics of transcendence in his philosophy of thought, being and action. In doing so, he was still thinking only as philosopher, but greatly expanding the metaphysical realm of philosophy as preamble to theology.

The Principle of Theology in Faith

All this being said about metaphysics as necessary preamble, however, we cannot say that theology follows simply from the rational affirmation of God in metaphysics, for God is affirmed as totally transcendent in metaphysics (in other words, as totally beyond the capacity of reason to enquire or to fathom). Medieval theologians spoke of this inability to fathom on the part of reason as an inability to know *what* God is by any natural light of reason. Even those who admitted a natural desire to see God as God is in Godself – as Aquinas did, for example, following directly from the metaphysical affirmation that God is – never admitted that this desire could be fulfilled by the pursuit of rational discourse alone. Nor did they think that revelation, even supernatural revelation in the human historical process, supplied what was missing for knowing *what* God is in Godself in this life, except possibly in some extraordinary, but ineffable mystical experiences. That would have been to realize the beatific vision here and now, in this life, something that we still cannot fathom even with religious faith in God and God's revelation.

Theology, as distinct from philosophy or metaphysics, is discourse about God. Aquinas puts this in the simplest of terms, when he asks himself what is the *subject* of theology, which he wants to treat in sacred teaching as a science. God is the *subject* of this science in a way that God cannot be the subject of any other science, not even metaphysics, whose *subject* can only be being as being, or *ens commune*, at best, not God, not in any strict sense of the term *subject of a science*. If subjects other than God are brought into the purview of theology, it is only as they relate to God, either as created by God, or as elevated, in God's providential design, and as returning to union with God (at least for the rational creature) through the mediation of Jesus Christ and the Church as his mystical body. Now this concrete relation of all things to God through Jesus Christ may be what is most real about them, but that is not known in metaphysics or in any other human science. That is known only as a matter of religious belief in a science that is grounded in religious belief or in the science God has of Godself, and not in any philosophical principles.

Aquinas also has a simple way of putting this in his discussion of how different sciences are subordinated to one another, with metaphysics as the first or the most foundational of the philosophical sciences, while theology is not subordinated to any of them. God, in God's total transcendence, cannot be the subject of any science other than God's own science of Godself. If there is to be any other science of God than this proper science God has of Godself, it can only be a derivative of this science – God's science of Godself – depending on how much of that science God chooses to communicate to spiritual creatures. Now, short of the beatific vision, in the historical context of Christian religion, this comes down to matters of Christian belief (or what Aquinas calls 'articles of faith'), which become new principles of inquiry into what metaphysics, or the highest form of philosophical enquiry, affirms but cannot fathom.

This means that, no matter how necessary metaphysics may be as preamble to authentic religious belief, it can never function as principle for theology, as it does for the particular natural and social sciences, including ethics. These sciences have their principles in the light of human reason enquiring into *what* things are in the world of humankind. Theology has its principles in the light of God's own science of Godself, as made manifest in articles of faith or religious beliefs. Believers can reason from these beliefs, seeking a better understanding of what it is they believe in, but never as from principles that are evident in the light of reason. Theology is thus above the loop that ties all the particular sciences to metaphysics, as science of first principles, but the loop itself is one that ties all things to the divine, including the highest achievements of culture and civilization. As such, theology is not dependent on any of the human sciences of nature or history, but neither is it in a position to simply replace or displace any of those sciences. On the contrary, it has to use them as handmaidens or as preambles in its own rational elaboration of the content of revelation or of religious belief concerning humankind and the world in their relating to God.

For this reason, we have to say that all the particular sciences are preamble, not just to metaphysics, but to theology as well, as distinct from metaphysics, but without subordinating theology to any one of them, even less than to metaphysics.

The Autonomy of Philosophy with Respect to Theology

We have also to say that theology is not in any position to judge the validity of any of these sciences, which remain autonomous in accordance with their own principles of rational enquiry, except perhaps in a negative way, when the sciences might be construed as saying something contrary to faith. When such seeming contradictions occur between human science and matters of faith, it is not the function of theology to overrule human science as such, but rather to show only that the seemingly contradictory affirmation or negation is not a matter of science, which, of course, presupposes that one knows something about scientific discourse as such. In such cases, a distinction is made in what purports to be preamble, so that it will remain a preamble and not become an obstacle to religious belief, or a preamble to atheism. Otherwise, in the more positive use of human sciences as preamble to coming to some understanding of religious beliefs, theology can only use these sciences in accordance with its own principles, which are of a different order than those of the natural order, or of natural and social science.

This does not mean that we have to posit two kinds of realism, one for natural science, and one for theology or supernatural science, but it does mean that, in the order of human learning, we always have to start from the lower form of scientific realism in order to rise to a higher form of scientific realism, in the spirit, one we have only by faith in things we hope for from the divine.

Recognizing how the metaphysical affirmation of the total transcendence of God serves as necessary preamble, not only to religious beliefs as such, but also to the rational elaboration of these beliefs in a theology seeking understanding of its beliefs, shows us how other human sciences can also serve as necessary preambles for understanding how God makes Godself manifest in religious beliefs. In communicating his truth and his life God has to relate to the human understanding of truth and life in the world. Otherwise, we could have no understanding whatsoever of what is revealed in religious beliefs. The narrative of God's word in Scripture and tradition would be meaningless to us. We would know that God is revealing something to us, but we would have no idea of what he is revealing, not even the truth that he *is* to begin with.

Without some understanding of personhood and of relation through generation and spiration, we would have no idea of the Trinity, Father, Son and Holy Spirit. Without some understanding of human nature and human action, we would have no idea of the Word becoming man in history. Without some idea of the cardinal virtues, we would have no idea of the theological virtues. All of this is a matter of preamble in the theological exploration of how creation relates to God as to its principle and its end. One could even say that development in the understanding of the preamble could affect development in the understanding of religious beliefs or dogma, always with the proviso that the truth of genuinely religious consciousness derives from a totally transcendent God affirmed rationally in metaphysics as totally mysterious to human understanding.

Theology, as discursive elaboration of religious beliefs, is more than just a metaphysics of being or of the world spirit operative in history. It speaks of a totally transcendent spirit that cannot be identified with any particular community, whether Greek, or German, or even nominally Christian. Even the visible Church, as mystical body of Christ, has universal ramifications for all cultures and civilizations. Even as more than a metaphysics of being or of spirit, however, theology is not a substitute for metaphysics, or for any other critical science of nature or society. Theology requires a robust sense of natural and social science as well as of metaphysics, for its own development as rational discourse on the divine mysteries. It has nothing to fear from the development of such science and metaphysics, and much to gain from it as rational discourse on supernatural life and grace in the world.

Conversely, philosophy, in the form of natural and social science as well as metaphysics, has nothing to fear from theology, even when it is used in the service of theology and religious consciousness. It cannot serve that purpose unless it remains free and autonomous. *Non adjutrix, nisi libera*, as Blondel put it so cogently in his *Letter on the Exigencies of Contemporary Thought in Matters of Apologetics*,[10] after having insisted that it is not free unless it assists in religion – *non libera, nisi adjutrix* – implying that philosophy must be a preamble for religion. This is what he tried to show in rather formal terms in his original philosophy of action in 1893, ending in a philosophy of the supernatural and, in much more elaborate concrete terms, in his final work on *Philosophy and the Christian Spirit*.

Theology cannot replace or displace metaphysics as discourse on being and on the reality of transcendence, since it needs it as

---

10 Cf. Maurice Blondel, *The Letter on Apologetics & History and Dogma*, tr. Alexander Dru and Illtyd Trethowan (Grand Rapids, MI: Wm. B. Eerdmans, 1994), p. 168.

preamble to its own discourse on the totally Transcendent. Nor can it exclude philosophy from drawing some light of its own from the mysteries made manifest in the discourse and beliefs handed down in religious traditions in matters of interest to philosophy, whether as psychology, ethics, or as metaphysics.

Philosophy, on the other hand, cannot hold back from matters of theology and religious belief, turn its back on God, so to speak, since that would be to verge into atheism or nihilism, or into what we would have to call a purely negative theology that says *no* to the God who is its principle and end. In short, philosophy, or the metaphysics of transcendence, calls for a positive theology that it cannot account for in any way, but that can be recognized as enhancing the rationality of human existence in the world, in a way that human reason alone cannot do. It is this necessary positivity of religious belief that modern and postmodern thought has been unable to recognize by reason of its failure to acknowledge the total transcendence of God as universal cause, both as principle and as end, of all that is other than Godself.

8. Truth, Time, Religion

PHILIPP W. ROSEMANN

While pre-modern thinkers were firmly committed to the view that truth is timeless, in the postmodern age, philosophers such as Martin Heidegger and Michel Foucault have argued the opposite position. There is no truth that could be abstracted from specific historical and cultural conditions: being reveals itself differently in different epochs. The postmodern position appears to preclude religious truth as commonly understood in the West, that is to say, as based upon an inerrant revelation received from God. But what is the exact relationship between religion and time? This paper intends to show that religious traditions do not have to be conceived as static and unchanging. Rather, they possess a temporality of their own, a rhythm which may be more fundamental than the time of the philosophers. Religions do, however, require a personal commitment that is, in a certain sense, absolute. Interpreted as an acknowledgement of human finitude, such an absolute commitment may not be a bad thing, even from the postmodern perspective.

A Short History of Time

Western philosophy long maintained that the relationship between truth and time is entirely extrinsic; indeed, that the two are irreconcilably opposed. Plato went so far as to posit a realm of immaterial and timeless 'forms' transcending the sensible world as we know it, and argued that it is this realm of forms which is 'really real', rather than the material and perceptible things that surround us. The latter constitute nothing more than faint images of the forms or ideas, in which they are said to 'participate'. Knowledge, on this account, requires us to leave the changeable world behind and to engage in the contemplation of the forms in their stable presence. Those who fail to pursue this philosophical quest are like prisoners in a cave who, unable ever to glimpse the light of the sun, stare at shadows projected on the cave wall and tragically but stubbornly mistake them for the real world.

While Aristotle rejects Plato's world of forms as a remnant of unwarranted mythical beliefs, he too identifies truth and being with those aspects of reality that endure, rather than with dynamism and change. Thus, Aristotle asserts a primacy of substances over the changing characteristics of such substances: if we desire to know the structure of reality and thus answer the question, 'What is being?' we need to analyse man, tree and house – not old, green and large. For a man grows old, rather than being constantly so; a tree may be green in the summer, yet it loses its leaves in the winter; and a house may well be large, but this is not a necessary characteristic of all houses. So Aristotle reduces the question of being to the question of substance, which he defines as that which underlies all change. Furthermore, although Aristotle recognizes that individual human beings die, just as trees do, and that houses too are not eternal, he believes that the 'form' of human being, the 'form' of tree and perhaps even the 'form' of house endure. In other words, there is a core in each substance which confers its essential identity upon it and does not perish when the individual substance does. There always were, always are and always will be human beings and trees – perhaps even houses. One quickly sees that Aristotle was no Darwin: the deep structure of the world is stability, not flux, dynamism and development.

Knowledge, according to Aristotle, consists in the attempt to capture this deep structure by identifying the necessary causes of things. Why is it that we get a continuity of form in the procreation of living things, so that 'human begets human' (and not horse)? Why is it that the heavenly bodies revolve in eternal, unchanging paths? These are scientific questions for Aristotle because they seek knowledge of what cannot be otherwise. Something that is merely contingent – such as a historical event – is not subject to

Truth, Time, Religion

scientific enquiry, which is why Aristotle has little time for historical truth.[1]

If we trace the hierarchy of causes back to increasingly general causes of greater and greater explanatory power, we will arrive at what Aristotle calls the 'Unmoved Mover' – God. The Unmoved Mover is that element of reality that keeps the other, inferior ones, in motion without itself being subject to any movement or change. The Unmoved Mover is the paradigm of being and substance, unaffected by the accident of time.

Why did the Greeks define truth in the way they did, that is to say, by construing it as opposed to time? Perhaps the Greek conception of truth has to do with the fact that, for them, reality was essentially *seen* – not heard, touched, smelled or tasted. It is striking that whenever Plato and Aristotle discuss processes involving the mind (and therefore processes that require metaphorical language since the mind is immaterial and cannot be described concretely), they invoke the metaphors of light and vision. Plato famously compares his highest form, that of the Good, to the sun in the *Republic*, and Aristotle employs the analogy of sight in his analyses of intellect in his treatise *On the Soul* (Bk. III, chap. 5). Both *idea*, Plato's term for 'idea', and *eidos*, which Plato and Aristotle use to designate form, derive from the root *vid-*, which indicates vision. This choice of metaphor is crucial: what we see has to possess a certain stability for us to be able to perceive it properly; indeed, we see most clearly those things that are passively laid out before us at an appropriate distance. These features distinguish sight from other senses, such as hearing or touch. What we hear is much more fleeting than what we see: the sound of a voice or of a bird's song cannot be captured, made stable and examined in the way a visible object can (especially before the invention of the tape recorder!). A voice requires us to

---

1 See Aristotle, *Poetics* 9, 1451b5–9: 'Hence poetry is something more philosophic and of graver import than history, since its statements are of the nature rather of universals, whereas those of history are singulars. By a universal statement I mean one as to what such and such a kind of man will necessarily say or do' (*The Complete Works of Aristotle: The Revised Oxford Translation*, ed. Jonathan Barnes [Bollingen Series; 71] (Princeton, NJ: Princeton University Press, 1984), 2: 2323).

be passive and attentive. Touch, for its part, lacks the objective distance of sight, affecting both the one who is touched and that which does the touching. No doubt the fundamental orientation of Western civilization would have been different had the Greeks chosen another root metaphor for the description of reality.[2]

The fact that *idea* and *eidos* are terms which have their etymological roots in visual processes might appear paradoxical, given that Plato and Aristotle use them precisely to refer to the deep structure of reality, not its surface appearance that lies open to sight. We can never 'see' a Platonic form or the essence of the human being according to Aristotle. Maybe the Greeks 'saw' differently than we do, then. In fact, Greek statues appear to confirm this impression. E. H. Gombrich has remarked that Greek statues do not represent the appearance of actual human beings – they are perfectly symmetrical, for example, unlike the two sides of the human body. And why do the statues of Greek males always look as though the relevant gods, heroes or discus throwers worked out daily at the gym? The answer that Gombrich suggests is that the Greek artist somehow saw 'through' the material appearance of actual human beings to an ideal, and that he attempted to capture the ideal rather than the reality; or, better, that the ideal *was* reality for him.[3]

Christianity should have subverted the Greek antagonism between truth and being, on the one hand, and time on the other. The Christian God is very different from a Platonic form or Aristotle's Unmoved Mover: he became man, and in doing so conferred a dignity upon particularity, materiality and time that was incomprehensible foolishness to the Greek mind. Nevertheless, the theological articulation of the Christian faith quickly adopted the language of Greek philosophy, with the consequence that a number of radical implications of the incarnation remained unexplored – the implication, most notably, that truth might be much more intimately connected with time than was conceivable within

---

2 On the metaphor of vision in the history of Western philosophy, see *Sites of Vision: The Discursive Construction of Sight in the History of Philosophy*, ed. David Michael Levin (Cambridge, MA: MIT Press, 1997).

3 See E. H. Gombrich, *The Story of Art*, 15th ed. (London: Phaidon, 1992), pp. 57, 69f.

the framework of Greek thought. Yet the Judaeo-Christian understanding of time was in one important respect so utterly incompatible with the Greek one that no theologian could fail to notice the difference: for the Greeks time was circular, whereas for the Old and the New Testaments it is linear. In other words, Judaeo-Christian time has a beginning – creation – and an end: Judgement Day. Greek time, by contrast, was an eternal return of the same. As Aristotle explains, civilizations rise, flourish and disappear almost without trace, in unending succession.[4] This conception allows us to understand, by the way, why Aristotle was not Darwin: the forms of living things have to remain stable throughout time because time describes a circle.

Circular time is quite naturally conceived as accidental, to use Aristotelian language (in the *Categories*, Aristotle describes time as an accident of substance). Since a circle of time cannot give rise to significant progress or decline – everything always comes back ultimately the same – time is easily (mis)understood as being devoid of metaphysical significance. Time that possesses a beginning and an end, by contrast, opens up the possibility of ascending and descending lines of development. In the narrative of the Old and New Testaments, the Judaeo-Christian tradition makes ample use of this possibility: creation, the Fall, the history of Israel and the Gospel accounts of the life and death of Christ elevate time to the status of salvation history. In other words, God uses time as the medium of his interaction with the human race. But not only the fate of humanity at large is decided in time; time is also crucially significant for the salvation of the individual soul. Whether a soul enjoys eternal life or suffers damnation depends solely on its actions in time, and not in some disincarnate other world (as is the case in Plato's Myth of Er, for example).

Nonetheless, until deep into the Middle Ages Christian thinkers continued to speak of time in Greek terms, Platonically contrasting the material world of change with the immaterial realm of eternal truth. Time stretched out, or 'distended', in the dimensions of past, present and future is but a faint image, Augustine argues in the

---

4 See especially the dialogue *Peri philosophias*, in *Aristotelis fragmenta selecta*, ed. W. D. Ross (Oxford: Clarendon Press, 1955), pp. 73–96.

Confessions, of God's eternal simultaneity. All that the Christian life is about is essentially an attempt to pull the three dimensions of time together through the exercise of speech and memory: to create a life so focused on the eternal God that it is no longer dispersed in a multiplicity of activities.

Why did Christianity not exploit the positive possibilities of biblical time more fully in its patristic and medieval theologies? The answer is simple: even if time was the medium of salvation, there was too little of it left to be of much interest.

It is well known that the apostles expected Christ to return and the world to end during their own lifetimes. Although the Second Coming did not occur as originally expected, Christian theology continued for many centuries to think of the present as the end-time. Thus, Augustine divided human history into six ages, according to the six days of creation. Since the first five ages corresponded to Old Testament events up to the incarnation, all of the remaining salvation history, from the life and death of Christ right to the end of the world, had to be crammed into the sixth age. Evidently, this conception of history was heavily slanted toward the past, as there was little room for the present, let alone the future, to unfold.

Augustine's view of salvation history dominated Christian theology until the thirteenth century, when many religious people – especially members of the recently founded Franciscan order – began to feel that they lived at the dawn of a radically new age. Bonaventure, minister general of the Franciscan order and one of the most original scholastic theologians, responded to this sense of newness by rethinking the traditional Augustinian scheme in light of some of the main insights of the principal proponent of this 'new age' theology, Joachim of Fiore. According to Bonaventure, salvation history no longer possesses six stages but two times seven: seven for the Old Testament and another set of seven, mirroring the first, for the New. The significance of this move consists in the fact that there is now much more room for properly Christian history to unfold: the Christ-event has been moved from the end of history, where it was located in the Augustinian scheme, to its centre. In Bonaventure's conception, there are seven stages from the birth of Christ until the Second Coming; in Augustine, there was one. Furthermore, Bonaventure rejects the Joachimite claim that we have already entered into the final, seventh age of the

Truth, Time, Religion

end-times; rather, we live in the sixth age, still awaiting the end of history.[5]

Through this reconfiguration of salvation history Bonaventure accomplished nothing less than the invention of the future: he pushed back the past, as it were, and by doing so opened up a space for the Christian present and future to evolve before Judgement Day. It accords well with this redistribution of emphasis from the past to the present and future that Bonaventure believed in the possibility of progress in theology. Revelation, for him, did not simply indicate the canonical body of Scriptures in which God was believed to have spoken to his people, but rather assumed the more dynamic meaning of the ongoing process of God's self-communication.[6] Such revelation could occur in the great thinkers of the theological tradition as their reading of Scripture uncovered new and hitherto unsuspected depths of meaning in God's word. Bonaventure employed the term *multiformes theoriae* to designate the seeds of such new insights in Scripture.[7]

As in so many other ways, then, the foundations for the modern understanding of time were laid in the scholastic age. The nominalist aversion to metaphysics, with its claim that the structures of reality allow us to make inferences concerning the being of the Creator, contributed further to the recognition that time is not extrinsic to truth but, rather, functions as the medium of its unfolding. For the nominalists, the only legitimate God-talk is based upon his self-revelation in time, that is to say, in the Scriptures and in the teachings of his Church. The Reformers embraced this part of the nominalist heritage, which accounts for the traditional division between Catholic theology, emphasizing

---

5 On Bonaventure's theology of history and its assimilation of Joachim of Fiore, see Joseph Ratzinger (Pope Benedict XVI), *The Theology of History in St. Bonaventure*, trans. Zachary Hayes, O.F.M. (Chicago: Franciscan Herald Press, 1989). About the controversy surrounding this book, one may read the interesting account in Joseph Ratzinger, *Milestones: Memoirs 1927–1977*, trans. Erasmo Leiva-Merikakis (San Francisco: Ignatius, 1998), chap. 8: 'The Drama of My *Habilitation* and the Freiburg Years', pp. 103–14.

6 Bonaventure inherited this 'open' view of revelation from the Fathers and the early Middle Ages.

7 See Ratzinger, *The Theology of History in St. Bonaventure*, p. 7.

metaphysics, and Protestant theology, which stresses the importance of salvation history while rejecting the 'Hellenization' of the Christian faith.

All these developments come to full fruition in Hegel. Hegel is the first philosopher whose entire thought revolves around the positive connection between truth, being and time. For Hegel, truth is not something statically possessed at any one point or by any one thinker (with the sole exception, somewhat amusingly, of Hegel himself). Rather, truth *is* history; that is to say, it is the growth of knowledge and self-consciousness in time. Everything that surrounds us, all of reality, including ourselves, including the past, is nothing but a manifestation of the process in which the ultimate principle, which Hegel calls Spirit, comes to know itself by externalizing itself, unfolding, spelling itself out. Hegel thus thinks God – for Spirit is God – within the horizon of time. Interestingly, although Hegel considered himself a Christian thinker, the Christian tradition, whether Catholic or Protestant, does not agree. In Hegel, God has become too incarnate, as it were, and Christianity too de-Hellenized, that is to say, too thoroughly purged from the Greek opposition between truth and time.

Contemporary philosophy is still entirely in Hegel's thrall. Nietzsche simply reversed Hegel's progress-scheme without challenging the fundamental assumption that undergirds it, namely, the assumption that truth and time are inextricably connected. For Nietzsche, Hegel's mistake consisted not in assuming that there is no truth outside time but in maintaining that truth *grows* in time: no, Nietzsche protests, we are deluding ourselves by seeing ourselves at the end of a long ascending line of history. The opposite is the case: Western civilization has suffered terrible decline since the days of ancient Greek tragedy, especially the tragedy of Aeschylus and Sophocles. These Greeks still recognized the profound dimension of suffering that characterizes human existence; Socrates, Plato and especially Christianity, by contrast, are marred by an infantile optimism – by a repression of the truth – for which humanity has had to pay a high price. In the contrast between Hegel and Nietzsche, we can discern two opposing forces that are still at work in contemporary culture: on the one hand, we often act like good Hegelians, believing in the possibility of unlimited economic and technological progress. We are disappointed when the media report that economic growth in a given year 'only' reached a certain percentage. The possibility that growth might not be, or cannot be, or should not be the ultimate direction of history does not occur to us. On the other hand, contemporary culture often regards the world as being in the throes of a mortal and painful disorder – especially, of course, moral disorder. This gloomy view corresponds to Nietzsche's scenario of decline. It is perhaps worth noting that not infrequently, the very same people subscribe to a Hegelian theory of economics and technology while having a Nietzschean outlook on morality.

Heidegger has in a certain sense overcome the opposition between Hegel and Nietzsche by renouncing – at least in his most thoughtful moments – the temptation to assign a direction to history. According to Heidegger, history is a succession of different ways in which human beings encounter reality or, as the philosopher himself puts it, in which time 'gives' being. In this succession, there is no epoch in which the ultimate mystery of existence – that there is anything at all rather than nothing – was not somehow obscured by human beings' more superficial concern to 'get things done', as it were; to make reality 'manageable', serviceable to our ends. Yet there is also no epoch in which humanity is so removed from the truth of being that it grasps nothing at all of it. Our own age, the age of technology, comes perhaps closest to a complete 'forgetfulness of being', so drunken are we with the delusion of finally having mastered reality and being the 'lords of the earth'. However, even in this perilous condition there is hope since 'where danger is, grows the saving power also' (as Heidegger notes quoting Hölderlin).[8] Thus, in sum, for Heidegger no period in history is 'better' or 'worse' than any other from a metaphysical point of view. It is not surprising, therefore, to find him point out the triviality of attempts to show that a particular philosopher had more valid insights than another: being manifested itself differently to Plato than it did to Hegel; Plato and Hegel responded differently to this gift of being in time; our task, consequently, is

---

8 Martin Heidegger, 'The Question Concerning Technology', in *Basic Writings*, ed. David Farrell Krell (San Francisco: Harper Collins, 1993), pp. 311–41, at p. 333.

not to judge Plato or Hegel, but to chronicle the dispensations of being in an attempt to discern their moving force.[9]

Against this background, it is understandable that post-Heideggerian philosophy has tended toward the condition of a history of ideas. Michel Foucault, certainly one of the most influential philosophers of the twentieth century, in his various works analyses the stages through which our contemporary conceptions and practices concerning madness, criminal justice, medicine and sexuality have emerged in the history of the West; he refrains from judgement on the superiority of any such stage over another. It has become extremely difficult for contemporary philosophy to offer moral guidance. In *Discipline and Punish*, Foucault suggests that it is a delusion to believe that modern-day practices of incarceration are more benign than quarterings performed in the marketplace.

Should we therefore reject contemporary philosophy? Has it gone too far in emphasizing the flux of time over against the ancient insistence that knowledge presupposes necessary and changeless objects? In attempting to answer this question, I would say that different systems of philosophy are not objects of choice like goods on the shelves of a supermarket. The various aspects of human culture form a whole: literature, music, religion, science, economic practices and also philosophy develop in tandem to form a larger cultural whole. Thus, defending, say, Platonic forms in the postmodern world is in a certain sense like worshipping Zeus or maintaining that the earth is a disc at the centre of the universe. We no longer encounter the world Platonically; we encounter it more

---

9 See Martin Heidegger, 'The End of Philosophy and the Task of Thinking', in *Basic Writings*, pp. 431–49, at pp. 432f.: 'Not only do we lack any criterion that would permit us to evaluate the perfection of an epoch of metaphysics as compared with any other epoch; the right to this kind of evaluation does not exist. Plato's thinking is no more perfect than Parmenides'. Hegel's philosophy is no more perfect than Kant's. Each epoch of philosophy has its own necessity. We simply have to acknowledge the fact that a philosophy is the way it is. It is not for us to prefer one to the other, as can be the case with regard to various *Weltanschauungen*.' For further reflection on Heidegger's philosophy of history, see my essay, 'Heidegger's Transcendental History', *Journal of the History of Philosophy* 40 (2002): pp. 501–23.

in the way Heidegger describes; that is to say, for us being is that which forms part of a complex economic and technological system in which everything, including ourselves, stands in danger of becoming a resource for 'progress'. To acknowledge that reality is important, precisely to create room for critical reflection about it. Platonism would be like a daydream suppressing the truth. More than that, however, Heidegger would argue that Platonism is ultimately responsible for our current predicament: its tendency to freeze being in the static presence of 'forms', to arrest reality before our gaze so that we may be able better to grasp and manage it, constitutes the distant ancestor of an attitude to reality that emphasizes exploitation.

Truth, Time, Religion

The question to which I now turn concerns the possibility and meaning of religion in the postmodern world. From a philosophical point of view, as we have seen, postmodernity designates – among other characteristic positions – the conviction that being, truth and time are inextricably connected, so that there is no truth outside time. On the contrary, truth is intimately time-conditioned, with the consequence that history becomes the master-science by chronicling the different forms that reality and truth have taken in different epochs and indeed different civilizations.

On the face of it, religion is not at all compatible with such a view. Religions typically claim to possess truths that are absolute, eternal, and therefore not subject to development and revision in time. Many Jews, Christians and Muslims, for example, strongly hold the belief that they possess written revelations from God that are inerrant.

In order to address the question of the possibility of religion in postmodernity, it will be a useful first step to ask if religious traditions are based upon a simple and irreconcilable opposition between eternity and temporal flux or if, by contrast, the temporality of religion allows for a more positive role of change and development. In other words, to what extent do religions need to claim that they possess unalterable truths that are unaffected by the limitations of time and history? To avoid the risk of irresponsible generalizations, I will in the following discussion concentrate on the example of the Christian tradition, although I will, within this example, draw attention to structures that may be typical of religions more generally.

The development of the Christian tradition in time forms the subject matter of much modern and contemporary literature, most famously perhaps John Henry Newman's *Essay on the Development of Christian Doctrine* (1845).[10] Less well known, on the other hand, is what I believe constitutes the very first treatment of this issue, which occurs in the prologue of a work by the fifteenth-century monk, mystic and theologian Denys the Carthusian. Here is the relevant passage:

> [T]he wisdom revealed at the time of the evangelical law is very splendid and great. [This wisdom was revealed] first by Christ, then by the mission and inspiration of the Holy Spirit, next by the glorious apostles and evangelists, then by the holy Fathers, and finally by the Catholic and scholastic doctors, excellently learned not only in the divine Scriptures but also in all philosophy . . . just as wisdom grew in the course of time before the coming of the Savior, so it also does in the meantime [since his coming]. And most of all from the time when Master Peter Lombard, bishop of Paris, collected his *Book of Sentences*, wisdom appears to have received much and great elucidation, growth, and abundant increase . . . And those things that were hidden have been brought forth into the light; the difficulties of the Scriptures have been unknotted; and points that can be objected to the Christian faith, and have been objected by the faithless, have been solved outstandingly. Indeed, the aforesaid Master and illustrious learned scholastics who have written famously on the *Book of Sentences*, have subtly discussed, magisterially made clear, and Catholically treated not only the more difficult places of Scripture, but also the words and writings of the holy Fathers, who have written much that is difficult and obscure in their expositions of the Scriptures and other

---

10 See John Henry Cardinal Newman, *An Essay on the Development of Christian Doctrine*, 6th ed. [Notre Dame Series in the Great Books] (Notre Dame, IN: University of Notre Dame Press, 1989).

treatises. Since it is known, however, that almost innumerable people have already written upon this *Book of Sentences*, and that moreover even today some are writing [on it] – perhaps even more than is useful, as due to some less illustrious writings of recent people, the more illustrious writings of the older ones are less attended to, read, and investigated – hence it is my intention in this work to prepare a kind of collection of extracts from the commentaries and writings of the most authoritative, famous, and excellent doctors, and to bring the reflection of these doctors back into one volume. For just as the very text of the *Book of Sentences* is gathered from the words and testimonies of the holy Fathers, so this work too is put together from the doctrines and writings of the aforesaid writers upon the *Book of Sentences*.[11]

Denys describes the Christian tradition as a movement of expansion and contraction involving several phases that are centred, appropriately, upon Christ. The first stage of the unfolding of the Christian tradition is the incarnation itself, that is to say, the fact that God revealed himself in person to humankind. Denys recognizes that Christianity is not primarily a body of doctrine; rather, a person stands at its centre. Religion frequently involves such a personal dimension, although religions differ on the precise theological status of their central figures: to be a Christian means to place one's trust in Christ the God-man; to be a Muslim means to trust that the prophet Muhammad received authentically divine revelations through the archangel Gabriel; and to be a Buddhist means to take inspiration from the spiritual discourses of Siddhārtha Gautama.

Denys the Carthusian describes the second stage in the development of the Christian tradition as the sending of the Holy Spirit – still we are not dealing with doctrine but with a person, the third person of the Trinity, as guarantor of the integrity of the Christian faith. In the third place Denys mentions the apostles and evangel-

---

11 D. Dionysii Cartusiani, *Commentaria in primum librum Sententiarum*, Doctoris Ecstatici D. Dionysii Cartusiani Opera Omnia 19 (Tournai, Belgium: Typis cartusiae S. M. de Pratis, 1902), prooemium, 36. The translation is mine.

ists, that is, the immediate followers of Christ, some of whom have bequeathed us testimonies that have become the textual foundation of Christianity. This textual foundation was then, fourth, developed and expanded upon by the Church fathers, whose personal holiness Denys emphasizes: in other words, they did not merely generate abstract theology but bore practical witness to their faith. The Catholic and scholastic doctors form a fifth layer in what one could call the 'onion' of the Christian tradition: a series of layers that form around Christ, whose message comes to be disseminated in wider and wider circles. Initially, this dissemination relies exclusively upon personal witness, but the further these circles are removed from the centre, the greater does the importance of texts become. Preserving the memory of Christ and his followers, these texts gradually grow into a body of doctrine, that is to say, theology: 'those things that were hidden have been brought forth into the light; the difficulties of the Scriptures have been unknotted; and points that can be objected to the Christian faith, and have been objected by the faithless, have been solved outstandingly.' Denys the Carthusian stresses the positive role that texts play in the growth of wisdom, although later in the passage on which I am commenting, he intimates the possibility that the multiplication of texts may also carry the risk of obscuring precious insights. Denys, therefore, has a very dynamic view of the Christian tradition: its wisdom unfolds fully only in time. Yet he does not subscribe to a Hegelian belief in unambiguous progress.

In Denys the Carthusian's account of the Christian tradition, Peter Lombard and his *Book of Sentences* occupy a privileged position – surprisingly perhaps for the modern reader who is not an expert in medieval intellectual history. Many will appreciate the historical importance of Augustine, Boethius, Peter Abelard, Bonaventure, Thomas Aquinas, Duns Scotus or William of Ockham; yet for Denys Peter Lombard's contribution to the tradition is strategically – if not doctrinally – more crucial than that of such much better known figures. For in his twelfth-century *Book of Sentences* Peter Lombard 'collected', as Denys says, the accumulated wisdom that preceded him. And indeed, the *Sentences* served as the standard textbook of theology from the thirteenth century until the end of the medieval period, making available to its readers a collection of passages from Scripture, the Church fathers, and medieval authorities; a collection systematically arranged as a coherent body of teachings. The word that Denys employs to characterize the nature of the *Sentences* – it is a work that Peter Lombard 'collected' – indicates that the *Sentences* do not, strictly speaking, constitute a further expansion of the tradition but rather a kind of 'folding back': a movement in reverse which ensures that the wisdom hitherto acquired is not lost in unstructured dispersal.

After this contraction, however, the tradition expanded once again, this time around the new core of the *Book of Sentences* – a textual core, however, not a personal one. Denys recognizes the enormous doctrinal progress that has been made by the many scholastics who have commented upon their standard textbook: they have 'subtly discussed, magisterially made clear, and Catholically treated not only the more difficult places of Scripture, but also the words and writings of the holy Fathers, who have written much that is difficult and obscure in their expositions of the Scriptures and other treatises'. Nevertheless, the mass of literature on the *Sentences* (which is the work of Christian literature to have elicited the greatest number of commentaries, except only for Scripture itself) has obscured these genuine insights. This is why it has become necessary, three centuries after Peter Lombard, to repeat the task of the *Book of Sentences*, that is, to bring the tradition 'back into one volume'. This task Denys the Carthusian has undertaken in his own *Sentences* commentary, from whose prologue the excerpt that I am interpreting is taken.

The principal elements, then, of Denys's theology of history are clear. History is the medium of doctrinal progress, of a gradual expansion of the wisdom that God revealed to humankind in Christ and, indeed, prior to him, in the Old Testament. This expansion, however, needs to be counterbalanced by periodic contractions, lest the newly acquired wisdom be lost in dispersal. Perhaps one of the aspects of this dispersal that Denys – an author with a strong mystical bent – has in mind is the fact that texts can never fully capture the personal dimension that is involved in faith. In other words, theology tends to suffocate the deeply personal message of a religion's founder in increasingly technical detail. This tendency needs to be counteracted.

Denys the Carthusian's theology of history – whose principles are rooted in a Neoplatonic metaphysics of emanation and return

– renders a remarkably accurate picture of the development of the Christian tradition through its apostolic, patristic and scholastic phases. Moreover, it is easy to apply Denys's insights to periods of history following him, such as the Reformation. The Reformers' desire to return the Christian tradition to scriptural principles could thus be read as the attempt to return Christianity to its centre, obscured by centuries of scholastic theologizing.

If it is compared with the philosophical theories of time that we examined in the first part of this chapter, the temporality of the Christian tradition occupies a position somewhere between the ancient view that time is circular, and Heidegger's conception of time as the medium in which being is at once given and its deepest mystery concealed. For on the one hand, the rhythm of Christianity is characterized by a kind of breathing movement: an expansion around its personal and scriptural core, followed by a contraction which returns the tradition to that core. On the other hand, this rhythm includes both the possibility of doctrinal progress and the risk of decline; indeed, perhaps the expansion around the core, which at once removes us from it and allows us to unfold its meaning and implications, is a revealing that cannot but conceal.

The temporal structure that we discovered in Denys the Carthusian's account of the development of wisdom is not limited, it seems to me, to the Christian tradition. Perhaps it applies to all traditions, including religious ones, that grow around an authoritative body of writing.[12] Until a certain point in history, for example, the Western literary tradition could be described not unreasonably as a movement of expansion and contraction around the textual core of ancient literature: Homer remains the model for Virgil, Dante 'baptizes' Virgil, the Renaissance attempts a return to the purity of these ancient sources, this return gives rise to a new wave of literary activity and so forth. American political life in many ways centres on the interpretation of the Constitution, which was for many years interpreted expansively so as to allow for new developments; currently we are witnessing a strong

---

12 This is the suggestion that I advance in the conclusion of my recent book, *The Story of a Great Medieval Book: Peter Lombard's 'Sentences'*. [Rethinking the Middle Ages; 2] (Peterborough, Ontario: Broadview Press, 2007), pp. 184–93.

tendency to return to the letter of the text. And interestingly enough, philosophy itself possesses the structure and temporality of a tradition – a tradition, moreover, not unconnected with the Homeric one. Plato in his writings is clearly engaged in dialogue with the Homeric tradition, in addition to offering critiques of the sophistic movement and of certain Presocratics, such as Parmenides. In a further expansion, Aristotle responds to Plato, the Neoplatonists attempt a synthesis of Plato and Aristotle, and so forth. But there are also crucial moments in the development of Western philosophy when thinkers endeavour to recover the 'pure' Plato or Aristotle, beyond the accretions of traditional interpretations. Thus, for instance, the so-called 'radical' or 'heterodox Aristotelians' of the thirteenth century defended an Aristotelianism purged of Christian elements. Even Heidegger develops much of his philosophy in a close rereading of the Presocratics, Plato and Aristotle.

If what I have been saying so far is true, there exists a certain rhythm or temporality of tradition that is more basic than the temporal scenarios described by the likes of Aristotle, Heidegger and Foucault. It undercuts their theories, as it were, by constituting the ground on which they are possible, or the medium in which they are developed in the first place. Moreover, this temporality is also that of religion.

Now one could go a step further and claim that the temporality of tradition does not only possess a certain theoretical primacy over other conceptions of time, but that it is important in our practical lives to hold on to religious conceptions of time. The theories of time that Hegel, Nietzsche and Heidegger defend represent the theoretical counterpart of the rhythm of modern and postmodern life. I have noted before how odd it is that it is often the same people who subscribe at once to beliefs in progress and in decline, only with regard to different objects. These people are technological and economic Hegelians and moral Nietzscheans, as it were. And are we not all frequently torn in our evaluation of our own times between admiration of the advances of technology and economics, on the one hand, and dread of the consequences produced by these very advances, on the other? Perhaps, then, as a result of this confusion, we adopt a Heideggerian position, according to which there is light and shadow in every age; we cannot really tell

Veritas: Belief and Metaphysics

whether we are worse or better off than the ancient Greeks or the medievals. Thus, we are temporally confused.

This confusion, I submit, is due to the fact that we have lost touch with the natural rhythm of time, which is circular. 'Natural' time is circular in that it consists of a stable alternation of day and night, summer and winter, waking and sleep, life and death, planting and harvest, and so forth. Up to a certain point in the development of human civilization, this natural time unalterably dictated the rhythm of human existence: when candles are expensive or light bulbs do not exist, one goes to sleep at night (rather than shopping or working); without air conditioning and effective heating, which create an artificial atmosphere of constant temperature, there are times of the year when it is simply too hot or too cold to engage in certain activities; when there is no global network of agricultural trade, certain fruits and vegetables become available only in particular seasons, and are cyclically replaced by other foods as the seasons change. By contrast, postmodern time lacks any such natural rhythm: poor shop attendants have to keep the pharmacy open at two o'clock in the morning so that we may shop for yoghurt and headache pills; we eat tropical fruit whenever we so desire, even when it is freezing outside; effective heating allows us to walk around in T-shirts in the middle of the winter. All these developments bespeak progress and are welcome – in a certain sense. Yet they also create human beings who, uprooted from their natural environment, can no longer receive any orientation and direction from it.

Religion elevates the rhythm of nature to a symbolic level, conferring spiritual meaning upon it. This sublimation of natural time enables us to live in accordance with natural rhythms of summer and winter, life and death, and so forth, while also creating a distance from them – a space in which authentically human meaning can arise that transcends merely natural cycles. Consider some of the major elements in the Christian liturgical year, which is essentially structured around Advent, Christmas, Lent and Easter. Advent is a period of preparation for Christmas, which marks the birth of Christ, that is to say, the beginning of a life-cycle. But this is more than a regular life; it is the life that Christians use as a pattern upon which to model their own existences. In this manner, they do not have to invent themselves from scratch, as it were, like

Nietzschean supermen, but are able transfer some of the burden of being upon other shoulders. For example, they will fast during Lent because Christ, too, fasted for 40 days, became very hungry and was tempted by the devil. Although it may be difficult for us to understand, given the overabundance of food that many of us experience every day, periods of fasting used to be part of the natural cycle of life. Sometimes droughts occur, crops fail, domestic animals succumb to disease, winters are too harsh and long – and food becomes scarce. There are of course still many parts of the world where such conditions continue to obtain. The Lenten practice of fasting transforms hunger from a mere condition of need into an opportunity for spiritual growth, thus conferring meaning upon an element of human life that would otherwise appear as nothing but deprivation. Finally, Easter performs a similar function with regard to the reality of death. We all die, but the religiously sublimated death is more than the cessation of life: it is a following in the footsteps of Christ who himself died, in the hope of rising again.

The point of these remarks is not to engage in Christian apologetics; I could have discussed the liturgical rhythm of other times apart from the Christian one. Jews and Muslims, for instance, live according to liturgical cycles that show structural similarities to Christian time. My point, rather, is to bring out the temporality of religion – not just of religious tradition but of religious everyday life. This temporality is cyclical, as we have seen, although not in the sense of an eternal return of the same. Rather, religious time – and especially the Christian time that I have analysed – is the medium of salvation in which individual, particular events acquire transcendent significance. This moment of meaning is what distinguishes liturgical time most clearly from technological time. The latter is the 'objective' time of our digital chronometers which is no longer based on cycles of nature – in particular, the rise and setting of the sun – but rather on the so-called caesium standard, that is to say, the radiation of caesium-133 atoms.[13] This time is completely

---

13 On the history of the technology of time-measurement and its place within Western civilization, see Gerhard Dohrn-van Rossum, *History of the Hour: Clocks and Modern Temporal Orders*, trans. Thomas Dunlap (Chicago and London: Chicago University Press, 1996).

homogeneous and empty, possessing no rhythm other than the infinite succession of seconds all of which are alike. As this time is gradually taking over our lives, replacing both natural and liturgical time, it extends its homogeneity to all aspects of human existence: not a good foundation for attempts to make sense of our lives.

There is a certain existential interest, therefore, in not completely ceding the ground to conceptions of time that eliminate difference. These conceptions include – paradoxically perhaps – the postmodern idea according to which history is a series of epochs that are all equally valid yet incommensurable, following each other without forming a meaningful pattern: a cycle, or an ascending or descending line. Furthermore, we have seen that the development of Western philosophy, of which postmodern thought is but the latest step, has the characteristics of a tradition. Traditions, in turn, possess a rhythm that shares many traits of the religious temporality. Perhaps we should conclude, then, that we have finally proven the superiority of religion over postmodern philosophy.

Upon closer scrutiny, however, such a proof might turn out to be too facile. Focusing particularly on the example of Christianity, we have found that religious traditions develop around a textual core. For such traditions to take root, as it were, the texts around which they unfold cannot just be any texts: they have to be sacred texts. 'Sacred' means that a community of believers attributes at least some degree of inerrancy to them: they represent the word of God; that is why they can form the starting point of a religious tradition in the first place. Such inerrancy is best interpreted very broadly, as contemporary biblical criticism has shown. Raymond Brown, one of the best-known contemporary biblical scholars, has affirmed that 'whether the words of the Bible reflect revelation received from God or constitute an account inspired by God, they remain very much human words, reflecting partial insight and time-conditioned vision'.[14] Nevertheless, even if one asserts that every word in Scripture is a human word, there is no way around the need to recognize that Scripture is also the word *of God*, in the

---

14 Raymond E. Brown, *The Critical Meaning of the Bible* (Ramsey, NJ: Paulist Press, 1981), pp. 20–1.

sense that it is an inspired word. The Christian faith requires this recognition, just as Judaism requires assent to the sacred status of the Hebrew Bible, and Islam, as a religious tradition, depends upon the belief that the Qur'ān represents God's revelation to Muhammad. But there can be no proof of such a claim. Muslims like to argue that there is an inimitability to the Qur'ānic language which is itself proof of the divine origins of the work. Such an argument, however, will convince only those who are already of the Muslim faith.

Indeed, the desire to *prove* the inspired or revealed status of a sacred text – and it is not only Muslims who succumb to this temptation – is a category mistake. A religious commitment is a deeply personal one, such that the textual foundation which many religions acknowledge can be misleading, suggesting as it does an 'objective' basis that is quite foreign to religion. Denys the Carthusian knew full well that Scripture and, even more so, Scripture commentaries and the theology resulting from them, function properly only as a trace of God's self-revelation as a person and the personal witness to that event by the apostles, evangelists and later saintly theologians. In older Catholic churches, the altar always contained a relic – a piece from the bones, clothing or belongings of a saint – since that is ultimately the only foundation on which religious practice can be built: personal witness. To demand proof of the personal core of religious faith is like asking someone to prove that his or her partner is worth loving, or to show reasons why that person should trust his or her best friend.

The absurdity of such a demand appears in even higher relief if we consider how we typically come to 'choose' our partners or best friends: it is a highly contingent and ultimately obscure matter. There is no *proof* that my partner deserves my trust. If there were such certainty, such an objective basis for trust in personal relationships, then why is this trust so often disappointed? And how could it be possible for a lover to come to trust a career criminal, as happens so often in prison romances? The situation is quite similar with regard to religion. Religious belief depends on rational choice only to a very limited extent. To be sure, a religion can disappoint me if it turns out to be run by crooks, incoherent in its tenets or incapable of helping me at crucial junctures of my life. However, the positive foundations of a person's faith usually lie in contingent factors such as that person's place of birth, personal upbringing or significant friendships. Had I been born in Saudi Arabia rather than in Germany, and to Muslim parents, there can be little doubt that I would be writing as a Muslim today.

The contingency of religious faith can appear shocking. Yet it is a most appropriate, and indeed religious, recognition of the radical finitude of human existence. We cannot invent ourselves from scratch but are, as Heidegger would say, 'thrown' into conditions that are not of our own making. These conditions we must assume and somehow derive meaning from them. Religion is one of the most important ways of making sense of the human condition. That there are many religions which are irreducible to each other proves that the postmoderns are right even while being wrong: that is to say, while postmodern thinkers such as Heidegger and Foucault appear not to have grasped the temporality of traditions, they were correct in maintaining that history is a complex series of irreducibly different ways for human beings to encounter reality.[15]

---

15 I do not wish to deny the possibility, maintained by Alasdair MacIntyre, that different traditions can 'compete' with each other and, in such competition, prove to be refutable. In the case of the great religious traditions, however, the likelihood of such refutation appears slight. See Alasdair MacIntyre, *Whose Justice? Which Rationality?* (London: Duckworth, 1988), esp. ch. 18: 'The Rationality of Traditions', pp. 349–69.

9. On the Power and Fragility of Belief: Updike, Deleuze and Lyotard

JAMES WILLIAMS

From 'Belief That' to the 'Withness of Belief'

> The eavesdropping clergyman, numbed by his sudden atheism, had half-intended to push open the swinging door and enter the fragrant brightness and let his unspeakable wound be soothed away by the blameless activity there, but he lost heart and turned away. He stood baffled, looking about the dining room for some exterior sign of the fatal alteration within him. *There is no God.* With a wink of thought, the universe had been bathed in the pitch-smooth black of utter hopelessness. Yet no exterior change of color betrayed the event.[1]

John Updike's novel *In the Beauty of the Lilies* is a detailed fictional account of the nature, power and fragility of belief through the twentieth century. Updike investigates how belief energizes and sometimes fails a series of characters as they struggle to make their way through a set of events and existential crises representative of a subset of American life. However, in the novel, belief does not take on familiar philosophical forms. We are not given simple cases of 'belief that', 'belief in' or 'belief about'. When thinking philosophically about belief it is common to think that it is a cognitive state, a 'propositional attitude'. These propositions can then

---

1 John Updike, *In the Beauty of the Lilies* (London: Penguin, 1996) henceforth abbreviated as IBL, p. 10.

relate to states of affairs, for example causally and/or in terms of dispositions (*the frost made her believe that the day would be fresh; she dressed warmly which led him to conclude that she believed it would be cold*). To 'believe that P' is then to have a mental content P or that tokens P: *A has the belief that Scotland is always sunny or holds the proposition P 'Scotland is always sunny'*. To 'believe in' would then be, more loosely and more generally, to hold a series of related propositions, in the sense of relying upon their structural relations to many wider propositions *I believe in the infallibility of my God* or *I believe in the power of science to lift the veil of dogmatic ignorance*. I have deliberately taken these voices from two structural beliefs around infallibility or inalienable power at either end of damagingly polarized and deliberately misleading contemporary debates about belief, religion and philosophical naturalism. Updike's book calls into question this polarization and the positions found at its extremes. In his resistance to simple oppositions and his call for tolerance of differing creeds based on sensibility and careful reflection, he rejoins William E. Connolly's arguments for pluralism in the field of beliefs or creeds:

> The relational modulation of faith, again, inserts an element of agony into faith. Something is received in return: You sacrifice the unquestioned demand for the hegemony of your faith to curtail the occasions when its very defense calls upon you to impose otherwise unnecessary violence or suffering on others. You accentuate a dimension of your faith: its call to tolerance unless it is subjected to intolerable provocation. You do so, however, by recomposing what counts as an intolerable provocation to your faith.[2]

According to the prevailing view about the nature of belief, even if there is an acceptance that beliefs are more complex and woolly than allowed by these thin definitions, it is still affirmed that belief conforms to a relatively simple cognitive form verifiable through dispositions or causal relations. This form also allows for the core

---

2 William E. Connolly, *Pluralism* (Durham, NC: Duke University Press, 2005) p. 33.

On the Power and Fragility of Belief

definition of knowledge as justified true belief: *I believe that Scotland is always sunny for these reasons and Scotland is in fact always sunny.* In the Beauty of the Lilies is striking because it extends belief in a series of unexpected directions that are hard to relate to propositions and to structures of propositions. As shown in the passage quoted above, Updike portrays belief as having a bodily aspect alongside its cognitive one – hence the numbing aspect of loss of belief and its appearance as physical wound. He repeatedly takes the internal proposition 'There is no God' rendering it in the familiar italics of the stream of consciousness and setting it alongside its bodily and perceptual effects. Whether in its emergence or its disappearance, in its effects and relations to other thoughts, the proposition 'There is no God' cannot be separated from affects and sensations. The proposition rests on bodily moments and triggers others: 'He was shaking, a look at his hands discovered. A slight lumpy soreness, as if after a mismanaged swallow, had intruded itself into his throat' (IBL, 11). This series of physical dependencies is not the realm of dispositions, or of simple propositions. Clarence, the clergyman, is capable of maintaining an appearance of belief and his dispositions do not at first betray the state within him. Later in the book, in its most horrifying moment and character – the child-murderer Jim – contradictory statements and dispositions sickeningly confound interpretation: 'Jim lowered its muzzle with that bunched expression on his mouth people use when they make a small mistake or eat something distasteful' (IBL, 483–4). At times, Jim says he does not believe but acts as if he does; at others, he shows signs of not believing while appearing to act on belief. Clarence, while stating and acting as if he has lost all belief, acts as if he believes and is killed by a belief he does not have – he is killed by an absence of belief or a negative proposition 'There is no God'.

Updike consistently resists the simple separation of the concern with the epistemological side of belief and its emotional and energetic side. He does this by allowing epistemological beliefs to run independently of deeper beliefs, while showing that these deeper beliefs are where the importance or power of belief lies. Despite the waxing and waning of belief the set of straightforward knowledge-based propositions remains unchanged ('No exterior change of color betrayed the event.'), yet a parallel set of propositions that

Veritas: Belief and Metaphysics

express our sentiments towards what we know are turned over ('a universe bathed in the pitch-smooth black of hopelessness'). In this chapter, I hope to show how this position is close to Deleuze's work on sense, where actual states and the propositions denoting them are brought into relation with flows of intensity, and also close to Lyotard's account of affects, where emotional and bodily affects are significant points of eruption of the unconscious and its different time structures that loop unpredictably and non-linearly within knowledge structures. Both of these thinkers are a better match for Updike's account than the analytic grounding of belief in propositions. It could be argued that these positions can be drawn close to one another, for example, in terms of theories about the map-like and strongly relational qualities of beliefs according to some analytic views, but my position will be that different starting points lead to radically different positions, despite possible refinements.

Though the analytic notion of degrees of belief could be seen as close to an interpretation of Deleuze or Lyotard in terms of degrees of intensity, this would have to be at the cost of imposing a sense of degree, as degree of probability, on theories that are explicitly resistant to such cognitive and comparative views of intensity. In this passage from his *On the Plurality of Worlds*, David Lewis argues for the mapping of belief systems on to probability distributions:

> A better response is to continue to treat a belief system as a precise numerical probability distribution, but then to say that normally there is no fully determinate fact of the matter about exactly which belief system someone has. There are a range of belief systems that fit him equally well, though it may be that none fits perfectly; and there is no saying that his real belief system will be one rather than another within this range[3]

It is this precision and capacity for forecasting that Updike, Deleuze and Lyotard call into question, seeing shifts in belief as novel events incommensurable with any pre-given distribution. Affects and sensibility are not indeterminate through a lack of

---

3 *On the Plurality of Worlds* (Oxford: Blackwell, 1986), p. 30.

factual knowledge about their states for a given case, but because they shift in non-linear and radically unpredictable ways. Part of this resistance lies in a definition of the body as a locus for novelty and transformation, for the expression of the waxing and waning of belief, beyond any inductive patterns. This is the drama of belief in Updike's novels and Deleuze's philosophy; it is also a valuable source of the humility of belief that does not need to be grounded in a relative lack of knowledge that could at some date be corrected. The drama and dynamics of belief cannot be captured through models of 'belief that' and, instead, we require an equally dramatic and dynamic metaphysical model for belief, a 'witness of belief' like Whitehead's 'witness of the body':

> When we perceive a contemporary extended shape which we term a 'chair,' the sense-data involved are not necessarily elements in the 'real internal constitution' of this chair-image: they are elements – in some way of feeling – in the 'real internal constitutions' of those antecedent organs of the human body *with* which we perceive the chair.'[4]

Updike's witness of belief is a parallel process for propositional beliefs to this extension of perception and sense-data into the body. The proposition is inseparably *with* the body and our unconscious and the events they extend into, to the point where an analysis of the proposition alone, or in relation to the independent matters of fact it is related to necessarily misses the reality and power of belief.

Belief, Policing and Holistic Tolerance

What is at stake in this opposition between an extension and a restriction of the nature of belief, between 'belief that' and the 'witness of belief'? The definition of belief and its relation to knowledge as justified true belief is at the centre of arguments about how to police belief. These arguments depend on judge-

---

4 A. N. Whitehead, *Process and Reality* (New York: The Free Press, 1978), pp. 64–5.

ments with respect to whether different beliefs are well-grounded and justified. Ill-grounded beliefs will be heavily policed as to their proper domains, which will be highly limited, whereas well-grounded beliefs will be subject to a politics of encouragement, for example, through the state in education or through different academic disciplines and their claims to police their own domains and those belonging to other disciplines. The division between well-grounded and ill-founded, or between different grades and degrees in certainty, privacy or universality of beliefs, thus allows for strategies for including or excluding beliefs from social and political activity, and for shaping beliefs in terms of information and learning. The specific definitions of belief, its kinds and types, guides the detail of the strategies, for example, in terms of education or acceptable location in social debates. This is why I use the term policing, in the wide sense of disciplining and punishment developed by Foucault, itself responding to the division of disciplines and faculties in part inherited from Kant's critical philosophy and critical of the normalization and power associated with policing and punishment: 'Actually, the problem is rather in the great rise in dispositions of normalization and the great extension of effects of power that they carry through the installation of new objectivities.'[5] To police belief is to lay out a set of practices, from learning, to acceptable form, to treatment, to its surveillance, and right on to the punishment of those who hold dangerous beliefs and rewarding those who do not (or who have the 'right' beliefs). The point of this essay will not be to take sides, for example, on the debate on whether having beliefs counter to rather defensive definitions of liberal democracy is itself reason for punishment, or on the debate around the right place for beliefs in education or academic research (and which beliefs). Instead, I am interested in the relation between different philosophical definitions of belief and possible strategies with respect to it. There is no doubt that this implies taking sides in the debates, but it is not something I want to develop explicitly here.

An example of the strategies I have in mind, currently growing in importance, attempts to draw belief away from an overly emo-

---

5 Michel Foucault, *Surveiller et punir: naissance de la prison* (Paris: Gallimard, 1975) p. 313, my translation.

tional impressionistic and irrational state to a purer one strongly related to logical structures of propositions that can be anchored in experience or, preferably, in the empirical sciences. A good example of the application of the strategy can be found in the spread of evidence-based practice in GP-based medicine since the 1990s. The strategy comes in response to the perception that some medicine failed to be anchored by evidence due to different combinations of the temptation to stick with the tried and tested, the confusion caused by a great profusion of different sources, time and work pressures, the rise in non-evidence-based forms of treatment or demand for such by patients, and the prevalence of prejudicial judgements or situations due to social conditions. It brings together a set of tactics designed to ensure that belief about the state of a patient and best treatment are grounded in evidence, where 'evidence' is in fact short-hand for the most up-to-date information about well-grounded treatments matched to an accurate evidence-based diagnosis. When looking at the nefarious influences on contemporary medicine listed above, we can see that the problem is not so much that evidence was not used earlier, but rather that a series of difficulties meant that it became harder to keep up with the best and most reliable evidence. Treatment was beginning to be detached from the best science itself defined as evidence-based, for example in terms of peer-reviewed papers based on randomized double-blind clinical trials published in respected and established journals. Here is a widely available pedagogical definition of evidence-based medicine for GPs:

> 'Evidence-based medicine is the conscientious, explicit and judicious use of current best evidence in making decisions about the care of individual patients' – Sackett et al.
>
> It is a process which combines the individual doctor's expertise, the best available external clinical evidence and the patient's preferences when making decisions about the patient's health care.[6]

---

6 http://www.gpnotebook.co.uk/simplepage.cfm?ID=1346109997& linkID=14742&cook=yes, citing D. L. Sackett, W. M. C. Rosenberg, J. A. M. Gray and W. S. Richardson, 'Evidence-based Medicine: What it is and What it is not', *British Medical Journal* 312 (13 Jan 1996), pp. 71–2.

Veritas: Belief and Metaphysics

It should be noted that this definition leaves considerable space for a more experience-based approach and that part of evidence-based medicine lies in knowing the limitations of the approach, for example, where evidence is lacking or when dealing with complex individuals, the 'whole' patient. Yet this apparent softening of practice in relation to evidence is in fact a strengthening of the overall strategy, where evidence and justified true belief set a direction by becoming a goal in itself, involving constant refinement, self-critique and suspicion of final truths, rather than the fixed body of knowledge and actions that form evidence-based practice at any given time.

When looked at from a point of view that combines 'the evidence-based strategy' and the 'knowledge as justified true belief standard', Updike's novel appears to bypass a critical approach to belief that its content seems to call for. This is due to Updike's failure to connect false beliefs with the correction afforded by the strategy, not only explicitly in judgements or contrasts between characters, but also in the space afforded to the reader in moving beyond the novel. While a morality tale is too much to ask for in writer who has sought to portray modern America as it is rather than assess or judge its lack of moral direction, in the sense of policing belief, is surprising. The novel has bookends that point strongly towards such a possible outcome by capturing two of the shibboleths of what I will loosely call the 'evidence-based movement'. *In the Beauty of the Lilies* begins with a loss of belief apparently triggered by argument and evidence usually associated with the loss of religious belief due to philosophical arguments (Nietzsche's, for instance) and to empirical evidence (the lack of evidence of Godly effects on social ills when compared to socialist struggles and defeats). The novel ends with an account that echoes the siege of the David Koresh-led Branch Davidians at Mount Carmel near Waco, Texas. The siege, or perhaps more accurately the stand-off, began on 28 February 1993 and ended on 19 April 1993 when 76 people including 27 children died during an assault led by the FBI. Accounts of the raid before the siege and of the later assault are extremely controversial and subject to careful management by opposed sides; in some ways, the parallels drawn through Updike's references to Waco in his afterword and the closeness of his account to the first accounts of the tragedy promote inaccuracies and disputed facts.

On the Power and Fragility of Belief

Given the reference to the debunking of nineteenth-century religious beliefs and his use of the Waco case, we could have expected Updike to side with an approach to religious belief based on gradually expelling it from realms where scientific theories have much stronger claims. Cases such as Waco and the Jonestown mass murders and suicides are often used to demonstrate the dangers of religious belief and the value of science and rational critique in avoiding them. To take an example from a key proponent of strategies based on judgements about true and false beliefs, Richard Dawkins, in describing the 'memes' and 'mind-viruses' that favour religious belief, draws on the example of Reverend Jim Jones and the Jonestown suicides: 'Admittedly, the Reverend Jones conned only a few thousand people. But his case is an extreme, the tip of an iceberg.'[7] For Dawkins, science is no such virus and indeed rests on virtues inimical to the kind of virus behind religious belief:

> Scientific ideas, like all memes, are subject to a kind of natural selection, and this might look superficially virus-like, but the selective forces that scrutinize scientific ideas are not arbitrary or capricious. They are exacting, well-honed rules, and they do not favour pointless self-serving behaviour. They favour all the virtues laid out in textbooks of standard methodology: testability, evidential support, precision, quantifiability, consistency, intersubjectivity, repeatability, universality, progressiveness, independence of cultural milieu, and so on. Faith spreads despite a total lack of every single one of these virtues.[8]

It is deeply questionable whether Dawkins is right about the lack of these virtues in the spread of religious thought, as any careful consideration of theological analysis will show, for example, in Augustine or Levinas, to name but two. Nonetheless, his statement captures the battle over belief and the implementation of different strategies for the selection of the 'right' beliefs. There is of course a very strong contrast between Dawkins's thin meme and virus

---

7 Richard Dawkins, *A Devil's Chaplain* (London: Orion Books, 2004), p. 168.
8 Dawkins, *A Devil's Chaplain*, p. 171.

theory and Updike's sensitive portrayal of the struggle at the heart of his characters. At least in fiction, testability and its relatives are present in inner turmoil and debate, whether religious, existential or truth-driven (in the Dawkins sense).

Updike is not unsympathetic to similar virtues to those listed by Dawkins. His critical writing frequently rests on them and, with similar concerns as Dawkins, through a desire to value and protect children from rogues, for instance. The last lines of *In the Beauty of the Lilies* rest with Teddy, the most humanistic and irreligious figure of the book, viewing television images of the aftermath of the post-siege fire:

> Then a concluding zoom of the four or so women with smoky faces coming out of this storm hutch like they're scared they're going to be shot, then stepping into the open, squinting, blinking as if just waking up, carrying or holding on to the hands of their children, too many to count. The children. (IBL, 491)

Similarly, Updike's recent review of Michel Houellebecq's books for the *New Yorker* ends with a severe reproach for the French writer:

> But how honest, really, is a world picture that excludes the pleasures of parenting, the comforts of communal belonging, the exercise of daily curiosity, and the widely met moral responsibility to make the best of each stage of life, including the last? The island possible to this airless, oppressive imagination has too few resources.[9]

To offer a counterbalance, the same passage was selected by Ted Pelton on the Now What collective blog (and by many other bloggers) for an equally severe, if amusing, judgement on Updike:

> Updike uses the New Yorker review to trash all [of Houellebecq's work], saving out only H's first novel 'Whatever,' which profits, according to Updike, by being 'less idea-driven.' Including

---

9 http://www.newyorker.com/critics/books/articles/060522crbo_books

Houellebecq's Platform and (H's greatest achievement) Elementary Particles in the judgment, Updike comes off as positively school-marmish: 'how honest, really, is a world picture that excludes the pleasures of parenting, the comforts of communal belonging, the exercise of daily curiosity, and the widely met moral responsibility to make the best of each stage of life, including the last?' John, it's ART. It is supposed to wrench us out of the everyday – JUST IN OUR HEADS, JOHN – so that we can regard the world anew. Updike shrinks from Houellebecq like he was confronting some strange abduction-minded hallucinogenic sex cultist. It's OK, John, it's OK. He's gone. You're safe again.[10]

However, this is to miss Updike's deep pragmatism that is holistic (in the sense of a sensitivity to whole beings within environments that shape them but that they can also shape but only within uncertain and fluid boundaries), individualistic (in the sense of awareness of unbreachable variety) and tolerant (in the sense of valuing respect for difference but also allotting an important place for debate and contact free of violence – as far as possible). This pragmatism informs Updike's writing, connecting him to William James and *In the Beauty of the Lilies* to *The Varieties of Religious Experience*:

> Ought it to be assumed that in all men the mixture of religion with other elements should be identical? Ought it, indeed, to be assumed that the lives of all men should show identical religious elements? In other words, is the existence of so many religious types and sects and creeds regrettable? To these questions I answer 'No' emphatically. And my reason is that I do not see how it is possible that creatures in such different positions and with such different powers as human individuals are, should have exactly the same functions and the same duties. No two of us have identical difficulties, nor should we be expected to work out identical solutions. Each, from his peculiar angle of observation, takes in a certain sphere of fact and trouble, which each

---

10 http://nowwhatblog.blogspot.com/2006/06/updike-end-of-authorship.html

must deal with in a unique manner. One of us must soften himself, another must harden himself; one must yield a point, another must stand firm – in order the better to defend the position assigned him.[11]

Like Connolly's pluralism gestured to earlier, James's pragmatism stresses the need for tolerance and a flexible pluralism in a world characterised profoundly by differences in context and background. Pelton misses the point that for Updike the most pressing questions are: Why is this connection of tolerance and variety breaking down? What is the role of media, economics, conflict and social relations that turns beings from a broad and multifaceted solutions to 'fact and trouble' to thin and desperate ones? Updike's concern is that it is not 'just in our heads' and this explains his charting of the rise of different media through the twentieth century in *In the Beauty of the Lilies*. Notwithstanding his innacuracy with respect to Mount Carmel, he is trying to understand and respond to the thread that links violent act to violent act through television coverage and documentary (for example, the thread that connects Mount Carmel to the bomber Timothy McVeigh). Updike is not opposed to belief, but he realizes that its withness has changed as our bodies have expanded into a world of virtual projections and simulations, as well as more sinister forms of manipulation and propaganda.

The Problem of Belief and the Circle of the Proposition

Softly, greedily squeezing, Emily had been taken unawares by her husband; her eyes, with their big movie-star whites, rolled upward to him in a glance of guilty surprise swiftly replaced by a watery plea that he ignore in her worship the something shameful.
'She's perfect,' she said apologetically.
'So are you,' he lied, and she left the baby and came into his arms

---

[11] William James, *The Varieties of Religious Experience* (Harmondsworth: Penguin), pp. 476–7.

for her hug, hard-earned reassurance. But this vision of her, plaintively crouched over the baby like that, was another that Teddy could never stop remembering. Such pain. (IBL, 226–7)

Updike uses propositions such as 'she is perfect' in *In the Beauty of the Lilies* in order to reveal a complex emotional and cognitive knot underlying apparently simple statements. The propositions resurface at different point in the novel with different force and changing meanings. They are vehicles for emotional investments and tensions that change through time and provide succour but also despair and disruption. When each proposition reappears it does so partially with the simplicity of a 'belief that', as if a belief about a state of affairs had arrived to make good a difficult situation, but, at the same time, the proposition confounds this first simple level by connecting belief to a web of unconscious influences. This is a witness of belief that must have the following properties in order to fit Updike's use of the proposition in his novel:

- Belief is a non-linear relation through time (and not mapped in terms of degrees or step changes).
- Belief is a relation to the unconscious (and not simply a matter of things we are temporarily not conscious of).
- Belief is hermetic and individual and connects only transversally (it is neither public, nor general).
- Belief is an inseparable relation of mind, body and unconscious desire (it cannot be accounted simply in terms of causal relations or interpreted through dispositions).
- Belief cannot be accounted for in terms of propositions (unless propositions are extended through a different sense of sense and a different idea of signs).

To understand the departure in terms of belief required by Updike's work, it is useful to turn again towards David Lewis's work on belief in *On the Plurality of Worlds*:

> Besides the fit of belief and desire to behaviour at a moment, there is also a fit over time. One way to think of this would be as a fit between successions of systems of belief and a stream of

evidence: the changes in belief are as they should be, given the evidence. But it is easier to think of it as a fit between the momentary system of belief and desire and present dispositions to follow contingency plans whereby future behaviour depends on what happens meanwhile.[12]

According to Lewis's treatment, belief must have a consistency over time as well as a correlation to behaviour. Whereas Updike's intuition is that beliefs have a secret life which breaks with this fit and this continuity and allows us to extend the nature of belief through an extension of the modes of propositions. To find an account of the proposition and of language supporting this latter view, I will now turn to Deleuze's work on propositions from his *Logic of Sense*.[13]

Two ideas situate Deleuze's philosophy of language. The first is that processes that we use to explain how language works with respect to truthful communication (denotation, manifestation and signification) form a 'circle'. How a proposition refers to something in the world depends on how it is qualified by the moment when it is written or spoken by someone, and this in turn depends on how its meaning is set, for example, according to dictionary definitions, but this is in turn incomplete without a reference. Each ground given for deciding on, say, truth, or meaning, or validity requires further grounding outside itself, to the point where no hierarchy or fixed order of the components of language can be set. For instance, it is not that we can refer to things in language and that this reference is crucial for deciding about the truth of a proposition, but somehow incomplete when we need to decide on its meaning (in a statement about a matter of fact, such as 'The book is on the table', for instance). It is rather that no aspect of denotation is complete without manifestation and without signification. The circling is the process of language, not the things positioned on the circle. The second idea is that sense breaks the circle and can be found in each of the processes set in the circling. We cannot escape the way we keep turning round and round from

---

12 *On the Plurality of Worlds*, p. 37.
13 *Logique du sens* (Paris: Minuit, 1969); trans. Mark Lester and Charles Stivale (London: Athlone, 1990).

On the Power and Fragility of Belief

denotation, to manifestation, to signification unless we refer to an extra process in language. This additional key component is sense, as distinct from the other terms, but also as the way to stop each one failing, where failing means coming up against paradoxes that block its functioning. Thus the proposition 'She is perfect' does not only have a referent (the child), the manifestation (its saying) and a signification (the meaning of she's perfect), it also has a sense (its significance or value that shifts through the novel).

Deleuze extends language into sense through an argument dependent on a series of paradoxes. His treatment therefore provides useful points of contact with other philosophies of language, but only as a way in to his fully original position that depends on the relation of structure, sense and event. The statements about the circle therefore have three functions: first, they give an impression of how Deleuze's philosophy relates to flaws in denotation, manifestation and signification; second, they allow for a set of critical arguments for the extension into sense through each of the elements of the circle; third, they lead into a different account of language based on sense and structure. Deleuze gives the following arguments for the extension of denotation, manifestation and signification into sense towards the end of the series on the proposition; he gives very similar arguments in a discussion of sense in *Difference and Repetition*[14] in a discussion of the sixth postulate for an image of thought. The main point is that sense cannot be identified with any of the three elements of the circle:

1. The sense of a proposition cannot be the denotation, because this appeal to a referent establishes the value of truth or falsity of a proposition, whereas propositions retain a sense independent of their truth or falsity, that is, they can have an effect independent of whether they are true or false (for example in the emotional function of the proposition 'There is no God' for Updike's Clarence).
2. The manifestation of a proposition cannot correspond to its sense because without sense or signification the manifestation becomes empty, that is, the subject of the proposition, the 'I' uttering it, must convey a meaning and alter a series of values

---

14 *Différence et repetition* (Paris: PUF, 1969).

or lose the identity required to manifest anything (it is because the proposition 'There is no God' carries such devastating meaning and emotional charge that its manifestation when Clarence utters it registers as important and noteworthy).

3. Sense cannot be the signification of the proposition because, if we define signification as the 'possibility for it to be true', that is, if we say that a proposition can only be true if it has 'meaning' and if we then define what form this meaning should take, then there must still be something in the proposition that allows it to be shown to be true or false in designation and to vary in its implied desires and beliefs in manifestation (so even if we can decide on the exact meaning of the proposition 'She is perfect' there still has to be some way of allowing its significance and designation to vary – in the way it does in the passage quoted in exergue at he start of this section). We need a third term, sense, between the deduced truth associated with signification and the values of true and false established by correspondence in denotation.

What this means for belief is that the connection between belief and evidence, its association with a given speaker and disposition, and its analysis according to an agreed meaning must be extended into processes that explain the significance and value of the proposition, that is, how it works on a given manifestation, undermines or devalues appeals to a given form of evidence, and extends meaning into individual and hermetic emotional and physical effects. So when we connect Deleuze's arguments for the extension of the proposition into sense defined as that which carries emotional significance in the proposition, to Updike's sensibility that belief must be about more than evidence, dispositions and meaning, we arrive at a view of belief in relation to the proposition that demands a shift from notions that belief is 'belief that X is the case' to belief as that which works with sense, that is, with processes that carry and convey significance: sense is part of the witness of belief.

On the Power and Fragility of Belief

Time and the Limits of Knowledge

> 'You believe, I know, and it is lovely in you. I envy you, I suppose. But I no longer can – if simply willing it or praying for it would do it, don't you think I would have? And the bitter fact is that my respect for the church is still enough that I do not intend to pollute its pulpit with hypocrisy.' (IBL, 63)

An example of processes that carry sense behind the structures of fact, dispositions, will and meaning in belief and propositions can be found in Lyotard's work on time and the unconscious in his essay 'Emma' in *Misère de la philosophie*.[15] His ideas allow us to explain the underlying unconscious shifts and movements that burst into Updike's characters infusing their beliefs with a force stronger than will, than the appeal to evidence and than powerful dispositions such as prayer. How can it be that belief resists our capacity to confront it with evidence, to seek to negate or confirm it through our actions and to analyse its meaning? In order to show the work of time on conscious thoughts or dispositions open to conscious analysis, such as belief, Lyotard divides time into a series of diverging but also interfering lines. There is not a single and united time, but many timelines running alongside each other with points of contact and capacities to transform one another. One line, the one we are most familiar with, stands for the way conscious recollection can return to earlier events. Such conscious recollections follow one another in the familiar linear manner, that is, according to a straight line passing from past, through present, to future. The forward momentum of this line, its 'passing away' and 'moving towards', describes a loss or insufficiency and a counter possibility for novel creation. This is because, when we remember earlier events, we do so in a manner that is necessarily limited, that is, the early event can never be entirely and accurately brought back. Instead, the earlier event has to be renewed in the present through a narration ('this is what happened . . .') However, another line departs from the same early event and drifts away from the straight line of successive conscious recollections and

---

15 (Paris: Galilée, 2000), pp. 55–96.

narrations. This other line describes the unconscious life taken on by aspects that escaped consciousness at the time of the event but that were nonetheless inscribed unconsciously. A very simple example of this would be cases of missed insults and slights. At the time of the initial injury we consciously perceive no sign of malevolence and hence have no evidence for later cognitive analysis or associated narration (we cannot say 'she did *it* to hurt', because there is no *it*) – to all intents and purposes nothing happened. But something did happen, and it returns unexpectedly, this time signified not by the actual injurious fact, but by a disturbing feeling ('Hold on minute! What did she say exactly?'). This feeling occurs on the familiar conscious line but sets it in relation to another unconscious one, where the unconscious event has bubbled away independent of our blithe conscious thoughts. Each of Updike's characters carries such slights, wounds and marks; they remain as critical parts of them long after they have been formed and have served their first functions: 'The kidding, the confidence were things he remembered how to do from an earlier time. Something pathetic had crept into his manner, a sickly need to ingratiate himself, even with his younger brother' (IBL, 225).

It could be assumed from the distinction drawn between conscious and unconscious times that we have only two lines and that the second can be folded back on to the first, but an important feature of the difference between the two times is that it sets up a wider fragmentation and incommensurability. This is because, first, each time the lines interfere they set off new divergences and, second, different aspects of the original event lie on different unconscious lines. An event fans out into a set of timelines which then fold back on to one another. Time therefore unfolds in a complicated manner, not as a simple stream, but as a series of connected but unpredictable whirls and eddies. Lyotard denies that conscious reflection or narratives can somehow regain full control of unconscious processes. He accepts that these processes must reappear in perceivable and knowable forms, but he points out that this return is particularly troubling and disruptive. The reappearance of something hidden involves an undoing of control through the disruption of current conscious lines of knowledge, understanding and narration in their relation to the past. This is why he is interested in Freudian psychoanalysis through its studies

On the Power and Fragility of Belief

of deep-seated neuroses triggered by the return of twofold past events. An event in the past is twinned with another later event and this twinning explains the particularly troublesome return in the present. It is not that a new fact occurs to be added to a set of ongoing accounts. It is rather that two combined and hitherto concealed events return to question and undermine those ongoing processes. So the unconscious returns with the power of a betrayal rather than as an innocent discovery. This return is doubly difficult to handle because it disrupts the accounts we have formed for our conscious recollections and resists further incorporations through its dual nature. We do not only have to handle one returning event but two apparently incompatible ones.

This series of unconscious lines and their power to disrupt chaotically yet with great intensity is detrimental to the claims of narrative, not in the sense of the modern novel, but in the sense of the kinds of narrative we tell to ourselves in order to bolster or explain current beliefs. Our conscious tales have the role of setting up identities over time against the necessary failure and waning of memory, but these narratives are themselves prey to different aggressions and failures in relation to unconscious events and timelines. It is crucial to note that throughout his work Lyotard viewed this fragility in relation to the return of the unconscious, as a positive platform for the resistance to false inclusions and exclusions. Narrative is reminded of its necessary limitations and injustices through the affects and feelings that express what has been unconsciously concealed. His philosophical essays can be seen as repeated efforts to conduct this unconscious power, not only in the name of justice, but also for the renewal of creative narratives themselves. This explains his concern with Freudian psychoanalysis and its work on suggested recollection or anamnesis, but it also explains why he criticizes and adds to this sense of recollection. Lyotard agrees that anamnesis is necessary, but once it is set as a specific practice with a set psychoanalytic theory, then it is constricted and misunderstood. There can never be a final theory of the unconscious, but only essays that attempt to express why there could be no such finality. This is not a dishonest attempt to 'say what cannot be said'. It is rather an attempt to think through the nature of our sources of knowledge and identity, to work out their limits, and therefore to see how we may begin to reflect on how to remind ourselves of those limits, given the precise nature of necessary forms of exclusion and forgetfulness. So according to this view of time and its relation to cognitive states in the present, such as beliefs, our knowledge of a present state must always be under threat, whether it is acquired through introspection, deduced from dispositions or constructed within a narrative. 'Belief that' is then hostage to unconscious processes that work away in time and extend belief back through our emotional, affective and subconscious history. This is of course also true for any account of what I have called 'the witness of belief'. However, the key difference is that if we hold to models based on 'belief that' we do not even have the space for explaining and working with the unconscious and its many interfering timelines. Whereas 'the witness of belief' makes space for the bodily and sensual aspects of belief, and thereby provides a portal on to these processes.

Conclusion

The aim of this chapter has not been to decide once and for all between different models for belief; rather, it has been to show that there are resources in the modern novel and the works of John Updike, in particular, that suggest that an extension of what we take belief to be can lead to an understanding that is more accurate and more productive. This extension is given a metaphysical framework in some works of contemporary French philosophy, notably, in Gilles Deleuze's development of the concept of sense and in Jean-François Lyotard's work on time in relation to knowledge and the unconscious. It has also been argued that the philosophical and social stakes of such an extension are high with respect to how belief is fostered and set in a legal context, for example, in terms of pedagogy within professional practice or through claims that some beliefs are fundamentally illegitimate. If we follow Updike's, Deleuze's and Lyotard's suggestions such clear-cut judgements or exclusive practices are called into question for they may be based on serious misunderstanding of the nature of belief in relation to language, time and human existence. There is no doubt that this then commits us to a more complicated world, where we cannot simply dismiss beliefs or justify practices that seek to control which ones we come to hold, but this 'price' must be weighed up against the much higher risks carried by acts based on a false model of reality.

10. Can Abraham be Saved? And: Can Kierkegaard be Saved? A Hegelian Discussion of *Fear and Trembling*[1]

VITTORIO HÖSLE

Translated by J. M. Miller

In this chapter I will attempt to answer two questions that appear to stand in tension with one another. First, *can Abraham be saved?* This question is posed by Kierkegaard with gripping intensity, and in so far as I take it up again, I at least recognize that the question *must* be asked, and that Kierkegaard demonstrates his greatness in asking it. On the other hand, my second question – *can Søren Kierkegaard be Saved?* – presupposes that Kierkegaard's philosophy is no less problematic than Abraham's behaviour itself. The tension between the two questions can be tolerated only in so far as one holds, *along with* Kierkegaard, that philosophy must reflect on Abraham, indeed, that it cannot ignore the difficulties which he poses, and if at the same time one believes, *against* Kierkegaard, that his own response is not only false, but also entirely unacceptable, and that it poses a new problem itself: How could a philosopher of Kierkegaard's merit have offered such a theoretically absurd and practically dangerous response?

The hope to make sense of both Abraham's deed as well as Kierkegaard's thought is all the more important the more one is convinced that the world, especially the historical world, does not

---

[1] This essay was first written in Norwegian. I am grateful to my colleague Audun Øfsti, who rendered the text into legible form.

lack an inherent rationality – that is, the more sympathy one has towards Hegel's notion of a system. It is well known that post-Hegelian philosophy is a strong argument against Hegel. This is evident not only if one analyses the concrete philosophical arguments that we find in writers like Feuerbach, Kierkegaard and Marx, and recognizes them (something that, in my view, is far more difficult than we think today; for Hegel's critics rarely argue on his level); the simple fact that both political and philosophical history continues after Hegel can itself be seen as an argument against him – at least if no logic can be found in such later developments. Anyone attempting to take Hegel's central ideas seriously therefore should avoid adopting a purely negative attitude toward Hegel's critics. One might state a slight paradox (and since Kierkegaard loved paradoxes, he would not protest): if Hegel were fully justified in spite of his critics, he could not be right; for in that case the history which followed him would make little sense. Only by granting that post-Hegelian philosophy had been aware of several problems that Hegel could not yet accommodate into his system, do we have the possibility of defending the basis of his objective idealism.[2]

I have both an objective as well as a subjective ground for focusing specifically on Kierkegaard among all of Hegel's critics. The objective ground is that Kierkegaard is undoubtedly the most fascinating of all such critics. His personality is one of the most enigmatic in the history of philosophy; were existential radicalism the most important criterion for determining the greatness of philosophers, Kierkegaard could claim first prize among them all. In our own century, only Wittgenstein can be compared to him. Indeed it is no coincidence that Wittgenstein admired Kierkegaard more than any other philosopher of the nineteenth century.[3] His life is characterized by a flawless purity, and in this life one finds a truly wonderful logic. Not only is his life, in a certain sense, a work of art; his philosophical writings are accomplished works of art

---

2 I refer here to my book *Hegels System. Der Idealismus der Subjektivität und das Problem der Intersubjektivität*, 2 volumes (Hamburg: Felix Meiner Verlag, 1987).

3 See Wittgenstein's letter to M. O'C. Drury, quoted in Alastair Hannay, *Kierkegaard* (London: Routledge & Kegan Paul, 1982), IX.

as well. One certainly cannot deny the poetic quality of Vico's language, or Hegel's. But their works are doctrinal writings, not new literary genres. By contrast, Kierkegaard discovered an entirely new form of expression for his philosophical thoughts; since Plato, no philosopher has been such a great poet. That does not mean, of course, that he can also be compared to Plato as a philosopher.

Thus, I come to the second reason for my disagreement with Kierkegaard. In my first book, which deals with the problem of the relationship between philosophy and the history of philosophy,[4] I investigate several structural analogies between various philosophers. In particular, I claim that such an analogy exists between Plato, the Neoplatonists, Cusanus and Hegel. As far as the first three are concerned, I agree with Egil Wyller, a Norwegian philosopher who exercised a great deal of influence on this book.[5] The agreement ended and the disagreement began with respect to Hegel. In Wyller's view, Hegel's predecessor, namely, Fichte, and later, his critic, Kierkegaard, were among those who carried on the tradition he termed 'henological'. Of course, the partial differences in our interpretation of the history of philosophy are a function of systematic differences, particularly with respect to the relation between philosophy and religion. My critique of Kierkegaard therefore focuses on *Fear and Trembling,* Kierkegaard's most provocative writing on this problem, rather than his more explicit arguments against Hegel in the *Philosophical Fragments* and, to a greater extent, in the *Unscientific Postscript*.[6] Perhaps this

---

4 *Wahrheit und Geschichte. Studien zur Struktur der Philosophiegeschichte unter pragmatische Analyse der Entwicklung von Parmenides bis Platon* (Stuttgart/Bad Cannstatt: Frommann-Holzboog, 1984).

5 See Egil A. Wyller, *Enhet og Annethet: En historisk og systematisk studie i Henologi. I-III* (Oslo: Dreyer, 1981); *Den sene Platon* (Oslo: Tano Forlag, 1984).

6 For Kierkegaard, and especially his critique of Hegel, see K. Nadler, *Der dialektische Widerspruch in Hegels Philosophie und das Paradoxon des Christentums* (Diss. Kiel, 1931); J. Collins, *Kierkegaard's Critique of Hegel* (New York: Fordham University Press, 1943); M. Bense, *Hegel und Kierkegaard. Eine prinzipielle Untersuchung* (Köln: Stauffen Verlag, 1948); N. Thulstrup, 'Kierkegaards Verhältnis zu Hegel', *Theologische Zeitschrift* 13 (1957), pp. 200–26; R. L. Perkins (ed.), *Kierkegaard's Fear and Trembling: Critical Appraisals* (University, AL: University of

Can Abraham be Saved? Can Kierkegaard be Saved?

approach can be validated by the fact that Kierkegaard himself viewed *Fear and Trembling* as the work that would be the most likely to outlive him;[7] it cannot be doubted, at least, that it is his 'most difficult writing'[8] which therefore requires above all others a philosophical analysis.

The following chapter is naturally divided into four parts. First, I will sketch an outline of Kierkegaard's argument. Then, I will attempt to show why this argument is unacceptable. Third, I will offer an alternative response to Kierkegaard's question. Finally, I will try to defend the intuition that I take Kierkegaard to be justified in holding against his own concrete formulations. As one can see, the structure is dialectical: the third and fourth parts are in a certain sense a synthesis of the first two. I believe, along with both Hegel and Kierkegaard, that the synthesis is stronger if the thesis and antithesis stand in the most radical opposition to one another. Thus, if my critique should be too severe, I beseech the reader's patience – it is not my last word on Kierkegaard.

Kierkegaard's Text

As with almost all of Kierkegaard's works, *Fear and Trembling* mixes a peculiar brand of poetic flourish with philosophical – that is, argumentative – analysis; and in this analysis, literary works play a major role. The subtitle of the work, 'Dialectical Lyric', indicates this relation between two forms of expression. Moreover, the pseudonym, *Johannes de Silentio*, behind which Kierkegaard con-

---

Alabama Press, 1981). The most important Kierkegaard bibliographies are: J. Himmelstrup, *Søren Kierkegaard. International bibliografi* (København: Nyt Nordisk Forlag, 1962); A. Jørgensen, *Søren Kierkegaard-litteratur 1961–70* (Aarhus: Akademisk Bokhandel, 1971); A. Jørgensen, *Søren Kierkegaard-litteratur 1971–80* (Aarhus, 1983).

7 See *Søren Kierkegaards Papirer*, Anden forøgede Udgave ved N. Thulstrup, Tiende Bind, Anden Afdeling (København: Gyldendal, 1968), p. 16: 'Oh, if I am dead – Fear and Trembling alone will suffice for an immortal name of an author. Then will it be read and translated into other languages' (September 1849).

8 E. Hirsch, *Kierkegaard-Studien*, 2 vols (Gütersloh: Bertelsmann, 1930–1933), p. 635.

ceals his identity, suggests that the main point of the text cannot be disclosed.⁹ And lastly, Hamann's motto indicates that an implicit meaning lies behind that which is said explicitly. After a rather polemical foreword, Kierkegaard describes the state of mind in which he approaches the tales of Abraham's temptation; he tells four variations on the story, all of which suggest a lack of faith on Abraham's part and thus must be distinguished from that which actually occurs. The 'Speech in Praise of Abraham' contrasts the true Abraham with the heroes of the fictitious variations. Following the 'Preamble from the Heart', the central text – the 'Problemata' – discusses three questions: 'Is there a teleological suspension of the ethical? Is there an absolute duty to God? Was it ethically responsible for Abraham to conceal his intentions from Sara, Elieser and Isaac?' It is not difficult to see a *climax* in the three questions: the first transcends the ethical; the second speaks expressly of God; and the third addresses silence as a necessary consequence of the absolute, more than ethical relation of the individual with God.

The starting point for Kierkegaard is the conviction that accepting Abraham's behaviour on the basis of our normal ethical understanding is no simple matter. 'The ethical expression for what Abraham did is that he was willing to murder Isaac; the religious expression is that he was willing to sacrifice Isaac; but in this contradiction lies the very anguish that can indeed make one sleepless' (29f./60).¹⁰ Neither the Church's interpretation of Christianity nor Hegel's philosophical discussion of Christianity can impart

---

9 Here I cannot address the problem of how Kierkegaard's pseudonyms relate to each other and to the author's intention.

10 Kierkegaard is quoted from the following edition: *Samlede Værker*, vols 1–20 (København: Gyldendal, 1963), with both Roman and Arabic numerals. When no Roman numeral is given, I refer to the fifth volume, which contains *Frygt og Bæven*, et al. A printing error in V 35 is corrected on the basis of another edition: *Frygt og Bæven. Sygdommen til Døden. Taler*. Tekstudgivelse, efterskrift og noter af L. Petersen under medvirken af M. Jørgensen (København: Borgen, 1989). For this translation of the chapter the standard English translation by A. Hannay is used: S. Kierkegaard, *Fear and Trembling* (Harmondsworth: Penguin, 1985); then also the corresponding pages in English are given after a solidus. One obvious oversight was corrected.

Can Abraham be Saved? Can Kierkegaard be Saved?

meaning to Abraham's willingness to sacrifice Isaac. What confuses Kierkegaard the most is not the fact that modern man is far removed from Abraham, but the fact that one continues to show hypocritical admiration for a man who must be condemned if one were only consistent in one's principles. In order to continue perceiving Abraham as a model, our ethical categories must be radically altered; if one is not willing to do this, one must distance oneself from Abraham. 'So let us either forget all about Abraham or learn how to be horrified at the monstrous paradox which is the significance of his life, so that we can understand that our time like any other can be glad it has faith' (49/81). Ironically, Kierkegaard depicts a priest, who praises Abraham in his sermons, but would be horrified if someone in his parish were to take him seriously (28ff.). Kierkegaard undoubtedly grasps a central feature of modern Christianity, which has become much more of a cultural than a religious phenomenon. As a Christian, one has several elements in his cultural repertoire that are not taken seriously, even though one lacks the courage to clear them from one's path. Such half-heartedness cannot satisfy Kierkegaard's notion of seriousness. 'But if one wants to market a cut-price version of Abraham and then still admonish people not to do what Abraham did, then that's just laughable' (50/82). Kierkegaard especially rejects any attempt to rationalize Christianity, for this would necessarily entail a decisive break from those moments in faith which are more basic than reason. While the Danish Hegelians want to go beyond faith with Hegel, Johannes de Silentio would be content if he could only arrive at faith (9ff.). For him, Hegel is easier to understand than Abraham (32). Johannes laments the absence of the force of passion in our own time (11, 40, 62, 68, 91, 109), yet he feels this very force in Abraham. He is the hero whose poet he wants to be (17f.).

What is faith? Kierkegaard develops this concept as a third step beyond that which one could call a commonplace philistine mentality, as well as resignation. We can already observe the triadic character of this and many other divisions. Kierkegaard – whose master's thesis, *On the Concept of Irony*, is one of the best books written in Hegel's spirit – also remains, in terms of his conceptual apparatus, a critic of Hegel in debt to Hegel to a much greater extent than he himself was aware. Since the first step is not analysed in greater detail by Kierkegaard, I will content myself here with a few remarks on the relation of resignation and faith. Resignation – which can result from rejection by a beloved woman – consists in the recognition that we cannot attain that which we desire in escaping to an internal world, in the dignity of subjectivity as opposed to the contingency of existence, and at the same time, in a melancholy relation to the outer world. 'The knight of resignation is a stranger, a foreigner' (47/79), because he has sustained endless suffering. In this way he has surely become invulnerable to harm.

> Infinite resignation is that shirt in the old fable. The thread is spun with tears, bleached by tears, the shirt sewn in tears, but then it also gives better protection than iron and steel. A defect of the fable is that a third party is able to make the material. (43/74)

Through resignation one experiences death, before one dies (43, 105); 'for only in infinite resignation does my eternal validity become transparent to me' (44/75), as it is expressed in a sentence that reminds us of Heidegger's notion of 'being-toward-death'.[11]

Faith presupposes all of this – without resignation one cannot become a believer. But faith finds the way back to the world and does not lose its trust in it, or in existence. Faith reverses the movement of the infinite resignation – 'having performed the movements of infinity it makes those of finitude' (36/67). 'Convinced that God troubles himself about the smallest thing' (33/64), faith returns from eternity to the temporal (19). This movement could be called *Katabasis*, corresponding to the *Anabasis* of resignation. Since the believer, like the philistine, is at home in the world, he can be confused with him (37ff.); perhaps for this reason 'the dialectic of faith is the most refined and most remarkable of all dialectics' (35/66). To have faith means 'to exist in such a way that my opposition to existence expresses itself every instant as the most beautiful and safest harmony' (47/78).

All of this explains Abraham's trust in God, and thus why he was willing to sacrifice Isaac without despair. The variations at the

---

[11] See M. Heidegger, *Sein und Zeit* (Frankfurt am Main: Klostermann, 1977), §§ 46 ff.

beginning of *Fear and Trembling*, on the contrary, offer a glimpse of the different forms that the knight of resignation can take. However, the moral problem is not thereby resolved: Did Abraham have the right to sacrifice Isaac? The difficulty of the question consists in the fact that Abraham is not simply sacrificing himself; he is willing to kill another human being. Had Abraham sacrificed himself instead of Isaac, he would have doubted; he would have been a hero worthy of our admiration – but Abraham does not doubt (21f.). It is equally impossible to say that Isaac's sacrifice takes place for the sake of a higher purpose, as in the case of a tragic collision. If Agamemnon, Jephthah and Brutus sacrifice their children to save their homeland, it is perceived as something terrible. But it can be rationally analysed with pure ethical categories – as a conflict between two values. Abraham's deed, however, cannot be justified in this way. The tragic remains within the realm of the ethical. Abraham, however, opens a new dimension – the religious dimension – which forms a third stage, beyond the aesthetic and the ethical. (While *Either/Or* does not yet explicitly mention this third stage, it receives careful treatment in *Stages on Life's Way*.) 'Abraham is therefore at no instant a tragic hero, but something quite different, either a murderer or a man of faith. The middle-term that saves the tragic hero is something that Abraham lacks' (53/85). Abraham cannot be understood if we do not give up the Hegelian notion, already present in Greek thought, that the ultimate purpose of the individual is 'to abrogate his particularity so as to become the universal' (51/83). Faith is something entirely different:

> Faith is just this paradox, that the single individual as the particular is higher than the universal, is justified before the latter, not as subordinate but superior, though in such a way, be it noted, that it is the single individual who, having been subordinate to the universal as the particular, now by means of the universal becomes that individual who, as the particular, stands in an absolute relation to the Absolute. This position cannot be mediated, for all mediation occurs precisely by virtue of the universal; it is and remains in all eternity a paradox, inaccessible to thought. (52f./84f.; 57f.; 64f.)

Veritas: Belief and Metaphysics

All religious people must experience this paradox, and must do so in anxiety – even Mary ('she is not at all the fine lady sitting in her finery and playing with a divine child' (61/94)); even the apostles: 'Was it not a fearful thought that this man who walked among the others was God? Was it not terrifying to sit down to eat with him?' (61/94). Thus one must admit, 'that those whom God blesses he curses in the same breath' (60/94).

Against both Kant and Hegel, Kierkegaard maintains that, although every duty is also a duty to God, there is also a direct duty toward God that cannot be reduced to a duty to other humans (63). The knight of faith 'addresses God in heaven as "Thou"' (71/105). We read now that for the faithful, 'interiority is higher than exteriority' (64/97). For this reason, communication about faith is impossible (even among the various knights of faith); in faith, the most radical form of egoism coincides with absolute devotion to God (66); the universal disappears in this exclusive relation between God and the soul. Thus the knight of faith cannot be assisted by the Church either, 'for qualitatively the idea of the Church is no different from that of the state' (68/102). Kierkegaard sees no danger that his theory could be misused. Such a fear can only torment him who does not know 'that to exist as the individual is the most terrifying thing of all' (69/102). He cannot be responsible for 'stragglers and vagrant geniuses' (70/103). All the same, Kierkegaard admits that the knight of faith is, in a certain sense, insane (70, 23, 96f.).

While the universal is apparent, the individual is 'concealed' (75/109). Thus it immediately follows that the third question must be answered in the affirmative: Abraham must keep his intentions to himself, for no one could have understood him. 'The relief of speech is that it translates me into the universal (102/137) – but we have already seen that Abraham is outside of the universal. Kierkegaard recognizes that the ethical demands candour, particularly because – and here he seems to anticipate the central thought of the discourse ethics – only an open discussion can ensure that we do not overlook any significant argument (79f.). He also recognizes that not every form of silence is good – it can be demonic. Silence is 'the demon's lure, and the more silent one keeps the more terrible the demon becomes; but silence is also divinity's communion with the individual' (80/114–15). We do not have space

Can Abraham be Saved? Can Kierkegaard be Saved?

here to discuss Kierkegaard's category of the demonic; let it suffice to say that it functions as a bridge concept. Just as the category of the 'interesting' mediates between the aesthetic and the ethical (75f.), the 'demonic' mediates between the ethical and the religious. 'In a sense there dwells infinitely more good in the demonic person than in a superficial person' (88/122). Both the demonic person as well as the religious leave the universal behind and close themselves up in their individuality; but the first does this without the authority of God, whereas the other does so in obedience to God. I cannot here analyse the narrative of Agnes and the merman, which illustrates a significant example of the demonic. As he so often does in his works, Kierkegaard again speaks in this fable of the dissolution of his engagement to Regine Olson. The merman's greatest pain is that he cannot disclose himself and thus must hurt the woman he loves in order to free her from a love that will only condemn her to unhappiness; if he is the cause of misfortune, it is he who suffers most from it. The demon cannot discuss his pain with others because he fears their compassion: 'A proud and noble nature can endure everything, but one thing it cannot endure, it cannot endure pity. Pity implies an indignity' (94/129).[12] The merman, however, can and should express himself. There is a solution to his dilemma: to disclose himself and marry Agnes. That is the difference between Abraham and himself. The demon commits a sin by keeping his silence; and 'an ethic that ignores sin is an altogether futile discipline' (90/124).

We need to distinguish the demonic from a case in which silence is ethically permitted. Kierkegaard, in contrast to Goethe, represents Faust as a sceptic who does not want to communicate his corruptive thoughts because he does not want to risk the deterioration of society (97ff.). He finds himself in an ethical dilemma; for on the one hand the universal demands of him that he speak; on

---

12 Cf. the related passage in Hegel's *Vorlesungen über Ästhetik* [*Lectures on Aesthetics*]: 'But the noble and great man does not want to be pitied and lamented in that way. For insofar as only the miserable part, the negative aspect of the misfortune is pointed out, there is a disparagement of the unhappy person' (XV 525; my translation). Hegel is quoted according to the edition: *Werke in zwanzig Bänden* (Frankfurt am Main: Suhrkamp, 1969ff.).

the other hand he has also the ethical duty not to disrupt the certainty of simpler folk. Kierkegaard's Faust thus stands between the tragic hero and Abraham; he must choose between two values, but one value is the negation of the universal, the disclosed. However, it is still an ethical value at stake. That distinguishes Faust from Abraham; and Kierkegaard can only repeat himself: 'Abraham cannot be understood, he can only be admired' (101).

A Refutation of Kierkegaard's Argument

Each of Kierkegaard's critics must recognize at least two of the philosopher's merits: a contempt for a lukewarm Christianity and an extraordinary depth of psychological analysis. Anyone wanting to understand the notion of anxiety, despair, etc. will always refer back to Kierkegaard.[13] Were it not for his phenomenological analysis of the unhappy subjectivity (developed further by Heidegger, Sartre and Jaspers in the twentieth century), we would be without one of the greatest philosophers in this philosophical domain. That does not imply, however, that Kierkegaard can be compared with those philosophers who can claim to have discovered new arguments; indeed, I fear that one cannot even regard him as among the greatest Christian theologians.

In order to begin my critique, it is clear that Kierkegaard always argues disjunctively: '*Either – Or*' is not only the title of his first and brilliant book, it is his general *forma mentis*. Either Abraham must be condemned or we must recognize the theory of the absolute relation of the individual to the Absolute – this is the central thesis of *Fear and Trembling*. I will show that we do not necessarily have to accept this alternative; if, however, we must accept it, a rational human being can only come to the conclusion that, because Kierkegaard's theory is absurd, Abraham must be condemned. In philosophy, it is not sufficient simply to establish implications or alternatives. The ultimate aim of philosophy consists in making categorical statements, as Plato taught, and as Fichte demonstrates quite convincingly in his work, *On the Concept of the Science of Knowledge*. Kierkegaard, on the other hand, contents himself with

---

13 See *The Concept of Anxiety* and *The Sickness Unto Death*.

offering only an alternative: Abraham's salvation is never proved; but only that he can be saved on the sole condition that we do not take ethics to have the final word. One could say that at least such an alternative is original, but not even that is true. Kierkegaard is not the first to note the difficulty that Abraham's behaviour poses for an ethics based on rationality; both Kant and Hegel were attuned to this much earlier.[14] Kant mentions Abraham in *Religion Within the Limits of Reason Alone*, and criticizes him in a parenthesis (VI 187). Also, in *The Contest of Faculties*, Kant argues that it is impossible to know whether or not it is God speaking to an individual, but that that person can exclude such a possibility if the supposed voice of God commands something which is immoral.

> An example may be the myth of the sacrifice that Abraham, acting on divine command, was going to carry out by slaughtering his own son and burning him (the poor child was unknowingly carrying wood for it). Abraham should have answered to this allegedly divine voice: 'It is certain that I should not kill my son, but that you who appear to me are God, I am not certain and cannot be certain,' even though the voice came down from (visible) heaven. (VII 63)

With this critique of Abraham, Kant plays a part in one of the most important trends of contemporary philosophy: the eradication of all superstition with theological implications. Abolishing superstition was extremely important on both theoretical as well as practical grounds: only thus could reason achieve autonomy, and only thus could the state demand obedience from its subjects. The inevitable consequence of allowing a tale of a divine voice to count as an instance against philosophical arguments or moral and positive laws would be intellectual and political anarchy. Indeed, one does not understand the reason why both Hobbes, in the *Leviathan*,[15] and Spinoza, in *Tractatus Theologico-Politicus*,[16]

---

14 Kant is quoted according to the edition: *Akadamie-Textausgabe* (reprint; Berlin: Georg Reimer, 1968); the translation is mine.
15 See *Leviathan* (Harmondsworth: Penguin, 1968), Chs. 2, 12, 32–47.
16 See *Tractatus theologico-politicus* (Heidelberg: C. Winter, 1925), Chs. 1 ff.

discuss prophets and miracles in such detail if one fails to understand that the modern state could not have developed without having rejected them. Every modern, constitutional state would exact punishment against anyone who behaves as Abraham – just as today, Jehovah's Witnesses are punished for letting their children die rather than undergo a blood transfusion that they consider forbidden by God.

But does a critique of purely subjective religious claims not imply the negation of every theology? One misunderstands the great rationalists if one fails to see that almost every one of them desired to be a rational theologian: Descartes, Spinoza, Leibniz and Hegel are deeply religious men – all of whom hold the conviction that God is best served if one rejects an irrational form of religion. For God manifests himself most clearly through reason. (Hobbes himself considers faith in divine voices a remnant of pagan demonology; he would have considered Kierkegaard, who always emphasized that his philosophy alone offered an advance over the Greeks, to be much more pagan than all the rationalists.) One can deny the project of the rational theologians, but certainly not their subjective religiosity: the critique of a voluntarist account of God, put forth by Leibniz, Kant and Hegel, is grounded in both logical argument as well as the sense that a God who cannot be conceived by reason cannot be loved, only feared. In the text just quoted from Kant we find a very significant passage – the parenthesis around 'visible'. By this Kant wants to suggest that the true heaven is not of the sensible realm; the true heaven, in which God resides, is the moral law. We find God when we listen to the moral law, and any excuse that detracts from the latter is irreligious, even when (or perhaps exactly when) they lay claim to a divine command. Kant therefore describes the story of Abraham as a 'myth'. (Incidentally, I want to point out that in this short text Kant expresses a deep sympathy for Isaac, while Kierkegaard never attempts to see the matter from Isaac's perspective; that is, he does so only in his variations on the story, which do not deal with the biblical Isaac.)

Kant does not yet try to understand how Abraham could believe that Isaac must be sacrificed – in his eyes, Abraham is himself a victim of superstition. By contrast, Hegel has a strong historical interest in the psychology of Abraham, even though he dislikes

Can Abraham be Saved? Can Kierkegaard be Saved?

him. In the first part of the *Spirit of Christianity and its Fate*, sometimes called the 'Spirit of Judaism', Hegel attempts to approach Abraham's values and those of Judaism. According to Hegel's interpretation, its fanatic form of monotheism fears nothing more than loving something more than God; thus Abraham must prove to himself that he can kill Isaac.

> He could not love anything; the only love that he had, namely, to his son and hope of progeny – the only way to extend his being, the only way of immortality he knew of and hoped for – could depress him, disturb his mind, which detached itself from all, and unsettle it, which once went so far that he wanted to destroy even this love and was reassured only by the certainty of the feeling that this love was only as strong as to leave him with the capacity to slaughter with his own hand his beloved son. (I 279)

We will see that Hegel's historical-psychological interpretation cannot be viewed as correct. But one can probably say of Kierkegaard that he was in no position to love another human being, which explains why he was so fascinated by Abraham. Hegel was wrong about Abraham, but not with regard to Kierkegaard. Moreover, we see here the most important difference between Kant and Hegel: Kant seeks the universal, the divine in the moral law, while Hegel seeks the universal in the world-historical evolution. Kant's philosophy of religion is an ethical theology, while Hegel's is a speculative philosophy of history.

I began by showing that Kierkegaard's alternative is not original. We have already seen that the alternative can be resolved: Abraham, as Kierkegaard understands him, must be condemned (or be seen as a lowly, irresponsible fanatic). Kierkegaard's theory that the religious can defeat the ethical as well as the rational must be rejected. Every claim to validity must be justified by reason; whoever denies this destroys all communication among rational human beings. Kierkegaard knows this; he asserts that his theory cannot be disclosed; he writes under the pseudonym, 'Johannes de Silentio'. Why then does he write at all? I do not wish to pursue the question here whether the fact that Kierkegaard drafts his journals in a public language presupposes that his writings can be communicated. In any case, it is clear that *Fear and Trembling* (which was published as a book) presupposes this, and that a performative contradiction consists in trying to communicate that which cannot be communicated and thinking that which cannot be thought. Presumably, that is an argument against negative theology as well; but it is of utmost importance to realize that Kierkegaard's view does not belong to negative theology. This view contains (perhaps unconvincing) arguments for the theory that the Absolute cannot be determined. The Neoplatonists never would have accepted that a definite commandment such as 'sacrifice Isaac' could stand in relation to the Absolute – for the abstract Absolute cannot legitimize any action, at least not an action that contradicts fundamental moral principles. Kierkegaard wants much more than negative theology can offer – he wants to justify the absurd. But the idea of justification already presupposes certain principles of reason; justifying their negation is logically impossible. On a practical level, too, society would collapse if we took seriously the absolute relation of the individual to the Absolute. For, by definition, such a relation cannot be distinguished from madness. Once more Hegel:

> By appealing to his sentiment, his inward oracle, that person is done with in relation to the other who does not agree; he must aver that he has nothing further to say to the person who does not find and feel the same in himself; in other words, he treads upon the root of humanity. For its nature is to insist on agreements with others, and its existence consists only in the achieved community of consciousnesses. The anti-human, the beastly, consists in limiting oneself to the sentiment and in being able to communicate through it alone. (III 64 f.)

Kierkegaard is a philosopher who is not able to think transcendentally or justify his claims as valid. He constantly confuses psychological inquiry with the question of validity. His phenomenological capability is not tied to a transcendental consciousness. Nevertheless, every phenomenological analysis presupposes categories; and Kierkegaard derives his categories (which are the basis of his classifications) primarily from Hegel, but without wanting to accept the systematic context that ascribes meaning to these categories. He is not the only one to do this (Marx is another famous example); all the same, it is always risky to saw off the branch upon which one sits – it avenges itself.

Kierkegaard's theory that the religious is not simply the ethical is of course correct; there are plenty of moral individuals to be found who are not religious. But he wants to say something more: He believes that an action that is morally prohibited can be justified if it is a religious deed. Even though Kierkegaard is convinced that he is less modern than, say, Hegel, his belief in the independence of the religious is indicative of the tendency of modernity toward autonomy. Modern capitalism does not want the economy to be evaluated on the basis of ethics – business is business. Nor does the modern artist want his art to serve 'the Good' – *l'art pour l'art*. And modern science recognizes no objections made on ethical grounds alone. Likewise, the modern religious man seeks the absolute autonomy of religion.[17] Kierkegaard's doctrine of the different stages could at first glance be compared to Scheler's value ethics.[18] For Kierkegaard's notion of the 'aesthetic' corresponds to the 'pleasant' in Scheler's hierarchy of values; the ethical corresponds to the just, and the religious corresponds to the holy. However, there is a major difference here: Scheler's values are all *moral* values, and the conflict between them is tragic in the Hegelian and Kierkegaardian sense. This implies that an objective criterion exists that can determine when an inferior value must give way to a higher. Also, if Scheler's concept of the holy is not particularly clear, he of course never would have accepted Abraham's action. Apart from that, it is remarkable that Kierkegaard's third *Problema* still makes use of the expression 'ethically responsible'. In truth, this makes little sense, for we have already seen that Abraham's action transcends the ethical. Does Kierkegaard perhaps mean to say that he is responsible in a more than ethical sense? In any case, the fact that Kierkegaard employs the word 'ethical' is an indication of the absoluteness of ethics.

---

17 J. Hellesnes ('Det socialhygieniska tänkesättet', *Ord & Bild* 3 (1991), pp. 93–100) has recently analysed scientism, moralism and aestheticism as three consequences of this process of emancipation. Accordingly, Kierkegaard's view could be called 'religionism'.

18 See M. Scheler, *Der Formalismus und die materiale Wertethik*, 6th edition (Bern/München: Francke, 1980).

Veritas: Belief and Metaphysics

Kierkegaard has a rather peculiar concept of faith. It is not difficult to see that he is working with two different concepts. On the one hand faith (in the 'Preamble from the Heart') is the third stage, after the philistine mentality and infinite resignation. On the other hand, faith implies a readiness to act against reason. The first concept is clearly not identical to the second. In order to understand the deeper meaning of the first concept, we must use a broader concept of resignation than Kierkegaard does. Resignation can be understood as a tension between the ego and the world. This feeling is a necessary consequence of philosophy, since philosophy involves, first and foremost, placing a question mark behind everything which had hitherto never been doubted. The peculiar capacity for abstraction that a philosopher must possess makes it particularly difficult to find one's way back to the world. Nonetheless, there are a few philosophers who claim they have succeeded in doing so, not only in thought, but also in life. The philosopher who makes this claim most energetically is Hegel. His concept of reconciliation corresponds to Kierkegaard's first concept of faith. We cannot investigate here whether Hegel's system actually achieves reconciliation with the world. At the very least, one must admit that, if one understands Hegel correctly, one comes to understand a great deal of the world in all its abundance. But if one understands Kierkegaard correctly, one has an important and original insight into the soul's abyss, but little else – neither nature nor history is better understood. If we compare the lives of Hegel and Kierkegaard – for Kierkegaard competes with Hegel on an *existential* rather than *argumentative* level – we see on the one hand a man who has a family, who is integrated into his society, and who clearly has a passion for life, even if we hardly perceive him as superficial. On the other hand, we see a talented, but curmudgeonly man who could never find his way back into the world. Kierkegaard is the knight of resignation, and Hegel the knight of faith. One does not risk too much in supposing that, precisely because he rejects Kierkegaard's second concept of faith, Hegel could have been a believer in his own life (in the sense of Kierkegaard's first concept of faith).

With regard to the second concept it is obvious that the naïvely religious person is not a believer in this sense. Faith, which is opposed to reason, is a concept of reflection; that is to say, only the individual who has lost immediate religious trust can begin to say that he believes, but does not know. Kierkegaard's concept of faith is possible only as a reaction to rationalist theology and ethics. Historically speaking, it is absurd to assume that Abraham actually could have said, '*Credo, quia absurdum*'. Only he who suffers from his own negativity can idealize faith in this way, as Kierkegaard does. The relation between Abraham and God cannot be called faith in Kierkegaard's sense; this relation is indeed more basic than the difference between faith and reason. We must therefore say that Kierkegaard's concept of faith is not only philosophically absurd, but historically absurd as well. One need not have studied hermeneutics to get the feeling that, between the Old Testament and Kierkegaard, or indeed, even between the New Testament and Kierkegaard, there lies an abyss – an abyss created by modern subjectivity.

It is of utmost importance that Kierkegaard does not claim to be historically accurate. Not only does he lack any historical inclination, he is also aware of this. He writes on several occasions that he has no interest in discussing the possibility that Abraham's deed might have a different interpretation within his own milieu than it would have in our day and age.

> Or perhaps Abraham simply didn't do what the story says, perhaps in the context of his times what he did was something quite different. Then let's forget him, for why bother remembering a past that cannot be made into a present. (30/60; 33, 50, 67)

Of course, Kierkegaard's critique of historicism is in a certain sense justified: one can learn from Lessing, Kant and Hegel that the historical problem of whether what is stated in the Bible actually took place is not important in answering the question of whether Christianity is relevant for us. The past must become the present – one must recognize, along with Hegel and Kierkegaard, that this is so. This does not imply, however, that we may read into the text only what we already feel or believe – such an interpretation would be historically false and systematically superficial: so much can already be gleaned from Spinoza's critique of Maimonides.[19] We

---

19 See *Tractatus theologico-politicus*, Ch. 7, 15.

need both: first, we must attempt, by way of historical method, to understand what is intended by the Bible's authors (or by the people about whom they narrate); then, we must try to find a meaning therein. Kierkegaard never attempts the first task. He finds in the story of Abraham something which keeps him constantly occupied, namely, his sacrifice of Regine. For that reason, Abraham (who likely would have had little appreciation for a modern existence such as Kierkegaard) can be seen as a precursor to Kierkegaard. I think along with Hegel that a historicist philosophy of religion is much worse than a speculative philosophy of religion; yet there is something still worse than what historicists have done — namely, Kierkegaard's approach. For even if the historicists do not rise to the universal that is given in reason, they at least find their way into the universal element of a culture's past; Kierkegaard, however, grasps only his own subjectivity. The twofold attack which Kierkegaard wages in *Philosophical Fragments* against both historicist and speculative philosophy of religion cannot be won,[20] even if the absolute individual naturally fails to recognize this, and instead despises those who cannot accept his doctrine: for being the absolute individual means rendering oneself immune to every form of criticism. I cannot give an analysis of the *Philosophical Fragments* here, but I would like to say that in a certain sense of the term Kierkegaard proceeds far more aprioristically than Hegel (or Spinoza); for Hegel knows that the correct historical interpretation often differs from the concept of speculative philosophy. Kierkegaard, on the other hand, claims to be able to discover actual historical truth in his own subjectivity (despite his repeated reminders that he is not interested in factual history). Kierkegaard commits the same error for which he reproaches both Socrates and Hegel: overestimating the value of

---

20 The fundamental contradiction in *Philosophical Fragments* consists in the fact that on the one hand Kierkegaard wants to defend historical facticity from the autonomy of reason, which, on the other hand, he has to use to attack historicism. 'It immediately becomes obvious that the historical in a more concrete sense is indifferent' (VI 56). But if it is truly the case that God could not favour anyone in a particular time, those who lived before Christ must have had the possibility of knowing God. Kierkegaard's ahistorical Christianity has substantially less content than Hegel's reconstruction in the *Lectures on the Philosophy of Religion*.

anamnesis and failing to come out of oneself. He never attempts to understand a historical figure as something different from modern subjectivity – even though this might have helped him understand himself better than the way in which he continuously revolves around himself.

The critique published in *The Corsair* is simply vindictive. But the famous caricature undeniably makes an important point: that the whole world revolves around Kierkegaard. F. W. Korff's ironic book, *Der komische Kierkegaard*,[21] fails to acknowledge Kierkegaard's greatness; but he is correct to point out that there is something grotesque to be found in Kierkegaard's attempt to use (or misuse) God, Abraham and many others to justify his problematic relationship with Regine. As with Rousseau and Nietzsche, Kierkegaard is one of those philosophers who cherish speaking about themselves; and one does not deny subjectivity all its rights if one prefers those philosophers who are more discreet, who lose themselves in their work, and who immerse themselves in the riches of a world that is far greater than even the most interesting modern subjectivity. (Indeed, Kierkegaard is without a doubt far more fascinating than the caricatures of him that we find in our century.) He himself writes: 'For he who loves God without faith reflects upon himself, while the person who loves God with faith reflects on God' (35/66). If this is true, one must say that Spinoza and Hegel love God faithfully, *but not Kierkegaard.*

One can regard Kierkegaard's view as morality in the Hegelian sense – he avoids traditional mores because he finds them banal and superficial. But he offers no rational alternative, aside from the claim that his own subjectivity is true. This position is immoral, even though Kierkegaard does not aim at mere pleasure, and even though he himself suffers most from a sense of isolation which is the necessary consequence of his critique of both history and rationality. But suffering does not imply that one is in the right – an inner joy is also expected, especially from a Christian, but which is conspicuously absent in Kierkegaard. It is clear that the absolute individual can never love another, or himself, since he has destroyed a necessary condition for intersubjectivity – that is, *rationality.* Even if Kierkegaard recognizes the 'deep secret', that

---

21 Stuttgart/Bad Cannstatt: Frommann-Holzboog, 1982.

'in loving another one should be sufficient unto oneself' (42/73), he nonetheless praises Abraham as 'great in that love which is hatred of self' (18/50). And it is but all too evident that Kierkegaard himself was great in exactly this kind of love. Jean Wahl's application of Hegel's category of the unhappy consciousness to Kierkegaard is well known;[22] and one can very well regard Kierkegaard as a far better example of the kind of psychological structure analysed in *The Phenomenology of Spirit* than the medieval Christianity which Hegel had in mind (III 163 ff.).

I want to say, therefore, that continuity between Kierkegaard and the major Christian tradition is hardly discernible: Christianity of the Middle Ages was far removed from Kierkegaard, both emotionally and intellectually. The view, *credo quia absurdum*, is found among only a few philosophers, even if not all of them were radical rationalists like Raimundus Lullus. A story Lullus tells in his autobiography can be described as 'anti-Kierkegaardian' *par excellence*.[23] He decides to travel to North Africa with the aim of converting Muslims, but at the last moment, he does not follow through with his intention. His failures plunge him into a deep, psychosomatic crisis; he believes he will die and thus requests holy communion. But then he hears a divine voice which instructs him otherwise, for in his sinful state he would only profane the holy sacrament. But Lullus deliberates the matter further and reaches the conclusion that he would appear a heretic if he died without having taken communion; and this would have a negative effect on the fate of all the books he had written with the intention of saving many souls. Thus he takes communion nevertheless, in spite of the fact that the voice becomes audible to him again and adds that he would face damnation for doing so. Lullus later interprets the voice as a temptation from God: and in choosing the redemption of others' souls over his own, he passed the test. Had he obeyed the voice, he would have demonstrated merely a radical religious egoism. Following reason rather than a voice that commands

---

22 J. Wahl, *Etudes Kierkegaardiennes* (Paris: F. Aubier, 1938).
23 See my analysis of the *Vita coaetanea* in my introduction to: R. Lullus, *Die neue Logik. Logica Nova*, ed. with textual criticism by Ch. Lohr, translated by V. Hösle and W. Büchel with an introduction by V. Hösle (Hamburg: Felix Meiner Verlag, 1985).

Can Abraham be Saved? Can Kierkegaard be Saved?

unreasonable things, is the greatest expression of religiosity. No doubt Lullus would have judged Kierkegaard to be someone who acts contrary to the essence of Christianity.

Also, if we analyse Kierkegaard's life, it is much easier to find a rather demonic element in his thinking than something of a distinctly Christian character. Kierkegaard belongs to those philosophers of the nineteenth century who feel that Christianity risks growing listless, and who, in their sincere character, can no longer bear the hypocritical culture of their day, a culture which is no longer Christian, but which still parades itself as such. Nietzsche belongs to this group as well, though the conclusions he draws stand in opposition to those of Kierkegaard. Juan Donoso Cortés might also be mentioned in this context. But Donoso Cortés, the great Spanish Catholic reactionary (1809–53), was at the same time very much active in the social sphere. In a state of grim despair over the crisis of Christianity, he worked tirelessly to fulfil Christ's commandment to the needy. Charity in him has something of a compulsive character. But Donoso Cortés is to be admired, while Kierkegaard's discourse on love comes across as compensation for a personality whose narcissism renders it impossible to assume responsibility for another. Christianity is a religion in which intersubjectivity plays a major role. Kierkegaard, who holds little interest for the social and political concerns of his day, hardly maintains any intersubjective relation aside from his relation with his father and Regine. With Kierkegaard, subjectivity destroys intersubjectivity: since one can never know whether another has faith (VI 93), a religious community is essentially impossible. Finally, Kierkegaard's battle against the Church demonstrates his lack of recognition for the moral duties which he ascribes to his Faust. While it is reasonable to insist that duty to truth be mediated by a duty to society, Kierkegaard attacks without any sense of tact the religious sentiments of individuals who could not afford his luxuriant subjectivity on account of their other responsibilities.

Kierkegaard's God belongs more to the Old Testament than the New; at any rate, his God is no *Deus caritatis*.

Can Abraham be Saved?

The last words in Ibsen's *Brand* are, as is well known, deeply ambiguous. On the one hand, they indicate that Brand's God is not the true God, and in a certain sense they are a condemnation of his life. On the other hand, it is clear that a God, understood as a *deus caritatis*, could not condemn; he must understand and recognize even those who are not capable of loving as he loves. We must therefore try to understand both Abraham as well as Kierkegaard better than we have done so far; if we are to be satisfied with our interpretation, Abraham must become something more than a murderer, Kierkegaard something more than a narcissist.

We want to accompany Abraham and Isaac once again to Mount Moriah. What takes place there is perhaps more important for the history of the relation of humans to God and God to humans than either Kant or Hegel believed. Along with Kierkegaard, we want to assume that this journey has a meaning for the modern individual, and indeed for all individuals. But in order to discover this meaning, one must avoid two of Kierkegaard's mistakes: we must adhere to the notion that human sacrifice can never be justified, and that God could never have commanded such a thing. We must recognize, moreover, that previous cultures could have held values different from our own, even though all cultures share common values as well. Kant's moral philosophy and Vico's philosophy of history should be the eyes through which we perceive this mythical journey.

Today we are experienced in reconstructing the past of humankind. Thus it cannot be at all surprising to suppose that Abraham can only be understood if we go beyond the text of the Bible, for the period in which the Elohist writes is long after that in which the sacrifice must have taken place;[24] and it is only likely that his interpretation does not capture what the real figure in an even more distant past must have intended to do.[25] Abraham, rather

---

24 For the sources of the Old Testament see, for example, W. H. Schmidt, *Einführung in das Alte Testament* (Berlin/New York: de Gruyter, 1979).

25 Cf. *Das Alte Testament Deutsch*, ... ed. by A. Weiser, Volume 2/4: Das erste Buch Mose. Genesis, translated and explained by G. von Rad,

than the Elohist (whom Kierkegaard perhaps did not interpret so incorrectly), should be our primary interest. In his novel, *Joseph and His Brothers*, Thomas Mann presents one of the most fascinating approaches to the Old Testament, whose psychological and metaphysical interpretation inspires my present analysis. Of course, we cannot know whether a person by the name of Abraham actually existed; we cannot rule out that he is a *universale fantastico* in Vico's sense of the term, in other words, that many historical personalities and many historical events are wrapped up into one literary figure. Mann's *Höllenfahrt* can bring us into that very mindset which we need in order to understand that this in no way detracts from the value of our story, but rather increases it.

In order to understand what must have taken place in the history of the Jewish religion, we must recall that human sacrifice was a common practice in almost all archaic cultures, and that the sacrifice of one's own children was quite widespread in Semitic culture – in Carthage, for example, it was practised up until the time of the Romans.[26] Even if such a practice cannot be justified, we do not want to overlook the idea of a deep moral truth manifesting itself in this terrible institution. Las Casas already understood that human sacrifice is not an expression of contempt for human life.[27] Quite the contrary: precisely because life is the

---

9th edition (Göttingen: Vandenhoeck & Ruprecht, 1972), pp. 188–194: 22, pp. 1–19, esp. 189: 'Auch diese Erzählung – die formvollendetste und abgründigste aller Vätergeschichten – hat nur einen sehr lockeren Anschluß an das Vorhergegangene und läßt schon daran erkennen, daß sie gewiß lange Zeit ihre Existenz für sich hatte, ehe sie ihren Ort in dem großen Erzählungswerk des Elohisten gefunden hat. So steht also auch hier der Ausleger vor jener nicht unkomplizierten Doppelaufgabe: Er muß einerseits den Sinngehalt der alten selbständigen Erzählung ermitteln, dann aber natürlich auch der schon verhältnismäßig früh vollzogenen gedanklichen Verbindung mit einem ganzen Komplex von Abrahamsgeschichten Rechnung tragen.'

26 Von Rad writes: 'Es mag deutlich geworden sein, daß die Erzählung in ihrer mutmaßlichen ältesten Fassung die Kultsage eines Heiligtums war, und als solche hat sie die Auslösung eines eigentlich von der Gottheit geforderten Kinderopfers durch ein Tieropfer legitimiert.' (193) Cf. Exodus 34.19 f.

27 See Las Casas, *In Defense of the Indians*, translated, edited and

greatest good, it is offered up to the gods; and precisely because one's own children are most precious, they are slaughtered. Only through fear and trembling, which the sacrifice sustains, can an archaic society overcome the centrifugal forces that threaten it – that is Vico's sociological interpretation. But on the moral level, it is equally clear that the sacrifice of something one loves is the clearest proof that one is not dependent on external factors, that one can separate oneself from the world. Without this capacity, a human being can hardly mature. A culture that has lost all sacrificial traditions has lost a central feature of humanity, and it is certainly important that such a culture be reminded of Abraham.

But if Abraham had only complied with the command to slaughter Isaac, he would not have been any more interesting than the Phoenician or Aztec fathers who did the same. He would have been a representative of archaic mores that we would regard, along with Hegel, Vico and Durkheim, with a certain sympathy if our disgust for modern subjectivity had become too strong. But his values would not be our own; and even the critics of morality must realize that there is something greater than traditional conduct within given mores. What is this 'something greater'? It is a conduct that overcomes earlier, more primitive mores and makes way for newer and better ones. Abraham is an example of precisely that; he is the first in a line of biblical figures characterized by inspired moral renovation – here we might think of the prophets, and last but not least, of Christ. Abraham can and must be admired, not because he was willing to sacrifice Isaac, but because he was the first to *abolish* the custom of sacrifice.

How, then, are we to understand the voice that initially commands Abraham to sacrifice Isaac, and subsequently, to spare him? After Hobbes, Spinoza and Vico, it is clear that the voice is not to be interpreted as an objective, acoustic phenomenon. (Kierkegaard himself once attempted to give a psychological explanation of the miracle of Isaac's birth.) Nor is it to be understood as some form of deception. And lastly, it would miss the point altogether if the voice were described as a subjective illusion. Insofar as the archaic individual hears God, he hears the moral law; and this has a much

---

annotated by S. Poole (De Kalb: Northern Illinois University Press, 1974), pp. 221 ff., esp. 234. Las Casas speaks expressly of Abraham.

higher reality than daydreams. On the long journey to Mount Moriah (lasting perhaps a thousand years), Abraham (or the various Abrahams) must have developed the profound belief that God could not will the sacrifice of an innocent child. The man who discovers a higher concept of God also enters a higher level of human moral development. He does not err in believing that he hears the voice of God; for the moral development of humanity is not merely subjective; in it, something manifests itself that is greater than a psychological phenomenon, namely, the moral law. The archaic individual can experience its objectivity only as an external power. But how terrible must have been the painful uncertainty over whether it was actually God renouncing the sacrifice due to him, or whether this renunciation was in fact a temptation. It is no simple matter to be a moral innovator, and it is likely even more difficult if the new voice suggests that which one secretly desires. Only someone with a deep loyalty to the other aspects of his mores could have attempted to do away with human sacrifice – only he who knows obedience can be taken seriously when he claims to have heard a new voice.

Why, then, does Abraham warrant more than a purely historical interest? Thank God human sacrifice is no longer practised today, and thus this history could be consigned to the past. But even if one considers this concrete question resolved, the conflict between the mores of a society and new moral commandments is eternal, for no society can realize everything that the moral law commands. In relation to this conflict, we must acknowledge that Kierkegaard grasps several ethical problems neglected by rationalist ethics, even if they do not constitute a general argument against rationalism. A rationalist ethics (as, for example, discourse ethics) insists on the universal, on the importance of discussion, and on what in Kantian terms can be referred to as the 'capacity of publicity'.[28] And as we have seen, it is true that whatever cannot in principle be communicated cannot be true. One should openly discuss ethical issues in order to find solutions to them. But that which discourse ethics does not fully appreciate – and what Kierkegaard over-appreciates – is that situations exist in which it is impossible (whether factually or ethically) to discuss publicly what should be done. I will not

---

28 Kant, *Zum Ewigen Frieden*, VIII 381.

attempt here to offer a typology of such situations; I will only mention the most important case – namely, when paradigmatic mores are no longer perceived as adequate by a developed moral conscience. One can certainly suppose that the old paradigm will be criticized from a number of persons at once; but it is not unthinkable that only one individual can be found who already stands on the ground of a higher paradigm. There must, of course, be objective arguments for the innovator's view – otherwise he would not be a moral revolutionary, but merely a dangerous criminal, or at best a mad narcissist. That does not mean, however, that he can discuss his insights with others. Nor does it mean that he has developed for himself a precise argument for his point of view – perhaps he has only a moral feeling that could later be articulated as an argument, but is not yet in a position to be developed in rational form. In this situation – and *only* this – can we speak of the absolute relation of the individual to the Absolute. The Absolute remains the universal and the rational; but it is the universal with respect to a future community, and with respect to rational argumentation – not, however, with respect to the norms of contemporary culture. Thus, the individual is completely alone, and it is no doubt an agonizing struggle he has with himself in which he gains the consciousness that he is right – 'To contend with the whole world is a comfort, but to contend with oneself dreadful' (102/138; 46). In terms of understanding the existential situation of this individual, Kierkegaard is of greater help to us than Kant – even if Kant alone manages to establish the objectivity of ethics.

I have already mentioned that the moral innovators, at least at the beginning of the history of our moral consciousness, could not have advanced any rational argument. Nonetheless, without them the moral never would have been raised to the level upon which ethical argument is made possible; and if we want to immerse ourselves in their moral struggle, we will always fall back on the Bible. Even if one does not believe in a verbal inspiration of the Bible, one must appreciate the fact that likely no other text contains so many splendid descriptions of the moral innovators' struggles. The Prophets are the most well known; but Abraham is the first to experience such a struggle, and his story will always empower those who feel that the mores of their culture stand in need of radical reform.

Can Abraham be Saved? Can Kierkegaard be Saved?

Can Kierkegaard be Saved?

It is not difficult to guess what Kierkegaard's objection to our reconstruction of moral history would be. He could well make the following criticism (not to mention many others): we seem to presuppose a moral superiority over Abraham in so far as we speak of a *development* of moral consciousness. But this is exactly the kind of thinking that Kierkegaard would not tolerate.

On one hand, Kierkegaard is mistaken. Vico and Hegel are not wrong in supposing that different cultures hold different values, and that not all of these values can be equally rational. There is progress in human mores, and it would be absurd to deny that the institutions and values that are realized in the modern constitutional state are 'higher' or 'better' than those which existed in Abraham's day. On the other hand, Kierkegaard suggests something of utmost importance, something which offers a key to properly understanding the rational core of his critique of Hegel. Even if, these days, every philistine adopts certain values that Abraham neither knew nor respected, it would be absurd, indeed blasphemous, to claim that the philistine is a greater moral character than Abraham. For if we evaluate the morality of a person, we not only analyse his or her behaviour, we must also situate those behaviours in the context of their respective culture. And the moral innovator is always more noble than his epigones, even though the latter adapt themselves more quickly to the new values than he himself could do, since he had first to discover them. Moral values are not only a function of a culture, they are perhaps even more the result of a subjective appropriation. Since those who are born at a later time enjoy the advantage of becoming familiar with higher ethical values earlier, they are far less dependent on the subjective work of appropriation; and precisely this is not only an opportunity, but rather a grave danger. For no one can relieve the individual of the subjective moral appropriation. For this reason, a later culture loses its superiority if, being proud of its superiority, it neglects the subjective appropriation. If the individual does not reiterate the *phylogenesis* in his *ontogenesis*, he can become no better than his predecessors, only the caricature of them. Reaching a decision after a prolonged struggle for particular values is not the same as donning oneself superficially with them; and if those who come later content themselves with the latter, they have no place to speak of progress.

> What then is education? I had thought it was the curriculum the individual ran through in order to catch up with himself; and anyone who does not want to go through this curriculum will be little helped by being born into the most enlightened age. (44/75)

Kierkegaard diagnoses precisely this situation in his own time. Even if his critique of Hegel is misguided from an existential point of view (for the young Hegel went through a phase of deep despair), one cannot doubt that the claim made by most Hegelians – that an absolute insight lies at their disposal – is in no way mediated by their existence, and therefore *grotesque* (92). One understands Kierkegaard's criticism of each and every professor who lectured on the meaning of doubt without taking on any intellectual or personal risk (58, 99), and it is certainly right to distinguish between Descartes, who must have expended a great deal of effort to carry out his methodical doubt, and his epigones (9f.).

> Conventional wisdom aims presumptuously to introduce into the world of spirit that same law of indifference under which the outside world groans. It believes it is enough to have knowledge of large truths. No other work is necessary. But then it does not get bread, it starves to death while everything is transformed to gold. (27/57–8)

It is much more important to ward off the confusion between the subjective appropriation of Christianity's commandments and the cultural Protestantism of Kierkegaard's time. Even if Martensen was on to something when he wrote that Christianity was our second nature,[29] Kierkegaard's critique hits upon an important point: that faith cannot be naturalized, and that the convictions of our society cannot replace the subjective choices for or against Christianity (VI 86 f.). To choose Christianity for oneself means

---

29 H. L. Martensen's text, which Kierkegaard criticizes in *Philosophical Fragments*, is called *Den christelige Daab* (København: Reitzel, 1843).

more than simply growing up in a Christian society (not to mention a society which can no longer be called Christian). This insight from Kierkegaard is the basis of dialectical theology. Admittedly, the dialectic between morality and mores constitutes one of the fundamental reasons why dialectical theology has nowadays become a part of the cultural Protestant tradition – one can of course cite Kierkegaard and Barth with the same absurd pompousness with which Hegel and Schleiermacher were treated after they had become established fixtures of our culture. Subjectivity is not the truth, but beyond my own subjectivity the truth can never be a truth *for me*. Kierkegaard is wrong to deny that human subjectivity is always a part of a culture; but he and all the existentialists are correct in pointing out that something exists which can never be undertaken by another, not even by the most advanced of cultures. *I* am the one who must always take a stance on truth, even if the truth can only be considered truth if there are objective arguments for it.

But Kierkegaard does not suggest simply that understanding something entails more than being aware of what others have said about it. He suggests also that even the deepest subjective understanding is by itself not yet sufficient. With this point we leave off Kierkegaard's critique of the Hegelians and turn to his critique of Hegel himself. While his central criticism that a concrete existence cannot be integrated into a system is certainly correct, it is also superficial. It was never Hegel's intention to systematize all contingencies relevant to an individual's existence, even if he never denies that the universal must exist as the individual. Hegel is convinced, along with Plato and Aristotle, that science and philosophy deal only with the universal. However, he knows, of course, that a universal characteristic of existence is to exist as individual. As a philosopher, Hegel would have lacked the patience to analyse Kierkegaard's concrete psychological problems, though he likely would have learned to appreciate his more general views. All the same, Kierkegaard recognizes a problem that Hegel could not resolve. Hegel is principally a defender of theoretical life; that is, for him the best approach to reality is the theoretical, contemplative approach. According to Hegel, the philosopher has withdrawn from the struggles of the world, transformed reality into theoretical propositions, and no longer needs to dwell on the question, 'what ought I to do?', but rather contents himself in discovering rationality in reality. Kierkegaard never realizes that this approach is a result of Hegel's theological premises (and that his own existentialism is more compatible with an atheist perspective than a theist): if the world is God's creation, it cannot be chaotic, but must be understood as a cosmos; nor can the historical world lack a hidden logic which transcends the intentions of active human beings. But even if one cannot deny that Hegel's (and Leibniz's) approach to the world is a justifiable position, it goes without saying that it is not the *only* possible position. We must also *live* in this world; we must shape it and form it without knowing beforehand the purpose that our actions serve in God's world-plan. Hegel abandons us if we attempt to live as finite beings with respect to a future unknown to us; for Hegel thinks only of the past. If we want to live 'forwards', the notion will not suffice; without *passion*, the concept is powerless. Philosophy cannot be content with mere retrospection; philosophy must be more than a theoretical approach. This is obvious in the case of ethics: the grounding of moral norms cannot replace the task of their appropriation; to have given a speculative justification of Christianity does not imply that one has become a Christian. The existential struggle is more than mere comprehension, even if without the effort of the concept it can only be untruth.

With this insight, Kierkegaard takes up one of the central convictions of Greek philosophy. Plato withholds his esoteric doctrine because he believes it would be lost on those whose personalities are not formed in a certain way; and in general, the Greek schools of philosophy always wanted to be more than just sites for learning true propositions. Plato writes dialogues in order to show what *kind* of individual one must be in order to understand certain truths. Plato does not explicitly instruct – not because he thought that truth could not be articulated propositionally, but because he was convinced that this manner of grasping truth would be of little help to anyone. Only if I discover truth for myself, by thinking through the interlocutors' arguments and considering the relation between these arguments and the characters defending them, can I appropriate truth. Philosophy discusses explicitly that which art suggests; but only by pointing out what a theoretical position holds for a person's own life can art motivate us to become one with philosophical truth. Perhaps we can say that, with Plato, one still finds a unity in that which for Hegel and Kierkegaard is distinct: Hegel represents objectivity, Kierkegaard subjectivity. The divine Plato develops a philosophy that does not appear to differ much from Hegel's in terms of its content, but in a form that is taken up again by Kierkegaard.

A great deal of modernity becomes intelligible, then, if one understands that Plato's synthesis is no longer possible. There exists a yawning abyss between the existential relationship of a disciple that links Socrates and Plato and the business-like structure of our philosophical institutions, and there is good reason to fear that the ideal of equality will gradually displace the education of character. Kierkegaard's (as well as Nietzsche's) existence is a deeply felt protest against this tendency. The end result of this tendency would be a culture that no longer knows what it means to be serious, a culture whose representatives lose sight of what it means to sacrifice themselves. Only by sacrificing himself could Kierkegaard wage a battle against this development – and not only by his teachings, but also by his existence. Only as an unhappy consciousness could Kierkegaard allow his creativity to unfold and say that which he can and must say better than all others. Regine was sacrificed, not on the altar of an irrational God, but on the altar of absolute Spirit; and indeed, on the basis of the simple truth that marriage is not always compatible with a creative life – even more so if the central idea of this life is sacrifice. Whether Kierkegaard's breaking of his engagement can be justified is not an easy question to answer. Nevertheless, one must recognize that Kierkegaard never stops loving Regine; few lovers have dedicated such a great literary-philosophical monument to their beloved with such loyalty.[30] Romantic subjectivity has found no greater expression than in Kierkegaard – therefore he too can be redeemed in the universal. For it is the universal itself that recognizes that truth must be reconciled with subjectivity.

---

30 This text was originally delivered as a lecture at the University of Oslo on 11 July 1991. In discussions after the lecture, Egil Wyller emphasized the importance of Kierkegaard's *Works of Love* in better understanding his concept of love.

11. From Copenhagen to Cambrai: Paradoxes of Faith in Kierkegaard and de Lubac

ERIC LEE

The concept of the paradox has a long history. For the purposes of this chapter, I will examine the role of paradox in the last two centuries as articulated in the works of Søren Kierkegaard and Henri de Lubac. Both wrote at length about the ironies, absurdities, and paradoxes of life while directing their audiences to the paradox of the God-Man in Jesus Christ to whom one looks to make a kind of 'sense' out of all these paradoxes. Christ is not received merely for the sake of resolving lacunae but is the one to whom one looks in *faith* with one's heart, soul and mind. As I will attempt to show, it is the paradox that, when completely entered into by faith, lifts the person up into the fullness of existence.

I will assess the critical diagnoses of Kierkegaard's and de Lubac's (and our own) times, show corresponding sympathies between their thought, and demonstrate that, despite the historical distance from these thinkers and from the historical event of Christ, contemporaneity with Christ by faith is that which draws the human into the mystery of the paradox. First, it may be helpful to describe definitions of the paradox in Kierkegaard and de Lubac before moving on to their individual critical accounts.

Paradoxes of Faith in Kierkegaard and de Lubac

Paradox: Peering into Existence

Paradoxes are on the one hand ineffable, yet on the other hand one knows that they are so. Roy Sorensen has said that, 'Paradoxes are questions . . . that suspend us between *too many* good answers.'[1] There is a kind of 'buoyancy'[2] that holds up the two poles of the equation in such a way that the arresting 'symmetry'[3] prevents certainty from ceasing the quest for answers. This may be because the journey itself, according to Sorensen, is in the questions.[4]

The paradox presents itself as such because it is contrary to reason alone. It is a contradiction; it is absurd. The contradiction is that with which one wrestles. One must not look down upon it, for this absurdity is not pitiable. Instead, it is that which drives our passions.[5] Kierkegaard, writing pseudonymously as Johannes Climacus, articulates the ultimate paradox of thought as the desire 'to discover something that thought itself cannot think'.[6] But what if, in the interruption of one's passions, one *does* look down upon the paradox?

---

1 Roy Sorensen, *A Brief History of the Paradox: Philosophy and the Labyrinths of the Mind* (New York: Oxford University Press, 2003), p. xii.

2 Sorensen, *Brief History*, p. 4.

3 Sorensen, *Brief History*, p. 5; cf. Henri de Lubac, *Paradoxes of Faith*, trans. Ernest Beaumont (San Francisco: Ignatius Press, 1987), p. 11.

4 Sorensen, *Brief History*, p. xi.

5 Søren Kierkegaard, *Philosophical Fragments*, ed. and trans. Howard V. and Edna H. Hong (Princeton: Princeton University Press, 1985), p. 37.

6 Kierkegaard, *Fragments*, p. 37. Curiously, despite Wittgenstein's penchant for *not* reading previous philosophers, in the preface to his *Tractatus Logico-Philosophicus*, trans. D. F. Pears and B. F. McGuiness (London: Routledge, 1978), he says, 'The book will, therefore, draw a limit to thinking, or rather – not to thinking, but to the expression of thoughts; for in order to draw a limit to thinking we should have to be able to think both sides of this limit (we should therefore have to be able to *think what cannot be thought*)' (p. 3, emphasis mine). True, this phrase may have been inspired from Kierkegaard after all, as a letter from Bertrand Russell to Ottoline Morrell insinuates. Ray Monk, *How to Read Wittgenstein* (New York: W. W. Norton & Company, 2005), p. 24 says that Russell 'was astonished when I found he has become a complete mystic. He reads people like Kierkegaard and Angelus Silesius, and he seriously contemplates becoming a monk.'

Veritas: Belief and Metaphysics

When the understanding between the person and the paradox ceases to be mutually received, then the absurd is no longer a cause for wonder but a cause for offence.[7] But is this the fault of paradox? Climacus resolutely says 'no': 'all offense is in its essence a misunderstanding of *the moment*, since it is indeed offense at the paradox, and the paradox in turn is the moment.'[8] In other words, the offence is not contained within the paradox; it remains outside of it, in relation to it.[9] If offence resided within the paradox, and it was offended at itself, the paradox could not exist as a suspension of two opposing poles; it would implode upon itself. To impose upon the paradox internal antagonism[10] is to parody its essence, and to do so would only flow out of and reveal one's own offence. 'The offense remains outside the paradox – no wonder, since the paradox is the wonder.'[11]

Reading 'objective' accounts of the paradox such as Sorensen's, one is often left with befuddling impressions, or the hope placed in 'progress' that will eventually solve present and past paradoxes in a new, unforeseen horizon.[12] Henri de Lubac, by contrast, says,

> Paradox is the search or wait for synthesis. It is the provisional expression of a view which remains incomplete, but whose orientation is ever towards fullness. Paradox has more charm than dialectics; it is also more realist and more modest, less tense and less hurried; its function is to remind the dialectician when each new stage is reaching the argument, that however necessary

---

7 Kierkegaard, *Fragments*, p. 49.
8 Kierkegaard, *Fragments*, p. 51.
9 Kierkegaard, *Fragments*, p. 52. Cf. Søren Kierkegaard, *Concluding Unscientific Postscript to* Philosophical Fragments, ed. and trans. Howard V. and Edna H. Hong (Princeton: Princeton University Press, 1992), p. 205: '... the eternal, essential truth is itself not at all a paradox, but it is a paradox by being related to an existing person.'
10 I would argue that the penal atonement theory does this as it pits the Father against the Son.
11 Kierkegaard, *Fragments*, p. 205. See also, p 65: 'But then is faith just as paradoxical as the paradox? Quite so. How else could it have its object in the paradox and be happy in its relation to it? Faith itself is a wonder, and everything that is true of the paradox is also true of faith.'
12 See Sorensen, *Brief History*, pp. 369–71.

this forward movement is *no real progress has been made*. As the scholars of old say, in a rather different sense, of eternal life itself, we are ever going from 'beginnings to beginnings'.[13]

Furthermore for de Lubac, 'Paradoxes are paradoxical: they make sport of the usual and reasonable rule of not being allowed to be *against* as well as *for* ... They do not sin against logic, whose laws remain inviolable: but they escape its domain.'[14] The fulfillment of the paradox, as in many of de Lubac's other themes, exists outside of the confines in which one speaks of the contradiction, always drawing creation toward the thing-in-itself of the paradox. This object, which is the object of faith, is the 'supreme Paradox' of the incarnation.[15]

However one attempts to analyse this faith, fuelled by a passion that can only remain in suspense between the two poles of nature and grace, Creator and creature,[16] culminating in God and humanity in the God-Man of Jesus Christ as the ultimate paradox, one will come to see that any dissolution of either side of the paradox leads to a legion of disintegrations in the form of foundationalisms, unnecessary certainties and heresies.

Paradox in Kierkegaard: Passion and Dissolution

Historically, when it has pertained to faith in Christ, to lean in any one direction concerning the paradox of the hypostatic union has led anywhere from Docetism on the one side of the 'equation' to Socianism on the other.[17] Kierkegaard, speaking from within his

---

13 De Lubac, *Paradoxes of Faith*, pp. 9–10, emphasis mine.

14 De Lubac, *Paradoxes of Faith*, pp. 11–12.

15 De Lubac, *Paradoxes of Faith*, p. 8. See also, p. 10: 'Paradoxes the word specifies, above all, then, things themselves, not the way of saying them.'

16 Dietrich Bonhoeffer, *Cost of Discipleship* (New York: Simon and Schuster, 1995), p. 298: 'God saw himself in Adam. Here, right from the beginning, is the mysterious paradox of man. He is a creature, and yet he is destined to be like his Creator. Created man is destined to bear the image of uncreated God. Adam is "as God". His destiny is to bear his mystery in gratitude and obedience towards his Maker.'

17 Cf. de Lubac, *The Mystery of the Supernatural*, pp. 167–8, 175.

birth-city of Copenhagen, was able to provide incisive critiques of what he observed in the cultural elites and academia[18] around him as well as the pervading Christendom that also tended to pull against the symmetry of the paradox.[19] It is notable that Kierkegaard concerned himself with the wide-ranging critiques of Hegelianism and Christendom, the critiques of 'objectivity' (vs. subjectivity), and with the 'occasion', the 'moment', and the 'halt' in which these dialectical expressions 'infinitely change everything'.[20]

These three emphases are intricately woven together within Kierkegaard's works. Contained within his critique of Hegelian thought lies a profound upholding of the subjective individual against world-historical process.[21] Similarly contained within his critique of 'objectivity' lies a strong regard for the utmost subjective truth, and within the 'moment' is the depth of the infinite as seen in the paradox that keeps the subject in dialectical suspension.

This truth, when one is in untruth,[22] can not be sought after – for

---

18 To professors, see Kierkegaard, *Fragments*, p. 38, n.3: 'Take the paradox away from a thinker – and you have a professor. A professor has at his disposal a whole line of thinkers from Greece to modern times; it appears as if the professor stood above all of them. Well, many thanks – he is, of course, the infinitely inferior.' To philosophers, see *Fragments*, pp. 123ff, esp. 164–5.

19 See Søren Kierkegaard, *Practice in Christianity*, ed. Howard V. and Edna H. Hong (Princeton: Princeton University Press, 1992). Also see Søren Kierkegaard, *Either/Or*, ed. and trans. Howard V. and Edna H. Hong (Princeton: Princeton University Press, 1987), p. 283: 'Just as God mocks the greatness of men by forging them into the law of the occasion, so a person in turn mocks by making the occasion into everything and the next moment into foolishness, whereby God then becomes superfluous, the concept of a wise Governance becomes a piece of folly, and the occasion becomes a wag who pokes fun at God just as much as at man, so that all existence ends in a jest, a joke, a charade.' This appears to foreshadow *Practice*.

20 Kierkegaard, *Practice*, p. 23: 'Halt now! But before what is one to halt? Before that which at the same moment infinitely changes everything . . . before that which is infinitely more important and infinitely more decisive: **the inviter**.'

21 Kierkegaard, *Postscript*, pp. 134–49, 154–61, 182–4.

22 Kierkegaard calls this sin, because it is one's own fault that one is in untruth, *Fragments*, p. 15.

one does not know for what one is searching; nor is one searching for this truth when one is in truth – for it has already been discovered.[23] Kierkegaard is not merely rehashing Meno's paradox[24] in the opening pages of *Fragments*, but is making a clear attempt to move beyond it – a move beyond Socratic recollection into the reception of not only the teaching but of the teacher.[25] As James K. A. Smith says, 'Kierkegaard provides an account of learning that which is Unknown – wholly other – only on the basis of *revelation*, a gift that must be *received*.'[26] Thus, when Climacus says, 'the understanding steps aside and the paradox gives itself,'[27] Smith rightly remarks that one does not 'know' or 'comprehend' the paradox, but instead one comes 'to an understanding *with* the paradox'.[28] But what happens when one attempts fully to know, grasp and comprehend this paradox? I will address Kierkegaard's response to this question in his assault upon objectivity, his critique of the essentializing of the past, the naturalization of the present, and their culmination as found within Christendom.

In his charge against objectivity, Kierkegaard says,

> Christianity . . . protests against all objectivity; it wants the subject to be infinitely concerned about himself. What it asks about is the subjectivity; the truth of Christianity, if it is at all, is only in this; objectively, it is not at all.[29]

If the subjective individual is not upheld by Christianity, then the individual finds him or herself at risk at becoming dissolved into the dialectic of history – absorbed into the objective process where

---

23 Kierkegaard, *Fragments*, p. 9.
24 Plato, *Meno* 80e.
25 Kierkegaard, *Fragments*, p. 111.
26 James K. A. Smith, *Speech and Theology: Language and the Logic of Incarnation* (London: Routledge, 2002), p. 161. See also John Milbank, *The Suspended Middle: Henri de Lubac and the Debate concerning the Supernatural* (Grand Rapids: William B. Eerdmans Publishing Company, 2005), p. 6: 'Yet by a symmetrical paradox the "more" demanded by nature can only be received from God as a gift.'
27 Kierkegaard, *Fragments*, p. 59.
28 Smith, *Speech and Theology*, p. 163.
29 Kierkegaard, *Postscript*, p. 130.

consequences are diminished or inflated directly proportional to one's 'objective' ethical worth in the world-historical arena.[30] Worse, the ethical is no longer original within the individual but instead is 'an abstraction from the world-historical experience'.[31] This spectre that appears is no longer truly human but is only abstractly so in the most pejorative way. Externalities pass themselves off for pious inwardness[32] as the objective measure of what purports to be inside, which, upon inspection, is found to be nothing. Communities, cities and nation-states parody the individual where only a simulacrum remains; no one seems to know who one is when the world-historical process has tyrannically dictated that one is a mere cog in the dialectical mechanism of being a Republican or Democrat, New Labour or Conservative, Capitalist or Communist. One no longer places one's passionate faith in the paradox, but instead first turns to the nation-state to act as mediator, contract provider and even saviour.[33] While the individual is incorporated into an abstraction larger than him or herself, ironically, the individual thus becomes *reduced* to a misrepresentation of who she truly is: somebody 'in general'.[34] As the reduction is prolonged, this world-historical perspective has the potential, over time, to amplify its own objective hubris.

One is bound to find lurking within this view an unnecessary privileging of the present over the past, thus making certain acts or trends in history a false necessity. Johannes Climacus warns against this tendency in *Philosophical Fragments*. He first describes the contemporary follower of the paradox of Christ,[35] which is followed with an explication of how the 'follower at second hand' (or third, fourth, etc.) is not in any way at a disadvantage or advantage in relation to the historical distance between themselves

---

30 Kierkegaard, *Postscript*, pp. 143–4.
31 Kierkegaard, *Postscript*, pp. 144, 148–9.
32 For instance, see Kierkegaard's ridicule of 'Christian art' in Kierkegaard, *Practice*, pp. 254–7.
33 See William T. Cavanaugh, 'The City: Beyond Secular Parodies', in *Radical Orthodoxy*, eds John Milbank, Graham Ward, and Catherine Pickstock (London: Routledge, 1999), pp. 182–200.
34 Kierkegaard, *Postscript*, p. 167.
35 Kierkegaard, *Fragments*, pp. 55–71.

and the paradox.³⁶ Sandwiched between these two sections is an interlude on the topic of the necessity of the past over the future, which I would argue is one of the key technical underpinnings of Kierkegaard's critique of Hegel's world-historical process. The principle question at hand is, 'Is this unchangeableness [of the past] the unchangeableness of necessity?'³⁷ The logical progression concerning what comes to exist ('becoming') is important to note: (1) precisely because what is possible has come into existence as actuality, 'possibility is *annihilated* by actuality';³⁸ (2) therefore, 'everything that comes into existence demonstrates that it is not necessary, for the only thing that cannot come into existence is the necessary, because the necessary *is*'.³⁹

When what has come into existence is necessary, the paradox of the coexistence of the temporal and the eternal is collapsed, by an eternalization of the historical. Thus, time is treated not as a gift but as a given. A handful of examples are in order.

When a call for a 'return to origins'⁴⁰ is made, inevitably one hears protests such as, 'But would you have us reject the current order in its entirety?' Yet, to hold either the present or past as the 'ground' is to make the same mistake of unnecessarily placing a primacy on something that contains no inherent necessity, as Kierkegaard argues. Also, the praise of 'progress' in objectivity – as it is found in historical knowledge and speculation over against the past (as opposed to an Irenaean development) – indicates an abstraction of humanity from one time to another that tends to regard the present at the belittling expense of the past and at the expense of the subject. Precisely the opposite is true.⁴¹ Again, the protesters: 'Humanity must have been extremely misinformed 500 years ago to think such things!' Once more, the individual is not only absorbed into the world-historical process but concomitantly rejects even the gift that *is* the past. Does one stand upon the

---

36 Kierkegaard, *Fragments*, pp. 89–110.
37 Kierkegaard, *Fragments*, p. 76.
38 Kierkegaard, *Fragments*, p. 74.
39 Kierkegaard, *Fragments*, p. 74.
40 I have in mind here specifically the *ressourcement* (a bit unhappily: 'return to the sources') characteristic of the *nouvelle théologie*, especially Henri de Lubac.
41 Kierkegaard, *Postscript*, pp. 80–1.

Veritas: Belief and Metaphysics

shoulders of others, or does one pierce their shoulders with sharpened cleats?

Indeed, Climacus shows us that the question about the difference between the followers at first and at second hand is the wrong one to ask.[42] The follower in the twentieth-first century has not only tended to essentialize his place in time, but also seems to be certain of the benefits and consequences of the paradox – so much so that it is believed that 'the advantage of the consequences . . . is supposed to have been *naturalized* little by little'.[43] Christ is emptied of his divinity; the paradox is explained away. What is an integral part of the story is removed, reduced and placed on the shelf as extraneous syrup, if at all.[44] Hence, for Kierkegaard, the stage is set for philosophers of immanence to exert their influence upon the interpretation of the occasion – philosophers who cannot understand it,[45] like the darkness cannot understand the light.[46]

Likewise, another outcome that manifests itself from the privileging of one's place in history with regard to the consequences received by the occasion is inherent in the catastrophe of Christendom. Here, Anti-Climacus declares,

> We have mutually fortified one another in the thought that by means of the outcome of Christ's life and the eighteen hundred years, by means of the results we have come to know the answer. As this gradually became wisdom, all the vitality and energy was distilled out of Christianity; the paradox was slackened, one became a Christian without noticing it and without detecting the slightest possibility of offense.[47]

---

42 Kierkegaard, *Fragments*, pp. 91, 104–5.
43 Kierkegaard, *Fragments*, p. 95.
44 I am indebted to Matthew Hambrick for this brilliant metaphor to help understand the extrinsicism of the concept of 'super-nature'. When posed that way, what does pure immanence want to do with syrup, anyway?
45 Kierkegaard, *Either/Or*, p. 283: 'The occasion is a finite category, and it is impossible for immanental thinking to grasp it; it is too much a paradox for that. We see this because that which comes out of the occasion is something quite different from the occasion itself, which is an absurdity to any immanental thinking.'
46 John 1.5.
47 Kierkegaard, *Practice*, p. 35. Cf. *Practice*, p. 112.

The occasion for the halt was removed because the occasion *itself* was

> taken, turned, and scaled down; [Christ] himself guaranteed the truth as a matter of course – a man whose life had had such consequences in history. Everything became as simple as pulling on one's socks – naturally, for in that way Christianity has become paganism.[48]

The consequences inherited from the paradox are subsequently held over against the paradox in such a way as to act under the assumption that the consequences can in fact retroactively modify the paradox itself.[49] 'But, humanly speaking,' rebuts Climacus, 'consequences built upon a paradox are built upon the abyss, and the total content of the consequences, which is handed down to the single individual only under the agreement that it is by virtue of a paradox, is not to be passed on like real estate' – or the putting on of one's socks! – 'since the whole thing is in suspense.'[50]

When the paradox is naturalized, objectified and reduced to mere *datum*, one prevents oneself from ever being offended. Modern-day minds see that

> signs and wonders are something exasperatingly annoying, something that in a very embarrassing way almost forces one to have an opinion, something that, if one does not happen to feel like believing, can be a burdensome thing to be contemporary with, especially since it makes existence far too strenuous, especially the more intelligent, developed, and cultured one is.[51]

The paradox of Christ no longer presents itself as the decision for the leap – one experiences it in untruth so as not to receive the paradox as gift. If one sees oneself as complete, then what bearing

---

48 Kierkegaard, *Practice*, p. 35
49 Kierkegaard, *Fragments*, p. 95: '. . . which would be just as acceptable as the assumption that a son received retroactive power to transform his father.'
50 Kierkegaard, *Fragments*, p. 98.
51 Kierkegaard, *Practice*, p. 41.

does the 'occasion' have upon the supposed totality of one's existence? Can the offence[52] elicited be reduced further than annoyance? Perhaps, but instead of intentionally collapsing everything into pure Stoicism, humanity creates institutions to catechize fellow humans into the thought that the mystery of existence has been discovered. Mapping the human genome, mapping the mind and even mapping the universe in endless speculation direct desires away from the 'how' to the 'what' of existence.[53]

On the contrary, Kierkegaard would have it in the following way:

> With respect to existing, there is only the learner, for anyone who fancies that he is in this respect finished, that he can teach others and on top of that himself forgets to exist and to learn, is a fool. In relation to existing there is for all existing persons one schoolmaster – existence itself . . .[54]

Henri de Lubac: Friend of the Transcendent Philosopher[55]

De Lubac's most sustained treatment on Kierkegaard is found within his *Drama of Atheist Humanism*, a somewhat fragmented collection of articles which, while not entirely genealogical in nature, do tell the very convincing 'end of the story'[56] in regard to nihilism.[57] Such a nihilism is no longer a set of mind games of

---

52 For more on offence, see the chapter titled 'The Categories of *Offense*, That Is, of Essential Offense' in Kierkegaard, *Practice*, pp. 75–144.

53 Kierkegaard, *Postscript*, p. 540.

54 Kierkegaard, *Postscript*, p. 621, n. 878. See also the conclusion, *Postscript*, pp. 621–3.

55 Henri de Lubac, *The Drama of Atheist Humanism*, trans. E. M. Riley, A. E. Nash, and M. Sebanc (San Francisco: Ignatius Press, 1995), p. 103: 'As he is the philosopher of transcendence, Kierkegaard is the theologian of objectivity.'

56 Milbank, *The Suspended Middle*, p. 10, n. 13.

57 For a more sustained and genealogical accounts of nihilism, see Michael Allen Gillespie, *Nihilism Before Nietzsche* (Chicago: University of Chicago Press, 1996) and especially Conor Cunningham, *Genealogy of Nihilism: Philosophies of Nothing & the Difference of Theology* (London: Routledge, 2002).

nothingness (if it ever was), but as Archbishop Javier Martínez has said, it has become a *practice*: a 'practice of suicide' against existence.[58]

After comparing the writings of Nietzsche and Kierkegaard in order to show their similarities and the importance of these two nineteenth-century thinkers,[59] de Lubac ponders whether or not *Concluding Unscientific Postscript* to Philosophical Fragments is Kierkegaard's masterpiece.[60] Succeeding a brief excursus to visit *Fragments* and Kierkegaard's own affinity for *Fear and Trembling*, de Lubac proclaims that *Postscript* is 'perhaps Kierkegaard's masterpiece and . . . one of the masterpieces of the philosophical and religious literature of all time'.[61]

The importance of *Fragments* and *Postscript* for de Lubac are, respectively, their philosophies of dogma and of faith.[62] De Lubac offers a concise, yet highly accurate overview of Kierkegaard's thought in *Postscript*, highlighting his emphasis on paradox, subjectivity and his fight against Hegelianism. Giving a nod to Kierkegaard's writing in *Practice in Christianity* and elsewhere, de Lubac sums up his efforts thus:

> And as, in the campaign he conducted, toward the end of his life, against the established Church of his country, he wanted to save that 'shocking' element which is essential to Christianity, so in his struggle against Hegelianism he wanted to save the element of 'paradox', which is no less essential.[63]

Indeed, no less essential because it is the paradox which gives rise to the 'shock' – to the 'halt'.

---

58 Archbishop Javier Martínez, '"Beyond Secular Reason": Some Contemporary Challenges for the Life and the Thought of the Church, as Seen from the West' (A talk given at the occasion of the Conference organized by the Foundation 'Russia Cristiana', together with the Synodal Theological Commission of the Moscow Patriarchate, on the topic: 'Orthodox Theology and the West in the XXth Century. History of a Meeting', Seriate, Bergamo (Italy), 30–31 October 2004), p. 6.
59 De Lubac, *Drama of Atheist Humanism*, pp. 95–101.
60 De Lubac, *Drama of Atheist Humanism*, pp. 101–2.
61 De Lubac, *Drama of Atheist Humanism*, p. 102.
62 De Lubac, *Drama of Atheist Humanism*, p. 103.
63 De Lubac, *Drama of Atheist Humanism*, pp. 106–7.

Veritas: Belief and Metaphysics

The critiques that de Lubac provides of Kierkegaard are short. First, he does wonder what a 'converted' Hegelianism would look like, if he were to make the effort. Second, there's also cause for concern that Kierkegaard's over-purified version of Christianity binds one to an 'inhuman solitude'.[64] Attempts at answering these questions are mostly relegated to footnotes.[65] Lastly, de Lubac rightly points out that Kierkegaard's writings are pervaded with a strong 'Lutheran flavor'.[66] While this can be clearly seen in his strong emphasis on the 'consciousness of sin',[67] de Lubac acquits him of the typical distortions found therein due to his strong emphasis on paradox. And in the end, despite these brief considerations, de Lubac holds up Kierkegaard as the 'herald of transcendence'.[68]

These concerns, however, belie the myriad similarities and convergences between Kierkegaard and de Lubac. Aside from their strong emphases on paradox (de Lubac's will be considered below), an interesting concurrence is their focus upon the dissolution of the individual within human abstractions or atheism. For Kierkegaard, Hegelian thought as figured in the world-historical narrative gave rise to angst; for de Lubac, 'The Dissolution of Man'[69] and the abstraction of the 'public' elicited strong critique.

De Lubac's assessment of the dissolution of humanity is centred on Feuerbach, Marx and Nietzsche. For Feuerbach, the existence or non-existence of God and humanity seemed directly proportional.[70] For Marx and Nietzsche, against the 'do-nothing' philosophers of their time, both desired revolution in order to transform the world.[71] This revolution is by no means utopian: Nietzsche proceeded to predict catastrophes, demolitions, upheavals and wars – all 'thanks to' him.[72]

---

64 De Lubac, *Drama of Atheist Humanism*, p. 107.
65 De Lubac, *Drama of Atheist Humanism*, p. 107, n. 108.
66 De Lubac, *Drama of Atheist Humanism*, p. 110.
67 Kierkegaard, *Practice*, pp. 67–8, 155.
68 De Lubac, *Drama of Atheist Humanism*, p. 111.
69 The chapter title found within the section on Feuerbach and Nietzsche, de Lubac, *Drama of Atheist Humanism*, p. 58.
70 De Lubac, *Drama of Atheist Humanism*, p. 59.
71 De Lubac, *Drama of Atheist Humanism*, pp. 61–4.
72 De Lubac, *Drama of Atheist Humanism*, p. 64.

'What,' asks de Lubac, 'has become of man as conceived by this atheist humanism?' He answers,

> A being that can still hardly be called a 'being' – a thing that has no content, a cell completely merged in a mass that is in the process of becoming: 'social-and-historical man', of whom all that remains is pure abstraction, apart from the social relations and the position in time by which he is defined. . . . There is nothing to prevent his being used as material or as a tool either for the preparation of some future society or for ensuring, here and now, the dominance of one privileged group. There is not even anything to prevent his being cast aside as useless . . . In reality there is no longer any man because there is no longer anything that is greater than man.[73]

One final intriguing commonality between the two is where de Lubac picks up on Kierkegaard's notorious use of the phrase 'infinite qualitative difference', in regards to the difference between God and humanity. Kierkegaard first develops this concept rather thoroughly in his *Sickness Unto Death*[74] and then later refines it in

---

73 De Lubac, *Drama of Atheist Humanism*, p. 66. Similarly, see also de Lubac's brief take on Marx's materialism in Henri de Lubac, *The Mystery of the Supernatural*, trans. Rosemary Sheed (New York: Crossroad, 1998), pp. 122–3.

74 Søren Kierkegaard, *The Sickness Unto Death*, ed. and trans. Howard V. and Edna H. Hong (Princeton: Princeton University Press, 1980), pp. 99, 117, 121, 126–7. See my appendix below for the quotations. There also appears to be a glimpse at another intriguing similarity when Kierkegaard says, 'In no way is a man so different from God as in this, that he, and that means every man, is a sinner, and is that "before God," whereby the opposites are kept together in a double sense: they are held together (*continentur*), they are not allowed to go away from each other, but by being held together in this way the differences show up all the more sharply, just as when two colors are held together, *opposite juxta se posita magis illusunt* [the opposites appear more clearly by juxtaposition]' (*Sickness Unto Death*, p. 121). Cf. Plato and Descartes vs. Thomas and Aristotle on uniting the body and soul in one substance in order to differentiate, 'unite in order to distinguish', de Lubac, *The Mystery of the Supernatural*, pp. 30–3. Cf. also the original working out of this idea in Henri de Lubac, *Catholicism: Christ and the Common Destiny of Man*,

Practice in Christianity, also labelling it the 'chasmic abyss'.[75] Its use is threefold: first, faithfully to ensure that God and humanity do not become pantheistically mixed; second, as an extension of the first, to show that it is due to humanity's sin that this distance is absolutely infinite; and lastly, to show that this infinite qualitative distance 'constitutes the possibility of offense'.[76] One sees this famous phrase quoted directly by de Lubac in *The Mystery of the Supernatural* without reference,[77] as well as paraphrases of it in his *Brief Catechesis on Nature and Grace*.[78] Kierkegaard maintained this infinite distinction for the non-pantheistic drama that brings one to a decisive 'halt'. De Lubac appropriates the language to maintain the distinction in unity of the natural and the supernatural. Yet, despite the minute differences in their language, we see that both have a similar task: their desire faithfully to maintain this infinite qualitative difference so that we may be united with the paradox[79] as we are drawn up into Christ in abasement,[80] 'crossing, by grace . . . an impassible barrier'.[81] It is to the specific sketches of the paradox in de Lubac that I will now turn.

---

trans. L. C. Sheppard and E. Englund (San Francisco: Ignatius Press, 1988), p. 328: 'The paradox is this: that the distinction between the different parts of a being stands out the more clearly as the union of these parts is closer' and pp. 328–33.

75 Kierkegaard, *Practice*, pp. 28–9, 63, 127–8, 131, 139–40, 170, 205, 251.

76 Kierkegaard, *Sickness Unto Death*, p. 127.

77 De Lubac, *The Mystery of the Supernatural*, p. 35.

78 Henri de Lubac, *Brief Catechesis on Nature and Grace*, trans. Richard Arnandez, F.S.C. (San Francisco: Ignatius Press, 1984), p. 32: 'infinite disproportion'; p. 49; and in a Hans Urs von Balthasar quotation, p. 75.

79 De Lubac, *The Mystery of the Supernatural*, p. 222: 'It is revelation which brings a final judgement to bear on all this human evidence: it condemns its *hubris*, estimates its deviations and brings to light its core of truth. Desire to see God, desire to be united with God, desire to be God: we find all of these, or similar phrases, outside Christianity and independent of it.'

80 Kierkegaard, *Practice*, pp. 259–62.

81 De Lubac, *The Mystery of the Supernatural*, p. 83.

Paradoxes of Faith in Henri de Lubac

> *Those who have never seen the sea believe that nothing is more monotonous – whereas nothing is more varied, nothing has more surprises in store.*[82]

De Lubac wrote two small volumes on the topic of paradox,[83] in which he turned the idea of paradox this way and that, always regarding it at a distance, the distance in which beauty is found.[84] John Milbank locates the paradox as one of the main 'axes' of de Lubac's thought.[85] One can clearly see that the heart of de Lubac's most central and sustained (and revised)[86] work, *The Mystery of the Supernatural*, contains four gears on this thematic axis: 'The Christian Paradox of Man', 'The Paradox Unknown to the Gentiles', 'A Paradox Rejected by Common Sense' and 'The Paradox Overcome in Faith'. Within these chapters, as well as the rest of the book, are the fruit of reflection upon the paradox. In truth, as I have attempted to show in the work of Kierkegaard and now with de Lubac, 'all the ideas that bear upon the reality of our being in relation to God'[87] are paradoxical.

The central thesis of de Lubac's work which draws heavily upon the writings of Thomas Aquinas – itself a paradox – is this: each human being, as the creation of uncreated God, has a natural desire for the supernatural which has been supernaturally given as a free and gratuitous gift[88] – that 'supreme gift' which is in no way under obligation from God[89] but is freely given as God's self 'at

---

82 De Lubac, *Paradoxes of Faith*, p. 191.
83 See de Lubac, *Paradoxes of Faith*; Henri de Lubac, *More Paradoxes*, trans. Anne Englund Nash (San Francisco: Ignatius Press, 2002).
84 For more on this topic excellently articulated, see David Bentley Hart, *The Beauty of the Infinite: The Aesthetics of Christian Truth* (Grand Rapids: Wm B. Eerdmans Publishing Company, 2003), pp. 18ff.
85 Milbank, *The Suspended Middle*, p. 2.
86 De Lubac's original *Surnaturel* provided much of the content for *Mystery*, and he was prompted by reviewers and friends to clarify some of his main points from the original.
87 De Lubac, *The Mystery of the Supernatural*, p. xxxiv.
88 De Lubac, *The Mystery of the Supernatural*, p. 167.
89 De Lubac, *The Mystery of the Supernatural*, p. 50. As David L. Schindler puts it, 'of the created spirit who desires God essentially, but without demanding anything' (*The Mystery of the Supernatural*, p. xix).

every stage of the giving of it.'⁹⁰ This gift 'is an infused grace,' says de Lubac, 'that raises up the essence of the soul to some divine *esse*, making it truly fitted for divine activities'.⁹¹

Like that 'something that thought itself cannot think', the human being is for de Lubac that creature who, while spun into the cloth of existence, desires the *whole* cloth and all of that which is beyond; every human thirsts for that which exceeds the fabric and yet, this is accomplished by the threads of one's own fabric.⁹² Drawing particularly upon the work of Augustine and Origen, de Lubac maintains the infinite qualitative difference between God and the human while showing that this desire to cross the chasmic abyss, received by our faith as the perfect, free gift (*donum perfectum*), cannot merely be deciphered naturally. He says that 'there is something in man, a certain capacity for the infinite, which makes it impossible to consider him one of those beings whose whole nature and destiny are inscribed within the cosmos'.⁹³ How can the fabric know purely within itself why it exists? Does not the fabric need to look to the artist who fashioned it?

De Lubac wonders why so many 'Thomistic' theologians could miss obvious statements made by Thomas himself about this topic.⁹⁴ This paradox of existence, however, is overlooked not only by 'Thomists'. Christians of all persuasions, in recent times, have more and more looked to the natural world for (panentheistic) 'signs' of the nature of God – a natural world whose end is perceived to be only in itself. One face of this phantasm is that 'pure reason' which attempts to subvert all discourse in its appeal to a 'common sense'⁹⁵ or the ideals of a nation-state to set the stage for 'reasonable' ('polite'?) communication that finds its virtue not in love but in 'objectivity'.

---

90 De Lubac, *The Mystery of the Supernatural*, p. 236.
91 De Lubac, *The Mystery of the Supernatural*, p. 86.
92 De Lubac, *The Mystery of the Supernatural*, p. 106.
93 De Lubac, *The Mystery of the Supernatural*, p. 110.
94 De Lubac, *The Mystery of the Supernatural*, p. 111.
95 I place this in quotes because I do not actually believe that such a thing, as it is intended in modern-day discourse to imply, exists. The truly sensible is only a reason suspended in faith and vice versa; see Cunningham, *Genealogy of Nihilism*, p. 274 for a lucid exposition of the 'imbalances' that arise when one aims for a [non-existent] 'pure' form of faith or reason.

'In the "purely natural world" where this creature lives,' de Lubac warns, 'all idea of God's free gift is lost.'[96] What masquerades as philosophy in the guise of 'pure metaphysics' may amount to nothing more than *description*, severing itself from the gift of the transcendent. In lieu of this gift, existence is treated instead as given.[97]

In 'The Paradox Unknown to the Gentiles', de Lubac offers a brief sketch of philosophical history which finds a helpful typology in the Averröes/Alexander duality. 'One held man to be a properly eternal being, while the other held him to be an individual destined wholly to die.'[98] From this, all others that follow vary upon this theme. The Marxist variation, for instance, 'returns to the idea of an eternal matter within which nothing really new is created, and in relation to which all the apparent advances of history are mere surface disturbances which will come and go indefinitely'.[99] In this way, the Heraclitean flux really does solidify into the Parmenidean stasis.[100] What is denied, then, is the opening up of the human to the new life by Christian philosophy which disallows either of the above extremes.[101] The paradox, when rightly received as gift, opens one up not to the purely (gnostic) eternal or to the purely

---

96 De Lubac, *The Mystery of the Supernatural*, p. 48.

97 See Conor Cunningham, 'Language: Wittgenstein after Theology', in John Milbank, Graham Ward, and Catherine Pickstock (eds), *Radical Orthodoxy: A New Theology* (London: Routledge, 1999), pp. 64–5. I would argue that this is one of the underlying errors in the polemics of Creationism (see in particular the video series, theme park, etc. of Kent Hovind), which proclaim at every opportunity that these particular fundaments (in the foundationalist sense) of creation are as 'fundamental' to one's faith as the proclamation of Christ crucified. Coincidentally, and of extreme interest here is de Lubac's theological defence of the evolutionary theory of his friend Teilhard de Chardin, see Henri de Lubac, *Teilhard de Chardin: The Man and His Meaning*, trans. René Hague (New York: Hawthorn, 1965). Instead, then, of offering an account of the creation story that emphasizes the goodness of creation as spoken into existence by the Triune God, new stories that amount to nothing more than a description of how God 'literally' created the cosmos are spun.

98 De Lubac, *The Mystery of the Supernatural*, p. 122.

99 De Lubac, *The Mystery of the Supernatural*, pp. 122–3.

100 The ailment suffered by the patients in the movie *Awakenings* (1990) starring Robin Williams seems to illustrate this effect.

101 De Lubac, *The Mystery of the Supernatural*, p. 124.

temporal, but to the temporal lifted up in eternity; time is not annulled, but completed in fullness.

De Lubac concludes his critical paradox-specific examination with a rejoinder to the rejection of the paradox founded upon 'common sense'. At heart, this term as it will be explored here refers to and is founded upon a fallacious teleological interpretation of nature. To sum up briefly de Lubac's cogent historical analysis on the matter, after Denys the Carthusian openly rejected Thomas's view on the finality of humanity, Cajetan later picked up on Denys's rejection and passed it off as a *commentary* on Thomas that effectively turned 'the objection into the answer'.[102] A misreading had thus become the standard interpretation *du jour*.

The thrust of the rationale given for this rejection of the paradox is that it is egregiously guilty of the sins of conceptual incoherence and near-flippant lexical abuse.[103] One can see the offence that erupts from the unreciprocated understanding between the champion of the 'obvious' and the paradox. Thus, attempts at watering down the chasm between God and the human are quick to follow. Or, the human merely becomes a 'natural being'[104] whose end is itself.[105] Against this, de Lubac calls for a Christian humanism: not a humanism that is merely 'baptized' in nominal fashion, but a Christian humanism[106] where the human is lifted up into God.

Thus, the gift of faith itself is that to which the human is called. It is this towards which the understanding of faith must be directed.[107] By itself, as purely 'given', the understanding gives rise to uneasy tensions that construct ontotheological realities which oppose nature and grace (or conflate the two), justice and mercy, and so forth;[108] whereas these are suspended in the gift of faith, their distance in unity remains as paradox. Assuredly, de Lubac states:

> For every statement of the faith is twofold; as regards us it necessarily consists of two views, the two apparent objects of

---

102 De Lubac, *The Mystery of the Supernatural*, p. xvii, 143–5, 160.
103 De Lubac, *The Mystery of the Supernatural*, p. 161.
104 De Lubac, *The Mystery of the Supernatural*, p. 163.
105 At this point the human *would* be a purely immanent 'it'.
106 De Lubac, *The Mystery of the Supernatural*, p. 162–3.
107 De Lubac, *The Mystery of the Supernatural*, p. 165.
108 De Lubac, *The Mystery of the Supernatural*, p. 166.

which seem at first glance to be opposed to each other, not to say contradictory. These two views tend to coalesce at an infinite distance upon a single object, but the intuition of this unity escapes us.[109]

De Lubac clearly saw, as did Kierkegaard in his observation of the 'slackening' of the paradox, that these easy solutions of understanding amount to a 'blur' of the paradox; and, like Kierkegaard's desire to see Christianity made difficult once again against those throughout Copenhagen who made faith as easy as the 'silly game'[110] of putting on one's socks, de Lubac likewise says, 'The resistance of dogmatic data to many of our hypotheses is an excellent thing for preventing our thought from being facile.'[111]

Fully Entering into the Paradox by Faith: Towards a Confessional Participation in Existence by Spontaneous Imitation

Kierkegaard, in *Postscript*, says that 'every human being has a strong natural desire and drive to become something else and more'.[112] The paradox, wherein the understanding comes up against its limit, is completely entered into faith. To reiterate de Lubac's articulation of this paradox, 'The desire to see [God] is in us, it constitutes us, and yet it comes to us as a completely free gift.'[113] Stamped upon existence is this 'truth that is beyond our depth'.[114] This truth, not as 'possessed by the light of reason', but when 'believed in the darkness of faith', suspends both love as a commandment and love as a free gift.[115]

Arriving at this truth begins with the idea of mystery. 'This idea of mystery,' says de Lubac, 'is perfectly acceptable to reason once

---

109 De Lubac, *Brief Catechesis on Nature and Grace*, pp. 72–3.
110 Kierkegaard, *Practice*, p. 67.
111 De Lubac, *Paradoxes*, p. 223. Cf. *Paradoxes*, p. 106: 'He who wants to have solutions for everything, must give up reflection, so as to have them ready made. But in that case they will not really be solutions for anything.'
112 Kierkegaard, *Postscript*, p. 130.
113 De Lubac, *The Mystery of the Supernatural*, p. 167.
114 De Lubac, *The Mystery of the Supernatural*, p. 167.
115 De Lubac, *The Mystery of the Supernatural*, p. 169.

one has admitted the idea of a personal and transcendent God.'[116] Thus, rightly understood, this idea can never be grasped in fullness, but paradoxically both regarded at a distance and in inwardness. When we do not hold this understanding between the transcendent and personal God and between the love as both a commandment and a free gift, the paradox as understood within us slackens; de Lubac says, 'When it is between two truths of faith that the ultimate harmony cannot be seen, to choose one and reject the other then becomes heresy properly so called.'[117]

Faith is that gift received that holds the paradox in dialectical harmony within us, the culmination of which is seen most truly in the fully divine and fully human nature of Jesus Christ. 'Blessed is anyone who takes no offence at me', he says.[118] The offence is abolished by faith; the infinite qualitative distance is traversed by 'the assurance of things hoped for, the conviction of things not seen';[119] the paradox, therefore, is entered into by faith.

In conclusion, I would like to offer a brief sketch of what this faith means as provided by the themes orbiting the paradox as demonstrated by Kierkegaard and de Lubac. Springing forth from their various expressions, I believe that it is imperative that we move towards a confessional participation in existence, supported by a daily spontaneous imitation of the Supreme Paradox.

First, the call to be confessional arises not only because we are commanded to be, but also because not to be places us at a false distance between one another and between ourselves and God. In this false distance, which is the same infinite qualitative distance between the imitator and the admirer,[120] we forget that we are guilty of those things of which we accuse others. De Lubac, again operating on the axis of paradox, is helpful here: 'One might even advance the paradox that the full realization of what sin is does not exist in the sinful Christian, however lucid he may be, but only in the repentant Christian.[121] And Kierkegaard:

---

116 De Lubac, *The Mystery of the Supernatural*, p. 171.
117 *The Mystery of the Supernatural*, p. 175. See also, pp. 167–8.
118 Matthew 11.6. This and all following references are in the NRSV translation.
119 Hebrews 11.1.
120 Kierkegaard, *Practice*, p. 251.
121 De Lubac, *Brief Catechesis on Nature and Grace*, p. 131.

each individual in quiet inwardness before God is to humble himself under what it means in the strictest sense to be a Christian, is to confess honestly before God where he is so that he still might worthily accept the grace that is offered to every imperfect person – that is, to everyone.[122]

As sinners, but never obsessing over our sin,[123] when we are able to admit that 'My enemies are men like me,'[124] we may accept that 'God proves his love for us in that while we still were sinners Christ died for us.'[125]

The second key aspect to picking up where Kierkegaard and de Lubac leave off is their call to participate in existence – in the necessary existence that is God. Kierkegaard wrote against the ontological objectifiers as well as those who chose to admire instead of imitate Christ, while de Lubac warned against a 'pure metaphysics' of description that would leave us on the sidelines of existence – reporting but never participating, or at best, merely reading along while the drama of existence unfolds in front of us. We must not be hearers who are deceived, but 'doers of the word', says the Epistle of James. 'For if any are hearers of the word and not doers, they are like those who look at themselves in a mirror; for they look at themselves and, on going away, immediately forget what they were like.'[126] This word to love God with all our being and to love our neighbour as ourselves must be the impetus for the participation in the life of Christ through the Spirit as we engage in the works of mercy, weekly being directed towards, oriented and shaped by the participation in the Eucharist.

And lastly, it is the Holy Spirit that guides us in imitation of Christ. Imitation of the 'Supreme Paradox' is not rigid, nor has it ever been, but has always been received in unexpected and surprising ways as a free gift. Bruce Ellis Benson's phenomenological concept of the 'premeditated spontaneity' of jazz musicians works out

---

122 Kierkegaard, *Practice*, p. 67.
123 De Lubac, *Brief Catechesis on Nature and Grace*, p. 134.
124 See the wonderful Derek Webb, 'My Enemies are Men Like Me', *Mockingbird* (2005), CD.
125 Romans 5.8.
126 James 1.22–5.

a paradox that can be extremely beneficial for the conception of the Christian tradition:

> As odd as it may sound, the musician who is most prepared – not only in terms of having thought about what is to be played but even having played various possibilities – is most able to be spontaneous. It is when one already is prepared that one feels free to go beyond the confines of the prepared (with the assurance that one can always fall back on them if necessary). In the same way that [Hans-Georg] Gadamer argues that the experienced person is most open to new experience, it is the experienced improviser – the one who has already thought a great deal about what is to be played – who is most able to play something surprising. Experience can turn into a rut, but it can also beget spontaneity.[127]

This approach may help the Church to be a body of spontaneous imitators in reception of the established dogma and the plentiful and varied theological voices over the ages. As 'premeditated spontaneous imitators' of the Supreme Paradox, there is hope for escaping the easy route of Christendom that reduces existence to bare ontology through endless description – a mode of being that tragically slackens the paradox in life.

Instead, along with Kierkegaard, a return to subjectivity as imitating participants in existence presents itself as paramount.[128] In doing so the distance between the twenty-first and first centuries is eradicated and by faith one's existence is doxologically oriented and bound up in contemporaneity with the God-man. And with de Lubac, Thomas, and countless others who continue to speak

---

127 Bruce Ellis Benson, *The Improvisation of Musical Dialogue: A Phenomenology of Music* (Cambridge: Cambridge University Press, 2003), pp. 142–3. Many thanks to Cynthia Nielsen for pointing this book out to me on her helpful and articulate weblog, see http://percaritatem.blogspot.com.

128 And, along with Kierkegaard in *Practice in Christianity*, I would caution against the idolatrous forms of [direct] communication with which the current popular Christian culture in North America is all too eager to engage. For Kierkegaard it may have been 'Christian art'; for us it may have mutated into the phenomena of the bumper sticker, etc.

across time as paradoxical inspiration-for-spontaneity, the completion of humanity that is affirmed in Christ continues to reveal itself in the natural desire for that which is beyond – that which is received as a totally free gift. It is only through the ultimate teacher – that Supreme Paradox – to whom Kierkegaard and de Lubac point that any descriptions are truly descriptive, any reason has any true sense, any paradox finally beheld, and any life can finally truly exist, but in the light and participation of he who is fully human and fully divine.

12. Heidegger's Approach to Aquinas: Opposition, *Destruktion*, Unbelief

SEAN MCGRATH

In a recent article, the German philosopher of religion Bernhard Casper outlines an interpretation of Heidegger's relationship to scholasticism inspired by his teacher and mentor, Heidegger's colleague and friend, Bernhard Welte.[1] Heidegger is read as an iconoclast who tears down the idols of metaphysics for the sake of facilitating an authentic religiosity. This reading of Heidegger has become a standard theistic *apologia* for Heidegger's ontology.[2] Casper builds his argument on the undeniable fact that Heidegger's critique of 'ontotheology' is rooted in his early theological objections to the formulaic rigidity of early twentieth-century neo-scholasticism. Casper argues that Heidegger's critique is not in itself opposed to philosophical theology, but only to a certain variety of it, 'the ecclesiastical neo-Scholasticism' which understands itself as 'a closed system and a timeless and a-historical

---

1 Bernhard Casper, 'Das theologisch-scholastische Umfeld und der anti-idolische Grundzug des Denkens des jungen Heidegger', in *Quaestio. Annuario di storia della metafisica*, vol. 1, *Heidegger e i medievali. Atti del Colloquio Internazionale Cassino 10/13 maggio 2000*, ed. Costantino Espossto and Pasquale Porro (Turnhout, Belgium: Brepols, 2001), pp. 11-22. Cf. Bernhard Welte, *Religionsphilosophie* (Freiburg i.Br.: Herder, 1978); Bernhard Casper, Klaus Hemmerle and Peter Hünerman (eds), *Besinnung auf das Heilige* (Freiburg i.Br: Herder, 1966).

2 See, for example, Laurence P. Hemming's position in his *Heidegger's Atheism. The Refusal of a Theological Voice* (Notre Dame: Indiana University Press, 2003).

Heidegger's Approach to Aquinas

ground of all knowledge'.³ Casper sees a religious *telos* unifying Heidegger's 'paths of thinking'. From his student writings to the later work, Heidegger's lifework is a one-pointed search for 'the ground', the theological foundation of thinking and being. Casper notes that already in the early student book reviews Heidegger is articulating a notion of thinking as a will to the ground (*der Wille zum Grund*), a directedness which ostensibly 'signifies [also] the desire for a knowledge of God'.⁴ The target of the ontotheology critique is, therefore, not philosophical theology as such, but any mitigation or foreclosure of questioning with a premature answer. The philosophy of the '*causa sui*' that Heidegger denounces as idolatry in *Identity and Difference* is the textbook scholastic theology, not the work of Aquinas, Bonaventure or Scotus.⁵

In this chapter I argue that this interpretation fails to make sense of Heidegger's readings of Aquinas. Heidegger rejects not only Aquinas's natural theology, but also his notion of the *desiderium naturale*, the human being as intellectually and volitionally directed to the Creator.⁶ In Heidegger's alternative ontology, the human being is so 'fallen' that it has no intimation of a Creator.⁷ Heidegger opposes the Thomistic principle of the analogical unity of the being of God and the being of creation, the *analogia entis*, not only because it introduces a philosophical figure for God, but also because it infects philosophy with theology. Even in his 1915 study of Scotus, Heidegger tends to reduce Scotus's *univocatio entis*, which has, of course, an infinite referent, to *esse intentionale*, the being that is proportionate to the human intellect.⁸ The

---

3 Casper, 'Das theologisch-scholastische Umfeld', p. 21.

4 Casper, 'Das theologisch-scholastische Umfeld', p. 13.

5 Casper, 'Das theologisch-scholastische Umfeld', p. 17. See Martin Heidegger, *Identity and Difference*, trans. Joan Stambaugh (New York: Harper & Row, 1969), p. 72. All references to Heidegger's works will be to English translations where they exist.

6 See Thomas Aquinas, *Summa Theologiae* 1, q.1, a.1: 'man is directed to God, as to an end that surpasses the grasp of his reason.'

7 I have argued this point at length in my *The Early Heidegger and Medieval Philosophy. Phenomenology for the Godforsaken* (Washington, DC, Catholic University of America Press, 2006).

8 In chapter two of the *Habilitationsschrift* Heidegger explores the phenomenological significance of the Scotistic doctrine of the converti-

Veritas: Belief and Metaphysics

opposition to any Divine ontological analogue motivates Heidegger's *Destruktion* of Aquinas's notion of *veritas* in 1923/24, and the *Destruktion* of Aquinas's distinction of *essentia* and *existentia* in 1927 and 1941.[9] Heidegger's mature position regarding philosophical theism amounts to what Aquinas would regard as philosophical atheism: God not only *does not show himself* in any way in nature or in human living, neither as effect nor as final cause of human desire, 'the hermeneutics of facticity' is only possible on the supposition that God does not exist. Heidegger's interpretation of being as 'time' is intended to make the *analogia entis* impossible, and with it, any philosophical knowledge of God. The assumption of time as the horizon of being is complexly related to the early Heidegger's appropriation of Luther. As such it has a theological underside. It is not only a hermeneutical-phenomenological

---

bility of being and truth (*verum*). That a being is true by virtue of its being means that being has an essential relationship to intellect, for truth is relation to intellect. Scotus ultimately relates being to the divine intellect. God grounds the truth of things by willing them to be. Through an immanent reading of the convertibility of being and truth, that is, without reference to God, Heidegger interprets the Scotistic convertibility of being and truth as an indication of the givenness for a finite subject of all that is or can be. See Martin Heidegger, *Frühe Schriften. 1912–1916*, ed. Friedrich-Wilhelm von Herrmann (Frankfurt a.M.: Vittorio Klostermann, 1978), pp. 267–8: 'Just as *unum* turns out to be the primordial form of the object in general, so too *verum* must be apprehended as a *formal relation*. The object is true object in regard to cognition. Insofar as the object is *object of cognition, it can be called true object*. The object shows the *fundamentum veritatis*. Transcendental philosophy has found the most precise expression for this relation: the object is only object as object of cognition: cognition is only cognition as cognition of the object. There is no object without a subject and *vice versa*.'

9 These three texts are the only sustained treatments of themes from Aquinas in Heidegger's works. Martin Heidegger, *Einführung in die phänomenologische Forschung, Gesamtausgabe*, 17 [1923/24], ed. Friedrich-Wilhelm von Herrmann (Frankfurt a.M.: Vittorio Klostermann, 1994), [hereafter *GA* 17], pp. 162–94; Martin Heidegger, *Basic Problems of Phenomenology* [1927], trans. Albert Hofstadter (Bloomington, Ind.: Indiana University Press, 1982), *GA* 24, pp. 77–121; Martin Heidegger, *Nietzsche*, II, *The Eternal Return of the Same* [1941], trans. David Farrell Krell (New York: Harper & Row, 1984), *GA* 6.2, pp. 4–24.

principle; it is also a declaration of what is and what is not theologically possible for the human being. The assumption of God-forsakenness (Aquinas's *desiderium naturae* trumped by Luther's *aversio Dei*) invites a radical theology of revelation to declare its unequivocal 'no' to philosophy.[10]

Pace Casper, I read Heidegger as on the track of something decisively non-Christian, a pre-Judaic experience of 'the holy' free of theistic associations and interpretations. The early Heidegger sets up the conditions for the possibility of such a post-Christian religiosity by first outlawing theism in philosophy, and then ransacking Jewish-Christian texts, formalizing their most characteristic features and declaring them the rightful property of philosophy. Others have noted that Heidegger frequently dismisses the very Christian sources which he himself so heavily relies upon. If occasionally the Christians hit upon something true, as for example, in the case of Augustine or Kierkegaard, they generally lack the power to follow the truth into its concealed ground, which in Heidegger's view is certainly not a sense for the Creator or the *imago Dei*. Aquinas's natural theology is symptomatic of the medieval forgetfulness of being; it represents a betrayal of the early

---

10 The question remains, to what degree has Heidegger left open the possibility of a philosophical approach to God 'beyond being'? See Jean-Luc Marion, *God Without Being. Hors-Texte*, trans. Thomas A. Carlson (Chicago: The University of Chicago Press, 1991). Whatever else this alternative philosophy of God would signify it would be anti-Thomistic if it rejects the *actus purus* of *esse*. However, it is not clear from Marion's own reflections on Aquinas that the 'being' meant in the title of his book is equivalent to *esse*. After debating with Thomists on the issue, Marion conceded the point that Aquinas's identification of God with being does not subsume God under a human measure. The *analogia entis* preserves the distance between infinite and finite being. See Marion's preface to the English edition of *God Without Being*, p. xxiii: 'Even when he thinks God as *esse*, Saint Thomas nevertheless does not chain God either to Being or to metaphysics. He does not chain God to Being because the divine *esse* immeasurably surpasses (and hardly maintains an *analogia* with) the *ens commune* of creatures, which are characterized by the real distinction between *esse* and their essence, whereas God, and He alone, absolutely merges essence with *esse*: God is expressed as *esse*, but this *esse* is expressed only of God, not of the beings of metaphysics. In this sense, Being does not erect an idol before God, but saves his distance.'

Christian breakthrough to facticity, the atheistic significance of which the early Christians could not grasp.[11]

Opposition

Although a large literature on Heidegger and Aquinas exists,[12] Heidegger has comparatively little to say about Aquinas or Thomism. His principle medieval sources are Augustine, Scotus, Eckhart, and Luther, all of whom stand in tension with, if not opposition to Aquinas on many points. In his three readings of Aquinas, which I examine in detail below, Heidegger appears to disregard a Thomistic notion with which he might be expected to sympathize, what the Gilson school has isolated as the existential moment in Aquinas's ontology, the irreducible givenness of *esse*.[13]

---

11 Jacques Derrida has remarked on the peculiar inauthenticity of Heidegger's treatment of his Christian sources. In *The Gift of Death* he writes: 'Heideggerian thought was not simply a constant attempt to separate itself from Christianity. . . . The same Heideggerian thinking often consists, notably in *Sein und Zeit*, in repeating on an ontological level Christian themes and texts that have been "de-Christianized." Such themes and texts are then presented as ontic, anthropological, or contrived attempts that come to a sudden halt on the way to an ontological recovery of their own originary possibility.' Jacques Derrida, *The Gift of Death*, trans. David Wills (Chicago and London: The University of Chicago Press, 1995), pp. 22–23.

12 See, for example, John D. Caputo, *Heidegger and Aquinas: An Essay on Overcoming Metaphysics* (New York: Fordham University Press, 1982); Gustav Siewerth, *Der Thomismus als Identitätssystem*, Gesammelte Werke, 2, ed. Wolfgang Behler and Alma von Stockhausen (Düsseldorf: Patmos, 1979); Johannes Baptist Lotz, *Martin Heidegger und Thomas von Aquin. Mensch – Zeit – Sein* (Pfullingen: Neske, 1975); John M. Deely, *The Tradition via Heidegger: An Essay on the Meaning of Being in the Philosophy of Martin Heidegger* (The Hague: Nijhoff, 1971); Hans Meyer, *Martin Heidegger und Thomas von Aquinas* (München: Schöningh, 1964); Bertrand Rioux, *L'Être et la verité chez Heidegger et Saint Thomas d'Aquin* (Paris: Presses Universitaires de France, 1963).

13 See Gerald B. Phelan, *The Existentialism of St. Thomas*, ed. Arthur G. Kirn (Toronto: Pontifical Institute of Mediaeval Studies, 1967); Etienne Gilson, *Being and Some Philosophers* (Toronto: Pontifical Institute of Mediaeval Studies, 1952); Jacques Maritain, *Existence and the Existent*,

Heidegger's Approach to Aquinas

The non-conceptual, non-substantive nature of *esse* was a topic of intense interest among German Thomists in the 1920s and 1930s. Three of Heidegger's most devoted students in the 1930s, Gustav Siewerth, Johannes Lotz and Max Müller, submitted *Habilitationsschriften* to the University of Freiburg drawing explicit connections between Heidegger's ontological difference and Aquinas's *distinctio realis*. Heidegger, a second examiner for Martin Honecker, the Chair of Christian Philosophy, dismissed these works, rejecting any attempt to build a bridge between Aquinas and his philosophy as a theologization of ontology.[14]

While Siewerth has made a strong case for interpreting Aquinas's notion of *esse* in non-ontic language,[15] the opposition between Aquinas and Heidegger runs far deeper than a quarrel over the interpretation of terms. Heidegger is diametrically opposed to the premise of Aquinas's ontology, the eternity and infinity of *esse*. In its place he posits *Sein* as a radically temporal and finite horizon of understanding. Aquinas holds that changing beings participate in that which never changes, *ipsum esse*, and are real to that degree; Heidegger holds that beings only *are* to the degree that they are temporalized by coming into 'the clearing' of *Dasein*'s 'care'. Aquinas grounds potency in act; Heidegger holds that 'higher than actuality stands possibility'.[16] Aquinas makes God the starting point for philosophy; Heidegger excludes God from ontology, for if being means time, God cannot be said to be. Heidegger's early notion of being as temporalizing pre-understanding projected by *Dasein*, or later, as *Ereignis*, the occurrence of being, which sends *Dasein* into a particular dispensation of *Seinsverständnis*,

---

trans. Lewis Galantiere and Gerald B. Phelan (New York: Pantheon, 1948).

14 Hugo Ott, *Martin Heidegger: A Political Life*, trans. Allan Blunden (London: HarperCollins Publishers, 1993), pp. 276–80.

15 See Gustav Siewerth, 'Das Sein als Gleichnis Gottes' in Gustav Siewerth, *Gesammelte Werke*, vol. 1, *Sein und Wahrheit*, ed. Wolfgang Behler and Alma von Stockhausen (Düsseldorf: Patmos, 1975); English translation: *Philosophizing with Gustav Siewerth – Das Sein als Gleichnis Gottes. Being as Likeness of God*, ed. and trans. Andrzej Wiercinski (Konstanz: Gustav-Siewerth-Gesellschaft, 2005).

16 Martin Heidegger, *Being and Time*, trans. Joan Stambaugh (Albany, NY: SUNY, 1996), [hereafter *BT*], p. 34.

represents a decisive break with Aristotelian-scholastic ontology. In his early and later writings Heidegger disassociates being from act. Aquinas compounds the distortion already at work in Plato, the identification of being with constant presence, with the causal derivation of all beings from the *actus purus*. Heidegger derives the primordial Greek notion of being, *physis*, from *phainesthai*, 'to appear', denoting withdrawal and hiddenness as much as emergence and presence. This temporal structure can still be seen at work in Aristotle's notion of *energeia*. With the scholastic translation of *energeia* into *actualitas*, that which is effected by a working activity, the temporal association in *physis* is forgotten. In medieval terms, Heidegger reduces *esse* to *natura*. In Heidegger's view, Aquinas is guilty of compounding the forgetfulness of being (*Seinsvergessenheit*) already underway in late antiquity by imposing theologically altered formulations of Greek notions upon philosophy. The elision of the temporality of the being of beings, which begins with the Platonic turn away from *physis* to *eidos*, is secured through Aquinas's identification of being with *actus purus*, the pure actuality of infinite *substantia*.[17]

Three historical figures are decisive to Heidegger's polemical approach to Aquinas: Duns Scotus, Wilhelm Dilthey and Martin Luther. Heidegger's turn to Scotus in 1915 is influenced by his theology professor, Carl Braig, in some respects an anti-Thomistic neo-scholastic. A few years later, Heidegger's reading of Dilthey, especially Dilthey's discovery of the breakthrough to facticity in early Christianity, leads him to read the whole medieval period as one of decline. Around the same time, Luther drives Heidegger to overturn the medieval theological paradigm, and purge philosophy of theological content, as Luther had purged theology of philosophical content. Each of these voices contributed to a prejudice in Heidegger, which made it difficult, if not impossible, for him to read Aquinas sympathetically.

---

[17] Thirty years ago Thomas Sheehan summed up the much-misunderstood conflict between Heidegger and Aquinas on the nature of being. His succinct but penetrating account still stands. Thomas J. Sheehan, 'Notes on a "Lovers' Quarrel": Heidegger and Aquinas', *Listening* 9 (1974), pp. 137–43.

Heidegger's Approach to Aquinas

The archival work of Hugo Ott and Theodore Kisiel,[18] and the publication of much of Heidegger's *Gesamtausgabe*, especially the lectures leading up to *Being and Time*, have greatly filled out the details of Heidegger's Roman Catholic origins. From grammar school Heidegger had been steeped in the philosophy and theology of medieval Catholicism. His philosophical education had been largely scholastic, from the seminary exercises in apologetics, to his study of ontology under Braig at the University of Freiburg.[19] His 1915/16 *Habilitationsschrift* on Duns Scotus, *Die Kategorien und Bedeutungslehre des Duns Scotus*, is the fruit of a long apprenticeship to the philosophical traditions of the Roman Catholic Church.[20] Heidegger admitted this theological provenance, however tersely: 'Without this theological start, I would never have come onto the path of thought. But our origins always lie before us (*Herkunft aber bleibt stets Zukunft*).'[21] Heidegger saw himself as a scholastic phenomenologist in 1915, and anticipated making a major contribution to a renaissance of interest in medieval philosophy and theology. In a grant application that year he solemnly dedicated himself to 'the task of harnessing the intellectual and spiritual potential of Scholasticism to the future struggle for the Christian-Catholic ideal'.[22] In the winter semester of 1909, Heidegger enrolled in the theological seminary in Freiburg, the *Collegium Borromaeum*, where he continued his theology studies until 1911. Here he came under the influence of Braig, who introduced him to the basic principles of medieval metaphysics and the possibilities for theology in conversation with modern philosophy. Braig belonged to the Tübingen school of speculative theology,

---

18 Theodore Kisiel, *The Genesis of Heidegger's Being and Time* (Berkeley: University of California Press, 1993).

19 See Heidegger's 1963 intellectual autobiographical essay, 'My Way in Phenomenology', in Martin Heidegger, *On Time and Being*, trans. Joan Stambaugh (New York: Harper & Row, 1972), p. 75.

20 On Heidegger's Scotus study, see S. J. McGrath, *The Early Heidegger and Medieval Philosophy*, pp. 88–119.

21 Martin Heidegger, *On the Way to Language*, trans. Peter D. Herz (New York: Harper & Row, 1971), p. 10.

22 Heidegger's 1915 grant application to the 'The Constantin and Olga von Schaezler Foundation in Honour of St. Thomas Aquinas'. Ott, *A Political Life*, p. 73.

Veritas: Belief and Metaphysics

which integrated the insights of German Idealism with scholasticism.[23] Later in life Heidegger remembered Braig as his first philosophical mentor:

> It was from his lips, when he let me walk with him sometimes, that I first heard of the importance of Schelling and Hegel for speculative theology, as opposed to the doctrinal system of Scholasticism. In this way the tension between ontology and speculative theology as the developmental structure of metaphysics entered the horizon of my search.[24]

If Franz Brentano's *Von der mannigfachen Bedeutung des Seienden nach Aristoteles* first drew Heidegger's attention to the question of the meaning of the word 'being', Braig's *Vom Sein. Abriß der Ontologie* was Heidegger's first exposure to a systematic answer to the question.[25] Braig's work is a synthesis of ancient and medieval sources into a systematic ontology, but the predominant influence is Scotus. With Scotus, Braig holds that Aquinas's *analogia entis* leaves theology vulnerable to philosophical agnosticism, for it fails to recognize the essential knowability of the first principle. Aquinas's real distinction leads to a problematic affirmation of the existence of absolute being (*ipsum esse*) in the absence of any knowledge of the divine nature. As an alternative, Braig advocates a Scotistic essentialism, with roots in Augustine. Our everyday understanding of being is made possible by a primal illumination, an innate understanding of absolute being.[26] The essential forms of being – unity, otherness, self-identity – are neither 'read off' of experience, nor deduced a priori from reason; they emerge from the encounter of the immaterial intellect with the beings of everyday experience. In our everyday acts of knowing, being 'appears as something non-sensible, something supported by

---

23 On Braig see Karl Leidlmair, 'Carl Braig', in Emerich Coreth, Walter M. Neidl and Georg Pfligersdorffer (eds), *Christliche Philosophie im katholischen Denken des 19. und 20. Jahrhunderts*, 1, Neue Ansätze im 19. Jahrhundert (Graz: Styria, 1987), pp. 409–19.
24 Heidegger, 'My Way in Phenomenology', p. 75.
25 Carl Braig, *Vom Sein. Abriß der Ontologie* (Freiburg: Herder, 1896).
26 Cf. Augustine, *De Trinitate*, 8, 3.

thinking and only determinable in thinking'.[27] This thinking of being is only possible on the basis of an implicit knowledge of 'the unconditioned being, which conditions particular forms of being'.[28] Braig writes, 'The ground of being is not found . . . in a sensible being,' yet it shines through sensible beings, penetrating them and making them possible.[29] Being is not a concept that is projected onto things, not a 'clear and distinct' idea, which could be defined or accessed through Cartesian introspection, but 'the first determination which a being must have in order to be'.[30] Every attempt to define being inevitably fails, substituting some attribute of a particular being for being itself.[31] Reason finds itself in a Socratic *aporia*: it must affirm being, for it has always already assumed it, but it cannot define what it is that it affirms. 'For reason being is an assumption essential to the perceptibility of the experiential object, as well the possibility of the thinkable'.[32] Yet this inevitable assumption is neither 'the name by which we indeterminately fuse all things,' nor 'the common source out of which things come'; but 'the unnamed N which by itself signifies nothing, but which can take on all the values of the real predicates of an essential something and does indeed take them on insofar as the thing is.'[33] 'Being is that which is highest, most universal and simple, that which is abstracted (*abgezogen*) from beings, the distinctive feature in all concepts immediately imposed by thinking itself.'[34]

Braig's notion of being is none other than the *univocatio entis* of Scotism, the univocal a priori notion, empty of content but applicable to everything, creature and Creator alike.[35] Braig modifies

27 Braig, *Vom Sein*, p. 5.
28 Braig, *Vom Sein*, p. 5.
29 Braig, *Vom Sein*, p. 5.
30 Braig, *Vom Sein*, p. 19.
31 Braig, *Vom Sein*, p. 22.
32 Braig, *Vom Sein*, p. 19.
33 Braig, *Vom Sein*, p. 19.
34 Braig, *Vom Sein*, p. 23.
35 See Augustinus Karl Wucherer-Huldenfeld, 'Zu Heideggers Verständnis des Seins bei Johannes Duns Scotus und im Skotismus sowie im Thomismus und bei Thomas von Aquin', in Helmuth Vetter (ed.), *Heidegger und das Mittelalter* (Frankfurt a.M.: Peter Lang, 1999), pp. 41–59.

Scotistic ontology with transcendental philosophy. In a move that foreshadows Division One of *Being and Time*, Braig presents an ontological answer to the transcendental question. Braig argues that the question of 'the condition of the possibility of knowledge', if properly put, leads, not to Kant's transcendental subjective synthesis, but to *ipsum esse*. Everything depends upon putting the question properly. Kant's problematic, which suspends all metaphysical and ontological judgements until first achieving a proper understanding of the rules by which reason operates, will never arrive at being in Braig's view, for being is not a 'category', which could be deduced a priori. Being is hidden by beings, but it first shows its hiddenness in beings. Being is always the being of a being, *das Sein des Seienden*, an expression that occurs more than once in his work, as John Caputo has pointed out.[36] Braig writes,

> There is no speculative, absolute, intuitive, simply, presuppositionless metaphysics, which could disregard experience and read philosophical knowledge off of 'empty' thinking, determining it out of 'pure' thinking, or producing it through 'creative' thinking – there is no scientific ground for such a metaphysics.[37]

Yet the non-empirical nature of being justifies a qualified transcendental turn, one that stays with beings, while investigating their conditions of possibility. Ontological knowledge is not a cognition of a being, but the thematization of a presupposed immaterial intellectual principle. To thematize the ground we must turn from the thing to the light which makes it knowable, the *lumen naturalis*, and ultimately, the light of God. The human being is turned toward being in its being, and by this directedness makes possible an understanding of beings.[38]

---

36 Caputo, *Heidegger and Aquinas*, p. 54.
37 Braig, *Vom Sein*, p. 8.
38 Carl Braig, *Vom Denken. Abriß der Logik* (Freiburg: Herder, 1896), p. 9; Braig, *Vom Erkennen. Abriß der Noetic* (Freiburg: Herder, 1897), p. 156. The following remark from Caputo seems doubtful: 'The idea of Being as a horizon of meaning projected by *Dasein*'s understanding, within which beings are set free to appear as beings, is totally foreign to Braig.' *Heidegger and Aquinas*, pp. 50–1.

Braig's Scotistic mediation of medieval and modern sources doubtlessly influenced Heidegger's choice of topic and method of approach in his *Habilitationsschrift* (written under the direction of the neo-Kantian Heinrich Rickert). Heidegger's first book is a transcendental-phenomenological retrieval of the contemporary relevance of medieval speculative grammar and Scotistic metaphysics. The young Heidegger approaches Scotus's metaphysics and Thomas of Erfurt's *De modis significandi* (until 1922 presumed to be a work of Scotus's) as undeveloped sources for phenomenology, traditions unburdened by the epistemological dichotomy of modern philosophy, and rich with phenomenological moments: being as the basic field of intentional acts (*ens logicum*), the primordial intention of givenness (*modus essendi activus*), and the unobjectifiable thisness (*haecceitas*) of historical life. In Scotus and Thomas of Erfurt Heidegger finds clues that he will develop in his phenomenological ontology: the intention of being in ordinary speech acts, the gap between the universality of concepts and the individuality of existing things, the difference between privations, possibilities and actualities. His enthusiasm for the Middle Ages sparks a short-lived investigation into the philosophical foundations of medieval mysticism.[39] The influence of Braig and Scotus on Heidegger raises a further question: to what degree is the ontology of *Being and Time* a critique of Braig's transcendental Scotism? Is the Scholastic paradigm of being polemicized in the introduction to *Being and Time* not the Scotistic notion Heidegger learned from Braig, being as empty universal, the univocal notion applied in every act of thinking: self-evident, necessary and all-applicable, but itself content-free and undefinable?[40] If this is the case, it proves that those Thomists who try to mediate Heidegger and Aquinas are not entirely misguided. Heidegger may not have Aquinas's *esse* in mind in *Being and Time*, Section One. Nonetheless, Aquinas falls under a more serious reprobation: Heidegger's denial of the infinity and divinity of being.

Between the years 1917 and 1919, the year he wrote his famous

---

39 See Martin Heidegger, *The Phenomenology of Religious Life*, tr. Matthias Fritsch and Jennifer Anna Gosetti-Ferencei (Bloomington, IN: Indiana University Press, 2004), [hereafter *GA* 60], pp. 230–54.

40 See *BT*, pp. 2–3.

Veritas: Belief and Metaphysics

letter to his priest friend, Engelbert Krebs, breaking with 'the system of Catholicism',[41] Heidegger's view of medieval philosophy and theology underwent a radical change. The change seems to be related to a religious crisis in Heidegger's personal life which resulted in a conversion from Catholicism to non-denominational Protestantism. On 23 December 1918, Elfride Heidegger, expecting her first-born, told Krebs that they would not baptize the child, as promised at their Catholic wedding the year before (over which Krebs had presided), because Heidegger had 'lost his institutional faith'.[42] Although she and her husband remained Christian, they could no longer keep their commitment to raise the child Catholic. In his notes from this period Heidegger shows an increasing suspicion that scholasticism betrayed early Christianity.[43] He was deeply impressed by Dilthey's thesis that in its effort to segregate itself from Greek philosophy, Christianity discovered 'historical consciousness', only to allow it to be buried once again under Scholastic metaphysics.[44] The young Heidegger regarded the life-consciousness of primordial Christianity (*urchristliches Lebensbewußtsein*), the God-intensified 'self-world' of Christian discipleship, which comes to acute expression in Paul and Augustine, as the site of a breakthrough to facticity. In the 1919–20 lecture course, 'Grundprobleme der Phänomenologie', Heidegger argues that the experience of early Christian conversion is 'the historical paradigm for the turn to the self-world', Early Christian experience is relentlessly concentrated on inner motivation and the historical singularities of personal life.

> The most profound historical paradigm for the noteworthy process of shifting the centre of gravity of factic life and the life-world into the self-world and the world of inward experience is

---

41 Ott, *A Political Life*, p. 106.
42 Ott, *A Political Life*, pp. 106–21. Husserl confirms that Heidegger had undergone a religious conversion in a letter to Rudolf Otto of 5 March 1919, quoted in *A Political Life*, p. 118.
43 See in particular the 1917 note entitled 'The Religious *a priori*', GA 60, pp. 237–9.
44 See Wilhelm Dilthey, *Introduction to the Human Sciences*, trans. Ramon J. Betanzos (Detroit: Wayne State University, 1988), pp. 228–39. Cf. Kisiel, *Genesis*, pp. 100–5; GA 60, 118.

given for us in the emergence of Christianity. The self-world as such enters into life and becomes lived as such. What comes forth in the life of the primal Christian communities signifies a radical reversal of the directional tendency of life. It is usually thought of as a denial of the world and asceticism. Here lie the motives for the development of completely new contents of expression which life fashions – even up to that which we today call history.[45]

Heidegger's appropriation of Dilthey's stark opposition between early Christianity and scholasticism marks his break with Braig and Scotism. Where the early Christians thematize historical being-in-the-world, the scholastics define *ens infinitum*. Where the early Christians develop a notion of conscience, the scholastics codify natural law. Where the early Christians proclaim faith as a mode of historical existence, the scholastics denigrate faith as a deficient mode of theoretical cognition. In his notes, the young Heidegger records the following passage from Dilthey:

It has been the tragic fate of Christendom to remove the holiest experiences of the human heart from the quiet of a personal life and to make them part of the motive forces of world-historical hypocrisy in the process. On the theoretical level it succumbed to a fate which weighed no less heavily on its further development. If Christianity wished to bring the content of its experience to full consciousness, it had to assimilate that content into the conceptual framework of the external world, which ordered it according to the relations of space, time, substance, and causality. Thus the development of this content in dogma was at once its externalization.[46]

It is in the context of his study of Dilthey that we must interpret Heidegger's profoundly anti-scholastic reading of Book 10 of

---

45 Martin Heidegger, *Grundprobleme der Phänomenologie*, *Gesamtausgabe*, 58, ed. Hans-Helmuth Gander (Frankfurt a.M.: Vittorio Klostermann, 1992), [hereafter *GA* 58], pp. 61–2.
46 Dilthey, *Introduction to the Human Sciences*, p. 233; See Kisiel, *Genesis*, p. 104.

Veritas: Belief and Metaphysics

Augustine's *Confessions* in the 1921 lecture course, 'Augustine and neo-Platonism'.[47] The point of the lecture is to demonstrate that Augustine's breakthrough to the historical self in the archaeology of *memoria* is eclipsed by the imposition of Neoplatonic axiology, the notion of God as the *summum bonum*, the highest value, which relativizes and devalues all temporal values. Although Heidegger only coined the term 'ontotheology' in his later writings,[48] the basic idea first appears in this lecture. Metaphysics betrays the factic when it traces the changing and the temporal to the unchanging and eternal. At the moment of the breakthrough to historicity Augustine's restlessness (*cor inquietum* – what in *Being and Time* Heidegger calls Angst) is resolved in the Neoplatonic being-toward-eternal-truth (*veritas aeterna*). The unique attributes of human being disengaged in the *Confessions*, restlessness, care, the being of the past in memory, and being toward the future, are denigrated to shadows, half-real, participated being – not positive phenomena, but privations of the fullness of being that God alone enjoys.[49] In the follow-up 1921 Augustine lecture course, 'Phenomenological Interpretations of Aristotle', Heidegger singles out the notion of infinite being as the principal obfuscation of the phenomenon of life in the history of philosophy. 'With this infinity, life blinds itself, annuls itself. Incarcerating itself, life lets itself go. It falls short. Factical life lets itself go precisely by expressly and positively fending off itself.'[50]

Dilthey leads Heidegger to the early Reformation, according to Dilthey, the moment when historical consciousness re-emerges from its dogmatic eclipse in the Middle Ages. Although we have little textual record of Heidegger's Luther studies, which we know occupied him in the years immediately following his *Habilitationsschrift* (1916–19), he left traces of his reading of Luther in occasional remarks scattered throughout the early Freiburg and

---

47 *GA* 60, pp. 113–227.
48 Heidegger, *Identity and Difference*, pp. 42–76.
49 *GA* 60, pp. 118, 194–5, 199, 212–13.
50 Martin Heidegger, *Phenomenological Interpretations of Aristotle. Initiation into Phenomenological Research*, trans. Richard Rojcewicz (Bloomington, IN: Indiana University Press, 2001), [hereafter *GA* 61], 108.

Marburg lectures.⁵¹ Piecing these references together we get a hint of what might be regarded as Heidegger's first 'history of being'. What is decisive for Heidegger is how Luther's polemic against the scholastic thesis of the analogy of being (*analogia entis*) brings about a retrieval of the repressed self-world of primordial Christianity. The factical self rises up in rebellion in the early Reformation, tearing down the constructs of scholastic science overlying it and retrieving historically saturated, authentic Christian faith. It is no exaggeration to say that Heidegger's early philosophy is constructed as a hermeneutical phenomenological complement to Luther's *theologia crucis*. In tandem with Luther, who maximizes the human being's need for transformative grace by underscoring natural life as an *aversio Dei,* Heidegger intensifies the uncertainty, difficulty, and Godforsakenness of human existence.⁵² Heidegger's retrieval of Luther is accompanied by

---

51 Luther's influence on Heidegger has long been known, if only recently textually corroborated. As early as 1955, the Luther scholar Edmund Schlink described Heidegger's philosophy as 'a radical secularization of Luther's anthropology'. Edmund Schlink, 'Weisheit und Torheit', *Kerygma und Dogma* 1 (1955), p. 6. See also Otto Pöggeler's 1963 reference to Heidegger's reading of Luther's *Disputatio Heidelbergae* in his *Martin Heidegger's Path of Thinking*, trans. David Magurshak and Sigmund Barber (Atlantic Highlands: Humanities Press, 1987), p. 28; Richard Schaeffler's 1978 examination of Lutheran themes in *Being and Time* in his *Frömmigkeit des Denkens. Martin Heidegger und die katholische Theologie* (Darmstadt: Wissenschaftliche Buchgesellschaft, 1978), chapter one. See also Karl Jaspers, 'On Heidegger', *Graduate Faculty Philosophy Journal*, 7 (1978), pp. 108–9. References to Luther in the *Gesamtausgabe* publications of Heidegger's *frühe Freiburger Vorlesungen* (all references given here to the German editions): *GA* 56/57, p. 18; *GA* 58, pp. 62, 204–5; *GA* 60, pp. 283, 310; *GA* 61, pp. 7, 182–3; *GA* 63, pp. 5, 14, 27, 46, 106. See Rudolph Bultmann's letter to Hans von Soden of 23 December 1923 praising Heidegger's Luther scholarship, quoted in Ott, *A Political Life*, p. 125.

52 Jean Greisch writes: 'Without directly saying it, he [Heidegger] suggests that the hermeneutics of facticity can make a pact with the theology of the cross.' Jean Greisch, *L'Arbre de vie et l'arbre du savoir: le chemin phénoménologique de l'herméneutique heideggérienne (1919–1923)* (Paris: Édition du Cerf, 2000), p. 247. On Heidegger's relationship to Luther see S. J. McGrath, 'The Facticity of Being Godforsaken: The Young Heidegger's Accommodation of Luther's Theology of the Cross',

savage critique of neo-scholasticism and Catholicism, all the more remarkable in the light of his devout orthodoxy a few years earlier. In a 1917 note, we read of 'dogmatic, casuistic pseudo-philosophies, which pass themselves off as such philosophies of a particular system of religion (for instance Catholicism) and supposedly stand close to religion and the religious'.[53] In a 1919 note, Heidegger polarizes the Protestant and Catholic experience of faith; the latter theorizes and distorts early Christian religiosity; the former vindicates it.

> Protestant faith and Catholic faith are *fundamentally different*. Noetically and noematically separated experiences. In Luther an *original* form of religiosity – one that is also not found in the mystics – breaks out. The 'holding-to-be-true' of Catholic faith is founded entirely otherwise than the *fiducia* of the reformers. . . . From there also the concept of 'grace' differentiates itself, and with it, the entire 'relationship' of grace and freedom, nature and grace; and the meaning of the phrase '*gratia supponit naturam*'; the doctrine of the '*iustificatio*' and the conception of the sacrament.[54]

Without denying the existence of personal religious motives, we can conclude that Heidegger's study of Dilthey and Luther precipitate his changed view of the philosophical value of scholasticism. The reversal is demonstrated through a comparison of the so-called 'Phenomenological Foundations of Medieval Mysticism: Notes to a Cancelled Lecture Course'[55] with the *Habilitations-*

---

in the *American Catholic Philosophical Quarterly*, 79: 2 (Spring 2005), pp. 273–90. See especially John van Buren's superb 'Martin Heidegger, Martin Luther', in Theodore Kisiel and John van Buren (eds), *Reading Heidegger from the Start: Essays in his Earliest Thought* (Albany, NY: SUNY Press, 1994), pp. 159–74.

53 GA 60, p. 237.
54 GA 60, p. 236.
55 GA 60, pp. 229–54. The precise dating of these notes is not found in the *Gesamtausgabe* edition, which misleadingly suggests that the notes were compiled in 1918–19 in preparation for a lecture on medieval mysticism. Some are at least as early as 1917. Only a few can be regarded as composed in preparation for the cancelled lecture course of 1919. I have relied on Alfred Denker's *Historical Dictionary of Heidegger's Philosophy*

schrift on the topic of the significance of medieval mysticism. In 1915, Heidegger argues *against* a dichotomy of medieval mysticism and medieval scholasticism. The false dichotomy is symptomatic of a flattening of the multiple domains of meaning to which the medieval mind is acutely sensitive. 'The two "antithetical pairs": rationalism and irrationalism, Scholasticism and mysticism do not coincide,' Heidegger writes in the *Habilitationsschrift*. 'As a rationalistic construct detached from life, philosophy is powerless; as an irrationalistic experience, mysticism is aimless.'[56] Mysticism is the spontaneous expression of the lifeworld of the Middle Ages; scholasticism is its science. Without mysticism, scholasticism would be empty and lifeless. Without scholasticism, mysticism would be blind. Two years later, Heidegger's notes express the opposite view, emphatically re-inscribing the scholasticism/mysticism dichotomy:

> Already in the strongly natural-scientific, naturalistic theoretical metaphysics of being of Aristotle and its radical elimination and misrecognition of the problem of value in Plato, which is renewed in medieval Scholasticism, the predominance of the theoretical is already potentially present, so that Scholasticism, within the totality of the medieval Christian world of experience, severely endangered precisely the immediacy of religious life, and forgot religion in favor of theology and dogma. And already in the early days of Christianity, these dogmas exercised a theorizing, dogma-promoting influence on the institutions and statutes of church law. An appearance such as mysticism is to be understood as an elementary counter-movement.[57]

John van Buren has shown us that Luther's most significant influence on the young Heidegger was the *theologia crucis*, the theological critique of the scholastic presumption of a natural and speculative access to God.[58] Luther attacks scholastic theology as

---

(Lanham, Maryland and London: The Scarecrow Press, 2000) for my dating.
56 *GA* 1, p. 410.
57 *GA* 60, p. 238.
58 John van Buren, *The Young Heidegger: Rumor of the Hidden King* (Bloomington: Indiana University Press, 1994), pp. 149–50.

the *theologia gloriae*, a Greek aesthetic theology, which presumes that God can be seen in nature. The scholastic appropriation of Greek metaphysics is motivated by a flight from the uncertainty, turmoil and temporality of authentic Christian discipleship. The scholastics substitute a philosophical principle, to which human reason is assumed to have constant and unhindered access, for the crucified God who can only be known in revelation. Faith for Luther means risking unconditional trust in the paradoxical manifestation of God in the Crucified, divinity revealed in a contradictory form, the Godforsaken's only possible access to God.[59] In the light of this radical Lutheran theology of fallenness, Heidegger denies theology the possibility of a philosophical access to the divine, and philosophy, a natural access to theology.[60]

Destruktion

The later Heidegger regards the Aristotelian-scholastic notion of being as *substantia* as the pivot of the forgetfulness of temporality in Western philosophy. *Substantia* is that which subsists and supports changes, that which can stand alone and bear properties, that which can be named. Yet 'being' is a verb before it is a noun. The Greek infinitive *einai*, 'to be', originally meant *parousia*, 'to be present'. From simple unmodulated presence, we arrive at the notion of coming into presence, arrival, advent. In this primordial word, 'there prevails, in an unthought and concealed manner

---

[59] See Luther's 'Heidelberg Disputation' and 'Disputation Against Scholastic Theology' in *Luther's Work*, p. 31, in *Career of the Reformer*, trans. Harold J. Grimm (Philadelphia: Mulenberg, 1957). See the lecture Heidegger gave in Rudolph Bultmann's seminar in 1924, 'The Problem of Sin in Luther', recently translated by John van Buren in *Martin Heidegger, Supplements. From the Earliest Essays to Being and Time and Beyond*, ed. John van Buren (Albany, NY: State University of New York Press, 2002), pp. 105–10.

[60] This is a central thesis of Heidegger's 1928 lecture 'Phenomenology and Theology', trans. James G. Hart and John C. Maraldo in Martin Heidegger, *Pathmarks*, ed. William McNeil (Cambridge: Cambridge University Press, 1998), pp. 39–54.

presence and duration – there prevails time'.[61] The temporal connotation is to some degree retained in the technical Aristotelian term *ousia* (the Greek root of *substantia*), which, in everyday ancient Greek, meant household goods, property, that which one has at one's disposal. Presence originally meant presencing in the present; as such it had an essential reference to emergence into presence. With the reification of being-present in *substantia*, the dynamism inherent in the infinitive *einai* is lost. The notion of that which appears in time is eclipsed by the concept of that which lies always present-at-hand, that which has no time because it does not change.

The Aristotelian-scholastic divinization of *substantia* elevates being above *physis* and precludes a phenomenological investigation of historical life on its own terms. When philosophy presumes access to an *ens infinitum* the answer to the question of the meaning of being is given in advance: being means God; all other beings *are* in so far as they participate in the *actus purus*. Factical life is interpreted in terms of nonfactical eternity. Temporality is excluded from the discussion, and theology substituted for the understanding native to life. The phenomenological maxim, 'back to the things themselves', is a call to hold thinking to life, to resist the perennial temptation to fly from time into 'eternal verities', and 'grasp factical life in its decisive possibilities of Being. . . . to make factical life speak for itself on the basis of its very own factical possibilities'.[62] Heidegger's antithesis to ontotheology – being *as* time – uproots the notion of *ens infinitum* and renders it impossible. Whatever else the divine might be, it is *not* being. From the outset of *Being and Time*, Heidegger excludes the possibility of knowledge of a nontemporal, immutable, and infinite being: 'Being is in each instance comprehensible only in regard to time.'[63]

The assumption that Aquinas's alleged ontotheology obstructs temporality colours the few sustained interpretations of Aquinas

---

61 Martin Heidegger, 'An Introduction to "What is Metaphysics?"', in Heidegger, *Pathmarks*, pp. 285–6.
62 Martin Heidegger, 'Phenomenological Interpretations with Respect to Aristotle (Indication of the Hermeneutical Situation)', *Man and World* 25 (1992), hereafter PIA: p. 393.
63 *BT*, p. 16.

Veritas: Belief and Metaphysics

which appear in Heidegger's works. In the 1923/4 lecture course *Einführung in die phänomenologische Forschung* Heidegger takes Aquinas to be a key figure in the scholastic movement that prepares the way for the modern methodological censure of temporality.[64] By securing the truth of things in the divine gaze (*verum transcendens*), Aquinas's ontotheology fixes being in the vicegrip of judgemental thinking. Truth is denied its own mode of being; truth *is* only to the degree that it stands in relation to a correctly judging intellect. Even transcendental truth, *verum transcendens*, is a relation to intellect: by thinking essences God invests them with the transcendental relation which makes them possible. The historical effect of Aquinas's ontotheological move is Cartesianism. Where in Aquinas the certainty of judgements is ultimately anchored in the absolute veracity of the eternal being, in Descartes the certainty of perception is anchored in the transparency of the *cogito*. 'The care *of* certainty is as a care *about* certainty at the same time a taking care in which temporality is excluded. That means however: the exclusion of *Dasein* as such. The care of certainty is the *displacement* of being.'[65] In Aquinas's five ways, the being of the world is conceived as caused, therefore secured in the care of certainty as calculable, measurable and predictable. According to Heidegger, it is a small step from here to the reductionist physics of the modern age.[66]

The famous 1927 Marburg lecture course, *Basic Problems of Phenomenology*, contains a lengthy analysis of the distinction between *essentia* and *existentia* in Aquinas, Scotus and Suarez. Heidegger argues that the distinction was known to the Greeks, if only in an undeveloped form. It remained for the scholastics, under the impulse of biblical theology, to fully elaborate the distinction. Through scholasticism the distinction became bound up with the metaphysics of creation. As a means for distinguishing uncreated from created being, the distinction eclipses the factic: if essence and existence, whatness and thatness, are presumed to exhaust the ontological field, *Dasein* must remain unexplored. *Dasein* is never a *what* or a *that*, but always only a *who*. 'The medieval period

---

64 *GA* 17, pp. 162–194.
65 *GA* 17, p. 283.
66 *GA* 17, p. 194.

shows no new approaches,' Heidegger writes. Heidegger undertakes a phenomenological genealogy of the distinction between *essentia* and *existentia* in order 'to establish the birth certificate of these concepts'.[67] Both have their roots in facticity (as do all genuine ontological notions), but their factical origins are concealed in the Latin terms. The factical ground of the distinction can only be accessed through a *Destruktion* of the Latin terms back to their Greek roots.

Heidegger follows Giles of Rome in interpreting Aquinas's *distinctio realis* as a distinction between two things. By thinking of the distinction between *essentia* and *existentia* as a distinction between two *rei* (*existentia* is added to *essentia* in the divine production of beings), Aquinas, in Heidegger's reading, displays not only his inability to think being in anything other than ontic terms, he also shows incoherence. If *existentia* is really distinct from *essentia*, then it must have a whatness proper to it by which it is distinguished. *Essentia* and *existentia* become two things conjoined by God in created beings. Yet an *existentia* that is a thing in its own right collapses the distinction between *essentia* and *existentia*. For in order to be a thing, *existentia* would have to have its own *essentia*.[68]

---

67 GA 24, p. 100.
68 To the contrary, Gilson shows that the *distinctio realis* cannot be taken to mean a distinction between two things. See his *Being and Some Philosophers* (Toronto: Pontifical Institute of Mediaeval Studies, 1952), p. 172: 'The very common mistake about this fundamental thesis of Thomism is always due to the same overlooking of the reciprocal character of efficient causality and formal causality. "To be" is not a thing distinct in itself from "essence" as from another thing. It is not, for the simple reason that taken in themselves, "to be" and essence are not "things." Their composition alone is what makes up a thing, but they both become, so to speak, "real" because "to be" then is to be a "being," just as "to be such" is to be "such a being." Actual existence, then, is the efficient cause by which essence in its turn is the formal cause which makes an actual existence to be "such an existence." Since they represent irreducibly distinct modes of causality, essence and existence are irreducibly distinct, but the reality of their distinction presupposes their composition, that is, it presupposes the actual reality of the thing. Existence is not distinct from essence as one being from another being; yet, in any given being, that whereby a being both is and actually subsists is "really" other than that

Veritas: Belief and Metaphysics

Aquinas's approach to the distinction typifies Christianity's distortion of Greek ontology with a theology of creation, which results in a reduction of being to product. 'That beings must be understood as created by God is adhered to as an unshakeable conviction. By this ontical declaration a putting of the ontological question is condemned from the start to impossibility.'[69] Heidegger traces *essentia* and *existentia* back to factical life by way of Greek categories derived from 'a productive comportment of *Dasein*' (*herstellendes Verhalten des Daseins*).[70] The distinction translates ancient concepts originally employed to describe the making of artefacts appropriated by medieval theologians to explain the theological dogma of creation. All production proceeds by way of an image that acts as the producer's model, the form or *eidos* in Aristotle's metaphysics, 'that which a thing already was' (*quod quid erat esse*). When a thing is produced, the *eidos* is actualized, given existence. The product is released into a state of independence from its producer and becomes a real thing. In Heidegger's view, the scholastic metaphysics of creation is modelled on production. God is distinguished from all that he produces in so far as he alone does not need to be produced. Things have a pre-existence in God – they are essences without existence – as the form of an artefact has a pre-existence in the mind of the artisan. The scholastics are following the Greeks in this regard. Because in a general sense goods are products, *ousia* (property) was originally understood by the Greeks within the horizon of production, the process of forming something on the basis of a preconceived model. The philosophical notion, *eidos*, the image by which a being is crafted or made, becomes the concept of eternal form.[71] The model which precedes the production is understood to be free of imperfections –

---

whereby it is definable as such a being in the order of substantiality.' See Aquinas, *De ente et essentia*, c. 5, l, 24–27. English translation, *On Being and Essence*, trans. Armand Maurer (Toronto: Pontifical Institute of Medieval Studies, 1968), p. 61. See also Joseph Owens, *The Doctrine of Being in the Aristotelian Metaphysics: A Study in the Greek Background of Mediaeval Thought*, 3rd rev. ed. (Toronto: Pontifical Institute of Mediaeval Studies, 1978), pp. 1–10.

69 GA 24, 100.
70 GA 24, p. 105.
71 GA 24, p. 151.

the idea in the mind of the craftsman is a vision of a flawless product. Consequently, *eidos* is interpreted as timeless being. Production externalizes *eidos* and releases the product into independent existence. Hence the genesis of the notion of being as object of intuition: that which shows itself as existing, independent of the perceiver. In this way, *ousia* came to mean *Vorhandensein*, objective presence.

In the 1941 Nietzsche lecture, the forgetfulness of being is pushed further back to Plato and Aristotle. The *essentia/existentia* distinction is interpreted as compounding the late Greek substitution of permanent presence for the Presocratic notion of being as emergence, *physis*. *Essentia* and *existentia* configure being as effected thing, work or present-at-hand entity, that which can be caused, made, calculated and manipulated. This metaphysics reaches its completion in the technological age. The scholastics are assigned their ignominious place in the history of being as the chief perpetrators of the forgetfulness of being in the modern age. The role is not one that the scholastics freely assumed, but one which they were given. Heidegger assumes a critical distance to his 1927 genealogical approach to the distinction of *essentia* and *existentia*; the distinction is no longer interpreted as a Latinization of Greek ontology, it is the epoch-making moment that makes metaphysics possible. 'The division into whatness and thatness does not just contain a doctrine of metaphysical thinking. It points to an event in the history of being.'[72] Heidegger shows how *existentia* is related to *actualitas*, which is derived from *agere*, 'to act'. To exist is to have an *essentia* which is given *actualitas* through efficient causality, to be brought into actual being from a prior state of possible being. In the modern age being sends itself as actuality (*Wirklichkeit*), that which is actual, effected, brought into being through a causal act. Only that *is* which acts or is capable of causally acting on another. Within the horizon of *actualitas*, being is reduced to the spatiotemporal nexus of causes thematized by natural science.

The later Heidegger traces the scholastic understanding of *essentia/existentia*, not to Greece, as he did in 1927, but to Rome, the culture of action and law. The scholastics perpetuate Roman

---

72 GA 6.2, p. 4.

Veritas: Belief and Metaphysics

totalizing rationality, ushering in the epoch of doing, making and producing. From Rome through Christendom to modernity, the rule of metaphysics as the ontology of *actualitas* holds sway. *Actualitas* finds its highest manifestation in God, the *actus purus*:

> The causal character of being as reality shows itself in all purity in that being which fulfills the essence of being in the highest sense, since it is that being which can never not be. Thought 'theologically,' this being is called 'God.' It doesn't know the state of possibility because in that state it would not yet be something. In every not-yet there lies a lack of being, in that being is distinguished by permanence. The highest being is pure actuality always fulfilled, *actus purus*. Effecting is here the persisting presencing of itself of what persists of itself. This being (*ens*) is not only what it is (*sua essentia*), but in what it is, it is always also the persistence of what it is (*est suum esse non participans alio*).[73]

The notion of God supplants unconcealment with constant presence; it is as such the metaphysical concept *par excellence*, the notion that makes *physis* impossible to think. No being spontaneously emerges when all is caused.

Unbelief

It is important to note how Heidegger's atheistic *Destruktion* of *essentia/existentia* remains consistent with his early phenomenology. In 1924 he argued that 'the philosopher does not believe'.[74] In 1935 he supplemented this by holding that the authentic theologian does not philosophize. As 'a thinking and questioning elaboration of the world of Christian experience, i.e., of faith' theology has little or nothing to do with philosophy.[75] The separation of

---

73 GA 6.2, p. 15.
74 Martin Heidegger, *The Concept of Time. Begriff der Zeit*, German-English edition, trans. William McNeill (Oxford: Blackwell, 1989), 1. Cf. GA 61, p. 197.
75 Martin Heidegger, *An Introduction to Metaphysics*, trans. Ralph Manheim (Garden City: Doubleday, 1961), p. 6.

philosophy from theology remains a leitmotif of Heidegger's later career. 'If I were to write a theology,' Heidegger said in Zurich in 1951, 'then the word *Being* would not occur in it. Faith does not need the thought of Being. When faith has recourse to this thought, it is no longer faith. This is what Luther understood.'[76] Philosophy does not believe because it has no *reason* to believe. God is not given in the world, not even as the unobjectifiable term of a human desire. Scholastic philosophical theology is a tissue of illusion, not only deceptive of our theological predicament, but also distortive of our philosophical situation. Philosophy must articulate the world as it is, not as it might appear to an intelligence illuminated by supernatural faith. Unlike theology, philosophy lives by questioning, and the spirit of questioning demands a radical detachment from already formulated answers. Such a stance is apparently compatible with a certain kind of religious faith. Indeed, in its uncompromising honesty, Heidegger holds that it is closer to the truth of religion than a safe and unthinking piety. Philosophy censures God-talk for it is this-worldly, 'the grasp of factical life in its decisive possibilities for being', as Heidegger puts it in the 1922 Natorp-Bericht.[77] Philosophy must stay with the most basic terms of life, even if this amounts to formal unbelief.[78] Heidegger pre-

---

76 Martin Heidegger, *Seminare 1951–1973*, Gesamtausgabe 15 (Frankfurt a.M.: Vittorio Klostermann, 1986), pp. 436–7.

77 PIA, pp. 355–93, at p. 367.

78 'First of all, if philosophy is not a contrived preoccupation with just any 'generalities' whatsoever, and with arbitrarily posited principles (a preoccupation which merely runs alongside life itself); but if it exists rather as a questioning knowledge, i.e., as research, simply as the genuine, explicit actualization of the tendency towards interpretation which belongs to life's own basic movements (movements within which life is concerned about itself and its own Being); and secondly, if philosophy intends to view and to grasp factical life in its decisive possibilities of Being; i.e., if philosophy has decided radically and clearly on its own (without regard for any bustling about with respect to world-views) to make factical life speak for itself on the basis of its very own factical possibilities; i.e., if philosophy is fundamentally atheistic and if it understands this about itself; – then it has decisively chosen factical life in its facticity and has made this an object for itself. . . . [Philosophy is] "atheistic," but not in the sense of a theory such as materialism or something similar. Every philosophy which understands itself in what it is must

supposes that factical life experience is nontheistic, that is, we have no worldly experience of God. Therefore a philosophy committed to 'research', not to generalities and world-views, but to going along with life in its spontaneous self-interpretation, that is, a hermeneutics of facticity, will not be theistic.

With two thinkers as diametrically opposed as Heidegger and Aquinas dialogue and debate are not possible. At issue here is not this or that argument or thesis but the basic horizon of thinking. One cannot resolve this *disputatio* without radically altering one of the opposed positions; one can, however, correct misrepresentations. Gustav Siewerth, Johannes Baptist Lotz and Ferdinand Ulrich, among others, have commented on Heidegger's repeated failure to grasp that *esse* in Aquinas is not a substance, but an act of emergence, as such not entirely unlike the Greek notion of *physis*, 'self-blossoming emergence'. The ontotheological charge, that the ontological difference is forgotten when being is causally reduced to a highest being, also seems to fall short of the mark in the case of Aquinas. God's creation is a kenotic self-differentiation, not a production. God is the paradigm for all emergence into being, the first instance of difference, making possible all subsequent differentiations. He is emphatically not a thing. The divine act by which he causes beings to be is not the production of a thing from a prototype, but a self-emptying. God empties himself into being, allowing there to be something other than himself. He allows for finite being by allowing for nothingness, and in doing so allows Himself, who is without limit, to be, paradoxically, othered.

The Gilson school argues that for Aquinas, the *esse* in which all things participate is neither a substance, nor a concept. As really distinct from *essentia*, *esse* is non-substantial and non-conceptual. 'In the mind of Thomas Aquinas, the notion of being underwent a

---

– as the factical *how* of the interpretation of life – know (and it must know this precisely when it still has some "notion" of God) that life's retreat towards its own self (which philosophy achieves) is, in religious terms, a show of hands against God. But only then is philosophy honest, i.e., only then is philosophy in keeping with its possibility free from misleading concern which merely talks about religiosity. [One may well ask] whether the very idea of a philosophy of religion (especially if it makes no reference to the facticity of the human being) is pure nonsense.' *PIA*, pp. 367, 393.

remarkable transformation,' Gilson writes. Being no longer meant form (*eidos*) as it did for Plato, or substance (*ousia*) as it did for Aristotle; it meant *esse*, the act signified by the verb 'to be'.[79] When form or *eidos* is no longer identified with being, essence becomes potency to a more fundamental act. *Essentia* is a limitation of *esse*, a contraction of the act of being to determinate structure. *Substantia* is a further contraction of *esse* to a particular this. In itself *esse* is infinite actuality, act without determination or limit. Containing within itself all formal differences, 'in a more excellent way than other things' (*modo excellentiori omnibus rebus*), *esse* is participated in by everything that exists, yet remains free of all generic, specific and individual determinations.[80] This dynamic non-substantive notion of *esse* does not seem to figure into Heidegger's *Destruktion*.

Esse is not found apart from things; it is something that a thing 'does' in some respect, but it is not itself a thing. It is not static, but the pure energy of be-ing (the participle understood here as a verb), the dynamic act of a thing's being posited outside the merely possible.[81] Aquinas says that *esse* is to *essentia* as light is to the illuminated. 'Being is always to be found in a thing, and is the act of a being, just as light is the act of the illuminated' (*esse in re est, et est actus entis, resultans ex principiis rei, sicut lucere est actus lucentis*).[82] The light metaphor shows that *esse* must be traced back to something other than *essentia*. In creation God releases an order

---

79 Etienne Gilson, *History of Christian Philosophy in the Middle Ages* (New York: Random House, 1955), p. 368.

80 Aquinas, *De ente*, c. 5, 35; English, p. 62.

81 Gerald Phelan argues: 'Things which "have being" are not "just there" (*Dasein*) like lumps of static essence, inert, immovable, unprogressive and unchanging. The act of existence (*esse*) is not a state, it is an act, the act of all acts, and, therefore, must be understood as act and not as any static and definable object of conception. *Esse* is dynamic impulse, energy, act, – the first, the most persistent and enduring of all dynamisms, all energies, all acts. In all things on earth the act of being (*esse*) is the consubstantial urge of a nature, a restless, striving force, carrying each being (*ens*) onward, from within the depths of its own reality to its full achievement, i.e., fully to be what by its nature it is apt to become.' Gerald B. Phelan, *The Existentialism of St. Thomas*, ed. Arthur G. Kirn (Toronto: Pontifical Institute of Mediaeval Studies, 1967), p. 77.

82 Aquinas, *In III Sent.*, d. 6, q. 2, a. 2, *resp.*

of essences, a dimension of himself, a possibility of divine thinking, into relatively independent existence. The release is not the production of one thing from another, but an act of self-limitation by which the being who has no other allows for another, allows the whole *esse/essentia* composite to emerge. Creation is God's pouring himself out. The creature has a nature proper to itself and so we speak of *essentia* as the thing's formal cause, that to which the thing owes its determinate structure. Yet without God, neither the thing nor the thing's essence would have *esse*.[83] *Esse* is not a thing that can be separated from another thing, not a thing that comes together with a second thing (*essentia*), to compose a third thing, the existing substance.[84] Things all have essences; *esse* has no essence, it is not a what, not a form, but an act that is in itself free of all determinate form.

Far from forgetting the difference between being and beings, it seems that Aquinas makes it a foundation for ontology.

What would Heidegger say to this? He would have to concede that Aquinas does not identify being and substance. However, he would point out that, by identifying being with act, Aquinas nonetheless de-temporalizes being. *Esse* is 'something fixed and at rest in being' (*aliquid fixum et quietum in ente*). To be means to be the being of that which subsists, that which persists through time. Being is the *actus essendi*, the act of an essence, that is, the act of subsisting. God, *ipsum esse subsistens*, is not an exception to this de-temporalization but its primary instance. The point of the distinction between the being of God and the being of every created thing is to emphasize that subsistence is most perfectly found in

---

83 See Etienne Gilson, *The Christian Philosophy of St. Thomas Aquinas*, trans. L. K. Shook (New York: Random House, 1956), p. 448, n. 30.

84 The interpretation of the *distinctio realis* as a distinction between two things originated two years after the death of Aquinas with the writings of Giles of Rome. According to Joseph Owens, Aquinas only uses the term *realis* to characterize the distinction between *esse* and *essentia* in three places. Generally Aquinas avoids the term because of its connotation of a distinction between two *res*. See Joseph Owens, *An Elementary Christian Metaphysics* (Milwaukee: Bruce Publishing Company, 1963), p. 104n. Thomas Aquinas, *In I sent.*, d. 19, q. 2, a. 2; *De Ver.*, 27, 1, ad 8m; *In se hebd.*, c. 2., *Cont. Gent.*, I, 20.

God and only secondarily found in creatures. God cannot be called a substance in the same way that all other beings are called substances because God is absolutely subsistent, that is, absolutely present. God imparts something of this ontological stability to every created thing. That which is perfectly fixed and at rest (God) is most properly called being; that which is relatively fixed and at rest (substance) has being in a secondary sense; that which is not fixed and at rest in any way, but requires another being in order to exist (accident) has being in a qualified and derivative sense. The hierarchy of being is established in terms of changelessness, fixity, freedom from time: being is properly attributed to the absolutely timeless standing-alone of God, with qualification to the relatively timeless standing-alone of created things, and in a derivative sense to everything that can only abide and stand with the support of other things.[85]

So in one sense, Aquinas is guilty as charged. He de-temporalizes *esse*. It is important to note, however, that the analogy of being allows Aquinas to maintain a finite sense of *esse*, which participates in eternal *esse*, but is not reducible to it. For Aquinas the

---

85 The following passage from Aquinas, *In I Periherm*, lect. 5, no. 22, shows that Aquinas differentiates the nominal and verbal sense of being and is, therefore, not guilty of substantializing it. Nonetheless, he identifies being with what Heidegger calls 'constant presence'. This, for Heidegger, is enough to prove that Aquinas is forgetful of being: 'For [is] means that which is understood after the manner of absolute actuality [*in intellectu per modum actualitas absolutae*]. For is, when it is expressed without qualification, means to be in act [*in actu esse*], and therefore it has its meaning after the manner of a verb. But the actuality, which is the principal meaning of the verb is, is indifferently the actuality of every form, either substantial or accidental act. Hence it is that when we wish to signify that any form or act actually inheres in any subject, we signify it by this verb "is," either simply or according to some qualification – simply in the present tense; according to some qualification, in the other tenses.' The primary meaning of *esse* is verbal, but the present tense of the verb takes pre-eminence. All other tenses are diminishments of *esse simpliciter*. To be for Aquinas is to be actual. Being is *actualitas*, presence in the present, capacity to abide all change and stand alone. Time is not the horizon of being, but as in Plato, a moving image of eternity (*Timaeus*), the theatre of actualizations, the drama of a 'now' that has no past and no future because it is in itself eternal.

finitization of being would mean both a denial of the existence of God and an affirmation of a univocal notion of being. Heidegger's finitization of being is an atheistic Scotism, a privileging of absence over presence, possibility over actuality, and a forgetting of the differences in being. Time could only be the horizon of being if there were no analogy between the being constitutive of human understanding and the being of God. Heidegger's medieval sources betray his antipathy to this line of thinking. Scotus believes that *analogia entis* denies us too much; Luther, that it presumes too much. But Heidegger goes much further than objecting to *analogia entis* on the grounds that it pushes God too far from philosophy (Scotus), or brings him too close (Luther). Heidegger wishes to remove the notion of the Creator from philosophy altogether. The Creator God neither grounds nor haunts philosophy. He is 'dead' for thinking, to be replaced by new notions of 'the holy', 'the fourfold', etc. In Aquinas's eyes Heidegger could only be an apostate, not even a heretic – one with whom one could debate because of shared foundations – but an unbeliever.

In the light of these opposed horizons, the numerous attempts to mediate Aquinas and Heidegger are problematic. Heidegger's insights could only be appropriated by Thomism by first being radically transformed, purged of the overlay of Scotism and Lutheranism, and disengaged from the founding assumption of the finitude of being. Of course, they would then no longer be recognizable as Heideggerian insights.

13. A Defence of Anti-Conceptualist Realism

E. J. LOWE

Introduction

Metaphysical realism is the view that most of the objects that populate the world exist independently of our thought and have their natures independently of how, if at all, we conceive of them. Metaphysical realism is committed, in my opinion, to a robust form of *essentialism*, that is, to the doctrine that there are mind-independent facts about the *identities* of most objects. 'Identity' in this sense means *individual essence*, which John Locke aptly characterized as 'the very being of any thing, whereby it is, what it is'. Many modern forms of anti-realism have their roots in a form of *conceptualism*, according to which all truths about essence knowable by us are ultimately grounded in *our concepts* – that is, in our ways of thinking about things – rather than in things 'in themselves'. This view has its historical roots in Immanuel Kant's critical philosophy, so that contemporary conceptualist anti-realism may, without undue distortion, be described as 'neo-Kantian' in spirit. This is despite the fact that one important way in which its adherents differ from the historical Kant is in their emphasis upon *language* as the medium of thought, as a result of the so-called 'linguistic turn' in philosophy that occurred in the early to mid-twentieth century.

My aim in the present chapter is to show that and why conceptualist anti-realism is an incoherent doctrine and why and how we can and must support metaphysical realism and robust essentialism, while still properly acknowledging the cognitive role of concepts in mediating our grasp of the nature of mind-independent reality. I shall begin with a sketch of the version of essentialism that I favour – a version that I call *serious* essentialism – and in the course of doing so I shall identify its three key principles. Then I shall try to explain why I think that conceptualism can provide no adequate substitute for this form of essentialism and inevitably collapses into an incoherent variety of global anti-realism.

Serious Essentialism

It is vital for my purposes in this chapter that the doctrine of *essentialism* be suitably understood. I say this because many contemporary *possible-worlds theorists* readily describe themselves as essentialists and propose and defend what *they* call essentialist claims, formulated in terms of the language of possible worlds. They will say, for instance, that an essential property of an object is one that the object possesses in every possible world in which it exists. And they will typically claim that some, but not all, of an object's actual properties are essential to it in this sense. But a doctrine of this sort is not serious essentialism in my sense, because it attempts to characterize essence in terms of antecedently assumed notions of possibility and necessity and thus – in my view – puts the cart before the horse. It is at best *ersatz* essentialism. So what is *serious* essentialism? To pursue this query, one might seek to ask *what essences are*. However, this question is already potentially misleading, for it invites the reply that essences are *entities* of some special sort. And, as we shall see, I want to deny that essences are entities. According to serious essentialism, as I understand it, all entities *have* essences, but their essences are certainly not further entities related to them in some special way.

So, what do we or, rather, what *should* we mean by the 'essence' of a thing – where by 'thing', in this context, I just mean any sort of entity whatever? We can, I suggest, do no better than to recall John Locke's perceptive words on the subject, which go right to its heart. Essence, Locke said, in the 'proper original signification' of the word, is 'the very being of any thing, whereby it is, what it

A Defence of Anti-Conceptual Realism

is'.[1] In short, the essence of something, X, is *what X is*, or *what it is to be X*.[2] In another locution, X's essence is the very *identity* of X – a locution that I am happy to adopt, provided that it is clearly understood that to speak of something's 'identity' in this sense is quite different from speaking of the identity *relation* in which it necessarily stands to itself and to no other thing. However, in order to avoid potential confusion about the meaning of locutions such as these, I think that it is important to draw, from the very start, a distinction between *general* and *individual* essence.[3] The key point to be emphasized in this connection is that any individual thing, X, must be a thing *of some general kind* – because, at the very least, it must belong to some *ontological category*. Remember that by 'thing' here I just mean 'entity'. So, for example, X might be a material object, or a person, or a property, or a set, or a number, or a proposition, or whatnot – the list goes on, in a manner that depends on what one takes to be a full enumeration of the ontological categories to be included in it.[4] This point being accepted, if X is something of kind K, then we may say that X's *general* essence is *what it is to be a K*, while X's *individual* essence is *what it is to be the individual of kind K that X is*, as opposed to any other individual of that kind.

Before I proceed, however, an important complication must be dealt with. It should be evident that we cannot simply assume that there is only ever a *single* appropriate answer to the question

---

1 See John Locke, *An Essay Concerning Human Understanding*, ed. P. H. Nidditch (Oxford: Clarendon Press, 1975), III, III, 15.

2 The historical source of this view lies, of course, with Aristotle, whose phrase το τι ην ειναι is standardly translated as 'essence': see Aristotle, *Metaphysics* Z, 4. Its more literal meaning is 'the what it is to be' or 'the what it would be to be'.

3 I do not attempt to offer here a *semantic analysis of* expressions such as 'what X is', 'what it is to be X' or 'the identity of X', though that is no doubt an exercise that should be undertaken at some stage in a full account of what I am calling *serious essentialism*. I assume that our practical grasp of the meaning of such expressions is adequate for a preliminary presentation of the approach of the sort that I am now engaged in.

4 For my own account of what ontological categories we should recognize and which we should regard as fundamental, see my *The Four-Category Ontology* (Oxford: Clarendon Press, 2006), especially Part I.

'What kind of thing is X?'. For instance, if 'a cat' is an appropriate answer to this question, then so will be the answers 'an animal' and 'a living organism'. So too, of course, might be the answer 'a Siamese cat'. It is important to recognize, however, that some, but not all, of these answers plausibly announce the fact that X belongs to a certain ontological category. In my own view, 'X is a living organism', *does* announce such a fact, but 'X is a cat' does not. I take it that the substantive noun 'cat' denotes a certain *natural kind* and consider that such kinds are a species of *universal*. Thus, as I see it, natural kinds, such as the kind *cat*, are themselves things belonging to a certain ontological category – the category of universals – but such a kind is not *itself* an ontological category, because ontological categories are not *things* at all, to be included in a complete inventory of what there is.[5] One upshot of all this is that I want to maintain that a certain sort of ambiguity may attach to questions concerning a thing's general essence, as I shall now try to explain.

An implication of what I have said so far is that if 'a cat' is an appropriate answer to the question 'What *kind* of thing is X?', then we may say that X's general essence is *what it is to be a cat*. But, while I don't want to retreat from this claim, I do want to qualify it. I should like to say that if X is a cat, then X's *fundamental* general essence is *what it is to be a living organism*, because that – in my view – is the most narrow (or 'lowest') ontological category to which X may be assigned. The reason for this is that it is part of the *individual* essence of the natural kind *cat* – of which X is *ex hypothesi* a member – that it is a kind of living organisms. Now, there are, I believe, certain essential truths concerning X which do not issue from its fundamental general essence but only from the fact that it belongs to this particular natural kind. These are essential truths concerning X which are determined solely by the individual essence of that natural kind.[6] Accordingly, I want to say

---

5 See further my *The Possibility of Metaphysics* (Oxford: Clarendon Press, 1998), ch. 8, and my *The Four-Category Ontology*, ch. 2.

6 I want to maintain that X's fundamental general essence determines what is *absolutely* metaphysically necessary for X, whereas the individual essence of the natural kind *cat* determines only what is metaphysically necessary for X *qua* member of that kind. Thus, in my view, *being a cat* is not an absolute metaphysical necessity for any individual living organism

that *what it is to be a cat*, while it is not X's fundamental general essence, is nonetheless what we might appropriately call X's *specific* general essence, on the grounds that the kind *cat* is the most specific (or 'lowest') natural kind to which X may be assigned.[7] However, I readily acknowledge that the distinction that I am now trying to draw between 'fundamental' and 'specific' general essence in the case of individual members of natural kinds is a controversial one that needs much fuller justification than I am able to give it here. Hence, in what follows, I shall try as far as possible to prescind from this distinction, hoping that the simplification involved in doing so will cause no damage to the overall thrust of my arguments.[8]

Why are Essences Needed?

I have just urged that all individual things — all entities — have both general and individual essences, a thing's general essence being *what it is to be a thing of its kind* and its individual essence being *what it is to be the individual of that kind that it is,* as opposed to any other individual of that kind. But why suppose that things must *have* 'essences' in this sense and that we can, at least in some cases, know those essences? First of all, because otherwise it makes no sense — or so I believe — to say that we can talk or think comprehendingly about things at all. For if we do not at least know

---

that is, in fact, a cat. To put it another way: I believe that it is *metaphysically* possible — even if not *biologically* or *physically* possible — for any individual cat to survive 'radical' metamorphosis, by becoming a member of *another* natural kind of living organism. See further my *The Possibility of Metaphysics*, pp. 54–6.

7 I take it here, at least for the sake of argument, that there are 'higher' natural kinds to which X may be assigned, such as the kinds *mammal* and *vertebrate,* but that Siamese cats — for example — do not constitute a distinct natural kind of their own.

8 One consequence of this simplification is that I shall often continue to speak of 'the' kind to which a thing belongs, without discriminating between 'kind' in the sense of *ontological category* and 'kind' in the sense of *natural kind,* and without explicit acknowledgement of the fact that the question 'What kind of thing is X' may be capable of receiving more than one appropriate answer.

what a thing is, how can we talk or think comprehendingly about it?[9] How, for instance, can I talk or think comprehendingly about *Tom*, a particular cat, if I simply don't know what cats are and which cat, in particular, Tom is? Of course, I'm not saying that I must know *everything* about cats or about Tom in order to be able to talk or think comprehendingly about that particular animal.[10] But I must surely know enough to distinguish the kind of thing that Tom is from other kinds of thing, and enough to distinguish Tom in particular from other individual things of Tom's kind. Otherwise, it seems that my talk and thought cannot really fasten upon *Tom*, as opposed to something else.[11]

---

9 Note that I ask only how we can *talk* or *think* comprehendingly about a thing if we do not know what it is – not how we can *perceive* a thing if we do not know what it is. I am happy to allow that a subject S may, for example, *see* an object O even though S does not know what O is. Seeing, however, is not a purely intellective act. Indeed, of course, even lower animals that cannot at all plausibly be said to understand *what* objects exist in their environment, may nonetheless be said to *see* or *feel* or *smell* some of those objects.

10 Perhaps, indeed, all I need to know about cats is that they are *animals* or *living organisms* and perhaps, likewise, all I need to know about Tom is which animal or living organism he is.

11 Of course, it is fashionable at present to suppose that our talk and thought have, in general, their *referents* in the 'external' world secured through the existence of appropriate *causal* links between certain constituents of our talk and thought – certain of our linguistic and mental 'representations' – and various extra-linguistic and extra-mental entities belonging to that world: links that can, and mostly do, obtain without our needing to have any knowledge of them. On this sort of view, it may be supposed, my talk and thought can fasten upon Tom because there is an appropriate causal link between the name 'Tom', as I have learnt to use it, and *Tom* – and an analogous causal link between a certain 'mental representation' of mine (perhaps a certain 'symbol' in the putative 'language of thought' supposedly utilized by my brain) and *Tom*. I will only say here that I cannot begin to understand how it might seriously be supposed that a linkage of this sort could genuinely suffice to enable me to *talk and think comprehendingly about Tom*, even if it is conceded that there is a (relatively anodyne) notion of 'reference' that could perhaps be satisfactorily accounted for by a causal theory of the foregoing sort. I should emphasize, then, that I am not presently concerned to challenge the so-called causal theory of reference, much less to defend in opposition to it some sort of

However, denying the reality of essences doesn't only create an epistemological problem: it also creates an ontological problem. Unless Tom has an 'identity' – whether or not anyone is acquainted with it – there is nothing to make Tom the particular thing that he is, as opposed to any other thing. Anti-essentialism commits us to anti-realism, and indeed to an anti-realism so global that it is surely incoherent. It will not do, for instance, to try to restrict one's anti-essentialism to 'the external world', somehow privileging us and our language and thought. How could it be that there is a fact of the matter as to *our* identities, and the identities of *our words and thoughts*, but not as to the identities of the mind-independent entities that we try to capture in language and thought? On the other hand, how could there *not* be any fact of the matter as to our identities and the identities of our words and thoughts? Everything is, in Joseph Butler's memorable phrase, *what it is and not another thing*. That has sounded to many philosophers like a mere truism without significant content, as though it were just an affirmation of the reflexivity of the identity relation. But, in fact, Butler's dictum does not merely concern the identity relation but also identity in the sense of *essence*. It implies that there is a fact of the matter as to what any particular thing is – that is, as to its 'very being', in Locke's phrase. Its very being – its identity – is what makes it the thing that it is and thereby distinct from any other thing.

Essences are apt to seem very elusive and mysterious, especially if talked about in a highly generalized fashion, as I have been doing so far. Really, I suggest, they are quite familiar to us. Above all, we need to appreciate that in very many cases a thing's essence involves *other things*, to which it stands in relations of *essential dependence*. Consider the following thing, for instance: the set of planets whose orbits lie within that of Jupiter. What kind of thing is that? Well, of course, it is a *set*, and as such an abstract entity

---

neo-Fregean theory of reference as being mediated by 'sense'. Rather, I am simply not interested, at present, in semantic questions or rival semantic theories, but rather in the purely metaphysical question of *how it is possible to be acquainted with an object of thought*: my answer being that it is so through, and only through, a grasp of that object's *essence* – that is, through knowing *what it is*.

that depends essentially for its existence and identity on the things that are its members – namely, Mercury, Venus, Earth, and Mars. Part of *what it is to be a set* is to be something that depends in these ways upon certain other things – the things that are its members. Someone who did not grasp that fact would not understand *what a set is*. Furthermore, someone who did not know *which things* are this set's members, or at least what determined which things are its members, would not know *which particular set* this set is. So, someone who knew that its members are the planets just mentioned would know which set it is, as would someone who knew what it is to be a planet whose orbit lies within that of Jupiter.[12] This is a simple example, but it serves to illustrate a general point. In many cases, we know what a thing is – both what kind of thing it is and which particular thing of that kind it is – only by knowing that it is related in certain ways to other things. In such cases, the thing in question depends essentially on these other things for its existence or its identity. To say that X depends essentially on Y for its existence and identity is just to say that it is *part of the essence* of X that X exists only if Y exists and *part of the essence* of X that X stands in some unique relation to Y.[13] Knowing a thing's essence, in many cases, is accordingly simply a matter of understanding the relations of essential dependence in which it stands to other things whose essences we in turn know.

---

12 There are, broadly speaking, two different views of what a set is: one which takes a set simply to be the result of – as David Lewis puts it – 'collecting many into one', and another which takes a set to be the extension of a property or of a concept. For Lewis's remark, see his *Parts of Classes* (Oxford: Blackwell, 1991), p. vii. I see no compelling reason why, in principle, our ontology should not accommodate sets in *both* of these understandings of what they are. But since I am using the example of sets only for illustrative purposes, this is a matter on which I can afford to remain agnostic here.

13 See further my *The Possibility of Metaphysics*, ch. 6, or alternatively my 'Ontological Dependence', *The Stanford Encyclopedia of Philosophy* (2005), ed. E. N. Zalta, http://plato.stanford.edu.

A Defence of Anti-Conceptual Realism

Essences are Not Entities

I said earlier that it is wrong to think of essences as themselves being *entities* of any kind to which the things having them stand in some special kind of relation. Locke himself unfortunately made this mistake, holding as he did that the 'real essence' of a material substance just *is* its 'particular internal constitution' – or, as we would now describe it, its atomic or molecular structure.[14] This is a mistake that has been perpetuated in the modern doctrine, made popular by the work of Saul Kripke and Hilary Putnam, that the essence of water *consists* in its molecular make-up, H_2O, and that the essence of a living organism *consists* in its DNA – the suggestion being that we *discover* these 'essences' simply by careful scientific investigation of the things in question.[15] Now, as we saw earlier, it may well be part of the essence of a thing *that it stands in a certain relation to some other thing*, or kind of things. But *the essence itself* – the very being of a thing, whereby it is, what it is – is not and could not be some further entity. So, for instance, it might perhaps be acceptable to say that it is part of the essence of water *that it is composed of H_2O molecules* (an issue that I shall return to shortly). But the essence of water could not simply *be* H_2O – *molecules* of that very kind – nor yet the *property* of being composed of H_2O molecules. For one thing, if the essence of an entity *were* just some further entity, then *it in turn* would have to have an essence of its own and we would be faced with an infinite regress that, at worst, would be vicious and, at best, would appear to make all knowledge of essence impossible for finite minds like ours. To know something's essence is not to be acquainted with some *further thing* of a special kind, but simply to understand *what exactly that thing is*. This, indeed, is why knowledge of

---

14 Thus, at one point Locke remarks: '[W]e come to have the *Ideas of particular sorts of Substances*, by collecting such Combinations of simple *Ideas*, as are by Experience . . . taken notice of to exist together, and are therefore supposed to flow from the particular internal Constitution, or unknown Essence of that Substance' *(Essay, II, XXIII, 3)*.

15 See, especially, Saul A. Kripke, *Naming and Necessity* (Oxford: Blackwell, 1980) and Hilary Putnam, 'The Meaning of "Meaning"', in his *Mind, Language and Reality: Philosophical Papers Volume 2* (Cambridge: Cambridge University Press, 1975).

essence is possible, for it is a product simply of *understanding* – not of empirical observation, much less of some mysterious kind of quasi-perceptual acquaintance with esoteric entities of any sort. And, on pain of incoherence, we cannot deny that we understand what at least some things are, and thereby know their essences.

Here it may be objected that it is inconsistent of me to deny that essences are entities and yet go on, as I apparently do, to *refer to* and even *quantify over* essences. Someone who voices this objection probably has in mind W. V. Quine's notorious *criterion of ontological commitment*, encapsulated in his slogan 'to be is to be the value of a variable'.[16] I reply, in the first place, that I could probably say all that I want to about my version of essentialism while avoiding all locutions involving the appearance of reference to and quantification over essences, by paraphrasing them in terms of locutions involving only sentential operators of the form 'it is part of the essence of X that' – where 'the essence of X' is not taken to make an independent contribution to the meaning of the operator, which might be represented symbolically by, say, 'E_X' in a sentential formula of the form '$E_X(p)$'. The latter is a kind of locution that I certainly do want to use and find very useful. However, I think that effort spent on working out such paraphrases in all cases would be effort wasted. If a paraphrase *means the same* as what it is supposed to paraphrase – as it had better do, if it is to be any good – then it carries the same 'ontological commitments' as whatever it is supposed to paraphrase, so that constructing paraphrases cannot be a way of relieving ourselves of ontological commitments. We cannot discover those commitments simply by examining the syntax and semantics of our language, for syntax and semantics are very uncertain guides to ontology. In other words, I see no reason to place any confidence in Quine's famous criterion.

---

16 See, for example, W. V. Quine, 'Existence and Quantification', in his *Ontological Relativity and Other Essays* (New York: Columbia University Press, 1969).

A Defence of Anti-Conceptual Realism

Essence Precedes Existence

Another crucial point about essence is this: in general, *essence precedes existence*. And by this I mean that the former precedes the latter both *ontologically* and *epistemically*. That is to say, on the one hand, I mean that it is a precondition of something's existing that its essence – along with the essences of other existing things – does not preclude its existence. And, on the other hand – and this is what I want to concentrate on now – I mean that we can in general *know* the essence of something X antecedently to knowing whether or not X exists. Otherwise, it seems to me, we could never find out *that* something exists. For how could we find out *that* something, X, exists before knowing *what X is* – before knowing, that is, *what it is* whose existence we have supposedly discovered?[17] Consequently, we know the essences of many things which, as it turns out, *do not* exist. For we know what these things *would be*, if they existed, and we retain this knowledge when we discover that, in fact, they do not exist. Conceivably, there are exceptions. Perhaps it really is true in the case of God, for instance, that essence does not precede existence. But this could not quite generally be the case. However, saying this is perfectly consistent with

---

17 Notoriously, Descartes is supposed to have claimed, in the *Second Meditation*, to know *that* he existed before he knew *what* he was – that is, before he grasped his own essence. But it seems to me that any such claim must be construed as being either disingenuous or else intended non-literally, if it is not to be dismissed as being simply incomprehensible. It might, for instance, be taken to imply merely that Descartes was certain that the word 'I' *had a reference,* before knowing what that reference was. To be accurate, though, what Descartes actually says is 'But I do not yet have a sufficient understanding of what this "I" is, that now necessarily exists': see René Descartes, *Meditations on First Philosophy,* trans. J. Cottingham (Cambridge: Cambridge University Press, 1986), p. 17. That is consistent with saying that Descartes *does* already grasp his own essence, but needs to clear his mind of confused thoughts concerning it. Query: might we not come to know what X is *neither before nor after* discovering that X exists, but *simultaneously* with that discovery? Well, I see no reason to deny this possibility in some cases. But that concession need not be taken to undermine the claim that, in general, we *can* know the essence of something X before knowing whether or not X exists.

acknowledging that, sometimes, we may only come to know the essence of something after we have discovered the existence of certain *other* kinds of things. This is what goes on in many fields of theoretical science. Scientists trying to discover the transuranic elements knew before they found them *what it was* that they were trying to find, but only because they knew that what they were trying to find were elements whose atomic nuclei were composed of protons and neutrons in certain hitherto undiscovered combinations. They could hardly have known what they were trying to find, however, prior to the discovery of the existence of protons and neutrons – for only after these sub-atomic particles were discovered and investigated did the structure of atomic nuclei become sufficiently well understood for scientists to be able to anticipate which combinations of nucleons would give rise to reasonably stable nuclei.

Here it may be objected that Kripke and Putnam have taught us that the essences of many familiar natural kinds – such as the kind *cat* and the kind *water* – have been revealed to us only a posteriori and consequently that in cases such as these, at least, it cannot be true to say that 'essence precedes existence', whatever may be said in the case of the transuranic elements.[18] The presupposition here,

---

18 The extent to which the Kripke-Putnam doctrine has become a commonplace of contemporary analytic philosophy is illustrated by the following remark of Frank Jackson's, which he makes simply in passing and without acknowledging any need to justify it: '[W]e rarely know the essence of the things our words denote (indeed, if Kripke is right about the necessity of origin, we do not know our own essences)': see his *From Metaphysics to Ethics: A Defence of Conceptual Analysis* (Oxford: Clarendon Press, 1998), p. 50. Yet, I would urge, it should strike one as being odd to the point of paradoxicality to maintain that we can talk or think comprehendingly about things without knowing *what it is* that we are talking or thinking about – that is, without grasping their essences. The charitable conclusion to draw would be that philosophers like Jackson do not use the term 'essence' in what Locke called its 'proper original signification'. Now, of course, Locke himself says that the 'real' essences of material substances are *unknown* to us – and the Kripke Putnam doctrine is recognizably a descendant of Locke's view, to the extent that it identifies the 'real essences' of material substances with their 'internal constitutions', many of which are certainly still unknown to us and may forever continue to be so. But Locke, at least, concluded – unlike

of course, is that Kripke and Putnam are *correct* in identifying the essence of water, for example, with its molecular make-up, H_2O. Now, I have already explained why I think that such identifications are mistaken, to the extent that they can be supposed to involve the illicit *reification* of essences. But it may still be urged against me that even if, more cautiously, we say only that it is part of the essence of water *that it is composed of H_2O molecules*, it still follows that the essence of water has only been revealed to us – or, at least, has only been *fully* revealed to us – a posteriori.

In point of fact, however, the Kripke–Putnam doctrine is even more obscure and questionable than I have so far represented it as being. Very often, it is characterized in terms of the supposed modal and epistemic status of identity-statements involving natural kind terms, such as 'Water is H_2O', which are said to express truths that are at once necessary and a posteriori. In such a statement, however, the term 'H_2O' is plainly not functioning in exactly the same way as it does in the expression 'H_2O molecule'. The latter expression, it seems clear, means 'molecule composed of two hydrogen ions and one oxygen ion'. But in 'Water is H_2O', understood as an identity-statement concerning kinds, we must either take 'H_2O' to be elliptical for the *definite description* 'the stuff composed of H_2O molecules' or else simply as being a *proper name* of a kind of stuff, in which case we cannot read into it any significant semantic structure. On the latter interpretation, 'Water is H_2O' is exactly analogous to 'Hesperus is Phosphorus' and its necessary truth reveals nothing of substance to us concerning the composition of water. If we are inclined to think otherwise, this is

---

modern adherents of the Kripke-Putnam doctrine – that 'the *supposition of Essences, that cannot be known*; and the making them nevertheless to be that, which distinguishes the Species of Things, *is so wholly useless . . . [as]* to make us lay it by' *(Essay,* III, III, 17) and he accordingly appeals instead to what he calls *nominal* essences. The correct position, I suggest, is neither Locke's nor that of the Kripke-Putnam doctrine, but rather (what I take to be) Aristotle's: that the real essences of material substances *are* known to those who talk or think comprehendingly about such substances – and consequently that such essences are not to be identified with anything that is *not* generally known to such speakers and thinkers, such as the 'particular internal constitution' of a material substance, or a human being's (or other living creature's) 'origin' in the Kripkean sense.

because we slide illicitly from construing 'H_2O' as a proper name to construing it as elliptical for the definite description 'the stuff composed of H_2O molecules'. Now, when 'Water is H_2O' is understood on the model of 'Hesperus is Phosphorus', its necessary a posteriori truth may in principle be established in a like manner – namely, by appeal to the familiar logical proof of the necessity of identity,[19] together with the a posteriori discovery of the co-reference of the proper names involved – but not so when it is construed as meaning 'Water is the stuff composed of H_2O molecules', for the latter involves a definite description and the logical proof in question notoriously fails to apply where identity-statements involving definite descriptions are concerned. Thus far, then, we have been given no reason to suppose that 'Water is H_2O' expresses an a posteriori necessary truth that reveals to us something concerning the essence of water. The appearance that we have been given such a reason is the result of mere sleight of hand.[20]

There is, in any case, another important consideration that we should bear in mind when reflecting on the frequently invoked analogy between 'Water is H_2O' and 'Hesperus is Phosphorus'. It is all very well to point out that the discovery that Hesperus is Phosphorus was an empirical one. But it was not *purely* empirical, for the following reason. The identity was established because astronomers discovered that Hesperus and Phosphorus *coincide in their orbits*: wherever Hesperus is located at any given time, there too is Phosphorus located. However, spatiotemporal coincidence

---

19 See Saul A. Kripke, 'Identity and Necessity', in M. K. Munitz (ed.), *Identity and Individuation* (New York: New York University Press, 1971). I express doubts about the cogency of this proof in my 'Identity, Vagueness, and Modality', in J. L. Bermudez (ed.), *Thought, Reference, and Experience: Themes from the Philosophy of Gareth Evans* (Oxford: Oxford University Press, 2005). However, for present purposes I set aside these doubts.

20 Here I note that it might be thought that 'Water is the stuff composed of H_2O molecules' follows unproblematically from the supposed empirical truth 'Water is H_2O' (construed as an identity statement involving two proper names) and the seemingly trivial, because analytic, truth 'H_2O is the stuff composed of H_2O molecules'. But the latter, when the first occurrence of 'H_2O' in it is interpreted as a proper name, is no more trivial than '*Water* is the stuff composed of H_2O molecules' – and this is how it must be interpreted for the inference to go through.

A Defence of Anti-Conceptual Realism

only implies identity for things of appropriate kinds. It is only because Hesperus and Phosphorus are taken to be *planets* and thereby *material objects of the same kind* that their spatiotemporal coincidence can be taken to imply their identity. But the principle that distinct material objects of the same kind cannot coincide spatiotemporally is not an empirical one: it is an a priori one implied by *what it is* to be a material object of any kind – in other words, it is a truth grounded in *essence*. It is only because we know that it is *part of the essence* of a planet not to coincide spatiotemporally with another planet, that we can infer the identity of Hesperus with Phosphorus from the fact that they coincide in their orbits. Thus, one must already know *what a planet is* – know its essence – in order to be able to establish by a posteriori means that one planet is identical with another.[21] By the same token, then, one

---

21 Here it may be asked: did astronomers know *which* planet Hesperus is – that is, know its *individual* essence – before knowing that it is identical with Phosphorus? It might seem that the answer must be 'No': for if they did, it may be wondered, how could they have been in any doubt as to its identity with Phosphorus? However, here we need to bear in mind that it is clearly not part of the essence of any planet that it has the particular orbit that it does: a planet can certainly change its orbit, and indeed could have had a quite different one. But what led to the discovery that Hesperus is the same planet as Phosphorus was simply that their orbits were plotted and found to coincide. And since one can know which planet a planet is without knowing what its orbit is, it is therefore perfectly explicable that astronomers should – and did – know which planet Hesperus is and which planet Phosphorus is without knowing that Hesperus is the same planet as Phosphorus. So how, in general, *does* one know which material object of kind K a certain material object, O, is? Well, one way in which one can know this, it seems clear, is *through perceptual acquaintance* with O that is informed by knowledge of the *general* essence of objects of kind K. (Recall, here, that perception of an object O does not *in itself* presuppose knowledge of what O is, so that the foregoing claim does not beg the very question at issue.) That is to say, it very often happens that one perceives an object O in circumstances that enable one to know that *what* one is perceiving, O, is a particular object of kind K. In such circumstances, one is thus in a position to know *which* object of this kind O is – namely, *that* one (the one that one is perceiving). And one can retain this knowledge by *remembering* which object it was that one perceived. I should emphasize, however, that this does not at all imply that it is part of O's individual essence that it is the object of kind

must already know *what a kind of stuff is* – know its essence – in order to be able to establish by a posteriori means that one kind of stuff is identical with another. It can hardly be the case, then, that we can *discover* the essence of a kind of stuff simply by establishing a posteriori the truth of an identity-statement concerning kinds of stuff – any more than we can be supposed to have discovered the essence of a particular planet by establishing a posteriori the truth of an identity-statement concerning that planet. So, even granting that 'Water is H_2O' is a true identity-statement that is both necessarily true and known a posteriori, it does not at all follow that it can be taken to reveal to us the essence of the kind of stuff that we call 'water'.

Be all this as it may, however, we still have to address the question of whether, in fact, we ought to say that it is part of the essence of water that it is composed of H_2O molecules. So far, we have at best seen only that the Kripke–Putnam semantics for natural kind terms have given us no reason to suppose that we ought to. I am inclined to answer as follows. If we are using the term 'water' to talk about a certain chemical compound whose nature is understood by theoretical chemists, then indeed we should say that it is part of the essence of this compound that it consists of H_2O molecules. But, at the same time, it should be acknowledged that the existence of this compound is a relatively recent discovery, which could not have been made before the nature of hydrogen and oxygen atoms and their ability to form molecules were understood. Consequently, when we use the term 'water' in everyday conversation and when our forebears used it before the advent of modern chemistry, we are and they were *not* using it to talk about a chemical compound whose nature is now understood by theoretical chemists. We are and they were using it to talk about a certain *kind of liquid*, distinguishable from other kinds of liquid by certain fairly easily detectable macroscopic features, such as its transparency, colourlessness and tastelessness. We are right, I assume, in thinking that a liquid of this kind actually exists, but *not* that it is part of its essence that it is composed of H_2O

K that one perceived on a particular occasion – for, of course, it will in general be an entirely contingent matter that one happened to perceive it then, or indeed at all.

molecules. At the same time, however, we should certainly acknowledge that empirical scientific enquiry reveals that, indeed, the chemical compound H_2O is very largely what bodies of this liquid are made up of. In fact, the natural laws governing this and other chemical compounds make it overwhelmingly unlikely that this kind of liquid could have a different chemical composition in different parts of our universe. But the 'could' here is expressive of mere physical or natural possibility, not *metaphysical* possibility.[22] Only an illicit conflation of these two species of possibility could reinstate the claim that water is *essentially* composed of H_2O molecules.

But, it may be asked, what about our supposed 'intuitions' in so-called 'Twin-Earth' cases – for example, the supposed intuition that if, on a distant planet, a watery stuff was discovered that was not composed of H_2O molecules, then it would not be *water*? In answer to this question, I would remark only that these supposed intuitions need to be interpreted in the light of the fact, just mentioned, that the natural laws governing chemical compounds in our universe almost certainly render such scenarios physically impossible. The supposedly 'watery' stuff on Twin Earth would be like fool's gold (copper pyrites): it would at best be *casually* mistakable for water and *that* is why it would not be water. The *chemical* explanation for this would be that fool's water, as we could justly call it, is not composed of H_2O molecules. But we cannot turn this perfectly legitimate chemical explanation into a logico-cum-metaphysical argument that genuine water is of *metaphysical* necessity composed of H_2O molecules – unless, once again, we conflate physical with metaphysical necessity.

Essence is the Ground of All Modal Truth

So far, I have urged that the following two principles must be endorsed by the serious essentialist: that *essences are not entities* and that, in general, *essence precedes existence*. But by far the most important principle to recognize concerning essences, for the

---

22 For extended discussion of the need to distinguish these two species of possibility, see my *The Four-Category Ontology*, ch. 9 and ch. 10.

purposes of the present chapter, is that *essences are the ground of all metaphysical necessity and possibility*.[23] One reason, thus, why it can be the case that X is *necessarily F* is that it is part of the essence of X that X is F. For example, any material object is necessarily spatially extended because it is part of the essence of a material object that it is spatially extended – in other words, part of *what it is to be a material object* is to be something that is spatially extended. But this is not the only possible reason why something may be necessarily F. X may be necessarily F on account of the essence of *something else* to which X is suitably related. For example, Socrates is necessarily the subject of the following event – *the death of Socrates* – because it is part of the essence of that event that Socrates is its subject, even though it is not part of Socrates' essence that he is the subject of that event. It is not on account of *what Socrates is* that he is necessarily the subject of that event but, rather, on account of *what that event is*.[24] This is not to say that Socrates could not have died a different death, only that no one but Socrates could have died the death that he in fact died. And what goes for necessity goes likewise, *mutatis mutandis*, for possibility. I venture to affirm that all facts about what is necessary or possible, in the metaphysical sense, are grounded in facts concerning the essences of things – not only of existing things, but also of non-existing things. But, I repeat, facts concerning the essences of things are not facts concerning *entities* of a special kind, they are just facts concerning *what things are* – their very beings or identities. And these are facts that we can therefore grasp simply in virtue of understanding what things are, which we must in at least some cases be able to do, on pain of being incapable of thought altogether. Consequently, all knowledge of metaphysical necessity and possibility is ultimately a product of the understanding, not of

---

23 Compare Kit Fine, 'Essence and Modality', in James E. Tomberlin (ed.), *Philosophical Perspectives, 8: Logic and Language* (Atascadero, CA: Ridgeview, 1994).

24 Note that analogously, then, it could be conceded that H_2O molecules necessarily compose water without it being conceded that it is part of the essence of *water* to be composed of H_2O molecules – for the necessity may be explained instead as arising from the essence of H_2O molecules.

How, for example, do we know that two distinct things of suitably different kinds, such as a bronze statue and the lump of bronze composing it at any given time, can – unlike two *planets* – exist in the same place at the same time? Certainly not by *looking very hard* at what there is in that place at that time. Just by looking, we shall not see that two distinct things occupy that place. We know this, rather, because we know *what a bronze statue is* and *what a lump of bronze is*. We thereby know that these are *different* things and that a thing of the first sort must, at any given time, be composed by a thing of the second sort, since it is part of the essence of a bronze statue to be composed of bronze. We know that they are different things because, in knowing what they are, we know their *identity conditions*, and thereby know that one of them can persist through changes through which the other cannot persist – that, for instance, a lump of bronze can persist through a radical change in its shape whereas a bronze statue cannot. These facts about their identity conditions are not matters that we can discover purely empirically, by examining bronze statues and lumps of bronze very closely, as we might in order to discover whether, say, they conduct electricity or dissolve in sulphuric acid.[25] Rather, they are facts about them that we must grasp *antecedently* to being able to embark upon any such empirical inquiry concerning them, for we can only inquire empirically into something's properties if we already know *what it is* that we are examining.

---

25 See further my 'Substantial Change and Spatiotemporal Coincidence', *Ratio* 16 (2003), pp. 140–60, and my 'Material Coincidence and the Cinematographic Fallacy: A Response to Olson', *The Philosophical Quarterly* 52 (2002), pp. 369–72, the latter being a reply to Eric T. Olson, 'Material Coincidence and the Indiscernibility Problem', *The Philosophical Quarterly* 51 (2001), pp. 337–55.

Essentialism and Conceptualism

At this point I need to counter a rival view of essence that is attractive to many philosophers but is, I think, ultimately incoherent. I call this view *conceptualism*.[26] It is the view that what I have been calling facts about essences are really, in the end, just facts about certain of *our concepts* – for example, *our concept* of a bronze statue and *our concept* of a lump of bronze. This would reduce all modal truths to conceptual truths or, if the old-fashioned term is preferred, *analytic* truths. Now, I have no objection to the notion of conceptual truth as such. Perhaps, as is often alleged, 'Bachelors are unmarried' indeed expresses such a truth. Let us concede that it is true in virtue of our concept of a bachelor, or in virtue of what we take the word 'bachelor' to mean. But notice that 'Bachelors are unmarried' very plausibly has a quite different modal status from an *essential* truth such as, for example, 'Cats are composed of matter'. In calling the former a 'necessary' truth, we cannot mean to imply that bachelors *cannot marry*, only that they cannot marry *and go on rightly being called 'bachelors'*. The impossibility in question is only one concerning the proper application of a word. But in calling 'Cats are composed of matter' a necessary truth, we certainly can't be taken to mean merely that cats cannot cease to be composed of matter *and go on rightly being called 'cats'* – as though *the very same thing* that, when composed of matter, was properly called a 'cat' might continue to exist as something immaterial. No: we must be taken to mean that cats cannot fail to be

---

26 Who, it might be asked, is really a conceptualist in the sense that I am about to articulate? That is difficult to say with any assurance, since most conceptualists are understandably rather coy about proclaiming their position too explicitly. However, among major analytic philosophers of the twentieth century, Michael Dummett very plausibly counts as one, so might David Wiggins, and also Hilary Putnam. See Michael Dummett, *Frege: Philosophy of Language*, 2nd edn (London: Duckworth, 1981); David Wiggins, *Sameness and Substance Renewed* (Cambridge: Cambridge University Press, 2001); and Hilary Putnam, 'Why There Isn't a Ready-Made World', in his *Realism and Reason: Philosophical Papers Volume 3* (Cambridge: Cambridge University Press, 1983). Further cf. my comments below at pp. 317f.

composed of matter *simpliciter*, that is, without qualification. Cats are things such that, *if they exist at all*, they *must* be composed of matter. The impossibility of there being an immaterial cat is not one that merely concerns the proper application of a word: it is, rather, a genuinely *de re* impossibility. That, I contend, is because it is one grounded in the essence of cats, inasmuch as it is *part of the essence* of a cat, as a living organism, to be composed of matter. In contrast, it is not part of the essence of any bachelor to be unmarried, for a bachelor is just an adult male human being who happens to be unmarried – and any such human being undoubtedly *can* marry. So, it seems clear, 'Cats are composed of matter' is certainly not a mere conceptual truth, and the same goes for other truths that are genuinely essential truths – truths concerning or grounded in the essences of things. They have, in general, nothing to do with our concepts or our words, but rather with the natures of the things in question. Of course, since concepts and words are *themselves* things of certain sorts, there can be truths concerning *their* essences. Indeed, what we could say about 'Bachelors are unmarried' is that it is, or is grounded in, a truth concerning the essence of the concept bachelor, or of the word 'bachelor'. We could say, thus, that it is part of the essence of the concept *bachelor* that only unmarried males fall under it, and part of the essence of the word 'bachelor' that it applies only to unmarried males.

At this point, I anticipate the following possible response from the conceptualist, challenging my attempt to distinguish between the modal status of the statements 'Bachelors are unmarried' and 'Cats are composed of matter'. *Both* statements, the conceptualist may say, express conceptual truths, and the difference between them lies only in the fact that, while the term 'cat' is a so-called *substance sortal*, the term 'bachelor' is only a *phase sortal*.[27] This, he may say, adequately explains why it makes no sense to suppose that something, by ceasing to be composed of matter, could cease to qualify as a *cat* and yet *go on existing* – for a substance sortal is precisely a term that, by definition, applies to something, if it

---

[27] For this distinction, see David Wiggins, *Sameness and Substance Renewed*, pp. 28–30.

applies to it all, *throughout* that thing's existence. To this I respond as follows. We need to ask, crucially, what determines whether or not a given general term should be deemed to be a substance sortal. If this is taken *simply* to be a matter of what *concept* it expresses for speakers of the language in question, rather than a matter of *what manner of thing it applies to*, then deeply anti-realist consequences immediately ensue. To see this, suppose that there is a community of speakers who speak a language very like English in most ways, except that in place of the term 'bachelor' they deploy the term 'sbachelor', where 'sbachelor' in their language is (supposedly) a *substance* sortal rather than a phase sortal, so that *they* would deem 'Sbachelors are unmarried' to be on a par, modally, with 'Cats are composed of matter' – the implication being that, for these speakers, a sbachelor *ceases to exist* if he undergoes a marriage ceremony and is replaced by a numerically different being, called (let us say) a 'shusband'. So, where ordinary English speakers would describe a certain situation as being one in which a certain *man* survives the transition from being a bachelor to being a husband, speakers of our imaginary community would instead describe *the very same situation* as being one in which a certain sbachelor ceases to exist and is replaced by a shusband. As far as I can see, the conceptualist cannot say that we ordinary English speakers describe this situation *rightly* and that the imagined speakers describe it *wrongly*: for the only standard of correctness to which the conceptualist can appeal is that provided by the *actual conceptual repertoire* of the speakers of any given language. That being so, since the two speech communities clearly *differ* over the question as to whether or not, in the envisaged situation, *something has ceased to exist*, the conceptualist seems committed to the conclusion that there is *no mind-independent fact of the matter* concerning such existential questions – and this position is blatantly anti-realist.[28]

But I said that conceptualism is ultimately *incoherent*. Indeed, I think it is. For one thing, as we have just seen, the proper thing to say about 'conceptual' truths is, very plausibly, that *they are*

---

28 In any case, it is relatively easy to think of other examples of modal truths which, even less controversially, cannot sensibly be taken to be merely conceptual truths – for example, 'Socrates is not divisible by 3'.

A Defence of Anti-Conceptual Realism

grounded in the essences of concepts. That being so, the conceptualist cannot maintain, as he does, that *all* putative facts about essence are really just facts concerning concepts. For this is to imply that putative facts about *the essences of concepts* are really just facts concerning *concepts of concepts* – and we have set out on a vicious infinite regress. No doubt the conceptualist will object that this complaint is question-begging. However, even setting it aside, we can surely see that conceptualism is untenable. For the conceptualist is at least committed to affirming that *concepts* – or, in another version, *words* – exist and indeed that concept-users do, to wit, *ourselves*. *These*, at least, are things that the conceptualist must acknowledge to have *identities*, independently of how we conceive of them, on pain of incoherence in his position. The conceptualist must at least purport to understand *what a concept or a word is*, and indeed *what he or she is*, and thus grasp the essences of at least some things. And if of *these* things, why not of *other* kinds of things? Once knowledge of essences is conceded, the game is up for the conceptualist. And it must be conceded, even by the conceptualist, on pain of denying that he or she knows what *anything* is, including the very concepts that lie at the heart of his account. For, recall, all that I mean by the essence of something is *what it is*.

I recognize, however, that conceptualism is deeply entrenched in some philosophical quarters and that conceptualists are consequently unlikely to relinquish their views very readily in the light of objections of the sort that I have just raised. Hence, in the next two sections of this chapter, I shall endeavour to undermine conceptualism in two further ways: first, by exposing the unholy alliance between conceptualism and scepticism and, second, by developing a more general argument to show how conceptualism leads to global anti-realism and why it is ultimately incoherent.

Conceptualism and Scepticism

Why is anyone ever even tempted by conceptualism, if it has such deep flaws as I maintain? My own view is that this temptation is the legacy of *scepticism*, particularly scepticism concerning 'the external world'. The sceptic feels at home with himself and with his words and concepts, but expresses doubt that we can ever really know whether those words and concepts properly or adequately characterize things in the external world. He thinks that we can know nothing about how or what those things are 'in themselves', or indeed even whether they are *many* or *one*. According to the sceptic, all that we can really know is how we *conceive* of the world, or *describe* it in language, not how *it is*. But by what special dispensation does the sceptic exclude *our concepts* and *our words* from the scope of his doubt? For are they not, too, things that exist? There is, in truth, no intelligible division that can be drawn between *the external world*, on the one hand, and *us and our concepts and our language* on the other. Here it may be protested: But how, then, *can* we advance to a knowledge of what and how things are 'in themselves', even granted that the sceptic is mistaken in claiming a special dispensation with regard to the epistemic status of our concepts and our words? However, the fundamental mistake is to suppose, with the sceptic, that such an 'advance' would have to proceed *from* a basis in our knowledge of our concepts and words – that is, *from* a knowledge of how we conceive of and describe the world – *to* a knowledge of that world 'as it is in itself', independently of our conceptual schemes and languages. This 'inside–out' account of how knowledge of mind-independent reality is to be acquired already makes such knowledge impossible and must therefore be rejected as incoherent.

But what alternative is there, barring a retreat to some form of anti-realism? Again, *knowledge of essence* comes to the rescue. Because, in general, essence precedes existence, we can at least sometimes know *what it is* to be a *K* – for example, *what it is* to be a material object of a certain kind – and thereby know, at least in part, what is or is not *possible* with regard to *K*s, in advance of knowing whether, or even having good reason to believe that, any such thing as a *K* actually *exists*. Knowing already, however, *what it is* whose existence is in question and that its existence is at least *possible*, we can intelligibly and justifiably appeal to empirical evidence to confirm or cast doubt upon existence claims concerning such things. By 'empirical evidence' here, be it noted, I emphatically do *not* mean evidence constituted purely by the contents of our own perceptual states at any given time, as though all that we had to go on is how the world in our vicinity *looks* or otherwise *appears* to be. That, certainly, is not the conception of 'empirical evidence' that is operative in scientific practice, which appeals rather to the results of controlled experiments and observations, all of which are reported in terms of properties and relations of mind-independent objects, such as scientific instruments and laboratory specimens. The growth of objective knowledge consists, then, in a constant interplay between an a priori element – knowledge of essence – and an a posteriori element, the empirical testing of existential hypotheses whose possibility has already been anticipated a priori. This process does not have a foundational 'starting point' and it is constantly subject to critical reappraisal, both with regard to its a priori ingredients and with regard to its empirical contributions. Here we do not have a hopeless 'inside–out' account of objective knowledge, since our own subjective states as objective inquirers – our perceptions and our conceptions – are accorded no special role in the genesis of such knowledge. Those subjective states are merely some among the many possible objects of knowledge, rather than objects of a special kind of knowledge which supposedly grounds the knowledge of all other things. But, to repeat, it is crucial to this account that knowledge of *essences* is not itself knowledge of *objects or entities* of any kind, nor grounded in any such knowledge – such as knowledge of our own concepts.

Conceptualism and Anti-realism

Recall that 'conceptualism', as I am using this term, is the view that, to the extent that talk about essences is legitimate at all, essences are purely *conceptual* in character. On this view, the essence of a kind of entities K is simply *constituted* by 'our' concept of a K – or, if not by 'our' concept, then at least by *some* thinking being's concept. But what exactly *is* a 'concept'? Well, 'concept' in the current context is a philosophical term of art, so it is partly up to us as philosophers to stipulate how we propose to use it. As I have already indicated, I myself regard a concept as being *a way of thinking of some thing or things*, and I take it that conceptualists can agree with me about this. However, as a metaphysical realist, I also want to say that not all of our ways of thinking of things –

not all of our *conceptions* of things – are equally good. Because I am a metaphysical realist, I believe that our conceptions of things may be more or less *adequate*, in the sense that they may more or less accurately reflect or represent the natures – that is, the *essences* – of the things of which we are thinking, or at least *attempting* to think. Thus it is open to me to stipulate further that, in *my* usage, a 'concept' is precisely an *adequate* conception of some thing or things, which accurately reflects the nature or essence of the things in question. For example, I can say that a child who conceives of a triangle merely as being a three-sided shape does not yet fully grasp the *concept* of a triangle, as a *planar* figure with three *rectilinear* sides. Clearly, however, it is not then open to *me* to say that the essence of *K*s is constituted by our *concept* of a *K*, because this would leave no room for me to say, non-vacuously, that the concept of a *K* is a conception of *K*s that *accurately reflects* the essence of *K*s. Essences, on my account, must be *mind-independent*, if the question can sensibly be put as to whether or not a conception of *K*s adequately reflects the essence of *K*s. But what can be said on behalf of the rival view – conceptualism as I call it – that essences are always *constituted* by concepts? First, it should be clear, if it isn't clear already, that conceptualism is a strongly *anti-realist* view. Second, I want to press home my complaint that conceptualism is a view that is ultimately *incoherent*. Let us deal with the first point first.

The following question, it seems to me, must be a deeply embarrassing one for the conceptualist: *in virtue of what*, according to conceptualism, can it truly be said that *there exist* entities that fall under, or satisfy, our concepts – including, most centrally, our *sortal* or *individuative* concepts? That is to say, what does it take for there to *be K*s, on this view? This is simple enough, it may be replied: there must be entities that possess whatever features they are that we have built into our concept of a *K*. So, for example, if *K* is *lump of bronze*, conceived, let us say, as a maximal connected aggregate of bronze particles, then there must be just such things. This will be the case if, sometimes, some bronze particles adhere to one another so as to form a maximal connected whole. Well and good: but remember that conceptualism is the doctrine that *all* essences are constituted by concepts. So, in particular, the doctrine must be taken to extend to the essence of *bronze particles* – what it *is* to be a bronze particle. (It must also extend to the essence of the relation of *adherence*, but I won't dwell on that equally important fact for the moment, for the concept of adherence is not an individuative concept.) Bronze particles, on this view, exist just in case there are some things that possess whatever features we have built into our concept of a bronze particle. However, either the concept of a bronze particle is relevantly similar to that of a lump of bronze, in that it characterizes the nature of such an entity in terms of properties and relations of entities of *other* kinds, or it is not. If it is, then the next question is just pushed back one stage. If it is not – and this is the next question – then what *does* it take for the world to contain entities falling under the concept? What, in this case, must *the world* contribute to the fact that entities of this putative kind exist? Since, according to conceptualism, all essences are *constituted* by concepts – where concepts are understood to be 'ways of conceiving' deployed by thinkers – the conceptualist cannot suppose that *how the world is*, in respect of *what kinds of entities it contains*, is something that is the case independently of what concepts thinkers deploy. On this view, *what it is* for the world to contain entities of a kind *K* just *is* for the concept of a *K* to have application, or be applicable. Consequently, an adherent of this view cannot cash out what it is for such a concept *to have application* in terms of there being in the world entities answering to the concept. For, as I say, on this view, there *being in the world* such entities just *is* a matter of the concept's 'having application'. So a quite different understanding of 'having application' must at least implicitly be in play.

What is this alternative understanding? I think that it can only be something like this: the concept of a *K* 'has application' just in case thinkers find it *useful*, or *convenient*, to conceive of the world as containing *K*s. This may require the concept in question to be logically consistent – thus ruling out, for example, the applicability of such concepts as 'round square cupola' – but otherwise the constraints would seem to be purely pragmatic. This, it seems clear, is a deeply anti-realist view. It is a view according to which, in Hilary Putnam's well-known words, there isn't a 'ready-made world'[29] – or, if you like, there isn't any truth about 'what is there

---

29 See Hilary Putnam, 'Why There Isn't a Ready-Made World'.

anyway', to use Bernard Williams's equally familiar phrase.[30] Or, yet again, it is a view according to which, to employ Michael Dummett's somewhat less felicitous metaphor, reality is an 'amorphous lump' – one that can be 'sliced up' in indefinitely many different but equally legitimate ways, depending on what 'conceptual scheme' we or other thinkers happen to deploy.[31] It *may* also be the view to which David Wiggins is committed, willy-nilly, by the doctrine that he calls 'conceptualist realism' – committed in virtue of the fact that the only notion of *individuation* that he admits is a cognitive one, whereby individuation is a *singling out of objects by thinkers*.[32] Not only is this view deeply anti-realist: it is also, as I have said, doubtfully coherent. For those who philosophize in these terms rarely stop to think about how their doctrine is supposed to accommodate *thinkers*, their *thoughts* and the *concepts* that they deploy. For these, too, are putative kinds of entities, whose essences, according the conceptualist doctrine, must like all others be constituted by 'our' concepts of them. It is at this point that the conceptualist manifestly paints himself into a corner from which there is no escape. There simply is no coherent position to be adopted according to which *all* essences are constituted by concepts, because concepts themselves are either *something* or else *nothing* – they either exist or they do not. If they don't, then conceptualism is out of business. But if they do, then they themselves have an essence – *what it is* to be a concept. The conceptualist, to be consistent, must say that the essence of *concepts* is constituted our *concept* of a concept. But what could this *mean*? And what could it mean, according to conceptualism, to say that the concept of a concept 'has application' – that *there are* concepts? I don't believe that conceptualism has any intelligible answer to such questions. The lesson, I take it, is that at least *some* essences must be mind-independent, in a way that conceptualism denies. Serious essentialism, as I call it, is my attempt to provide such an account of essence.

---

30 See Bernard Williams, *Descartes: The Project of Pure Enquiry* (Harmondsworth: Penguin, 1978), p. 64. Williams himself, of course, is not a conceptualist anti-realist, holding that what he calls an 'absolute conception' of reality is possible.
31 See Michael Dummett, *Frege: Philosophy of Language*, 2nd edn, p. 563.
32 See David Wiggins, *Sameness and Substance Renewed*, p. 6.

A Defence of Anti-Conceptual Realism

Some Implications for Reductionism and Theories of the Self

In this concluding section, I want make some brief remarks applying some consequences of the preceding arguments to other important issues in philosophy, focusing on two in particular: *reductionism* and *theories of the self*. We have in fact touched on both of these issues in passing in earlier sections. Thus, reductionism was at issue in our brief discussion of the example of the bronze statue and the lump of bronze on pp. 309–10. The reductionist will say that he cannot understand how we can suppose the statue to be anything *different* from the lump of bronze, given that they exactly coincide, are composed of exactly the same bronze particles, and share exactly the same observable characteristics throughout the period of time in which the one is said to be 'made of' the other. For a similar reason, he will say that he cannot understand how a human person could be supposed to be anything *different* from his or her biological body. However, we can now see that the reductionist was *looking in the wrong place* to understand the nature and ground of these distinctions. That a lump of bronze has different identity conditions from those of a bronze statue, and that a human person has different identity conditions from those of a biological organism, are certainly not facts that we could discover purely empirically, by examining very closely the properties and relations of bronze particles or human cells. Merely by examining such things, we shall never *discover* that such entities compose other objects of certain kinds. Rather, only if we *already* possess a grasp of what a statue or a person *is*, including a grasp of its identity conditions, will we be able to discern the existence of such a thing in a place occupied by bronze particles or human cells. Possessing such a grasp, we shall also know how such things *differ* in their identity conditions from other things that can be composed of bronze particles or human cells, such as lumps of bronze and human bodies.[33]

In short, the reductionist's urge to reduce *different* things to the *same* thing – bronze statues to lumps of bronze, or human persons

---

[33] I say much more about what I consider persons to be in my *Subjects of Experience* (Cambridge: Cambridge University Press, 1996), ch. 2.

to human bodies – arises from a mistaken assumption that any complexity or diversity in the world must be entirely determined *from the bottom up*, so that where we can see no difference between the component parts of things and their arrangement at any given time, as in the case of the bronze statue and the lump of bronze, there can be no difference between what things those parts compose. This reverses the proper order of understanding. We *start* with an understanding of what, for instance, a bronze statue and a lump of bronze *are*, which includes an understanding of the differences between their respective identity conditions. This then enables us to understand how, given those identity conditions, two such things, while being different, can at one and the same time be composed of the same bronze particles arranged in the same way. And we can also see why, at *other* times, that same bronze statue may be related in the same way to a *different* lump of bronze, since it can undergo a change with respect to which bronze particles compose it, whereas a lump of bronze cannot. Mere observation of the aggregate behaviour of bronze particles, in the absence of such prior understanding, could never have enabled us to acquire that understanding. The reductionist's error is to suppose that nothing that could not be deduced from the aggregate behaviour of bronze particles in such a case could constitute genuine knowledge of anything. More generally, his error is to suppose that nothing that could not be deduced from the aggregate behaviour of *the fundamental particles of physics* could constitute genuine knowledge of anything.

I have just explained my opposition to reductionism in general, appealing to the theory of essence developed earlier in this paper, and I have made it clear that my opposition extends to reductionism about *persons* in particular – that is, to reductionist views of *ourselves*. What can we say, positively, about the essence of human selves – about *what we are*? I mentioned, in footnote 17, Descartes's famous engagement with this question, and his apparent claim to know *that* he existed before he knew *what* he was. I queried that claim as being either disingenuous or else non-literal, on the grounds that I could not make sense of it if it was intended to be taken literally. Perhaps 'disingenuous' was too strong a word, however. Descartes was partly engaged in an educative exercise, designed to reveal to his readers what, if they reflected hard enough, he thought they already possessed the resources to know. On the question of his essence, his final verdict is famously that he is essentially *a thinking thing*. He certainly doesn't believe that empirical information is needed in order to grasp this fact – indeed, if anything, he thinks that empirical information has hitherto obscured this fact for him. Now, I certainly agree that it is at least *part* of my essence that I am a thinking thing. Indeed, I hope that I have already made it clear that, in my view, it is part of my essence that I am a being that can *grasp the essences of at least some things* – since, without such a grasp, it is not possible to think comprehendingly *about* anything, and thought that is not about anything would not be genuine thought at all. Furthermore, since I can patently think comprehendingly *about myself*, I must to that extent grasp *my own* essence. Where I part company with Descartes is over his opinion that I am essentially an *immaterial* thing. I suspect that he is guilty of a relatively simple error in the logic of essence. From the claim – which I accept – that I am *not* essentially a purely material thing, such as my body, he infers that I am essentially a purely *non*-material thing. The error here is one that modern logicians would describe as involving the *scope* of a logical operator, in this case the negation operator, 'not'. Formally, the error is one of inferring '*a* is essentially not *F*' from '*a* is not essentially *F*'.

To be fair, there is a perhaps little more to Descartes' argument than this, for it is a principle of his overall metaphysical system that each fundamental kind of substance can possess only *one* leading attribute – *thought* and *extension* being such attributes and accordingly properties that cannot be possessed by one and the same substance. Given this further assumption, the mere fact that I possess the attribute of thought excludes the possibility that I also possess the attribute of extension. However, it is hard to see what could motivate this assumption, other than the following line of argument: if *a* is a substance and *F* and *G* are different attributes, such as thought or extension, then (1) if *a* is *F*, then *a* is *essentially F* (for instance, if I am a thinking thing, then I am essentially a thinking thing), (2) if *a* is essentially *F*, then *a* is *not* essentially *G* (for instance, if I am essentially a thinking thing, then I am not essentially an extended thing), and (3) if *a* is not essentially *G*, then *a* is not *G* (for instance, if I am not essentially an extended thing, then I am not an extended thing). For, clearly, if (1), (2) and (3) are true, this immediately follows: (4) if a is F, then a is not G (for instance, if I am a thinking thing, then I am not an extended thing). Now, I myself have no particular quarrel with (2), but I do with (1) and (3) – which, it should be noted, stand or fall together, since the contrapositive of (1) has exactly the same form as (3). Let us focus, then, on (3). Now, of course, what is indisputably correct is this: (5) if a is essentially *not* G, then a is not G (for instance, if I am essentially a non-extended thing, then I am a non-extended thing). The suspicion must be, then, that Descartes is trading on a confusion between this indisputable truth and the supposed truth of (3). Thus, we are back to what I originally said was the source of his error, a confusion about the scope of the negation operator. For the difference between (3) and (5) lies in their antecedents which are, respectively, 'a is not essentially G' and 'a is essentially not G', which differ precisely with regard to the scope of the word 'not'.

I conclude, then, that Descartes has done nothing to convince me that, just because I am essentially a thinking thing, I cannot *also* be an extended thing, possessing physical properties of shape, size and weight – even though I am not, for reasons discussed earlier, simply identifiable with the living biological organism that is my human body.

14. Realism in Theology and Metaphysics[1]

MICHAEL C. REA

Over the past decade or so, increasing attention has been paid in two separate disciplines to questions about realism and ontological commitment. The disciplines are analytic metaphysics on the one hand, and theology on the other. In this chapter, I shall discuss two arguments for the conclusion that realism in theology and metaphysics – that is, a realist treatment of doctrines in theology and metaphysics – is untenable.[2]

---

1 Versions of this chapter were read at the 2006 'Belief and Metaphysics' Conference, sponsored by the University of Nottingham's Centre of Theology and Philosophy, the 2007 Pacific Regional Meeting of the Society of Christian Philosophers, and the 2007 Midwest Regional Meeting of the Evangelical Philosophical Society. I am grateful to audiences on those occasions for helpful discussion. I would also like to thank the participants in my 'Metaphysics and Christian Theology Seminar' (especially Alex Arnold, Andrew Bailey, Adam Green, Nate King, Jenny Martin, Luke Potter and Chris Tucker), and participants in the University of Notre Dame Center for Philosophy of Religion reading group (in particular, Robert Audi, Alicia Finch, Tom Flint, Don Howard, Alan Padgett, J. Brian Pitts, Kevin Sharpe and Nick Trakakis) for very helpful discussion of the ideas in this chapter and for comments on an earlier draft.

2 By 'theology' in the present context I have primarily in mind those sub-disciplines of theology that go by such labels as 'systematic theology', 'dogmatic theology', 'philosophical theology' and the like. The arguments of this chapter do not (to my mind, anyway) have any obvious bearing on (say) historical and biblical theology or the various kinds of biblical criticism that are practised in contemporary theology departments.

Veritas: Belief and Metaphysics

'Realism' is variously defined in the literature. For purposes here, I shall adopt the following characterizations:

- Where 'x' is a singular term, *realism about x* is the view that there is a y such that x = y.
- Where 'F' is a putative kind-term, *realism about Fs* is the view that there are Fs *and* that F is a genuine kind-term.
- Where 'T' refers to the linguistic expression of some claim, theory, or doctrine, to *interpret or treat T realistically* is (a) to interpret T as having an objective truth value (and so to interpret it as something other than a mere evocative metaphor or expression of tastes, attitudes, or values); and (b) to interpret T in such a way that it *has realist truth-conditions* – in other words, it is true only if realism about the xs and Fs putatively referred to in the theory is true.
- Where 'D' refers to a discipline (like metaphysics or theology), *realism in D* is or involves interpreting the canonical statements of theories or doctrines in D realistically.

Thus, one way to be an anti-realist about God, say, is to affirm explicitly that there is no such being as God; but another way to be an anti-realist about God is to say, for example, that 'God exists' expresses a truth, but that the truth it expresses *isn't* that there is an x such that x = God. Likewise, one way to be an anti-realist about beliefs, say, is to affirm explicitly that there are no such things as beliefs; but another way to be an anti-realist about beliefs is to offer paraphrases of belief-talk according to which 'there are beliefs' expresses a truth, but the term 'belief' doesn't pick out a genuine kind of mental state. Furthermore, in light of the above characterizations, theists and atheists alike can interpret the same theological claims realistically. Indeed, their disagreement will most perspicuously be expressed as a disagreement over the truth value of the claim 'God exists' *realistically interpreted*.

One motivation for doubting that we should interpret doctrines in metaphysics or theology realistically is the vague worry that practitioners of both disciplines are spinning out theories with no reliable way of determining which of the competing theories is true. The worry is that the practitioners of each discipline are simply talking past one another, that their 'debates' lack substance, and that their theories don't tell us anything of interest about the world or its inhabitants. In short, theorizing in both disciplines is but idle word play; and so it is doubtful that the theories in either discipline have objective truth values or truth values with realist truth conditions.

Those caught in the grip of this worry then face the question of what to do with metaphysics and theology. In the case of metaphysics, the verdict is often that we should simply view it as a game and either stop playing it or else leave it to weekends and spend our day jobs on more serious activities – like, perhaps, philosophy of science. Theology is more complicated because many of the objectors still want to maintain that there is some value in religion, and they recognize that the sentences typically taken to express the core doctrines of religions like Christianity still have some value even if they can't be taken with literal seriousness. Indeed, whereas the objectors to metaphysical realism tend also to be objectors to metaphysics in general, the objectors to theological realism often style themselves as people interested in *saving* religion from the pernicious influence of modernism, fundamentalism, ontotheology or other villains. Still, for many of us, theology is of far lesser interest and import if the anti-realist verdict is allowed to stand. If, in the end, the theories produced by theology are not fitting objects for belief, it is hard to see why we should take the discipline very seriously.

In this chapter, I want to examine two ways of making the vague worry more precise. In *God and Realism*,[3] Peter Byrne offers an argument against realism in theology that is readily modified to cut against realism in metaphysics as well. And in *The Empirical Stance*,[4] Bas van Fraassen offers an argument against the very practice of analytic metaphysics that is both readily seen as an argument against realism in metaphysics and easily adapted into an argument against realism in theology. In what follows, I will examine these two arguments and defend four conclusions: first, that Byrne's argument is answerable; second, that van Fraassen's argument is unanswerable if we adopt what he calls the 'empirical stance'; third, that there is (and can be) absolutely no reason why

---

3 Aldershot: Ashgate, 2003. Hereafter referred to as GR.
4 New Haven: Yale University Press, 2002. Hereafter referred to as ES.

metaphysicians or theologians *ought* to adopt the empirical stance; and, finally, that for those who don't adopt the empirical stance, van Fraassen's objections can be answered in precisely the same way as we answer Byrne's.

The chapter will have three sections. In the first, I briefly present and respond to Byrne's argument against theological realism. In the second, I present van Fraassen's argument against analytic metaphysics and I show how, if sound, it constitutes a reason to reject both metaphysical and theological realism. Finally, I show how van Fraassen can be answered. Obviously what I am doing here falls far short of a full-blown defence of realism in either metaphysics or theology. But the objections raised by van Fraassen and Byrne are tokens of a type of objection that I think is rather widely endorsed among those who are suspicious of these two brands of realism. Thus, responding to those objections constitutes an important first step in the direction of a defence.

Byrne's Argument

Peter Byrne sums up his argument against theological realism as follows:[5]

(1) All disciplines of thought that can be interpreted realistically show the accumulation of reliable belief.
(2) Theology does not show the accumulation of reliable belief.
(3) Therefore, theology cannot be interpreted realistically.

Byrne declares that this argument is 'simple' (GR, p. 162) and 'decisive' (GR, p. 161). As a matter of fact, however, it is no simple matter at all to figure out precisely what Byrne means by terms like 'interpreted realistically' or 'show the accumulation of reliable belief'; nor is it a simple matter to figure out why exactly he thinks that the two premises of the argument are true. Since time will not permit the sort of detailed exegetical discussion it would take to sort out the terminological issues, I will simply offer glosses that I think are faithful to what Byrne was aiming at. I will then try to

---

5 GR, p. 162.

reconstruct as best I can his defence of the premises. Readers who think that the resulting product is not something Byrne would be happy with are welcome to take the argument of the present section as one of my own invention (albeit inspired by the work of Byrne and others) and offered primarily as a prelude to the discussion of van Fraassen.

Byrne seems to think that to *interpret a discipline of thought realistically* is just to see it as the sort of discipline whose methods of enquiry are successfully aimed at truth, whose theories are grounded in and responsive to evidence, and whose conclusions are intended to tell us the literal, objective truth about the world.[6] Thus, those disciplines which we can interpret realistically in Byrne's sense are presumably just those disciplines whose theories we can sensibly interpret realistically in my sense.

Byrne also seems to think that a discipline *shows the accumulation of reliable belief* just in case it generates an increasing number of statements that we can rationally expect not to be contradicted by future well-established theories in the discipline.[7] Reliable beliefs in a discipline D are just those beliefs that can be expected to remain permanently sanctioned by D's theoretical apparatus.[8]

---

6 Cf. GR Chapter 1, *passim*, and especially pp. 155–9. On p. 159, Byrne offers what might appear as an outright definition of what it is to interpret a discipline of thought realistically. He says: 'We have reached the conclusion that to interpret a discipline of thought realistically is to see its evolving conclusions as the outcome of real-world influences.' But, of course, this offers us nothing by way of precision; for, after all, superstitions, prejudices, fears and ambitions, peer pressure and other sociological influences, and so on are all 'real-world influences'. *Every* discipline – from biology and chemistry on the one hand to astrology and iridology on the other – is such that its 'evolving conclusions' are the outcomes of 'real-world influences'. But, of course, this can't be what Byrne has in mind. To find out what he has in mind, however, we have to look elsewhere and then offer a gloss; and my own view is that if we do this, and if we do it in the most charitable way possible, we arrive at something like the gloss that I have just offered.

7 Cf. especially GR, pp. 159–61.

8 Note, however, that this definition of reliable belief leaves open the possibility that reliable beliefs in one discipline might be contradicted by reliable beliefs in another discipline. If we were looking for *sufficient* conditions for the realistic interpretation of a discipline, we would want to

To say that a belief is reliable, then, is *not* to say that it is likely to be true (though it might in fact turn out that the reliable beliefs of a discipline are just the ones that are likely to be true). Rather, it is just to say that it is unlikely to be overturned by future evidence or theoretical developments.

Given all of this, Byrne's argument might be restated as follows: Consider some discipline D. We can take D's theories as worthy of belief and as aiming to tell us the literal truth about the world only if the practice of D over time generates an increasing number of statements that we can rationally expect not to be contradicted by future well-established theories in D. But we don't find such an increase of 'reliable belief' in theology. Thus, we should not treat theological theories as worthy of belief or as aiming to tell us the literal truth about the world. And, we might add, what goes for theology also goes for metaphysics: we don't find the accumulation of reliable belief in that discipline either. Thus, we should not be realists about theories in metaphysics either.

So much for the argument. Now, what shall we think of the premises? Let us begin by observing that *neither* of the premises is obviously true. A relatively narrow discipline that hits on the truth right at the outset will show no *accumulation* of belief at all; but that by itself is not obviously a reason to doubt that it is to be interpreted realistically. Thus, there is prima facie reason to think that premise (1) is false. Moreover, many branches of theology within Christendom seem clearly to have shown the accumulation of reliable belief (as defined above) over the centuries. In the Catholic Church, for example, the Nicene Creed and the Canons and Decrees of the Council of Trent – to name just two of a variety of doctrinal standards within Catholicism – are not at all likely to be contradicted by future developments in (official) Catholic theology. The Nicene Creed and the Canons and Decrees of the Council of Trent are explications of and elaborations on doctrines that the Catholic Church claims to have found in Scripture. They were needed precisely because their contents were not explicitly part of Christian belief prior to their formulation – so, in other

---

rule this out. But since Byrne is concerned to show that theology fails to meet a *necessary* condition for being interpreted realistically, I doubt that this problem will cause much trouble for present purposes.

words, they constitute genuine theoretical developments rather than being, like the Scriptures, mere *sources* for theological reflection. Though plenty of Roman Catholics, including Roman Catholic theologians, disagree with them in part or in their entirety, the Catholic Church is set up in such a way that we can be virtually certain that they will not be contradicted by future established theories in official Catholic theology. Likewise, and for similar reasons, it is highly unlikely that either the Nicene Creed or the Westminster Confession will be contradicted by future developments in (traditional, orthodox) Presbyterian theology – here not because the Presbyterian Church is set up so as to guarantee that those doctrinal standards will be preserved, but rather because theology as it is practised by those with a traditional, orthodox bent is not at all revisionary in the way that certain other brands of theology might be.[9] And, of course, similar things might be said for various other sectarian theologies. Thus, there is prima facie reason to reject premise (2) as well.[10] What then are Byrne's arguments for these premises?

Premise (2), oddly enough, is offered without any argument at all. Byrne simply declares that it is obviously true, and then follows

---

9 Moreover, even the revisionists in the Presbyterian camp will likely agree on permanence of conditional claims to the effect that, given an appropriately strong view of the inspiration and infallibility of the Bible, the doctrines expressed in the Nicene Creed, the Westminster Confession and various other doctrinal standards are true.

10 Is it really fair, though, to treat *official Catholic* theology, or *traditional, orthodox Presbyterian* theology as disciplines in their own right, rather than as branches of a single discipline – theology? It is hard to see why not; but, in the end, nothing hinges on treating them as such. For surely Byrne would not countenance *this* sort of reply to his argument: 'Granted, we cannot interpret theology realistically. But that doesn't matter; for all I claim is that we *can* interpret the distinct theory-building enterprise of *Catholic* theology realistically.' But so far as I can tell, the only *argument* he has against this reply is an adapted version of the argument currently under discussion: i.e., a theory-building enterprise can be interpreted realistically only if it shows the accumulation of reliable belief; but in these various theory-building enterprises there has been no accumulation of reliable belief. If this *is* the argument he would use, then my reply is as above: these theory-building enterprises have shown the accumulation of reliable belief after all.

Veritas: Belief and Metaphysics

that declaration with remarks that effectively just restate and elaborate on it. Thus, he writes:

> Consider this question: do we know anything more about God than we did at the dawn of Christian theology nearly 2,000 years ago? Answer: No. During that period many theological theories have come and gone in Christian thought, but there has been no accumulation of insight and discovery whatsoever. The stock of reliable beliefs about the Christian God, about its attributes and plans, has not increased one iota . . . Theology has not possessed intellectual traditions and modes of discovery [analogous to those in science] to enable its practitioners to be open to influences from divine reality and its practitioners have not been put in cognitive contact with divine reality. The academic discipline of theology is simply not productive of reliable beliefs about God – or about anything else for that matter. It cannot be understood realistically. QED. (GR, p. 162)

But why should we believe any of this? The stock of reliable beliefs about the Christian God has not increased *one iota*? Again, it is hard to take this claim at all seriously in light of what we know of the histories of Catholic theology, traditional Presbyterian theology, and any of a number of other sectarian theologies within Christendom. The 'QED' at the end of the paragraph seems, to put it mildly, a bit premature.

Premise (2), then, is a natural target for resistance. But for present purposes I want to waive worries about premise (2) and focus instead on premise (1). Here Byrne does want to offer argument; though what the argument amounts to, exactly, is rather hard to tell. What he says explicitly in favour of (1) is just this: 'Premise (1) has been established through consideration of the example of science' (GR, p. 162). What we find, however, upon reviewing his consideration of the example of science is that, really, he has defended not (1) but (1a):

(1a) Disciplines that show the accumulation of reliable belief are to be interpreted realistically.

And what he offers in support of (1a) is just a version of the familiar 'no miracles' argument for scientific realism. In his words:

> The story of science is a human story, but one which is comprehensible only if we assume that human theory and practice are being in part, at least, shaped by what the world is really like. If there is a progressive, cumulative structure to the development of science, this strongly suggests real-world cognitive contact and influence; otherwise the accumulation of reliable belief would be the merest accident. (GR, p. 156)

A generalization on this argument yields (1a); but it yields nothing close to (1).

Nevertheless, there is an argument for (1) lurking in the neighbourhood. Suppose we endorse the following premises:

(1b) For any discipline D, there is no initial presumption that D is to be interpreted realistically.

(1c) There can be no evidence supporting a realistic interpretation of a discipline apart from the accumulation of reliable belief.

(1d) Absent an initial presumption for interpreting a discipline D realistically, and absent evidence that D is to be interpreted realistically, D cannot rationally be interpreted realistically.

If we do endorse (1b–1d), and if we are persuaded by Byrne's argument for (1a), then we have a ready argument for (1).

The idea, then, is something like this: For any discipline D, the practitioners of D aren't entitled simply to adopt, without argument, a realist interpretation of D. Rather, if we want to interpret D realistically, we need to do so on the basis of evidence – evidence that D is really putting us in touch with the truth about things. But what evidence could we possibly acquire? In the case of science, we have (allegedly) the accumulation of reliable belief. And it is, one might think, very hard to explain how we could have that if science weren't putting us in touch with the truth about things. But absent the accumulation of reliable belief, what other evidence could we have for interpreting science realistically? What other phenomenon would be best explained by the supposition that science, or any other discipline, is putting us in touch with truth? Apparently none. Thus, the only disciplines that we are entitled to interpret realistically are those that show the accumulation of reliable belief – which is just to say that premise (1) is true.

The trouble with this line of reasoning is just that, if it were sound, we would face the threat of global scepticism. Let D be the discipline of Detecting Reliable Beliefs (DRB). (If you prefer, you could treat it as the discipline for detecting success, and then fill in your favourite criterion for success. But since we're talking about Byrne, we'll focus on his.) Practitioners of DRB – all of us, I suppose, to some extent or another – are engaged in the enterprise of trying to find out which, if any, of their beliefs count as reliable. Moreover, if Byrne is correct about the criteria for interpreting a discipline realistically, realism about any other discipline is predicated in part on a realist interpretation of DRB. That is, unless we assume that the claims of DRB have objective truth values (and, indeed, that they tell us the objective truth about things), we will not be entitled to believe that any discipline has shown the accumulation of reliable belief.[11] And if we are not entitled to believe that any discipline has shown the accumulation of reliable belief, then (by Byrne's lights), we cannot interpret any discipline realistically.

---

11 Suppose you think that some claim of DRB has a truth value, but that the truth value is not objective. Thus, suppose you think something like this: 'It is true, but only true-for-me, that $B_1 - B_n$ *are reliable beliefs in discipline D.*' Given our understanding of reliable belief, this would seem to be equivalent to the view that you, but not necessarily anyone else, can rationally expect that $B_1 - B_n$ will be permanently sanctioned parts of D's theoretical apparatus. But isn't this claim self-undermining? Note that the claim *isn't* equivalent to the (perhaps perfectly sensible) claim that you have evidence E that (for all you know) nobody else has, and that given this, it is *objectively* rational for you (but not necessarily for anyone lacking E) to believe that $B_1 - B_n$ will be permanently sanctioned parts of D's theoretical apparatus. Rather, if it is really *only* true-for-you that $B_1 - B_n$ are reliable beliefs in D, the idea is that *even people in your same epistemic position* might not rationally be able to expect that $B_1 - B_n$ will be permanently sanctioned by D. But this fact by itself counts as good reason to question whether practitioners of D will continue to sanction $B_1 - B_n$. Thus, in affirming that it is only true for you that $B_1 - B_n$ can rationally be expected to be permanently sanctioned by D, you acquire a defeater for the belief that $B_1 - B_n$ will always be sanctioned by D; and so it becomes *irrational* for you to expect that $B_1 - B_n$ will be permanently sanctioned by D.

Realism in Theology and Metaphysics

So can we interpret the theories of DRB realistically? Well, following Byrne's reasoning, in order to assess this question we should ask: Has DRB itself shown the accumulation of reliable belief? There are two ways of trying to answer this question. Practitioners of DRB might assume from the outset (until given reason to do otherwise) that the methods they employ in practising DRB are successfully aimed at truth; and, on the basis of this assumption, they will likely say 'yes, DRB has shown the accumulation of reliable belief'. Note, however, that these practitioners of DRB are interpreting DRB realistically, and they are doing so not *on the basis* of its success, but rather *in advance* of any awareness of its success. Indeed, their assessment of DRB's success *depends* on their realist interpretation of DRB. On the other hand, practitioners of DRB might refrain from interpreting DRB realistically until they have independent evidence that DRB has shown the accumulation of reliable belief. But this will be a long wait; for, after all, any mode of detecting whether DRB has shown the accumulation of reliable belief will itself fall under the scope of DRB.

The upshot, then, is this: If you can't interpret a discipline realistically until it has shown the accumulation of reliable belief, then you won't ever be able to interpret DRB realistically. And if you can't interpret DRB realistically, then you can't interpret any discipline realistically. But Byrne acknowledges that some disciplines can be interpreted realistically. Thus, he must concede that at least some disciplines can be interpreted realistically even if they haven't shown the accumulation of reliable belief. In the case of DRB, it seems, in fact, that there is a rational initial presumption that DRB is to be interpreted realistically, contrary to (1b) above. And, for all we know, there might be other disciplines for which there is evidence, but of an entirely different sort, that supports a realist interpretation of the discipline – contrary to (1c). Absent (1b) and (1c), however, there is no clear argument for (1). And so Byrne's argument fails – even ignoring worries about (2).

One might object that there is no such discipline as DRB; thus, my argument against Byrne – which apparently rests on the supposition that there is such a discipline – fails. I admit that it seems odd to characterize DRB as a discipline. After all, it is hard to imagine awarding university degrees in DRB, or applying for NEH or NSF funding to pursue DRB. But, really, the objection does not rest in any important way upon the supposition that the criteria for discipline individuation allow us to treat DRB as a discipline. For whatever else DRB happens to be, it is, at the very least, a theory-building activity. And what the argument just presented shows is that at least some theory-building activities *must* be interpreted realistically in the absence of the accumulation of reliable belief. But if that is right, then the door is open for thinking that other theory-building activities – including, for all we know, full-blown disciplines (whatever exactly a 'discipline' amounts to in Byrne's usage) can be interpreted realistically in the absence of the accumulation of reliable belief.

In closing this section, I would like to note a connection between my argument here and some conclusions that I have defended elsewhere. In *World Without Design: The Ontological Consequences of Naturalism*,[12] I argued that, assuming we want to form beliefs on the basis of evidence, we cannot avoid treating at least some sources of evidence as basic sources, where a source is treated as basic just in case it is trusted as reliable *in the absence of evidence for its reliability*. The reason is simple: in order to acquire or appreciate evidence for the claim that a source S is reliable, one must either invoke evidence from some distinct source S*, or one must invoke evidence from S itself. Since we do not have infinitely many sources of evidence, it follows that at least one of our sources is such that some, if not all, of the evidence we have in support of its reliability comes from the source itself. But in such a case, our disposition to trust the source *precedes* our having evidence for its reliability. Thus, our trust in the source does not depend on the evidence – even if, in the end, our *belief* that the source is reliable does depend (circularly) on the evidence. So, assuming it is rational for us to trust any of our sources of evidence as reliable, it must be rational to treat at least one of them as basic.

But if all that is right, then (*ceteris paribus*) it will be rational to interpret realistically any discipline that can be practiced just by relying on basic sources, and furthermore, it will be rational to do so in advance of any evidence of success. Suppose, for example, we (rationally) treat source S as basic. Then, from our point of view, source S is a *reliable* source of evidence. Other things being equal,

---

12 Oxford: Clarendon Press, 2002.

then, it will be rational for us to form beliefs on the basis of evidence garnered from source S. In other words, propositions supported by evidence from S will be fitting objects of belief for us. But then, of course, it follows that (*ceteris paribus* – in other words, absent counterevidence from other sources, strange circumstances, and so on) the conclusions of any discipline that can be practised just by relying on S will be fitting objects for belief. In other words, it will be rational for us to believe those conclusions as expressions of the literal, objective truth about the world. Thus, by definition, it will be rational for us to interpret the discipline realistically.

Of course, one might try to oppose realism in theology or metaphysics by arguing that these disciplines inevitably rely on evidence from sources that are not rationally treated as basic, or by arguing that they are in some other way defective; but those would be very different arguments, and ones that have yet to appear in the literature in any sort of developed form.

Van Fraassen

I now want to turn to a different sort of challenge: an objection to the very enterprise of metaphysics that, if sound, carries over to theology as well. The objection is raised by Bas van Fraassen in the opening chapter of *The Empirical Stance*.

According to van Fraassen, analytic ontology – which, for purposes here, I am taking to be identical to the discipline of metaphysics – aims to answer questions that science doesn't ask, and to do so in the same way that science answers its questions. What does this mean exactly? Primarily, it means that metaphysicians *posit* things to do explanatory work, and then they try to justify the acceptance of their explanatory posits by appeal to the sorts of virtues that justify the acceptance of scientific explanations – not virtues like predictive success and increased ability to control nature, however; rather, virtues like explanatory power, simplicity, elegance, conservatism, and the like. (For convenience, I shall refer to the latter sorts of virtues as 'explanatory virtues'. In doing so, however, I do not mean to make any presuppositions about whether or to what extent the virtues that I am calling 'explanatory' can be distinguished from putatively non-explanatory virtues like empirical adequacy; nor do I mean to make any presuppositions about whether the allegedly different explanatory virtues can be distinguished from one another.)

Thus construed, analytic ontology is open to two objections.

The first objection is that relevant differences between science and ontology cast doubt on the justification for accepting the ontologist's explanatory posits. Van Fraassen lays out the objection as follows:

> You will have understood me correctly if you now see science and analytic ontology caught in a Pascalian wager ... If the wager is on a choice of theories or hypotheses, then from a God's-eye view, success consists in selecting the true and failure in choosing the false ... As in all success and failure, however, although there is value in winning as such, there are also collateral value and damage that win and loss bring along with them ... In science, the stakes are great for all of us: safety, food, shelter, communication, all the preconditions for life in peace and justice that a successful science can enhance. The risk of acquiring some false beliefs matters little in comparison. *Most important for us, here, the acquisition of false beliefs by itself, apart from their practical empirical consequences, is no great matter in its contrast class of practical risk and gain.*
>
> That is very far from how it is in metaphysics. There the gains to be contemplated are those of having true beliefs ... and of being in a position to explain ... The risk is precisely that of acquiring false beliefs ... Where is the metaphysician who shows us how likely it is that inference to the best explanation in ontology will lead to true conclusions? Why is he or she missing? Where is the metaphysician who makes the case that the gain of explanatory power outweighs the risk of ending up with a tissue of falsehoods? (ES, pp. 15–16; emphasis mine)

The argument, in sum, seems just to be this: false belief, as such, is to be avoided; and there is no *evidence* that explanatory virtues lead us to true belief. Thus, we are justified (*if at all*, one might add) in forming beliefs on the basis of best-explanation arguments only if the gain from doing so outweighs the risk. In science, we might have a case for the conclusion that gain outweighs risk; but not in metaphysics.[13] Thus, absent some argument for the conclusion that inference to the best explanation in metaphysics is likely to lead us to the truth (and given that there is something rather absurd about constructing metaphysical theories while at the same time withholding belief in them and suspending judgement about their explanatory status), one ought not to engage in metaphysics at all.

Of course, one might note that there *are* arguments in the literature for the conclusion that explanatory virtues are truth-indicative. But such arguments typically focus on the status of explanatory virtues as criteria for theory choice in *science* rather than metaphysics; and, more importantly, they typically reason from the premise that this or that feature of science is hard to *explain* apart from the assumption that choosing theories on the basis of certain explanatory virtues is a reliable way of reaching the truth to the conclusion that, therefore, the assumption in question is true. But according to van Fraassen, the demand for explanations is precisely what good empiricists aim to resist.[14] In other words: if one is already committed to the metaphysical enterprise, one will take seriously the demand for explanation, and, in doing so, one may well be led to the conclusion that choosing theories on the basis of their explanatory power (among other virtues) is a reliable way of getting to the truth. But if the question is *why we should be committed to the metaphysical enterprise in the first place*, then arguments that presuppose a need for explaining things will be impotent. Thus, the empiricist will be completely unmoved by the usual arguments for the claim that explanatory virtues are truth-indicative.

But, one might wonder, why should metaphysicians care whether empiricists are moved by replies to their objections? As it turns out, I think that they should not care; and I think that, in the end, van Fraassen's objections against metaphysics are, at best, grumblings

---

13 Here I take it that van Fraassen is suspending, for the sake of argument, his view – defended at length in *The Scientific Image* (Oxford: Clarendon Press 1980) – that explanation is not the aim of science, and that believing that scientific theories provide true explanations is to take an objectionably metaphysical view of science.

14 On this, see (for example) van Fraassen's reply to Richard Boyd in Paul Churchland and Clifford Hooker (eds), *Images of Science* (Chicago: University of Chicago Press, 1985).

that *express* the empiricist distaste for metaphysics but that will not and should not convince the unconvinced that the distaste ought to be shared. Showing this, however, will take a bit of argument – argument that is best left until after van Fraassen's second objection has been presented.

The second objection is that the procedure of explanation via theoretical posit results in the creation of 'simulacra' which then replace the real things that we aim to be theorizing about and thereby make our theoretical activity into an idle exercise in wordplay. So, for example, van Fraassen argues that when philosophers ask the question 'Does the world exist?' what they inevitably do is to make the question rigorous with technical definitions of 'world' and related terms that map on to some but not nearly all uses of the term 'world' and then stipulate that the world exists if, and only if, the world *as they have defined it* exists. He notes that one might just as well introduce a new technical term – 'Sworld', for example – and then ask whether the Sworld exists. The trouble, of course, is that we wouldn't really care about the answer – unless we had reason to think that 'the world exists' means the same thing as 'the Sworld exists'. But therein lies the rub; for, after all, it doesn't, exactly. As van Fraassen puts it:

> 'Sworld' is intelligibly related to 'world,' taking over a carefully selected family of uses, regimenting them, and is then used to make new, logically contingent, fully intelligible assertions. If we are careful not to let other usages of 'world' creep back into our professional discourse, then 'the world exists' is a perfectly good way of saying 'the Sworld exists.'
>
> The unfortunate negative verdict forced on us by this . . . line of reasoning, which grants sufficiency to such lenient standards [of meaningfulness], is that it is very easy, all too easy, to make sense. We can sit in our closets and in a perfectly meaningful way, kneading and manipulating the language, create new theories of everything and thereby important contributions to ontology. In other words, to put it a little more bluntly, this 'word play' we [are engaged in] is merely idle world play; although shown to be meaningful, it is merely idle world play nevertheless. (ES, p. 27)

In sum, then, ontologists who try to answer the question 'Does the world exist?' in the way just described inevitably replace talk of the world with talk of a simulacrum – the Sworld. But the simulacrum isn't what we care about when we ask the question the ontologist is trying to answer; and so the ontologist is engaged in a project that is somewhat removed from our real interests and concerns.

So go van Fraassen's objections against metaphysics. I'll consider responses in a moment; but first I want to comment briefly on how these objections might carry over to theology. It is clear that van Fraassen thinks that they do – or, at any rate, that they carry over to some kinds of theology – for some of the examples he uses are examples drawn from the philosophy of religion. I take it that, as applied to theology, the objections are just these: (a) there are no empirically detectable pay-offs for the procedure of explanation by theoretical posit in theology, and (b) the God that is talked about in that part of theology that resembles or overlaps with analytic philosophy of religion is a simulacrum – either different from the real God, or else simply stipulated to be identical to the real God. Obviously not all of theology is indicted by these objections. But at least two kinds probably will be: so-called *perfect being theology*, an approach adopted by many medieval and contemporary analytic philosophers that attributes properties to God (such as simplicity and changelessness) on the basis of intuitions about perfection; and systematic and philosophical theology, at least in so far as these activities involve a certain amount of explanatory postulation in the effort to build detailed theories out of the data provided by divine revelation and religious experience. And, again, the objection will be that perfect being theology results in the creation of a simulacrum (one which privileges for theological purposes the characterization of God as *perfect* over characterizations of God as our parent, our employer, our shepherd and so on), and that the explanations offered by systematic theology have no pay-offs that outweigh the risks associated with treating explanatory power as a theoretical virtue.

But now what shall we think of these objections? Let us begin with the 'simulacrum' objection. And here, I think, it will be helpful to begin by considering a rather simple-minded response to van Fraassen. The objection, again, is that metaphysicians aren't talking about things that we care about: they talk about the Sworld rather than the world; they talk about the God of the philosophers rather than about God; and so on. But, one might wonder, how do we *know* that the Sworld isn't the world? How do we know that the God of the philosophers isn't God? How, in other words, do we know that these things are just simulacra? It seems, in fact, that we can't know unless we already have a metaphysical story to tell about the nature of the world or about the nature of God. But, of course, to have a metaphysical story to tell, we'd have to do some metaphysics.

But the response isn't quite right. It's *not* true that the *only* way to know that you've constructed a simulacrum is by comparing the object of your discourse with the *real* thing. The other way to know that you've constructed a simulacrum is by knowing that constructing simulacra is pretty much *all* you can do. And here, I think, we start to get at the real objection in van Fraassen's text. As I see it, the concern is just this: metaphysicians are in the business of offering explanations by postulate. We postulate definitions, entities, properties and the like; and we use our postulates to build theories that explain the world to us. Our postulates are by their very nature props and models – 'simulacra', if you will, that may or may not manage to represent the things they are about in a full and accurate way. And – this is the concern – precisely because we have no evidence that explanation by postulate is a reliable way of reaching the truth, we have no way of knowing the extent to which simulacra represent the things that they are about. To the extent, then, that we try to force our talk about (say) God or the world to conform to our idea of the God of the philosophers or of the Sworld, we change the subject from something we know and recognize to something that, for all we know, may be (and probably is) at best a shadow of the thing we actually care about.

Two Stances

Suppose we grant that the, or a, defining characteristic of analytic metaphysics (and of certain theological enterprises as well) is a willingness to engage in explanation by theoretical postulate. How shall we address the sceptical worry raised at the end of the previous section – the worry, in short, that we have no evidence that

Realism in Theology and Metaphysics

the methods of metaphysics are reliable and therefore we have no reason to think that the simulacra we construct bear any important relation to the things we care about? The answer, so I shall argue, just depends on which of two 'stances' we adopt: the empirical stance or the metaphysical stance.

According to van Fraassen, empiricism is a philosophical position that involves, in addition to a familiar sort of respect for science, empirical investigation, undogmatic theorizing, and the like, the following two values, tendencies, or attitudes:

(a) a rejection of demands for explanation at certain crucial points, and
(b) a strong dissatisfaction with explanations (even if called for) that proceed by postulation.

It is (a) and (b), he thinks, that separate empiricists from metaphysicians. Moreover, empiricism, on his view, is not a belief or a philosophical thesis. Rather, it is a stance: an 'attitude, commitment, approach, a cluster of such – possibly including some propositional attitudes such as beliefs as well' (ES, pp. 48–9). To adopt empiricism, or the *empirical stance*, then, is to adopt the characteristic attitudes, commitments, and so on of the empiricist tradition – including (a) and (b). And we might go on to say that, in contrast with the empirical stance there is also a *metaphysical stance* – a stance characterized in part by a willingness to embrace demands for explanation and to be satisfied with explanations that proceed by postulation.

So far as I can tell, those who adopt the empirical stance can have no answer to van Fraassen's objections against metaphysics. We have already conceded for the sake of argument that metaphysics involves offering explanations by postulation; and, so far as I can tell, apart from the sorts of explanatory arguments already in the literature, there is no argument forthcoming for the conclusion that selecting theories on the basis of explanatory virtues is, in general, a reliable way of reaching the truth. And, of course, *explanatory* arguments will be of no use in persuading an empiricist to take metaphysics seriously; for those are precisely the sorts of arguments of which empiricists are most suspicious. From within the empirical stance, then, it is hard to find any resources for answering van Fraassen's objections.

Veritas: Belief and Metaphysics

On the other hand, the objections are readily answerable from within the metaphysical stance. Indeed, those who adopt the metaphysical stance may simply adapt the reply I offered to Byrne. We know that some sources of evidence have to be taken as basic. Even the empiricist must acknowledge as much for, lest she fall into global scepticism, she will be forced to take at least sense perception and logical reasoning as basic sources. But then why not take the methods and sources of evidence employed by metaphysicians as basic sources as well? There are, to be sure, arguments in the literature for the conclusion that some of these sources – intuition, for example – are unreliable or unworthy of being treated as basic sources. But, notoriously, these arguments are not decisive – in no small part because (as is often pointed out) it seems impossible to *run* the arguments without presupposing the reliability of intuition. In any case, however, they are not the arguments that van Fraassen has offered; and to the extent that his objections depend on them, they are all the weaker for that dependency. My suggestion, then, is that van Fraassen's scepticism about metaphysics ought to be treated in precisely the way that Byrne's theological scepticism ought to be treated: both are rightly ignored.

Matters would be different, of course, if there could be some *argument* for the conclusion that it is more rational to adopt the empirical stance than to adopt the metaphysical stance. Is there such an argument? More pertinently, is there any such argument that those who have already adopted the metaphysical stance will be rationally bound to accept? It is hard to see how there could be. For, after all, the two stances are distinguished in part by different views about what constitutes good argument and rational theorizing; and, unless the standards and sources characteristic of the metaphysical stance are self-defeating, there is no reason to think that those adopting the metaphysical stance ought to be persuaded by *empiricist arguments* for the conclusion that it is irrational to adopt the metaphysical stance. And so far as I am aware, there is no argument forthcoming for the conclusion that the standards and sources characteristic of the metaphysical stance are self-defeating. At any rate, no such argument has been offered by Byrne or van Fraassen.

Interestingly, van Fraassen does seem to have a *pragmatic* argument for adopting the empirical stance. The pragmatic argument is just his first objection against metaphysics: namely, that the payoff we gain from believing the theories we choose on the basis of explanatory virtues is too small to offset the risk of false belief. In fact, however, the pragmatic argument seems unsound. Granted, food, shelter and safety are not at stake in metaphysics. But other things are.[15] Metaphysics impinges on morality; it also impinges on our very conception of ourselves. Are we free? If not, does it follow that we are not morally responsible? Can a person existing now be the same person as one existing a thousand years from now? If not, as Derek Parfit seems to suppose, is there any point in taking steps – as both scientists and religious believers do in various different ways – to try to prolong our lives significantly? The list of questions might well go on; and to the extent that our metaphysical views do impinge upon our moral lives and upon our self-conception, they will impact our intellectual and emotional lives, our social interactions, and a variety of other aspects of life. Indeed, many religious believers have thought that one's metaphysical beliefs – particularly one's theological beliefs – make the difference between eternity in heaven and eternity in hell. For those who think this, the risk of false belief and reward of true belief rise exponentially. So, contrary to what van Fraassen argues, false belief in metaphysics can be a serious risk; true belief can be an important reward. And the reward of getting it right might well justify taking the risk.

Van Fraassen will almost certainly be unmoved by the response just offered on behalf of metaphysics. But really that doesn't matter. For plenty of people *will* be moved. That is, plenty of people will agree that the potential reward of true belief in metaphysics *does* outweigh the risk. And for those people, there will be ample pragmatic justification for adopting the metaphysical stance.

---

15 Some of the points here, particularly the point about free will, are borrowed from Alicia Finch's discussion of van Fraassen's objection in her review of *The Empirical Stance*, in *The American Catholic Philosophical Quarterly* 77.2 (Spring 2003), pp. 302–7.

Conclusion

In this chapter, I have examined two objections against realism in theology and metaphysics, and I have concluded that practitioners of metaphysics and theology ought simply to ignore these objections. In a very important sense, both objections are simply instances of 'preaching to the choir'. Those who are already sceptical of theology or metaphysics or both will find in the objections plenty to agree with. But they should not convince the unconvinced.

15. Deification as Metaphysics: Christology, Desire, and Filial Prayer

PATRICK RICHES

> God always makes me yearn for what he wants to give me.
> *St Thérèse of the Child Jesus*

In an address delivered two years before he was elected pope, Joseph Ratzinger, discussing the nature of the human person, said: 'Man is not satisfied with solutions beneath the level of divinization. But all the roads offered by the "serpent" (Gen. 3.5) . . . fail. The only path [to divinization] is communion with Christ.'[1] His claim posits anthropology in terms of an irreducible human desire, a self-transcending desire for deification that underpins both human sin and salvation. In this framework, it is possible to claim that communion in the incarnate Logos not only redeems, but fulfils, by purifying Adam's perverted desire to 'grasp' divinity. So that in Christ, the serpent's false promise is recapitulated into a true prophecy of the authentic pattern of deiform desire, now made possible by the ecclesial abiding of the Holy Spirit who liturgically re-presents the formal pattern of the Son's *theandric* gift of himself. In this way, desiring into the Sequela of Christ is the substance of prayer: the mystery of human desire plunging into the depths of the Trinity.

---

1 Address given in Rome, 2000, 'The New Evangelization: Building the Civilization of Love', http://www.ewtn.com/new_evangelization/Ratzinger.html

Veritas: Belief and Metaphysics

'*Hos*': The Conjunction of Christic Recapitulation

The Sequela of Christ is not a contradiction of the desire of Adam but rather its purified fulfilment. Christ recapitulates the sin of Adam by healing the false-sequela of death from within. He enters into its anguish and absorbs it into his way of deification. Jean Daniélou writes: 'recapitulation consists in Christ's reproducing the story of Adam on a higher plane.'[2] The higher plane of the Sequela[3] of Christ is the gift of love the Son makes when he willingly hands himself over to the *nihil* of Adam's sin. The God-Man, who is by nature what Adam was meant to become by grace, undoes the fall into death by opening a way of *theosis* through the

---

2 Jean Daniélou, *A History of Early Christian Doctrine Before the Council of Nicaea*, vol. 2, *Gospel Message and Hellenistic Culture*, trans. John Austin Baker (London: Darton, Longman and Todd, 1973), p. 180.

3 *Sequela Christi* means 'the following of Christ'. The Sequela of Christ can be understood as the mystical assimilation of the human into the divine personhood of Jesus, who in the incarnation offers the narrative of his life as the patterned way of christoform union/deification. What I intend to invoke with the term is something of a blending of ontology and narrative, something suggestive of an ontology of the 'patterned repetition' of the narrative of Christ's life. In this way I want to combine the injunction of Christ – 'If any one serves me, he must follow me [*me sequatur*]; and where I am, there shall my servant be also; if any one serves me, the Father will honour him' (John 12.26) – with the Pauline theology of pressing on, through the *pattern* given in Christ, in order to attain the heavenly goal in him (cf. Phil. 3.12–17). This 'patterned repetition' is liturgical in the deepest sense: it is a repetition of the *mystery* of the narrative of Christ into the pieties, politics and the social diversifications of the Church's communal-life-of-doxology. Although the Sequela can be thought to mean something along the lines of *mimesis*, it is a more open (and non-identical) notion of narrative repetition: rather than perfectly duplicating the 'pure original', it aims at something convertible with the diverse participations of the non-identical narratives of the communion of saints in the union of Christ's divine personhood. As Ratzinger writes in 'The New Evangelization': 'Christ offers himself as the path of my life. Sequela of Christ does not mean: imitating the man Jesus [as a mimesis of a pure original]. This type of attempt would necessarily fail – it would be an anachronism. The Sequela of Christ has a much higher goal: to be assimilated into Christ, that is to attain union with God.'

kenotic pattern of not counting equality with God a thing to be grasped (cf. Phil. 2.6).[4]

The adamic-will to be *hos theos* (LXX Gen. 3.6) is recapitulated through the christic-will to be *hos anthropos* (Phil. 2.7). In this way the formal pattern of Christ's being *hos anthropos* effects an ontological restoration by 'unwinding' the narrative of sin and death issuing from Adam's will to grasp divinity.[5] In this, the incarnation reveals that deification and death both turn on a simple conjunction: *hos*. Giorgio Agamben (in a different context) has argued that this particle '*hos*' is deployed in the New Testament as a term of messianic expectation, of comparison and juxtaposition. As a messianic conjunction, it is for Agamben a conjunction between 'the time that remains' and 'the eternal-time in God'.[6] '*Hos*' can be read as the term between the fall into death and the glory of deification. In this way it is the conjunction of christic-recapitulation: not simply a term of similitude, but rather a tensive term of difference that opens a new semantic field of meaning and identity.[7]

In the present context, the semantic field opened up by '*hos*' is itself the theandric field of incarnation and resurrection, of *theosis* through *kenosis*. In this semantic community of difference, this

---

4 On Philippians 2, the Adam/Christ theme and Gen. 3:6 see Morna D. Hooker, 'Adam *Redivivus*: Philippians 2 Once More', in Steve Moyise (ed.), *The Old Testament in the New Testament: Essays in Honour of J. L. North* (Sheffield: Sheffield Academic), pp. 220–34. I am indebted to Prof. Maurice Casey for pointing this article out to me and for conversations on this topic.

5 David Bentley Hart writes: '[T]he Irenaean language of *anakephalaiosis* . . . describes with extraordinary felicity the necessary logic of all Christian soteriology. It is because Christ's life effects a narrative reversal, which unwinds the story of sin and death and reinaugurates the story that God tells from the foundation of the world – the story of the creation he wills, freely, in his eternal councils – that Christ's life effects an ontological restoration of creation's goodness.' Hart, *The Beauty of the Infinite: The Aesthetics of Christian Truth* (Grand Rapids: Eerdmans, 2003), p. 325.

6 See Giorgio Agamben, *The Time that Remains: A Commentary on the Letter to the Romans*, trans. Patricia Daily (Stanford: Stanford, 2005), pp. 23–5.

7 Agamben, *The Time that Remains*.

excess of meaningful distance between creature and Creator, sin and salvation, the Sequela of Christ opens a way between death and deification, a pattern of meaning into the ecclesial reality of resurrection. But if the Sequela of Christ is a way *between* death and deification it points *beyond* death by passing *through* death. The tension of the Sequela is that it is in the between of sin: 'unless a grain of wheat falls to the earth and dies, it remains alone; but if it dies, it bears much fruit' (John 12.24).[8] In the recapitulation of the Adamic-story, the reproduction of the false-sequela 'on a higher plane' is paradoxically grounded in the depth of the soil in which sin was sown. Thereby Christ, through the false-sequela of death, becomes the Sequela of resurrection into deification by grace. The divinity Adam sought to take by force and by a misguided logic is, in Christ, revealed to be what God eternally wills the human to receive as gift. In revealing this, Christ reveals the true Adam.

Le *Surnaturel* and the Double Mediation of Desire

'Christ the new Adam, in the very revelation of the mystery of the Father and of his love, fully reveals man to himself and brings to light his most high calling.'[9] This sentence from *Gaudium et spes* echoes one of the most important passages of Henri de Lubac's first book, *Catholicisme: les aspects sociaux du dogme*.[10] In the

---

8 I am here indebted to a conversation with Chris Hackett.

9 *Gaudium et spes*, 22.

10 De Lubac, *Catholicism: Christ and the Common Destiny of Man*, trans. Lancelot C. Sheppard and Sister Elizabeth Englund, O.C.D. (San Francisco: Ignatius, 1988), p. 339. De Lubac's original reads: 'By revealing the Father and by being revealed by him, Christ completes the revelation of man to himself. By taking possession of man, by seizing hold of him and penetrating to the very depths of his being Christ makes man go deep down within himself there to discover in a flash regions hitherto unsuspected. It is through Christ that . . . man emerges definitively from the universe, and becomes conscious of his own being.' These words, as paraphrased in *Gaudium et spes*, are particularly linked to the pontificate of John Paul II, who quoted this sentence more frequently than any other from all the Conciliar Documents. The first time he quotes the sentence is in his programmatic first encyclical, *Redemptor hominis* (II.8). On the

Deification as Metaphysics

original, de Lubac went on to write that by revealing the human to himself, Christ had penetrated the depths of the human mystery, into 'regions hitherto unsuspected'. In the incarnate Son 'man emerges definitively from the universe, and becomes conscious of his own being'.[11] The knowledge of the human revealed in Christ is, for de Lubac, the revelation of the *surnaturel*. In *Le mystère du Surnaturel* de Lubac sums up this mystery by quoting Marie-Dominique Chenu's claim that in the human there is 'a depth, a living response, a natural desire, a "force" upon which freely given grace finds something to work'.[12] This force of natural desire is, for de Lubac, correlative with both the 'heart' and 'will' of the human person. This means that the 'will' is *not* a mere faculty (and so not discrete from intellect), but rather the 'will' is the fundamental depth of substance of the human person, a depth in which desire and reason are united.[13] For de Lubac 'heart' and 'will'

---

interrelation between the anthropology of John Paul and de Lubac see Paul McPartlan (who to my knowledge was the first to point out the de Lubacian paraphrase in *Gaudium et spes*, 22), 'Henri de Lubac – Evangelizer', *Priest and People* (August-September 1992), pp. 343–6. Further cf. David L. Schindler, *The Heart of the World:* Communio Ecclesiology, Liberalism, and the Liberation, (Grand Rapids: Eerdmans; London: T&T Clark, 1996), pp. 51–3, esp. p. 51 n. 9. More generally cf. Tracy Rowland, *Culture and the Thomist Tradition: After Vatican II* (London: Routledge, 2003); and Angelo Scola, '"Claim" of Christ, "Claim" of the World: On the Trinitarian Encyclicals of John Paul II', *Communio*, 18 (1991), pp. 322–31.

11 De Lubac, *Catholicism*, p. 339.

12 De Lubac's *surnaturel* thesis can be characterized as a sensibility of concrete theological fidelity to the revelation of the reality of this 'force' in the human, this *something* (depth, living response, natural desire) which God already gives of himself to human nature, in order that he may find in the human 'something to work', a 'grace' before grace. This would be what *Gaudium et spes* calls the 'intimate and vital bond of man to God' (19). M.-D. Chenu, O.P., *L'Évangile dans le temps* (Paris: Cerf, 1965), p. 676, as quoted by de Lubac in *Mystery of the Supernatural*, trans. Rosemary Sheed (New York: Crossroads, 1998), p. xxxvi.

13 In *Pic de la Mirandole* de Lubac describes the will as, 'la substance foncière de l'être humain' (p. 173). As the substantial depth of the human (which itself must be revealed), the heart of the human-as-'will' is pre-eminently irreducible to a mere faculty: 'Elle définit le fond même de l'être [humain], saisi en se point central où il n'est pas encore question de

Veritas: Belief and Metaphysics

correlate with the Pauline language of human 'spirit'/'*l'esprit*' or *pneuma*.[14]

In *Petite catéchèse sur Nature et Grâce*, de Lubac writes: 'We can scarcely do without this word [*pneuma*] if we wish to explain

---

distinguer les deux 'facultés' de l'intelligence et du vouloir' (*Mystery of the Supernatural*, p. 174). In 'Mysticism and Mystery' he reiterates: 'the will is not a mere "faculty", but the most profound element of being' (pp. 61–2); in the essay he also talks of 'mystical union' with God as a 'union of will'. In *Pic de la Mirandole*, de Lubac explicitly associates the human 'will' (the freedom in which the human is created to love) with paragraph 19 of *Gaudium et spes*, with the *mark* of the human as *imago Dei* called to communion with God (p. 173). See de Lubac, *Pic de la Mirandole* (Paris: Aubier-Montaigne, 1974); and 'Mysticism and Mystery' in *Theological Fragments*, trans. Rebecca Howell Balinski (San Francisco: Ignatius 1989), pp. 35–69. Also see John Milbank, *The Suspended Middle: Henri de Lubac and the Debate Concerning the Supernatural* (London: SCM Press, 2005), p. 28. For a much expanded discussion of the 'will' along these lines in Balthasar and Aquinas cf. David C. Schindler, 'Towards A Non-Possessive Concept of Knowledge: On the Relation Between Reason and Love in Aquinas and Balthasar', *Modern Theology* 22 (2006), pp. 577–607.

14 The *pneuma* of the human person functions, for de Lubac, within his insistence on a tripartite anthropology, rooted first in the Pauline trichotomy of spirit, soul and body (1 Thess. 5.23) and correlated with the Mosaic command of tripartite love (Deut. 6.5). On de Lubac's view, *pneuma* is the core of the fullness of human life and communication with God. But *pneuma* is also a radically ambivalent term for de Lubac. Accordingly even as *pneuma* is the very heart and deepest reality of what it is to be human, *pneuma* is paradoxically *not* an entirely constituent 'part' of the human person. That is, *pneuma* is at once the deep reality of the human person, and yet it is irreducible to the human and so not simply 'human'. De Lubac writes: 'Thus what par excellence makes a man, what constitutes man in his worth among the beings of this world, much more, what makes him a being superior to the world, would be an element that, rather than being "of man", would be "in man".' So *pneuma* is the '*force*' upon which Chenu reads God finding *something* to work in all human life. It is the heart of the human but it is something of God, a gift or grace that *precedes* grace. See the articles collected under the title 'Tripartite Anthropology' in *Theology in History*, trans. Anne Englund Nash (San Francisco: Ignatius, 1996), pp. 117–200 (especially pp. 117–29 and pp. 178–200), the quotation here is at p. 129. On the convertibility of the will and *pneuma* see de Lubac, *Pic de la Mirandole*, pp. 170–83.

Deification as Metaphysics

the "longing for God", which is basic to man.'[15] But for de Lubac, in as much as *pneuma* is constitutive of the human, and even as there is a living response to grace in every person and culture, only in Christ is the meaning of this mystery fully manifested.[16] Human desire is a content that must be revealed.[17] De Lubac argues that in Christ 'the knowledge that is revealed to us of that calling . . . leads us to recognize within ourselves the existence and nature of that desire'.[18] Apart from Christ, the human remains hidden from himself, and that desire, which is constitutive of his very nature, remains an enigmatic-desire-without-object: 'a desire which might not merely mistake its object, but even pursue quite worthless objects'.[19]

Only Christian revelation makes possible the recognition of the 'indications' and 'meaning' of human desire – and this, not only because Jesus is the authentic pattern of human willing, but also because, as the perfect image of the Father, he fully reveals the object of desire's intellection (cf. 1 Cor. 11.7 and 2 Cor. 4.4).[20] The Sequela of Christ is both the way and the end, both the object and the formal pattern of genuine human longing.

In a manner not unlike the temporal tension of Agamben's *'hos'* conjunction, de Lubac comes metaphysically to occupy what Hans Urs von Balthasar names his 'suspended middle'.[21] This 'middle' is the unity of nature and the supernatural in the depths of the human heart, the reality of what can be called a pneumatic anthropology: *L'esprit est donc désire de Dieu.*[22] This is 'the Christian paradox

---

15 De Lubac, *A Brief Catechesis on Nature and Grace*, trans. Brother Richard Arnandez F.S.C. (San Francisco: Ignatius, 1984), p. 27.
16 De Lubac, *The Mystery of the Supernatural*, p. 273.
17 De Lubac, *The Mystery of the Supernatural*, p. 265.
18 De Lubac, *The Mystery of the Supernatural*, p. 259.
19 De Lubac, *The Mystery of the Supernatural*, p. 266.
20 Cf. De Lubac, *The Mystery of the Supernatural*, p. 273.
21 Hans Urs von Balthasar, *The Theology of Henri de Lubac: An Overview*, trans. Joseph Fessio S.J., Michael M. Waldstein and Susan Claments (San Francisco: Ignatius, 1991), p. 15; and Milbank, *The Suspended Middle, passim*, see p. 11. I owe a conceptual debt here to a conversation with Melissa Riches.
22 De Lubac, *Surnaturel: Études historiques* (Paris: Desclé de Brouwer, 1991), p. 483.

of man'.²³ Balthasar describes the de Lubacian paradox as 'the absolute ordination to the end, which also was and remains the origin, that lies within creatureliness as such'.²⁴ This absolute desire – this paradoxically self-transcending constitutive desire – is, for de Lubac, the supreme term of mediation: neither purely immanent nor transcendent, it is the term of the 'between' of created and uncreated. It is the transcendent horizon of immanence: *quaerere Dominum*. For Balthasar, de Lubac's *surnaturel* thesis is the truth of a 'third domain': a term *in addition to* 'nature' and supernatural 'grace'. Or better, it is a domain of nature that does not emerge until illumined by grace.²⁵ By recovering and positing this domain (not properly the subject of revelation and yet unintelligible without it), de Lubac offers what John Milbank describes as a kind of 'non-ontology'²⁶ – a metaphysical sensibility radically 'between the field of pure immanent being proper to philosophy . . . and the revelatory event proper to theology'.²⁷

---

23 De Lubac, *The Mystery of the Supernatural*, pp. 135–53.

24 Balthasar, *Theo-Logic*, II, *Theological Logical Theory*, trans. Adrian J. Walker (San Francisco: Ignatius, 2004), p. 96. I owe a debt here to Chris Hackett who pointed me to this passage in Balthasar.

25 Balthasar here invokes Romano Guardini: 'There are realities that in themselves belong to the "world", to the whole of immediate existence, and thus are in principle capable of being grasped by refined and deepened experience but de facto are grasped only within the encompassing grasp [*Übergriff*] of the corresponding realities of revelation.' Guardini, *Welt und Person* (Würzburg: Werkbund, 1952), p. 67, as quoted by Balthasar, *Theo-Logic*, II, p. 96.

26 Milbank is here playing on François Laruelle's notion of 'non-philosophy', see Laruelle, *Principes de la Non-Philosophie* (Paris: PUF, 1996); and cf. Milbank, *The Suspended Middle*, pp. 95–6.

27 Milbank, *The Suspended Middle*, p. 5. This leads Milbank to go on to suggest that 'the *surnaturel* thesis *deconstructs* the possibility of dogmatic theology as previously understood in modern times, just as it equally deconstructs the possibility of philosophy *tout court*. For now, on the one hand, doctrine remains "extrinsic", arbitrary, and incomprehensible unless interpreted in accordance with an innate, radically given human nature . . . on the other hand, this "given" human nature is only manifested to philosophy as paradoxically exceeding itself . . . Philosophy then appears to require the transcendent supplement of theology, yet theology equally requires the (consequently non-available) foundation of philosophy' (p. 11).

Deification as Metaphysics

This anthropology of the between turns on the phrase: *le désir naturel du surnaturel*. The phrase can be translated either 'the natural desire *of* the supernatural' or 'the natural desire *for* the supernatural'. The fourth section of *Surnaturel* (1946) opens with a 'historical note' that bears the phrase as its title. In this 'note', de Lubac places the ambiguity of his own phrase within the field of flux of St Thomas Aquinas, between *desiderium naturale* (natural desire) and *desiderium naturae* (desire of nature).[28] This suggests that the ambiguities of desire are, for de Lubac, inherent to the *inquietum cor* of the human person, and so the longing of the human spirit is necessarily an aporetic play of desire both 'of' and 'for' the supernatural. It means that the question de Lubac poses to Maurice Blondel – 'How can a conscious spirit be anything other than an absolute desire for God?'[29] – is equally a question concerning the absolute ingression *of* God himself in the middle of every human longing *for* God. There is a double exigence suspended in *le désire naturel du surnaturel*.

One way of clarifying this double interplay in the *surnaturel* thesis is through the philosophy of William Desmond, and his notion of metaxological desire.[30] For Desmond, being in the

---

28 De Lubac, *Surnaturel*, pp. 434–8; and cf. *The Mystery of the Supernatural*, p. 85.

29 The question is posed in a letter de Lubac wrote to Blondel, on 3 April 1932, a letter he afterwards describes as a 'sketch of what would latter become my book *Surnaturel*'. The letter and relevant ensuing correspondence with Blondel are printed in the first appendix of de Lubac, *At the Service of the Church: Henri de Lubac Reflects on the Circumstances that Occasioned his Writings*, trans. Anne Elizabeth Englund (San Francisco: Ignatius, 1993), pp. 183–8, quotes here at p. 183 and p. 184. The question is quoted by Milbank as an epigraph to *The Suspended Middle*.

30 Metaxological desire is a desire of the metaxological community of being, developed by Desmond through a 'four fold sense of being' in which the metaxological is contrasted with (but also contains) three other senses of being: the univocal, the equivocal and the dialectical. The metaxological derives from the Greek *metaxu* and *logos*, the *metaxu* meaning middle/between and *logos* meaning discourse/speech. More specifically, Desmond's metaxological is, as Christopher Simpson puts it, a sense of being 'situated between the totalizing closure of rigid univocal thinking and the fragmented discontinuity of equivocal thinking – "between"

metaxu is being mindful of our 'self-transcending openness to transcendence',[31] which is a double movement in metaxological being: *ad exterioribus ad interioria, ab inferioribus ad superiora.*[32] In the first movement we come to know 'the *dunamis* of our openness', moving us 'from the exterior to the interior'. Next we discover the self-transcending urgency of our desire where we find an opening to a superior other: this moves us 'from the inferior to the superior'. Desmond writes: 'We are the interior urgency of ultimacy, this [other whom we meet in our inferiority] is ultimacy as the superior.'[33]

The superior found in our interior, is, for Desmond, an authentic other who is not synonymous with our own being. He writes:

---

utter lack of understanding and absolute, full comprehension'. But if, on the one hand, the metaxological is *between* the perfect grasp of univocity and the total loss of equivocity, on the other hand it is crucially *beyond* the self-mediation of the dialectic. This means that the metaxological is 'an overdeterminate intermediation in excess of any single self-mediating (dialectical) whole'. These quotations are from Christopher Ben Simpson's paper, 'Divine Hyperbolic: Desmond, Caputo, and Postmodern Theology', delivered at the conference Belief and Metaphysics, presented by the University of Nottingham's Centre of Theology and Philosophy, Instituto de Filosofía Edith Stein, Granada, Spain (15 Sept. 2006). See Desmond, *Being and the Between* (Albany: SUNY, 1995), pp. 118, 196, 418 and 451.

31 William Desmond, *Perplexity and Ultimacy*, (Albany: SUNY, 1995), p. 11.

32 Augustine, *In Enarratio in Ps.*, 145.5 (*Patrologia Latina* 37.1887), as quoted by Desmond in *Perplexity and Ultimacy*, p. 11. Desmond originally culls this phrase, Augustine's own description of his search for God, from Étienne Gilson, *History of Christian Philosophy in the Middle Ages* (New York: Random House, 1955), p. 77. There Gilson writes: 'however different in their details, all Augustinian itineraries of the soul in quest of God are substantially the same: they go from the exterior to the interior, and from the inferior to the superior; *ad exterioribus ad interioria, ab inferioribus ad superiora.*' Desmond quotes the phrase in his early essay, 'Augustine's *Confessions*: On Desire, Conversion and Reflection', *Irish Theological Quarterly* 47 (1980), pp. 24–33, at p. 30, and p. 33 n. 21. Further to this essay and *Perplexity and Ultimacy* see: *Desire, Dialectic, and Otherness: An Essay on Origins* (New Haven: Yale, 1987), pp. 13–14; and *Is There a Sabbath for Thought?* (New York: Fordham, 2005), pp. 8–9.

33 Desmond, *Perplexity and Ultimacy*, p. 11.

> This superior ultimate is not identical with our erotic self-mediation; it is irreducible to us and mediates with us – the inferior – through the agapeic excess of its own unequalizable plenitude. So, in fact, this second movement also allows the possibility of a double mediation: our own erotic quest of the ultimate; the ingression of the ultimate as a superior other that interplays with the middle out of its own excessive transcendence.[34]

For Desmond, this double mediation of desire in the metaxological is inclusive of, but more expansive than, the self-mediating desire of the dialectic. Therein the first mediation is dialectical, a relation to the alterity of being as a means of self-relation, self-constitution and self-understanding (the echo of Hegel is explicit). Yet the double mediation is a first *plus* a second: it is mediation *between* and *beyond*. This means that in the desire of being there is a relation, an intermediation, in addition to the merely immanent-erotic (as self-oriented): there is a mediation of desire beyond the self that *makes possible the first mediation*.

This mediation of desire beyond the self is an agapeic mediation of transcendence, a communication with a genuine other, an agapeic ultimate.[35] This agapeic intermediation is not opposed to the erotic, for, on Desmond's view all forms of love 'have the promise of the agapeic in them'.[36] Which means both intermediations are agapeic, especially in so far as the second intermediation is a communication with the source of the plenitude that makes possible the first mediation of desire.

The natural desire of/for the supernatural is therefore neither unitary nor perfectly immanent, but rather is suspended in double mediation, in the intermediation of created and uncreated. This

---

34 Desmond, *Perplexity and Ultimacy*, p. 11.

35 This 'agapeic ultimate' should be situated within the larger sense of Desmond's notion of transcendence. Transcendence for Desmond is a community of others that he thinks in terms of three transcendences: the exterior transcendence of beings that are not the self, the interior transcendence of the self, and the superior or ultimate transcendence of God. I am indebted to Christopher Simpson for this clarification.

36 From personal correspondence; on this theme see two essays from Desmond's *Is There a Sabbath for Thought*: 'Caesar with the Soul of Christ: Nietzsche's Highest Impossibility', pp. 200–37; and 'Enemies: On Hatred', pp. 289–311.

Veritas: Belief and Metaphysics

makes the present reading of the *surnaturel* thesis a reading committed to discerning, as inherent to the thesis itself, both an immanent openness and a transcendent ingression at the heart of natural human desire. Further, it is to put forward a reading that explicitly resists the tendency to unbalance the aporetic 'middle' of the *surnaturel* thesis by resolving the aporia of *natural* desire in the direction of a pure immanent openness or a *potentia obedientialis*.[37] If

---

37 Unbalancing the aporetic 'middle' of the *surnaturel* thesis in the direction of 'immanent openness'/'*potentia obedientialis*' can be thought of in terms of a narrow reading of Karl Rahner's 'supernatural existential'; and this, as it is expressed in Rahner's first intervention in the debate on the supernatural: 'Concerning the Relationship between Grace and Nature', in *Theological Investigations*, vol. 1 (Baltimore: Helcon, 1963), pp. 297–318. His essay is an attempt to steer a middle course between the so-called '*nouvelle théologie*' and neo-scholasticism, between the *surnaturel* thesis and the neo-Thomist 'doctrine' of *natura pura*. Here Rahner seeks to articulate a way of both retaining the neo-scholastic commitment to the 'obediential potency' of pure nature, while at the same time embracing de Lubac's deconstruction of the dualism and extrinsicism to which this theology tended. Rahner posits *natura pura* as a 'remainder concept' (*Restbegriff*) – as a tool of thought rather than as an existential reality – and so the means by which the neo-scholastic language of 'obediential potency' can be redeployed in talk of humanity's supernatural ordering (Rahner, 'Grace and Nature', p. 313). Rahner argues that God wills for human nature a concrete end that is at once supernatural and unexacted, and for Rahner (here in agreement with de Lubac) there is a disposition in nature for the supernatural, what he calls a 'supernatural existential'. But for Rahner (now in disagreement with de Lubac) the disposition itself is categorically figured apart from the quiddity of human nature qua nature (p. 308). And so, on Rahner's view, there are two ways of speaking of human nature: first, in the sense of human nature existentially encountered (ordered to the beatific vision); and second, 'nature in the technical, *theological* sense' (Karen Kilby, *Karl Rahner: Theology and Philosophy* London: Routledge, 2004, p. 54), that is human nature as *natura pura*, technically (but abstractly) bracketed from the supernatural end. And so to speak of human nature as 'supernatural existential' is to speak of it, not in its 'pure' sense, but in its *existential* reality. In this light one could say that for Rahner the *natural human desire* (as for de Lubac) is always first a desire *of* the supernatural; but for Rahner (unlike de Lubac) there is technically no natural desire *for* the supernatural, instead the second desire is another desire *of* the supernatural, now 'existentially' *in* nature but never intrinsic to the quiddity of human nature itself. In this way de Lubac's

the human is not satisfied beneath the level of divinization, this dissatisfaction implies that the divine telos is yet interceding for – and

---

of/for is refigured as desire *of/in*. In this Rahner can be read as unbalancing the double exigency of desire in the direction of a single-double-modality of the supernatural, from which nature in its 'purity' always stands apart. The risk here is that the 'supernatural existential' may tend to shift the *surnaturel*, away from the aporetic 'middle' in which there is a *positive desire* in the *ordo naturalis*, now towards a *purely passive* immanent openness. And so for Rahner (at least in this initial stage) human nature is characterized – not so much by *desire* – but by *potency*. As Rahner puts it: 'this "potency" is what is inmost and most authentic in him [the human], the centre and root of what he is absolutely' (Rahner, p. 311). The point at which the 'supernatural existential' becomes a significantly problematic reduction of the *surnaturel* thesis is the point at which one takes this particular Rahnerian version of the 'supernatural existential' as a *necessary qualification* of de Lubac. To do this is to risk installing the 'potency' of *natura pura* in place of the concrete 'desire' of the *ordo naturalis* (as apprehended in the light of the incarnation). Resolving the aporia of de Lubac's 'middle' by shifting entirely to the potency of immanent openness in place of any positive desire of the *ordo naturalis* is a serious reduction of the *surnaturel* thesis. At the very least it is fair to acknowledge that this first intervention of Rahner does risk circumscribing desire within the pure potency of passive immanence. But it needs further to be stated that this is Rahner's *first* intervention in the debate, not his last, and so should not be read as his univocal position. Karen Kilby has shown that Rahner's position on the relation of grace and nature was very much a process of thought, and that 'Concerning the Relationship between Grace and Nature' is but *one* version of Rahner's 'supernatural existential'. In this case it may be possible to articulate a version of the 'supernatural existential' which is more convertible with de Lubac, and indeed falls less prey to the passive limitation that here risks extrinsicism. Such an alternative reading of the 'supernatural existential' ought, following Kilby, to begin with the fourth chapter of the *Foundations of Christian Faith*, where Rahner tends to eschew the language of *potency* as the foundation the 'supernatural existential'. In these terms a version of the 'supernatural existential' may emerge which can be read in terms that maintain the 'middle' of the *surnaturel* thesis. See Kilby, *Karl Rahner*, pp. 53–8. Cf. Rahner, *Foundations of Christian Faith: An Introduction to the Idea of Christianity*, trans. William V. Dych (New York: Crossroad, 1978, 2005), pp. 116–37. Also cf. Milbank, *Theology and Social Theory*, 2nd edition (Oxford: Blackwell, 2006), pp. 206–56 (especially pp. 222–5 on Rahner); and Fergus Kerr O.P., *Immortal Longings: Versions of Transcending Humanity* (London: SPCK, 1997), pp. 159–84.

participating within – the pneumatic longing of every human nature. The proleptic gift of receptivity in the transcendent ingression makes possible the desire of the *metaxu* itself: 'desire is the gift of the anticipation of gift.'[38]

Here we arrive at what can be called the Chalcedonian heart of de Lubac's Christological anthropology.[39] In Christ, 'Nature and the supernatural are . . . united without in any sense being confused.'[40] The real implication of the *surnaturel* thesis, therefore, is the undoing of every immanent humanism, every attempt to think the human person outside the revelation of Jesus Christ, the True Man who is very humanity and very divinity. In the God-Man humanity is revealed to be *theandric*, and so, paradoxically, the human can only be fully revealed by the One who is fully divine. Therefore the only tenable humanism this side of the incarnation is a christocentric-humanism of pneumatic longing.[41]

---

38 Milbank, *The Suspended Middle*, p. 38.

39 For a discussion of de Lubac's *surnaturel* and Christology see Susan Wood, 'The Nature-Grace Problematic within Henri de Lubac's Christological Paradox', *Communio*, 19 (Fall, 1992), pp. 389–403.

40 De Lubac, *The Mystery of the Supernatural*, p. 132.

41 See de Lubac, 'Tripartite Anthropology' in *Theology in History*, p. 129. The question of humanism and the claim that Christianity is the integral humanism is arguably the governing idea of de Lubac's work. At the close of 'Tripartite Anthropology', de Lubac makes his own these words of Jean Daniélou: 'There is in us a certain root that plunges into the depths of the Trinity. We are these complex beings who exist on successive levels, on an animal and biological level, on an intellectual and human level and on an ultimate level in those very abysses that are those of the life of God and those of the Trinity. This is why we have the right to say that Christianity is an integral humanism, which is to say, which develops man on all the levels of his experience. We must always be in defiance of all the attempts to reduce the space in which our existence moves. We breathe fully in the measure to which we do not let ourselves be enclosed in the prison of the rational and psychological world but to which a part of us emerges into these great spaces that are those of the Trinity. And this is what creates the incomparable joy of existence in Christianity.' Daniélou, *Mythes païens, mystère chrétien* (Paris: Fayard, 1966), p. 103, as quoted in de Lubac in 'Tripartite Anthropology', in *Theology in History*, p. 200. Hence Milbank's claim: 'Christianity is a humanism, else it is misunderstood. On the other hand, secular humanism is the absolute antithesis of the Gospel' (*The Suspended Middle*, p. 5). And his suggestion in *Theology*

Dyothelite Christology and Dyothelite Mediation

By vindicating the dyothelite Christology associated with St Maximus the Confessor, the Third Council of Constantinople (680–1) made it doctrine that the work of salvation is a labour divinely willed through a human will.[42] In this way the Council doctrinally specified a mode of 'theandric unwinding' of the false-sequela of Adam's wilful grasp, a mode by which the divinity Adam sought to take might be received as gift. And so what Christ wills *hos anthropos*, he wills in order that the human might be accomplished as *truly human*, accomplished in the gift of being *hos theos*.

Conor Cunningham has characterized the logic of the fall as the attempt 'to have a-part of the world apart from God'.[43] Following Cunningham, the fall can be thought of as 'the attempt to be a god apart from God'.[44] Which means that Adam's sin is not his desire; rather, the sin is all in the grasp. And so the attempt to 'be a god a-part' literally turns the immortal longing to death, to that one

---

and Social Theory that twentieth-century French theology is essentially a 'recovery of a pre-modern sense of the Christianized person as the fully real person.' *Theology and Social Theory*, p. 207.

42 For the text of the *Terminus* of the Third Council of Constantinople (in Greek and Latin with English translation) see Norman P. Tanner S.J. (ed.), *Decrees of the Ecumenical Councils*, vol. 1, *Nicea I – Lateran V* (Georgetown: Sheed and Ward, 1990), pp. 124–30. Cf. Michael Sharkey (ed.), *International Theological Commision: Texts and Documents 1969–1985* (San Francisco: Ignatius, 1989), 'Select Questions on Christology', pp. 185–206.

43 Cunningham, *Genealogy of Nihilism* (London: Routledge, 2002), *passim*, quote here at p. 172. Cunningham's logic of the fall and Adam's 'grasp' has led him more recently into the study of the perverted attempt to grasp humanity in a certain 'thin' (and heterodox) Christian opposition to Darwinism, cf. Cunningham's essay in this volume, 'Trying my Very Best to Believe Darwin', and his forthcoming book, *Evolution*, Interventions (Grand Rapids: Eerdmans, 2008).

44 Cf. Augustine: '[The first parents] could better have become . . . [gods] if they had through obedience adhered to their highest and true ground and not through pride set themselves up as their own ground. For created gods are gods not by any true being of their own but by participation in the true God' (*De Civitate Dei*, 14.13).

thing Adam can properly grasp apart from his Maker: the *nihil* from which he was made.[45] This cosmic reversion upon the *nihil*, issuing from Adam's sin, is precisely the contingency into which the incarnation descends. Having taken upon himself the depth of what Adam has become through sin, Christ turns precisely *this* into the salvation of filial obedience, even unto death (cf. Phil. 2.8).

Maximus the Confessor's dyothelite theology is especially formed through a sustained reflection on Christ's prayer at Gethsemane: 'Father, if it be possible, let this cup pass from me; nevertheless, not as I will, but as thou wilt' (Matt. 26.39, cf. Mark 14.36 and Luke 22.42).[46] The *resistance* in Christ's prayer (the petition to the Father

---

45 Thomas Aquinas writes: 'Each created thing, in that it does not have existence save from another, taken in itself, is nothing' (*ST* I-II, q. 109, a. 2; as quoted by Cunningham). In this way the fall is the reality of created being taking self-sufficiency into itself. If God is the one in whom creation lives and moves and has its being (cf. Acts 17:28), then desiring to be a god a-part from God is desiring nothing at all (because there is no 'god' apart from God). This means that the fall is Adam's *failure in desire*. Cunningham, 'Being Recalled: Life as Anamnesis', in Harm Goris, Henk Schoot and Herwi Rikhof (eds), *Divine Transcendence and Immanence in the Thought of Thomas Aquinas*, Publications of the Thomas Institute Utrecht (Louvain: Peeters, 2007), typescript, p. 22.

46 The main texts of Maximus's dyothelite reading of Gethsemane are: *Opusculum* 3 (PG 91:45B-56A), *Opusculum* 6 (PG 91:65A-68D), *Opusculum* 7 (PG 91:69B-89B), *Ad Thalassium* 21 (PG 90:312-317A) and *Disputatio cum Pyrrho* (PG 91:288A-353B). English translations of these texts can be found in the following: *Opusculum* 6 and *Ad Thalassium* 21 in *On the Cosmic Mystery of Jesus Christ: Selected Writings from Saint Maximus the Confessor*, trans. Paul M. Blowers and Robert Louis Wilken (Crestwood: St Vladimir's, 2003), pp. 173-6 and pp. 109-13; *Opusculum* 3 and 6 in *Maximus the Confessor*, Selected English Translation, trans. Andrew Louth (London: Routledge, 1996), pp. 193-8 and pp. 180-91; and *Disputatio cum Pyrrho* translated by Joseph P. Farrell, *The Disputation with Pyrrhus of our Father Among the Saints Maximus the Confessor* (South Canaan: St Tikhons Seminary Press, 1990). All my quotations of Maximus are from these translations. For various secondary discussions of the correspondence of wills in Maximus see: Ivor J. Davidson, '"Not My Will but Yours be Done": The Ontological Dynamics of Incarnational Intention', *International Journal of Systematic Theology*, 7 (2005), pp. 178-204, especially pp.190-7; F.-M. Léthel, *Théologie de l'Agonie du Christ: La liberté du Fils de Dieu*

Deification as Metaphysics

to let this cup pass from him) is, for Maximus, central to both the theandric union of wills and the soteriological ontology of the prayer. For Maximus – following St Gregory Nazianzen[47] – Christ's human will, being perfectly deiform by nature, must already be perfectly united with the will of the Trinity. In *Opusculum* 6, Maximus suggests that precisely in Christ's 'not what I will' there is a kind of icon of 'perfect harmony and concurrence' between the created and uncreated wills (*Patrologia Graeca* 91:65B–68C). The *resistance*, on Maximus's reading, is a *resistance* in the reality of Christ having become *like us in all things* but sin (PG 91:68C).

This point is made also in *Ad Thalassium* 21, when Maximus responds to the question of how the sinless one can put on the passions that result from Adam's sin. Here Maximus argues that only by putting on these passions has Christ 'inaugurated a complete restoration' (PG 90:313C). Only in assuming the depth of temptation, the liability of vulnerability and the corruption of the fallen body can Christ heal Adam's wound.

---

et son importance sotériologique mises en lumière par saint Maxime le Confesseur (Paris: Beauchesne, 1979), pp. 29–49 and pp. 86–99; Paul M. Blowers, 'The Passion of Jesus Christ in Maximus the Confessor: A Reconsideration', *Studia Patristica*, 37 (2001), pp. 361–77; Lars Thunberg, *Microcosm and Mediator: The Theological Anthropology of Maximus the Confessor*, 2nd Edition (Chicago: Open Court, 1995), pp. 208–30; and Hans Urs von Balthasar, *Cosmic Liturgy: The Universe According to Maximus the Confessor*, trans Brian Daley (San Francisco: Ignatius, 2003), pp. 256–71.

47 Gregory Nazianzen, commenting on John 6.38 ('I have come down from heaven not to do my own will but the will of the one that sent me'), states: 'Certainly had these words not been spoken by the very one who "came down" we should have said the language bore a stamp of a mere man like us, not that of the Savior we know. *His* will is not in the least degree opposed to God, is totally dependent upon God. Our merely human will does not always follow the divine; it often resists and struggles against it. This is the way we interpret: "Father, if it be possible let this cup pass from me, but not what I will – let your will prevail"' (*Oration* 30.12). This text is given important and repeated attention by Maximus in his writings on Gethsemane, and it is also central to the *Terminus* of the Third Council of Constantinople. My quotation is from the translation in *On God and Christ: The Five Theological Orations and Two Letters to Cledonius*, trans. Frederick Williams and Lionel Wickham (Crestwood: St Vladimir's, 2002).

Veritas: Belief and Metaphysics

In the *Disputatio cum Pyrrho* (still with Gregory in the background) Maximus argues that the *resistance* of the human will in the prayer at Gethsemane is the labour of *purification*. That is, the *resistance* of Gethsemane is precisely the theandric work by which the human will of the Son *purifies* the anguish of death and the fear of suffering (PG 91:297B). Balthasar argues that for Maximus, salvation consists in Jesus wilfully subjecting the passions of the fallen nature to the divine will of God.[48] This is how Christ takes the very wage of Adam's sin and offers *it* as the pattern of recapitulation: Christ transfigures Adamic-death into God's own glory.[49] 'He represents our rebellion in himself.'[50] In this way the Son assumes the suffering of death and the loneliness of the *nihil* in order that the false-sequela of the sinful grasp might be recapitulated through his prayer into the Sequela of salvation, that being *hos anthropos* might be perfected into the gift of becoming *hos theos*. And this divine work of filial devotion is accomplished through the human will: 'having become like us for our sake, he was calling on his God and Father in a human manner, when he said, *Let not what I will, but what you will prevail*' (PG 91:68D).

Joseph Ratzinger points out that this is central to the incarnational descent: 'the Logos so humbles himself that he adopts a man's will as his own and addresses the Father with the I of this human being.'[51] Thereby the prayer of Gethsemane 'transforms

---

48 Balthasar, *Cosmic Liturgy*, p. 263–7. And here Balthasar quotes from one of the *Opusculum*: 'Our vulnerability [passion] has two aspects: that of punishment and that of guilt. The former is characteristic of our nature as such; the latter simply disfigures it. The former was freely and ontologically taken on by Christ along with his human existence; through this act, he gave strength to our nature as it is and freed it from the curse that lay on us. But he made the latter aspect his own in the course of salvation history, through his love for humanity, in that he took it up to destroy it, as fire consumes wax or the sun the mists of the earth, so that in its place he might bestow on us his blessings' (PG 91:237B), as quoted at p. 267.

49 In these sentences I am indebted to a conversation with Keith Starkenburg.

50 Balthasar, *Cosmic Liturgy*, p. 267–8.

51 Ratzinger, *Behold the Pierced One: An Approach to Spiritual Christology*, trans. Graham Harrison (San Francisco: Ignatius, 1986), p. 41. For Ratzinger's thought on this subject, additional to *Behold the*

human speech into the eternal Word, into his blessed "Yes, Father".⁵² Through Gethsemane, Jesus purifies the anguish of humanity into filial love for the Father and transforms human speech into the Word of God. By this double recapitulation, Christ opens a liturgical pattern into his own filial life in 'wilful-communion' with the Father.⁵³

Further to this, the dyothelitism of Constantinople, in giving doctrinal status to the notion of salvation as an act of divine willing through a human will, concretely specifies a mode of *mutual indwelling* of divinity and humanity in the person of Christ.⁵⁴ It is therefore possible to claim that in this specification, whatever

---

Pierced One, see *A New Song for the Lord: Faith in Christ and Liturgy Today*, trans. Martha M. Matessich (London: Crossroads, 1996), pp. 3–34, and esp. pp. 7–11.

52 Ratzinger, *Behold the Pierced One*, p. 41.

53 This phrase 'wilful-communion' is taken from a quotation de Lubac makes of his friend Pierre Teilhard de Chardin, a quotation used in order to explicate Pico della Mirandola's theology of the human 'will' in union with God: 'Oh! Si je pouvais vous résister si peu, Maître, que vous n'arriviez, pour ainsi dire, plus à me distinguer de Vous [. . .] si parfaitement nous serions unis dans la communion de la volonté!' See de Lubac, *Pic de la Mirandole*, p. 174.

54 This mode of *mutual indwelling* is perhaps most evocatively expressed through Maximus's reflection on Denys the Areopagite's notion of the *theandric energy* of Christ. Denys, in his Fourth Epistle, writes that Christ 'did not do divine things divinely, or human things humanly, but as God made man, he manifested, as he lived in our midst, a certain new *theandric energy*' (PG 3:1072C). This *theandric* reality is, in Maximus, understood more concretely in terms of the will: Christ wills divine things humanly and human things divinely. For Maximus this becomes a specification of the circumincession of the natures, the reality of Christ's *theandric* personhood. In *Opusculum* 7, Maximus writes: 'And again it appears that as God, being also a human being in essence, he wills to fulfill the economy of the Father and work the salvation of us all. It made clear that as man, being by nature God, he acts humanly, willingly accepting the experience of suffering for our sake. And it is again made clear that as God, who is human by nature, he acts divinely and naturally exhibits the evidence of his divinity' (PG 91:84C). The translation from Denys is my modification based on Andrew Louth's in *Denys the Areopagite* (New York: Continuum, 2001), p. 75. The translation of Maximus is by Louth; see n. 46 above.

Veritas: Belief and Metaphysics

binary logic may have been retained in Chalcedonian Christology is, through the *Terminus* of Constantinople, decisively overcome – at least this is Ratzinger's position.[55] He argues that in Christology 'the affirmation of true humanity and true divinity can only retain its meaning if the mode of unity of both is clarified'.[56] The *Terminus* states that, 'the two wills and principles of action are reconciled in correspondence for the salvation of the human race'.[57] By this, argues Ratzinger, Constantinople 'abolishes all dualism or parallelism of the two natures',[58] and does so through the doctrine of a communion of created and uncreated love in the person of Jesus:

> The metaphysical two-ness of a human and divine will is not abrogated, but in the realm of the *person* . . . the fusion of both takes place, with the result that they become *one* will, not naturally, but personally. This free unity – a form of unity created by love – is higher and more interior than merely natural unity. It corresponds to the highest unity there is, namely, trinitarian unity.[59]

The mutual indwelling of divinity and humanity happen in this way as a *personal* communion of love within the person of Jesus. This is the 'wilful-communion' that reveals the fullness of the human person in terms of the circumincession of mutual communication with God in the triune life.[60]

---

55 Ratzinger, *Behold the Pierced One*, pp. 37–42.

56 Ratzinger, *Behold the Pierced One*, p. 38.

57 See Tanner, *Decrees of the Ecumenical Councils*, vol. 1, *Nicea I – Lateran V*, p. 129–30. The translation from the Greek is my own.

58 According to Ratzinger this binary logic was not overcome in the doctrine of Chalcedon, for him Chalcedon requires the clarification of Constantinople. He writes: 'The so-called Neo-Chalcedon theology which is summed up in the Third Council of Constantinople (680–681) makes an important contribution to a proper grasp of the inner unity of biblical and dogmatic theology, of the theology and religious life. Only from this standpoint does the dogma of Chalcedon (451) yield its full meaning.' *Behold the Pierced One*, p. 37.

59 Ratzinger, *Behold the Pierced One*, p. 39, italics his. And cf. Rowan Williams (whose view is rather similar to Ratzinger's), '"Person" and "Personality" in Christology', *Downside Review*, 94 (1976), pp. 253–60.

60 This corresponds with de Lubac's claim in *Pic de la Mirandole* that

Deification as Metaphysics

For Ratzinger, another particular benefit to this Christological doctrine of mutual indwelling is that it offers to humanity the prayer of the Son as the hinge of participation in the redemptive work of incarnation.[61] From this we can claim a doctrinal resource in the dyothelitism of the *Terminus* of Constantinople by which to articulate a theology of divine-humanity not confined to the head, but rather liturgically extending into the body. This is to read the *Terminus* in the direction of what John Milbank has called an 'ecclesiological construal of Christ's divine personhood'.[62] For here, in the Christological indwelling of difference in the correspondence of personal desire – this 'wilful-communion' – one discovers a language by which to speak of humanity's desiring into the Sequela of Christ as itself a liturgical repetition of the salvific act of divine willing through a human will. Further, it is possible to

---

'une doctrine de la volonté [. . .] [est] une doctrine de l'amour' (p. 174). From which de Lubac goes one to explicate Pico's theology of the union of the human will with the divine will, which is crucially realized in terms of St Paul's theology of unity of spirit with God. De Lubac writes: 'L'union du vouloir humain au vouloir divin déborde les deux zones encore extérieures où elles e'exercent pour se réaliser dans ce que saint Paul appelai l'unité d'esprit avec Dieu. Or, par sa doctrine, Pic de la Mirandole appartient à cette famille spirituelle. Il rejette tout "actus tyrannicus voluntatis"' (p. 174–5). All this, moreover, is evocative of de Lubac's notion of *pneuma* as 'the depth of human communication with God'. See n. 13 and n. 14 above.

61 Ratzinger, *Behold the Pierced One*, pp. 41–2.

62 Milbank's argument for an 'ecclesiological construal of Christ's divine personhood' is meant to emphasize the repetition of the ecclesial pattern of Christ rather than the imitation of Jesus as a 'pure original'. And so Jesus is here figured as the 'founder' of a new polis, the Church, whose life is to be *wholly* re-narrated, repeated and re-realized in the life of the new community (p. 157), of which Jesus is the first in a repeatable series, which means that every member of the polis is called to be an *alter Christus*. As I intend this should also be linked with Kenneth Surin's notion of a 'Trinitarian poetics of the church'. See Milbank 'The Name of Jesus', in *The Word Made Strange: Theology, Language, Culture* (Oxford: Blackwell, 1997), pp. 145–68, here p. 150 and p. 157; and Surin, '"The weight of weakness": intratextuality and discipleship', in *The Turnings of Darkness and Light* (Cambridge: Cambridge University Press, 1989), pp. 201–21, see especially 213–21. And cf. Donald Mackinnon, *The Borderlands of Theology* (Lutterworth: London, 1968), p. 63.

Veritas: Belief and Metaphysics

articulate this correspondence of desire as an indwelling double mediation of a particularly pneumatological desire. In this way, the correspondence of desire reads as a work and ingression of the Holy Spirit playing out of the middle of human longing. The created will figures as the 'erotic quest of the ultimate' while the uncreated will is read as an agapeic ingression of pneumatic-transcendence.

The Sequela of Christ, then, is the pattern into which human desire is drawn; it is a pneumatologically suspended ecclesial dyothelitism, a communion of filial return in Christ. The Sequela is the pattern of participating into the heart of Christ's life in Love for the Father: 'I have come down from heaven, not to do my own will, but the will of him who sent me'(John 6.38).[63]

The Holy Spirit and the Filial Prayer of the Son

The Church's liturgy could be said to rise and fall in the correspondence of created and uncreated desire. In her liturgy, the Church learns by gift to call God 'Father', and thereby she is drawn into Christ's filial way of *being for* his paternal source. This then is deification: the transformation of the human into God through the communication of God to the human of God's own inner life in the filial adoption by which God loves the human with a fatherly love. The labour of this incorporation of humanity into the filial Sequela of *theosis* is traditionally attributed to the person of the Holy Spirit.[64] It is the Spirit who anoints us, making us *christos*, 'gods

---

63 This is the central biblical reference for the dyothelite articulation of the *Terminus* of Council of Constantinople. The quotation and the commentary by Gregory Nazianzen in *Oration* 30.12 are cited in both Maximus and in the *Terminus*. See Tanner, *Decrees of the Ecumenical Councils*, vol. 1, *Nicea I – Lateran V*, p. 128; and n. 47 above.

64 For example Basil the Great, in *De Spiritu Sancto*, writes that the Spirit makes humans 'spiritual', which for him is deification: the 'endless joy in the presence of God, becoming like God, and the highest of all desires, desiring to be God' (9.23). For more on the tradition of attributing the work of deification to the person of the Spirit see Norman Russell, *The Doctrine of Deification in the Greek Patristic Tradition* (Oxford: OUP, 2005), pp. 194–7; and Jules Gross, *La Divination du chrétien d'après les Père grecs* (Paris: Gabalda, 1938), pp. 239–44.

Deification as Metaphysics

... [and] sons of the Most High' (Ps. 81.6).⁶⁵ It is the Spirit who adopts us into the divinized life of the Son who is 'the first among many brethren' (Rom. 8.29). It is the Spirit who deifies us into the Son's theandric prayer.

Filial adoption is bound to the theology of prayer, to the gift of the *Pater Noster*, which is the gift of entry into the Son's trinitarian communication, the pattern of his filial disposition. According to Adrienne von Speyr the words of the *Pater Noster*, 'live from the Son's substance, which have received something of him that remains in them'.⁶⁶ In this way, to utter the *Pater Noster* is to be mystically united with the Son's mode of being, which means that to participate in the Son's filial prayer is metaphysically much more than a merely 'semiotic' repetition. On the contrary, prayer is the ontology of being *caught up into* the Son's divine life. Prayer is the divine, and divinizing, work of pneumatological adoption: it is receiving what St Paul calls the 'spirit of sonship' (Rom. 8.15).

Prayer, as Paul articulates it in Romans 8, is the reality of the life of communal coinherence in the resurrection of the Son.⁶⁷ 'If the Spirit of him who raised Jesus from the dead dwells in you, he who raised Christ Jesus from the dead will give life to your mortal

---

65 This is my translation from LXX (Ps. 82 in the Hebrew numbering).

66 Von Speyr, *The World of Prayer*, trans. Graham Harrison (San Francisco: Ignatius, 1985), p. 134.

67 This reading of Romans 8 is intended to resonate with something of the ethos of von Speyr's little book, *The Victory of Love: A Meditation on Romans 8*, trans. Sister Lucia Wiedenhöver, O.C.D. (San Francisco: Ignatius, 1990). The reading is firstly indebted to the sure influence of Eugene F. Rogers Jr, whose graduate seminar on the Holy Spirit and the Trinity I attended as a Masters student at the University of Virginia in the autumn of 2003. On the Pauline theology of prayer, in addition to von Speyr's *The World of Prayer*, Rogers had his students read some essays by Sarah Coakley that had particularly influenced his own reading of Romans 8. For Rogers see: *After the Spirit: A Constructive Pneumatology from Resources outside the Modern West* (Grand Rapids: Eerdmans, 2005), especially pp. 214–22. For Coakley see: 'Why Three? Some Reflections on the Origin of the Doctrine of the Trinity', in Sarah Coakley and David Pailin (eds), *The Making and Remaking of Christian Doctrine: Essays in Honour of Maurice Wiles* (Oxford: OUP, 1993), pp 28–56; and 'Can God be Experienced as Trinity?', *The Modern Churchman*, 28 (1986), pp. 11–23.

bodies also through his Spirit who dwells in you' (Rom. 8.11).[68] Prayer is the adoptive participation of creation in the christic-passover of call and response, the resurrectional-passover from death to deified life at the right hand of the Father. This pneumatological communication begins, for Paul, with the realization that 'we do not know how to pray as we ought' (Rom. 8.26). 'Not knowing how' is the disposition of openness to the co-operative act of the Spirit's intercession with the created spirit, drawing creation into the filial life by crying out to the Father on our behalf (Rom. 8.15–16, and cf. Gal. 4.6). As Jean-Louis Chrétien writes:

> This is the circularity of prayer: the man praying prays in order to know how to pray, and first of all to learn that he does not know how, and he offers thanks for his prayer as a gift of God.[69]

The gift of prayer is the person of the Spirit through whom humanity takes the place of the Son: 'When we cry "Abba! Father!" it is the Spirit himself bearing witness with our spirit that we are children of God . . . and fellow heirs with Christ' (Rom. 8.15–17). In

---

68 What is true about the resurrection becomes true of prayer; in this way prayer is entering into the Trinitarian communication by which the Father summons the resurrectional-response of the Son's dead body to the alighting of the Spirit. Cf. von Speyr: 'As Spirit of the Father, the Holy Spirit has raised up the Son in the Father's name. Here the unity between the Father and the Spirit becomes tangible. We touch here the Father's action through the Spirit in the Resurrection as closely as in the overshadowing of the Mother. The Spirit formed the Son's life in her. He carried the Father's seed as the expression of his will to her. And here again it is the Spirit of the Father as Holy Spirit in inseparable unity who acts in the Father's name: to bring life to give back to the Father the living Son. The Son's body is fit for this resurrection; it belongs to the Father to such a degree that it answers the summons at once . . . *everything is done in God and through God* [my italics].' Von Speyr, *The Victory of Love*, p. 37. This axiom of *everything being done in God and through God* is as true of prayer as it is of resurrection.

69 Chrétien, 'The Wounded Word: Phenomenology of Prayer', in Dominique Janicaud and Jean-Francois Courtine (eds), *Phenomenology and the 'Theological Turn': The French Debate*, trans. Jeffrey L. Kosky and Thomas A. Carlson (New York: Fordham, 2000), pp. 147–76, here p. 157.

Deification as Metaphysics

this way prayer is the pneumatological call and response of/for creation paternally recognized through the Son.[70]

The communicative labour of prayer is reflexive, an allocution of what Chrétien calls an 'enveloping and intertwining of the human and divine call'.[71] Here God's call interplays out of the response of the voice that prays. As Paul Claudel puts it: 'It is He who through our heart and our mouth invokes Himself.'[72] This interplay of God in our middle (praying on behalf of the one who does not know how to pray) is for St Paul the reality of the adoption whereby the human puts on the 'spirit of sonship' (Rom. 8.15) and becomes caught up by the Spirit into Christ's own prayer. The Spirit re-presents the Son's abiding in the 'middle voice' of a phenomenal 'between' at once passive and active, weak and infallible.[73] This 'middle voice' of prayer is the ecclesial/liturgical continuation of Christ's theandric life. As von Speyr writes:

---

70 Von Speyr writes: 'Recruited by the Son for the same state, we can now become with him sons, chosen and adopted sons. The Spirit of the Father is so infinite that he can accept and recognize us also in the Son's place. This recognition however, which is a gift, demands a response from us. We should be quite sure of this. We must not hanker for our old place [in the flesh] and stubbornly live in fear. Our response is to cry out together with Christ: *Abba! Father!* The response is recognition; it is also obligation, it is responsibility, faith. Faith within love, in the new hope given by the state of sonship.' Von Speyr, *The Victory of Love*, p. 48.

71 Chrétien, 'The Wounded Word: Phenomenology of Prayer', p. 164; cf. Coakley, 'Can God be Experienced as Trinity?'.

72 Claudel, *La rose et la rosaire* (Paris, 1947), pp. 156–7; as quoted by Chrétien, 'The Wounded Word: Phenomenology of Prayer', p. 164. Cf. von Speyr: 'The Spirit mediates and takes the initiative, because we in our weakness have entrusted ourselves to him. He takes up his dwelling in us not in appearance only: he is at home. And God listens to the Spirit because it is his Spirit. He recognizes his voice, even when we pray together with him, even when we say the words the Spirit inspires in us.' Von Speyr, *The Victory of Love*, p. 76.

73 This terminology of 'middle voice' is Catherine Pickstock's, borrowed of course from Ancient Indo-European languages, in which verbs can be conjugated in either the active, middle or passive voice. See Pickstock, *After Writing: On the Liturgical Consummation of Philosophy* (Oxford: Blackwell, 1997), *passim*.

The Son does not turn away from us, he does not leave us behind in uncertainty, or merely with the promise of the Cross or with the grace given to the Church: *he takes part. He continues, and his part is prayer*. This makes our prayer suddenly come to life, for *in prayer we do nothing else but what the Son does*; we do it in our weakness, but supported by his infallibility . . . We were created for him, but now we have become cosharers in his prayer; he takes over the whole greatness of prayer, the perfect conversation with the Father, he gives it the divine meaning of his intercession and invites us to pray with him.[74]

The deifying adoption of the human into Christ is becoming a 'cosharer' by the Spirit in the perfect pattern of the Son's communication with the Father, a communication of 'divine reflexivity'.[75]

In prayer God plays in the middle; the created spirit is suspended in the transfiguring agape of the uncreated Spirit's ingression. In this way creation comes into the filio-form life of the Son. The act of prayer, through the willed submission of the created spirit to the uncreated Spirit, participates in the Son's own *kenosis* and filial obedience: his willing surrender of himself in doxological adoration to the Father. We are thereby incorporated into the triune life by the christic handing-over of ourselves to the Spirit out of pneumatic love of our paternal source.[76] Herein we learn to cry 'Abba! Father!' We learn to say: 'Thy kingdom come, Thy will be done' (Matt. 6.10). Herein our lips bear 'the weight of the double Yes' spoken by the human spirit and the Spirit of Christ.[77] To be sure

---

74 Von Speyr, *The Victory of Love*, p. 100; the italics are mine.

75 Sarah Coakley writes: '[Prayer] is not a simple communication between an individual and a distant and undifferentiated divine entity, but rather a movement of *divine* reflexivity, a sort of answering of God to God in and through the one who prays.' Coakley, 'Can God be Experienced as Trinity?' p. 21.

76 This points to what David Hart calls the 'different kind of substantial presence' posited by Christianity: 'one that *is* only in being handed over in love, surrender and given anew.' See Hart, *The Beauty of the Infinite*, p. 327; this can be read as linking up with von Speyr's above quoted claim that the words of the *Pater Noster* 'live from the Son's substance'. Von Speyr, *The World of Prayer*, p. 134.

77 Von Speyr, *The Victory of Love*, p. 34.

this 'weight of the double Yes' is the weight of the dyothelite reality of prayer. On this view, the interplay of wills in the pneumatic correspondence of dyothelite prayer is the deiform opening to the double mediation of desire. Here the alterity of the uncreated/superior is welcomed into the created/inferior heart. To speak the *Pater Noster* authentically is to perform an act of 'genuine will' in a community of others that refuses the grasp of self-closure and is therefore open to a transcendent alterity.[78] Herein we come to *give ourselves as Amen* to the prayer which is the heart of the Church: the Eucharistic Prayer sung to the Father on our behalf, sung in the unity of the Holy Spirit, sung by the priest *in persona Christi*.

The Spirit is the way of our pneumatic self-transcendence. He is the divine person who draws us into the heart of who we are, into the exigency of our being. And he perfects our human longing into the communion of the Son's prayer. Here the mystery of human desire plunges into the depths of trinitarian love. Now we live for the Father in the formal pattern of the Son's theandric gift. We are deified by the Spirit who intercedes with our spirit, who interplays with the middle of our erotic longing out of the agapeic plenitude of God's own unequalizable gift of Godself.

---

78 Here I am appropriating something of what William Desmond writes of in a different context: 'The doubling of the will might be seen as the upsurge of the exigence of the double mediation required by the metaxological sense of being: both self-mediation and intermediation with the other. What happens in the doubled will is the struggle to overcome the temptation to reduce this twofold mediation to a shut-in process of singular self-mediation. In mediating with itself, the genuine will opens up to the appeal of the other; and thus it may live the double mediation in an ethically affirmative sense; the good will may instantiate respect both for itself and for the community of others. By contrast, the will at war with itself fights the closure of its own self-mediation completely in itself; for this closure is also a closing down of the second intermediation with the other. Such self-closure is a refusal of the metaxological community of being and the open intermediation with the other which its requires.' Desmond, *Beyond Hegel and Dialectic: Speculation Cult and Comedy* (Albany, NY: SUNY Press, 1992), pp. 212–13.

Conclusion: Towards a *totus Christus* Christology

The recapitulation of creation into Christ is the pneumatological return of creation to the Word through whom it was spoken: it is the telos of every human desire and of the Church in the *totus Christus*. In the middle of this *theandric eros* ecclesiology and Christology meet in the communion of the double mediation of desire in the filial prayer to the Father. Here the unity in difference, which is the communion of the Trinity, is reflected in a second unity of indwelling difference: the communion of the members of Christ's deified body. As *Gaudium et spes* puts it:

> The Lord Jesus, when He prayed to the Father, 'that all may be one . . . as we are one' (Jn 17:21–22) opened up vistas closed to human reason, for He implied a certain likeness between the union of the divine Persons, and the unity of God's sons in truth and charity. This likeness reveals that man . . . cannot fully find himself except through a sincere gift of himself. (24)

In this way deiform life is coming to live by *Gift*. It is finding oneself in the love of giving oneself to another, and gracefully receiving oneself out of the fullness of another's generosity.

St Irenaeus of Lyon answers the question of why God fashioned the flesh of Jesus out of the flesh of Adam instead of creating anew from the dust: 'In order that it may not be another form of being, nor another being to be saved, but rather that the *same might be recapitulated*, and the similitude of being be kept.'[79] What Christ recapitulates is not another desire, but the original human desire of the Father's handiwork.[80] The Sequela of Christ, in order for it to disclose the true desire of divine-humanity, must re-enact – *in truth* – the whole pattern of the Adamic-parody. In order to purify and redeem the sin of the first desire, Christ must enact and reveal the

---

[79] Irenaeus, *Adversus haereses*, III.11.10; PG 7:955B. English translation: *Irenaeus: Against Heresies*, ed. and trans. Alexander Roberts and James Donaldson, in *Ante-Nicene Fathers*, vol. 1 (Henderson: Peabody, Massachusetts, 2004).

[80] Cf. Irenaeus, *Adversus haereses*, V.14.2; PG 7:1162.

Deification as Metaphysics

truth of the first sin: Adam's desire to be God. Christ *makes all things new* because he never makes anything twice.[81]

The Lord's mercies are new each morning (cf. Lam. 3.22–23). And the false road offered by Satan in the Garden – the promise that we would be *like gods* – was always a prophecy of the one divine end we have in Christ Jesus.

---

81 I owe this turn of phrase to Conor Cunningham. Cf. Jean Daniélou, *A History of Early Christian Doctrine Before the Council of Nicaea*, vol. 2, *Gospel Message and Hellenistic Culture*, p. 180.

16. Wittgenstein's *Leben*: Language, Philosophy and The Authority of the Everyday

NEIL TURNBULL

Wittgenstein and the Meaning of 'Life'

As is now well known, Wittgensteinian philosophers generally oppose traditional conceptions of the overall purpose of philosophy, especially those conceptions that view philosophy as a general intellectual discipline, requiring a technical or esoteric mode of thinking capable of delivering insights into the ultimate nature and/or purpose of human existence. Thus in orthodox interpretations of his later work,[1] Wittgenstein is widely recognized as a proponent of a strong 'counter-philosophical' thesis, namely, that philosophy is a symptom of the 'bewitchment of the intelligence by means of language' and that philosophers can only articulate highly conventional truths with which 'we' are, in some sense, already familiar. In this way, the later Wittgenstein is often

---

1 Clearly any attempt to define 'an orthodox view' of Wittgenstein's philosophy is fraught with many difficulties, especially as there is a real disagreement among Wittgensteinian philosophers as to whether the later Wittgenstein is a 'realist' or an 'anti-realist' philosopher. However, it seems clear that, notwithstanding these differences, there is an incipient orthodoxy in Wittgensteinian studies, and it is that Wittgenstein was a reformer of the 'analytic tradition' who attempted to show that meaning is not logical or experiential but fundamentally grounded in social and cultural competences of various kinds.

viewed as having claimed that philosophers cannot make any general 'theoretical' assertions about the nature of the world, but can only propose what he termed 'reminders for a particular purpose' – reminders that the everyday conversational world, the world 'right under our noses' and a world that, in his view, is easily recognized and understood once we pay attention the social function of our everyday linguistic practices, is the only world that there is. As Wittgenstein states:

> it is true to say that our considerations could not be scientific ones. It was not of any possible interest to us to find out empirically 'that, contrary to our preconceived ideas, it is possible to think such and such' – whatever that may mean ... *And we must not advance any kind of theory*. There must not be anything hypothetical in our considerations. We must do way with all *explanation*, and description alone must take its place. The problems are solved not by the giving a new information, but by arranging what we have already known.[2]

However, at the same time, it is also frequently recognized that the later Wittgenstein did not reject the possibility of *philosophizing* as such, but simply positioned himself against conceptions of philosophy that understood it to be an intellectual pursuit of general theoretical truths, or, more specifically, a mode of intellection that is in someway continuous with, yet rival to, modern science – or a search for 'a metaphysics' in the traditional sense of the term. Thus not only is Wittgenstein often viewed as a critic of modern Western philosophy, but he is also frequently understood to provide us with an alternative way of 'doing philosophy' founded upon a new 'way of seeing' familiar and mundane truths; a way of seeing that he famously termed *'Übersicht'*, or a 'global synoptic overview'. In orthodox accounts, *'Übersicht'* is understood to be a 'generalized vantage point' from which the fundamentally 'practical' significance of human meaning-making practices can be 'clarified', for those in the grip of the various forms of intellectual perplexity that the later Wittgenstein believed

---

2 Ludwig Wittgenstein, *Philosophical Investigations* (Oxford: Blackwell, 1958), 109; italics added.

to lie at the root of all forms of philosophical enquiry.[3] Thus in orthodox accounts of his later work, Wittgenstein is seen as a proponent of the thesis that the central problem of philosophy is not the nature of knowledge or subjectivity *per se* – the problematic that had defined most modern philosophical endeavours from Descartes onwards – but the problem of *commanding a clear view* of our 'entanglement' in the ordinary, taken-for-granted, rules that shape and guide our linguistic practices. Thus Wittgenstein, in the main, is understood to have claimed that the role of the philosopher is to develop perspicuous global representations of the interconnections between human practices, and as such he is often viewed as advocating a version of 'social holism'.[4]

However, it is also widely acknowledged that Wittgenstein's anti-philosophical stance stems from his advocacy of a pragmatic account of meaning, especially his infamously gnomic idea that 'meaning is use' – and in orthodox accounts of his later work it is this dimension of his thinking that largely predominates. Thus according to many, the later Wittgenstein is to be read as arguing that meaning and understanding are not expressions or syntheses of underlying intellectual schemes or processes, but are, in essence, modes of *action* – simple 'doings' – guided by tacit a priori rules; rules that are, ultimately, expressions of customs or traditions. Thus the later Wittgenstein is widely viewed as claiming that in order for speakers and listeners to be able to understand the meaning of 'a word', they must be able to deploy that word in a way that is guided by the accumulated habits of individual and collective pasts – habits that express themselves as taken-for-granted dispositions that allow words to perform specific 'social functions' in particular social situations. Thus in orthodox accounts, the later Wittgenstein is often viewed as a Kantian; a philosopher who tried to show that 'concepts without customs are blind', and that input from the 'empirical given' is neither necessary nor sufficient for understanding the meaning of words and, more generally, the nature of language in general. So in these same orthodox accounts,

---

[3] *Philosophical Investigations*, 122; J. Genova, *Wittgenstein: A Way of Seeing* (London: Routledge, 1985).

[4] See David Pears, *The False Prison: A Study of the Development of Wittgenstein' Philosophy* (Oxford: OUP, 1987).

Wittgenstein's Leben

not only is the later Wittgenstein viewed as a social holist, but he is also generally conceived as a second wave sociological neo-Kantian, concerned with exploring the limits of human understanding through a series of reflections on the hermeneutic significance of what Crispin Wright has termed 'the background of unreflective custom';[5] a background that guides practice as 'a remote instauration of a calculus we are meant to perform without reflection or responsibility'.[6]

This chapter challenges this orthodox, social holist/neo-Kantian, account of the significance of Wittgenstein's later philosophy of language (that positions him at the intersection between Kant, Hegel and Frege). More specifically, this chapter claims that these orthodox views fundamentally misread the wider philosophical and political significance of one of the later Wittgenstein's key philosophical terms of art – 'forms of life' – and that this is the result of a failure to consider the centrality of the question of the meaning of 'life' – *'Leben'* – in the work of the both the early and the later Wittgenstein.[7] In so doing, I argue that orthodox accounts overlook the extent to which Wittgenstein's later philosophy stands as a key moment in the evolution of the tradition of *Lebensphilosophie* that formed the vanguard of the *Mitteleuropean* conservative counter-revolution against Kantianism, Hegelianism and positivism in the first two decades of the last century.[8] The argument offered here is quite specific: if one pays

---

5 C. Wright, 'Wittgenstein on Mathematical Proof' in A. Phillips Griffiths (ed.), *Wittgenstein: Centenary Essays* (Cambridge: CUP, 1991), p. 98.

6 J. Roberts, *The Logic of Reflection: German Philosophy in the Twentieth Century* (New Haven: Yale, 1992), p. 154).

7 Thus Wittgensteinian orthodoxies have obscured a very important philosophical theme that draws both Wittgenstein's early and later work into a common metaphysical frame of reference.

8 Although the influence of *Lebensphilosophie* on Wittgenstein's thought has, to some extent, been touched upon elsewhere (see D. Bolton, 'Life-Form and Idealism' in G. Vesey (ed.), *Idealism Past and Present* (Cambridge: CUP, 1984), pp. 269–84), much of the analysis on offer seems to equate *Lebensphilosophie* with 'naturalism'; more specifically with the idea that meaning is a form of cognition that is ultimately grounded in an evolved human nature. In these accounts, the orthodox neo-Kantian thesis is countered with the claim that the later Wittgenstein

close attention to Wittgenstein's account of the relationship between *Leben*, 'linguistic meaning' and the nature of philosophy, then his famous counter-philosophical definition of philosophy must be understood against the backdrop of the wider, and more general, problematic of the significance of *Leben* in his work; and that in many ways Wittgenstein's later philosophy amounts to a strong philosophical defence of the epistemological and ontological significance of *Leben* against sceptical and idealist modes of philosophizing that reduced life and its meanings to the level of 'the idea' via a subject-centred logic of the concept.

Lebensphilosophie: Wittgenstein's Intellectual Context

Lebensphilosophie, or 'life philosophy', has its origins in European romanticism, especially the naturalistic holism of Goethe and Schleiermacher. The philosophical works of these two thinkers were to give impetus to a new approach to philosophical problems that viewed *Leben* as a wider vital context within which all concepts and modes of understanding emerge as meaningful and significant – that is, as 'living symbolisms'. At the ontological level, within *Lebensphilosophie* '*Leben*' is conceived as an ineluctable flow, a series of becomings, and as such something fundamentally different form the forms of scientific naturalism that had defined the *Weltanschauung* of the early modern period.[9] Although questions surrounding the significance of *Leben* fell out of favour among European philosophers after World War One – the ideas

---

was much more concerned with situating the problematic of meaning within what he was to term 'the natural history of human beings' than he was with finding quasi-transcendental conditions of possibility for linguistic meaning. However, in what follows my argument is that in the work of the later Wittgenstein *Leben* is not synonymous with 'human nature' and thus Wittgenstein was not a naturalist in this strict philosophical sense of the term. *Leben* is not human nature, but human *life*. Moreover, this kind of naturalism is entirely compatible with Kantian thinking, especially as the naturalistic Kantianism of contemporary cognitive science amply demonstrates.

9 Cf. S. Lash, 'Life', in *Theory, Culture & Society* 23:2-3 (2006), pp. 323-9.

Wittgenstein's Leben

of Heidegger, in particular, moving quickly to replace '*Leben*' through an appreciation of the 'deeper primordialities' of 'Being' – in the early decades of the last century the philosophical significance of *Leben*, and its associated political problematics, became a central concern for many European philosophers and sociologists. Schopenhauer, Nietzsche and Dilthey were the main philosophical figures in early *Lebensphilosophie*. The sociologists Simmel and Tarde were also influenced by *Lebensphilosophie*, as were Freud and Jung. Essentially, the life philosophers claimed that 'life and meaning' form a unity, and that life is essentially meaningful because in its very 'essence' it is 'productive of meaning' through the bare fact that it is 'lived' by individuals and groups. More generally, '*Leben*', for the life philosopher, is always 'lived', and as such always experienced and 'self-interpreted'.

This idea was to go on to form the basis for Husserl's critique of the 'one-sided rationality' of positivism. As Husserl observed, 'life gives', and in his view this is the 'principle of all philosophical principles', the starting point for all forms of philosophical enquiry.[10] As Nietzsche argued, 'life is no argument';[11] and the idea that life is the real, authentic, object of philosophical contemplation and that 'thinking', in the formal intellectualist sense of this term, is a symptom of the degeneration and the emaciation of human vitalities, stand as important socio-political motifs in twentieth-century *Lebensphilosophie*.

One of the most significant influences on the development of *Lebensphilosophie* was Dilthey's famous critique of positivism. In Dilthey's philosophy, positivism was criticized for advocating a conception of thought divorced from 'life'. The overall purpose of *Lebensphilosophie*, according to Dilthey, is to counter the continual drift of concepts into the realms of the sciences, by translating them back into the vital *working context* from which they originate.[12] Dilthey recognized that once *Leben*, and not *thought*,

---

[10] Cf. also M. Heidegger, *Towards the Definition of Philosophy* (London: Continuum, 2000), p. 94.

[11] Cf. F. Nietzsche, *A Nietzsche Reader* (Harmondsworth: Penguin 1984), p. 202.

[12] Cf. T. Kiesel, *Heidegger's Way of Thought* (London: Continuum, 2002), p. 91; my emphasis.

is viewed as the beginning of philosophical enquiry, then the nature and significance of human activities can only be understood *from within human life itself*; that is, human action can only be understood in terms of the meanings and plans that organize *Leben* into a coherent liveable whole. Thus in his view, meaning and understanding do not require some special act of intellectual *gnosis*, as both classical and modern philosophers had hitherto claimed, but simply a 'sympathy for life': and for him it is this vital dimension, the tacit dimension of intuitive feeling for the temporally and spatially organized ebbs and flows of human life, that stands as the tacit condition of possibility for the more abstract forms of theoretical knowing that we now associate with 'modern science'. However, it was Dilthey's suggestions that the main source of insight into the nature and significance of human conceptuality is an understanding of its 'working context' – *Wirkungszusammenhang* – that was perhaps the most philosophically resonant idea to emerge out of his version of *Lebensphilosophie*. This idea seemed to imply that 'understanding' is an event that occurs in the lived contexts of practical activity; something that in the first instance 'happens' as we practically engage with the world and interact with each other. Thus for the Diltheyan *life philosopher* 'the beginning of all understanding', as Goethe observed, is an understanding of the nature and significance of 'the deed' – and as such *'Leben'*, as, first and foremost, purposeful practical activity, must be conceived, philosophically, as *a dynamic social metaphysics of objects and persons*.

It is this conception of *'Leben'* that was eventually developed into a coherent social philosophy by a conservative thinker who was to exert a dominating influence over the development of Wittgenstein's thought: Oswald Spengler. Many Wittgensteinians now recognize that Spengler was a key influence on Wittgenstein's later thinking.[13] As is now well known, Spengler's work is generally associated with the mood of cultural pessimism that took hold of European intellectual circles in the early decades of the last century, and Wittgenstein's later philosophy was certainly affected by the Spenglerian *'Stimmung* of decline'. However, more signifi-

---

13 Cf. A. Turalni, 'Wittgenstein and Spengler *vis-à-vis* Frazer', in *Philosophy and Social Criticism* 31 (2005), pp. 69–89.

cant in this context are the resonances between Wittgenstein's and Spengler's general philosophical aims and aspirations. There are significant noticeable similarities between Wittgenstein's idea of 'perspicuous representation' and Spengler's idea of *Weltanschauung* – but similarities of a more 'fundamental', metaphysical, nature can also be clearly discerned, especially in a late work of Spengler's *Man and Technics*.[14] In this work, Spengler's analysis begins from a key assumption of *Lebensphilosophie*: that 'life' is not a naturalistic Darwinian struggle for survival, but something that is revealed only through 'unsophisticated living with it, through the inwardly felt relationship of Ego and Tu, which is known to every peasant and to every true artist and poet'.[15] However, for Spengler, this shows that *Leben* is not only a vital dynamic ontological movement, but necessarily *ordinary*. According to Spengler, life is always 'our common life together' and as such it is something shared, taken for granted and altogether familiar. It is what is shared whenever humans relate and is always something in excess of conscious thought.

Perhaps more important in this context is Spengler's claim that ordinary life is a form of play between people and things directed towards wider collective/social ends. And according to Spengler, language must be seen as a phenomenon of *Leben* in just this sense. For him, language is not a system of representation, but part of what he terms 'the wider tactics of living'. In his view, language is what enables life to 'work as it raises life to a higher social power: the power of collective action'.[16] Language is conceived as the micro-instrument that makes possible a macro *collective doing by plan*;[17] and for Spengler, putting the matter in a very Wittgensteinian way, 'the inner form of language, the grammar, is the *command*. The primordial aim of all speech is *the carrying out of an act*, and it is only later that "thinking" gains independence from language and activity, and sets itself up *against* life as a power in itself.'[18]

---

14 Cf. Oswald Spengler, *Man and Technics: Contribution to a Philosophy of Life* (University Press of the Pacific, 2002).
15 Spengler, *Man and Technics*, p. 20.
16 Spengler, *Man and Technics*, p. 27.
17 Spengler, *Man and Technics*, p. 51.
18 Spengler, *Man and Technics*, p. 57.

This aspect of Spenglerian *Lebensphilosophie* echoes strongly in Wittgenstein's later philosophy. Spengler's idea of language as 'play', and life as a 'collectively organized game', were to eventually provide Wittgenstein with the basis for a new *life-philosophical* lexicon with which he was to develop his critique of the individualist 'metaphysics of the subject', that had up to then formed the starting point for modern forms of philosophical enquiry. As with Spengler, language, for Wittgenstein, is also 'a game', but only in so far it is a form of life – that is, a way through which life is organized into meaningful routines. Thus 'the rule that gives meaning' for later Wittgenstein, is not a Platonic entity, but is simply 'life itself' – more specifically, the only 'rule' that there can possibly be 'for us', in his view, is the self-evidence and necessity that accompany the everyday *habitus* that allows us to act, to 'go on', in specific concrete situations (and so in a real sense Wittgenstein assumes that life is its 'own rule'). Therefore at the ontological level, there is simply no easy way, in his view, in which language can be divorced from life: 'You must bear in mind that the language-game is so to say something unpredictable. I mean: it is not based on grounds. It is not reasonable (or unreasonable). It is there – like our life' (*wie unsere Leben*).[19] Hence for him to imagine a language is to imagine a form of life.[20] For Wittgenstein the *life-philosopher*, language is able to 'command', to impose itself on human life, because it is a phenomenon entirely immanent to *unsere Leben*.

Clearly, it is this conception of the nature of language that underlies Wittgenstein's famous example of the 'builders': the putative paradigmatic 'language-gamers' that he introduces at the start of the *Philosophical Investigations*. Wittgenstein's builders are clearly meant to indicate that language, at root, is a mode of *tactical organization* that gives direction to 'our lives', but only because that organization is, in a non-mechanistic way, entirely 'natural' (not in the biological sense that the natural sciences have given to this term, but in the sense of being in accordance with what Wittgenstein refers to as our 'natural history', the history of '*Leben*' understood 'from within'). Thus the later Wittgenstein

---

19 Ludwig Wittgenstein, *On Certainty* (Oxford: Blackwell, 1969), p. 559.
20 Wittgenstein, *Philosophical Investigations*, 19.

departs from the main tenets of *Lebensphilosophie* in one key respect: for him all forms of linguistic meaning presuppose the recognition of the *authority* of '*Leben*' rather than a recognition of its dynamic and somewhat anarchic and antinomial contingency. And therefore in his view, in order to be able to understand language, one must accept/trust in the authority of the form of life within which any language 'commands' us to conform to its perlocutionary and illocutionary demands. More generally, 'life' in the form that it has taken for us, is the ultimate philosophical standard for the later Wittgenstein – it is the 'bedrock' that ends analysis with the assertion 'well, this is simply what we do'. Or perhaps better, 'this is how we live'.

Lebensformen, Language and Life in the Later Wittgenstein

Of course, to make this claim is to challenge many of the definitions of 'form of life' found in the orthodox literature. There seem to be four competing definitions of 'forms of life' in orthodox accounts of the later Wittgenstein: 'behaviourist', 'naturalist/organismic', 'linguistic' and 'quasi-anthropological'.[21] Thus according to some commentators, *Lebensformen* are simply ways of acting or behaving, but for other philosophers they must be read 'organismically', as referring to something like biologically evolved 'human nature' or biological life,[22] while sociologists understand them as historically specific socio-cultural formations.[23] Perhaps the more preva-

---

21 Cf. N. Grier, *Wittgenstein and Phenomenology: A Comparative Study of the Later Wittgenstein, Husserl, Heidegger and Merleau-Ponty* (New York: SUNY Press, 1981); N. Garver, *This Complicated Form of Life: Essays on Wittgenstein* (Chicago: Open Court, 1994); M. Ter Hark, 'Patterns of Life: A Third Wittgensteinian Concept', in D. Moyal-Sharrock (ed.), *The Third Wittgenstein: The Post-Investigations Works* (Aldershot: Ashgate), 2004; Winch, 'Understanding a Primitive Society', in D. Z. Phillips (ed.), *Religion and Understanding* (Oxford: Blackwell, 1967).

22 Cf. also R. McDonagh, 'Wittgenstein, German Organicism, Chaos and the Centre of Life', in *Journal of the History of Philosophy* 43.3 (2004), pp. 297–326.

23 Cf. H. M. Collins, *Artificial Experts: Social Knowledge and Intelligent Machines* (Cambridge, MA: MIT Press, 1991).

lent view in orthodox accounts is the 'linguistic definition' – that 'forms of life' are synonymous with 'spoken languages', because for some 'talking is the human form of life'.[24]

According to Norman Malcolm, 'form of life' is perhaps the most significant philosophical concept for the later Wittgenstein.[25] However, a close reading of Wittgenstein's key texts forces us to question the extent to which 'forms of life' were as significant to Wittgenstein as such orthodox commentators have claimed. If we take the Wittgensteinian *oeuvre* as a whole, he refers as often, if not more often, to *Gewöhnliche Leben* ('ordinary life'). In fact, there are only four references to '*Lebensformen*' in *Philosophical Investigations*, and in other texts, especially the later remarks published as *On Certainty*, *Zettel* and *Remarks on Colour*, he seems to prefer the expressions '*im Leben*' and '*unser Leben*' – 'in life' and 'our life'. Thus in the *Remarks on Colour*, Wittgenstein observes that concepts stand 'the middle of our life'[26] to the extent that meaning and understanding are not 'a matter of the *words* one uses or what is one is thinking when one is using them, but rather the difference that they make at various points in life'.[27] Even in the *Investigations*, the place where Wittgenstein deploys the term '*Lebensform*' most often, he see claims that words have sense only they become interwoven with the 'weave of our lives'.[28]

Thus it should come as no surprise to discover that Wittgenstein's reflections on the philosophical significance of *Leben* are also deployed to answer epistemological questions. Wittgenstein's

---

24 Cf. Stephen Mulhall, 'Avoiding Nonsense, Keeping Cool: Nielsen, Phillips and Philosophy in the First Person', in K. Nielsen and D. Z. Phillips (eds), *Wittgensteinian Fideism* (London: SCM Press, 2001), p. 72.
25 Cf. Norman Malcolm, *Wittgenstein and Idealism*, in G. Vesey (ed.), *Idealism Past and Present* (Cambridge: CUP, 1984), pp. 249–67.
26 Ludwig Wittgenstein, *Remarks on the Foundations of Mathematics* (Oxford: Blackwell, 1998), p. 302.
27 Wittgenstein, *Remarks on the Foundations of Mathematics*, p. 317. See p. 128, where he talks about 'life' being akin to 'psychological atmosphere' and something to be valued, to the extent that a lifeless thing 'lacks something'. More generally, for the later Wittgenstein, words only possess meaning to the extent that they are 'brought to life' – that is stand in vital relation to living human beings.
28 Wittgenstein, *Philosophical Investigations*, II, 174.

anti-sceptical philosophy can be seen as grounded in the claim that epistemological doubts can be of no real significance to 'us', because they make no difference to the direction of 'our lives'.[29] This is because, in his view, with epistemological language the background of ordinary *Leben* is missing, and as a consequence this mode of language remains 'lifeless' – devoid of any connection to the patterns of *unsere Leben* that could provide it with a real human sense and/or significance. Thus for Wittgenstein to doubt, say, the existence of the 'external world' is to doubt 'life itself' and as such is 'radically incoherent', because 'doubting' only has 'significance' in the context of '*Leben*' (and so for Wittgenstein, famously, such a doubt, that doubted everything, would not even be a doubt). Thus again in *On Certainty,* Wittgenstein comments that '[m]y life shows that I know or am certain that there is chair over there, or a door and so on'.[30] Hence he points out that ordinary mundane beliefs about 'this and that' are in some contexts 'unshakeable convictions' whose fixity and incorrigibility stems not from logical ideas of necessity or self-evidence but from their being immersed 'in life'. Thus Wittgenstein asks, against the sceptic 'do I, in the course of my life, make sure I know that here is a hand – my own hand, that is?'[31]

Interestingly, Wittgenstein's interest in the philosophical significance of *Leben* first began in the *Tractatus Logico-Philosophicus.* Many now recognize that the *Tractatus* was not primarily an exercise in formal semantics and/or philosophical logic, and is certainly no homage to neo-Kantianism. It is primarily a work of *ethics*; and questions surrounding the meaning of *Leben,* especially the relationship between '*Leben*', 'the world' and 'the metaphysical subject', are perhaps the most significant philosophical issue to arise from this work. Here, Wittgenstein famously claimed that 'the world and *life* are one',[32] and for the early Wittgenstein, meaning is entirely immanent to the world/life in that, ontologically,

---

29 Wittgenstein, *On Certainty*, p. 338.
30 Wittgenstein, *On Certainty*, p. 7.
31 Wittgenstein, *On Certainty*, p. 9.
32 Cf. Martin Stokhof, *World and Life as One: Ethics and Ontology in Wittgenstein's Early Thought* (Stanford: Stanford University Press, 2002).

there is nothing but the world/life. But the answer to 'the riddle of life' – the riddle that lies behind all philosophical forms of enquiry – lies not 'in the world/life but in the inexpressible realm of the 'the mystical' (and thus there is certain tension between 'life' and 'mystical revealed truth' in the work of the early Wittgenstein). In metaphysical terms, the world/life for the early Wittgenstein is a transcendentally subjective space that circumscribes 'the totality of facts' and 'all that is the case'[33] and as such provides the conditions of possibility within which 'something can be said'.

In the later work, this residual positivism drops out of the picture, and *Leben* is no longer valued as the inexpressible transcendentally subjective context for all logically legitimate assertions, but is conceived as objective, external and intrinsically meaningful. Rather than a space organized by a logical subjectivity from 'within', *'Leben'* becomes the external impersonal ground for all notions of logical self-evidence and all ideas of necessity. Life – the wider holistic context of the earth below, the sky above, human beings, with their comings and goings, trials and tribulations – is simply self-evidently *there* for the later Wittgenstein. For him, this idea of life stands as the antidote to all forms of metaphysical speculation and epistemological doubt. Consider the following passage from *Philosophical Investigations*:

> Look at the blue sky and say to yourself 'How blue the sky is!' – When you do it spontaneously – without philosophical intentions – the idea never crosses your mind that this impression of colour belongs to *you*. And you have no hesitation in exclaiming that to someone else. And if you point at anything as you say the words you point at the sky. I am saying: you have not the feeling of pointing-into-yourself, which often accompanies 'naming the sensation' when one is thinking about a 'private language'. Nor do you think that you really ought not to point to the colour with your hand, but with your attention (Consider what it means to 'point to something with your attention'). (275)

Of course one of the key questions is, to whom is Wittgenstein referring here? Who is Wittgenstein's 'we'? More specifically to

---

33 Cf. Ludwig Wittgenstein, *Tractatus Logico-Philosophicus* (London: Routledge and Kegan Paul, 1981), 1–1.1.

whom does *Leben*, in the last instance, belong? When read historically, it is possible to read Wittgenstein as making a conservative claim – that the 'we' is the collective pronoun of early twentieth-century *Mitteleuropean* high culture, a culture where life was understood as something devoid of the intellectual problems that were then becoming the fashionable province of modernist thinkers.[34] Wittgenstein's philosophy, when conceived in this way, is fundamentally satirical in that, like Musil, his arguments seem to poke fun at the modes of theorization and speculation that were central to the *Zeitgeist* of twentieth-century modernism. But there is clearly more to Wittgenstein's argument than this. This can be seen if we consider his famous ethnographic thought-experiments – his imaginative references to the practices of other tribes and 'other forms of life'. Wittgenstein uses these tropic scenarios in order to demonstrate the fundamental contingency of all *forms* of life; more specifically that life can evolve into new forms that 'we', given our current customs and traditions, may struggle to understand (for example, Wittgenstein asks us to imagine a tribe that does not possess the concept 'all', merely the concept 'all but one'. We could understand this tribe, but only because we already understand how the word 'all' is used in our lives).[35] More important however, is Wittgenstein's use of these thought-experiments in order to test our intuitions about '*Leben*' – to show that meaning and '*Leben*' form a unity, that is to show us that where we see '*Leben*' we always see meaning, even if that meaning is not readily understandable from our own point of view. Thus he states that in order to understand the meaning of a word spoken by a member of 'another tribe' one must 'imagine the details of their life *and* their language'.[36]

---

34 Cf. Jacques Bouveresse, '"The Darkness of this Time": Wittgenstein and the Modern World', in A. Phillips Griffiths (ed.), *Wittgenstein: Centenary Essays* (Cambridge: CUP, 1991), pp. 11–39.
35 Cf. Wittgenstein, *Remarks on the Foundations of Mathematics*, p. 43.
36 Cf. Wittgenstein, *Remarks*, p. 421.

Philosophy: The Demand for a Life 'Less Ordinary'

To conclude: for Wittgenstein *Leben* is not, in essence, conceptual and as such it is not open to forms of scientific theorization and metaphysical imagining. *Leben* 'happens' before it is thought or articulated and therefore 'meanings', for Wittgenstein, are not cognitive/hermeneutic acts of any kind, but simply events that occur within life. As he states, '[o]ne doesn't *take* what one knows as cutlery at meal *for* cutlery; than one ordinarily tries to move one's mouth as one eats, or aims at moving it.'[37] For him, concepts only possess significance in terms of their relationship to human life, and as such human conceptuality is necessarily complex and multiform. We can only understand another form of life as long as we can recognize it as *life* – that is, as the characteristic pattern of 'ego' and 'tu' that comprise *unsere Leben*.

Thus *Leben* takes on a strangely humanist form for the later Wittgenstein, in that *Lebensformen* must possess a mundane and familiar pattern that 'we recognize', not as 'nature' or 'process', but as *living a life*. Thus Wittgenstein saw himself as a philosopher who attempted to relocate philosophical reflection within a new metaphysical horizon – the space of ordinary life – and he believed that philosophical problems will disappear once they are placed in this context. Once we look at philosophical problems from the 'point of view of life', we can see them for what they are – pseudo language games without a living purpose or context. Moreover, '*im Leben*', it may be 'unwise' to speculate and to doubt excessively, and in valorizing 'life' Wittgenstein is taking the point of view of what might be termed of ordinary popular *phronesis* – the perspective required for the forms of everyday wisdom that we deploy in order to keep 'hold of life' and avoid nonsense, red herrings and useless speculation. The self-evidence of *Göwohnliche Leben* is thus derived from an understanding of, and a sympathy for, an idea of life as something that is 'lived' rather than 'thought', 'done' and 'endured' rather than 'constructed' or 'created'. Wittgenstein's understanding of 'life' is in one sense an aristocratic fantasy of the mundane *vie quotidienne* – of the 'everyone' that stands out-

---

37 Wittgenstein, *Philosophical Investigations*, II, 195; original emphasis.

side and opposed to the world as it has been uselessly conceived by philosophers – but in another sense it is an attempt to allow philosophy to speak from a vantage point entirely immanent to life, so that it can claim for itself a stake in the forms of ordinary practical wisdom that modern science and philosophy, with their championing of technical reason, seem to have relegated to the hermeneutic sidelines.

Thus the key to understanding Wittgenstein lies in his claim that *'Leben'* cannot be captured by philosophical discourse, but only by those practices that emerge from within *Leben* itself. Thus Wittgenstein notes in *Culture and Value* that wisdom – the traditional aim of the philosopher – is grey; whereas *life* and religion – the practice that attempts to articulate the meaning of 'life' from within itself – are *full of colour*.[38] But a question emerges here: why did Wittgenstein claim that philosophy itself was not, and cannot, be a thread in the weave of our lives? Why did he view philosophy as symptom of *Leben's* desire to 'substantialize' itself – to conceive of 'life' as comprised of a basic, mysterious and intellectually problematic entities and processes? *Why from the point of view of life does it appear that philosophy does not belong to it?* Wittgenstein's suspicions of philosophy clearly turn on his understanding of the 'ordinariness of life'. Perhaps we can state that for the later Wittgenstein in particular, philosophy is not of this 'ordinary life', of 'our life', and as a result lacks a significant relationship to any context that that could provide it with relevance and/or wider significance – and in this respect his ideas are in accord with those historians of classical philosophy who note that classical Platonism, but also Stoicism and Epicureanism, were preparations not for *life*, but for *death*.[39]

But there is a more general point to be made (and one wonders about the extent to which his claim can be sustained today), when philosophical forms of questioning are no longer the prerogative of the closeted and cloistered intellectual, and when many philosophical forms of wonderment and metaphysical curiosity are now

---

38 Ludwig Wittgenstein, *Culture and Value* (Oxford: Blackwell, 1994), p. 62.

39 Cf. Pierre Hadot, *Philosophy as a Way of Life: Spiritual Exercises from Socrates to Foucault,* trans. Michael Chase (Oxford: Blackwell, 1995).

important part of 'everyday lives'. We now live in times when philosophical ideas form the background to many aspects of popular culture – not only in the proliferations of what might be termed 'vernacular philosophies' providing advice on 'how to live', but also in the New Age thinking and other forms of 'cosmological consciousness' that are now a prominent feature of today's High Street. It seems that philosophy has become 'more ordinary' than it was in Wittgenstein's time (when 'ordinariness' was either dismissed as 'false consciousness' or associated with highly romanticized notions of 'peasant simplicity'). For many people today, reflecting on what constitutes 'the good life', and perhaps reflecting upon global epistemological grounds for belief – through, say, sceptical doubts about the veracity of, say, political information conveyed through the media – are a reasonably routine aspect of 'our life'. In 'our lives', there is a growing demand for the 'extraordinary' and philosophical questions and modes of reflection are often called upon to meet this demand. Thus although, as one commentator has put it, in the age of philosophical instrumentalism and the diminution of philosophy by the special sciences, it may now be derisory to call oneself a philosopher,[40] today many desire answers to the riddles that life poses and with that 'calling' are inevitably drawn back into the orbit of philosophy. Philosophy, it seems, still fascinates, because 'ordinary life' is, in some way, experienced by most as radically incomplete. As Theodore Adorno was to famously claim, '[p]hilosophy, which once seemed obsolete, lives on because the moment to realise it was missed.'[41] Thus contrary to the intentions of some Wittgensteinian philosophers, philosophy has not been vanquished, but still haunts the late-modern world as a spectral promise of personal and collective 'self-realization'. Wittgenstein, writing for the future, seemed to be dimly aware that philosophy could realize itself again, but he could not see that there are 'potentials' within everyday life that could realise this state of affairs far sooner than he could have hoped for.

As a consequence, it is important to examine the historicity of

---

40 Philippe Lacoue-Labarthe, *Heidegger, Art, and Politics: The Fiction of the Political*, trans. Chris Turner (New Haven: Yale, 1990), p. 1.

41 Cf. Theodor Adorno, *Negative Dialectics*, trans. E. B. Ashton (London: Routledge, 2000), p. 3.

all intuitions of the 'ordinariness' of life, and thus to situate Wittgenstein's *Leben* within a particular historical context. And Wittgenstein, in his last writings, seemed to be aware that our basic conceptions of *Leben* (what he termed our *Sätze*), are in a constant state of flux; and that, in a Quinean way, what was once self-evidently 'there', like our life, may later become a matter for empirical investigation and theoretical reflection.[42] Looking back, we can now see that Wittgenstein was no wrecker of philosophical visions and perspectives but a *reformer* of the Western philosophical tradition, and his lasting intellectual significance resides in his call for the philosopher to return to 'life' – that philosophy 're-enliven' itself at a time when philosophical enquiry is becoming ossified and subject to increasing professionalization and governmental administration. For Wittgenstein, philosophy needs to rediscover its connections to a certain kind of vision, to a way of seeing that brings *Leben* back into philosophical focus – and in so doing rediscover its relationship to art and to religion as 'transforming powers' that can allow us to develop the forms of wisdom that can put us in a position to see the world 'aright'.[43] In this sense, Wittgenstein turned the philosophical conceptions of the positivists against themselves. For positivists such as Waismann, '[p]hilosophy is many things and there is no formula to cover them all. But if I were asked to express in a single word what is its most essential feature, I would unhesitatingly say: vision . . . the piercing of that dead crust of tradition and convention, the breaking of those fetters that bind us to inherited preconceptions, so as to attain a new and broader way of looking at things.'[44] For Wittgenstein, this philosophical vision was turned back on itself in order to reveal the 'world' pushed aside by the positivist, the ordinary world of *Leben*: a world that is not the end of philosophy, but simply its new beginning. It is a world that is fundamentally and necessarily *Heimlich* – the site where words possess a 'meaning' to the extent that meaning presupposes 'being at home' in, and a 'knowing one's way about', the complex patterns, routines and

---

42 Cf. Wittgenstein, *On Certainty*, p. 97.
43 Cf. Wittgenstein, *Tractatus*, 6.54.
44 F. Waismann, 'How I See Philosophy', in A. J. Ayer (ed.), *Logical Positivism* (New York: Free Press, 1959), pp. 345–91, at p. 375.

activities that make up *'unsere Leben'*.[45] For Wittgenstein, like Nietzsche, the 'honest philosophical thinker' is forced to recognize that philosophy must leave life 'as it is', and in so doing speak for life and those, like 'us', who live it.

---

45 Cf. N. Scheman, 'Forms of Life: Mapping the Rough Ground', in H. D. Sluga and D. G. Stern (eds), *The Cambridge Companion to Wittgenstein* (Cambridge: CUP, 1996), pp. 383–410.

17. Plato against Ontotheology[1]

PAUL TYSON

Introduction

For Heidegger, Western metaphysics from Plato to Nietzsche epitomizes abstract intellectual hubris. On his view, the Western metaphysical tradition is synonymous with ontotheology – an idealized and theoreticized false capture of Being and God by an 'all too human' philosophy. This chapter will affirm Heideggerian critique in so far as it applies to the philosophical hubris of the great current of Western secular metaphysics and speculative theology from the fourteenth century to the twentieth century. However, I shall argue that Heidegger – bound as he is to the nineteenth-century counter-Enlightenment tradition – is far too sweeping in his dismissal of the history of Western metaphysical belief, and in particular in his lack of sensitivity to the religious depth of Plato's metaphysical position.[2] So that while Heidegger's 'ontotheology' is very important in the context of twentieth-century modernism and its counter-Enlightenment critique, this chapter seeks to bring a nuance to bear upon the totalizing tendency of the Heideggerian critique of ontotheology, particularly in

---

[1] I would like to acknowledge Merold Westphal's very valuable feedback on the reading of an earlier version of this chapter in Granada, 2006.

[2] To argue that Plato's metaphysics makes a pretentious and delusional religion out of philosophy (i.e. Plato's metaphysics is ontotheology) is a very different thing from arguing that Plato's religious outlook implies a set of metaphysical beliefs (i.e. Plato's 'philosophy' is essentially doxological, and not philosophy at all in a secular, discretely rational or empirical manner).

relation to its rejection of Western metaphysics *in toto*, as ontotheologically infected 'footnotes to Plato'.

I shall attempt to make this case via two avenues of pitting Plato against ontotheology: first, Plato is viewed in sympathy with Heidegger's opposition to ontotheology. Because Plato never was modern, he does not suffer from the epistemological foundationalism, the egocentric subjectivism and the nominalist sacred/secular divide that leans modern metaphysics and theology so easily towards ontotheology.

Second, and more profoundly, Plato is viewed in opposition to the anti-metaphysical stance of the counter-Enlightenment. Plato's 'philosophy' is completely premised on a small family of allegorical, yet substantive, metaphysical beliefs – beliefs Plato finds necessary for reason, morality, craft and natural philosophy, but beliefs in no way established by human thought, morality, craft or observation. Hence, the rejection of metaphysical belief itself is mere sophistic babble to Plato. Given Plato's very strong grasp of the necessity of divinely given allegorical belief as the grounds of human reason, Plato rejects the totalizing scope of the critique of ontotheology, and challenges the believability and rationality of the counter-Enlightenment stance of metaphysical unbelief.

So Plato is of interest to us now if we seek to uphold the useful critique of modern reason brought forward by the counter-Enlightenment, and he is of interest to us now if, in a post-secular manner, we are a bit 'over' the forceful dismantling of all metaphysical beliefs, and are prepared to try tentative restorative moves towards meaningful beliefs concerning truth and reality.

However, in deference to the counter-Enlightenment, I wish to point out that I am making a limited claim in this chapter for Plato's antagonism towards ontotheology. I am not claiming that Plato cannot be read in an ontotheological manner, nor am I denying the general claim that the long Western traditions of metaphysics and theology have often demonstrated ontotheological tendencies. For I believe that ontotheology – as idolatry – is a perennial tendency in 'normal' human belief. But I intend to suggest that by giving careful attention to how we read Plato, it can be persuasively argued that Plato himself was not a Platonist.[3]

---

3 This is not as cheeky a comment as it may at first sound. Consider a

Further, in the traditions of the classical and medieval appropriation of Plato by Christian theological saints, I think Plato can be read very convincingly as a proto-Christian advocate of spiritual humility, of the epistemology of revelation and faith, and within the contemplative stance of worshipful devotion to God. That is a tradition of 'doxo-ontological'[4] belief – from Justin, Origen and Augustine through to Bonaventure and Aquinas – that has no truck with ontotheology. This is the tradition of contemplation as *worship*, and it does 'dance and sing'. And this is a tradition of belief that I think it would now be profitable for us to carefully re-explore.

A Post-Secular Appropriation of Heidegger's critique of Ontotheology

Heidegger is, at least, a counter-Enlightenment aesthetic existentialist of the Void. His opus grapples with a profound sense of crisis in the truth and reality belief traditions of nineteenth- and

---

parallel between Plato's dialogical mode of communication and Kierkegaard's pseudonymous mode of communication. Kierkegaard makes it quite clear that his pseudonyms are to be taken seriously. Not that they do not reveal something about what Kierkegaard believed, but rather that the matter Kierkegaard's 'indirect communication' is concerned with has no interest in whether good scholars can academically speculatively reconstruct what Kierkegaard believed, but is concerned with how you, the reader, grapple with your own beliefs in the light of the stimulus to question and explore that Kierkegaard puts forward. Hence, Kierkegaard specifically excludes the idea that there can be disciples of Kierkegaard, a Kierkegaardian system of belief, and hence, Kierkegaard was not a Kierkegaardian. Plato, at least the only Plato we now have access to, is – more so than Kierkegaard – a master of indirect communication, and while a spectrum of speculative Platonisms can be constructed from certain features of his work, it seems that taking his corpus as a whole, it is very hard to discern a single watertight, tied down system of belief (Aristotle may be more of that ilk), and that the point of his dialogical mode of communication is likewise to stimulate the reader to question, think and believe for themselves. Plato, it seems, had very little interest in Platonism.

4 This is Michael Hanby's valuable term. See his *Augustine and Modernity* (London: Routledge, 2003), p. 67.

twentieth-century Europe. He tries to re-create the absence of twentieth-century Western epistemological, metaphysical and theological belief adequacy as a positive existential virtue, and styles this re-creation as a recovery of Presocratic thought. Heidegger thus finds his own historical grounding in Western thought salvageable, via his poetic pre-classical restitutionism. This being the case, Heidegger has a very complex relationship with classical thought.

He maintains a crisis stance of profound inadequacy towards all Western theological and metaphysical traditions from Plato to the present, and yet a continuous interest in what went wrong with that heritage preoccupies him. On the one hand, his crisis stance often makes his interpretation of classical thought hermeneutically incredible;[5] on the other hand, his very philosophically deep speculative analysis of the classical and pre-classical worlds of thought, recontextualized as a medium for his penetrating contribution to twentieth-century thought, makes it impossible simply to dismiss his wild interpretative claims. This complexity is probably why so few serious critical studies of Heidegger's understanding of Plato have been undertaken.[6] Further, such studies are simply not that profitable for Heideggerian scholarship where his reading of Plato is primarily a window onto Heidegger's thought; and such

---

5 Collingwood and Gadamer, for example, come to mind as far more careful interpreters of the meaning of thought in its historical belief context than Heidegger.

6 In *Heidegger and Plato* (Evanston, IL: Northwestern University Press, 2005) editors Catalin Partenie and Tom Rockmore note the obvious fact that 'Heidegger's views of Plato are extremely complex' (p. xix). Further, Partenie and Rockmore note: 'With rare exceptions, Plato scholars are not usually interested in discussing Heidegger's admittedly unorthodox views' (p. xxiv). Yet, there is some penetrating critical work in this area. See Hans-Georg Gadamer, 'Plato', in *Heidegger's Ways*, trans. John W. Stanley (Albany, NY: SUNY Press 1994), pp. 81–94; see Adriaan T. Peperzak, 'Did Heidegger Understand Plato's idea of Truth?' in *Platonic Transformations* (Lanham, MD: Rowman & Littlefield, 1997), pp. 57–112. In terms of the manner in which Heidegger misreads philosophy in the Middle Ages, and hence that era's theological and Christian appropriation of Plato, Sean McGrath's *The Early Heidegger and Medieval Philosophy* (Washington, DC: The Catholic University of America Press, 2006), is outstanding.

studies are also more or less irrelevant to serious classical scholarship on Plato, which has no commitment to Heidegger's distinctive, somewhat a-historical interpretive stance.

For the above reasons, this essay does not enter into a serious engagement with Heidegger regarding his controversial reading of Plato, and does not explore the often fascinating and profound nuances of Heidegger's ontotheological critique; I will take up here only one merit and one failure of Heidegger's ontotheological critique. The merit of ontotheology is its insight into the delusional hubris of all reductively philosophical and distinctly modernist truth constructs. The failure of Heidegger's critique of ontotheology, however, is Heidegger's post/modernist blindness to the role of faith in non-reductively philosophical, non-post/modern, non-secular truth and reality beliefs. This is a critical failure in relation to Plato, for, as I hope to demonstrate, Plato is a deeply religious thinker and his thought is premised on faith. If this can be demonstrated then Plato is of far more interest to us when read in a post-secular context than he is read merely in a postmodern context. Following a post-secular line of interest then, this chapter draws what it finds of use from the concept of ontotheology not directly from Heidegger, but from Merold Westphal's distinctly faith-concerned appropriation of Heidegger's critique of philosophical and theological hubris.

Westphal's appropriation of Heidegger's ontotheological critique is sympathetic to Heidegger, based on strong scholarship, and – unlike Heidegger – very clear in its substantive belief implications. Most importantly for the post-secular stance of this chapter, Westphal's argument is grounded in religious faith. That is, it is an appropriation more able to understand Plato's thought as rising from proto-religious faith than our post-Enlightenment secularistic assumptions about philosophy typically allow.[7]

---

7 Westphal has no interest in Plato in *Overcoming Ontotheology*. Rather, Westphal in this text is interested in showing where the critique of philosophical hubris aligns with Christian doctrine. Yet in his paper 'The Use and Abuse of Metaphysics for the Life of Faith' (read at the University of Nottingham's Centre of Theology and Philosophy's 2nd annual conference, Granada, September 2006), Westphal makes it clear that faith must have an aspect of substantive belief content that is metaphysical, though faith and ontotheology are anathema. Again, his Granada paper makes no

Veritas: Belief and Metaphysics

In *Overcoming Ontotheology*,[8] Westphal convincingly argues that the hermeneutics of human finitude and suspicion underpinning Heidegger's critique of ontotheology, are philosophically very powerful and can be profitably aligned with the Christian doctrines of human createdness and the fall. As creatures, we have no direct access to a God's-eye view of reality; all aspiration to a knowledge of final truth, constructed in terms of purely human framing and limits, are hubristic. As fallen creatures, our fellowship with the divine person who alone can give us truth, is always to some extent incomplete – even where we are caught up in the redemptive and sanctifying grace of God – so any total vision of truth is pretentious, and our fallen capacity for self-deception must be assumed to be at least partially active at all times. Yet, in the broader context of Christian belief, placing no confidence in human truth constructs does not imply that belief in God's powers of revelation are excluded when it comes to true beliefs – be those beliefs about physics or metaphysics. While all human beliefs are indeed constructed in the terms of human history/language/culture and framed by the epistemological limits of our thinking perceptions, such constructs and limits need not imply the absence of truth, but – given divine inspiration – can furnish the grounds for valid working metaphors of truths that are, indeed, in some measure, of Reality.

So the concept of ontotheology I am drawing from Westphal savagely attacks the pretensions of any notion of a divinely unaided grasp of truth, and limits any divinely aided grasp of truth to the realm of partial metaphor, rather than total knowledge capture. This stance holds that the humility of faith is central to any view of truth and reason, but rejects the self-defeating assertion that all views of truth and reason are false.

---

reference to Plato, but the stance, 'oppose philosophical hubris, embrace metaphysical belief by faith' is clear in Westphal, and it is that stance that I apply to Plato in this chapter.

8 Merold Westphal, *Overcoming Ontotheology* (New York: Fordham University Press, 2001).

Plato and the Apophatic and Personalist Tradition of the Greeks

In order to reframe Plato outside of the belief limits of a counter-Enlightenment crisis stance – let us first see if we can think of Plato as a philosopher who is not, in any purely philosophical sense, an idealist.

MacMurray's fascinating work, *Persons in Relation*,[9] links true knowledge to the mode of our existence, the personal mode. In this he is somewhat following the theological vision of Martin Buber,[10] somewhat following Kierkegaard's analysis of the self and of knowledge as relational,[11] and is somewhat followed, in the philosophy and sociology of science, by Michael Polanyi.[12] Truth understood in the existential mode of personhood is 'rational' in the manner that persons as a whole think (i.e. including the logic of human emotion, physicality and spirituality). In this line of thinking, to think of truth in terms of discretely objective empirical knowledge or of supposedly pure intellectual formulations is a hopeless reductionism and simply unreal. This line of thought seeks to recover truth in the mode of the person, and I hope to suggest, Plato was no abstract idealist but was also very aware of the personal mode of human existence and knowledge. Christos Yannaras finds apophatic Greek thought embedded in this personal and humble existential mode, so why should this mode not apply to Plato?

Yannaras states:

> In the case of the Greek philosophical tradition, from Herakleitos up to Gregory Palamas, we may characterise apophaticism as the denial that we can exhaust truth in any formulation, the

---

9 John Macmurray, *Persons in Relation* (London: Faber and Faber, 1961).
10 Martin Buber, *I and Thou* (Edinburgh: T & T Clark, 1937).
11 S. Kierkegaard, *The Sickness Unto Death*, trans. Hong & Hong (Princeton, NJ: Princeton University Press, 1980) and S. Kierkegaard, *Concluding Unscientific Postscript*, trans. Hong & Hong (Princeton, NJ: Princeton University Press, 1992).
12 M. Polanyi, *Personal Knowledge* (Chicago: University of Chicago Press, 1962).

recourse, in other words, to the symbolic-iconological manner of expressing truth, as well as the adoption of the dynamics of *relatedness* (in the sense of the Herakleitean κοινωνειν, i.e., 'being in communion') as the criterion for the verification of knowledge.[13]

If one reads Plato within this apophatic tradition,[14] then one sees both halves of Plato – his doubts and his beliefs – rather than finding hubristic idealism to be what he is really on about and 'Socratic ignorance' either an early phase of Plato's thought, or a mere ruse.[15] That is, it seems reasonable to hold that Plato's approach to truth – both his caution and his belief – can be more easily understood in terms of Greek symbolic-iconological and relational participatory modes of belief, than it can be understood

---

13 Christos Yannaras, *On the Absence and Unknowability of God, Heidegger and the Areopagite* (London: T&T Clark International Ltd, 2005), p. 117.

14 In this work (Yannaras, *On the Absence and Unknowability of God*, 2005, p. 105) Yannaras finds Platonism to be guilty of the idealism Heidegger attributes to it. So Yannaras, it seems, does not situate Plato within this Greek apophaticism, even though he finds apophaticism common to much pre-Socratic and Classical Greek philosophy. Yet, Yannaras's reading of Plato's *eros* as idealism is, I think, debatable, even though Plato obviously has – from the perspective of Christian doctrine – a weak appreciation of matter and flesh as creation, and hence does indeed tend to disembody and intellectualize desire. Yannaras equates Plato's spiritual desire for Beauty with abstract, impersonal idealism based on a reading of *Symposium* 211b7–c9, even though Plato in 212a explains that this desire is the path of (Jowett) 'becom[ing] the friend of God'. So I do not think it is fair of Yannaras to equate Plato's de-sensualized 'love of beauty for its own sake' with some passionless, impersonal, ideal 'love' outside of relational participation in God.

15 With John M. Cooper (ed.) in his introduction to *Plato, Complete Works* (Indianapolis: Hackett, 1997; pp. xii–xviii) I find the interpretative device of a distinct chronology – early, middle and late Plato – to be fraught with difficulties. In reading the entire dialogues as one work I found a profound unity of approach underlying the often sharp differences in 'doctrine' that can be found between and within each dialogue. So no doctrinally discrete chronology, no Plato I, II & III, is assumed in this chapter.

in more recognizably modern, theoretical and reductively rationalistic modes of belief.

While eternal Ideas and the capacity of the human mind to receive some vision of truth from beyond the flux and contingency of our spatio-temporal context *are* central to Plato's philosophy, his mode of belief concerning Ideas and Reality is not aligned with reductively philosophical or recognizably modern idealism.[16]

Is Plato, in Westphal's Terms, an Ontotheologian?

Plato is, of course, no Christian. But for his work to escape Westphal's Christian critique of ontotheology, it needs to demonstrate a proper appreciation of human finitude and be appropriately suspicious of the innate purity and goodness of human reason.

Plato and human finitude

In keeping with the mode of human existence, Plato pursues wisdom via a carefully calibrated integration of the transcendent with the immanent. This delicate and complex double move is characteristic of all of his dialogues. If one seeks to distil the transcendent kernel from the dramatic, immanent contextual husk in Plato, he appears to be the archetypal hubristic ontotheologian. And yet, if one only focuses on the immanent in Plato, his transcendent oracles appear as mere unsubstantiated fancy, and the contingent specificity of context alone grounds his work. Both of these views are one-eyed. Plato writes synoptically, and the vision of truth he offers has the outer eye grounded in the immanent and the inner eye probing the transcendent; the resultant combination of the inner and the outer, the visible and the invisible, the tangible and the intangible, is the 'view' he seeks to communicate. The transcendent cannot be reduced to the immanent, and yet, we can

---

16 See S. Gersh and D. Moran (eds), *Eriugena, Berkeley and the Idealist Tradition* (Notre Dame, IN: University of Notre Dame Press, 2006) for some refreshingly careful distinctions on a range of very different belief stances commonly lumped together under the heading 'idealist'.

only seek to grasp and articulate what the transcendent is in terms of our immanent context, a context not, in its own terms, suited to this aim. Plato sits with this uneasy tension and never tries reductively to resolve this tension. So while he does indeed favour the permanent reality of the transcendent over the transitory expressions of that reality in the immanent, he never tries to articulate the transcendent without reference to the limitations of the immanent.

After the cultural dominance of the totalizing and reductive metanarrative of rationalistic and objective scientific truth, grounded in epistemological subjectivism, and authorized by modern secular philosophy,[17] we have become accustomed to viewing Plato though our own reductive, egocentric and totalizing assumptions about truth. But this is our error, not Plato's. We have become so accustomed to reading Plato as a rigidly dogmatic idealist, that we miss the extent to which he couches all of his propositions in pseudonyms, in metaphors, in poetic myth, in the terms of humble and dependent religious devotion, in spiritual eroticism and in 'Socratic' irresolution. We do not even notice that Plato's voice only comes to us via the suggestive, specifically contextualized, personalized, temporally defined, open-ended drama of the everyday.

The banquet in *Symposium*, for example, reveals Plato's literary genius. Plato revels in sensitive dramatic descriptions of the particular specificities of character, time and place. But this context is no mere backdrop for the dialogue, but rather, delight in company and in the pleasures and desires of body and mind shared in the banquet reflect the themes of conviviality, passionate searching and inebriated disappointment that drives the religious love quest of philosophy itself through the dialogue. This synoptic mode of communication – immanently grounded and transcendently concerned – fails if one only sees the 'philosophical' point of the dialogue, or only revels in the literary genius of its particular culturo-historical construction.

In *Theaetetus*, the mind grasps, by a mysterious power of her own, intellectual truth,[18] but this truth is not a product of the

---

17 See J-F. Lyotard, *The Postmodern Condition* (Minneapolis: University of Minnesota Press, 1979).

18 Plato, *Theaetetus*, 185, trans. Benjamin Jowett, 3rd edition, *The*

human mind, and is not – remember the sun in the cave metaphor[19] – containable by the human mind in any thing more than mere shadows or poor reflections, but is from *beyond* the human mind. In *Meno*, the human mind must have some affinity with divinity and have some derivative or pre-existent participatory association with *Nous* in order to have the ability to grasp truth at all,[20] but this in no manner gives human *nous* the grasp of Truth that the divine *Nous* both has and generates. Epistemological humility, as in *Theaetetus*, is seen here in Plato as expressly unable to identify how the mind grasps genuinely intellectual truths, and in truth itself not being a product of the human mind. Further – as diagrammatically demonstrated in *Meno* – while the human mind grasps universal mathematical truths, yet this truth is only expressible by the human mind in concrete examples tied to the realm of contingence, transience and flux in which we live. That is, the pure reality of eternal and unchanging truth is always only expressible by us via the terms of the imperfect realm in which we live. Truth itself is never fully revealed to us via those specific and temporal modes of conceptual mediation in which we must know 'our' own

---

Dialogues of Plato (Oxford: Oxford University Press, 1892) ('Jowett' hereafter): [Theaetetus] '. . . the mind, by a power of her own, contemplates the universal in all things.'

19 Plato, *Republic*, Book VII, 516, Jowett: 'Last of all, he will be able to see the sun . . .' After a long process of spiritual growth, the seeker after truth can move from giving first attention to the shadows of truth cast by our temporally bound perceptions, to an indistinct vision of the real things (not visible in perceptual shadows themselves) that cause those shadows. From here the quest moves to seeing real things more clearly by the light reflected from them, and from there to a search for the source of light itself. It is clear from *Phaedo* that Plato does not envision the higher quests of truth to be possible to mortal men, but that our challenge in this brief life is to get as good a start on the eternal road to truth as we can manage.

Critically, the light of intellectual truth is not generated in the human mind for Plato; rather the glory of the human mind is its potential to absorb and to some measure reflect that intellectual light of truth, in which all perfection is found. Perfection is only in immortal reality, and beyond that, in the light itself, and is not found in any human reflection of truth, and is certainly not contained within the human mind for Plato.

20 Plato, *Meno*, 82, Jowett: '. . . there is no teaching, but only recollection.' Plato, *Meno*, 86, Jowett: 'And if the truth of all things always existed in the soul, then the soul is immortal.'

thoughts. Truth itself remains essentially beyond conceptual grasp, essentially not egoistically ours, and our approach to its understanding – for we understand only as a result of the self-giving relationship divinely initiated between us and the divine – remains essentially unknowable in Plato.[21] He attempts to give us no humanly and temporally defined epistemological certainties and for this reason he totally escapes the critique of epistemologically foundationalist, egocentric, totalizing hubris assumed in secular scientific and philosophical reason that Lyotard finds – in my view validly – so profoundly inadequate. Plato has no ontotheological methodology in relation to how we know truth, and makes no claims to have a humanly expressible complete and certain knowledge of truth.

Plato affirms that we need a symbolic-iconological vision of reality cast beyond the necessary limits of our culturo-sensory knowledge in order to take belief seriously, but we cannot let go of the fact that our attempts to conceptually describe such a vision is not reality. It is a source of constant surprise that Plato's clear grasp of both our need for a metaphorical vision of reality, and the fact that our metaphorical vision is not reality, is not obvious to all his readers. The cave metaphor is, expressly, a metaphor.[22] It is

---

21 Yet, this is, using Yannaras's terminology, a Greek 'apophaticism of the person', not a Western rationalistic 'apophaticism of essence' (*On the Absence and Unknowability of God*, p. 29). The interpersonal knowledge, the love of friends, is never a total knowledge about the person – the essence of any person is beyond human knowledge – but this knowledge through personal energies is the knowledge of love, and this is the deepest and truest knowledge. Plato, in worshipful contemplation, knows the divine Good as Mind (Person), in the terms of love, and this is not terms that can ever be conceptually sounded out – not even between ordinary people – by theoretical or rational or scientific knowledge. Henri Crouzel describes Origen's epistemology, fully within this Greek tradition, saying 'knowledge is for him the same thing as union and love.' (Crouzel, *Origen*, Edinburgh: T & T Clark, 1989, p. 99).

22 Plato, *Republic*, Book VII, 517, Jowett: '[I have expressed the meaning of] this entire allegory ... according to my poor belief ... whether rightly or wrongly God knows.' The same passage in Plato, *Republic*, trans. Desmond Lee, 2nd edition (Harmondsworth: Penguin, 1974): '[regarding] this simile ... the truth of the matter is, after all, known only to god.'

Plato's feeble attempt to articulate his vision of reality. Plato's forms are allegorical. Does every tiny hair, Plato asks, have its perfect eternal form?[23] In *Parmenides* Plato marshals powerful arguments that warn against taking Plato's own theory of forms too literally. Plato recognizes where his metaphors break down. This does not negate the appropriateness of metaphor itself for Plato's purposes, but the difficulties that lead to the end of medieval realism seem largely the result of mistakenly treating Plato's religious metaphors as if they were intended as doctrinal certainties, or scientific theories, or strict logical treatise. Seeing universals – after Abelard's logic – as mere manners of speaking is to reduce the spiritually suggestive metaphors of universality and unchangeability beyond particularity and change, to a simple logical conundrum. It is to seek to define universality and unchangeability within the terms of particularity and change, and then to think one has achieved something profound by showing that such things are impossible. Such reductionism misses Plato's point about eternal forms entirely.[24]

---

23 Plato, *Parmenides*, 130 c,d, John M. Cooper (ed.), *Plato, Complete Works* ('Cooper' hereafter):

[Parmenides asks] 'And what about these, Socrates? Things that might seem absurd, like hair and mud and dirt, or anything else totally undignified and worthless? Are you doubtful or not whether you should say that a form is separate for each of these too, which in turn is other than anything we touch with our hands?'

'Not at all', Socrates answered. 'On the contrary, these things are in fact just what we see. Surely it is too outlandish to think there is a form for them. Not that the thought that the same thing might hold in all cases hasn't troubled me from time to time.'

Plato goes on to chide Socrates through Parmenides that in distinguishing between the dignified and the undignified the young Socrates is influenced not by philosophy but by the opinions of others. Even so, it seems clear that the spiritually upward drawing and unchangeable intellectual nature of divine form itself is not meant by Plato to give us a detailed explanation of empirical observations. His interest in form is more religious than scientific.

24 See Peter King, 'The Metaphysics of Peter Abelard', in Jeffrey Brower and Kevin Guilfoy (eds), *The Cambridge Companion to Abelard* (Cambridge: Cambridge University Press, 2004), pp. 65–125. In no manner do I mean to suggest that Abelard is anything other than one of

Veritas: Belief and Metaphysics

Plato and human fallenness

Plato's metaphysical analogies are deeply religiously premised, and deeply sceptical of human nature, as exemplified in *Apology*. Socrates is in trouble with the Athenians *because* he finds human wisdom worthless, but also seeks to serve divine wisdom.[25] The terms of human wisdom look solid and concretely grounded on first contact, but Plato's Socrates finds they are in fact delusional, and so generally accepted human authority, morality and dignity are harmless veneers in humble and charitable people, but the masks of oppression and evil in the proud, the ruthless and the self-interested. However, Socrates does not abandon wisdom because of this, but serves the god of wisdom in all the difficult to grasp, socially embarrassing, morally troubling and politically confronting pathways down which a devotion to divine truth leads one. It is the call to humility before divinity, and the subversive suspicion of all human knowledge and power constructs that an admiring Plato rightly discerns positions Socrates as a dangerous opponent of the Athenian status quo.

So, if we understand ontotheology, through the lens of the

---

the most innovative and brilliant thinkers of Western culture. However, the unhooking of Aristotelian logic from Platonistic participation, and the unhooking of language from participation in reality (and the resultant reduction of language to self-contained logical and conceptual games) can be traced, in the West, to Abelard's highly sophisticated nominalist irrealism. This move totally redefines classical and Augustinian logic in such a manner to make that logic look stupid. But it is the redefinition of Augustinian participation to operate within a non-Platonist, non-participatory view of Aristotelian logic that makes medieval realism look stupid, not Augustinian participation itself.

25 Plato, *Apology*, 23 a,b, in *Plato, The Last Days of Socrates*, Hugh Tredennick (Harmondsworth: Penguin, 1969): 'But the truth of the matter, gentlemen, is pretty certainly this: that real wisdom is the property of God, and . . . that human wisdom has little or no value. . . . when I think that any person is not wise, I try to help the cause of God by proving that he is not . . . [thus] my service to God has reduced me to extreme poverty [and public odium].' {Same translation, *Apology*, 29d}: 'Gentlemen, I am your very grateful and devoted servant, but I owe a greater obedience to God than to you.' {Same translation, *Apology*, 39b}: 'When I leave this court I shall go away condemned by you to death, but they will go away convicted by Truth herself of depravity and wickedness.'

Plato against Ontotheology

Christian doctrines of creation and the fall, as the presumption of a total grasp of truth by human knowledge, and as the assumption of the intrinsic intellectual goodness of humanity, then Plato is no ontotheologian.

If the case for Plato and his metaphysics being opposed to ontotheology is strong, then it has some interesting implications for us in our typically post-counter-Enlightenment metaphysical unbelief context. I would like to touch on these implications below.

A Skeletal Christian and Platonistic Critique of the Critique of Ontotheology

Westphal points out that the hermeneutics of finitude and suspicion characteristic of Heidegger's critique of ontotheology are powerful and much needed negative tools that echo the negative side – the humble appreciation of human limitations – of the theologies of creation and fall. However, unlike these Christian theologies, the hermeneutics of finitude and suspicion have no positive side – no view of Divine unlimitedness or human redemption – and therein is their fatal weakness. If all one has is finitude and suspicion, then all limited truth claims within the bounds of finitude and suspicion are mere assertions that must be undercut by their own hermeneutic. And indeed, the complex aesthetic linguistic games of the postmodern masters of textual manipulation revel in this double undercutting of not only their epistemologically naïve totalizing opponents, but of themselves as critics too. Maybe the Presocratic sophists are back. But if this is indeed the case, then Plato, slayer of Presocratic sophism, may yet prove to have some of the best positive responses to the vacuum of serious belief generated by postmodernism that we are likely to find.

On the negative side, Plato believes that we can have no conceptual truth in any final or total sense, but on the positive side, Plato equally believes that unless we *believe* that the person of divine truth (*Nous*) can grasp us, we should abandon the very idea of reason.[26] For this reason, he finds that the sophists are in the end,

---

26 See *Phaedo* 65–66 in conjunction with *Phaedo* 97–100. *Phaedo* 65–66 describes how the senses can give no truth, so the soul must rely on

just not serious thinkers. They are linguistic game players.[27] Plato

---

the mind alone for truth when seeking knowledge of those transcendent glories such as absolute beauty and absolute good. Our earthbound epistemological powers cannot be believed in relation to truth, and hence truth cannot be proven in terms of our natural epistemological powers. In 97–100 Socrates explores Anaxagoras' conception of the ontic and cosmological primacy of Mind with great and hungry interest, but is disappointed by Anaxagoras' inability to give persuasive accounts of the goodness and meaning of why all things – as the product of purposeful, good, rational Mind – are. That is, Anaxagoras cannot make good on his claim to demonstrate the rational, moral and aesthetic meaning of everything that is created by Mind. But, as Plato sees mind as the essence of the soul (personhood), Plato seeks this person beyond all appearance whose intelligence is distantly communicated in all Plato experiences. Putting the two cited passages together we may say that Plato believes that someone akin to Anaxagoras' Mind must indeed be the source of all that is – and this gives our minds whatever powers of reason we do have, and links reason deeply to personhood – but there can be no proof for this belief that is constructed in terms demonstrable to the senses, or contained by merely human conceptual logic. Hence, Greek apophaticism is present here; true essence is inexpressible in human speech, only iconic symbols of truth can be communicated by human language. Yet, unless one assumes that truth beyond the transitory, contingent and often meaningless world revealed via normal perception exists, reason (logos) – the human minds derivative intellectual kinship with Mind – is mere illusion too. A tacit participation of our mind in Mind, that cannot be proven or even expressed in the terms of the perceptual manifold and spatio-temporal existence, is everywhere assumed in Plato. Plato assumes that truth beyond our mind, in some measure, grasps our mind directly. This assumption is more explicit in the Neoplatonists and then Augustine – where the Christian terms of faith, belief and God easily take over from intellectual apprehension, reason and Mind – but the commonality between these different sets of terminology is in no manner forced.

27 Plato, *Sophist*, Cooper, 231d: '[The sophist is] an athlete in verbal combat, distinguished in his expertise in debating.' Plato, *Sophist*, Cooper, 233d: 'the sophist has now appeared as having a kind of belief knowledge about everything, but not truth.' Plato, *Sophist*, Jowett, 268c,d: 'He, then, who traces the pedigree of his art as follows – who belonging to the conscious or dissembling section of the art of causing self contradiction, is an imitator of appearance, and is separated from the class of phantastic which is a branch of image making into that further division of creation, the juggling of words, a creation human, and not divine – any one who affirms the real Sophist to be of this blood and lineage will say the very truth.'

Plato against Ontotheology

does not answer a fool according to his folly, so while he can be as playful as the most able dialectician (and indulges in showing this facility off from time to time), his advice is let the players play, and let those who take reason seriously have faith.[28] If we tried answering the positive belief void of postmodernism in this manner today, we would find humble religious metaphysics may indeed give us a philosophical renaissance that could make serious belief itself, worth doing again. And since it is very unlikely that consumerist irrealism will give people anything worth believing,[29] and since it is very unlikely that people can, in the long run, get on without serious belief,[30] such a renaissance may be sorely needed.

So ontotheology as the tacit absolutizing of finitude and a totalizing of suspicion to the exclusion of belief (relational adherence) in the divine person of truth, beyond human conceptual grasping, stands in direct opposition to reason itself in Plato. Plato's balance between scepticism towards human reason and participatory trust in divine revelation is necessary for any meaningful belief in truth itself, and it is this balance that makes Plato so easy to appropriate in Christian classical and medieval contemplation. Historically, we are now enough out of the shadow of the Enlightenment to understand the nature of our loss of this Christian Platonist tradition quite clearly. A post-secular understanding of how viable this lost tradition still is, is now emerging.

---

28 For example, when Plato argues like this: (*Phaedo*, 100b, Jowett) 'assume that there is an absolute beauty and goodness and greatness, and the like: grant me this, and I hope to be able to show you the nature of the cause, and to prove the immortality of the soul' – his 'proof' relies entirely on the willingness of his interlocutor to have the passionate existential personal interestedness in that which cannot be scientifically or logically demonstrated; this Kierkegaard calls faith. (See S. Kierkegaard, *Concluding Unscientific Postscript*.) There is an existential leap of trust involved in serious belief formation, that cannot be avoided, and it is the failure of the sophists to have that existential belief courage that renders them unable to take any belief, or truth itself, seriously. Reason – as anything other than a sophistic and political manipulative game – depends on faith so understood.

29 See Harry G. Frankfurt, *On Bullshit* (Princeton, NJ: Princeton University Press, 2005).

30 See Peter L. Berger, *Facing Up To Modernity* (Harmondsworth: Penguin, 1977).

Veritas: Belief and Metaphysics

A Very Quick Sketch of the Faithless Genealogy of Metaphysical Unbelief

Paul Tillich notes a profound historical shift – started with Abelard and locked down with William of Ockham – in the philosophy of religion underpinning Western culture.[31] It is the shift away from an ontological participatory understanding of religious belief, and to a cosmological and nominalistic understanding of religious belief. The return of Aristotle to the West at the same time that medieval realism was fading, gave self contained human logic and perception dependent observation unprecedented belief formation powers. It is here that the 'idea' of God first becomes a plaything of secular philosophical speculation, of secular scientific models, and of rationalistic and systematic theology. Here is where modern religious unbelief and the inevitable collapse of any meaningful metaphysical vision starts. Milbank makes a parallel argument in finding secular Western reason to be a nominalist Christian heresy that cannot fail to produce the collapse of both faith and reason in Western culture.[32] Thus the origin of truth shifts away from God and comes to reside in the mind of Man.[33]

It is strange how we tend to think of the end of Ptolemaic astronomy as replacing an anthropocentric cosmology with a radically decentred cosmology, when in fact, it is the replacement of a theocentric cosmology with a profoundly anthropocentric, nay, egocentric, cosmology that this cosmological belief-shift to modernity

---

31 Paul Tillich, 'The Two Types of Philosophy of Religion', in *Theology of Culture* (Oxford: Oxford University Press, 1964), pp. 10–29.

32 John Milbank, *Theology and Social Theory* (Oxford: Blackwell, 1990).

33 'Man', in the generic symbolic sense of the word, is sexually inclusive, and yet, as I am using it, it does have distinctly 'masculine' connotations. Those connotations – inherent in Ockham's proto-modern idea of dominion – are intended here to convey the voluntarist, dominating, autistic, hubris that fallen humanity in general is sadly prone to (outstanding examples of this can be found among both men and women). I prefer to think of humanity as feminine – as the Bride of Christ, for instance – as this portrays a redemptive love-centric outlook, responsiveness to the divine, and an inherently relational mode of human existence (outstanding examples of this can be found among both women and men).

signifies. Descartes' only solid foundation of belief is the existence of his own ego, and hence the explicitly human faculties of thought and perception, referenced to nothing outside of one's own ego's knowledge limitations,[34] becomes the horizon of human meaning within which Kant must work. The West has never been more anthropocentric, and it is this modern egocentricism that makes the pragmatic consumer irrealism of hypermodernism work for us. Self-worship, self-indulgence, self-constructed and commodified identities – these are the natural cultural outcomes of our modern egocentric cosmology.[35]

Before this nominalist egoism, Plato's faith in Divine Mind as the transcendent source of all meaning and truth that human minds can – iconologically – apprehend, gives rise to Aristotle's natural science and universal logic. Because Plato's faith in timelessly true, yet temporally and metaphorically revealing *Nous* has defeated the endlessly non-valent imaginative games of Presocratic sophistry, serious human reason is able to take off. Ironically, it seems that the great successes of nominalistic Aristotelian[36] reason and observation since William of Ockham, have led to hubris and a cutting off of reason from the essentially religious grounds in which it sits, and this returns us quite neatly to a sophistic frivolity towards reason and reality itself. So, far from science and faith, or religion and reason being polar opposites, the real opposition is between faith, reason and science on the one hand, and dogmatic doubt, secular Man, and sheer meaningless irreason on the other hand. It is only the strange desire to either separate or integrate nominalist Christian supernaturalism with secular scientific naturalism that makes faith and reason look opposed. Metaphysics, after Plato's model, as a humbly held, religiously received belief framework in which both the transcendent and the immanent are

---

34 Note: Yannaras, *On the Absence and Unknowability of God*, 2005, p. 24. 'Descartes . . . instituted the subject as the absolute determinative source of all knowledge and being, and subjected God to absolutized man . . .'

35 Christopher Lasch, *The Culture of Narcissism* (London: Norton, 1991).

36 See Llody P. Gerson, *Aristotle and Other Platonists* (Ithaca, NY: Cornell University Press, 2005) for a persuasive case that a non-Platonist (i.e. nominalistic) reading of Aristotle is a faulty reading.

synoptically united, alone seems to give human belief any true reason and meaning. Plato's metaphysical attitude may be well suited to the most pressing needs for meaningful belief in our times.

Conclusion

In this essay I have sought to demonstrate two things: first, that Plato can be validly read in sympathy with an ontotheological critique of modernist secular truth; second, that Plato's proto-religious metaphysical stance is not touched by the critique of truth and reality that falls out of the counter-Enlightenment 'disenchantment of reason'.[37]

If this case is strong, it has some striking implications for the importance of the contemporary study of Plato in our post-secular context, and for a renewed level of interest in the metaphysical tradition of the doxo-ontological appropriation of Plato by Christian classical and medieval thinkers. Maybe – via Plato's humble, iconological and participatory belief mode – we can still have meaningful beliefs about truth and reality; and maybe – as Plato suggests – we need to believe in divinely revealed meaningful reality in order to be distinctly human and, at least aspirationally, reasonable.[38]

---

37 I have borrowed this evocative phrase from the title of Paul Harrison's fascinating work on the nineteenth-century treatment of Socrates by Hegel, Kierkegaard and Nietzsche. See Paul Harrison, *The Disenchantment of Reason* (Albany, NY: SUNY Press, 1995).

38 Plato, *Phaedo*, Jowett, 90e: 'Let us . . . be careful of admitting into our souls the notion that there is no truth or health or soundness in any argument at all; but let us rather say that there is as yet no health in us . . .'

18. Lacan, Metaphysics and Belief

MARCUS POUND

What is the status of metaphysics and belief for the French psychoanalyst Jacques Lacan? In this chapter, I explore, first, Lacan's thought regarding metaphysics, his distrust of ontotheology, and the consequent impact upon the direction of treatment. Second, I consider the way Christian belief operates within his work.[1] I contend that Lacan cannot escape the logic of his own argument that we are born into existing and determinative symbolic structures, and as such his unconscious desire has been profoundly shaped by the wider biblical narrative. What transpires is that Lacan's distrust of metaphysics is co-extensive with a far more intense identification with Christ and Christianity, and for this reason Lacan's work constitutes an 'inherent transgression', an overstepping which reinforces the very thing it opposes. I shall begin by exploring Lacan's views on God and metaphysics.

Metaphysics

For Lacan, the fundamental metaphysical gesture occurs when one allows a part to function for the whole. In other words, when one term is elevated above all others, becoming the fundamental deadlock such that if it were to be unlocked, all other terms in the field of reference would lose their meaning. Like the madman in Nietzsche's *The Gay Science* who observes, 'we have drunk up the

---

[1] This topic has been ably treated by Slavoj Žižek, *On Belief* (London: Routledge, 2001).

sea and wiped away the entire horizon, unchaining the earth from its sun',[2] Lacan sums up his own position regarding the status of metaphysics in his enigmatic claim: 'there is no Other of the Other'. That is to say, there is no external legislative authority that secures the system as a whole. Indeed, in his seminar on *The Names-of-the-Father*, Lacan refuses outright the God of onto-theology, the *causa sui* which sustains being as a whole: 'That God affirms himself as identical to Being leads to pure absurdity.'[3] God is simply the idea of an uncastrated and perfect being, the condition of desire, an imaginary projection of wholeness, retroactively posited to make sense of a beginning that is by definition too traumatic to represent.

Where then does this leave the goals of psychoanalysis, which Lacan calls 'traversing the *fantasme*'? What is at stake is not so much being reconciled to castration – in other words, recognizing that we cannot be the object of desire for the mother – but rather, through an anxiety-provoking encounter with immanence, coming to recognize the non-existence of the Other. That is to say: recognize that the big Other through which we organize desire does not actually exist.

As the indefatigable Larval-Subject puts it:

> The concept of immanence is ultimately very simple, yet it proves very difficult to accept in its implications. To affirm immanence is to affirm that the world is sufficient unto itself, that we need not refer to anything outside of the world to explain the world such as forms, essences, or God, that the world contains its own principles of genesis.[4]

But why precisely should it prove so traumatic? By way of a

---

2 Nietzsche, *The Gay Science*, trans. By J. Nauckhoff (Cambridge: Cambridge University Press, 2001), pp. 119–120. I thank Larval-Subject whose blog has been a constant source of clarity. http://larval-subjects.blogspot.com/2006_01_larval-subjects_archive.html

3 Jacques Lacan, *Television: A Challenge to the Psychoanalytic Establishment*, trans. J. Mehlman, ed. J. Copjec (New York & London: W. W. Norton & Company, 1990), p. 85.

4 http://larval-subjects.blogspot.com/2006_01_larval-subjects_archive.html

thought experiment, consider the horrors of the Nazi regime. To accept that the executioners of the final solution were touched by a radical evil, as if it were a substantially present thing in those men and women, is relatively easy. What is far more unsettling is Hannah Arendt's thesis concerning the banality of evil: the perpetrators of the Nazi crimes were in fact ordinary people like you or me. In other words, the principle trauma we experience is not to be located in some occluded or dark source exterior to ourselves; rather, it is the possibility that there is no cause; we are our own immanent executioners.

To clarify the above, one should recognize two points regarding immanence. First, to speak of immanence in this way is to speak of relations, and whether in our dealings we primarily relate *to* something, remaining distinct as subject (that is, relations of transcendence); or *in* something (that is, immanent relations). To affirm the latter is to affirm the 'alreadyness' from which we speak, that we are already always begun, or what Heidegger referred to as the 'givenness' of *Dasein*. And this constitutes Lacan's major thesis of the 1950s – the period in which he was reading Heidegger and Lévi-Strauss – that we are born into an existing language or symbolic structure, a circuit which can determine in advance our desires, actions, or motivations such that 'it is perhaps only our unawareness of their permanence that allows us to believe in freedom of choice'.[5] Lacan concedes that 'Man speaks' but only because 'the symbol has made him man'.[6]

For this very reason Lacan, affirmed *and* gave novel expression to the doctrine of hereditary sin. As he says:

> the unconscious is the discourse of the other ... Not the discourse of the abstract other ... it is the discourse of my father for instance, in so far as my father made mistakes which I am absolutely condemned to repeat ... because I am obliged to pick up again the discourse he bequeathed to me, not simply because I am his son, but because one cannot stop the chain of discourse.[7]

---

5 Lacan, *Écrits*, trans. Bruce Fink (New York and London: W. W. Norton, 2006), p. 229.

6 Lacan, *Écrits*, p. 229.

7 Lacan, *The Seminar of Jacques Lacan, II: The Ego in Freud's Theory and in the Technique of Psychoanalysis, 1954–1955*, edited by Jacques-

In other words, to affirm the doctrine of hereditary sin is to affirm precisely the thought from which metaphysics flees: we are already begun. As Gillian Rose has suggested, it is possible to see here the beginnings of anxiety, because anxiety is precisely that which flees from beginnings, choosing instead a mythical past to retreat into, or precedence in, a previous experience to be repeated, rather than confront the possibility that, despite intention, we will fail in our actions, fall prey to unconscious desire, make mistakes, repeat the sins of the father, precisely because we cannot extricate ourselves from the wider cultural discourse.[8]

Second, as a corollary of the above, it follows that to affirm immanence is to state something specific about the self: one cannot be self-possessed; we cannot own ourselves. This was the basis of Lacan's tireless critique of ego-psychologists. Early interpreters of Sigmund Freud, such as his daughter Anna, Harry Guntrip or Heinz Hartmann, all argued that the self was in origin a bundle of self-seeking drives, the primary expression of nature, a chaos which needed to be brought into social conformity through the rationalizing principle of the ego.[9] Hence when Freud said *Wo es war, soll Ich werden* [Where it was, I shall become]', these ego-psychologists took it to imply the imperialism of the ego: 'Where the id was, there the ego shall be',[10] or 'the ego must dislodge the id'.[11] In other words, the aim of analysis was to develop strong fortifications against the anarchy of the drives, thereby securing the autonomy of the ego.[12]

Alain Miller and translated by Sylvana Tomaselli (London & New York: W. W. Norton & Company, 1991), p. 89.

8 Gillian Rose, *The Broken Middle: Out of Our Ancient Society* (Oxford: Basil Blackwell, 1992), p. 85.

9 For a brief overview of Ego-psychology, see Harold P. Blum 'Ego-Psychology and Contemporary structural theory', *International Psychoanalysis*, 2 (1998), available online at: http://www.ipa.org.uk/newsletter/98-2/blum1.htm; David Rapaport, 'A Historical Survey of Psychoanalytic Ego-Psychology', *Psychological Issues*, 1.1 (1959), pp. 5–17.

10 Lacan, *Écrits*, p. 247.

11 Lacan, *The Seminar of Jacques Lacan, XI: The Four Fundamental Concepts of Psycho-analysis*, (1964), edited by Jacques-Alain Miller and translated by Alan Sheridan (London: Vintage, 1977), p. 44.

12 Lacan, *Écrits*, p. 347; Lacan, *The Seminar, XI*, p. 44.

David Macey has suggested that this interpretation was motivated by the Jewish experience of totalitarianism. For example, Bruno Bettelheim, a survivor of Dachau, writes,

> If the author [Bettelheim] should be asked to sum up in one sentence what, during all the time he spent in the camp, was his main problem, he would say: *to safeguard his ego in such a way that, if by any luck he regain liberty, he would be approximately the same person he was when deprived of liberty.*[13]

But arguably a stronger incentive was the more general climate of political liberalism that grew out of Thomas Hobbes. In other words Freud was read as a kind of psychological supplement to support the existing political project of liberalism which placed such a high regard on autonomy. For example, like Hobbes, man passes from nature to society through a contractual agreement; only now the ban is explicitly directed towards the sexual relation. Ego-psychology was therefore a profoundly conservative project aimed at helping the subject adjust to a reality defined in advance by a wider secular and political programme.

In Lacan's work, by contrast, the ego is understood principally as an alienating structure (albeit an essential one), and emphasis falls on *Das Es*. What is at stake in Lacan's revision is not the usual argument that to cling too tightly to false images of unity is to encourage the excesses of totalitarianism, but that we *never* possessed such unity in the first place, and hence we can *never* escape the unconscious play of language returning in dreams and slips of the tongue. For this reason Lacan takes Freud to be saying '*Here, in the field of the dream, you are at home*'.[14] In other words, we do not and cannot possess our-selves in the manner of the autonomous liberal individual; we exist, in the 'equivocation of the middle', already begun.[15] And this makes beginning or assuming agency traumatic, because any beginning can only ever be a

---

13 Bruno Bettelheim, *Surviving the Holocaust* (London: Flamingo, 1986), p. 74, quoted in David Macey, *Lacan in Contexts* (London: Verso, 1988), p. 276 n. 165.
14 Lacan, *Seminar, XI*, p. 44.
15 Rose, *The Broken Middle*, p. 85.

Veritas: Belief and Metaphysics

temporary arresting of the flow of signs, a violent imposition. Neurosis is therefore any thought which tries to get rid of the difficulties of beginning or thinking from the equivocal middle.

How then should we approach Lacan's most direct statement against religion? Speaking on the relations between religion and psychoanalysis, he says:

> [they] are not very amicable. In sum, it is either one or the other. If religion triumphs as is most probable – I speak of the true religion and there is only one which is true [i.e. Roman Catholicism] – if religion triumphs, this will be the sign that psychoanalysis has failed.[16]

Why does Lacan think that religion will triumph over psychoanalysis? Because religion is 'capable of giving a meaning, one can say, to anything at all – a meaning to human life for example'.[17] Yet meaning implies unity, and the singular feature of the unconscious is discontinuity. This is the form in which it (*Das Es*) appears: a forgotten word or a slip of the tongue, a bungled action or break in the normal flow of speech, or what Freud called the *parapraxis*.[18]

No wonder Lacan was wary of religion: to posit God as the *causa sui* risks 'drowning'[19] life in meaning. It would, as William Richardson says, close the chain of signification in upon a centre that would hold the signifier and signified together to become the absolute foundation of meaning.[20] And this is why Lacan says that the true formula of atheism is not God is dead, but '*God is uncon-*

---

16 William Richardson, 'Psychoanalysis and the God Question', *Thought*, 240 (1986), pp. 68–83, at p. 75. From Lacan, 'Conference de Presse du Dr Lacan', *Lettres de l'Ecole Freudienne* (Bulletin interieur de l'Ecole Freudienne de Paris, 1974).

17 Richardson, 'Psychoanalysis and the God Question', p. 75.

18 'Act whose explicit goal is not attained; instead this goal turns out to have been replaced by another one.' Jean Laplanche, and Jean-Bertrand Pontalis, *The Language of Psychoanalysis* (London: Karnac, 1988), p. 300.

19 W. Richardson, '"Like Straw": Religion and Psychoanalysis', in *The Letter: Lacanian Perspectives on Psychoanalysis* 11 (1997), pp. 1–15, at p. 12.

20 Richardson, '"Like Straw"', p. 11.

scious'.[21] In other words, to affirm the death of God is to affirm the slippage of meaning and the role of unconscious desire in shaping our actions; it is to affirm that we find our gods too easily.

At this point a pressing concern arises. What remains of ethics and politics? After all, the cultural exigency in which Greek metaphysics first developed was the necessity of a secure ground for political concepts of justice. Hence in the *Meno*, Plato's teaching concerning the eternity or transmigration of the soul arises out of a discussion of the virtues. Metaphysics was therefore concerned with the actuality of political struggle and hence ethical action was principally understood in terms of agency, an agency seemingly undermined by Lacan.

One response is to adopt what I call a sentimental or romantic reading of Lacan, as exemplified by Mark C. Taylor or Charles Winquist.[22] These theologians herald the end of metaphysics as an end to an age of mastery. They read Lacan in terms of the apophatic tradition, a 'mystical *a*/theology' which prompts a constant process of decentring, releasing both God and ourselves from the clutches of concepts.[23] And herein lays the thrust of its ethics: ethics concerns the experience of alterity; the recognition that all our saying is also a non-saying, and this becomes the basis of an ethical relation to the other, a sort of letting others be in their otherness. The trouble with this approach is, as Gillian Rose has argued, that alterity can easily slip over into *absolute* alterity, giving way to the crippling anxiety of what one is to be before this absolute Other.[24] In such circumstances, act gives way to indecision and a barrier is

---

21 J. Lacan, *Four Fundamental Concepts of Psychoanalysis* (London: Vintage, 1998), p. 59.

22 See Mark C. Taylor, 'Refusal of the Bar', and Charles Winquist, 'Lacan and Theological Discourse', in Edith Wsychodgrod, David Crownfield and Carl Raschke (eds), *Lacan and Theological Discourse* (Albany: SUNY, 1989), pp. 39–58, 26–38.

23 Catherine Clément, *The Lives and Legends of Jacques Lacan*, trans. Arthur Goldhammer (New York: Columbia University Press, 1983), p. 144, quoted in Elizabeth A. Castelli, Stephen Moore, Gary A. Phillips and Regina M. Schwartz (eds), *The Postmodern Bible* (New Haven & London: Yale University Press, 1995), p. 209.

24 Gillian Rose, *Judaism and Modernity: Philosophical Essays* (Oxford: OUP, 1993), p. 8.

erected which paradoxically absolves us of having any relation to the Other.

But this was certainly not how Freud initially understood psychoanalysis. As Elizabeth Danto has recently argued, far from being a prudish Victorian practising in the closeted world of the female bourgeoisie, Freud was a modernist reformer, a social activist caught up in the social democratic movement sweeping across Europe in the wake of World War One; and the newly discovered psychoanalysis was a crucial tool for social change. During the 1920s he and his first wave colleagues envisaged establishing a new kind of community based on free clinics, clinics committed to helping the poor and disenfranchised, cultivating good and productive individuals. Anna Freud, Erik Erikson and Wilhelm Reich all made psychoanalysis accessible to farmers, office clerks, teachers, domestic servants, public school teachers and so on. Psychoanalysis was therefore deeply political.[25]

Little wonder then that Lacan took Antigone as the paradigm of the ethical act. The daughter of Oedipus, her conflict with Creon over her brother's burial stages the dispute between family and state, between two passionately held principles of right. And while the Chorus puts Antigone's misfortune down to the hand of fate, compelled as it were by the discourse in which she circulates, Lacan nonetheless ascribes to her a moment of supreme agency in which she takes responsibility for that discourse, if at the expense of her own life. It is as if, given her hand by Oedipus, she is forced to play; but while she has little choice in the matter, she can nonetheless play the hand to its bitter end. And of course, by assuming the desire for death – manifesting in the symbolic that which by definition cannot be represented – she becomes the sublime image of splendour. Hence, what marks Antigone out is her *fidelity to her desire* at the expense of her own life. This is why Lacan says: the only thing one can be guilty of is 'giving ground relative to one's desire', and 'the ethics to which psychoanalysis leads us [is] the relation between action and desire'.[26] So while

---

25 Elizabeth Danto, *Freud's Free Clinics: Psychoanalysis and Social Justice, 1918–1938* (Columbia: Columbia University Press, 2005).

26 Lacan, *The Seminar of Jacques Lacan, VII: The Ethics of Psychoanalysis, 1959–1960*, edited by Jacques-Alain Miller and translated by Dennis Porter. London: Routledge, 1999), pp. 321, 313.

psychoanalysis starts from the primacy of dispossession, it is not understood as a form of crippling scepticism, but paradoxically the very condition of a politically engaged act.

Belief

In a review of Gillian Rose's work, Rowan Williams asks: how do 'we come to think of thinking in the framework of dispossession'?[27] According to Williams, 'certain models of thinking come to be available because of the presence of certain narratives about God and God's people, narratives that insist on speaking of divine displacement in one sense or another'[28] – for example, a God who articulates his action through that which is other to the divine, or a God who dies on the cross and resurrects; moreover, this becomes the model of apostleship in which the subject abrogates the self in order to represent the non-interest of God. Should we not enquire then as to how psychoanalysis has been unconsciously shaped by this fundamental narrative of the death and resurrection of meaning?[29] In other words, should we not enquire into the ways psychoanalysis was already begun unconsciously shaped by the Jewish-Christian narrative?

According to Ernest Jones, Freud's enthusiastic biographer, the precedence for such a claim is already to be found in Freud: 'Freud spoke of having been greatly influenced by his early reading of the bible.'[30] And of course, Freud's identification with Moses and Jacob (the *name-of-his-father*) has been well documented – both figures in whom are condensed many of Freud's principle themes such as Judaism, law, dreams, struggles, redemption, etc.[31] And

---

27 Rowan Williams, 'Between Politics and Metaphysics: Reflection in the Wake of Gillian Rose', in *Modern Theology* 11.1 (1995), p. 18.

28 Williams, 'Between Politics and Metaphysics', p. 20.

29 Williams, 'Between Politics and Metaphysics', p. 20.

30 Ernst Jones, *The Life and Work of Sigmund Freud*, ed. by L. Trilling and S. Marcus (Harmondsworth: Pelican, 1964), p. 48.

31 Emanuel Rice, *Freud and Moses: The Long Journey Home* (Albany, NY: SUNY 1990); Richard Bernstein, *Freud and the Legacy of Moses* (Cambridge: CUP 1998); Peter Gay, *A Godless Jew: Freud, Atheism, and the Making of Psychoanalysis* (New Haven and London: Yale, 1987).

despite his professed atheism, it would appear he ended his life on the side of caution; choosing the Day of Atonement, *Yom Kippur*, upon which to commit suicide.

So the question remains: to what extent has Lacan's return to Freud been motivated by a Christian unconscious? This question has been rigorously researched by Mario Beira,[32] according to whom Lacan had an unresolved trauma revolving around what Lacan calls the *Name-of-the-Father* (E 66/278), the basis of symbolic function, the creative principle that unlocks language's potential as a whole – what Lacan would call a *point de capiton*. It is a 'name/s' because it determines a function of language, and it is the 'father' because the father initiates law in which the body of the mother is substituted for language (thus while Lacan rejects the idealist stand of metaphysics he nonetheless recognizes the necessity of the metaphysical gesture as the minimal condition of meaning).

According to Beira, Lacan's unconscious desire was shaped by a key event concerning the father: he was the only one of his three siblings not to have been born on Christmas day; unable as it were to assume the position of the Christ child for the father.[33] No wonder he positioned himself with regard to Freud the way he did, ensuring, in a parody of John's Gospel, 'No one comes to the father [Freud] except through me' (John 14.6). Moreover, by shortening his name from Jacques-Marie to 'Jacques', he was able to cut the umbilical chord to the Madonna, and assume the position of Christ, an exiled prophet to redeem his Moses (Freud) against a Jewish establishment who would ultimately sacrifice him by refusing him membership of the body Freud created: the International Psychoanalytical Association. Lacan would later comment: 'I am not saying – but it is not out of the question – that the psychoanalytic community is a church. But without doubt, the question arises if we are dealing with the echo of a religious practice.'[34]

He would find a Pauline ally in Jacques-Alain Miller, his son-in-

---

32 Mario Beira, 'Lacan, Psio-análisis y el Dios de Moisés', in *Lacan en Estados Unidos* (Sante Fe, Argentina: Homo Sapiens), pp. 121–38.

33 Elisabeth Roudinesco, *Jacques Lacan*, trans. Barbara Bray (London: Polity Press, 1999), p. 460.

34 http://web.mit.edu/sturkle/www/dolto.html

law, someone to formally systematize, interpret and proclaim his work to the world. Indeed, one way to express Lacan's endeavour is to take the 'I' (*das Ich*) out of 'I am' which in the French would involve omitting the 'i' out of *je suis*: *Jesus*.[35] This would also make sense of his request in a personal correspondence for his brother Marc-François, a Benedictine monk, to intercede with papal authorities in the hope of gaining Catholic approval, thereby doing 'homage to our common Father'.[36] It is little wonder the members of the International Psychoanalytical Association referred to Lacan as a 'mystical theologian'.[37]

The paradox to emerge here is that Lacan's atheism more fundamentally affirms an identification with Christ and the biblical narrative, his life and work parodying the redemptive work of creation through dispossession of the ego. Is this not the perfect example of what Žižek calls the '*inherent transgression*', a seeming act of transgression which merely serves to reinforce the very thing it opposes, not directly but paradoxically through its apparent overturning?[38] As Žižek says, 'The deepest identification that holds a community together is not so much an identification with the law that regulates its 'normal' everyday rhythms, but rather identification with the specific forms of transgression of the law'.[39] In other words, the law itself is split, operating both as a written

---

35 This point was made by Mario L. Beira in private correspondence.

36 Lacan, in a letter to his brother, quoted in Roudinesco, *Jacques Lacan*, p. 205. There is no further indication of the content of Lacan's letter in Roudinesco's work. Roudinesco, a historian of the psychoanalytic movement in France writes 'Lacan was not really renouncing atheism, but he knew that his way of reading Freud in the light of philosophy and from a non-biological point of view might attract a lot of Catholics, who didn't accept the "materialistic" aspect of the master's own teaching. When they read Lacan they felt on familiar ground, that of a Christian evaluation of human personality' (p. 205). The indication is that traditional analysis – and by this Lacan would have in mind ego-psychology – reduced the subject to the status of the scientific object making it antithetical to theologians.

37 Roudinesco, *Jacques Lacan*, p. 259.

38 Slavoj Žižek, *The Universal Exception: Selected Writings, Vol. 2*, ed. R. Butler and S. Stephens (London & New York: Continuum, 2006), p. 339.

39 Žižek, *The Universal Exception*, p. 28.

public law and through its obscene underside commanding us to transgress the law as the very means to secure it. Perhaps, then, Lacanian psychoanalysis is the obscene other or supplement of Christianity, which in the very act of overturning metaphysics, becomes an ethical practice to redeem creation.

The inherent transgression

If this is so, then where does it leave metaphysics? Lacan endorses an end of metaphysics, where metaphysics implies some transcendental extra, brought in to justify any particular given commitment. Indeed, my argument has been that to confront the anxiety of immanence, that is, to *traverse the fantasy*, is to situate oneself in the middle, a place of dispossession and failure because it confronts us with the fact that we are already begun. But if metaphysics means, as Rowan Williams suggests, that which provides the 'underlying intelligible structure'[40] or 'an overall proposal concerning the character of reality as known by agents',[41] in short, how we account for any given action as being more than purely arbitrary, then I have suggested that Lacan's work is indebted to Christian metaphysics, playing out the narrative of loss and redemption that is to be found in the passion. In other words, I have tried to show how psychoanalysis occupies precisely this middle ground in regard to theology, or that it is already positioned by a particular theological narrative.

All of this should impact on the future relations between the disciplines, because it invites us to reject the established relations between theology and psychoanalysis. In the old mode, characterized by Paul Ricoeur, theology might borrow the odd concept from psychoanalysis to think through a particular problem, such as whether our love is pathological or not; treating psychoanalysis as fire one must pass through as one might a coin to test its true value. Alternatively one might look to clinical practice, as a means to underpin the church's pastoral work with scientific credibility, such that theology may remain theology, and psychoanalysis remain psychoanalysis. What both approaches leave intact is the

---

40 Williams, 'Between Politics and Metaphysics', p. 6.
41 Williams, 'Between Politics and Metaphysics', p. 7.

very distinction itself between a realm of theology (grace) and a realm of psychoanalysis (nature), and hence the distinction between God from creation. Instead, just as Lacan transposes the old metaphysical split between man and his transcendental support into man; one needs to transpose the split between psychoanalysis and theology into theology itself. In other words, we need to recognize that Lacanian psychoanalysis is *already* theology. And hence only when it becomes theology proper, can it inversely become psychoanalysis proper; that is, a genuine non-ego-centred psychoanalysis, yet one which does not lead to the resigned despair offered up by the post-metaphysical age, because the 'alreadyness' or 'giveness' of immanence may be reinscribed as gift, and the dispossession of the ego, a participatory action in the redemptive work of creation.

19. The Politics of Fear and the Gospel of Life

DANIEL M. BELL, JR.

Recently I was shocked to learn from my mortgage company that it was not a matter of *if* but *when* a natural disaster was going to destroy my home. This startling revelation came on the heels of the morning's paper announcing that a flu pandemic was inevitable, and a radio show featuring an expert's claim that such a pandemic would have horrific effects comparable to those of nuclear war. As I turned toward my fridge in search of consolation I caught myself just in time, recalling a recent report raising serious safety concerns about refrigerated foods, and of course there is mad cow disease, and all those bacteria and the lead leaching into the tap water from the pipes and . . .

Fear abounds. From colour-coded alerts and militarized train stations and airports, to runs on gas masks, Cipro[1] and duct tape we are immersed in what Barry Glassner has aptly called a 'culture of fear'.[2]

Awash in fear, armies and security forces are mobilized, secret interrogation facilities are erected, resources are diverted from more pacific needs, suspects are rounded up, civil liberties and jurisprudence fall by the wayside – all in the pursuit of one overriding and all consuming concern: 'Nothing matters more to me right now than the safety of my home and the survival of my home-

---

[1] Cipro is a popular antibiotic that became a household name in the USA as a treatment for anthrax.
[2] Barry Glassner, *The Culture of Fear* (New York: Basic Books, 1999).

land.' So says a leading light among that novel political force, 'security moms'.[3]

Fear abounds, but so what? Who would be crass enough to challenge the legitimacy of this fear? Granted, there may be grounds for questioning the form taken by some of the concrete practices that have been promoted by this fear in response to the various and manifold threats that abound. We can, for example, debate the appropriateness of torture or the necessity of curtailing civil rights or the proper limitations of presidential powers in the midst of a war on terror, but who could challenge the underlying, primordial fear? Remembering the horror of Ground Zero, Madrid, London, surely only liberal elites ensconced in their ivory towers, sheltered (some would say 'alienated') from the real world and real people by the moribund moat of academia would dare dismiss wholesale this culture of fear and the politics it produces. And in so doing, they would expose not only the callousness of their souls toward vibrant human emotion and feeling but also their myopia, their failure to appreciate the conditions of possibility of their own lives. This is to say, such a critique could arise only from a failure to appreciate the ways in which the modern liberal political order itself is a response to fear. Thus, to challenge the culture of fear is not only to attack a principal human emotion, but it is also to assault the foundations of the very political order that keeps terror at bay.

So we are left wondering not simply, 'Is there a way beyond the culture of fear?' but perhaps more importantly, 'Should we even desire an alternative to the culture of fear?' What is wrong with fear? With a culture of fear? Moreover, fear's apologists remind us, the alternative to fear is typically apathy and decadence, a culture that is lifeless and listless, selfish and slothful.[4] Whatever a culture of fear's deficiencies may be, such an alternative can hardly be celebrated as an improvement.

---

3 Michelle Malkin, 'Candidates ignore security moms at their peril', *USA Today* (21 July 2004), 11A.

4 See, for example, David Brooks, 'The Age of Conflict', *The Weekly Standard* 7:8 (5 November 2001); Frank Rich, 'The Day Before Tuesday', *New York Times* (15 September 2001), p. A23; David Brooks, 'Facing Up to Our Fears', *Newsweek* (22 October 2001), pp. 66–9.

Veritas: Belief and Metaphysics

Any alternative to the culture of fear must address these concerns, and so they shape the account that follows. I begin by considering liberalism and fear. The dominant account of liberalism is that it is a political order designed to diffuse a pre- or extra-political fear and ward off terror, which it does by means of the construction of complex space (federalism, robust civil society, etc.). Drawing upon Hobbes, Foucault and Deleuze, I will show that the dominant account misconstrues both fear and liberalism's relation to fear. Indeed, their analyses suggest that fear is not a primordial instinct that swells fully formed from the human breast, prior to any political discipline and immune to political manipulation. To the contrary, modern political liberalism is revealed to be not about dissipating a pre-political fear but about the production and manipulation of fear. Liberalism is a politics of fear; thus, for the denizens of liberal political orders there can be no end to fear.

The relief of our fears will require a different order, a different politics, a politics of life. What are the contours of this politics? Here the constructive moment begins with Alain Badiou's treatment of St Paul. According to Badiou, Paul announced Christ as a truth-event that instantiates being-for-life by means of a break or rupture with the being-for-death that simultaneously animates and eviscerates political liberalism. Yet, such a politics stands or falls on the truthfulness of the claim that Christ's labour was one of pure affirmation, without a shadow of negation. Can such a claim stand at the foot of the cross? This prompts consideration of Christ's work of atonement. I argue in an Augustinian and Anselmian vein, that Christ's labour of atonement is not a matter of negation. Christ, and the life of fidelity to the truth-event that is Christ, is indifferent to crucifixion, suffering, and death. Thus displaced, death gives way to life, to the pure affirmation that is resurrected life. Christ gives the gift of life, a gift that founds a politics of resurrection. The final move anticipates objections that such a gift constitutes a politics at all by taking up Augustine's vision of the city of God.

The Politics of Fear and the Gospel of Life

Liberalism and Fear

The introductory defence of the culture and politics of fear follows the lineaments of what passes today for the canonical account of both the nature of fear and modern political liberalism's relationship to fear.

The origin and end of fear (I): the standard account

The intellectual pedigree of the dominant account of fear and liberalism's relation to fear can be traced back through thinkers such as Arendt, Tocqueville and Montesquieu, and it finds expression in an array of contemporary thinkers as diverse as Elshtain, Shklar, Rorty and Ignatieff.[5] According to this account, fear is a pre- or extra-political impulse. This is to say, it is a primordial, irrational force the cause of which lies prior to or outside of the political order. Think, for example, of the oft-repeated explanations of the motives of the terrorists who struck on 9/11 and who have since continued to inspire fear. It is said that they are persons bent simply on pure evil, and as such they have neither political motive nor political goal; their aim is solely destruction, pure and simple. Thus the fear they arouse is distinctly extra-political in origin. Fear's source is similarly located by prominent theorists of liberalism. According to Montesquieu, echoing earlier thinkers such as Hobbes and Locke, fear was born of a desire for security of person and goods. Specifically, fear, according to Montesquieu, was grounded in the threat of despotic tyranny and terror. For Tocqueville, fear was a generalized or mass anxiety prompted by a rapidly changing environment that washed away fixed reference points and established meanings. According to Arendt, the source of fear was the radical evil of totalitarian terror, a terror that threatened the integrity of the self. The thread that unites these and similar liberal accounts of fear is that in each instance, the source of fear is located outside the properly political realm, be it in a

---

[5] The treatment of liberalism and fear that follows is drawn from the masterful study of Corey Robin, *Fear: The History of a Political Idea* (Oxford: Oxford University Press, 2004).

generalized anxiety, an anti-political despotism, or a primordial retraction from death.

If fear's origins are extra-political, the response such fear elicits, according to the architects of liberalism, is distinctly political. Liberalism is born out of fear in the expectation that the liberal political order can keep terror and its consequent fear at bay. The standard narrative of liberalism's birth is the narrative of a political order founded with the intent to ward off terror, thereby dissolving the source of fear. Thus Montesquieu lays out a political order characterized by complex space – governing authority dispersed among separated powers with checks and balances coupled to a robust and pluralistic civil society where the self has opportunity to be enmeshed in a web of relations that can bolster it in resisting despotic intrusions. Likewise, in a similar vein, Tocqueville asserts that the growth and strengthening afforded civic associations and institutions under liberalism provides the best defence against the free-floating insecurity of the masses unhinged by a rapidly changing environment. Once again, it is the complex space of liberalism's political order, the proliferation of local institutions and social hierarchies in civil society, that tethers the individual in the midst of a changing world and so inhibits the spread of fear. Finally, Arendt, acknowledging the influence of both Montesquieu and Tocqueville,[6] argued that totalitarian terror advances by means of the creation of smooth or simple space that leaves the individual denuded, isolated before power, whereas liberalism's complex space protects the individual by providing the cover of diverse civic associations such that individuals need not be so exposed before terror. Again, the consistency that traverses the various accounts of liberalism's relation to fear is clear: Liberalism is a political response to an extra-political fear that wards off terror and fear by means of the construction of complex space – dispersing governing authority and providing the individual cover among a plethora of civic institutions and associations.

---

6 Robin, *Fear*, p. 99.

The origin and end of fear (II): Hobbes, Foucault and Deleuze

In the standard account, liberalism is cast as the end of fear and civil society, in particular, as a space of liberty. This account is not without its challengers. In particular, there are those who take issue with the claim that liberalism establishes a space of freedom from fear. Specifically, it is argued that far from warding off an extra-political fear, liberalism actually thrives on fear, generates it and governs by means of that fear. Liberalism is, in effect, a politics of fear.

Hobbes, for example, would certainly agree with those who suggest that liberalism is established on a foundation provided by fear. However, he would disagree sharply with the suggestion that the fear that underwrote the political project of the commonwealth was a pre-political passion. While acknowledging that persons do experience a pre-political sense of fear, Hobbes noted that that aversion in and of itself was insufficient to sustain the kind of commitment to self-preservation on which the sovereign commonwealth depended. In fact, Hobbes observed, fear often gives way to other passions, such as the desire for glory and honour, thus diminishing the motivating force of self-preservation. Consequently, in order for the commonwealth actually to unite under the sovereign, fear had to be promoted as a virtue in the service of a morally legitimate concern for self-preservation, while the moral stature of virtues such as courage had to suffer a corresponding reduction. As Corey Robin puts it,

> Hobbes . . . thought about the fear of death and the demand of self-preservation not as a description of an already existing reality – of how human beings actually behaved in the world – but as a project of political and cultural reconstruction, requiring the creation of a new ethos and a new man.[7]

But how, pray tell, was this new ethos to be constructed and this new person birthed? Addressing this question, Hobbes proved himself a much more astute political thinker than Machiavelli,

---

7 Robin, *Fear*, pp. 37–8.

who encouraged his prince to induce fear with the rather blunt instrument of stately violence. Hobbes realized that no prince possessed sufficient force to instil the requisite fear. Moreover, he recognized that fear alone, without a concomitant sense of investment or benefit, would not sustain obedience. In other words, what was needed was a way for citizens to participate in, and a reason for them to collaborate with, this induction of fear. For this, Hobbes turned to civil society. He thought that the leaders of civil society, particularly preachers and teachers (who had certainly shown themselves adept at inciting rebellion during the English civil war), could play a central role in the fostering a culture of fear. Legitimizing the moral elevation of self-preservation on the grounds that if one were dead, one could not pursue any goods, civic leaders could persuade the populace that it has a moral stake in perpetuating fear and moral grounds for collaborating in the establishment and maintenance of the sovereign's authority.

Hobbes's vision provides a blueprint for the modern state erected on the negative moral foundation of fear. This fear, however, is not extra-political but rather the thoroughgoing production of political processes. Moreover, it is the product of a collaboration between the sovereign and civil society, thus calling into question the extent to which civil society is rightly understood as a space of liberty from fear.

But, alas, what does this prove? After all, Hobbes's connection with liberalism is hotly contested. As Judith Shklar pointedly observes, the mere fact that Hobbes propounds a social contract theory of the state and loathes Catholicism does not make him the father of liberalism.[8] Furthermore, is not the claim that fear is used to bolster the sovereign state a rather antiquated one, given the contemporary geopolitical horizon, where, it is widely acknowledged, the sovereignty of states faces erosion by the global capitalist economic order? In other words, Hobbes's analysis may provide more heat than light simply because he was not dealing with liberal states undergoing capitalist stress. For this reason, we turn now to more contemporary analyses, beginning with Michel

---

8 Judith N. Shklar, 'The Liberalism of Fear', in Stanley Hoffmann (ed.), *Political Thought and Political Thinkers* (Chicago: University of Chicago Press, 1998), p. 6.

Foucault's account of governmentality and the modern liberal state.[9]

Governmentality, according to Foucault, is simply the art of government, the conduct of conduct. Although on the surface such a concept appeared decidedly unremarkable, as it is developed by Foucault, it encompasses much more than meets the eye. Governmentality includes within its scope disciplinary power, which was paradigmatically set forth in *Discipline and Punish* and for which Foucault is widely known. Disciplinary power is that rather overt and direct power whereby the state extends its dominion and enforces its sovereignty over those whom it renders its subjects. The most prominent example of this kind of power is, of course, the sword in the form of the penal power of the state, but it extends beyond blunt force to include the full range of the state's juridical reach.

Of course, at this point, Foucault has not succeeded in moving us much beyond Hobbes's analysis of the absolutist state. Indeed, Foucault acknowledges that the disciplinary power of the sovereign state is perhaps most clearly on display in the absolutist state that Hobbes theorized and which, according to Foucault's genealogy, slid into crisis not long after Hobbes's death. Yet it is precisely at the moment of the passing of the absolutist state and emergence of the liberal political order that the illuminating power of Foucault's account of governmentality is most profoundly manifest.

According to Foucault, the absolutist state went into crisis as it was confronted by a host of forces and events – wars, rebellions, financial difficulties, demographic, commercial and agricultural expansion – that simply exceeded the governing capacity of sovereignty and its disciplines. In response to this crisis, the art of government underwent a mutation and the liberal state was born. What is striking about the advent of the liberal state is that the link between maximal governmental effectiveness and maximal

---

9 A more detailed treatment of governmentality in Foucault, with appropriate textual pointers, can be found in Daniel M. Bell, Jr, *Liberation Theology After the End of History* (New York: Routledge, 2001), pp. 19–32. See also Graham Burchell, Colin Gordon and Peter Miller (eds), *The Foucault Effect: Studies in Governmentality* (Chicago: University of Chicago Press, 1991), which includes several essays by Foucault.

government itself is broken. Whereas sovereignty attempted to monopolize government, forging an identity between government and state apparatuses, liberalism extends or diffuses government beyond the state proper across the entire social field. Thus, notwithstanding popular rhetoric to the contrary, liberalism does not juxtapose government and freedom. Rather, liberal government is government *through* freedom. Civil society is rightly set against the state but not in the sense that civil society marks a space of liberty *simpliciter*. Rather, civil society is set apart from the state only in the sense that it embodies a different modality of government. In Foucault's language, liberal government combines macro level disciplinary power exercised through the state with what he calls biopower – power exercised at the micro level by means of what he calls technologies of the self. Biopower is the power operative in and through the private initiatives to mould the self into a particular kind of subject that proliferate throughout society apart from, and even frequently in apparent opposition to, the state as such. In this regard it may be helpful to think of various privately led campaigns of moralization/normalization, often associated with health, education, philanthropy or religion that flourish in civil society. These campaigns participate in the art of government as they promote specific techniques of the self, notwithstanding their character as private initiatives. For example, by encouraging practices of saving or the acquisition of insurance or particular parenting roles or the habits of cleanliness, sobriety, fidelity, self-improvement, responsibility and so on, such campaigns exert a biopower, essential to government, that ensures an individual's freedom is exercised in a manner commensurate with the state's interests.[10]

The proliferation of various technologies of the self in civil society as a form of 'private' government does not exhaust the extent to which liberal civil society is a space of government through freedom. Alongside the proliferation of techniques of the self, the expansion of liberalism's civil society was also accompanied by the decentralization of disciplinary power. The disciplinary power that under the absolutist regime was monopolized by

---

10 I owe these examples to Graham Burchell, 'Liberal government and techniques of the self', *Economy and Society* 22 (1993), p. 272.

the sovereign, under liberalism is now 'outsourced', dispersed across society, put in 'private' hands, particularly by means of the various human sciences. Hence, according to Foucault, it is no mere coincidence that with the dawn of liberalism we begin to see the state licensing what were formerly independent fields like medicine, psychiatry, psychology, criminology, pedagogy and so forth. In these ways, disciplinary techniques proliferate outside the state under the liberal governmentality.

Foucault's account of governmentality redeems Hobbes from being a mere historical curiosity, suggesting that while the absolutist state of Hobbes may differ from the liberal political order in important ways, with regard to government and fear, the difference is not as stark as is frequently supposed. Liberalism differs from Hobbes's absolutism only in the *modality* of governmental power. Liberalism is government *through* freedom, with both disciplinary and biopower dispersed across civil society. Thus, the very features that the architects of the standard account trumpet as erecting a dyke against fear and terror thereby clearing a space of liberty are revealed to be quite adept instruments of fear and terror. In other words, Foucault unmasks the complex space of liberalism, revealing that in itself complex space does not preserve or protect; to the contrary, by means of the decentralized disciplines and a variety of technologies of the self, complex space can facilitate our surrender and our immersion in a culture of fear even more effectively than naked sovereign power.

There is yet another lesson to be learned regarding the contemporary culture and politics of fear from Foucault's account of liberal governmentality. 'Governmentality' also sheds light on Hobbes's observation that for fear to work, people must be invested in it; they must be induced to believe in its benefits, while the counterposed virtues are marginalized. This is to say, Foucault helps us make sense of our collaboration with the production and perpetuation of a culture of fear. After all, if fear is not an extra-political intrusion but thoroughly political and if power is not the sole possession of a sovereign but instead is always already dispersed in its various forms (disciplines, technologies of the self, etc.) across the socius, then it will not do to argue that the culture of fear is simply imposed from on high by an imperial sovereign upon a repressed and captive population. (No one takes those colour-coded alerts that seriously.) After all, as the account of governmentality suggests, there is no 'on high' where power accumulates, leaving a vacuum 'below'. Nor, for the same reasons, will it suffice to assert a vast cabal of powerful institutions and persons. While it can hardly be denied that there are indeed powerful institutions and persons with vested interests in the perpetuation of fear, such an assertion is insufficient as an explanation in that it fails to appreciate the lesson of governmentality: fear is not merely *reflected* but is also *produced* and *reproduced* by civil society. This is to say, the security moms are not mere dupes of powerful men, but are themselves invested in fear and so reproduce it in their communities and children and so forth.

In this regard, Foucault once remarked that we have come 'to desire the very thing that dominates and exploits us'.[11] His account of governmentality exposes the fact that we do not live in fear because we have been beaten down. We are not simply crushed – although some are; the disciplines have not suddenly disappeared, only dispersed, like secret prisons around the globe. Rather, by means of a host of technologies of the self, our desires are so shaped that we come to long for the very goods that are bound up in the perpetuation of fear. We gain by fear. What do we gain? What goods are bound up with fear? Hobbes argued that fear was linked inextricably to the good insofar as survival was the condition of possibility for the pursuit of any and every good. John Locke held that fear was 'the chief, if not only spur to human industry and action'.[12] Likewise, Judith Shklar asserts that fear is the source of life's vitality,[13] while Michael Ignatieff believes that fear can nurture a new universal humanism.[14] After 9/11 a host of pundits echoed similar sentiments, proclaiming in essence that peace is dangerous and that fear alone can awaken the noblest that is within us. Nor should we forget the disconcerting insight offered

---

11 Michel Foucault, 'Preface', to Gilles Deleuze and Félix Guattari, *Anti-Oedipus: Capitalism and Schizophrenia* (Minneapolis: University of Minnesota, 1977), p. xiii.
12 John Locke, *An Essay Concerning Human Understanding* (Oxford: Clarendon, 1894), 2.20.6 (cf. 2.20.10; 2.21.34).
13 Shklar, 'The Liberalism of Fear', p. 11.
14 Michael Ignatieff, *The Warrior's Honor* (New York: Metropolitan Books, 1997), p. 18.

by Arendt, later in her life, in the course of exposing the banality of evil. Fear presents a host of opportunities for careerists, for the ambitious.[15] Lastly, we should not overlook the possibility that fear is desired simply because it provides an adrenaline rush, pulls us out of the undertow of the terminal boredom that weighs life down in the modern technocratic West.

If Foucault's account of governmentality shows how fear can be a political product of liberal political orders and their complex space of civil society, it does not appear to address the current situation where the power of the liberal state is being steadily eroded by the global capitalist market. For a clearer picture of the relation between the nation-state, the assembly of fear, and the capitalist order we turn to Gilles Deleuze.[16]

Like Hobbes and Foucault, Deleuze holds that life is constituted by motion; specifically by the active power that is desire. Moreover, this desire in a 'state of nature', if you will, is not reactive; it is not fearful. Rather, it is anarchic, creative, harmonic. This active, playful power that is desire only becomes reactive, fearful or, in Deleuze's terms, paranoid, as it is acted upon, as it is captured or seduced by reactive and fearful forces, which is precisely what the state-form attempts to do. The state-form assembles desire, forms and shapes it so that it is paranoid and fearful, and in so doing, the state promotes the promise of its own existence: surrender and be safe.

Deleuze's focus, however, broadens beyond the state-form to consider the contemporary political horizon as it is constituted by global capitalism. He positions his account of desire and the state-form within a universal history of capitalism. According to

---

15 Hannah Arendt, *Eichmann in Jerusalem* (New York: Penguin, 1994).

16 A more detailed treatment of Deleuze in this regard, with appropriate textual pointers, can be found in Daniel M. Bell, Jr, *Liberation Theology After the End of History*, pp. 12–19; 29–32. See also Gilles Deleuze and Félix Guattari, *Anti-Oedipus: Capitalism and Schizophrenia* (Minneapolis: University of Minnesota Press, 1983); Gilles Deleuze and Félix Guattari, *A Thousand Plateaus: Capitalism and Schizophrenia* (Minneapolis: University of Minnesota Press, 1987), pp. 424–73; Gilles Deleuze, 'Postscript on the Societies of Control', *October* 59 (1992), pp. 3–7.

this genealogy, the history of capitalism's advent is the story of the state-form's slow subsumption by or becoming immanent to economy. Hobbes's absolutist state of sovereignty was able to channel all desire through the bottle-neck of the state and its mercantile economy. Yet, as Foucault noted, eventually desire exceeded the ability of the sovereign to control and contain it, and as a result the state-form mutated into the liberal state. What is novel about the liberal state is that its art of government neither requires that all desire be funnelled through the state (civil society is fine, as per Foucault's governmentality) nor demands that desire be subordinated to the ends of sovereignty. In this sense, liberal government is distinctly economic government; it is government that strives to further not its own ends (what an earlier political tradition called 'reason of state') but the ends of capitalist economy. The liberal state is immanent to the larger economic field, and its task is primarily that of minimizing intervention and interference in the workings of that field.

Yet, we might ask, have we not crossed a new threshold in recent decades as capitalism has increasingly undermined the governing authority of even the liberal economic state? Does not global capitalism mark a crisis of the liberal state? After all, it would appear that capital's ability to eclipse national sovereignty is approaching the point of rendering the liberal state unnecessary, a point where passports can be replaced by credit cards and citizenship replaced by membership in trade alliances and associations. According to Deleuze, we have entered a new era, but the state-form has not been rendered obsolete. Rather, it is undergoing another mutation, a shift toward a much more active or aggressive advocacy of capital. No longer is the state satisfied with merely minimizing intervention in economy; now it actively pursues the extension of economy into every fibre and cell of human life. The state has become a model of realization for capital.

More specifically, and more immediately relevant to the matter of the culture and politics of fear, the state has become a war machine. Whereas it was once the case that states appropriated war machines; today states constitute a war machine. Specifically, they are capitalism's war machine. The capitalist state is the 'small state, strong state' that we see evolving all around us in response to the dictates of the global capitalist order – states long on disciplinary power and short on welfare capacity. Furthermore, the object of this machine is no longer, as it once was, war in the traditional sense of the term. Here we might recall the ways the 'war of terrorism' was described at its initiation. It is a 'ghost war', occurring not at the frontiers of society but, like a fog and in a manner synonymous with governmentality, permeating or blanketing society. And it is waged against a spectral enemy – be it terrorists with dirty bombs, microbes, or superpredator youths[17] – by means equally spectral: stealth forces, renditions, disappearances, electronic eavesdropping, invisible break-ins, snooping librarians, truck driver informants and so forth.

This war machine, moreover, does not simply fight *in* society, but rather it has society, peace, politics, the world order as its object. As Deleuze observes, with this latest permutation of the state-form, Clausewitz's famous formula has been inverted: War is no longer the continuation of politics; politics is now the continuation of war.[18] We are already living in the midst of World War Three, Deleuze wrote almost 30 years ago. Politics, culture, peace, civil society are the object of this war. Thus we are submerged in a state of permanent war; permanent emergency, a permanent state of exception where the laws and civic-political associations that once offered some degree of liberty are suspended indefinitely and foreclosed.[19]

Moreover, in waging this war against peace and politics, the state-form, in a move reminiscent of Orwell's *1984*, promotes and installs a very special kind of peace: a terrifying peace, the peace of absolute terror, a culture and politics of fear. Security is now conceived as war, as organized insecurity, as distributed and programmed universal catastrophe. War is peace and freedom is preserved only by sacrificing it and we all have a stake in this as we desire the goods that this fear makes possible.

And what goods are those? According to Deleuze, this state of

---

17 See Glassner, *The Culture of Fear,* and Marc Siegel, *False Alarm: The Truth About the Epidemic of Fear* (Hoboken, NJ: John Wiley & Sons, 2005).

18 Foucault makes a similar argument for different purposes in *Society Must Be Defended* (New York: Picador, 2003).

19 Deleuze's analysis helps make sense of the claim that we are now in a 'post-political' situation.

permanent war, this culture of fear has as its goal the deterritorialization of desire, the separation of the productive force of desire from anything that would stand between it and the capitalist market and the concomitant rendering available of this desire to this market. Thus, the culture of fear is not in service to the state per se, but the market. The threat of terror paves the way for capital and the goods it promises to provide. So, after 9/11 the president instructs us, not to seek out our neighbours and embrace them, but to shop, to seek out commodities and purchase them. Shortly thereafter, the US trade representative to Latin America wielded the threat of terrorism to cajole reluctant nations to fall in line with trade pacts. Likewise, homeland security and terrorism have been invoked to crush domestic labour actions, as well as popular movements against the expansion of the capitalist market. The invasion of Iraq, while falling far short of its lofty rhetoric with regard to the welfare of the Iraqi people, has gone a long way toward privatizing oil resources, abolishing unions, lowering wages, etc. – in short, furthering capital's extension in the region. Likewise, Hurricane Katrina was used to repeal a host of labour and environmental laws that stood in way of the market and talk persists of rebuilding New Orleans in a manner that is decidedly market-friendly. The list of examples of how fear and terror are used to promote the capitalist order could go on and on.

With Deleuze, we reach the end of our survey of liberalism and fear. The politics and culture of fear that envelop us is not the intrusion of an extra-political force kept at bay by the liberal political order. To the contrary, liberalism needs fear and so it produces it, and it does so not simply by the imposition of the heavy, disciplinary hand of the state and its apparatuses, but by the velvet touch (one that we even desire!) of the vast array of technologies of the self that constitute the complex space of civil society. Moreover, by means of this liberal governmentality, we come to desire our own domination and participate in a kind of political cannibalism whereby we want the very things that undercut the liberties liberalism purports to secure.

Thus, as we examine the culture of fear, we are looking as if into a mirror and glimpsing the truth of our liberal soul. Liberalism is founded on fear. As Judith Shklar has said so well, liberalism does not offer a *summum bonum* toward which all should strive; nor does it rest upon a theory of moral pluralism as many are wont to proclaim. Rather, its foundation is much more barren. Liberalism is erected on the sheer negative, the fear of a *summum malum*. As she says, 'to be alive is to be afraid.'[20] But in this way the contradiction at the empty heart of liberalism is exposed: the promise of liberalism – recall Montesquieu et al. – was freedom from terror and fear; yet this it cannot and it dare not deliver. For without fear, liberalism's *raison d'être*, even the very barren surface into which it sinks its sickly roots, erodes as if into nothing. Therefore, under liberalism, there can be no end to fear. Even death is not its terminus, but only its culmination and even its return, for death does not relieve our fears. Rather, as Hobbes insightfully discerned, face to face with death we are reminded that whatever meagre goods we seek out in the midst of this vale of tears – career, family, friends, etc.– are contingent upon actually surviving to pursue them.

For an end to fear, for a politics that finally is not cannibalistic of either liberty or life and so holds forth the hope of nurturing human communion/community (the root meaning of politics), for a more generous politics beyond the (anti-)politics of colour-coded insecurity and perpetual war with our neighbours, both foreign and domestic, we will have to look elsewhere. To this alternative we now turn.

The Gospel of Life

Even as we wander in liberalism's fields of fear, trying desperately to tend to the goods that constitute our lives – friends, families, neighbours, vocations – a word of hope, as if from on high, catches our ear: 'Do not be afraid.' The Christian gospel is frequently introduced in this way by both angelic messengers and Jesus. Juxtaposed to liberalism as a politics that begins by heightening fear, this gospel prelude is striking. Here we have the advent of a different and truer politics, a politics of life, and it begins with the dispersion of fear. To make sense of this gospel and its politics, we turn first to Alain Badiou's work on St Paul.[21]

20 Shklar, 'The Liberalism of Fear', p. 11.
21 Alain Badiou, *Saint Paul: The Foundations of Universalism* (Stanford: Stanford University Press, 2003).

Being for death and being for life: Badiou on St Paul

Badiou's work is about the recovery of a philosophical politics in the midst of an age disfigured by the monumental destruction of all politics. Against the ravages of the present age, Badiou posits a philosophy of the truth-event, which is nothing less than the unexpected irruption of a new way of being in the midst of the status quo characterized by what he calls imperialism, democratic totalitarianism, absolute injustice and more recently, 'the disjunctive synthesis of two nihilisms', by which he means the politics of fear in both of its prominent contemporary manifestations – fascist terrorism and the Western war on terrorism.[22] What attracts Badiou to St Paul is that in Paul Badiou discerns a fellow traveller who, under the shadow of the Roman Empire, witnessed a similar destruction of all politics.[23] In the midst of these destructions both ancient and contemporary, Paul stands as the militant herald of a truth-event that ruptures being-for-death with the possibility of pure affirmation, being-for-life.

According to Badiou, Paul sets forth the truth-event that is Christ in terms of two subjective paths, that of the flesh and the spirit, of death and life. Actually, Christ does not present two paths. Rather, as a truth-event, Christ is a break or rupture with the surrounding site or situation, an interruption, an absolute beginning, an act of creation *ex nihilo*. Accordingly, Christ makes possible a path other than that of the surrounding situation. In other words, where there was only fear and being-for-death, with the truth-event of Christ there issues forth the possibility of life and being-for-life.

What distinguishes these two paths, these two ways of being in the world? Being-for-life is characterized by love, which is a matter of pure affirmation and universal filiation. As universal filiation it is about the extension of the self in the direction of others. As pure affirmation, it is the denial of negation. It is indifferent to death. In contrast, being-for-death is life that is centred on death, that

---

22 See Alain Badiou, *Ethics: An Essay on the Understanding of Evil* (New York: Verso, 2001), p. lv, and Badiou, *Infinite Thought* (New York: Continuum, 2005), p. 118.
23 Badiou, *Saint Paul*, p. 7.

revolves around death, that leads inextricably toward death as its orienting point, even as that life-headed-toward-death may be consumed with resisting that destiny and slowing that descent.[24] (In this regard, think of the practice of contemporary medicine, which draws its orientation not from health, but from illness and death.) Being-for-death is a labour of negation, whether it is confronting others or facing death. As such, it is either pure negation – as in nihilism – or the negation of negation – as in a dialectical vision that ineluctably tethers affirmation to negation, thereby ensuring that negation is never finally left behind but instead always lingers as the trace that is affirmation's condition of possibility. Theologically, this being-for-death takes shape in a vision of redemption that finds its centre in Christ's death and the redemptive necessity of sacrifice and suffering.

If Badiou reads Paul correctly,[25] then the Christian gospel announces an interruption of the culture and politics of fear. It holds out the promise of a life that does not revolve around death and its warding off. However, it is not clear that Badiou does read Paul or the Christian vision of salvation rightly. After all, is it accurate to say that Christianity is decidedly indifferent to death, that salvation does not revolve around the redemptive significance of sacrifice and suffering? What, then, are we to make of the central artefact of the faith: the cross of Christ – not to mention the cross of all those who would follow in fidelity to the truth-event that is Christ?

Perhaps Christianity is not simply a matter of affirmation, but is a vision of the negation of negation. Which returns us to the question: Fear abounds, so what? Death is, after all, the enemy. Perhaps Christianity, while abjuring the crass production and manipulation of fear that currently plagues us, nevertheless does not offer a politics that is truly oppositional to the culture and politics of fear so much as it presents an alternative vision, a truer

---

24 See, for example, Ernest Becker, *The Denial of Death* (New York: Free Press, 1997).

25 For more on Badiou's use of Paul and its problems, see Daniel M. Bell, Jr. 'Badiou's Faith and Paul's Gospel: The Politics of Indifference and the Overcoming of Capital', *Angelaki: The Journal of the Theoretical Humanities* 12.1 (April 2007).

culture and politics of fear. After all, the fear of the Lord is the beginning of wisdom (Prov. 9.10).

Christ crucified and resurrected: the gift of life

In 1 John we are told that perfect love casts out fear (4.18)[26] and Paul reminds the church at Corinth, in an almost mocking tone, that death has been swallowed up, has lost its sting (1 Cor. 15). Here we have the signposts of a politics beyond fear and death, a politics of life, of pure affirmation. As Paul says, 'The Son of God, Jesus Christ, whom we proclaimed among you ... was not "Yes and No"; but in him it is always "Yes"' (2 Cor. 1.19). Here we behold a textual marker for a culture and politics that is finally so shockingly indifferent to death that if it is wrong, its inhabitants are of all people most to be pitied (1 Cor. 15.19) if not dealt with in a harsher manner.

Such a claim, however, runs up against the undeniable presence of the cross, sacrifice, suffering and death at the centre of the Christian narrative of salvation. As Paul says, 'we proclaim Christ *crucified*' (1 Cor. 1.23). Hence, does not the cross stand in the way of any attempt to construe Christianity as pure affirmation? Is it not the paradigmatic instance of negation, and the resurrection a reciprocal act negating the negation? Consider a widely popular rendition of Christ's work of atonement on the cross. Frequently attributed by the more theologically astute to St Anselm, but with an evident pedigree reaching back to Paul's letter to the Romans, the prevailing account of the cross goes something like this: Human sin is an offence against God's honour and God, as one who must uphold justice, cannot simply forgive sin but must

---

26 To be clear, this chapter juxtaposes two forms of life: one oriented by fear and death, the other by life. The crux of the argument is this fundamental orientation. Given more space, an account of the place of the passion called 'aversion', or what Aquinas calls 'the gift of fear' could be developed that would, for example, provide a way of accounting for such well-known texts as 'the fear of the Lord is the beginning of wisdom' (Prov. 9.10; Ps. 111.10) and so forth without in any way undermining the force of my argument. In this regard, see Scott Bader-Saye, 'Thomas Aquinas and the Culture of Fear', *Journal of the Society of Christian Ethics* 25.2 (2005), pp. 95–108.

enforce a strict rendering of what is due. Yet sinful humanity cannot fulfil the debt, so the God-man, Christ, steps forward to pay/negate the debt through his substitutionary suffering and death on the cross.

In this commonplace reading of Christ's work, death – the sacrifice that is the loss of life, the suffering that is redemptive – is the unmistakable fulcrum of salvation. Moreover, the unspoken subtext of this account is fear – the fear of eternal damnation that is avoidable only by a death. Furthermore, the resurrection is marginalized, as evidenced by the fact that this tale could be told without any reference to the resurrection at all. At best it is given a secondary or supporting role, becoming a kind of confirmation that the substitutionary death worked, that the sacrificial suffering was redemptive, that the negation was successfully negated.

Hence, the commonplace reading is not a tale of life but of fear and death and as such it does not hold forth the promise of deliverance from the culture and politics that currently afflict us. (Thus, it is unsurprising that many contemporary theological figures see in the liberal political order the proper analogue to the gospel.) Yet, the commonplace reading is also a profound distortion of Christ's work, the product of the transposition of the gospel of life into an alien and fundamentally negative key. For Christ's work does not find its centre in the death suffered on the cross but in the life of the resurrected. This is to say, Christ's work of atonement is the gift, not of death, but of resurrected life: Being-for-life. Christ's work was not that of negation – submitting to negation, and overcoming negation with an act of negation. Rather, Christ came not because he must die but so that we might live. Christ's work of atonement is a labour of sheer affirmation.

This affirmation upends the commonplace account of Christ's work. To begin with, human offence – sin – does not call forth divine negation.[27] The cross is not an instance of divine negation.

---

[27] A full treatment of this claim would necessarily consider the practice and meaning of judgement in the Christian life. For such a treatment by way of an engagement with Gilles Deleuze, see Daniel M. Bell, Jr., 'Only Jesus Saves: Toward a Theo-political Ontology of Judgment', in Creston Davis, John Milbank and Slavoj Žižek (eds), *Theology and the Political: The New Debate* (Durham, NC: Duke, 2005), pp. 200–27.

As the much-aggrieved Anselm noted long ago, it is not possible that human insurrection could thwart divine creative intent[28] and as the more esteemed Augustine forces us to concede, there is finally nothing – which is after all the substance of sin, death and rebellion – to be negated. Instead, as Anselm insisted and Scripture (including Paul) constantly affirms, the atonement proceeds according to the divine intentionality of/for life. In the face of human rebellion, God's honour will not let the breach stand but desires that humanity be restored to the life – to participation in the abundance of the divine life – that from the beginning God intended for humanity. Therefore, the Father sends the Son, who goes willingly to continue the labour of love that is the gift of life. Christ's labour is chiefly that of resurrecting life, not simply suffering death. The heart of Christ's atoning work is resurrection, the taking up of humanity into the life of charity shared by the blessed Trinity (*theosis*, deification), the effecting of ontological union with life.

But, of course, there is no evading the cross. The cross is the site of this truth-event. Yet, recall that the truth-event that is Christ is a break, a rupture, with the surrounding site. Hence, while the cross is the site of the resurrection, it is not its condition of possibility. The resurrection, in Badiou's terms, is a subtraction, not an addition, to the situation it breaks open. There is a disjunction between death and resurrection. The Gospels say as much when they testify that the response to the empty tomb is one of puzzlement and bewilderment. There is no way, beginning from death, being-for-death, that one can make sense of the resurrection. Resurrection is not the proper and expected encore to death in accord with some dialectical, rational protocol. This is the case because the resurrection does not answer death or even defeat death – both moves of dialectical negation that reify what they purport to overcome. Frankly, if the resurrection were simply

---

28 For a reading of Anselm against his modern detractors, see Daniel M. Bell, Jr., 'Forgiveness and the End of Economy', *Studies in Christian Ethics* 20.3 (December 2007); David Bentley Hart, 'A Gift Exceeding Every Debt: An Eastern Orthodox Appreciation of Anselm's *Cur Deus Homo*', *Pro Ecclesia* 7 (1993), pp. 333–49; Hans Urs von Balthasar, *The Glory of the Lord, Volume II* (San Francisco: Ignatius Press, 1984).

the negation of death, then Lazarus, a resuscitated corpse, which, incidentally, amazed but did not bewilder, would be our hope.[29] In contrast, the resurrected one stands starkly, blindingly alive – life's startling, naked interruption of death.

As the interruption of the site of death, the resurrected Christ does not merely defeat death or tame it or subdue it, all of which presume a relation to death, entail something with which one can be in relation. Such a presumption reifies death and being-toward-death. It grants death a substance, a reality and hence a permanence that it lacks. For this reason, the Scriptures speak of death destroyed (1 Cor. 15.26), of death 'being no more' (Rev. 21.4). For this reason, Paul speaks of the resurrected Christ as raised into being (Rom. 6.4), with the implication that death and being-toward-death are in fact not being at all; they are nothing. The offer of resurrected life unmasks death and being-toward-death as the absence of power, a void, nothing.[30] Hence, Badiou rightly observes that being-for-life is indifferent to death, because death precisely as nothing is nothing that can be taken into account. As nothing, death cannot make a difference. Hence, death makes no difference to Christ's fidelity nor to those who would be faithful to the event of Christ and obedience even to the point of death only sounds like foolishness, only presents a stumbling block, to the unredeemed still in thrall to death, being-for-death. To the redeemed, the resurrected, death is no obstacle, no thing, nothing at all and thus no longer concerns us (cf. Matt. 8.22) nor is it to be feared (Matt. 10.28).

At this point we can see the cross for what it is, neither the satisfaction of a divine demand for death nor even a divine instrument for negating sin. Rather, the cross stands as the nadir of sin; it is the deepest depth of human rebellion. Granted, the cross is a negation, or at least an attempt at such, but it is not a negation that God imposed; rather it is the last futile human effort at negation. We refuse the gift of life and attempt to negate it. But, alas, God refuses to accept our negation. After all, since all that is only is by

---

29 Lazarus, one should note, will die again, thus proving the point that a dialectical overcoming of death always reifies that which is attempts to escape.

30 See Augustine, 'Of True Religion', §22.

participation in affirmation, negation cannot be accepted because finally it does not exist. Thus, God actually refuses nothing; conversely there is nothing in our refusal for God to accept. (In fact, as the precepts of medieval theology make clear, God has never been estranged from humanity.[31]) So, Christ is faithful, obedient to the labour of life, even to the point of suffering our absurd attempts at negation. This is the work of atonement: Jesus is the gift of God's redemption, not because he endures divine negation in our stead, but because he embodies the divine refusal to negate humanity in its sin, a refusal that endures even to the point of death on a cross. And this divine refusal is nevertheless pure affirmation as the resurrected one returns to those crucified him with the offer of life.

Similarly, just as Christ's labour of affirmation reveals death to be nothing and the cross the last futile stand of an eternally foreclosed rebellion, suffering is now seen to be neither redemptive nor necessary. Whereas the commonplace account of Christ's labour tends to privilege suffering, as in what makes Christ uniquely redemptive is that he suffered more than anyone (some responses to Mel Gibson's *The Passion of the Christ* come to mind), we now see that suffering too is nothing, that what is redemptive in Christ's labour is his fidelity to life, his refusal to depart from this divine mission by repealing the offer of life in the face of suffering. In light of the surpassing glory, the life that is ours in Christ, suffering is unmasked as nothing (Phil. 3.8). Hence the supernatural calmness on display in the accounts of so many of the martyrs. In this regard, what is so remarkable about the martyrs is not their deaths, but their unflinching refusal to surrender their witness (the meaning of the Greek term, *martyr*) to life. Our perverse fascination with the manner of their deaths notwithstanding, what distinguishes the martyrs is their eternal life, on display with particular contrastive force at the moment of their death.

Furthermore, it is clear that suffering is not necessary. The divine affirmation of life is an act of creation *ex nihilo*. It requires no preliminary or contrastive negation. Consequently, what suffering there is is revealed in the light of Christ to be the contingent effect of sin. Suffering is a contingent, historical consequence of sin

---

31 See, for example, Augustine, 'On the Gospel of St John', tractate II, §8.

and rebellion and not of the liberative and redemptive heart of God. Hence, it is only temporal, temporary, passing and finally nothing. (In this regard, there is no such thing as radical evil whose effects persist, threatening the peaceful ontology of life.[32]) That one faces suffering and crucifixion points not to the necessity of suffering as the path of redemption but to the stubborn persistence of sin's refusal of affirmation and the brutal resilience of the culture of fear and death in producing both crosses and executioners.

Finally, as is the case with both the cross and suffering, sacrifice is transformed as it is repositioned within the theologic of affirmation or of being-for-life. Typically sacrifice is viewed as pernicious. This is to say, it is usually linked with negation. Sacrifice is understood as reductive, necessarily entailing a loss – a loss of self, a loss of dignity, a loss of identity, a loss of life. Pernicious or reductive sacrifice is always a giving-up or a surrender of the lesser to the greater – the present to the future, women to men, men to the state/corporation, all to the greater good (that is, the market). Thus, morality under the sign of modernity oscillates between egoism and altruism, between self-preservation and self-sacrifice. And, perhaps unsurprisingly, modern Christian ethics has tended to embrace altruism and 'self-sacrifice'. In so doing, however, it rightly earns the censure of liberationists and others, for such pernicious sacrifice does not open a path to affirmation and life but only reinforces our capture by the logic of negation, loss and death. It remains an instantiation of being-for-death.

In contrast, the truth-event of Christ initiates a non-reductive sacrifice that entails neither negation nor loss. Christ's sacrifice is one of pure affirmation. It should be clear by now that what is offered in Christ is not a death, but life itself. The substitutionary sacrifice Christ offered at the site of the cross is the fidelity and praise (the return of love) of the Son to the Father. Christian sacrifice is a *living* sacrifice (Rom. 12.1). In this way, the Christ-event ruptures the smooth space produced by our contemporary culture and politics of fear and death, with the result that sacrifice becomes gain (Luke 9.24) and we can give ourselves in love as a

---

[32] See John Milbank, *Being Reconciled: Ontology and Pardon* (New York: Routledge, 2003); Badiou, *Ethics: An Essay on the Understanding of Evil*.

gift of life to our neighbours without end and without loss (Matt. 22.39; Mark 12.31). In Christ's sacrifice nothing is lost and everything is gained. Through his sacrifice sin, which as *privatio* is precisely nothing, is lost. Through being joined to his sacrifice, the 'nothing' that we lose is the terrified, fearful self that only has the eyes to see and ears to hear the sacrifice of love as loss.

The 'nothing' that is overcome is the contemporary fantasy of absolute security, the pursuit of which only entrenches us more deeply in insecurity, terror and fear and leads us (willingly!) to surrender those very goods (life, love, liberty) such security purportedly promises to preserve and protect. The 'nothing' that is lost is the illusion that the politics of fear can ever deliver us from terror, conflict and death. The 'nothing' that is dispelled is the 'fog of war' that deceives us into thinking that the war against terror can be anything other than a war without end – a permanent emergency, perpetual war, that offers neither peace nor hope but only grief intensified as loss is compounded by loss.

What is gained in Christ's sacrifice is abundant life, the possibility of living life as pure affirmation, as ceaseless non-reductive giving (and receiving) the gift of life. In other words, Christ's sacrifice creates the possibility of facing others without armed suspicion as well as non-reductively sacrificing oneself to and for others that life might be extended. Put concretely and too concisely, Christ's sacrifice clears a space for a politics of life, a politics of relentless affirmation, of ceaseless giving even in this midst of terror. Christ's sacrifice creates the possibility of a politics that fearlessly pursues justice not as an act of counter-terror, torture and death but as a work of mercy whose end is the extension of communion.[33]

We have now come full circle. Christ is pure affirmation, the resurrection of life. And this gift of life is the love that casts out fear enabling us to live in peace with and service to our near and distant neighbour. Because finally no negation, loss or even death stands – they are all revealed to be nothing – in Christ we are freed from culture of fear and politics of terror and death it underwrites and

---

[33] See Daniel M. Bell, Jr., 'Justice and Liberation', in Stanley Hauerwas and Sam Wells (eds), *The Blackwell Companion to Christian Ethics* (Malden, MA: Blackwell, 2003), pp. 182–95.

so can give our life to and for others without fear of loss, in expectation only of the gain that is filiation and communion.

Writing to a community at the very heart of the anti-politics that dominated his age, a community that no doubt felt the pressures of the surrounding culture and politics of fear and death, Paul assures them that nothing is able to separate them from the love of God that is theirs in Christ (Rom. 8.39). Neither imperial rulers nor terrorist powers, neither vague threats in the present nor speculative threats of things to come, neither microbes nor mad cows, neither hurricanes nor hate. In Christ, sharing in his resurrection, they have received the gift of life.

And, of course, this is no gift of sentimental solitude (more accurately, 'resignation') nor an otherworldly consolation. This is the love that has always moved saints and martyrs – like the Christian Peacemaker Teams – to risk all (in the fear of losing nothing) for the sake of breaking down the dividing walls of hostility and in the midst of terrified and fearful individuals, create communion, community.

This gift of love, this gift of life, this resurrected life, is our political hope. In the midst of a world that purports to have attained its end in political liberalism,[34] which is a world of war without end, a world where we discover no end either to fear or death, into this world Christ enters, a truth-event that ruptures the culture of fear and the politics of death with the gospel of life. And where the gospel of life inflames saints to make true sacrifices, which are works of mercy that relieve distress and spread the joy of communion, there we are set free from fear and death and being-for-life is made possible. There, in the midst of the smouldering rubble of a terrified and terrifying post-political age, politics – the possibility of human community – is being born again.[35]

---

34 See the well-known thesis of Francis Fukuyama, 'The End of History?' *National Interest* 16 (Summer 1989), pp. 3–18 and his *The End of History and the Last Man* (New York: The Free Press, 1992).

35 I am grateful to Jeffrey Robbins and Peyman Vahabzadeh for their helpful comments on a draft of this essay, which appeared in the *Journal for Cultural and Religious Theory* 18.2 (April 2007).

20. Only Theology Saves Metaphysics: On the Modalities of Terror[1]

JOHN MILBANK

The End of the End of Metaphysics

The twentieth century, on one characterization, might be regarded as the age of the anti-metaphysical. Analytic philosophy initially sought to show that metaphysical speculation, and the invention of metaphysical entities, was based on logical and linguistic confusion. Phenomenology, for its part, claimed to displace ontology with a strict science of appearances. In either case, a claim was made to be able to establish certain finite bounds of the knowable, whether in terms of transcendental categories of meaning, or else transcendental categories of the fundamental kinds of things that can be shown to us. Certain ethical hopes were invested in this enterprise: if there can be a consensus around the nature of the

---

1 This title deliberately inverts that of my earlier essay 'Only Theology Overcomes Metaphysics', in John Milbank, *The Word Made Strange* (Oxford: Blackwell, 1997), pp. 36–55. However, this denotes no change of heart. The 'metaphysics' that is overcome in the former piece is the ontotheological science of transcendental ontology that has prevailed at least since Suarez. The 'metaphysics' that is saved in the present piece is the perennial 'realism' that lasted from Plato to Aquinas and then was reworked by Eckhart and Cusanus. Here, characteristically, being is not a transcendental framework that includes even the divine; rather being as God is identified as the transcendent source in which all else participates.

limits of our understanding, then perhaps a chastened human solidarity should result. From henceforwards human beings would pursue together what can be pursued and not seek through reason the ineffable. Since such a quest is impossible, it is all too likely to engender cruel dissent and finally bloodshed.

Of course, the history of the twentieth century was in part one of unparalleled state terror, of unbridled economic, international and inter-ethnic conflict. But this is naturally no proof that the anti-metaphysical endeavour was in any way the cause of these things, nor even that it was an impotent salve in the face of such violence. To the contrary, one could claim that the mood of sober finitism which prevailed in twentieth-century philosophy was intended in part to counteract ideologies that stemmed from nineteenth-century idealist narratives about the necessary direction of history, and even more from positivist ideas about a new era in which physical science would supplant metaphysics by usurping its role and providing a new, scientific, all-encompassing world-view. From this perspective, one can see Marxism as a Comtianism of the left, and Fascism as a Comtianism of the right.

Despite the complicity of many famous twentieth-century philosophers in fostering these naturalistic ideologies, one could argue that, by and large, twentieth-century philosophy in both its major currents was as adverse to naturalistic reduction as it was to metaphysical or quasi-religious speculation. This is shown, above all, in Frege and Husserl's shared refusal of psychologism, or the view that the supposedly objective 'reasoning' carried out by 'mental process' is merely an epiphenomenon of the contingent physical operations of the brain of the human animal organism.[2]

Perhaps, in consequence, the overwhelming mood of twentieth-century philosophy was neither atheism nor religiosity but rather agnosticism.[3] Indeed one could claim that it was just this agnosticism that distinguished it from nineteenth-century philosophy. This was exhibited in two ways: the one philosophical, the other religious in tone. Philosophically it was shown by what Quentin

---

2 See Martin Kusch, *Psychologism: A Case Study in the Sociology of Psychological Knowledge* (London: Routledge, 1995).

3 This is asserted by Quentin Meillassoux in his *Après la Finitude: Essai sur la Nécessité de la Contingence* (Paris: Seuil, 2006), pp. 39–69.

Meillassoux calls 'correlationism'. For this perspective, the non-speculative idealist view that our thought is indeed about a world external to us is balanced by an equal stress that the only world we know is the world *as* it is known to us.[4] (Of course there are many exceptions to this, but as a generalization it holds good.) The overall tone of twentieth-century philosophy was Kantian in the sense that epistemology not ontology dominated, but an epistemology of a quasi-realist bent. Dogmatism about how the world is in itself was largely eschewed, but likewise eschewed was any hypostasization of human thinking-processes themselves.

Such a philosophical agnosticism encourages also a religious agnosticism. And here Wittgenstein was not atypical but rather representative in suggesting that there may well be a realm of mystery that can disclose itself to an awareness in excess of the rational. In social and political terms this view did not favour the intrusion of the religious into the public and political realm, seen as governed by norms of free, open, rational discourse, but it did favour a respectful tolerance of private belief, and even, in Wittgenstein's case, a sense of the importance of a religious social space of ritual and collective ethical activity. Again, Meillassoux is not without warrant in speaking of a new sort of 'plural fideism' here, still linked, as are all fideisms, with a certain measure of rational scepticism. However, this is no longer the committed fideism of, say, Pierre Bayle in the past – totally sceptical and indeed almost nihilistic by dint of his reasonings, committed Huguenot in Dutch exile by bent of his faith. This is now rather a more general formal recognition of the validity of faith as an idiom – a kind of faith in faith, if you like. Hence one has a general rational acknowledgement of the possibility of many approaches to the one mystery, or else of a myriad private modes of access to rival mysteries.

One could contend, by contrast, as I have already suggested, that the terror of the twentieth century in fact sprang from a nineteenth-century hangover: from the persisting influence of idealist and positivist ideologies – and so from both metaphysical speculation and also from an unwarranted scientistic claim to take the place of this speculation. From such a viewpoint, 1990 saw the

---

4 Meillassoux, *Après la Finitude*, pp. 13–111.

final defeat of a certain reading of Hegel, besides the defeat of Marx, Comte and Spencer. The twin agnostic thrust of both phenomenology and analysis could be regarded as entirely in keeping with this moment. Hence the reputations of Frege, Wittgenstein, Husserl and even Heidegger (despite everything) naturally survived it. Thus it might be argued that the final arrival of a post-ideological era was fully in step with the anti-metaphysical thrust of twentieth-century philosophy. (I hasten to say that I regard this verdict as an overstatement, but, for the moment, let it stand.)

As we now know, the end of history lasted, if that is not an oxymoron, for about eleven years. Since 9/11 we have been confronted with the apparent displacement of ideological terror by religious terror, whether perpetrated by small groups or by nation states. (Or at least we can speak of state and anti-state terror that is in part propelled by religious belief.)

In the face of this situation, Quentin Meillassoux argues that we should become less sanguine about the anti-metaphysical and 'correlational' character of twentieth-century philosophy. Is its modest, bounded humanism really as bland as it seems? Or does the self-limiting abjuration of the speculative tend to leave the field free for the voices of religious fanatics, whose rival claims a plural fideism is powerless to adjudicate? It is all very well for philosophy to forswear any talk about ultimate reality, final truth and the nature of the good, but are there not social exigencies which tend inevitably to require at least implicit collective stances on these matters? Where reason has retreated, there, it seems, faith has now rushed in, often with violent consequences.

So if Meillassoux is right, the contemporary 'return of religion' is not evidence of either atavism or recidivism. Rather, we are talking about a fideism that is the inevitable complement of a modern, post-Kantian rationalism. And to Meillassoux one needs to add, I think, a further point: the 'modesty' of modern epistemology can, of itself, be a source of terror. For in a neo-liberal world, where there is only consensus as to formal procedures that promote narrowly defined utilitarian benefit combined with negative freedom of choice, all positive preferences, including fideistic ones, have to be simultaneously encouraged and yet severely policed if they are not to invade the rights of others. For plural fideism is inherently unstable – by insisting that the public sphere lie under the governance of transcendental reason, one cannot rule out the claims of religious belief, and yet these same claims, in their traditional forms, are most unlikely to accept their exclusion from the public forum, since their faith perspectives include strong views as to how this realm should be both constituted and conducted.

Hence the more anti-metaphysical modernity encourages pure faith, the more it must also rein back its socio-political intrusions through the deployment of excessive policing; the more also it must strictly confine the public realm to the procedural and the pragmatically measurable. But the more it seeks to do these things, the more it must perforce generate a new sort of liberal totalitarianism involving constant surveillance and ever more exhaustive indexing and categorizing of all citizens and all their activities.

There are, therefore, some good reasons for now being concerned about a style of philosophy that eschews the business of trying to determine the ultimate categories of being (or of reality) and the fundamental ways in which they may be said – to put it in Aristotelian terms. Is it enough, by contrast, to try to determine merely the ultimate presuppositions of our human mode of thinking about the world and of living within it? For this can still leave the way open to a species-relativism that brackets the questions of an objective truth and goodness and thereby leaves them to be answered by the assertions of irrational cults. Do we not after all need a public rational discourse about substantive truth, goodness and beauty which will rescue these universal and necessary concerns from the hands of fanaticism?

Were this perception to take hold (and perhaps it is already beginning to do so), then it is possible that twenty-first-century philosophy will revert to something more like a nineteenth-century battle between naturalism on the one hand and religiously-inclined speculations on the other.

But it is not precisely the case that we face the prospect of a new 'return of metaphysics'. For it is now time to qualify certain statements made above. The substitution of epistemology for metaphysics could itself sometimes bend back into the metaphysical. So, for example, in the case of both Russell and the early Wittgenstein, logical atomism became the basis for an ontology that could declare that 'the world is everything that is the case'. And Heidegger's relation to Husserl essentially repeated Hegel's

Only Theology Saves Metaphysics

relation to Kant. The latter (to oversimplify) restricted valid theoretical philosophy to a listing of the fundamental modes under which we can know; Hegel turned this critique of speculation into a new sort of speculation by giving ontologically absolute status to the human process of knowing and its historical unfolding. Somewhat similarly, Husserl restricted philosophical knowledge to the exploration of the fundamental modes of givenness in appearance; Heidegger later turned the givenness of being to problematic human awareness and practice (*Dasein*) into a disclosure, again unfolding through history, of Being itself.

At times, therefore, in twentieth-century thought, agnosticism was somewhat breached, by hypostasizing the epistemological. In both of the two cases cited, however, it was at the same time confirmed. Wittgenstein offered a purely immanent ontology which still reserved 'the mystical'; Heidegger, while mostly plundering and usurping (dishonestly) the theological legacy,[5] in order to articulate a new sort of quasi-religious ontology of his own, nevertheless left open a Lutheran space for a positive discourse of revelation that might possibly break through the field of 'being in general'.

And in both cases one appears to have a speculative excess which exceeds the inherent scope of either the logical or the phenomenological. Respectively – how can the discourse of what there can be pronounce on what there most fundamentally is? How can the discourse of the modes of appearance say how being itself ineluctably appears to us, much less what being in itself may be?

So one is left after all with a confirmation of the anti-metaphysical agnostic character of twentieth-century thought. But for the reasons we have seen, should not this idiom be questioned in the face of religious and neo-liberal violence – both the terror of pure faith and the terror of pure reason, whose collusional purity agnosticism helps to promote and preserve? Should not both its correlationism and its encouragement of plural fideism be called into question?[6]

---

[5] See, for example Phillipe Capelle, 'Heidegger, Lecteur de Saint Augustin', in *Finitude et Mystère* (Paris: Cerf, 2005), pp. 155–68.

[6] This question can be seen as the spirit of Pope Benedict's Regensburg address.

Veritas: Belief and Metaphysics

However, the agnosticism of twentieth-century thought, as we have seen, charted a mid-course between naturalism and religious speculation. So it would seem that if one questions it, then one must veer either to the left or to the right. And there is considerable evidence that this is already happening. One reaction, in part, to (understandable) fear of neo-religiosity is to espouse again a scientism of the Dawkins or Hawkings variety where, essentially, science itself does the work of metaphysics and offers a comprehensive vision of all of reality. A large public readership for difficult works expounding such views suggests that this scientism fulfils an immense social and psychological need. Meanwhile, within philosophy itself, there are many endorsements of this physicalism or else what one might describe as expositions of a kind of 'neo-Pythagoreanism'. By this I mean the view that the only categories of the real presupposed by the physical sciences are those of mathematics: physical reality is then regarded as the aleatory instantiation of pre-existing mathematical possibilities. At times Quine seemed to suggest that mathematics itself supplied an ontology; much more recently, in terms of a philosophy that somewhat bridges the analytic/continental divide, Alain Badiou has attempted to present set theory as an ontology, and category theory as the link between the ontological ground and the realm of actual appearances.[7] Badiou's political alliances are specifically Marxist and Maoist, and his tolerance for revolutionary terror as a temporary measure of the state leaves one fearful that his mode of evading an agnosticism that colludes with fideistic violence merely passes one back into the arms of an equally dangerous naturalistic ideology.

For all that, Badiou and his follower (in some measure) Meillassoux make two important points about the post-Kantian metaphysical legacy which broadly run in favour of the pre-Kantian and yet already modern metaphysical approaches of Galileo, Descartes, Spinoza and Leibniz. The first point is Badiou's: Kant's (and later Wittgenstein's) finitism is at variance with the specifically modern discovery of the immanence of the

---

7 Alain Badiou, *Being and Event*, trans. Oliver Feltham (London: Continuum, 2005); *Logiques des Mondes: L'être et l'événement*, 2 (Paris: Seuil, 2006).

Only Theology Saves Metaphysics

infinite with Cusanus, the primacy of the infinite (over the finite) with Descartes, the calculability of infinite quantities with Leibniz and finally the plurality and non-totality of the infinite with Cantor (who, as Badiou points out, was in many ways a Thomistic philosopher and theologian). For this reason, it is not that a speculative use of mathematics by philosophy is arbitrary; it is rather that mathematics has itself made a controlled speculation about the infinite newly possible. (One can agree with Badiou about the primacy of the infinite while still insisting that Nicholas of Cusa's more 'negative' understanding of this priority – the infinite is projected by us as in-finite, is preferable to the Scotist-Cartesian tendency to say that we can grasp infinity 'clearly and distinctly' as a 'positive' notion, even if we cannot fully comprehend it.)

The second point is Meillassoux's, in part after Jean-René Vernes.[8] Ever since Galileo and Descartes, and still more since Darwin, modern science has presumed to speak of the way that physical reality really is, in itself, independently of human observation. But the post-Kantian 'correlationist' view, which transcendentally restricts us to talk about how the world is for us only, is again at variance with this. One can add here, that this is based in Kant upon a wholly dubious claim to be able to intuit a priori extra-logical necessities (the doctrine of a priori synthesis). Without this claim, the Kantian 'middle' of critical idealism is surely derailed.

This second point, however, is not as clearly defensible as the first. Meillassoux exaggerates his case, by playing down the role of the divine observer in Galileo and Descartes, as guaranteeing the objectivity of external reality. Moreover, his supporting claim that correlationism especially breaks down with respect to the non-human past seems entirely doubtful. Why do evolutionary theories as developed by strictly scientific techniques of tested hypothesis (in so far as such theories do, indeed, respect such protocols) necessarily imply the strongest mode of realism as Meillassoux avers? Surely they only require the minimum philosophical assertion that they establish (approximately) how the pre-human natu-

---

8 Jean-René Vernes, *Critique de la Raison Aléatoire, ou, Descartes contre Kant* (Paris: Aubier Montagne, 1982).

ral world would have appeared to human beings had they been present to observe it.

Nevertheless, Meillassoux has a point. Modern science is scarcely epistemologically neutral, in the way that strict correlationism requires. Rather, it has an innate drive towards situating humanity in terms of the cosmos and not the inverse – a drive to 'round upon' the human subject itself in explanatory terms, even if certain branches of science, like quantum physics, may have discovered in objective, 'cosmological' terms that the bounds of human perspective is itself an aspect of a perspectival and relativized physical reality. And it does seem that Kant was essentially at odds with this constitutive thrust of the modern scientific outlook. Thus, for example, the supposedly over-speculative Christian Wolff supported the enterprise of an experimental psychology which the supposedly critical Kant eschewed in the name of a (fantasized) a priori rigour.[9] (It is surely possible to suppose that experimental observation of human mental workings will reveal certain patterns contingently rooted in our physicality, even though one would have problematically to allow for cultural variation and one should not dogmatically expect that this approach will by any means account for all or even much of the behaviour of a free and rational animal. But even pre-modern theology allowed for the empirically observable influence of the physical humours upon the human mind.)

As against Meillassoux, one may validly doubt the competence of natural science to encompass all of even our material reality (since it is not entirely predictable and controllable) and one might wish to argue (with both Aquinas and Descartes, in different modes) that philosophical realism requires an extra-human presence in the cosmos, since in truth we cannot hope to speak of 'how things are in themselves' as somewhat manifest in 'the way they are shown to us' unless we allow that 'the way they are shown to us' is irreducibly an appearance of things to *consciousness*, a being aware of things which we cannot in any way elide from our sense of 'thing' as such. To this degree, no spiritual metaphysics has ever avoided some sort of 'hypostasization' of the correlational,

---

9 See Frédéric Nef, *Qu'est ce que la Métaphysique?* (Paris: Gallimard, 2004), pp. 101–30.

Only Theology Saves Metaphysics

although older realisms, as opposed to speculative idealisms, posited rather a participation of our mode of correlation in a higher, hidden one, as opposed to an absolutization of our cognitive situation or its gradual development.

However, as with the contrast between Kant and Wolff just given, it remains the case that Meillassoux is right in so far as Kant's attempt to give science an anthropomorphic shape (which sometimes went to almost anthroposophical lengths, as with his absolutization of left- and right-handedness, on which his entire doctrine of absolute space depends), rather than an immanently cosmic or transcendently theological one, is in conflict with the basic thrust of the scientific enterprise.

But to these points of Badiou and Meillassoux concerning the post-Kantian correlationism that dominated twentieth-century philosophy, one can add three further ones, which considerably qualify their Galilean and Cartesian orientations.

The first is that the correlationist enterprise does not concern real constitutive relations between being and thinking. Such relations would involve the Aristotelian idea that finite being in some sense 'realizes' itself as human thought, and equivalently that the thought of a thing is so really related to that thing that in some sense it is identical with it. The ontological basis for this in Aristotle is, of course, the notion that the same form can exist in one mode as materially instantiated, and in another, more abstract mode, within a human or other sort of mind. By contrast, the 'correlation' of mind and world in twentieth-century philosophy is more one of accidental conjuncture ultimately determined by physical causality. Here the mind 'represents' to itself elements of the world with which it can by no means become identical, or at least it represents the appearances of these elements. To sustain a 'correlation' here, involves showing how the a priori structured thought-processes of the mind can be somehow 'matched' with empirical information. In exhibiting this connection one must first of all show the separation: both the 'givenness' on the side of the transcendental categories of understanding, and the equal 'givenness' of items of information that instance these categories in some measure or idiom.

Analytic philosophy in its classical guise depended upon this dividing and ruling, this Kantian benign synthesis of rationalism and empiricism. However, a post-analytic phase was inaugurated after the deconstruction of 'the myth of the given'. Sellars and then Quine and finally Rorty showed that the analytic is always already selectively synthetic, that the empirical is always already overdetermined by an interpretative application of the categorial. Inversely, the latter is but contingently constructed through an approximate and often culturally specific sense of the general culled from a selective empirical trawl.

In this way, within post-analytic thought, metaphysical and transcendental presuppositions, along with the practice of empirical observation, were once more historicized, in an effective reversion to the position of Collingwood. For this new outlook, one could say that the strange and yet basic ideas which we must presuppose in order to think at all (and which thereby supply the 'grammar' of normal 'empirical' ideas which are ideas of 'things' in an everyday, common-sense fashion) may indeed be to a large extent those fundamental ideas ('transcendental', 'metaphysical', whatever) which humans as such must presuppose. But since we can only reason by deploying the linguistic terms that we inherit, and we can never fully 'round upon' these terms to assess their own fundamental presuppositions – since they themselves are what we must most basically assume as the only terms which permit us to think at all – we cannot perfectly isolate metaphysical from cultural presuppositions, even if we rightly wish to eschew any relativistic counter-dogmatism.

In this way, the 'linguistic turn' itself finally defeated not only the reductive analytic programme, but also any merely transcendentalist or phenomenalist construal of the significance of this turn. Instead, one might say that those post-Baroque 'metaphysicians of language', namely Vico, Lowth, Hamann and Herder, were retrospectively vindicated: the linguistic turn, most radically understood, is *not* a 'linguistic idealism' which merely treats the fundamental grammar of human language (whether cultural or universal) as though it were a linguistification of the Kantian a priori categories of pre-linguistic thought. In terms of the latter, we 'inwardly' construct a human world by theoretically and imaginatively organizing sensory information according to permanently constrained norms. In the linguistified version of this, the constraints of language force us to construct within the space of interpersonal culture our human version of pre-given nature. However, language belongs surely within our primary artisanal interaction with the external world, such that we only reflexively possess an 'interiority' as a result of this interaction – this was perhaps the later Wittgenstein's most crucial message. And clearly this interaction is always both receptive and *externally* constructive (as of matter by the moulding of the hand, not of sensation by mind), such that it is impossible to disentangle the two components. The world is how we take it, yet what we take and modify is always the real world and always involves us in real relations to that world. (Trees are seen and are at once seen as shelter; they are buildings before buildings, while wooden buildings allow us to see both trees and shelter anew, and then to observe the trees now more for themselves and for the other relations in which they stand. Far down the line of human history, the British World War Two De Havilland Mosquito fighter-plane revealed anew the suppleness of the ash tree – of which it was constructed – beyond even anything that had been disclosed by Anglo-Saxon spear-shafts. Likewise, water observed is already water drunk and traversed and channelled, while fountains show us new and symbolic aspects of this liquid foundation for our lives.)

Thus our ideas of what is there involve always material symbols which historically became gradually abstracted into the spoken and written signs of language. In consequence, any word at once denotes a fact and an interpretation, in such a fashion as to render both empiricism and even a Kantian, critical idealism impossible. For we always arrive too late to disentangle what we have received from what we have constructed or what we have constructed from what we have stumbled upon. (The manipulation of wood discovers new properties of wood and 'arrives' at the actuality of the realized wooden dwelling.) For this reason, if the natural is always already for us cultural, the cultural never exits the natural and what is 'fundamental' for culture remains an attempt to discern what is 'fundamental' for nature.

Inevitably, then, the dissolution of the 'myth of the given' led to a revived pragmatism. Variants of the latter, however (continuing the blindness of William James in this respect) have usually failed to see that 'what works', pure and simple, remains too much on the empiricist side of the divide, whereas we can only define the *pragmata* that we seek in all their variety beyond mere utility, in terms of our obscure *theoremata,* which remotely anticipate 'what they will look like'. Nevertheless, it remains inversely the case that we can only explicate our 'theorems' by imagining in advance, and later pursuing in practice, all their consequences and implications. In other words, a non-reductive pragmatism, free of the myth of the given, would still require a mode of metaphysical speculation whose form cannot be dictated simply by 'pragmatic criteria' (as even Peirce perhaps too much presupposed).

The second further point to be made in criticism of any form of modern transcendentalist correlationism is that, if we cannot perfectly isolate metaphysical from historical presuppositions, then this goes along with the fact that we also cannot ever perfectly separate 'grammatical' category from 'empirical' content. A necessary vagueness pervades the meaning of categories like 'substance' or 'accident', or 'quality' or 'attribute' or 'relation', such that they are not just exemplified in particular empirical instances (as, for example, 'roundness' is by a circle), but also further interpreted as categories by these exemplifications, even though the examples cannot ever exhaust their range. It is partly for this reason that philosophers can never agree upon a fundamental list of categories – for example, is 'relation' irreducibly categorial, or is it shorthand for the relative constancy of merely accidental and contingent conjunctures? Is there an irreducible category of 'quality' as denoting something that must be 'attached' to a 'substance', or are there in reality only accidental 'bundles' of particular items, or indeed bundles of particularized attributes, sometimes today termed 'tropes'? The most reduced ontology would perhaps only admit the category of *res* taken as a univocal transcendental, thereby denying that reality must occur within any framework of 'natural necessity' (for example, always within some combination of the categorial terms listed by Aristotle) or else that it can only be known by us within the bounds of 'transcendental necessity' (for example, Kant's a priori conditions of understanding). Thereby reality is exiled from any mode of necessity whatsoever, other than that of logical necessity, which can itself be reduced to the various modes of consistency that follow upon the adoption of diverse initial axioms.

If, by contrast, one embraces some notion of 'natural' or else

Only Theology Saves Metaphysics

'transcendental' necessity, then can one come up with an incontrovertible and exhaustive list of fundamental categories? Here it should be remarked that there is something of a divide at the outset of the history of metaphysics. Aristotle sought to provide a definitive repertoire of categories, and so to give a complete list of all the basic 'hows' under which things fall. (How does such and such exist? As quantity, accident, relation and so forth.) Plato, on the other hand, was very unclear and fluctuating about the number of forms, and exactly what range of finite kinds of things required formal exemplars. While Neoplatonism sometimes sought to be more specific here, one might argue that this unclarity has to do with a sense that the boundary between the 'grammatical' and the 'empirical', while recognizable, is also murky. And of course this murkiness is most of all shown in Plato's controversial view that actual things in this world exist as 'participating' in their formal exemplars, while inversely the latter are not simply terms of art, nor just shadowy 'universal' aspects of real substantive things as for Aristotle (though also for Plato, in so far as forms are reflected within the material world), but themselves 'things' in the most eminent possible sense. (This was of course perpetuated by Christian theology in terms of the notion of divine ideas for which, for example, 'the tree' in God is far more tree than any created trees – as Aquinas affirms.)

Aristotle's providing of an exhaustive list of the modes of 'how' things can be, is itself linked to his marked concentration on the question of 'how'. This concentration provides us with a second important point of contrast with Plato, who is much more interested in the question of derivation or origination of things and so in the 'why' as well as the 'how', and even proffers the thesis that the answer to the 'why' alone fully describes the 'how'.

Aristotle's relative neglect of the issue of 'why' notoriously gives rise to a lacuna in his thought, as Adrian Pabst has recently pointed out.[10] Within his metaphysics, the formed substances that emerge in the course of time are lured forward by the first mover to their actualization, but not clearly generated by the first mover in the

---

10 In an as yet unpublished Cambridge doctoral thesis, entitled *Creation and Individuation: Theology and Politics in Patristic, Medieval and Early Modern Thought*.

first place. Likewise, the distinct modes in which being occurs (which give rise to the ways in which 'it may be said') apparently just *are*, and do not proceed from each other – privative being from motion from quality from substance from thinking substance, for example (as in Neoplatonism).

By contrast, in Plato the finite 'hows' only exist in terms of the causal 'whys' – by participation in the forms. But this priority of the 'why' is nonetheless made far clearer within the Neoplatonic synthesis of Plato with Aristotle, which provided a much more complete account of how hyper-substantive form engenders formalized material thing, and also allowed (from Plotinus onwards) that there is in some sense a form of everything that exists. For now participation is also a hierarchical generation from the One: first of all of the formal categories themselves and then successively of particulars – a *schema* that dominates (via the Syriac and Arabic transmissions) most of the 'Aristotelianism' of the early to high Middle Ages. Here, because the 'how' is always led back to the question of 'why' and only fully answered through this reduction, there is a kind of continuum between 'grammatical' category and 'empirical' content and a division of the two more in terms of degree than in terms of fundamental kind: qualitative division is subordinate to the 'quasi-quantitative' of the quasi-mathematical *series*. And indeed it is Platonism's greater attention to the mathematical paradigm for all identity and difference that permits this: for a number is ambivalently an empirical 'thing' and a category or 'set' of kinds of things. (For example, '2' is both an empirical position, and a definition of numbers occurring within a particular set – the set of all '2s'; likewise two apples are really there, but also only really there as a 'sorting' of these apples.) And arguably, Aristotle is not so much less tyrannically dominated by this mathematical paradigm (a common view) as less attentive to the implications of a paradigm that he, also, embraces, as in his recognition in the *Metaphysics* that *eidos* is, in one fundamental aspect, number.[11]

---

[11] See John Milbank, 'The Thomistic Telescope: Truth and Identity', in *American Catholic Philosophical Quarterly* 80.2 (Spring 2006), pp. 193–226.

Only Theology Saves Metaphysics

Now I wish to suggest something that might seem bizarre, but which I think merits consideration. There may be a certain structural homology between the Neoplatonic tracing of the how back up to the why on the one hand, and the historicist qualification of metaphysics on the other (and again, this is perhaps a very Collingwood-like thought). For in either case, one claims that one can only fully describe something in terms of origin. In either case also, this 'tracing back' only appears fallacious ('the genetic fallacy') if one assumes that a static synchronic functionality has priority over a dynamic process of becoming which constantly shifts the relations and emphases within a synchronic system – so in effect begging the question. Of course, in the one case one is speaking of a transcendent origin, in the other of an origin within historical time. Nevertheless, historicism, because it avers that the humanly universal and the culturally categorial are not readily separable, tends to have a Platonic bias towards the 'confusion' of the grammatical with the empirical. It will tend to see humanly assumed universals as vague in their generality and also as self-unfolding through empirical exemplification and as themselves partially generative of particulars through the course of their self-explication. (Of course one can see something like this in Hegel and Schelling; but one can borrow this from them while still prescinding from their account of necessary agonistic logical processes or their privileging of identity and will, respectively.)

And if modern historicism often reveals a certain Platonic affinity, then one can also conversely suggest that the requirement in Plato for a very concrete, specific encounter with an event in time as needed in order to 'trigger' our recollection of the forms (whereas in Aristotle there is no forgetting of the categories and so no need for the arrival of new events to stimulate our remembering of them), suggests a certain kind of proto-historicism. This was, indeed, augmented by the 'theurgic' reading of Plato's writings after Iamblichus, for which philosophical speculation can only be completed by the eventful descent of the divine into ever-renewed human ritual enactments. Augustine's modifications of Plotinus's 'interiorization' of the Platonic tradition should be seen (against most usual views) as parallel to this: the route to his 'remembering' of God lay through his biography and its recollection, which both involved crucial events of renewed 'illumination', penetrating within. Furthermore, the Christian disclosure of our total dependency on God as created from nothing and hence the drastic consequences of our sinful separation from God allow Augustine newly to make all of human history central for philosophy: the record of truth as the record of recollection is now indeed the 'hypertheurgic' account of the divine descent into time which shapes a worshipping community that offers a true sacrifice first as Israel, and then as the Church. The latter arises after the full meaning of this descent (of which Israel was a foreshadowing) has been revealed in the incarnation and God's own fulfilment of atoning sacrifice through the offering of re-created innocent humanity to himself by fully combining this offering with the eternal 'return' of the Son to the Father. Indeed, in the *Confessiones,* it is only the recollection of time which ensures that the meaning of time for the soul ceases to be a nihilistic 'dispersal', and can become instead a 'musical' integration of past, present and future which shadows the eternal. Thus Augustine's new 'historicization' of both theology and philosophy, while dependent wholly upon a biblical vision, nonetheless also augments certain latent features of the Platonic legacy. (I would also argue that it is this parallel to the theurgic that assists a later blending of Augustine with Dionysius and the consequent Maximian tradition – directly indebted to pagan theurgy via Proclus – in both Eriugena and Aquinas.)

I shall return to the analogy between Platonism and historicism presently. For now, a third further point needs to be made about the post-Kantian legacy of modern philosophy. This concerns the shift in treatment of the transcendentals which links to the priority of the possible over the actual, rather than the reverse. It is all very well to say that 'ontology' concerns the main modes in which being must be uttered (as Aristotle declared), but, as Aquinas realized beyond Aristotle (having absorbed Boethius's more rigorously logical and Neoplatonically influenced reflections on *esse*), being is not only transcategorial, it also transcends the contrast between category and content, just like that other transcendental *Unum* (also extremely important for Aquinas who stresses the divine simplicity as much or more than the divine *esse*), which, significantly is hyper-mathematical. (The number 'one' both most absolutely is only itself as complete, and at the same time is what most 'numbers', allows one 'to count' at all, because it is the very

Only Theology Saves Metaphysics

paradigm of all singular identity. Of transcendental 'unity' this is even more true.)

Being transcends the contrast between category and content: substance is, but a mouse equally is, and the dirt that the mouse has today picked up on its fur equally is also. For Aquinas, this opened the path to saying that beings, especially the higher sort of beings, are more defined by the actuality of what they do ('second act' or 'second perfection') and by the actual ends which they reach ('third perfection'), than by the initially given characteristics of their inert substantial being ('first act' or 'first perfection'). Just for this reason, he sometimes defines substance in its fullness, following Proclus, as a 'return to itself'.[12] All this means, in effect (as argued by Michel Corbin and Phillip Rosemann) that Thomas's metaphysics of *esse* itself opens out the excess over any pre-given essentialist ontology of the occurrence of the event, and itself confounds the priority of ontology over history, yet without simply reversing this priority.[13]

Similar considerations apply to other transcendental and trans-categorial terms like *ens, res, aliquid, unum, verum, bonum* and *pulchrum* (to list the major medieval examples). A particular and a universal both in some sense 'are'; they are both in some sense 'things'; they are both also 'some-thing' in such a mode that to be at all they must have some mark of distinction from all other things.[14] Likewise, the empirical can be as unified as much as the abstracted; a thing may (for Aquinas) be as 'true to itself' as we are

---

12 *ST* I, q.14, a.3 ad 1 and See Phillip W. Rosemann, *Omne Ens est Aliquid: Introduction à la Lecture du 'Système' Philosophique de Thomas d'Aquin* (Louvain/Paris: Peeters, 1996), pp. 52–65. Rosemann points out that this principle is already present in Aristotle, but that he confines it to the horizontal plane of outgoing and return within the same level of being, as, for example, humans always generate humans. The Neoplatonists, however, extended this principle to the vertical dimension of outgoing and return across diverse levels of being. Aquinas adopted the principle in this extended form.

13 For all the above paragraph see John Milbank and Catherine Pickstock, *Truth in Aquinas* (London: Routledge, 2001) in general but esp. 34 and Rosemann, *Omen Ens est Aliquid,* also in general but esp. pp. 13–48. See also Thomas Aquinas, *ST* I, q.6, a.3 resp; I.II, q.3, a. Resp; III, q.9, a.1 resp; *In Boeth. de Trin.* q.5, a.3.

14 On this, see Rosemann, *Omne ens est aliquid*, pp. 13–48.

to it; excellence may be shown in the flourishing of anything and not just in correct practical judgement. Finally, our sense of beauty is forced to hover between vague general norms (proportion, integrity, radiance, partial disclosure, etc.) and specific exempla that can never be definitive (such that the history of art is in part the history of the discovery of new and surprising modes of beauty – tending to prove that it is, indeed, a transcendental).

The above statements are, I think, in keeping with ordinary common sense. And yet the entire Kantian and post-Kantian enterprise depends upon a wholly questionable (and yet not perhaps demonstrably 'wrong', for all its counter-intuitivity) handling of the transcendentals which, by rendering them more subjective than objective (reduced to the main 'aspects of all things for us'), ensures that they become entirely 'grammatical' and not at all (in however obscure and problematic a sense, as the Middle Ages admitted) 'empirical', and thereby sink to the level of the quasi-categorially general and cease to be genuinely transcategorial. Thus, for example, for Kant, a flower in its entirety, cannot now be true as 'true to itself', but can only be related to the category true in so far as it is known about, just as it is only aspects of the flower which for Aristotle would fall under the categories of form, substance, accident and so forth (since categories are not for him or for Aquinas 'transcendentals' which apply to anything whatsoever and so to the totality of any particular thing).

A further consequence of this limitation of the meaning of 'transcendental' (which begins long before Kant, as far back as Duns Scotus) is that the full 'convertibility', the total overlapping of all the transcendentals grounded in divine simplicity – such that these paradoxically perfectly coinciding 'aspects' or *passiones* are only distinguished by our *modus cognoscendi* – is now compromised (beginning again with Scotus).[15] For since, in Kant, 'the good', for example, concerns only a certain way in which we subjectively take things, things as good need no longer necessarily be beautiful or true, or even 'be' as such at all.

---

15 For most of the points about Scotus in this essay, see Catherine Pickstock, *After Writing: On the Liturgical Consummation of Philosophy* (Oxford: Blackwell, 1998), pp. 121–67 and 'Duns Scotus: his historical and contemporary significance', in *Modern Theology* 21:4 (October 2005), pp. 543–74.

Only Theology Saves Metaphysics

But this reduction of the transcendentals to the quasi-categorial then has a de-historicizing consequence. In Aquinas, an entirely contingent, freely chosen deed of charity exercised on one particular unique day in time 'is' in one sense as much as anything else (even though 'things' in their totality may exhibit degrees of participation in being). It is also a 'thing' and 'some-thing' as much as anything else, and is likewise fully an instantiation of the integrally unified, the true, the good and the beautiful. But in post-Kantian thought, an event can only be a subordinate empirical instance 'for us' of quasi-categorial unity, difference, truth, goodness or beauty. This means that the 'feedback loop' from event to category is now lost: a particular work of charity as performed by a saint or by Jesus can now no longer redefine for us our whole sense of good as such, since this is exhaustively and formally defined by the categorical imperative; a strangely beautiful person or painting can likewise no longer reconfigure our entire sense of beauty, since this is also formally and entirely defined as the experience of the ineffable co-ordination of all the faculties.

Hence event has now sunk to the level of the 'illustrative' and while Hegel of course questioned this, he still, by articulating a material logic of becoming, ultimately folded back the contingent into the categorial, or else reduced it to the indifferently random. This applies also to Kant's treatment of 'being', although this point may be less immediately obvious. Certainly Kant, as inheriting from late scholasticism the thesis of the univocity of being, thinks that anything that is, from the highest to the lowest, equally and fully 'is'. So it might then appear to be the case that for Kant 'being' is much more of a genuine transcategorial transcendental in the traditional sense. And it is relevant here that the *Critique of Pure Reason* mainly concerns the topics of 'special metaphysics' – God, the soul and the cosmos – in the Suarezian tradition as transmitted via Wolff, and not the topic of 'general metaphysics' – *ens* as such, and its divisions. For Kant's implicit and elsewhere more articulated general ontology somewhat crosses the critical divide: both phenomena – experienced only by the positing of 'the transcendental object' as that obscure 'thingness' which binds appearing properties together – and noumena equally are (even if the former do not reliably disclose the latter), and practical reason *rationally* establishes the existence of the noumena.

Veritas: Belief and Metaphysics

However, Kant's famous view that 'being is not a predicate' sustains a post-Scotist reduction of even being to quasi-categoriality, the status of a quasi-genus. This is precisely because, if being is not an attribute, it is in reality for Kant a supposed bare, 'colourless' attribute of mere existence as such. If the 1,000 thalers exist, then their 'thalerness' has nothing to do with their existing and therefore their 'existence' is like the most thinned-out generic property imaginable – something you can see as being there (if you choose to insert a Scotist formal distinction) yet cannot see as possessing any characteristics – like looking at the most limpid imaginable water. For this reason, existence – taken as formally distinct from essence – teaches us nothing, save that an essence has been exemplified. We know all there is to be known about the 1,000 thalers if they are merely fictional; hence the fact that they exist – their event-status – is once more reduced to the merely illustrative.

By contrast, for Aquinas, as for Aristotle, the possible 1,000 thalers would be regarded as a possibility only gleaned from the fact that, in actuality, there has really arisen such a currency, sometimes traded in terms of such an amount, and only valid because real metals have been taken as valuable and have been stamped with the head of a certain monarch. This modal priority given to the actual means, for Aquinas (if not for Aristotle), that being is not a 'bare attribute' to which other purely essential qualities are super-added, but rather that all the qualities of, say, a coin, are primarily there not as possibilities but as actualities, as new manifestations of being as such, instances of further participation in being. In this way, for Aquinas, a new actuality can reveal to us 'more' of *esse* and there can be a hierarchy of more or less intense disclosures of *esse*. Thus while, for example, an accident 'is' in one sense as much as substance, the latter is a more primary site of being, and existential unities of substances, accidents, qualities, etc. can be arranged hierarchically: humans existing more richly than stones, and humans who reach their true *telos* through acts of charity more richly than their egotistic fellows.

Therefore, with the shift in meaning of 'transcendental' and especially of the transcendental *esse* from Scotus through to Kant and beyond, actuality is modally subordinated to possibility and in consequence the *event is reduced to the status of the illustrative*. The delusion of Protestant historicism (Hegel, Schelling, etc., ultimately rooted in Protestant scholasticism) is to imagine that a prizing of novelty favours the possible over the actual, whereas a genuinely Catholic historicism (Augustine, Aquinas, Cusanus, Pico, Bérulle, Vico, Ballanche, Péguy, Dawson – yet also the confessionally Lutheran Herder) grasps that the reverse is the case. For the possible can only be either the logically predetermined or else the reserve of sheer power and blind will, whereas the actual alone can present us with a genuinely new possibility (and open out yet further ones, in the way that an original work of art can give rise to an entire new genre), since it can show us a truth or a beauty or a goodness inseparable from its own contingent enactment. If the actual only illustrates the possible, then the only novelty it can exhibit will be that of the arbitrary and so of the violent. But if the possible is rather only ever abstracted from the actual (and how can we know what even logic would be if we lived under entirely different material circumstances?) then it is truly possible that we may always enjoy an expanded sense of possibility.

In short, post-Kantian philosophy, including twentieth-century philosophy, has been mostly committed to essentialism and to the priority of the possible over the actual, in such a way as to subordinate event to category. In this lineage, an affirmation of 'existence' is seen as merely the punctilinear confirmation that such and such an essence has been here instantiated, rather than as the acknowledgement of a contingently arriving actuality that might redefine for us what a particular thing is, what it is capable of and how it might be in the future. In the same fashion, as we have seen, after Kant the fundamental modes of truth and goodness and the experience of beauty became sedimented in an a priori fixity. Ludger Honnefelder has shown that this is basically because Kant had inherited, in a long lineage from Duns Scotus, a redefinition of a transcendental term as specifying in advance the exact formal 'range' of our access to goodness, truth, beauty and so forth, rather than, as for Aquinas, opening out for us an unlimited and but obscurely anticipated horizon of meaning which is real and objective and yet inexhaustible.[16] This is in part the reason why Aquinas

---

16 Ludger Honnefelder, *La Métaphysique comme Science Transcendental entre le Môyen Âge et les Temps Modernes*, trad. Isabelle Mandrella et al. (Paris: PUF, 2002).

says that everything is more true in God than it is for us, implying that, for him, to say something true regarding anything whatsoever, is first of all to identify with that thing and then, as it were, together with that thing to attempt to intimate something of its infinite depth of significance. Of course this appears 'wild' to modern philosophy – which is why it is ludicrous for the likes of Anthony Kenny to claim to be Aquinas's even remote progeny.

The line that stretches from Scotus to Kant attempts to tame this wildness. But the taming depends upon our being able in advance to determine the formal range of transcendental and perfection terms like 'being' and 'goodness'. Such a claim is itself arguably a form of metaphysical dogmatism that lacks even Aquinas's mystical alibi. At least the latter, one could say, is critically on the side of the inherently wild 'vagueness' of transcendental terms. This inherent vagueness tends to encourage, even if it does not rationally legitimize, the understanding of these terms as ontologically generative in a realist sense, and as raising the instance of the event to ontological equality with general circumstances. (One should, of course, acknowledge that Heidegger in his own albeit questionable mode – due to his contorted dishonesty about his theological sources of inspiration – achieved just these insights.)

One can claim then, that twentieth-century philosophy, defined as anti-metaphysical correlational agnosticism, has collapsed or is collapsing for five major reasons – some more recognized than others. These are: (1) renewed attention to the implications of the modern priority of the infinite over the finite; (2) likewise to the implications of the 'non-humanist' bias of modern science towards mind-independent reality; (3) the deconstruction of givenness; (4) the resurgence of concern with the category of the event; and finally, (5) the new genealogical tracing by many intellectual historians of modern philosophy back to its roots in post-Scotist scholasticism, which exposes certain buried metaphysical and theological presuppositions that may well remain open to a Thomistic critique.

One should add that variants of these critical questionings apply to phenomenology as well as to analysis. Heidegger, too, was committed to the priority of the possible over the actual and since he meant this in a non-logicist sense, it helps to foment a nihilistic tone in his *opus*. Similarly, the critique of 'the myth of the given' can be matched by a deconstruction of the notion of reduction to a fundamental donation of archi-phenomena (descendants of the Scotist *esse objectivum*, whose 'objectivity' for the understanding does not necessarily disclose any external reality)[17] to the human mind, as carried out by Derrida against Husserl in his surely (despite attempts) irrefutable *Voice and Phenomenon*. The continued later isolation of fundamental categorial donations, supposedly free of speculative decision, in the mode of Levinas, Marion and Henry, appears to be a sleight of interpretative hand. One can agree, instead, with Alain Badiou, that there can only be a plural phenomenology of various contingent natural and cultural 'worlds' with their own dominant logics of manifestation, always liable to historical revision.[18] By the same token, if there are no *foundational* donations after the manner of Husserl or even Heidegger, then nothing justifies the idea that the appearances of things do not belong to the real 'transcendent' exterior world rather than to our interior constitution of such a world, as in Husserl's transcendentally idealist idiom.

So it would seem that now, in the early twenty-first century, we are in a post-analytic and post-phenomenological situation. Correlationism has been deconstructed through exposure of the myth of the given, while agnosticism designed to ward off fanaticism appears now to foment it both directly and indirectly. Thus we see a return, in reaction, to a naturalistic 'metaphysics of the left'. However, this return, as in the case of Dawkins, seems to hold out a prospect of radical intolerance of religion which would surely undermine all human freedoms as such. Likewise, a return, with Badiou, to a materialist version of 'neo-pythagoreanism' holds out a new prospect of renewed state terror in the name of an implausibly arriving utopia.

So what of the metaphysically 'rightwards' alternative (which I hasten to say I do not in any way correlate with political conservatism)? Do we not now need again a rational discourse regarding the mysterious and the transcendent if we are to judge, as we must,

---

17 See André de Muralt, *L'Unité de la Philosophie Politique: de Scot, Occam et Suarez au Libéralisme Contemporain* (Paris: Vrin 2002), pp. 19–26, 61, 70, 106.

18 See Badiou, *Logiques des Mondes*.

between faith and faith and to enable a dialogue to take place between them? That would mean a recovery of metaphysics as 'wisdom', which is one of the terms used to describe this discourse from Aristotle onwards.

Faith, Reason and Terror in the Twenty-first Century

The answer to that is broadly yes, but I must enter some important caveats. This is not an appeal for a restored natural or rational theology. Indeed the latter, a purely post-Kantian early-modern phenomenon, is part of the post-Kantian problem, whether through its perpetuation or through a reaction against it which confuses it with a genuine metaphysics or theological ontology. Pure reason that purports to arrive at God or the soul or an ordered cosmos is deluding itself, and so only further assists the cause of agnosticism or atheism. Moreover, the conclusions that it reaches are so thin that they have to be supplemented with those of faith or revelation. And the deluded idea of an uninflected reason without arational assumptions or emotional bias encourages, inversely, the notion that faith commitments are simply 'beyond reason'. In this way, natural theology, still more than scepticism, is the ally of a partial fideism.

Likewise, all attempts to identify a common rational core between different religious faiths, or even to try to isolate a shared method of reading texts and shared criteria for authentic religious practice, to serve as the basis of dialogue, paradoxically foment fundamentalisms.[19] For beyond the shared core, the differences tend to become a no-go area, in such a fashion that they are all equally validated in their supra-rationality. It is perfectly possible that a religious fundamentalist will acknowledge in an interfaith context a shared rational theological core and yet still insist dogmatically upon the least justifiable aspects of his version of his own tradition – in the Islamic case, for example, on the divinely dictated-to-the-prophet and unerring character of the Qur'ān.

Instead of 'natural theology' and a 'common religious core',

---

19 Despite much common ground with what I am saying here, this is perhaps the case with so-called 'scriptural Reasoning'.

what we rather need to recover is a sense that philosophy itself, as for the Greeks, for the Indians, for the Muslim Iranians and for the modern Russian Orthodox tradition, can be rooted in a rational reflection upon religious commitments. Inversely, we need to recall that for Augustine and the Greek Church fathers, as for Philo and for several mystical Shi'ite and Sufi philosophers, revelation does not basically provide us with new information, but is rather a reflection upon events in performance and in utterance that are deemed to reconfigure our perception of transcendental being as such – or in the case of the event of the incarnation in Christianity, actually to reconfigure the real ontological relation of finite to infinite being. In Augustine, as in Aquinas, ontology itself was theologically modified in a way that acknowledged the openness of finite being to the possibility of incarnation and the descent of the Spirit, besides that of the human spirit to the deified reception of the beatific vision of the Trinity in the life to come. Accordingly, participation of finite being in God is now expressed in terms of remote relation to a triune God whose nature is obscurely hinted at by every level of the creation. Aquinas's understanding of finite individual act as advancing from substance to operation to finality is an example of this Trinitarian revision of the Aristotelian and Neoplatonic inheritance.

One could illustrate the point I am trying to make here about philosophy and revelation in the following way. Our modern assumptions would lead us to suppose that, for the Neoplatonic philosopher Proclus, proximity to the divine was achieved finally by knowledge, whereas for the Apostle Paul it was attained by faith. But as a matter of textual record the opposite pertains: Proclus says that the sage advances beyond *gnosis* to *pistis*, whereas Paul says that in the end faith falls away and we are left with the direct knowledge of God, albeit in the light of charity.[20]

The point is that our modern divisions, which are inherited from Christian scholasticism, are inaccurate for antiquity. Faith, grace, revelation, sacrament and conversion are categories that emerge as much or more from a Greek cultural legacy which also permeated philosophy, as from the Hebrew Bible, and sometimes the use of

---

20 See David Bradshaw, *Aristotle East and West: Metaphysics and the Division of Christendom* (Cambridge: CUP 2004), p. 151.

them by John or Paul is as 'philosophical' as it is 'religious', as has been increasingly recognized in (serious, not the general run of 'biblical critical') Pauline studies since Stanislas Breton's innovative little book on this subject.[21] Conversely, revelation is understood in the New Testament and by the Church fathers as an event that 'raises the capacity' of the human mind and extends the reach of its reasonings. A good illustration of this point can be taken from Duns Scotus, who is often rightly taken as a crucial figure in the genesis of the sundering of reason from revelation. Despite that fact, Scotus held that the truth of the univocity of being – often regarded as lying at the core of his proto-secularizing intellectual moves – was *more* apparent to human beings as a consequence of the incarnation, which had reminded humans again of the existence and primacy of the infinite. Fallen humans, he held, were more likely to assume that the first object of the mind is material being, and not to see that the mind, by force of its proper created nature, is orientated first to being which, with univocal indifference, may be infinite or finite as well as spiritual or material.[22]

So arguably, the true twenty-first-century alternative would be the encouragement of modes of reflection that integrate faith and reason on the lines of Augustinianism, a properly understood Thomism, the modern Russian Orthodox sophiological tradition or the Hasidic Jewish and mystical Islamic ones. All these traditions encourage the mutual interaction of faith and reason, besides a certain sacramental conveyance of spirit by matter and revelation by tradition and interpretation. It should surely be noted, in contrast, that it is an over-purist monotheism that wishes to cut down all the sacred groves and which has abandoned the mediations of sacrament, tradition and reason which appears today to generate the worst religious violence – whether we are talking about Muslims, Israelis or American evangelicals.

---

21 Stanislas Breton, *St. Paul* (Paris: PUF 1988).
22 See Pickstock, 'Duns Scotus: his historical and contemporary significance'.

The Return of the Metaphysical

To what I have said so far, it could easily be objected that I have neglected to mention the resurgence of metaphysics within analytic philosophy, in varieties that do not necessarily or always involve naturalism, and only in rare cases a pointing towards religious commitments. How is one to position this trend? As a continuation of correlational agnosticism or as a break with it? As analytic or post-analytic? I think the answer is that it hovers somewhere in the middle.

Thus, for example, if one is considering the influential 'plural worlds ontology' of the late David Lewis, one could compare the relation of Lewis to Quine to that of Hegel to Kant or of Heidegger to Husserl that I have already spoken of.[23] For all his 'modal realism' he did not contest Quine's suspicion of a logically modal definition of necessity that would cash-out in terms of ontological essence, rather than stipulating the conditions under which a relation that may effectively be deemed one of necessity might be identified. But where, in Quine, this confines modal considerations to pragmatic interactions with appearances, Lewis hypostasized just these interactions (like Fichte or Hegel hypostasizing transcendental understanding, or Heidegger hypostasizing the appearance of being to *Dasein*). For Lewis, the modal necessities which we generally recognize are those of our contingent actual world, which happens to fall under certain transcendental norms, and to have undergone a certain contingent but irreversible history, but there are other possible worlds which sustain an ontological equality with our own. Indeed the primacy of possibility over actuality was for Lewis so strong that for him these other possible worlds must be considered not as pure fictions, nor even as collections of fragmentary 'ersatz' surrogates shadowing our own world, in the mode of Jaakko Hintikka, but rather as themselves fully actual from their own point of view: this is exactly what defines 'modal realism'. (Nonetheless, Lewis was teasing about whether *we* can say that other worlds really exist and his main point was to argue

---

23 David Lewis, *On the Plurality of Worlds* (Oxford: Blackwell, 1986); on analytic metaphysics in general see also Nef, *Qu'est ce que la Métaphysique?*, pp. 415–783.

that this was an *unimportant* question; this indifference surely amounted to a nihilistic downgrading of actuality.) It is as if for him, as for Avicenna, the possible 'insists' itself into being, but now in multimondial fashion such that 'actuality' has itself been relativized to the point of view of but one possible world, on analogy with the perspective of a single conscious individual.[24] Frédéric Nef is surely right to say that Lewis in this way sought finally to consummate the post-Scotist overthrow of Aristotle's actualism.[25]

Within plural worlds ontology, the issue of whether or not there are stable essences then generally gets reduced to questions about which things in one world could appear as themselves to things in another world, or which things in one world might have counterparts in another, or finally which things in one world might actually migrate to another one. (I will confess here to preferring C. S. Lewis to David, along with Phillip Pullman, or Kieslowski's film *The Double Life of Veronique*; fiction just seems to handle all this with greater philosophical subtlety.)

David Lewis, following Quine, refused the perspectives of Saul Kripke and others which reduced such issues of identity to purely semantic ones which would seem to allow the usage of the name 'Plato' in one world, in fact to refer to 'Socrates' in another. At the same time, he also agreed, in effect, with Leibniz against Kripke, that one cannot sustain the same literal identity across all possible worlds: he saw the opposite view as an over-extension of the primacy of the criteria for a logical truth as sustaining itself in any possible world whatsoever. And it was for just this sort of reason that Lewis regarded ontology as more primary than logic: for in his view ontology had to do, not first of all with the principle of consistency, but with the imagining of diverse contingent sets of compossibilities. These different worlds were nonetheless for Lewis, as Nef puts it, 'federally united' in so far as some worlds other than ours can resemble ours in some or many respects and yet contain no items identical to the items in our worlds. Therefore they contain 'counterparts' which amount to little more than proximities along certain interlocking transcendental *spectra*: for example between the man who misses the number 84 bus in one

---

24 Lewis, *On the Plurality of Worlds*, pp. 92–7.
25 Nef, *Qu'est ce que la Métaphysique?*, pp. 675–7.

world and catches it in another, remembering that it cannot really be the same bus.[26]

However, for all the apparent 'return to metaphysics' here, at the seeming expense of the primacy of logical or semantic analysis, to suppose that these thinkable 'real fictions', federally conjoined within a Borgesian Babylonian library, enjoy ontological primacy with the actual world we know about is, in reality, merely to accord primacy to a more anarchic sense of the logically possible than that with which logic usually purports to deal.

Therefore what might well be asked at this point, is whether, having once gone so far in prioritizing possibility in all its infinite variety, one should not logically go in Badiou's 'neo-Pythagorean' direction. After all, the most elaborately abstracted as well as the most creatively free disquisitions (outside the normative axiomatizations of logic) on what one might term 'the actuality of possibility' and on migration from one organized world to another, are provided by the *mathematics* respectively of sets and of categorial 'bundling'. Hence it is arguable that the metaphysics of possible worlds, based upon logic, is but a weak version of speculative naturalism, whose most rigorous exponents lie within the French Cartesian tradition of reduction of the material to the mathematical (and so absolutely measurable).

By contrast, however, there are other contemporary analytic metaphysicians who accord a certain normative status to the actualities of the world we live in and recognize, beyond the occurrence of contingent bundles of properties, certain genuinely constant essences, irreducible ways in which properties 'belong in' substances, universals in excess of mere abstracted resemblance and even modes of constitutive relation. One can mention here, for example, David Armstrong and Jonathan Lowe.[27] In either case one can again speak to some extent of the 'post-analytic', since clearly the collapse of the 'myth of the given', or the duality of discrete a priori and a posteriori sources of knowledge must encourage philosophy to speak of real essences or real 'meanings'

---

26 On all this see Nef, *Qu'est ce que la Métaphysique?*, pp. 629–781.
27 See the latter's contribution in this volume, 'A Defence of Anti-Conceptualist Realism'.

(as John McDowell avers) out there in the world and not just resulting from a mental processing of empirical fodder.[28]

Such a recognition places this mode of philosophy nearer to certain traditional metaphysical discourses within the Western faith traditions before the onset, within Christendom, of the terminist revolution. However, thinkers like Armstrong and Lowe are basically trying to argue that the regularity of items and processes known to natural science, as well as to ordinary observation, involves certain necessary co-belongings or sequences. A defence of 'natural necessity' would seem to be implied here, in a way that it is not for the plural worlds theorists. While the latter indeed often speak of items like the constitution of water (as two parts hydrogen, one part oxygen) that might remain the same in different possible worlds, this only amounts to a constancy of definition across possible worlds, not to a real constancy of essence, since different but perhaps analogous contingent factors in different worlds might land up producing the same local result. And in general the positing of 'trans-world constancies' (as with 'counterparts') has to do with the impossibility of imagining another world *in every respect* different from our own.

So to read, with Lowe, this constancy of definition as a constancy of essence seems questionable. Fundamentally, he supposes that the regularity of composition in our world of water and so forth derives from the regularity of scientific laws which he deems to embody 'necessity' and not merely the recording of the entirely contingent normative regularities of the world we happen to inhabit. But nothing within secular reason, it seems to me, warrants this conclusion. Hume was right: within the framework of naturalism the only necessity that one should acknowledge is of the logical kind.

To support my contention here, it is worth considering briefly the history of thought about 'natural necessity'. First of all, the 'natural necessities' which Aristotle recognized in the cosmos were tied to his acknowledgement of the spirituality and (in some sense)

---

28 David Armstrong, *A World of States of Affairs* (Cambridge: CUP 1997); E. J. Lowe, *The Four-Category Ontology: A Metaphysical Foundation for Natural Science* (Oxford: OUP, 2006); John McDowell, *Mind and World* (Cambridge, MA: Harvard UP 1994).

eternity of form, which he espoused as much as Plato, even though he held that forms only occurred as incarnate in matter. The reality of forms as spiritual and in some sense eternal was then in turn inseparable from his obscure doctrine (which required, as we have seen, Neoplatonic revision) of the calling-forth of forms through the stimulation of the first mover.

In the case of Aristotle, the mode of 'necessity' involved here, which is certainly of an ontological valency, would seem ultimately to be linked to a pagan sense of fate. This is one reason why some Franciscan theologians in the Middle Ages, and later the nominalists, wished to pare down and ultimately (with Ockham and D'Ailly) to get rid of all non-logical necessity – thereby, perhaps, promoting a culturally dangerous sort of theological nihilism. For the nominalists, who were sometimes more extreme than Hume, not only is natural necessity unfathomable by us, it simply does not exist, regularities in nature being but the deposits of the divine will.

In the case of Bonaventure and Aquinas, however, the necessity of fate mutated into a notion of the divine election of the most 'convenient', or we should say the most 'beautiful' ontological patterns. The 'necessities' of the creation could for them be seen as harmonies which reflect the divine infinite harmony. God elects what is the most beautiful as he is, in himself, hyper-eminent beauty. Here necessity is neither fate nor sheer force of will, but nor is it is yet the Leibnizian divine calculus of the best possible world as that which will present the most complexity through the deployment of the most economy, according to the calculations of an infinite *mathesis* inaccessible to us, but still delivering (in our, univocal sense) a mathematical selection that is then confirmed by an act of pure choice, and not an aesthetic judgement. One could say here that Leibniz combines fate and the will, the pagan element with the nominalist-voluntarist one.

But from this briefly summarized history it can be concluded that, historically, natural necessity and, indeed, essences, universals, real relations and real inherence of qualities in substance have been always undergirded by *either* fate *or* divine beauty *or* divine will *or* divine *mathesis*. Once one has rejected all four of these things, then Hume is surely right, and, indeed, as Meillassoux argues, not radical enough. Without God, without spiritual substance, without form, the order of this world must be seen as a merely contingent given order, whose regularity is not 'unlikely' in terms of pure chance, since, after Cantor, there is no 'total' sum of possibilities within which, at the ultimate level, we can calculate (like Leibniz's God) even probabilities, or the very contrast between likely and unlikely chances.

It should be noted here that the critique of Hume by Thomas Reid of Aberdeen depended ultimately upon Reid's theism, since he was only able to move from a pragmatic to an ontological defence of realism by positing a divinely appointed link between our 'common sensing' and the essential inherence of qualities within things and the reality of cause.[29] This account of a realist theory of understanding was, in fact, more ineffable than that of Aristotle, since it lacked the immanent mediating factor provided by the Aristotelian notion that 'form' can migrate from material substance to 'intellectual being' as the scholastics later put it. And ultimately it is only this doctrine of knowledge 'by identity' which secures metaphysical realism at all, since if forms do not become universal within our minds (or, one might now say, within our linguistic expression) by virtue of a teleological ordering, then our mere 'representation' of how things are, including the apparent instance of constant essences, by a kind of 'mirroring', reduces either to a mere registering of appearances or else of an accidental world that might have been in every respect otherwise.

From this contention, negatively in favour of Hume, another one follows. Aristotle, notoriously, claimed in Book E of the (later named) *Metaphysics* that the 'first science' (which tradition came to describe as 'metaphysics') concerns *both* Being qua Being and its fundamental idioms *and* those entities that abide beyond the moving things described by physics: these are form and substance as relatively stable, separated spiritual substances (gods, later angels for the biblical traditions) and finally the first mover. Because the first three are somehow linked to the first mover, metaphysics is also, as he says, 'theology'. Neoplatonism later resolved the resulting *aporia* of which then comes first, Being or God, by deriving all being from a One beyond being or else later (in an

---

29 Thomas Reid, *An Inquiry into the Human Mind on the Principles of Common Sense*, ed. Derek R. Brookes (Pennsylvania: Penn State Press, 1997): see for example, Chapter 6, section 20, pp. 170–1.

Only Theology Saves Metaphysics

anonymous commentary on the Parmenides probably *not* by Porphyry – it is now thought – whose influence seems to have passed to Boethius and so eventually to Aquinas) a God who was himself being 'in the infinitive' (*esse*), being that is 'entirely verbal', being fully 'in act'.[30]

During the course of the Middle Ages however, beginning back in the twelfth century but then dominantly from 1300 onwards, most theologians indeed lapsed into 'ontotheology' by making being the prime object of metaphysics and God in some sense an object of study within the field of being. Rather like modern analytic philosophers, they tended to regard being as a surd property-less transcendental presupposition of all of reality, such that being *as such* had and required *no cause*.[31] Only finite being as created required a cause. Of course infinite being as uncreated did not require a cause and this might be seen (as by Scotus) as the most primary and paradigmatic instance of being, but the further and subtle point being made here is that for the dominant later medieval viewpoint it was also true that 'transcendental being' in itself, neutral as between infinite and finite, did not require a cause. So God created all finite 'thereness', but there was a kind of residue of 'thereness' which God did not create and which even his own infinite existence in some sense presupposed. This was primarily a logical presupposition, but also one given a certain ontological valency to the extent that infinite and finite started to be seen as both 'equally' and univocally existing: that is to say, as both occupying a 'transcendental' space of being that exceeds the space of formal logic. It was rather (in Scotus, who is the clearest here) a 'formal' space, hovering between the sheerly real and the merely logically modal (meaning here the *modus* in which we must perforce conceive things).

It was especially in terms of this new concept of the transcendentality of being that metaphysics became independent of theology and transcendentally prior to it, in the course of a long process that culminated with Suarez in the early seventeenth century. But here Aquinas (although he was later followed in this respect by the German Dominicans, by Pico and by Cusa) stands out as a quirky

---

30 See Bradshaw, *Aristotle East and West*, pp. 101–2.
31 Nef, *Qu'est ce que la Métaphysique?*, pp. 324–34.

exception: he, quite singularly, avoided ontotheology, because he almost uniquely saw metaphysics as having 'being' for its primary field of concern, and yet did *not* include God as an object of study within this field. Instead, for Aquinas, metaphysics could but dimly reason to God as the *cause* of its own subject-matter, God himself being properly the subject of a higher science, namely his own self-knowledge, in which we can participate only through the grace-given raising of humanity to supernatural life, which, however, is paradoxically never lacking from human nature as such, taken in its concrete specificity.[32] In a highly subtle and complex fashion for Aquinas, the bare theological conclusions which metaphysical reason itself gives rise to always already exceed themselves (for example, in terms of a universal pointing of all human thought and history to Christ, who is alone adequate finite truth)[33] in the direction of *sacra doctrina*, that knowledge of God's own higher science which we dimly receive through the mysteries of revelation.

But the important point to register here is that because, for Aquinas, the 'how' of being as such taken in the abstract (*ens commune*) is *entirely referred* to the 'why' of a higher cause, namely God who is substantively *esse* – and the non-abstract coincidence of being with essence – this means that existence as such, as we know it as abstractable (in real distinction from essence), *does* have a cause, and not simply a cause qua finite being. So for Aquinas, 'being' denotes not a surd transcendental fact, as for much of medieval (as well as nearly all modern) thought, but rather a Neoplatonic series of actualizations, taking 'actualization' to be convertible with 'perfecting'. This is one reason why 'analytic Thomism' makes about as much sense as, shall one say, 'market socialism'.

So for the 'majority report' of later medieval theology, metaphysics tended to become exclusively ontology, such that a complete description of the 'how' of the being of finite things might be provided without reference to the 'why' of their derivation. God

---

32 See Milbank and Pickstock, *Truth in Aquinas,* pp. 19–59.

33 See S-Th. Bonino, 'La théologie de la vérité dans la *Lectura super Joannem* de saint Thomas d'Aquin', in *Revue Thomiste, Veritas* special issue (January–June 2004), pp. 141–66.

himself had then to be situated within the transcendental ontological field in one way or another. In the case of Scotus he is so located through the a priori demonstrable primacy of the infinite over finite being, and this displaces the initial causal invocation of God, following the Dionysian tradition, as a 'requisite' source of contingent existences. For Aquinas, by contrast, metaphysics was yet more exclusively ontology rather than theology in the sense that (in contrast with Aristotle), God did not himself fall as an object of study within the ontological field.[34] Nevertheless, this field for Aquinas is radically fractured in its apparent completeness, such that it points in its entirety beyond itself towards a higher science, of whose reality we require to be fully assured by revelation. This fracturing means that the 'how' of *ens commune* is only fully accounted for by the displacement of all description towards the 'why' of derivation, such that God is concluded to within metaphysical ('rational') theology as a required cause of all being (if things are to make any ultimate sense and we are to avoid an infinite regress) and as an Averroist source of all motion, rather than as an Avicennian a priori demonstration of the primacy of infinite being within the field of being as such. For as the ineffable simple coincidence of being with essence, God lies 'beyond being' as we know it, namely as something contingently 'superadded' to essence, which always might or might not be (as Ibn Sina had already concluded, but with a bias towards the priority of essence).

It follows that while, in one sense, Aquinas avoided ontotheology by making metaphysics to be yet more exclusively ontology, in another he avoided the idea that ontology is transcendentally exhaustive, including even God within its scope. Hence, unlike many other medieval theologians, he also avoided a reduction of the Aristotelian hesitation between God and Being to an exclusive favouring of being, subordinating God, and rather made metaphysics to be about being in such a way that it was also problematically about God, in that it had to rationally subordinate its own positive knowledge of being to a hesitant, negative knowledge of the deity, since it concluded that God was entirely the source and 'explanation' of being, taken as abstractly general (*ens commune*).

The next crucial point to grasp is the link between these

---

34 See Milbank, 'Only theology overcomes metaphysics'.

ontotheological issues on the one hand, which have been mostly explored by 'Continental' historians of thought, and 'modal' issues (actuality and possibility, necessity and contingency – on which I have already touched) on the other hand, which have been mainly explored by 'analytic' historians (Finnish, British and French, though a scholar like Alain de Libera bridges this divide).

For the same shift towards metaphysics as primarily ontology ('containing' the theological) and not also, problematically, as theology in excess of ontology, also encouraged the rise of possibilism at the expense of actualism.

For Aristotle, the actual was primary in terms of definition, time and substance. We can define things because we encounter them; some things are possible only because other things are already actual; things that are actual are more real than things that are merely possible; ideas cannot of themselves give rise to things and finally the possible is defined by its tendency to the realization of an actual *telos*.

I would argue that this outlook is basically in keeping with commonsense. It was taken over and even augmented by Aquinas – for reasons which we shall see presently. For he understood the contingency of the created world in terms of the dependency of its *partial* actualization (and so its partial *perfection*) upon the divine simple and infinite actuality. In this manner the relative 'necessities' of the created order are just as contingent as its apparently more accidental or aleatory features.

For many of the Franciscan theologians however, as I have already mentioned, including Duns Scotus, this paid too much tribute to pagan fatality – although arguably, they only thought this because, for reasons of conceptual paradigm shift, they were *reinterpreting* the biblical legacy, and not because they were attending to it more precisely.[35] Instead of the notion of a partial created reflection of eternal glory, they preferred to stress the sheer electedness of the created order. Hence the very notion of 'contingency' started to be redefined, with papal backing at Avignon

---

35 This is a comment that I would want to make on Emmanuel Perrier OP's fine article, 'Duns Scotus facing reality: between absolute contingency and unquestionable consistency', in *Modern Theology* 21.4 (October 2005), pp. 619–43.

Only Theology Saves Metaphysics

and archepiscopal backing at Canterbury, as pure possibility that might have been otherwise. For Aquinas, as for Aristotle, an actuality realizes a possibility, but does not *continue* to be synchronically shadowed by a real possibility that is a hypostasized logical possibility, because for Aquinas an actuality fulfils in some measure a divinely intended good. By contrast, for Duns Scotus, the contingency of a finite actual moment is only guaranteed by the *persistence* in some sense of the real possibility that things might equally have been otherwise.[36] One could say that this view ignores the non-punctuality of events: the way in which, for a single actuality to have been different, everything would have had to have been different back to the beginning of time. But this is just why, with Leibniz, Scotist modalism shifts into the idiom of possible-worlds theory – the compossibles of the world are perennially shadowed by the compossibles of infinite other worlds. An entirely aleatory construal of this situation, however, is prevented in Leibniz by his Avicennian view that essence of itself 'urges' towards existence, that being is still, as for Aquinas, a perfection, and that God chooses the best of all possible worlds.[37]

However, the real point to note here is the link between attitudes towards the existential on the one hand and attitudes towards the modal on the other. If metaphysics on the post-Scotist view is about being and being concerns just the bare given instance of 'something as opposed to nothing', then actuality can no longer be construed as a rising order of perfections, and the complete 'nature' of a thing is fully determined, not by the arriving 'gift' of the event of actuality, but by preceding possibility. Thus metaphysics defined as the science of univocal being quickly becomes in effect or even in name the science not so much of every *ens* but rather of every *res* whether actual or possible, with priority given to the possible – and so to logic, to a sheerly indeterminate notion of will and choice and eventually, as with Kant, to knowledge over being, since knowledge has prior access to possibilities.

This gradual slide melds exactly with the shift in meaning of 'transcendental'. If being is merely the instantiation of possible being, then it exemplifies a predetermined range for being, as also

---

36 See Nef, *Qu'est ce que la Métaphysique?*, pp. 314–71.
37 See Nef, *Qu'est ce que la Métaphysique?*, pp. 379–415.

for unity, truth and goodness – now taken, after Scotus, not as fully convertible with each other, but as formally distinct on pain of losing their separate meanings, since it is now held that we have a *full and complete insight* into these meanings. This alliance of the redefined transcendental with the priority of the possible then continues to shape most of post-Kantian philosophy and in the twentieth century was just as prevalent within phenomenology as within analysis. (Cognitively speaking, we remain 'medieval' and are likely to remain so.)

In this way, the idea that natural necessities, essences, inherent formal meanings (*eid?*) and so forth, arrive only with actualization as 'gift' from God is therefore lost sight of. Instead, one has a doubly arid mere *givenness* without tint of generosity or gratitude. Possibilities are just 'there' without real receiving, while actuality is a non-predicamental existential instantiation of essence, equally sheerly 'there' without the 'why' of donation.

If, however, metaphysics secularized as transcendental ontology must perforce also be possibilistic, and if, as we have seen, possibilism without God points in all rigour towards a kind of nihilistic Pythagoreanism as articulated by Badiou (though with Badiou this is but half the story),[38] then it is fair to conclude that the *destiny* of metaphysics without theology is to be reduced to speculative materialism.

So my first contention is that 'natural necessity' can only be upheld by an Aristotelian belief in the spirituality of form, ultimately supported (beyond Aristotle) by the origin of form in God. And my second contention is that the Scotist and then nominalist-voluntarist turn from actualism to possibilism also reduces to speculative materialism, once the voluntarist God has been removed from the picture.

If these conclusions are correct, then the crucial intellectual issue of our time is the following: is the emancipation of metaphysics from theology as pure ontology, with the concomitant rise of possibilism, a tribute to critical progress – or was this shift rather initially to do with *theological* as well as philosophical preferences and then later to do with the ungrounded elective preference for a

---

38 See John Milbank, 'The Return of Mediation, or the Ambivalence of Alain Badiou' in *Angelaki* 12.1 (April 2007), pp. 127–43.

Only Theology Saves Metaphysics

materialist ontology? (Here one should mention that Alain Badiou generously, honestly and fully acknowledges that he has taken an initial axiomatic *decision* in his materialist reading of post-Cantorian mathematics, and that a theological reading, in the wake of Cantor's own Catholicism, remains a possibility.)

The first case, namely that secularized metaphysics has triumphed by force of argument, has been most comprehensively presented by the French analytic philosopher Frédéric Nef, in his at once monumental and fascinatingly meandering tome, *Qu'est-ce que la métaphysique?* He offers us here a history of metaphysics in a sophisticated analytic idiom that is reasonably sensitive to historical context. And he rightly urges *historical* reasons against the 'melodrama', as he sees it, of the Heideggerean narration. The trouble with the latter is that it exaggerates or misconstrues historical breaks like that between the Presocratics and Plato or – along with the entire modern German tradition up until the revisionist intellectual historiography of Honnefelder – that between supposedly pre- and post-critical (Kantian) thought. It also concentrates too much on big names and holistic systems, too little on minor figures and the continuous history of certain problems, in parallel with the history of mathematics. It especially fails to realize that the empiricists also offered their own metaphysical pictures, and partly for this reason it does not grasp that the issue of construal of modality (necessary and contingent, actual and possible) is as big or almost as big a constant theme as the treatment of being.[39]

With all this one can agree, and yet it is striking that, after all his cavils against a history of ruptures and genealogies of the *longue durée*, Nef himself unmistakably makes Duns Scotus and not Kant newly pivotal in the history of philosophy, in a manner that coincides both with Honnefelder's conclusions and with the revisions to Heidegger's historiography made by several French phenomenologists (primarily Courtine, Marion and Boulnois) who now generally see Duns Scotus and not Plato, nor even Aristotle, as the instigator of ontotheology (for reasons to which I have already alluded).

And yet, throughout his book, which tells the somewhat whig-

---

39 See Nef, *Qu'est ce que la Métaphysique?*, pp. 31–81.

gish story of the gradual but inexorable rational victory of possibilism, Nef polemicizes against the very notion of 'ontotheology' as used by Heidegger, and the idea that this notion should structure the recounting of the history of metaphysics. In resisting this metanarrative, he is also resisting the idea that metaphysics is a kind of contingent cultural invention, born of later Greek aporetic confusion, whereby God is defined in terms of being as 'a being' and yet being is itself, with a sort of vicious circularity, defined in terms of the exemplarity of the supreme being. Instead, Nef sees metaphysics as a perennial scientific possibility, one that was also pursued by Indian culture, within which it is surely impossible to trace any sort of 'ontotheological' conundrum. Picking up again on an earlier thematic, one might say that Nef sees the history of metaphysics in terms of 'how' certain problems have been tackled, where Heidegger saw it in genetic terms of asking just 'why' the question of being and the question of God had been problematically taken together within the Western legacy.

Which perspective is right? I suggested earlier that human beings inhabit both universal natural presuppositions and also inherited cultural ones, and that while it makes no sense perfectly to identify these two, we can never perfectly separate them either. Thus it seems to me sensible to say that yes, in India there has been something very akin to Western metaphysics and that *nevertheless* the legacy of Socrates' revision of Greek religion, and then the legacy of monotheism both pagan and biblical, has shaped all of Western philosophy, including Islamic philosophy, in a way that marks it out from Hindu philosophy in certain decisive ways (for example a dominant interest in both being as actual and the ultimate as goodness).

When it comes to the vexed question of 'ontotheology', then it seems that, at the minimum, we cannot deny that, since Aristotle, the question of being and the question of God (as manifest to both reason and revelation) have been taken together in a culturally specific way. In this sense, the question of 'how' arguments have been made and still more of 'how' questions have been posed is inseparable from the question of 'why' questions have been posed and answered in culturally specific fashions. After all, the big story which Nef himself tells is of the emancipation of ontology from theology to achieve a supposedly purer metaphysics, free of the distorting notions of the primacy of act which are linked to ideas of an actual originating deity. In this way he negatively acknowledges the historical importance of the link between God and Being.

His case, of course, is that ontology frees itself from theology and possibility from actuality by progressive force of argument alone. But in making this claim, one can notice that he commits some interpretative sleights of hand which sometimes make it seem as if the germs of later developments lay there all along. Above all, the orientation of metaphysics towards the knowledge of separate substances in Aristotle and (even) in Aquinas is reduced by Nef to an orientation towards the knowledge of abstractable universals alone (although these fall, for Aristotle, short of full separability). Accordingly, Aristotle's assertion that were there *no* separate substances and a final mover in existence then *physics* would be the first philosophy is ignored.[40] It is then falsely claimed by Nef that Aristotle locates God within the field of being, whereas he leaves him in an aporetic unclarity that nevertheless falls short of an ontotheological circle.

Equally, Nef misreads Aquinas as espousing an orientation of human beings to an independent philosophical beatitude (as affirmed for example by Siger of Brabant), whereas it is clear to the contrary that he thinks this can only be fulfilled through the grace-given beatific vision and its anticipations, as spoken of by St Paul.[41]

Finally, Nef's treatment of Olivier Boulnois' ontotheological construal of Scotus is shoddy: Scotus does indeed see God as transcendentally located within being and yet at the same time (with a kind of vicious circularity), being as itself paradigmatically instanced by the infinite being of God, which 'formally' precedes all his other attributes. It is true that Scotus does not as yet simply see God as 'a being', albeit supreme, but Nef ignores the way in which univocity of being opened the way for later theologians idolatrously to describe God as 'an individual'.

In these ways, Nef underplays the ruptures in the history of philosophy concerning the relationship between God and being; this then assists him in too easily concluding that the decisive

---

40 Cf. Aristotle, *Metaphysics*, 1026a20–34.
41 See Milbank and Pickstock, *Truth in Aquinas*, pp. 19–59.

rupture in modal considerations which he *does* acknowledge was a fundamentally philosophical break and not, as I would argue, a theological-philosophical *causura*, and one which moreover involved considerations belonging properly to *sacra doctrina* as well as those belonging to that 'theology' which is entertained by metaphysics itself.

My own main arguments against Nef's view that the emancipation of ontology and the possible from theology and the actual was a victory for good argument are, in outline the following.

First of all, as we have seen, it is only theology (rational and revealed) which, in the last analysis sustains a subject matter for metaphysics beyond the physical realm; otherwise one can more coherently transcendentalize physical or mathematical notions. It is here relevant that only with Suarez was 'general metaphysics' as initial ontology clearly separated from 'special metaphysics' dealing with God, the soul and the cosmos. (The contrast here, say with Neoplatonic modes of metaphysics which begin with God and return to him, is clearly stark.)

Suarez' division meant that questions of 'how things are' now transcendentally preceded questions of 'why things are'. By contrast, in the main traditions of Christian metaphysics and notably in Aquinas, the 'general' descriptions had also involved (Neoplatonically) 'generative' narrations – hence in Aquinas, *esse* was explained as that hyper-general reality in which all participate (beyond the abstractable created generality of *ens commune*) only in terms of its dynamic descending supervenience upon the created restrictions of *essentia*, existing in this mode or in that.

But nothing objective seems to justify the later sundering of the metaphysical 'how' from the metaphysical 'why'. Rather it rests upon a *decision* to read reality in cold terms as doubly given – once as possibility, second as existentiality and not in warm terms as the receiving of a gift – such that only the arriving actuality of a thing fully defines it as what it is: actuality fully realizing formal essence.

The 'cold' reading of reality effectively construes *all* of being as merely like instances *within* being. Thus, within the bounds of existence, a bicycle in a shop-window might present to the spectator the possibility of a gift to be given, whereas its later handing-over to a child (after purchase) is the actuality of donation. At first the potential gift is just a 'given' in the window, while its later

Only Theology Saves Metaphysics

becoming a gift is a second 'given' fact of actualization. Likewise, the cold transcendental ontology regards that being in general which is exhibited in finitude as simply the 'matter of fact' given instantiation of a previously 'given' (and not in any sense donated) possibility of finite being. The same dual givenness applies to the specific general arrangements of the world which we happen to inhabit.

But surely the religious sensibility tends to read existence as such as only *definable* in terms of gift – as if the bicycle had never first appeared in the window and never had to be bought, but was miraculously conjured up only in that instance when it first appeared to the child on the morning of his birthday (and as if we could only receive and ride bicycles which were presents).

And yet, despite this, the shift from interpreting being as created gift to interpreting it as uncreated givenness *did not* first occur mainly in terms of an exercise of purely philosophical reason. Instead, certain modes of reasoning were adopted in terms of a religious attitude which wished to protect absolute divine freedom beyond even the scope of its generosity, by insisting that God, in relation to the world, mainly considers a range of 'given' possibilities and then, as 'a matter of fact' makes a certain decision as to which ones will be actualized. Here, Aquinas's alternative religious vision, according to which God is himself 'compelled' in creating by the aesthetic 'glory' of his own intellect in the Paternal uttering of the *Verbum*, and the discriminating selective aesthetic judgements which he makes as to the contents of our world, is dogmatically, not rationally, abandoned. (It should nonetheless be noted here that *actus* in the infinite God does not denote exactly that 'termination' of possibility in act that finite act does; hence one could argue that for Aquinas the divine infinite act fulfils as sustaining the 'active possibility' that is *virtus*, even if it infinitely fulfils it. This is clearer in Nicholas of Cusa for whom, in God, the contrast of act and possibility is overcome as *possest*. But even his later *posse ipsum* surely denotes an 'active possibility' and not the reserved absolute power of the nominalists.)

In the second place, it would seem that there are at least equally good reasons in favour of the priority of the actual as of its reverse. Does not this principle alone conserve a strong realism and indeed a kind of radical empiricism, as G. K. Chesterton divulged? For if we do not first know the fundamental patterns of the world and the kinds of things in it by encountering them in existence, then, as I have already argued, we can never encounter anything radically new, which seems counter-intuitive. All that we could meet with would be instantiations of essences we already knew about, or could in principle imagine, trivially varied. Of course, there is the problem of how we can recognize radically new things or search for unknown ones, but Plato and Augustine recognized that our strange anticipation of the unknown is radically aporetic, and requires an appeal to transcendence (in terms of recollection or illumination), on pain of denying the arrival of the new as something still rationally coherent.

This is the positive argument for the priority of the actual. The negative argument is that, just as we can ask the idealist, with Jonathan Lowe, 'but what is the reality of your thinking?', so also with the possibilist we can ask (as he does not realize), 'but what is the actuality of your pre-given range of possibilities?' Surely they are only the possibilities that we have abstracted by affirmation or else by counterfactual contrast from this actual world, such that to sustain possibilism one would have to argue, in a nihilistic fashion, that the possibilities which *we* can glean are only the faintest degree of the actuality of this world, which itself only instantiates possibilities from a further range of hidden and to us radically counter-intuitive ones. And nihilism itself is forced to speak in paradoxical terms of the void or the repertoire of the sheerly aleatory *as if* they also were actual.

Philosophy habitually describes a possibility that is non-actual as 'fictional', but fictions, especially novels, rather show us that thickly-imagined alternative possibilities possess some degree of actuality of their own, because one can only grasp, say, the 'logic' of *Bleak House* by treating its world *as* a complex actuality and not at all as a mixture of essential possibilities blended together in varying combinations with certain diverting but inessential variations. Such a reduction of the book to predictable manipulations of structure would simply lose the specificity of the novel and its precondition of narrative genius. This is partly why Chesterton thought that the 'other realities' of fictions, especially fairy tales, revealed by indirection the 'magical' and unfathomable curious necessities ('limitations') of our own world, which are inseparable from its actuality, yet which can now, through this indirection, be seen as more than arbitrary, but rather as strangely necessary for the achievement of a life that bears aesthetic weight and moral solemnity.[42]

In these ways the bias of common sense runs towards the priority of the actual. However, I have already indicated that the counter-intuition of possibilism cannot readily be rationally refused, although it is forced to go to the lengths of nihilism. Hence the bent of the natural mind within this particular world can only be confirmed through resort to the theological. Agnosticism and atheism will rather, for the good Humean reasons which I earlier set out, favour the priority of the possible.

The Two Rival Metaphysics are Rival Christianities

All that I have said so far tends to suggest that the living viable forms of metaphysics are four in number.

First, there is theological realism inspired by Plato and Aristotle, which takes many different varieties within the three monotheistic faiths.

Second, there is the Scotist or Ockhamist version of Christian belief, still alive and well, for example, among many modern Franciscans and within the current Oxford theology department. This version allies philosophical possibilism (and so rationalism) with theological voluntarism (and so formalism and extrinsicism).

Third, there is an agnostic non-theological metaphysical realism of the type espoused by Armstrong or Lowe.

Fourth, there is post-metaphysical speculative materialism as approached by David Lewis but much more systematically realized by Alain Badiou.

The fourth option rests upon a rationally possible decision – but it too readily opens the way again upon positivistic secular terror. The third option offers much with which the theological realist will sympathize, but fails to see that metaphysical realism is

---

42 See John Milbank, 'Fictioning things: Gift and Narrative', in *Religion and Literature* 37.3 (Autumn 2005), pp. 1–37.

Veritas: Belief and Metaphysics

impossible without theology and likewise fails fully to see that this realism favours actualism, not possibilism.

So one is left with the two theological options for metaphysics which I would contend correspond to two rival Christianities. Here a couple of final considerations are in order, with respect to the question of Christianity and actualism.

First of all, as David Bradshaw has shown, *energeia* (which becomes Latin *actus*) dominates in Christian thought not just philosophically because of Aristotle, but also theologically because of St Paul. The latter for the first time spoke of God as giving the gift of his *energeia*, his activity, which is also his *energetic power*, such that our acts are synergically fused with acts that *go out* from God, and yet also *are* God. Later, a parallel fusion of human with divine *energeia* is found in pagan magical and theurgic texts (as Bradshaw further points out), whose suggestions are later fused with the Pauline ones by Dionysius the Areopagite. (Bradshaw follows recent scholarship in insisting, beyond Daniélou and Balthasar, on the crucial importance of this incorporation of the theurgic for later Christian theology.[43]) Only within this Christian tradition does Aristotelian being become emphatically also supreme actuality as supreme *act*, which, like light after Plotinus, goes out from itself while remaining within itself. Although his dubious Palamite biases unfortunately prevent Bradshaw from seeing this (a great pity, since it would much more fit the general thesis of his book), Aquinas is the supreme consummator of this entire tradition.[44]

In the end, this tradition is based on the incarnation, and this is the crucial reason why, if 'only theology saves metaphysics', we are talking about *sacra doctrina* as well as purely philosophical theology. Judaism and still more Islam tend to be suspicious of the capacity of image to disclose God, whereas they both consider law to be supremely disclosive of God. But Christianity is somewhat suspicious of law as the prime disclosure of God (Paul declared that it is 'preceded' by faith) and testifies that one supreme image (Christ) fully manifests God, such that all other images are in some degree sanctified.

---

43 See Ysabel de Andia, *Henosis: L'Union à Dieu chez Denys l'Aréopagite* (Leiden: Brill, 1996).

44 Bradshaw, *Aristotle East and West*, pp. 45–73; 119–53.

Now law prescribes in advance. While it would be utterly crass to say that pre-modern law wholly favoured possibility over actuality (since it relied greatly upon precedent, narrative and legal fiction), nonetheless law as a category in general does so more than image as a category in general. The primacy of image also entails the primacy of actuality (*this* realized picture beyond any pre-given formula rather than another), whereas any shift towards making law and will the most central considerations will tend also to favour the priority of the possible.

Here it is notable, as Pope Benedict indicated in his Regensburg address, that the post-Scotist stress upon possibility and the viewpoint of the now 'representing' subject (sundered from Aristotelian 'knowledge by identity') stems eventually from the lineage of the Muslim Ibn Sina.[45] (Though clearly it might have been politically wiser if the Pope had pointed out that there are other currents of Islamic philosophy at variance with this and in some ways closer in spirit to Aquinas: the work of Ibn El Arabi, for example.) Ibn Sina's essentialism in turn derived ultimately from Plotinus, who (unlike Iamblichus and Proclus who reacted against him) started to bend Platonism towards a philosophy of the a priori. It is also notable that the hypostasization of logical possibility as the foundation of ontology derives not so much from a reading of Aristotle directly as from a reading of Plotinus's student Porphyry, transmitted via Boethius. Here Gilbert of Porreta's work is also crucial and it must be noted that his work preceded the decisive Islamic influence.[46] Nevertheless, the encouragement of possibilism in the dominant currents of Islamic philosophy can certainly be connected to a religion that makes divine will and divine law the fundamental focus. Therefore one can, indeed, with Pope Benedict XVI, speak of the dominant post-1300 tendencies within Christian thought as involving a certain dubious 'Islamification' of the West – a tendency also reflected in the turn to political absolutism. (It is fair to speak in these terms, since a fideist version of the Sunni tradition has been overwhelmingly dominant in Islamic history.)

---

45 Benedict XVI, 'Faith, Reason and the University', delivered in the Aula Magna of the University of Regensburg, Tuesday 12 September 2006. For the text see on the web at http://www.vatican.va/holy_father/Benedict_xvi/speeches/2006/September/documents

46 Again, see the unpublished dissertation of Adrian Pabst.

Hence to deny the primacy of the actual is to deny the primacy of the image and the exceeding of the law by the incarnate Christ. This is why one can argue that Scotism and nominalism are diminished Christian theologies.

The second consideration again alludes to Duns Scotus. Emmanuel Perrier, OP is right to say that Scotus implicitly saw the question of the 'why' of creation as settled by dogmatic theology, and so focused, philosophically, on the 'how' of the way things synchronically are, thereby providing the grounds for the emergence of modern philosophical autonomy.[47] But we have already seen how this loses Being understood as gift, and so the right of theology (dogmatic and rational, inseparably) as queen of the sciences, fundamentally and finally to exhibit how things are. Moreover, the post-Scotist assumption (not quite so crudely fully fledged in Scotus himself) that dogmatic theology has already answered the key questions, loses the sense that revelation only provides answers as further mysteries and conundra. It is not an accident that Scotus explicitly abandoned the *via negativa*. In doing so, and in equally abandoning the sense that dogmatic theology involves a raising of discursive reasoning towards a fuller reason that is more intellectually intuitive (so anticipating the 'all at once' of the beatific vision), he inaugurated the reign of fideism which, as I argued at the outset, opens the gateway to religious terror. Terror has a specific modality and it is always that of the priority of the possible, whether this be religious or naturalistic – both being facets of modernity.

If Christianity, because of its exaltation of the image, appears to be the tradition most unambiguously committed to metaphysical realism, then certain currents within mystical Islam (Al Ghazali, Ibn el Arabi, Mulla Sadra), mystical Judaism and even Hinduism, together with Mahayana and Shin Buddhism, should also be acknowledged as so committed, albeit in a lesser degree. It is in this varied perenniality, which traces the how of things to the eternal why, and yet acknowledges both the varieties and the mergings of our diverse cultural whys as shaping our metaphysical hows, that the main hope of the twenty-first century must lie.

---

47 Perrier, 'Duns Scotus Facing Reality'.

Appendix

An Interview with John Milbank and Conor Cunningham

This text was transcribed from interviews conducted by Luiz Felipe Pondé, Professor at the Pontíficia Universidade Católica de São Paulo with Professor John Milbank and Dr Conor Cunningham. The interviews were given at the Centre of Theology and Philosophy's International Conference, Belief and Metaphysics, *presented in partnership with the Instituto de Filosofía Edith Stein de Granada, in September 2006.*

Luiz Felipe Pondé: *My first question is for Professor Milbank. What do you think of liberation theology?*

John Milbank: This is a question that I perhaps have to answer with a certain amount of caution, because it could well be that in terms of politics I am on the same side as the liberation theologians, but nonetheless I often have a lot of problems with them in theological terms.

I think that by far the best book of this school remains Gustavo Gutiérrez's *A Theology of Liberation*. There he makes a very important challenge to the consensus that, since Vatican II, tended to cordon-off politics to a sphere apart from theological discourse. He quite rightly pointed out that, on the one hand, Vatican II was proposing a kind of fluidity between the roles of nature and the supernatural, but, on the other hand, it was trying to make a very sharp division between the world of politics and the world of Church. This is Congar's 'distinction of planes' model. The Council fathers understandably tended to reject the old mode of Catholic reactionary politics and the 'orthodoxies' that supported authoritarian regimes, and at the same time they were trying to come to terms with a post-war liberal context. However, in doing so they surrendered too uncritically to liberal norms, and Gutiérrez was the first one to see the real inconsistency here.

Veritas: Belief and Metaphysics

In advocating a greater integration of grace and nature in the social sphere, however, Gutiérrez opted for a Rahnerian account of our natural orientation to the supernatural, rather than the account favoured by Henri de Lubac and Hans Urs von Balthasar. There is a significant difference between the two. For Rahner, there is at once too much stress on nature aspiring to grace and as predetermining the way it can be received and *also* on the specific superadded anticipation of grace as discontinuous with nature ('the supernatural existential'). De Lubac and Balthasar, by contrast, are much more abruptly paradoxical: all true nature is obscurely orientated to the beatific vision, and yet grace transforms nature (without destroying it) down to its very roots. In sociopolitical terms this suggests a much greater haziness between the secular and the religious and a greater capacity for theology to reinterpret social realities.

So I believe that one would in fact extend Gutiérrez's critical project further if one were to develop a political theology based more on the de Lubacian-Balthasarian, rather than the Rahnerian, model. And in a sense my political theology and that of Radical Orthodoxy (although its theology is by no means confined to the 'political') is an extension that attempts to do just this. Such a political theology wouldn't point in a strictly 'conservative' political direction; on the contrary, de Lubac wrote a critically appreciative book on Proudhon, and was profoundly sympathetic to a certain kind of non-statist socialism that has deep roots in the English as well as the French tradition.

What I find odd about liberation theology (and obviously this is difficult for me to say because I am talking about people who are struggling in situations vastly more difficult than anything I have ever experienced, and I very much sympathize with their struggle) is that often it doesn't seem to refer to earlier traditions of Christian socialism as they were formed both in Europe and in the Americas. (Here one might mention the work of Charles Péguy, Dorothy Day, Conrad Noel and Simone Weil, for example.) It seems to me that within liberation theology these long-standing traditions of Christian socialism have been too readily dismissed or passed over. I suspect that the reason for this is that liberation theology has tended to support a broadly Enlightenment form of logic, along with the normativity of secularization. Indeed it does so to such a degree that the first political move of liberation theology has tended to be the acceptance of a theology in which secularization is basically understood as 'good' and as an (if not 'the') authentic application of the gospel itself. And if part of the problem here has been liberation theology's relationship to Marxism (but I think this issue is entirely secondary to its prior endorsement of secularization), I would point out that there are other Christian (critical) engagements with Marxism that don't necessarily begin with this poor secularizing move.

So the problem with liberation theology, as I see it, is its enormous confidence in modernity and its location of theology within this normative framework: it is possible that this is the consequence of the normativity of the modern (curious as this may sound) within Iberian culture, which basically commences with the baroque in a way that it is not true of more northerly Western Europe. I feel that, by contrast, the earlier tradition of Christian socialism was much more critical of Enlightenment and modernity, and concomitantly tried to develop its version of socialism more directly out of theological resources than liberation theology has done.

The ethical consequence of this was that it much more sustained the idea that justice is only fulfilled as love, mercy and forgiveness than liberation theology has done, even though it also insisted that there is an *ordo amoris* in love, that love itself must be distributed justly. Liberation theology by contrast too often surrenders to a relativism of supposed circumstance in making justice primary, whereas if one insists on the universal primacy of charity and the attainment of real substantive social reconciliation, one can in fact make a more radical – because theological – challenge to current social conditions.

The political consequences of the greater theological stress of earlier Christian socialism were often an advocacy of co-operative or guild socialism with less of a role for the state and an insistence on the importance of intermediary associations, the widest possible distribution of private property (which remains valid) in the interest of the common good, and decentralization wherever this is most appropriate. All these emphases mean that true Christian socialism is a kind of 'left' version of Catholic social teaching – an important body of reflection which, in my view, liberation theology often dismisses far too quickly. But it may well be that I am ignorant of many new developments within Latin American political theology.

Luiz Felipe Pondé: *My second question is for Dr Cunningham. As the author of* Genealogy of Nihilism *what, if any, connection is there between nihilism and the social sciences?*

Conor Cunningham: In one sense, the social sciences can be understood as employing a methodological version of nihilism just to operate. In other words, in a manner reminiscent of the life sciences, they in some sense presume that the object under investigation does not have an irreducible integrity. Or, better put, their analysis can only ever go in one direction, so that, for instance, from the get-go religion is presupposed to be unable to illuminate the social sciences themselves. One could here perhaps imagine a scenario wherein an anthropologist hailing from Mars arrives on Earth and begins to investigate a rather strange practice found on this little planet, namely, 'religion'. Fair enough, one might be inclined to say, but never do we hear of a similar anthropologist coming and studying another strange practice also to be found on Earth, namely, 'anthropology'. In this way the social sciences are bereft of any reflexive awareness. And this is fine, on one level. As with the other sciences, or naturalism in general, difficulties arise when this methodological, analytic unilateralism lapses into an ontology. And so, as I see it, it is now the case that such sciences do not pay any attention to what such practices might say to them, because if they did the particular science would simply not work, in a purely utilitarian sense. Rather there is no counterfactual possibility of this ever happening, because the object or practice that is under the gaze of analysis is now not simply examined in terms of its parts, but is reduced to them. The object or practice is then denied any ontological integrity. At this point, I would argue, the sciences (social or otherwise) become vehicles for nihilism.

Appendix

Luiz Felipe Pondé: *How should the West deal with Islamic fundamentalism?*

John Milbank: First of all I want to say I think the recent policies of both the state of Israel and the United States may be just as big a problem. While I understand Israel's fear of the fact that still far too many Muslims do not accept her right to exist, her current behaviour only tends to confirm their arguments. Meanwhile, the imperialist ambitions of the United States are enormous and the link between capitalism and Protestant fundamentalism is increasing and is heavily deployed to undermine other cultures, including those of Latin America.

Second, I am suspicious of 'Islamic fundamentalism' as a blanket term. I think it tends to obscure the complexities of all kinds of different Islamic groups and traditions – for example, the regime in Iran is an attempt to have a kind of Islamic socialism, although it is also true that this has taken on what one can loosely call a 'fascistic' colouring. More crucially, though, 'fundamentalism' is a very difficult term in relation to Islam because to some extent the orthodox Islamic attitude to the Qur'ān is inherently 'fundamentalist'. Islam as such regards the language of the Qur'ān itself as the literal and unmediated word of God, even though traditionally this allows for allegorical readings built upon the literal sense. Furthermore, legitimization of any practice within Islam tends to rely upon an attribution directly back to the life of the prophet by reference to the numerous extra-Qur'ānic Hadiths. Whereas Christians regard Jesus as the Son of God and yet know little about his life and accordingly cannot build everything upon a literal *imitatio Christi*, Muslims see Muhammad as only a prophet and yet claim to know a very great deal about his life and to build almost everything upon his example and legal authority.

The crucial point here is that the incarnate God came to extend this incarnation in a certain way to the Church and to give his Spirit to the Church. Whereas instead of founding something like a church, Muhammad bequeathed a perpetual crisis: what new single authority is to replace the one prophetic authority that has revealed the word of the one God? This is why Islam has tended constantly to generate both tyrannies and dangerous charismatic rebellions. It is also why it lacks concepts of social space between the individual person and sovereign central authority: the idea of the corporation or free association which in the West has only been enabled by a sense of the formation of the body of Christ. Even Islamic cities, as the Islamist Malise Ruthven notes, tend to be ramshackle intersections of essentially private spaces and lack the sense of a public forum.

Accordingly, while one may agree with many aspects of the Islamic critique of Western decadence and Western consumerism, Islam does not in reality possess many resources with which to challenge this and has itself become yet more decadent than the West in terms of the loss of the riches of its own tradition. Among these riches, mystical Shi'ite and Sufi associations come nearer to providing a sense of a 'church' space which could challenge both the free market and State power. But these realities have long been in decline and 'political Islam', especially in its Wahabite version, is in a way all too modern – focused on developing centralized states and promoting Islam as a rigid law code unqualified by traditional mystical and Gnostic dimensions.

How should the West deal with political Islam? My views on this have evolved since I returned from the USA. I now think that in some ways Bush and Blair have taken us into a wrong and disastrous war in Iraq partly because they *underestimated* the danger of Islam and not the reverse. Of course, the war is essentially geopolitical and to do with the oil/guns equation, but also I think there was some genuine hope that a more Westernized regime could be established in Iraq. But there simply is no tradition of Islamic democracy. Moreover, the USA and Britain have themselves helped to sustain the most pernicious of all modern Islamic regimes in Saudi Arabia. Perhaps then the problem with Bush and Blair is the reverse of what the liberal left normally supposes – the problem is not that they fight Islam instead of 'terrorism' but rather that they claim to fight 'terrorism' in general rather than political Islam (which takes many forms, most of them not terroristic but most of them dangerous) in particular.

Before liberals scream at this point, they should consider that attacking a nebulous 'terrorism' is precisely convenient for our masters, who wish to strip away civil rights and preserve order by keeping us in a constant state of anxiety and under unnecessary surveillance. Of course, we should treat terrorists as criminals and

Appendix

not warriors and they should receive the full rights of criminals – Guantanamo is a horrific shame that is linked, as Giorgio Agamben has argued, to the new need of globalized order to identify an abjected enemy. However, it is also dangerous to our liberty to ignore the fact that most global terrorists are now indeed part of political Islam and that other manifestations of this also threaten the West. This is because the majority Islamic religious view that political law and the political state are full aspects of a religious order is not compatible with Christian religious views. There can be no 'dialogue' about this. To the contrary, this constitutive aspect of Islam does in fact need to be defeated – as peacefully as possible. That is because Christians are committed from the outset in the Gospels and in St Paul to the view that the state aspect of order is relatively secular in character in so far as it must resort to compromises that do not mediate to us the sacred, unlike the practices of charity and reconciliation within the Church. The aspiration to the full realization of the latter as a harmonious community beyond coercion and the law (which can only limit evil and not overcome it, as St Paul says) is a crucial part of Christianity. The post-Christian secular world is also committed to the secularity of the State – but what it now begins to realize is the degree to which this depends on a Christian religious vision. Suddenly the idea that we do indeed have to defend 'Christendom' seems not entirely ridiculous to all those in the West who think clearly and rigorously.

For to a certain degree, it is indeed plausible to say that the arrival of Islam in Europe is a danger and to say this has, of course, nothing to do with racism. It is a threat in population terms, and in terms of the will of Islam to establish Islamic legal norms and increasingly to impose through the sanctions of various threats an Islamic normativity about the historical origins of the Qur'ān, the treatment of women and so forth. We cannot give way to this – for example in terms of what happens in Islamic schools, public swimming baths, etc. At this point we have to realize that Europe and the Americas simply *are* Christian worlds, and that most secular standards are rooted in a Christian past. The alternative to being Christian is not to be neutrally secular, because either a substantively secular or else some particular religious viewpoint will prevail, even within a properly 'procedurally neutral' public space.

So the alternative could even eventually become Islamic, as G. K. Chesterton, with astonishing perspicuity, already warned in *The Flying Inn*. By not realizing this, we are also betraying many more secular and mystical Muslims who are very near to our Christian or Christian-derived standards.

On the other hand, all of what I have just said risks giving far too one-sided a picture. In reality I suspect that the 'Islamification' of Europe is incredibly unlikely even if we should not become sanguine. As David Ford and others have suggested, much more probable is that a different and unique European Islam eventually will emerge – which means, if we are honest, that in the long run Islam in Europe will take on a far more Christian character. Alongside the dangerous leadership of many Muslim organizations in Britain for example, one has to set the fact of a great many Muslims whose knowledge of their faith is already becoming thin, or who look to an authentic Christianity to protect them from the fiercest blasts of secularism. Moreover, in terms of the birth rate it is also the case that Christians are now having more children than the non-religious who, of course, often don't know why to have them.

In practical terms I think we need to get as many Muslims as possible studying the history of Islam from their own best teachers and from teachers in the West in order that they can recover the better – mystical Shi'ite and Sufi – aspects of their own tradition and blend this with a Western constitutional (and in that sense 'liberal') politics. In the very long term I suspect that we will see a gradual Christianization of Islam, along with a gain in Christian theological understanding from Islamic mystical traditions, especially concerning the role of the imagination in religious thought and experience – which can sometimes enable us to understand better things in Christian doctrine itself.

Luiz Felipe Pondé: *How, more generally, does a theologian interpret religious fundamentalism?*

Conor Cunningham: Leaving aside the issue of Islamic fundamentalism particularly, the two most prevalent forms of religious fundamentalism generally, one might say, are various forms of creationism and secularism, both of which share a common understanding of matter, matter as inert and inimical to the spiritual. And nothing of course could be further from the truth. The pathology that has gripped the secular mind in its bid to be rid of the divine has led us to inhabit a world devoid of first-person language. To invoke G. K. Chesterton again, he said something to this effect: 'I know a man who has such a passion for proving that he will have no personal life after death that he falls back on the position that he has no personal existence now ... The secularists have not wrecked divine things; but the secularists have wrecked secular things.' And the Siamese twin of this pathology is its religious equivalent that in light of such absurdity elects to fill the void left by reductionism as an *ersatz* metaphysic. In their view if we are going to speak of selfish genes, or are going to prohibit first-person language (it being mere folk psychology – and so the equivalent of saying 'the sun rises', when astronomy tells us it neither rises nor sets), then their own brand of unmediated, extreme religiosity is just as consistent. Here we can see that religious and secular fundamentalism are two sides of the same coin. Theology challenges both, because it includes a crucial level of mediation: mediation offered by history, other intellectual disciplines, and so on. And I might add that this element of *mediation* is perhaps precisely what John Milbank has just suggested as the beneficial remedy to fundamentalism in Islam by attention to the mediated traditions of mystical Shi'ite and Sufiism.

Luiz Felipe Pondé: *Is secularism the problem?*

John Milbank: Yes I think it is a problem, but this doesn't mean that I think the Church as an institution should be in control of everything. I think what we need is a culture with a sense of the sacred. If we are to live in a Christian culture this needs, in a subtle way, to pervade everything, it must not to be a mere superaddition. The point is that when things are secularized, they get fragmented – the individual is usually left to pursue private ends of subjective gratification, and this works to destroy communal coinherence, the pursuit of genuine happiness, just as it also tends to destroy nature. In my country, Britain, for example, it seems that people have two ways of understanding time. They are either using it to make money or using it to enjoy themselves in increasingly frantic and anarchic ways. And so you have got an excess of alcohol, rather crude and joyless, essentially private, unskilful and unharmonious forms of dancing. By contrast, here at the conference we had Flamenco dancers performing last night after dinner, and I was thinking to myself: this is sexy beyond anything we can now imagine. Why is it genuinely erotic? Because it is also *metaphysical*, because it is not just sexy, it is connecting us to the cosmos, both in its anguish and its ecstasy. This is real religiosity, if you like: it is precisely what we've lost. Secular culture is banal. It is *sad* and increasingly desperate.

Luiz Felipe Pondé: *You talk like Berdyaev, the Russian philosopher.*

John Milbank: Yes, I am very sympathetic to Russian thinking, because they never make the divisions between faith and philosophy that Western thought has tended to make. They preserve a kind of integral wisdom. Sergei Bulgakov is, however, actually the Russian thinker whom I would prefer to cite.

Luiz Felipe Pondé: *What does theology have to say today?*

Conor Cunningham: In light of all that we have just been saying, and of course what is perhaps the conviction at the very heart of our Centre of Theology and Philosophy at Nottingham, is that theology has more to say today than it ever has. And if it is the case that theology has more to say now than ever, this is because without theology the common-sense world, indeed the division of different disciplines dissolves under the onslaught of a pernicious reductionism. It is no longer (if it ever was) a question of asking 'do you believe in God?', with its usual Western correlative reply: 'no, but I do believe in being good to people.' For the fact is, that in the absence of theology, as we see very clearly in the academy, terms such as 'the good' or 'people' are no longer viable. And this is illustrated by the quotation we have taken from Paul Churchland for this conference: 'Could it turn out that nobody has ever believed anything?' Why would he ask such a thing? Quite simply, in light of the ontology now prevalent in the West, belief, *any* belief is no longer tenable, because the intentional lives we suppose we live are fictitious – that is, they are epiphenomenal, a mere shadow, cast by the grey meat of neurons and atoms that resides inside our skull. A situation compounded when we witness a biological theory such as Darwinism being universalized, becoming instead an all-encompassing philosophy. Arguably, theology today is the only viable antidote to such virulent reductionism. As David Chalmers says, you cannot have your materialist cake and eat your consciousness too! So, only a robust metaphysics holds hope for a richer account of existence.

Here one could invoke Wilfrid Sellars's phrase, the 'myth of the given', as a guide for theology, especially in relation to creation. By this I mean that Christians can very easily fall into the temptation of positing a pure nature over and against which they set the supernatural – here I would argue that only a *theological* disposition can guard against this. Such a disposition might reveal that there are a good many 'anonymous atheists' (to corrupt a phrase of Karl Rahner's) who attend churches, believe in God, and so on. An example of such 'anonymous atheists' might be those who advocate 'intelligent design'. It seems clear to me that such a notion is scientifically wrong (because it's not science, for one) and theologically pernicious, in so far as if 'intelligent design' were true and naturally 'provable' it would amount to one of the most potent arguments for atheism ever! And yet having said this (and here I am risking all my cultural bourgeois and liberal credentials), it must be admitted that 'intelligent design' nevertheless signals a significant cultural reaction against the hegemony of secular scientism, as well as the wilful corruption of evolution by secularists. But conversely, 'intelligent design' is itself guilty of scientism, as it too presumes that science is the sole criterion of truth. So 'what does theology have to say today'? It must begin by saying something radically otherwise. And in this context it would be something grounded in the doxological reality of the liturgical account of creation in Genesis, which is wholly irreducible to the secular, to the atheist worship of science (whether by Darwinians, creationists or the advocates of 'intelligent design').

Veritas: Belief and Metaphysics

Luiz Felipe Pondé: *But how can theology concretely help us? In Brazil, for example, theologians either go to liberation theology (as a Marxist thing) or move towards a kind of self-help theology. Do you think theology can talk to us in a different way in order to make us see something authentically outside secularism?*

John Milbank: I think the way one would want to reach both those groups is by developing a very strong ecclesiology. In other words, one must come to see the Church itself as the project of the redeemed society (sometimes liberation theology has done this, but rarely). If you see the Church in this way you come to see it as existing beyond the state, beyond the market, as the place of true human community. At this point perhaps you can start to integrate those personal concerns about self-realization with questions about social justice, because they can't be taken in isolation from each other. The trouble sometimes with Marxism is that it doesn't have any real lasting account of the human good. Equality, yes, but what is it that we are sharing? One of my consistently strong emphases is that you cannot have equality unless there is a certain consensus about what it is we should be sharing in common. Because we don't have that consensus, this is perhaps one of the reasons why we have the total dominance of the market, because all we can say is people deemed to possess completely 'neutral' wills should have choice and yet more choice.

It is only something like a religious culture that can provide the shared sense of what things should be valued as ultimate goods. Those things that people pursue for themselves as individuals, but also all that they pursue along with others, must be integrated into a notion of the sharing of the ultimate good if we are to begin thinking about family life, community life or our relationship to nature.

Luiz Felipe Pondé: *Professor Milbank, how do you read the last 25 or so years of the Catholic Church? And how do you view our new Pope, Benedict XVI?*

John Milbank: I suspect I prefer Pope Benedict to John Paul II as a theologian. In certain ways, this is because his theology is very much informed by de Lubac and Balthasar. I also think one needs here to acknowledge that the social documents for which he was responsible as Cardinal Ratzinger, when he was head of the Congregation for the Doctrine of the Faith, were in fact quite good. By no means – just because he has criticized liberation theology – does this mean that he thinks the Church can dispense with social justice or the preferential option for the poor. It is very clear that Benedict does think those things are important. And I must say that since he has become Pope, I've been extremely impressed. It seems to me he is trying to be very human, for one thing. For example, he says things like: 'You mustn't worry about your work if you don't get it all done. You must take breaks and refresh yourself.' This, it seems to me, is an incredibly important thing to say, one which is a profound challenge to the secular market economy.

I thought that *Deus Caritas Est* was a remarkable encyclical, especially for the way it tried not to be too controversial. The Pope seemed to be successfully leading the conversation on the erotic back to theology; it was a very theological document, a theological treatment of love, sexuality, justice and so on. It was, to my mind, also an ecumenical gesture, because it meant that a lot of people who might disagree with the details and concrete moral issues could nevertheless accept that this was a good starting point. I felt what he was saying is: 'Let's first of all look at the fundamentals.'

What I particularly like about his interventions, so far, is that he tends to be more theological than the previous Pope. And he seems also to have insisted that there is no easy boundary between reason and revelation.

When he was still a cardinal, he actually wrote to one of my pupils, Catherine Pickstock, because he had read her book *After Writing*, which is partly about liturgy. He seemed to like some of the things that she was saying about a too-ready acceptance of a kind of modernist understanding of what liturgy is, and liked her account of a richer theory of liturgy, blending both theological and ethnographical considerations. Also, in my theology and the theology of people associated with me, usually named either 'the Cambridge Movement', 'Radical Orthodoxy' or now sometimes 'the Nottingham School', we have insisted that you can't simply see the Greek philosophical legacy culminating in Plato and Aristotle as a kind of accidental context for Christianity, but, on the contrary, that it enters into the henceforth timeless constitution of Christianity through the Wisdom Literature, the Septuagint and the New Testament and then through the thought of the fathers of the first few centuries. Obviously, Christianity is developing the Jewish tradition, but the Jewish tradition itself had already become highly Hellenized and even Romanized. It is simply untrue to imagine that we could equally adopt, for example, Hindu or Chinese philosophy as a prolegomenon to Christianity even if Christians can learn new and important things from encounters with these other traditions. We have said that for some time, and so here, too, we are in agreement with the Pope.

We are also at one with Benedict in suggesting, like many other people, that things started to go wrong from the Middle to late Middle Ages, when you start to get the emergence of univocal ontologies, a separation between will and intellect and between faith and reason, and start also to get too positivistic an understanding of divine revelation, too extrinsicist an understanding of grace and so on.

This does not mean we would necessarily agree with Pope Benedict about all aspects of ecclesiology nor on every aspect of questions concerning women, gay men and women and so forth. On those issues, we are probably rather more complicated and also there are different shades of opinion within Radical Orthodoxy, which may well be to the good – as these matters cannot as yet perhaps be clearly resolved. However, one crucial novelty of Radical Orthodoxy is that we are trying to combine an orthodox theological vision with radical and counter-cultural political attitudes – although ones which tend to qualify a non-statist socialism with certain 'conservative' thematics, like respect for tradition – here we are in the tradition of John Ruskin who declared himself 'the reddest of communists and the bluest of Tories'! In this respect we also try to combine orthodoxy with a somewhat more liberal attitude on certain sexual questions than many orthodox Christians might hold; though we fully uphold the Catholic Church's desire to maintain the natural link between the human sexual act and procreation: this is absolutely crucial, and I, for one, am certainly opposed, for example, to any experimentation on embryos. But in general we suspect that much Christian rigidity and puritanism about sex since the early modern and especially the

Appendix

Victorian period is but weakly rooted in the authentic tradition – which has lay as well as priestly witnesses.

I have to make this point about a relative liberalism on sexual and gender issues with a fair degree of caution, because I think we certainly need a critique of the current banalization of sex as merely physical, healthy and releasing, as merely diverting and experiential and so forth. To the contrary, we need to recover a sense of the psychic risk and danger, the 'terribleness' of physical union with another (as Phillip Rosemann has said) if we are also to recover a sense of sexual value. If we do that then I think we will understand better why people aspire, as they still in fact overwhelmingly do, to reciprocally loving, faithful sexual relationships – to 'marriage' in fact.

Luiz Felipe Pondé: *From Brazil, looking at the Anglican Church and the Catholic Church, the feeling we have nowadays is that if a woman wants to be a priest, she becomes Anglican. We have a woman as an Anglican Archbishop in Brazil, for example.*

John Milbank: That is very interesting. I have to answer this on a personal level, because I am myself what is known in England as an Anglo-Catholic. Although I am, for mainly historical and cultural reasons an Anglican, theologically my thinking is almost identical with that of a Roman Catholic (though also with many Eastern Orthodox influences), including an acceptance of transubstantiation, for example. If pushed, however, I probably think that often the conception of the authority of the Papacy since the late Middle Ages has been 'all too modern', and that the main ecumenical need is to recover and develop a more authentic view of papal authority which all orthodox, sacramentally based Christians can accept.

I think part of the cultural – and yet also theological – reason why I remain an Anglican in England is that in England the parish churches are Anglican. Catholicity has for me something to do with the parish and the idea that the parish is there as the fundamental sociopolitical unit and it is for everyone and it is rooted in a territory. Somehow, the Roman Catholic Church in England is inevitably more congregational (and perhaps sometimes more 'sectarian') – that is, it is more a gathering of people who happen to be Catholics.

Veritas: Belief and Metaphysics

This theme is doubly important to me because my wife is currently an Anglican deacon, and will be ordained priest next year. She is an illustration of your point: I think that she remains an Anglican in part (though there are other reasons) because by doing so she can become a priest. Then you have the ironical situation that many women priests in the Anglican Church are very orthodox Catholic in their outlook. I would challenge Catholics who don't accept women priests to come and see women priests operating in the Anglican Church and then ask themselves in what sense they are not exercising a priesthood.

I think it is perfectly possible for a woman to act and preside at the Eucharist. And this is not because I think that gender difference is irrelevant. Rather, the priestly role is essentially Marian as well as Christological: the priest eucharistically 'delivers' Christ to us. Thus often in the Middle Ages Mary was presented in priestly garb and only in modern times has this kind of depiction been banned. I think we have tended to exaggerate the extent that the priest should be seen simply as Christ over against the laity, rather than as having authority by personifying the Church receiving Christ sacramentally. You need both symbolisms – just as the layperson is also Christ as well as Mary, especially Christ in his kingly aspect. At bottom this is to do with the paradox that for Christianity to exercise active power is always to be more receptive to the divine, and for this reason I would disagree with Balthasar about the Petrine and Marian aspects of the Church – to the contrary, they are the same aspect and that is crucial. So having both men and women reminds us of this Marian-Christic reality of the priesthood – though obviously one must not be inertly wooden even about this symbolism. Men can also be Marian, Christ in his self-giving and fertile authority has also been seen as a mother within the tradition. What I think we are currently failing to see on both the 'conservative' and 'liberal' sides is that the Middle Ages had *both* a strong sense of gender difference *and* a sense that this could be relativized in relation to the soul. This doesn't mean though that gender difference is merely penultimate. To the contrary, it concerns the complex beast-angel ontology of the human as described by Pascal. As souls we constantly exceed gender, yet as bodies who will be resurrected we also constantly return to it. And so even though it is transcended, sexual difference will also eschatologically remain – and sexual relationships, too, however transfigured. Does not the full logic of resurrection require that? Here I suspect that D. H. Lawrence might have been somewhat more orthodox than 'orthodoxy'.

I know many very orthodox Catholic theologians (for example, Jean-Yves Lacoste) who say, like Edith Stein in the recent past, that they can no longer understand what the theological objection to women in the priesthood is, and that most of the objections dreamt up are suspiciously novel in character. I think there must at the very least be a discussion on the issue, because the issue has never been before been raised. There is no tradition of understanding why women can't be priests: only a tradition that they have not been priests – which is not the same thing, and blind, reasonless tradition is not a Christian concept.

Luiz Felipe Pondé: *Professor Milbank, what do you think about the homosexual issue?*

John Milbank: This is a difficult question for me to answer because my opinions on the issue are extremely and perhaps unsatisfactorily complicated. That is because an honest reflection on my experience of homosexual friends does not leave me with any simple answers. I am sorry if this sounds just not good enough! I know some gays in very stable relationships that one must judge to be good by the fruits which they bear. It seems to me these relationships are sometimes exemplary and that they manage to live out the gospel in ways other people cannot. It may well be that certain people are simply biologically orientated in a way that does not follow the heterosexual norm. On the other hand, I still suspect that there is in some cases also a contingent, cultural dimension, and I definitely reject the idea that we are all really bisexual and that a free-floating sexuality is a good thing. The latter view is based on the suspicion of all substantive natural differences and the different roles that these differences imply. But I would have to say, equally based upon observation, that it does seem to me that homosexuality is too often linked to a kind of narcissism and a distorting of desire. I think homosexuality does, at its core, bring into a yet more intense play a desire based upon rivalry and so upon sameness, in the way René Girard has suggested. In this sense, I think one must not support a simply liberal opinion that says that homosexuality is an equally good option for all human beings. I think to the contrary that the sexual norm is heterosexuality and that this must be promoted as the norm. If you imagined, just for the sake of argument, a world where homosexuality was normative, it would be catastrophic for human bonds because it would vastly increase the rivalry/desire complex pertaining between men and women. The heterosexual logic is an easier and more relaxed one: one group of people you naturally sympathize with, the others are people you potentially desire. Where everyone within one gender is both, then, I submit, human association becomes more problematic. And still more problematic and sinister is the fact that, in a homosexual logic, the opposite sex are people that you *neither* desire nor most naturally sympathize with, despite certain gestures of camp pretence, and yet who *can be* also your rivals! This is even more dissolving of human bonds and respect for human personhood.

In addition, I absolutely agree with feminists like Luce Irigaray who argue that sexual difference is real and that humanity comes as either male or female. I do think there is a strong difference between men and women, although it is a mystery and hard to describe. So I also think that justice towards men and women has to recognize that difference. Furthermore, if you say that heterosexuality and homosexuality are equal, then in fact you are saying homosexuality is superior because you are saying that difference is indifferent, sexual difference doesn't matter.

Therefore, I think our attitude has to be a complex one. We need to be alert to the evidence (despite the dominant denials) that homosexuality can arise as a cultural or psychological distortion and we need to discourage this. On the other hand, there seem to be cases where you simply can't say that. It seems to me that we have to accept there are people who are simply born homosexual and that this appears to be a divine intention. In such cases it is, I believe, utterly wrong to deny such people sexual fulfilment. The Church needs to find a way to recognize their relationships, as was already envisaged by the great Russian Orthodox theologian Pavel Florensky, and more recently by Rowan Williams, the Archbishop of Canterbury.

Because it blends theological conservatism with a (critical) social radicalism, I hope that the mission of Radical Orthodoxy can be something of a mission of peace in mediating between liberal groups and conservative ones.

Luiz Felipe Pondé: *The American philosopher, Richard Rorty, told me that theology was dead as vocabulary and repertory. He of course is a neopragmatist, and he said that theology was dead in so far as it was a possible description of reality. Of course you don't agree with that.*

John Milbank: Of course [*laughter*]! Well it is very dangerous to adopt pragmatic criteria because there are no pragmatic criteria for doing so! Let what works flourish! But anything works! Pure pragmatism is formal emptiness, even though every theory has a practical implication – to that degree I am a pragmatist. But inversely, only theories define the nature of practices. Pure American pragmatism is already over. But not theology!

Conor Cunningham: It is not theology but humanism that is dead! And only theology can resurrect it. Indeed, there never was such a thing as humanism, as it was never more than a 'rich, spoilt kid, living off its parents' wealth', taking all its terms or concepts from them.

Luiz Felipe Pondé: *I come from a department called The Sciences of Religion in a Catholic University. There, the tendency is to see sociology, anthropology, psychology, natural sciences as sciences and theology as nothing but an object, not an agent in the dialogue. Do you think theology can still participate in the intellectual debate?*

John Milbank: I do, and I also would make the observation that in the last 20 years, theology has definitely moved back into the public sphere a little bit more. Take, for example, French phenomenologists like Jean-Luc Marion and Jean-Louis Chrétien. Marion often makes divisions between when he is being a theologian and when he is being a philosopher that I think in the end have much more to do with French academic life than anything else and perhaps don't best reflect what he himself is trying to do. Chrétien, though, doesn't do that to the same extent. Meanwhile in Anglo-Saxon countries, philosophers like Alasdair MacIntyre and Charles Taylor have increasingly engaged with theology.

I think that this is happening because we have recovered a different kind of theology, a theology that isn't simply a reflection on biblical texts or an exposition of dogmas. Rather this recovered and extended theology tends to explore what difference the tradition of the Bible makes to rational discourse, the kind of thing that in fact the Church fathers were always doing – Augustine, for example. Again, it is a question of not having a separation between theology and philosophy, which is very much the Nottingham model, exactly what our Centre of Theology and Philosophy is trying to achieve. We pursue theology and philosophy together, at the same time, not simply aspects of either discipline. I think if you do this, you bring theology back into the centre of crucial cultural debates – for example, concerning what a person is.

In Britain (and to some extent when I was in Virginia), we do have departments that comprise theology and religious studies. One cannot however simply collapse these two discourses together. Religious studies is about the history of religion and theoretical reflections upon this history. Theology is a thinking of God that involves reflection on revelation in relation to reason. On the other hand, I think the two things fertilize each other and it is very good to have them both in the same department. We don't need a meta-theory of how they combine, but they do in practice combine to mutual benefit.

For theology does need to reflect on the history of religions, but equally the study of religion needs to take seriously the internal accounts that faiths provide of their own practices, and it needs to sustain what Rowan Williams (speaking of secularity in general) describes as a 'procedural' neutrality as between these accounts on the one hand and reductive secular accounts of religion on the other. I think that if it privileges a priori the critical secular account of religion then it is just an ideology, and unfortunately a lot of people in religious studies do support that approach. In fact religious studies in the United States is full to bursting with second-rate ideologues.

Appendix

Luiz Felipe Pondé: *For example, let us think of the sociology of religion. The only book of yours we have translated into Portuguese is* Theology and Social Theory . . .

John Milbank: That was the first translation of that book into any language. It is now being translated into French, and I am very grateful. I have visited Portugal but I should still like to visit Brazil!

Luiz Felipe Pondé: *Professor Milbank, could you talk a little bit about what we might call your 'criticism' of sociology?*

John Milbank: The funny thing is that when I wrote *Theology and Social Theory*, my position on sociology seemed very counter-intuitive. Now that bit of the book seems almost the least controversial. I know a lot of people who are, formally speaking, sociologists who now say: yes, the very paradigm of sociology now seems to us to be ideological and outdated. But I suppose what I was trying to show was that sociology itself either inherits a particular theological standpoint – for example, Weber is related to the liberal Protestant tradition; or else, it is trying to self-displace religion, so that the content of religion is redescribed as being really about the social whole – regarded as a kind of a-historical universal. And this standpoint is very questionable, especially in terms of the priority it gives to the synchronic over the diachronic, since it tends to posit the social whole as something outside historical contingency.

One of the arguments of the book – an argument already made by Robert Spaemann in Germany – is that sociology in France was constituted as an inversion of some rather conservative but totally modern (because sceptical and voluntarist) Catholic thinking in de Maistre and de Bonald, an inversion that nonetheless preserves some of their assumptions, so that you tend to get the idea that society, together with language, is not a human invention, but rather a kind of quasi 'divine revelation'. This gets secularized by Comte as a thesis about the priority of the social. Comte connects it with a kind of totally immanentized religion and he set up, indeed, a Comtian church of positivism. Durkheim, despite the denial of many commentators, still gives a version of the Comtian project. In the end Durkheim's work is a theory of civil religion; it is trying to say why we should now worship the French state, if you like.

My thesis is that, in the end, sociology *stricto sensu* is still reducible to the kind of project I've just described. Therefore, you can deconstruct it this way. And this means that the idea that it is a neutral discourse that theology needs to take account of no longer appears to be the case. There is no such neutral space after all. A deepening of modern critique into postmodern critique rescues theology from the more extreme pressure of the modern.

Luiz Felipe Pondé: *So we don't have to study sociology?*

John Milbank: I'm not saying that at all, or rather I'm not denying that one needs to study synchronic as well as diachronic social realities. Indeed my idea of the religious is that it is in itself social, although not reducible to a hypostasized and spatialized a priori 'society'. Indeed, part of my criticism of sociology is that ironically it tends to think of religion too much as a kind of private psychological attitude.

My case would be that because religion and society are so mixed up with each other we can't abstract a social factor and say: 'Oh, here this the social factor that comes before the thinking factor.' Think of what Foucault says about a prison. It is at once a building and an order of discourse: therefore there is no formally isolatable social dimension any more than there is a formally isolatable natural human dimension. (And André de Muralt has now shown that what one has here is, indeed, a mode of thinking that can be traced back, step by step, through Montesquieu and so on, to the Scotist formal distinction; hence my critique of social theory is, in a rigorous sense, a Thomistic critique.) If sociology simply means that you are talking about a synchronic dimension in interplay with the diachronic dimension, then it is fine, but as Paul Veyne, the French historian and theorist says, one should rather describe this as *historie totale*.

I'm also saying that there are no clear boundaries between secular reflection and theological reflection. One reason why *Theology and Social Theory* builds up to Augustine is he has a very theological reading of history, even though it is also an empirical reading – indeed in more ways than I mention in that book.

Appendix

Luiz Felipe Pondé: *Do you think we still have room to think of the sacred as a possible category? Is it relevant to ethics – which is nowadays so disputed and problematic?*

John Milbank: I think people who discuss virtue ethics are opening our way back to a richer sense of ethics, although I also think that the Christian ethics of charity exceeds the bounds of an ethics of virtue. Here I think we need to qualify MacIntyre with Spaemann. If Christian virtue is finally charity, then this transcends the Greek sense of self-realization into something more ecstatic and relational, a kind of exchange that involves at once the realization of happiness for oneself and a concern for the other – a joy in and with the other in fact. In this context sanctity is very important for ethics.

For sometimes I think that in ethical discourse we are talking too much about abstract prescriptions that we need to live up to. As if we were saying to people: 'Well, you have got to be completely different from who you are.' Yet it is rather the case, as MacIntyre stresses, that people are habitually shaped, first of all, by the social role they have to play; and so the primary moral question is: what is the point of this social role? What is it tending to achieve as a state of affairs? Probably for an awful lot of people social roles are not very ethical or sacred, for after all, people have to make money. We need to start thinking much more about that, about what social roles are appropriate for Christians to perform and indeed for human beings to perform. What goals are they aiming at, what goods should be desired by the human will for it truly to function as a free will? But if we believe in this way in a teleology, then this also means that our cultural, political and ecclesial character is not accidental in relation to some sort of (post-Scotist!) abstracted pure animal nature or pure animal sociality or even pure political being untouched by grace. And to imagine that as an animal we have a more than animal goal is inevitably to do with the sacred. It is also true, as Spaemann argues, that only if we think humans have a *telos* – which ultimately must be a supernatural one – will we also affirm the teleology of animals and of all of nature, because here teleology only makes sense as an obscure hint of the next stage: the animal of the human, the plant of the animal, the crystal of the plant. In the same way humans only make sense to themselves as an obscure hint of the angelic, the deified.

Veritas: Belief and Metaphysics

The other thing in relation to the starting point in given character is that to some extent we all have a naturally given kind of character we can't help. We need to get away from an ethics that suggests you should become totally different from how you have been created. Let me put it this way: it is as if God has obscurely assigned us a role in the cosmic plot. We can't swap this for another role, so that if, for example we are ferocious and tempestuous by nature, our main aim should be to become meek and mild. William Blake was right to suggest that this is not really the gospel at all. No, the kind of approach for ethics that says: 'stop being ferocious and tempestuous!' is to some extent wrong. It might be much more that you have to say to yourself that if you are like this, how exactly are you to direct this ferocity towards the common good? To be sure this might well mean some tempering of this ferocity in an Aristotelian way – but the Pauline vision of division of moral labour in diversity of gifts points also beyond Aristotle. For Christianity there is a wider range and also a more open range of character that may fully succeed in attaining to the 'ethical'. Indeed Kierkegaard was right to imply that the good as practised is always different, even if he underplayed the importance of ecclesial co-ordination of these differences.

I think at that point also, there is a link between ethics and sanctity. Because sanctity has something to do with that sort of intangible quality of integrity that shines forth from the good person that goes beyond simply an observation that he performs deeds that fall formally into the category of good deeds. There is a way of doing these things, an art about the mode in which the good person performs an action that is unique to that person. That is what a saint is. A saint has an unforgettable personality, an energy that is nonetheless directed towards the good. St Paul says one can give everything, be a martyr, and yet lack charity. Surely this should give us pause for thought. For this saying implies that charity is an obscure, mysterious quality of self-giving and receiving from the other to form a unique blend. Charity is always singular both as spontaneity and response.

Appendix

Luiz Felipe Pondé: *Is Radical Orthodoxy neoconservative?*

Conor Cunningham: Radical Orthodoxy suspends the usual political dichotomies. It does, because both 'left' and 'right' are infected by the 'myth of the given' (to borrow Sellars's phrase again). And this given is the world they take to be there in an unproblematic fashion, a world construed in terms of presupposition of scarcity, and so, consequently, both 'left' and 'right' predicate their respective political philosophies on the notion of scarce resources, a cake to be cut up this way or that. Theology thinks radically otherwise. A theological political philosophy first and foremost is grounded in the logic of the Eucharist, where the phenomenon of consumerism is rendered impossible. In receiving the sacred body and blood of Christ we do not, and cannot, deplete it in any way. In this we are reminded that the world is *Gift*, and not a given. And this means that an authentically *theological* political imagination will move within a fearlessness – within a hope – to which the scarcity of secular politics will always be blind. As the Jewish poet Paul Celan said, 'the world is gone, I have to carry you.' This, arguably, is the politics of Radical Orthodoxy. Theology, like orthodoxy, is a thrilling 'romance', as Chesterton said, for we can never rest on our philosophical laurels. Just as when Christ endlessly tells us to feed the poor, and then when his feet are bathed with perfume by the woman, in response to protests at the apparent waste, he tells us that we will always have the poor. To which Judas – here, the father of *morality* – balks! Again, the 'left' and 'right' wings of politics are suspended: we build cathedrals decked in silver and gold because we should and must feed the poor.

Luiz Felipe Pondé: *What then does Radical Orthodoxy really mean?*

John Milbank: I think, very briefly, three things. First of all, we are an ecumenical theological movement that stresses the orthodoxy of the creeds and the ecumenical councils as a true reading of the Bible, the essential role of bishops and of the sacraments, and in addition the intellectual traditions of Augustine, of Maximus the Confessor (synthesizing the Cappadocians and Dionysius) of Eriugena, Aquinas and Nicholas of Cusa. All these things embody the most radical ideas that you can imagine. They challenge human assumptions most fundamentally. For they point towards the joining of humanity with divinity, and towards the transformation of society in the direction of a just and beautiful order, and a harmonious relationship with nature, even though these things can only be fully achieved at the eschaton.

The second thing is that Radical Orthodoxy stands for an extension of the *nouvelle théologie* programme of seeing faith and reason as belonging integrally together, but we want to develop further the metaphysical implications of that project. Rather than phenomenology alone, we favour a re-thought realist metaphysics, indebted especially to Neoplatonic ontologies of participation (which we regard as closely akin to the vision of the Bible) which would include much more attention than was given in the Middle Ages to history, to culture and to the role of the imagination.

The third thing is that at the outset of Radical Orthodoxy, the reaction to postmodernism was important, because I think we were saying: 'OK, don't just see the attack on humanism, the attack on pure reason as bad. On the contrary, see this as a deconstruction of the secular; see this as saying that humans as finite don't really have access to a fully determinate and complete knowledge.' But then say: 'Why does postmodern thought assume that this indeterminacy points toward nihilism? Might it not just as easily point towards an irreducible createdness, and yet participation in the creative divine source, the fact that we can only have a provisional source of determinacy if we have faith in God and seek to increase our participation in his life?' One may say that there is always a gap between our truths, truths that can only be partial truths, truths that are only true at all because they are a very small step on the way to expressing the full reality of things that exists in God. If one links traditional analogy to a post-Renaissance sense of the human shaping of culture and being shaped in turn by culture one has in that way a kind of theological postmodern re-reading of our current intellectual plight: the relativity of culture cannot be sidestepped, yet the formation of culture is in itself a striving towards the infinite fullness of the Son who is 'Word' and the infinite exchange of the Spirit who is 'Gift'.

Appendix

Luiz Felipe Pondé: *In the opposite way to that of nihilism.*

John Milbank: In the opposite way to that of nihilism, so that, just like the Russian sophiologists (Soloviev, Dostoyevsky, Florensky, Bulgakov), we are saying: forget about humanism and the Enlightenment. Don't think you have to defend that as a sort of halfway stage that trusts in the autonomy of reason as a foundation for faith . . . Instead, the real modern debate lies between theology and nihilism!

Name and Subject Index

9/11 terrorist attacks, 429, 436, 440, 455

Abelard, Peter, 174, 405, 406n24, 410
Abraham, 152, 204, 208–217, 219, 221–224, 226–231
actuality, 77, 79–80, 85–87, 117n69, 243, 265–266, 283–284, 287, 289n85, 290, 419, 463, 469, 472–473, 479–481, 488–490, 493–494, 496–499
adaptationist programme, 111, 118
Adorno, Theodore, 390
aesthetics, 5, 44, 46, 48. 60–61, 63; theological aesthetics, 44, 48–49, 60–61, 63–64
Agamben, Giorgio, 347, 351, 507
Agamemnon, 211
Agape, 17, 33, 37–38, 355, 366, 370–371
agnosticism, 268, 453–454, 457–458, 474–476, 479, 497
alterity, 51, 55–56, 60, 355, 371, 419,
analogia entis, 41, 48–49, 51, 53–64, 261–262, 263n10, 268, 275, 290
analytic philosophy, 41, 302n18, 339, 452, 461, 479
anamnesis, 201, 223,

Anaxagoras, 408
anthropological turn, 46
Antigone, 420
anti-realism, 291–292, 297, 312–318, 324–325, 374n1
anti-Semitism, 119
apophaticism, 42, 56n35, 399–400, 404n21, 408, 419
aporia, 67, 69, 269, 356–357, 484
Aquinas, St. Thomas, 2–3, 9–10, 43, 48, 50–52, 54, 58, 60–64, 68n5, 69, 71, 75–98, 113, 129, 131, 144, 156–157, 174, 249n74, 251–252, 254, 258, 261–266, 271, 279–282, 286–290, 353, 360n45, 395, 444n26, 452n1, 460, 465, 468–474, 477, 483, 485–489, 493–495, 498–499, 525
Aristotle, 2–3, 44–45, 47, 50, 56, 60, 66–70, 72, 77, 81, 162–165, 177, 233, 249n74, 266, 274, 277, 282–283, 287, 293n2, 302n18, 394n3, 410–411, 461, 464–470, 472, 476, 480, 482–484, 487–493, 497–499, 513, 524
Armstrong, David, 481–482, 497
atheism, 111, 119, 141, 147, 151, 154, 158, 160, 183, 248, 262, 264, 284, 285n78, 290, 418, 422–423, 453, 476, 497, 511
Augustine, St., 5, 10, 43, 50,

Name and Subject Index

54–55, 60–61, 64, 165–166, 174, 191, 252, 263–264, 268, 272, 274, 354n32, 395, 408n26, 428, 446, 467–468, 473, 477, 496, 520, 522, 525
autonomy, 3–5, 19, 26–27, 30, 43n5, 44, 157, 159, 215, 219, 416–417, 500; of reason 13, 20, 47, 222n20, 527
Averröes, 253
Avicenna (see Ibn Sina)

Badiou, Alain, 107, 120, 428, 441–443, 446, 458–459, 461, 475, 481, 490–491, 497
Baker, Lynne Rudde, 109
Barth, Karl, 8, 41, 49, 56–60, 233
Bauer, Bruno, 20
Baumgarten, Alexander Gottlieb, 46
beatific vision, 151, 156–157, 356n37, 477, 493, 500, 502
Beira, Mario, 422
Benedict XVI, Pope, 457, 499, 512–514
Benson, Bruce Ellis, 257
Berdyaev, Nikolai, 510
Berkeley, George, 107
Bettelheim, Burno, 417
biology, 105–106, 111–112, 122, 124–125, 131–132, 139, 142, 327n6
Blondel, Maurice, 7, 143–144, 154–155, 159, 353
Boethius, 174, 468, 485, 499
Bonaventure, St., 2, 166–167, 174, 261, 395, 483
Booth, Edward, 67, 69
Boulnois, Olivier, 491, 493
Bradshaw, David, 498
Braig, Carl, 266–271, 273
Branch Davidians, 190
Brentano, Franz, 268
Breton, Stanislas, 478

Brutus, 211
Buddhism, 173, 500
Bulgakov, Sergei, 510, 527
Bunge, Mario, 139
Butler, Joseph, 297
Byrne, Peter, 325–334, 342

Cajetan, St., 51, 55n35, 254
Calvin, John, 41
Cambridge Platonists, 4
capitalism, 219, 437–438, 505
Caputo, John, 270
care, 265, 274, 280
Casper, Bernhard, 260
castration, 414
categorical imperative, 114, 471
Catholicism, 328, 418, 432, 491
causation, 41–42, 58, 76, 121n87
Chalcedon, 68, 358, 364
Chalmers, David, 115, 121n87, 511
Chartres Platonists, 61
Chenu, Marie-Dominique, 349, 350n14
Chesterton, G.K., 100, 106, 109, 110n34, 115, 124n99, 495–496, 508–509, 525
Chrétien, Jean-Louis, 368–369, 519
Christian gospel, 165, 358n41, 441, 443, 445–446, 451, 503, 507, 517, 524
Christian humanism, 254
Christianity, 41, 44, 47, 62, 149–150, 164, 166, 168, 173–174, 176, 180, 208–209, 214, 217, 221, 222n20, 224–225, 232, 234, 241, 244–245, 247–248, 250n79, 255, 264n11, 272–273, 277, 282, 325, 358n41, 370n76, 413, 424, 443–444, 477, 498, 500, 507–508, 513–514, 516, 524

Name and Subject Index

Christology, 358n39, 359, 364, 372
Church Fathers, 43, 174, 477–478, 520
Churchland, Paul, 107–108, 510
civil rights, 427, 506
civil society, 428, 430–432, 434–440
Clark, Stephen R. L., 44
Clarke, W. Norris, 52
Claudel, Paul, 369
Clausewitz, Carl von, 439
Collingwood, R.G., 396n5, 462, 467
common sense psychology (CSP), 108
conceptualism, 291–292, 310, 312–313, 315–318
Connolly, William E., 184, 194
conscience, 230, 273
consciousness, 3, 5, 46, 112, 115, 120–121, 128–129, 143–144, 149, 151, 159, 168, 185, 200, 218, 224, 230–231, 235, 248, 272–274, 390, 460, 511
Continental philosophy, 120, 458, 488
Cortés, Juan Donoso, 255
cosmology, 62, 105, 410–411,
cosmos, 9, 63n50, 120, 234, 252, 253n97, 460, 471, 476, 482, 494, 510
Council of Trent, 328
counter-Enlightenment, 393–395, 399, 407, 412
Courtine, Jean-François, 491
Crane, Tim, 116
creation, 2, 9, 51–53, 55, 58–59, 61, 63–64, 66, 71, 73–78, 80, 91, 97–99, 128, 130, 141, 155, 158, 165–166, 199, 234, 239, 251, 253n97, 261, 280, 282, 286–288, 338–339, 347n5, 360n45, 368–370, 372, 400n14, 407, 408n27, 423–225, 430–431, 477, 483, 500, 511; *ex nihilo*, 55, 130n119, 442, 448; doctrine of, 42, 49–51, 59, 76n1; metaphysics of, 71, 280, 282
creationism, 73–74, 97, 115, 253n97, 508, 511
credit, 15–18, 20, 22, 25, 438
Crick, Francis, 108, 112n44
Cunningham, Conor, 59n.40, 246n57, 253n97, 359, 360n45, 373, 501, 503–504, 508, 510
Cusanus (see Nicholas of Cusa)

d'Ailly, Pierre, 483
Dachau, 417
Daniélou, Jean, 436, 358n41, 498
Dante, 176
Danto, Elizabeth, 420
Darwin, Charles, 100–105, 110–111, 132–133, 136, 140, 162, 165, 459
Darwinism, 73, 105–106, 110–111, 114–115, 117, 119, 132–133, 135, 137, 138n152, 359n43, 511; ultra-, 107n24, 110, 114, 119–120, 126, 128, 132–133, 135, 139
dasein, 57, 148, 150, 152–153, 265, 270n38, 280, 282, 287n81, 415, 457, 579
Dawkins, Richard, 101n5, 108n28, 111–112, 115, 117–120, 125, 128, 131, 134–138, 191–192, 458, 475
Day, Dorothy, 502
de Bonald, Louis Gabriel Ambroise, 521
de Maistre, Joseph, 521
Deacon, Terrence, 139
deconstruction, 36, 153, 356n37, 462, 474–475, 526
deification, 345–348, 366, 446

Name and Subject Index

deism, 58
Deleuze, Gilles, 186, 197, 428, 437–440
Democritus, 107
Dennett, Daniel, 105, 139
Denys the Areopagite (see Dionysius)
Denys the Carthusian, 172–176, 181, 254
Derrida, Jacques, 264n11, 475
Descartes, 1, 30, 41, 46, 115, 216, 232, 249n74, 280, 301n17, 320–322, 376, 411, 458–460
desire, 3, 7, 11, 37, 156, 162, 176, 178, 181, 192, 195–196, 210, 237, 250–252, 255, 261–262, 285, 345–346, 349, 351–359, 360n45, 365–366, 371–373, 389–390, 400n14, 411, 413–414, 416, 419–420, 422, 427, 429, 431, 436–440, 514, 517–518; natural, 3–4, 156, 251, 255, 349, 353, 355–356
Dewey, John, 105
dialectic, 22, 24, 57, 210, 233, 241, 353n30, 355,
Dilthey, Wilhelm, 266, 273–274, 276, 379,
Dionysius, 61, 363, 468, 525
Diotima, 46
Dobzhansky, Thodosius, 130
Docetism, 239
doctrines, 15, 35, 50, 173, 323–325, 328, 329n9, 398, 407
dogmatic theology, 41, 323n2, 352n27, 364n58, 500
Dostoyevsky, Fyodor, 527
doubt, 110, 211, 232, 314, 385–386, 388, 411, 460
doxological, 370, 393n2, 511
duck/rabbit, 122
dyothelite theology, 359–360, 366n63, 371

economics, 16, 142, 169, 177, 194
ecstasis, 36
Eddington, Sir Arthur, 106
El Arabi, Ibn, 499–500
Elshtain, Jean Bethke, 429
emanation, 67–68, 71, 175
empiricism, 19, 341, 462–463, 495
Enlightenment, 21–22, 24, 30, 32n13, 46, 409, 502–503, 527
epistemology, 1, 7, 56–57, 66, 395, 404n21, 454–456
Erikson, Erik, 420
Eriugena, Johannes Scotus, 468, 525
erotic, 2, 33n14, 355, 366, 371, 402, 510, 513
essentialism, 57, 102, 268, 291–292, 293n3, 297, 300, 318, 473, 499
eternal return of the same, 165, 179
ethics, 5, 113, 141, 157, 160, 212, 215, 219, 221, 229–230, 234, 385, 419–420, 449, 523–524
Eucharist, 1, 127, 155, 257, 516, 525
exchange, 15–16, 61, 149, 523, 526
existentialism, 57, 74, 234

faith, 1, 4–10, 15, 19–22, 24, 27, 34, 36, 42, 47n11, 48, 57, 76, 111, 128, 132, 142, 144, 152, 156–158, 164, 168, 172–175, 181–182, 184, 191, 208–212, 216, 220–221, 223, 225, 232, 236, 238n11, 239, 242, 247, 252, 253n97, 254–259, 272–273, 275–276, 278, 284–285, 369, 395, 397–398, 407n26, 409–411, 443, 453–457, 476–478, 482, 498, 508, 510, 514, 526–527

Name and Subject Index

Fall, 165, 346–347, 359, 360n45, 398, 407
falsification, 109
fanaticism, 217, 455–456, 475
fascism, 442, 453, 505
Feuerbach, Ludwig, 205, 248
Fichte, Johann Gottlieb, 4, 206, 214, 479
fideism, 37, 454–455, 457, 476, 500
Florensky, Pavel, 518, 527
Ford, David, 508
form, 52, 60–62, 64, 66, 69, 83, 86–87, 89, 91–96, 103, 130, 139, 148, 151, 155, 157, 162–164, 261n8, 276, 282, 287–288, 289n85, 381, 383, 388, 405, 461, 466, 470, 483–484, 490
Foucault, Michel, 161, 170, 177, 182, 188, 428, 433, 435–438, 439n18, 522
Fourth Lateran Council, 52
free will, 108, 343n15, 523
freedom, 27, 33, 59, 63, 74–75, 99, 276, 289, 249n13, 415, 431, 434–435, 439, 441, 455, 475, 495
Freud, Anna, 416, 420
Freud, Sigmund, 125, 200–201, 379, 416–418, 420–423
fundamentalism, 15, 126, 128, 325, 476, 505, 508–509

Gadamer, Hans-Georg, 5, 258, 396n5
Galileo, 107, 458–459
Gaudium et spes, 348, 349n12, 372
geometry, 17–18,
German Idealism, 47, 268
gift, 9–10, 16–17, 24, 37, 54, 63–64, 99, 130, 136, 169, 241, 243, 245, 251–258, 345–346, 348, 350n14, 358–359, 362, 366–368, 369n70, 371–372, 425, 428, 444n26, 445–448, 450–451, 489–491, 494–495, 500, 524–526
Gilbert of Porreta, 499
Gilbert, Walter, 128
Gilson, Etienne, 52, 264, 281n68, 286–287, 354n32
Glassner, Barry, 426
Gnosticism, 126, 130
Godfrey-Smith, Peter, 131
Goethe, Johann Wolfgang, 213, 378, 380
Goodman, Nelson, 119
Grant, Sara, 71
great chain of being, 103
Gregory of Nyssa, 43, 54, 65
Gregory the Nazianzen, 361n47, 362, 366n63
Griesemer, James, 134
Grotius, Hugo, 97
Guardini, Romano, 8, 352n25
Guntrip, Harry, 416
Gutierrez, Gustavo, 501–502

Hamann, Johann Georg, 208, 462
Hartmann, Heinz, 416
Hegel, Georg Wilhelm Friedrich, 4–5, 10, 13–14, 22–24, 30–33, 53, 115, 141, 144, 146–152, 154, 168–170, 174, 177, 205–209, 211–212, 213n12, 215–224, 226, 228, 231–235, 240, 243, 247–248, 268, 355, 377, 412n37, 455–457, 467, 471–472, 479
Heidegger, Martin, 5, 9–10, 41, 49, 57n38, 58, 141, 152–153, 161, 169, 171, 177, 182, 214, 260–261, 263–268, 271–283, 285–286, 288, 289n85, 290, 379, 393, 395–397, 400n14, 415, 455, 457, 474–475, 479, 492

Name and Subject Index

Henry, Michel, 120, 125, 475
Heraclitus (Herakleitos), 259, 399
hierarchy of being, 58, 63, 103, 135, 289, 472
Hintikka, Jaakko, 479
Hobbes, Thomas, 215–216, 228, 417, 428–429, 431–433, 435–438, 441
Homer, 176–177
homosexuality, 517–518
Honecker, Martin, 265
Honnefelder, Ludger, 77n3, 473, 491
Hösle, Vittorio, 132
Houellebecq, Michel, 192–193
humanism, 142, 146, 249, 254, 358, 436, 455, 519, 526–527,
Hume, David, 19, 41, 482–484, 497
Hurricane Katrina, 440
Husserl, Edmund, 56, 147, 272n42, 379, 453, 455–457, 475, 479

Ibn Sina, 68–69, 83, 480, 487, 499
Ibsen, Henrik, 226
idealism, 47, 205, 268, 400–401, 459, 461–463
identity, 51, 54, 65, 68, 90, 105, 108, 114–115, 117–118, 136, 150, 162, 198, 201, 268, 291, 293, 297–298, 303–306, 309, 319–320, 347, 449, 466–467, 469, 480, 484, 499
Ignatieff, Michael, 429, 436
imago Dei, 263, 349n13
immanence, 11–12, 19, 24, 79–80, 115, 155, 244, 352, 356n37, 414–416, 424–425, 458
incarnation, 42, 47–48, 130, 150, 154–155, 164, 166, 173, 239, 346n3, 347, 356n37, 358, 360, 362, 365, 468, 477–478, 498, 505

individuation, 115, 119, 136, 310n26, 318, 334
infinity, 63, 210, 265, 271, 274, 459
intellect, 2, 76, 81–90, 92–96, 98, 103, 111, 129, 163, 261, 268, 280, 349, 495, 514
Irenaeus of Lyon, St., 372
Isaac, 208–211, 216–218, 226, 228,
Islam, 181, 498, 500, 505–509
Israel, 165, 468, 505

Jacob, 421
Jacob, François, 124
James, William, 10, 193–194, 463
Jaspers, Karl, 214
Jehovah's Witnesses, 216
Jesus Christ, 68, 150, 154–156, 236, 239, 256, 346n3, 351, 358, 362–364, 365n62, 367, 372–373, 423, 441, 444, 448, 471, 505
Joachim of Fiore, 59, 166, 167n5
John of the Cross, 60
Jonas, Hans, 117, 126, 131
Jones, Ernest, 421
Jonestown massacre, 191
Judaism, 149, 151–152, 181, 217, 421, 498, 500
Jung, Carl, 379
Jüngel, Eberhard, 360

Kant, Immanuel, 1, 4–5, 7, 9, 11, 13, 19–21, 32n13, 56, 77n3, 212, 215–217, 221, 226, 230, 291, 377, 411, 457, 459–461, 470–474, 479, 489, 491
Keats, John, 61
Kenny, Anthony, 76, 474
kenosis, 59, 130, 286, 346–347, 370
Kierkegaard, Søren, 5, 152, 204–210, 212–237, 239–244,

Name and Subject Index

246–251, 255–258, 263, 394n3, 409n28, 412n37, 524; as Anti-Climacus, 244; as Johannes Climacus, 237, 242
Kieslowski, Krzysztof, 480
Kisiel, Theodore, 267
Koslowski, Peter, 114, 117n69,
Krebs, Engelbert, 272
Kripke, Saul, 299, 302–303, 306, 480
Kroff, F.W., 223

Lacan, Jacques, 413–420, 422–425,
Lacoste, Jean-Yves, 517
Las Casas, Bartolomé de, 227
Lash, Nicholas, 42
law, 27, 149, 172, 216–217, 228, 232, 240, 273, 277, 283, 421–424, 498–500, 506–507; divine, 141, 499; moral, 216–217, 228–229
Lawrence, D.H., 517
Leibniz, Gottfried, 10, 216, 458–459, 480, 483, 489
lent, 178–179, 384
Lessing, Gotthold Ephraim, 5, 221
Levering, Matthew, 43
Lévinas, Emmanuel, 113, 191, 475
Lévi-Strauss, Claude, 415
Lewis, C.S., 53, 110
Lewis, David, 186, 298n12, 479–480, 497
Lewontin, Richard, 106
Libera, Alain de, 488
liberalism, 417, 428–432, 434–435, 440–441, 451, 515; neo-, 455, 457
liberation theology, 501–503
lifeworld, 272, 277
Lindbeck, George, 41
linguistic turn, 41, 291, 462
liturgy, 128, 179–180, 345, 346n3, 363, 365–366, 369, 511, 513
Livant, Bill, 108
Locke, John, 106–107, 116n59, 291–292, 297, 299, 302n18, 429, 436
logical positivism, 41, 120
Lombard, Peter, 172, 174–175
Lotz, Johannes Baptist, 265, 286
love, 10, 29, 35, 37–40, 64, 149, 155, 213, 217, 223–225, 235n30, 252, 255–258, 346, 348, 349n13, 355, 362n48, 363–364, 366, 369n70, 370–372, 400n14, 402, 404n21, 403n21, 410n33, 424, 442, 444, 446, 449, 450–451, 503, 513; of God, 8, 37, 451
Lowe, E.J., 103n10, 121, 123, 481–482, 496–597
Lullus, Raimundus, 224–225
Luther, Martin, 41, 262–264, 266, 274–278, 285, 290
Lyotard, Jean-François, 186, 199–202, 404

Macey, David, 417
Macintyre, Alasdair, 182n15, 520, 523,
MacMurray, John, 399
Maimonides, Moses, 71, 221
Malcolm, Norman, 384
Malebranche, Nicholas, 4
Malthus, Thomas, 101
Manichees, 50
Mann, Thomas, 227
Marcel, Gabriel, 7
Maréchal, Joseph, 7
Marian theology, 516
Marion, Jean-Luc, 153–154, 263n10, 475, 491, 519
Marks, Jonathan, 124
Martínez, Archbishop Javier, 247
martyr, 448, 451, 524

Name and Subject Index

Marx, Karl, 205, 219, 248, 249n73, 455
Marxism, 253, 453, 458, 503, 512
mathematics, 81, 403, 458–459, 466, 468, 481, 491, 494
Maximus the Confessor, 43, 359–362, 363n54, 525
McDowell, John, 129, 482
McVeigh, Timothy, 194
mechanism, 38, 109, 242
mediation, 90, 147, 155–156, 211, 271, 352, 355, 366, 371–372, 403, 478, 509
Meillassoux, Quentin, 454–455, 458–461, 483
meiosis, 112
Mellor, David, 116
memes, 118–119, 133, 191
Merleau-Ponty, Maurice, 127
metaphysical realism, 291, 325, 484, 497, 500
metaxology, 11, 13–14, 34, 36, 353–355, 371n78
metaxu, 34, 353n30, 354, 358
Milbank, John, 50, 61, 251, 352, 358n41, 365, 410
Miller, Jacques-Alain, 422
mind-body problem, 109
monotheism, 9, 76n1, 217, 478, 492, 497
Montesquieu, 429–430, 441, 552
Moses, 128, 421–422
Moss, Lenny, 138
Muhammad, 173, 181, 505
Müller, Gerd, 139
Müller, Max, 265
Muralt, André de, 522
mysticism, 37, 156, 175, 237n6, 271, 276–277, 346n3, 349n13, 367, 386, 419, 423, 457, 474, 477–478, 500, 506, 508–509,
mythology, 10, 42, 43n3, 73, 132, 140–141, 162

Nagel, Thomas, 74, 106, 109–111, 120, 122, 139
narrative, 41, 144, 158, 165, 200–202, 248, 346n3, 347, 413, 421–424, 430, 444, 453, 496, 499
nation-state, 242, 252, 437
natural selection, 102, 110–111, 124n98, 130–131, 136, 138, 191
natural theology, 41, 57–58, 144, 261, 263, 476
naturalism, 73–74, 97, 109, 115–117, 132, 184, 377n8, 378, 411, 456, 458, 479, 481–482, 504
naturalistic fallacy, 100n2
Nef, Frédéric, 480, 491–494
negative theology, 53, 57, 59, 147, 160, 218
neo-Kantian, 271, 291, 377, 385
Neoplatonism, 2, 9, 175, 177, 206, 218, 274, 407n26, 465–468, 469n12, 477, 483–484, 486, 494, 526
neo-scholasticism, 260, 266, 276, 356n37
Neumann-Held, Eva, 137
Newman, John Henry, 50, 172
Newman, Stuart, 139
Newton, Sir Isaac, 104, 107
Nicholas of Cusa, 9–10, 206, 452n1, 459, 473, 485, 495, 525
Nietzsche, Friedrich, 11, 14, 30, 41, 50, 168–169, 177, 179, 190, 223, 225, 235, 247–248, 283, 379, 392–393, 412n37, 413
nihilism, 12–13, 34, 47, 73, 101, 141, 146, 152–153, 160, 246, 442–443, 483, 496–497, 504, 526–527
Noel, Conrad, 502
nominalism, 1, 4, 104, 167, 394,

Name and Subject Index

405n24, 410–411, 483, 490, 495, 500

O'Callaghan, John, 129
O'Hear, Anthony, 107, 114
Oedipus, 420
ontic, 56–57, 264n11, 281–282, 408
ontotheology, 49, 145, 152, 260–261, 274, 279–280, 325, 393–395, 397–398, 401, 406–407, 409, 413–414, 485–487, 491–492
Origen, 43, 252, 395, 303n21
Orwell, George, 439
Ott, Hugo, 267

Pabst, Adrian, 465
Palamas, Gregory, 399
panentheism, 9, 252
pantheism, 9, 152, 250
paradox, 197, 205, 209, 211–212, 236–245, 247–248, 250–259, 278, 351–352, 423, 516
Parmenides, 10, 170n9, 177, 405, 485
participation, 13, 17, 38, 46, 51, 55n35, 61, 64, 67, 71, 130n119, 256–257, 346n3, 359n44, 365, 368, 400n14, 405n24, 407n26, 446, 448, 461, 466, 471–472, 477, 526
Pascal, Blaise, 17, 336, 516
Paul, St., 43, 54, 130, 272, 346n3, 350, 365, 367–368, 428, 441–444, 446–447, 451, 477–478, 493, 498, 507, 524
Péguy, Charles, 473, 502
Pelton, Ted, 192
Perrier, Emmanuel, 488n35, 500
Peterson, John, 115
phenomenological reduction, 46
phenomenology, 5, 56, 147, 152–153, 271, 284, 452, 455, 474–475, 490, 526
physicalism, 109, 116–117, 121, 127, 458
physics, 81, 92, 96, 98, 107, 109n31, 122n88, 126n109, 142, 280, 320, 398, 460, 484, 493
Plato, 2, 10, 13, 44–45, 47, 50, 56, 66, 102, 152, 161, 163–164, 168–170, 177, 206, 214, 233–235, 249n74, 266, 277, 283, 287, 289n85, 393–397, 399–409, 412, 452n1, 465–467, 480, 483, 491, 496–497, 513
Plessner, Helmut, 131
Plotinus, 2–3, 10, 67–69, 71, 466–467, 498–499
Polanyi, Michael, 399
Portin, P., 138
possible worlds, 292, 479–483, 489
post-metaphysical, 41, 57, 425, 497
postmodernism, 12–14, 29–30, 41, 49–50, 57, 62, 120, 141, 160–161, 170–171, 177–178, 180, 182, 397, 407, 409, 522, 526
post-secular, 394, 397, 409, 412
potentiality, 55, 86, 117n69
poverty, 23, 36, 406n25
practical reason, 19–20, 471
pragmatism, 41, 193–194, 463–464, 519
presence, 7, 44, 73, 95, 127, 129, 162, 171, 266, 278–279, 283–284, 289n85, 290, 370n76, 421, 444, 460
pre-Socratic philosophers, 92
prime matter, 91
prime mover, 45, 66–67, 69
Proclus, 69, 468–469, 477, 499
Proudhon, Pierre-Joseph, 502

Name and Subject Index

Provine, William, 111
Przywara, Erich, 48–49, 51–61, 64
pseudo-Dionysius, 54, 59
psychoanalysis, 200–201, 414, 418, 420–421, 424–425
Pullman, Phillip, 480
pure reason, 56, 252, 457, 526
Putnam, Hilary, 75, 299, 302–303, 306, 310n26, 317

Quine, W.V.O., 104n13, 119, 300, 391, 458, 462, 479–480

Radical Orthodoxy, 502, 513–514, 519, 525–526
Rahner, Karl, 356n37, 502, 511
rationalism, 19, 229, 277, 455, 461, 497
Ratzinger, Cardinal Joseph, 345, 346n3, 362, 364–365, 513
Rea, Michael, 116
real distinction, 51, 53–54, 63, 263, 268, 486
Reformation, 41, 176, 274–275
reformers, 167, 176, 276
Reich, Wilhelm, 420
Reid, Thomas, 484
Renaissance, 176, 526
return of religion, 455
revelation, 2–4, 8, 42–43, 46–48, 54, 60, 69–72, 144, 146, 156–157, 161, 167, 171, 173, 180–181, 241, 250n79, 263, 278, 339, 348–349, 351–352, 358, 395, 398, 409, 426, 457, 476–478, 486–487, 492, 500, 513–514, 520–521
Richardson, William, 418
Rickert, Heinrich, 271
Ricoeur, Paul, 5–6, 424
Rieppel, Olivier, 104
Robin, Corey, 431
Rorty, Richard, 429, 462, 519

Rose, Gillian, 416, 419, 421
Rousseau, Jean-Jacques, 223
Rousselot, Pierre, 7
Ruse, Michael, 111, 113–114
Ruskin, John, 514
Russell, Bertrand, 124n100, 237n6, 456
Ruthven, Maline, 506

scepticism, 19, 21, 23, 41, 46, 110, 141, 313, 332, 342, 409, 421, 454, 476
Scheler, Max, 56, 219
Schelling, Friedrich Wilhelm Joseph, 4, 47, 268, 467, 472
Schleiermacher, Friedrich, 233, 378
scholasticism, 2, 57, 147, 260, 267–268, 272–273, 276–277, 280, 471, 473–474, 477
Schopenhauer, Arthur, 379
scientism, 120, 219n17, 458, 511
Scotus, John Duns, 2, 10, 77, 79, 81–82, 84–88, 90, 152, 174, 261, 264, 266–268, 271, 280, 290, 470, 472–474, 478, 485, 487–491, 493, 500
Searle, John, 100
second coming of Christ, 166
secular, 59n40, 73, 79, 109, 131, 154–155, 358n41, 393–394, 397, 402, 404, 410–412, 417, 478, 482, 490–491, 497, 502–503, 507–513, 520–522, 525–526
Sellars, Wilfrid, 106, 462, 511, 525
Sherrington, Sir Charles, 101
Shklar, Judith N., 429, 432, 436, 440
Siddhārtha Gautama, 173
Siewerth, Gustav, 265, 286
Siger of Brabant, 493
Simmel, Georg, 379

simulacrum, 242, 339–340
sin, 213, 239, 240n22, 248, 250, 256–257, 345–348, 359–362, 372–373, 415–416, 444–448, 450
Smith, James K.A., 241
social contract, 432
socialism, 486, 502–503, 505, 514
sociology, 399, 519, 521–522
Socrates, 45, 112, 168, 222, 235, 308, 312n28, 405n23, 406, 407n26, 412n37, 480, 492
Soloviev, Vladimir, 527
sophiology, 478, 527
sophists, 407, 409n28
Sorensen, Roy, 237–238
Spaemann, Robert, 126n105, 521, 523
Spencer, Herbert, 102, 455
Spengler, Oswald, 380–382
Speusippus, 45
Spinoza, Benedict de, 9, 154, 215–216, 221–223, 228, 458
Stein, Edith, 517
stoicism, 2, 43, 246, 389
Stroud, Barry, 116, 127n110
Suárez, Francisco, 51n20, 77, 80, 152, 280, 452n1, 471, 485, 494
subjectivity, 75, 210, 214, 221–223, 225, 228, 233, 235, 240–241, 247, 258, 376, 386
sublime, 62–65, 420
substance, 9, 66–67, 78, 86, 88, 90, 92–94, 96–97, 162–163, 165, 249n74, 273, 286–289, 299, 302n18, 303, 311–312, 321, 345, 349, 367, 370n76, 446–447, 464–466, 469–470, 472, 477, 481, 483–484, 488, 493
Sufi Islam, 477, 506, 508–509
supernatural, 2–4, 58, 74, 109, 142–144, 156, 158–159, 250–251, 285, 352–353, 355, 356n37, 358, 411, 448, 486, 501–502, 511, 523
supernaturalistic fallacy, 106, 109, 120, 122, 124
survival of the fittest, 102
suspended middle, 55, 351

Tarde, Gabriel, 379
Taylor, Charles, 520
Taylor, Mark C., 419
teleology, 208, 254, 484, 523
Térèse of the Child Jesus, St., 345
terrorism, 20, 439–440, 442, 506
Tertullian, 43
Thales, 115
theism, 44, 111, 151, 262–263, 484
theological aesthetics, 44, 48–49, 60–61, 63–64
theological realism, 325–326, 497
theosis, 346–347, 366, 466
Third Council of Constantinople, 359, 361n47, 364n58
Thomas of Erfurt, 271
Thomism, 7, 88, 264, 281n68, 290, 478, 486
Tocqueville, Alexis de, 429–430
torture, 39, 427, 450
transcendence, 2–3, 7, 24, 42, 51, 54, 57, 64, 79, 130, 144–147, 150–151, 153–156, 158–160, 246n55, 248, 354–355, 366, 371, 415, 496
transcendentals, 46, 468, 470–471
Trinity, 10, 50, 59, 146, 150, 155, 158, 173, 345, 358n41, 361, 364, 365n62, 367, 368n68, 371–372, 446, 477
truth-event, 428, 442–443, 446, 449, 451
tyranny, 34, 429, 505

unconscious, 186–187, 195,

Name and Subject Index

199–202, 413, 415–419, 421–422
univocity, 15, 18–19, 23, 36, 51, 52n23, 90, 98, 152, 261, 269, 271, 290, 353n30, 356n37, 464, 471, 478, 483, 485, 489, 493, 514
unmoved mover (see prime mover), 3, 163–164
Updike, John, 183–187, 190–200, 202

van Buren, John, 277
van Fraassen, Bas, 325–327, 335–343
van Inwagen, Peter, 115
Vatican II Council, 501
Vernes, Jean-René, 459
Veyne, Paul, 522
Vico, Giambattista, 206, 226–228, 231, 462, 473
Vienna Circle, 41
violence, 35–36, 146, 184, 193, 432, 453, 457–458, 478
Virgil, 176
virtue ethics, 523
void, 13, 395, 447, 496, 509
von Balthasar, Hans Urs, 8, 10, 44, 48–49, 56, 63n50, 349n13, 351–352, 362n48, 498, 502, 512, 516
von Speyr, Adrienne, 367, 369, 370n76

Wahl, Jean, 224
Waissmann, F., 391

Wandschneider, Dieter, 130
war, 101, 371n78, 426–427, 432, 438–442, 450–451, 506
Weil, Simone, 502
Weinandy, Thomas, 68
Weismann, August, 112, 133
Welte, Bernhard, 260
Westminster Confession, 329
Westphal, Merold, 393n1, 397–398, 401, 407
Whitehead, Alfred North, 119–120, 187
Wiggins, David, 310n26, 318,
will to power, 38, 41
William of Ockham, 123, 174, 410–411, 483, 497
Williams, Archbishop Rowan, 364n59, 421, 424, 518, 520
Williams, Bernard, 318
Wilson, E.O., 113–114, 132, 136
Winquist, Charles, 419
Wittgenstein, Ludwig, 41, 205, 237n6, 374–392, 454–458, 463
Wohlman, Avital, 70
Wolff, Christian, 77, 79, 460–461, 471
Wright, Crispin, 377–378, 380
Wyller, Egil, 206, 235n30

Yale school, 41
Yannaras, Christos, 399, 400n14, 404n21
Yeats, W.B., 107

Žižek, Slavoj, 413, 423
Zwingli, Ulrich, 129